The Co-Teacher Files—*A Word to the Student*

As a novice teacher, you will undoubtedly need resources to help you plan and evaluate classroom interactions. This book has been designed to be virtually your CO-TEACHER—to help you get ready for your first teaching experiences and to guide you through your first years of teaching.

It offers you an array of background information and practical advice to help you become a prepared, confident, and resourceful beginning teacher.

Moreover, this book includes three special resources that will function as a unique set of on-the-job CO-TEACHER FILES:

Suggestions for Teaching in Your Classroom

Applying Technology to Teaching

Resources for Further Investigation

These resources are easily located throughout this book. To enhance their visibility and utility, each of these three types of "files" for use now and later is tabbed and coded with its own color code. In addition, if you turn to the inside back cover of this text, you will find indexes for these three resources, listing the page numbers where they appear in the text.

For more information about how these and other qualities of this book can help you become a better teacher, see pages 7-10 in Chapter 1.

PSYCHOLOGY APPLIED TO TEACHING

Brief Contents

Contents

Preface

The hallmark of *Psychology Applied to Teaching* is its usefulness to teachers. It is written for students enrolled in an introductory educational psychology course, and is at once a basic source of information for prospective teachers and a resource for their future use as classroom teachers.

Special Features of the Text

This seventh edition of *Psychology Applied to Teaching* has been written to be used in three ways: (1) as a text that provides a review of scientific information organized and presented so that it will be understood, remembered, and applied; (2) as a source of practical ideas about instructional techniques for student teachers and beginning teachers; and (3) as a means for teachers to improve their effectiveness as they gain experience in the classroom.

Features of the Revision

Because of its central role in American society, education is a dynamic enterprise. Tens of thousands of people—including classroom teachers, school administrators, state education officials, politicians, and educational and psychological researchers—are constantly searching for and trying out new ideas in an attempt to increase student achievement. This searching about for ways to improve education is especially true of educational and psychological researchers. Since the last edition of *Psychology Applied to Teaching,* significant new developments have occurred in the areas of social, emotional, and cognitive development (particularly among adolescents), theories of intelligence, computer-assisted instruction, problem-solving, transfer of learning, classroom measurement and evaluation, and classroom management. The seventh edition has been extensively revised and comprehensively updated to incorporate these and other new developments. In developing *Psychology Applied to Teaching,* seventh edition, we were very much aware that this is a book for the 1990s—and beyond.

A key change in the seventh edition is the inclusion of a new chapter on cultural diversity and multicultural education programs. Titled "Understanding Cultural Diversity," Chapter 6 points out that the United States is no longer seen as a "melting pot" in which people of various cultures divest themselves of their unique cultural characteristics and take on a uniform set of "American" characteristics. Instead, the current metaphor is that of the salad bowl. People with different cultural backgrounds work toward the achievement of basic common goals while retaining and emphasizing their unique cultural characteristics. This chapter describes how students from different cultural backgrounds differ from one another and how these differences can be productively integrated into instructional programs. In addition, coverage of multicultural concerns, issues, and perspectives has been integrated wherever relevant throughout the text to better prepare prospective teachers for the growing cultural diversity of our schools and classrooms.

A second major change in the seventh edition is the inclusion of a new feature in each of the learning chapters (8, 9, 10, and 11) titled "Applying Technology to Teaching." Written to reflect the increasing use of technology in classrooms, particularly computer-assisted instruction, this feature describes ways in which teachers can use computer technology to enhance what students know, how they think, and how they solve problems.

In addition to a new chapter on cultural diversity and a new feature on using technology, almost every chapter has been revised to reflect other important new developments. Chapter 1, "Applying Psychology to Teaching," discusses the benefits of becoming a reflective teacher and introduces a topic that reappears in two later chapters—the constructivist approach to teaching and learning. Chapter 2, "Stage Theories of Development," summarizes current research findings on sex-role stereotyping and identity formation, discusses the significance of Lev Vygotsky's zone of proximal development concept for cognitive development, and outlines Carol Gilligan's theory of female identity and moral development. Chapter 3, "Age-Level Characteristics," features current research findings on the nature and causes of delinquency, sex differences in cognitive abilities, learning styles, emotional development of adolescents, sexual behavior among adolescents, psychiatric disorders of adolescence, and employment patterns of teenagers. Chapter 4, "Assessing Pupil Variability," contains new material on carrying out non-discriminatory assessments and guidelines for interpreting standardized test scores to parents. Chapter 5, "Dealing with Pupil Variability," summarizes current research on the prevalence and effectiveness of ability grouping, discusses alternatives to ability grouping, summarizes current research on the effectiveness of mainstreaming, and describes recent amendments to PL 94-142, the Education for All Handicapped Children Act. Chapter 8, "Behavioral Learning Theories," includes current research on the effectiveness of computer-assisted instruction and behavior modification techniques and an expanded discussion of social learning theory. Chapter 10, "Cognitive Learning Theories and Problem-Solving," contains a new section on how to use constructivism to foster meaningful learning as well as a current view of transfer of learning. Chapter 13, "Measurement and Evaluation of Classroom Learning," contains new sections on alternative assessment methods and how teachers can improve their classroom grading practices.

A final change that deserves mention is perhaps the most subtle and underappreciated since it does not appear in any specific location. As anyone who has studied psychology or taught students at any level can attest, human behavior is the end result of many factors that interact with one another. We have tried to sensitize the reader to this fact both by pointing it out explicitly (see the introduction to Chapter 9, for example) and by making cross-references to other chapters wherever possible. The topic of learning strategies, for example, is discussed primarily in Chapter 9 but is also mentioned in conjunction with the writing of instructional objectives (Chapter 7), helping students clarify their values (Chapter 11), and measuring classroom learning (Chapter 13).

Special Features of the Text

The following features, many of which were introduced in various earlier editions, have been selected, improved, and augmented to make this seventh edition more useful and effective than its predecessors.

Key Points   At the beginning of each chapter, Key Points are listed under major headings. They also appear in the margins of pages opposite sections in which each point is discussed. The Key Points call attention to sections of the text that are considered to be of special significance to teachers and thus serve as instructional objectives.

Suggestions for Teaching in Your Classroom   Most chapters include summaries of research findings and principles relating to a particular topic. These are followed by detailed descriptions of various ways in which the information and concepts might be applied in classrooms. Numerous examples of applications at different grade levels are supplied, and readers are urged to select and record applications that will fit their own particular personality, style, and teaching situation in a Personal Handbook. The Suggestions for Teaching are intended to be read while the book is used as a text *and* referred to by future teachers and in-service teachers after they have completed course work. For ease in reference, these suggestions are printed in a different typeface from that used in other parts of the book and are highlighted by a colored screen background. Suggestions for Teaching are also indexed inside the back cover of the text.

Mid-Chapter Reviews   This feature summarizes research-based information, principles, and theories presented in the first part of most chapters. These reviews strengthen understanding of points that serve as the basis for the Suggestions for Teaching in Your Classroom presented in the second part of most chapters. The Mid-Chapter Reviews include coverage of Key Points and are intended to serve as an effective learning aid for students preparing for examinations.

Handbook Headings and Becoming a Better Teacher: Questions and Suggestions   These two features facilitate the preparation and use of a personal handbook for teaching. Readers are urged to use the Handbook Headings, which appear in the margins, to prepare a personal set of guidelines for reference before and during the student teaching experience and during the first years of teaching. The questions and suggestions in the Becoming a Better Teacher section are intended to help in-service teachers to analyze strengths and weaknesses and to plan how to improve their effectiveness as instructors. A guide for setting up and using these resources is included in Chapter 15: "Becoming a Better Teacher."

Applying Technology to Teaching   New to this edition, this special feature suggests ways that teachers can use computer technology to enhance their students' learning. It appears near the end of each of the four learning theories chapters in Part 3.

Resources for Further Investigation   At the end of each chapter an annotated bibliography is presented offering sources of information of topics of interest to teachers. Some chapters also include within these suggestions instructions for carrying out simple scientific and observational studies and experiments.

Summary   A numbered set of summary statements appears after the Resources for Further Investigation. This feature is intended to help students review the main points of a chapter for upcoming examinations or class discussions.

Key Terms   Appearing after the Summary is a list of topics that are key aspects of the chapter. Understanding these topics is an essential part of understanding the chapter as a whole. To facilitate use of this feature, the page where each term is initially defined and discussed appears in parentheses.

Discussion Questions   This feature appears after the Key Terms. Because understanding and retention of new information is enhanced when learners actively relate it to known ideas and experiences, the Discussion Questions ask the reader to reflect on how previous experiences (or possible future experiences) relate to the chapter material. These questions can serve as the focus for in-class discussion and out-of-class discussion.

Glossary   A glossary of key terms and concepts is provided at the back of the book as an aid in reviewing for examinations or classroom discussion.

Indexes   In addition to the detailed name and subject indexes at the end of the book, indexes to Suggestions for Teaching in Your Classroom, Applying Technology to Teaching, and Resources for Further Investigation are included inside the back cover.

Instructional Components That Accompany the Text

Study Guide   The Study Guide for the seventh edition of *Psychology Applied to Teaching* was designed to help students formulate and carry out a strategy for mastering the Key Points. Students are provided general guidelines for analyzing their resources and learning materials, planning a learning strategy, carrying out the strategy, monitoring their progress, and modifying their strategy if they are dissatisfied with the results. As an integral part of the suggested tactics for learning, original "concept maps" are supplied for each major section of each chapter. Concept maps are schematic representations of how major topics, subtopics, and Key Points of a chapter relate to each other. Also included in the Study Guide are exercises designed to help students enhance memory and understanding of Key Point material, and two sets of review questions (multiple-choice and short-answer) to support student efforts at self-monitoring. New to this edition are rejoinders for each multiple-choice response, explaining to students why each choice is either correct or wrong and referring students to specific pages in the text for additional information.

Instructor's Lecture Enrichment and Resource Manual This teaching aid provides for each chapter a detailed lecture outline with supplementary teaching suggestions, coverage of Key Points, supplementary discussion topics, student activities, extra references, listings of films and videotapes, reproduction of the Study Guide's concept maps, and "Approaches to Teaching Educational Psychology," a compendium of teaching tactics from professors across the country.

Test Bank The thoroughly revised Test Bank includes 1255 test items consisting of 790 multiple-choice items in alternate forms, 395 short-answer questions, and 70 essay questions. Consistent with this text's long-standing emphasis on mastery, each multiple-choice and short-answer question reflects a Key Point and either the knowledge, comprehension, application, or analysis level of Bloom's taxonomy. Feedback booklets allow instructors to point out misconceptions in students' reasoning.

Test Generator This component is an interactive computerized version of the Test Bank.

Transparencies An extensive set of eighty transparencies in one, two, and four colors consisting of figures, charts, and instructional aids in the text, is available upon adoption of the text.

Acknowledgments A number of reviewers made constructive suggestions and provided thoughtful reactions at various stages in the development of this manuscript. Thanks go out to the following individuals for their help:

Tom Boman, University of Minnesota, Duluth
Lenore S. Brantley, Andrews University
Albert C. Ciri, Bridgewater State College
Paul Erickson, San Diego State University
Lynn Fox, San Francisco State University
Christine Cassatt Givner, Trinity College
Mark Grabe, University of North Dakota
Jerry Gray, Washburn University
David Jeffrey, Stephen F. Austin State University
Martha S. Jones, University of Texas, San Antonio

Thomas McCaig, University of Wisconsin, Stevens Point
Anne Nardi, West Virginia University
Kenneth R. Romines, San Jose State University
Mary R. Sudzina, University of Dayton

Finally, I would like to acknowledge several other individuals for their invaluable contributions to this book:

I am indebted to the editorial and production staff of Houghton Mifflin Company, particularly Susan Granoff and Carol Newman, for helping make this text more accurate, more readable, more useful, and more attractive than I could have made it myself.

I am indebted to Linda Patrick and the staff of the Operations Support Center at Southern Illinois University at Carbondale for turning my rough manuscript into high-quality finished manuscript in such timely fashion that I never missed a deadline.

And last but not least, I am indebted to my wife, Ruth, for her encouragement, patience, and understanding (particularly for her understanding); to my daughter, Andrea, for expressing an interest in psychology and in writing as she heads off to college (perhaps she will succeed me at this task one day); and to my son, Jeffrey, for teaching me more about adolescence that I could learn from several journals and books.

J.S.

PSYCHOLOGY APPLIED TO TEACHING

PSYCHOLOGY APPLIED TO TEACHING

Chapter 1

APPLYING PSYCHOLOGY TO TEACHING

As you begin to read this book, you may be asking yourself, "What will this book tell me about teaching that I don't already know?" The answer to that question depends on several factors, including your previous experiences with teaching and the number of psychology courses you have taken. Since you have been actively engaged in the process of formal education for at least twelve years, you already know a great deal about learning and teaching. You have had abundant opportunities to observe and react to over one hundred teachers. You have probably read several

A teacher's perception of what takes place in classrooms is often very different from the perception of students. (1991 Jeff Smith/The Southern Company)

hundred texts, finished all kinds of assignments, and taken hundreds if not thousands of examinations. Undoubtedly, you have also established strong likes and dislikes for certain subjects and approaches to teaching.

Yet despite your familiarity with education from the student's point of view, you have probably had limited experience with education from the teacher's point of view. As you read this book (and as you interact with pupils), you will discover that the teacher's perception of what takes place in classrooms is often substantially different from the perception of students. As a student, for example, you have probably resented certain assignments and examinations. You may have brooded about the weakness of a teacher who was unable to inspire students to learn and had to resort to coercion. However, you probably have not had the experience—yet—of attempting to arouse and hold the interest of one or more groups of students, nor have you been faced with the problem of assigning grades that must be backed up by evidence.

One type of information about teaching that you don't already know, therefore, takes the form of descriptions of classroom practice as seen from a professional educator's point of view. Such descriptions make up a substantial part of this book, since its primary purpose is to acquaint you with information about teaching that is derived from the discoveries of psychologists. Psychologists use the methods of science to study behavior, and if you have taken any courses in psychology, you are already familiar with the nature of knowledge in this field. However, this book differs from other books in psychology that you may have read because it stresses ways you might *apply* psychological knowledge to teaching. Psychologists have discovered many things about human behavior, and they have established principles and theories to summarize and clarify their insights. You may already be familiar with many facts and theories in psychology but probably have not tried to convert this knowledge into classroom applications. As you read this book, you will be frequently urged to think of ways you might use what you learn. To grasp how you might make applications, you should become aware at the very outset that this book has been designed to be used in three different ways. The simplest and most direct way to begin to explain the distinctiveness of this book and how it can be used is to relate a frustrating but enlightening experience.

"WHAT THEY DIDN'T TELL US"

A few years after the "senior" author of this book began teaching a course in educational psychology, a student-teacher chapter of the state teachers' association was formed on campus. The leaders of this group, who were scheduled to do student teaching the following September, decided to present a panel discussion at the last meeting of the year, in May. They invited five recent graduates who were just completing their first year of teaching to discuss the provocative topic "What They Didn't Tell Us." Since "they" included professors who taught educational psychology and since the professor who is writing these words was just beginning to think about getting to work on a text, he decided to go to the discussion and take notes. The meeting was very well attended, and the panelists had the audience of future student teachers on the edge of their seats much of the evening. When the meeting finally broke up, most of the audience left the room with a sense of satisfaction. They had picked up all sorts of valuable tips straight from the horse's mouth. The professor and would-be author, on the other hand, was bothered and bewildered.

The college the panelists had graduated from was quite small at that time, and all of them had taken his course in educational psychology just two years before. Several of the bits of information that the panelists had told the student teachers to be sure to pick up somehow or other before they entered a classroom had been discussed (directly or indirectly) in the ed psych text they had read. Yet these former students—who had successfully answered test questions and earned high grades in educational psychology—now talked as if they had never heard of such a course.

During the question-and-answer period that followed the panelists' presentations, the professor thought about asking to be recognized, standing up, and saying something like "This discussion really ought to be called 'What We Forgot.'

I *did* tell you some of the things you are talking about, but you didn't remember them." Since he tends to be timid about speaking in public, he squirmed silently in his seat in the back row and fumed and brooded. Later that night, after having had time to think things over, he was glad that he hadn't sounded off because he concluded that he (along with the author of the text he had used) was more to blame than were his former students for their failure to remember and use what they had learned.

At that early stage of his career, the professor made up tests similar to most of those he had taken all through his college years. After announcing that an exam would be given, he went through the assigned chapters of the text. When he found a section that impressed him as important *or* looked as if it could easily be converted into a test question, he wrote a multiple-choice item. Much of the time, it must be confessed, the information stressed in the questions was selected more for test-ability than for importance or significance. After they had taken the first exam, students figured out that the most sensible way to study for subsequent exams was to try to put themselves in the place of the person writing the questions. That is, they skimmed through the book and selected for study sections that impressed them as likely to appeal to someone making up items for an exam. Since they studied primarily to answer test questions, they naturally assumed that what they had learned had served its purpose as soon as they completed an exam. And since there was no longer any reason to remember it, they forgot it.

While the kinds of test questions used undoubtedly contributed to the tendency for students to fail to remember what they had learned, the text on which the questions were based also deserved part of the blame. The author made no attempt to illustrate how the material under discussion might be applied. His philosophy seemed to be "My job is to tell you about facts, principles, and theories. Your job is to figure out what to do with what I tell you." Since the students realized that their primary responsibility during the course was to pass exams, they had no inclination at that time to try to figure out how to apply what they read. And since the book offered no classroom applications that impressed them as being readily accessible for future use, they sold their texts at the end of the semester. Without the book to refer to a year or so later when they engaged in student teaching or two years later when they began to teach on their own, they had to rely on what they remembered. And since they remembered little or nothing about what had been covered in their course in educational psychology that could be converted into classroom applications, it was not surprising that they talked about "What They Didn't Tell Us."

These more or less inescapable conclusions were a source of great dismay to the professor since he was, and continues to be, convinced that educational psychology is potentially the most valuable course in a teacher preparation program. Teachers can benefit in hundreds of ways from the insights and discoveries of behavioral scientists—provided they comprehend, remember, and apply what has been reported and discovered. They can also benefit by frequently functioning as behavioral scientists themselves in their classrooms. So the professor who suffered the agonizing experience at the panel discussion decided to write a book about educational psychology that would correct the limitations of the text he had been using. Taking into account what he had learned from the "What They Didn't Tell Us" experience, the professor-author kept this list of goals on his desk as he wrote:

1. Try to reduce students' tendency to conclude that information about educational psychology should be learned only to answer test questions.
2. Emphasize and illustrate classroom applications of the scientific principles discussed so that students will become aware of the many ways that psychology can be applied to teaching.
3. Organize the book so that it functions not only as a text but also as a reference to be kept and used during student-teaching and first year–teaching experiences.

Letters from former students supported the conclusion that *Psychology Applied to Teaching* (as the book came to be called when it was eventually published) often achieved all three goals. Many students reported that they did come to realize that psychological principles can be applied in the classroom. Moreover, they kept the book after the course had been completed, and they referred to it both when the time came to student teach and during their first years of teaching.

A survey carried out two years after the book was published provided more systematic evidence of success. The student-teacher association sent questionnaires to one hundred recent graduates who were just completing their first year of teaching, asking them to evaluate the education courses they had taken. Over 60 percent of the respondents rated educational psychology as the most valuable and useful of all the courses (including general and specific methods) they had taken in their credential programs.

Subsequent editions of *Psychology Applied to Teaching* introduced new features designed to improve its usefulness. This seventh edition incorporates the best features of the previous editions. In order to achieve maximum value from this book, though, you should become aware of three ways of using it.

USES OF THIS BOOK

As just noted, this book has been written so that it can be used in three ways. First, it is a text for a course in educational psychology intended to help you master an organized sampling of scientific knowledge about development, learning, objectives, motivation, evaluation, and classroom management. Second, it is a source of practical ideas and suggestions to be converted into specific techniques you might use during the time you serve as a student teacher and during

This book has been written so that you can use it as a student in a course in educational psychology, as a student teacher coping with all the new experiences of an "apprentice," and as a first-year teacher interested in perfecting instructional skills. (Left: D. Degan/H. Armstrong Roberts; bottom: Bachmann/The Image Works, Inc.; facing page: Bill Luster/Matrix)

your first years of teaching. Third, it is a reference work to be consulted when you want to analyze certain aspects of instruction as you gain experience as a teacher.

Using This Book to Acquire Scientific Information

A substantial amount of scientific knowledge is of potential value to teachers. This book offers a selection of information from this pool of knowledge, organized so that you can learn and remember what you read as easily and effectively as possible. Chances are that your instructor will present lectures, organize discussions, show videotapes, and perhaps arrange field trips that will tie in with what is discussed in assigned chapters of this text. Depending on the purposes and organization of the educational psychology course you are taking, this book may also serve as the basis for examinations and/or other types of evaluation.

The primary reason for reading this book, then, is to become well acquainted with an organized body of scientific information in the field of educational psychology. Since this book presently functions as the text for a course, you may be asked to learn some sections well enough to be able to answer test questions. Tests do, after all, function as incentives that motivate students to read with care, and they provide information about how well students understand what they have read. It is particularly desirable for you to read this book carefully during this quarter or semester so that you will become well acquainted with the second way of using the book.

Using This Book as a Source of Practical Ideas

A second way this book can be used is as a source of practical ideas on how to teach. In addition to acquiring knowledge and learning principles that will serve as a general, all-purpose background for teaching, you should think of specific ways in which you might apply what you learn. Sooner or later you will engage in student teaching. You may be student teaching at the same time you are taking educational psychology. But it is more likely that you will student teach after you finish this book and that you will take one or more additional courses in methods of teaching. Your performance as a student teacher will probably be one of the most important factors to be considered when you apply for a teaching position. Furthermore, once you secure a job as a teacher, your performance in the classroom will be the major factor considered when your supervisors decide if you will be offered a contract for a second year. Therefore, you will be eager to function as a prepared, confident, resourceful student teacher and first-year teacher. This book has been designed to help you get ready for your first teaching experiences and to make it possible for you to find quick solutions to problems as they occur.

Using This Book to Become a Better Teacher

In addition to getting ready to teach, you will want to perfect your instructional techniques *as* you gain experience. Because you cannot anticipate all the problems you will encounter in any classroom, you will continually need to make adjustments and engage in a process of trial and error. To make this process as constructive as possible, you should systematically analyze strengths and weaknesses in your teaching. The third way you can use this book, then, is to analyze specific facets of your instructional techniques and plan how to correct errors and perfect successes.

THE NATURE AND VALUES OF SCIENCE

The various features of this book all summarize information supplied by psychologists. In addition, the observations of individuals not classified as psychologists will sometimes be mentioned. Indeed, people with many different kinds of backgrounds have taken an interest in education, and their ideas are occasionally noted at appropriate places in the chapters that follow. The primary purpose of this book, however, is to offer suggestions on how *psychology* (the scientific study of behavior and mental processes) might be applied to teaching. This text is based on the premise that information reported by scientists can be especially valuable for those who plan to teach. Some of the reasons for this conviction become apparent when the characteristics of science are examined.

The values of science become clear when one understands some of the limitations of casual observation—and of unsystematic applications of such observations to behavior—and sees how the scientist tries to correct these weaknesses.

Limitations of Unsystematic Observation

▶ Unsystematic observation may lead to false conclusions

Those who make unsystematic observations of human behavior may be easily misled into drawing false conclusions. For instance, they may treat the first plausible explanation that comes to mind as the only possible explanation. Or they might mistakenly apply a generalization about a single episode to superficially similar situations. In the process, they may fail to realize that the reactions of an individual in a given situation are due primarily to unrecognized idiosyncratic factors that may never occur again, or that the behavior of one person under certain circumstances might not resemble that of other persons in the same circumstances. In short, unsystematic observers are especially prone to noting only evidence that fits their expectations and ignoring evidence that does not. Ignorance of what others have discovered may cause such individuals to start at the same point when confronted with a problem—and to make the same mistakes others have made as they struggled to find solutions.

A clear example of the limitation of unsystematic observation is the practice of retaining children for a second year in a given grade because of poor achievement. Grade retention has long been used as a way of dealing with individual differences in learning rate, emotional development, and socialization skills. According to one estimate, 15 to 19 percent of all schoolchildren in the United States are retained in any given year (Smith & Shepard, 1987). In some school districts the retention rate for a given grade-level is reported to be as high as 50 percent (Schultz, 1989). The widespread use of retention in the United States and Europe continues despite the fact that most research clearly shows that low-achieving children who are promoted learn more the following year, have a stronger self-concept, and are better adjusted emotionally than similar children who are retained (Bracey, 1988; Holmes, 1989; Smith & Shepard, 1987).

▶ Grade retention policies influenced by unsystematic observation

Why is grade retention so popular when the evidence against it is so overwhelming? Recent studies indicate that teachers and parents, for a variety of reasons, strongly believe in its usefulness. Mary Lee Smith and Lorrie Shepard (1987), for example, found that teachers usually invoke one or more of the following poorly supported reasons to explain why they recommend retention:

1. *Teachers' beliefs about retention.* Many teachers believe that retention allows students to excel academically the following year, that retention in the early grades prevents retention later on, and that retention is free of cost and risk. These beliefs are typically based on personal experiences with one or a few children, limited follow-up, and no knowledge of the fate of similar children

Observing these children industriously coloring pictures may tempt you to conclude that they have been motivated by their teacher, but to reach a more trustworthy understanding of their behavior, you would need to study it systematically. (Terry Vine/Tony Stone Worldwide)

who were promoted. Controlled studies with large representative samples of retained and nonretained children clearly show that the effects of retention are seldom positive.

2. *Teachers' beliefs about child development.* Many teachers believe that certain children have not developed intellectually, socially, and emotionally enough to profit from normal classroom instruction. In addition, they believe that changes in the curriculum or in the teacher's instructional methods are not likely to be of much help. Such children, they feel, simply need time to mature. Yet research on peer tutoring (high-achieving students teaching low-achieving students of the same age), cross-age tutoring (high-achieving older students teaching low-achieving younger students), and computer-assisted instruction, to name just a few techniques, suggest otherwise.

3. *Teachers' beliefs that children should learn more and learn it sooner.* According to this view, the purpose of kindergarten is to master basic literacy and numeracy skills in preparation for more advanced work. Children who

cannot keep up become candidates for retention (instead of the curriculum becoming a candidate for change). As you will see in Chapter 2, when we take up Jean Piaget's theory of cognitive development, the research is not clear about the lasting benefits of pushing five- and six-year-olds to master too many aspects of reading, writing, and arithmetic.

4. *Teachers' beliefs about homogeneous classrooms.* Most teachers believe that instruction is more effective, and certainly more efficient, when classrooms are made up of children who are more alike than they are different. Retention is viewed as one way of producing more homogeneous classes. Once again, however, research findings on the effects of ability grouping are largely negative.

Beliefs about retention are, of course, modifiable. Just how modifiable was a question that Roy P. Doyle (1989) sought to answer. Doyle asked elementary school teachers, community leaders, and undergraduate education majors how strongly they subscribed to six beliefs that contribute to retention decisions. Three beliefs concerned the effect of retention on subsequent achievement, class variability, and motivation. The other three beliefs were more abstract in that they dealt with the need to maintain minimum grade standards, the integrity of eighth-grade diplomas, and promotion as a reward for earned accomplishment. Doyle then made a presentation to each group in which he used several lines of scientific evidence to argue against retention. Finally, he reassessed the strength of each group's beliefs. Doyle found less of a change in the beliefs associated with standards, integrity, and reward than in the beliefs associated with the effects of retention on children. Because of this difference, Doyle felt that it may be easier to convince people that retention is harmful than it is to persuade them to abandon the practice. One bright spot that surfaced in Doyle's study was that the education majors disagreed the most with all six beliefs after his presentation.

We are not saying here that most teachers are ignorant of or unwilling to accept scientific findings; indeed, we know many teachers whose attitudes and actions are informed by research. Rather, we are simply trying to illustrate the dangers of basing instructional practices on unscientific observations or opinions.

Strengths of Scientific Observation

▶ Scientific methods

Those who study behavior and mental processes scientifically are more likely to acquire trustworthy information than a casual observer is, and they are likely to apply what they learn more effectively because they follow certain procedures:

▶ Sampling

In most cases, a representative sample of subjects is studied so that individual idiosyncrasies are canceled out.

▶ Control

An effort is made to note all plausible hypotheses to explain a given type of behavior, and each hypothesis is tested under controlled conditions. If all factors but one can be held constant in an experiment, the researcher may be able to trace the impact of a given condition by comparing the behaviors of those who have been exposed to it and those who have not.

▶ Objectivity

Observers make special efforts to be objective and to guard against being misled by predetermined ideas, wishful thinking, or selected evidence.

Observations are made in a carefully prescribed systematic manner, which makes it possible for observers to compare reactions.

▶ Publication

Complete reports of experiments—including descriptions of subjects, methods, results, and conclusions—are published in professional journals. This dissemination makes it possible for other experimenters to replicate a study to discover if they obtain the same results.

▶ Replication

The existence of reports of thousands of experiments makes it possible to discover what others have done. This knowledge can then serve as a starting point for one's own speculations.

STUDYING BEHAVIOR AND MENTAL PROCESSES: COMPLICATING FACTORS

Although the use of scientific methods makes it possible to overcome many of the limitations of unscientific observation, the application of knowledge acquired in a scientific manner is subject to a number of complicating factors.

The Limited Focus of Research

Behavior is complex, changes with age, and has many causes. A student may perform poorly on a history exam, for example, for one or more of the following reasons: poorly developed study skills, inattentiveness in class, low interest in the subject, a poorly written text, low motivation to achieve high grades, vaguely worded exam questions, and/or difficulty with a particular type of exam question (compare-and-contrast essays, for example).

In order to understand how these factors affect performance on school-related tasks, research psychologists study at most only a few of them at a time under conditions that may not be entirely realistic. For example, a researcher who is interested in the effect on comprehension of note taking versus rereading may recruit subjects who are equivalent in terms of social class, prior knowledge of the topic of the reading passage, and age; randomly assign them to one of the two experimental groups; give them a brief passage to read; and examine the effects of note taking and rereading on several types of comprehension items.

▶ Research focuses on a few aspects of a problem

As a consequence, most research studies provide specific information about a particular aspect of behavior. More comprehensive knowledge, on the other hand, is acquired by combining and interrelating separate studies that have looked at different aspects of a common problem.

Individual Differences in Perception and Thinking

As we mentioned in the preceding paragraph, researchers equate subjects in an experiment on one or more major characteristics (such as age, ability, gender, or prior knowledge) in order to draw unambiguous conclusions about the effect of a particular variable or procedure on a particular outcome. This scientific tactic does not always produce clear-cut results, however, because of unforeseen differences between individuals.

To illustrate, consider the following experiment (Wenestam, 1978; cited in Marton, 1988). A brief passage on the nature of the Swedish social welfare system was read by fifteen Swedish men and women. The main point of the passage was that the social welfare system does more harm than good in trying to solve all of society's problems. Instead, it should focus on particular problems that are more solvable. To illustrate the point, the passage briefly described the Jansson family. Erik Jansson, the father, gets involved in fights and abuses alcohol. Mrs. Jansson suffers from a stomach ulcer and is often irritated with her three children. The eldest child skips school and belongs to a group that steals cars for fun. After reading the text, each person described what they thought it was about. About two-thirds of the subjects described the passage as being primarily about the nature of the social welfare system. The other one-third, however, saw something quite different. For them, the passage was primarily about the problems of the Jansson family. The relationship between the family's problems and the goals of the social welfare system was never mentioned by this latter group of subjects.

The constructivist view of learning holds that individual differences in such factors as age, gender, race, and ethnic background lead to differences in what people perceive and how they form ideas. (Kindra Clineff/The Picture Cube)

Such differences in perception and thinking have been described and explained by some of the greatest minds in education and psychology. The educational philosopher John Dewey and the developmental psychologist Jean Piaget (whose work we discuss in detail in Chapter 2), for example, both saw individual differences in perception and thinking as arising from a process that today is referred to as *constructivism.* In brief, the constructivist view of thinking holds that ideas are not given from one person to another like so many packages but, rather, are actively constructed by each person (Blais, 1988; Brooks, 1990; Wheatley, 1991). Many factors affect the form that an idea takes or whether it comes into existence at all. Some of the factors that are likely to play a role (and which we will discuss at various points in the text) include age, gender, race, ethnic background, prior knowledge, problem-solving skills, and motivation. Because different factors come into play for different people and the same factors affect people differently, two people can read the same passage yet construct entirely different interpretations of its meaning. (If you're having some difficulty grasping the notion of constructivism at this point, fear not. We will discuss it again in Chapters 2, 10, and 12.)

> Constructivism: individuals differ in what they perceive and how they form ideas

Selection and Interpretation of Data

The amount of scientific information available on behavior and mental processes is so extensive that no individual could examine or interpret all of it. Accordingly, researchers learn to be highly selective in their reading.

In addition, conclusions about the meaning of scientific results vary from one researcher to another. As you read this book, you will discover that there are differences of opinion among psychologists regarding certain aspects of development, motivation, and intelligence. Opposing views may be based on equally scientific evidence, but the way in which the evidence is selected and interpreted will vary. Just because a topic is studied scientifically does not necessarily mean that opinions about interpretations of the data will be unanimous.

> Differences of opinion due to selection and interpretation of data

New Findings Mean Revised Ideas

Scientific information is not only voluminous and subject to different interpretations; it is also constantly being revised. A series of experiments may lead to the development of a new concept or pedagogical technique that is highly successful when it is first tried out. Subsequent studies, however, may reveal that the original research was incomplete, or repeated applications of a technique may show that it is less effective once the novelty has worn off. But frequent shifts of emphasis in education also reflect the basic nature of science. A quality of science that sets it apart from other intellectual processes is that the discoveries by one generation of scientists set the stage for more complete and far-reaching discoveries by the next. More researchers are studying aspects of psychology and education now than at any previous time in history. And thousands of reports of scientific research are published every month. As our knowledge accumulates, it is inevitable that interpretations of how children learn and how we should teach

> Accumulating knowledge leads researchers to revise original ideas

Because educators are sometimes pressured to quickly adopt new teaching meth-
ods or institute new conditions, unsound practices may develop. To prevent the
development of fads, base instructional decisions on the latest research findings.
(James Wilson/Woodfin Camp & Associates)

will continue to change. We know more about development, learning, and teaching today than ever before; but because of the nature of some of the factors just discussed—and the complexity of human behavior—answers to many questions are tentative and incomplete.

You should be aware, of course, that fads occur in education (just as they occur in other fields). Occasionally, national and/or international events cause changes in our political and social climate. These changes often result in pressures on education to "do something." And when large numbers of educators embrace a new practice without waiting for or paying attention to research findings, fads develop (see Slavin, 1989, for an example). One of our objectives in writing this text is to help you avoid contributing to fads by demonstrating the importance of basing your practices on principles that have some research support.

In the last few pages we have asked you to consider some of the values of science, the strengths of scientific observation, and a few of the factors that complicate the scientific study of behavior and lead to frequent changes of emphasis in teaching techniques. These considerations help to explain why this book stresses how psychology might be applied to teaching; they also support the position that information reported by scientists can be especially valuable for those who plan to teach. At the same time, our intention has been to acquaint you with a few of the limitations and sometimes unsettling by-products of science.

The science of psychology has much to offer educators, but a scientific approach to teaching does have its limits. Research on teaching and learning gives you a systematic, objective framework for making instructional decisions. But, for the reasons cited above, it cannot give you a prescription or a set of rules that specify how you should handle every situation. Often you will have to make on-the-spot, subjective decisions about how to present a lesson, explain a concept, handle mass boredom, or reprimand a student. This contrast between an objective, systematic approach to planning instruction and the need to make immediate (yet appropriate) applications and modifications of those plans calls attention to a question that has been debated for years: Is teaching primarily an art or a science—or a combination of both?

TEACHING AS AN ART AND A SCIENCE

Some educators have argued that teaching is an art that cannot be practiced—or even studied—in an objective or scientific manner (Dawe, 1984; Flinders, 1989; Hansgen, 1991; Highet, 1957; Rubin, 1985). For example, Gilbert Highet, a distinguished critic and professor of literature, argued in *The Art of Teaching* that successful teaching must be considered an art because it involves two things that cannot be objectively and systematically manipulated—emotions and values. In Highet's view:

> Teaching is not like inducing a chemical reaction: it is much more like painting a picture or making a piece of music, . . . like planting a garden or writing a friendly letter. You must throw your heart into it, you must realize that it cannot all be done by formulas, or you will spoil your work, and your pupils, and yourself. (1957, p. viii)

Examples of the emotions and values referred to by Highet include believing that teaching is one of society's most valuable and rewarding activities, that teaching must be done as well as possible every day, that it is important to get students excited about learning, and that there is no such thing as an unteachable student. When Highet states that teaching cannot all be done by formulas, he is urging you to be flexible. Flexibility, which can be thought of as a "feel" for doing the right thing at the right time, can take many forms. First, it means using all the knowledge and techniques at your disposal to formulate effective lesson plans. It means knowing, for example, when to present a formal lesson and when to let

*Creativity and flexi-
bility will always be
important parts of the
art of good teaching.*
(Susan Lapides)

students discover things for themselves, when to be demanding and when to make few demands, when to be encouraging and when to criticize, when to give direct help and when to give indirect help. Second, flexibility entails the communication of emotions and interest in a variety of ways. David Flinders (1989) describes a teacher who, when talking to students, would lean or step in their direction and maintain eye contact. At various times she would raise her eyebrows, nod her head, smile, and bring the index finger of her right hand to her lips, indicating serious consideration of the student's comments. A third aspect of flexibility is the ability to improvise. When a lesson plan falls flat, the flexible teacher immediately thinks of an alternative presentation that recaptures the student's interest. Expert teachers actually plan improvisation into their lessons. Instead of writing out what they intend to do in great detail, expert teachers formulate general mental plans and wait to see how the students react before filling in such details as pacing, timing, and numbers of examples (Livingston & Borko, 1989). Obviously, this type of high-wire act requires a great deal of experience and confidence. A fourth aspect of flexibility is the willingness and resourcefulness to work around impediments. Teaching does not always occur under ideal circumstances, and teachers must sometimes cope with inadequate facilities, insufficient materials, interruptions, and other difficulties.

▶ Teaching as an art:
emotions, values,
flexibility

In summary, **teaching as an art** involves emotions, values, and flexibility. Because these characteristics are intangible, they can be very difficult, if not impossible, to teach. Teachers must find these qualities within themselves.

The argument for **teaching as a science** is equally persuasive. Scholars such as Paul Woodring (1957), Nathaniel Gage (1984), David Berliner (1986), and Lee Shulman (1986) agree that the science of teaching, as such, does not currently exist. But they contend that it is possible and good to have a *scientific basis* for the art of teaching. By drawing on established research findings, both prospective and practicing teachers can be taught many of the prerequisites that make "artistic" teaching possible. Also, as Robert Slavin (1989) persuasively argues, working from a scientific basis helps teachers avoid the pitfall of subscribing to the latest fad. This argument, of course, rests on the existence of a usable body of research findings, which educational psychologists believe does exist. As evidence, you might consult "The Quiet Revolution in Educational Research" (Walberg, Schiller, and Haertel, 1979) and "Productive Thinking and Instruction: Assessing the Knowledge Base" (Walberg, 1990). In both articles, Herbert Walberg identifies dozens of research-validated instructional practices that have been shown to improve achievement. For example, twenty-four of twenty-five studies found that giving teachers more instructional time—that is, giving students more time to learn—leads to higher achievement. (This finding is often used to support proposals for a longer school year.)

> Research provides a scientific basis for "artistic" teaching

Other studies have demonstrated the benefits of alerting students to important material through the use of objectives and pretests, getting students involved in a task through the use of questions and homework, and providing corrective feedback and reinforcement with written comments, verbal explanations, and praise. Another example of usable research can be found in the work of Berliner (1986) and Shulman (1986) on the characteristics of expert teachers. One reason some teachers are experts is that they can quickly and accurately recall relevant knowledge from two large areas: subject-matter knowledge and knowledge of classroom organization and management. From the research being done in this area, we are learning how expert teachers acquire this knowledge, recall it, and use it appropriately.

Look back at the heading of this section. Notice that it reads "Teaching as an Art *and* a Science," not "Teaching as an Art *Versus* Teaching as a Science." Our choice of wording indicates our belief that good teaching is a skillful blend of "artistic" and "scientific" elements. The teacher who attempts to base every action on scientific evidence is likely to come across as rigid and mechanical—perhaps even indecisive (when the scientific evidence is lacking or unclear). On the other hand, the teacher who ignores scientific knowledge about teaching and learning and focuses only on the need to excite and inspire students runs the risk of using methods and principles of teaching that are ineffective.

> Good teachers combine "artistic" and "scientific" characteristics

BECOMING A REFLECTIVE TEACHER

This blending of artistic and scientific elements can be seen in recent discussions of what is called **reflective teaching** (see, for example, *Educational Leadership,* March 1991; *Journal of Teacher Education,* March/April 1989; Schon, 1987; and

Reflective teachers think about what they do and why

Shulman, 1987). Reflective teachers think about the worthwhileness of the educational goals they are trying to achieve, the nature and effectiveness of the instructional techniques used to reach those goals, the assumptions behind the choice of instructional means and ends, and the extent to which scientific evidence supports their choice of means and ends. Jere Brophy and Janet Alleman (1991) illustrate the importance of thinking about long-range goals by pointing out how the choice of goals affects content coverage and how content coverage affects teachers' choice of classroom activities. If, for example, one goal is for students to acquire problem-solving skills, students would likely be engaged in activities that call for inquiring, reasoning, and decision-making. Debates, simulations, and laboratory experiments are just three examples of activities that might be used to meet such a goal. If, however, the goal is for students to memorize facts and information, students will likely be given activities that call for isolated memorization and recall. Worksheets and drill-and-practice exercises are typically used to meet this type of goal. The point, of course, is that effective teachers think about these issues as a basis for drawing up lesson plans.

Becoming a reflective teacher is not difficult, although it does require practice. As you try out various teaching techniques or wonder why certain pupils fail to respond to instruction, formulate hypotheses (tentative explanations) and then try to test them. You will rarely be able to do this in a completely controlled way, of course, but you can often set up what amount to simple experiments. If most of the students in your class tend to act restless and bored whenever you present

Reflective teachers set aside time to think about what they do in class, why they do it, and how their methods affect student performance. (1992 Bob Sacha)

a particular topic, for instance, you might test some hypotheses such as these, in an effort to do something about it:

Students will be less bored and restless if I arrange for them to be more active as they learn.

Providing a list of specific objectives to be achieved by the end of a thirty-minute study period will lead to more concentrated effort than simply telling students to read the text until the bell rings.

Reflective teachers
play roles of artist
and scientist

Once you establish one or more hypotheses, you can test them by trying out techniques that you think will work. As you use these techniques, play the role of artist and be enthusiastic and committed. Then play the role of scientist: Be objective when analyzing the results. If you find that your students respond more positively, or that test scores go up, or that projects improve, you have evidence to substantiate your hypothesis. If student behavior remains unchanged or deteriorates, however, formulate another hypothesis and test it.

One way to begin developing this reflective capacity is to follow our suggestion for compiling a personal Handbook of Teaching. The notion of a personal Handbook was introduced in the preface and is described in more detail in Chapter 15, "Becoming a Better Teacher." The section in that chapter entitled "Becoming a Better Teacher: Questions and Suggestions" contains a list of questions and suggestions organized by Handbook Headings that may help you identify and overcome weaknesses in your teaching technique. You can treat the questions as hypotheses and the suggestions that follow the questions as ways to test them. As you try them out, you can record the results and your personal reaction in your Handbook. Studies have shown that keeping a personal journal that focuses on the thoughts and feelings associated with particular teaching behaviors is an effective way to increase reflectiveness (e.g., Bolin, 1990).

THE CONTENTS OF THIS BOOK

In speculating about ways that psychology might be applied to teaching, a number of theorists have proposed what are often referred to as theories of instruction or models of learning (for example, see Mager, 1975; Carroll, 1963; Glaser, 1976; Bloom, 1976). The purpose of such theories or models is to provide a basic strategy for instruction.

Several theories of instruction will be discussed in subsequent chapters of this book. For now, however, note that these theories emphasize a basic four-step sequence that teachers might follow to make instruction as effective as possible:

1. Take into account what students are like and how much they know.
2. Specify what is to be learned.

3. Provide instruction by taking advantage of what has been discovered about learning, cognitive strategies, and motivation.

4. Determine if students *have* learned.

(Some models of learning suggest that the first step is to specify what is to be learned. While this is often a logical place to begin when dealing with college students, it may not be the best first step when dealing with younger students of various ages. Indeed, younger students tend to benefit when teachers initially consider their personal traits—how much they already know, their cognitive characteristics, how they behave in classrooms, and so forth.)

The contents of this book are arranged with reference to the sequence just described. Chapters 2 through 13 are grouped (as described below and diagrammed in Figure 1.1) to reflect and illustrate the four phases of the model of learning featured in this text. Chapters 14 and 15 provide additional helpful material on effective classroom management and improving teaching skills.

Part 1 Considering Student Characteristics

Chapter 2, "Stage Theories of Development," outlines and analyzes the most highly respected stage theories of development.

Chapter 3, "Age-Level Characteristics," describes the nature and pedagogical significance of selected characteristics of pupils at different grade levels.

Chapter 4, "Assessing Pupil Variability," discusses the nature of pupil variability and the role of standardized tests in its assessment.

Chapter 5, "Dealing with Pupil Variability," examines recent developments in the education of exceptional pupils and describes techniques for teaching pupils who require special educational provisions.

Chapter 6, "Understanding Cultural Diversity," describes cultural differences in perception, attitudes, values, and behavior, and how instructional practices can accommodate such differences.

Part 2 Specifying What Is to Be Learned

Chapter 7, "Devising and Using Objectives," offers suggestions for devising and using various kinds of instructional objectives.

Part 3 Providing Instruction

Chapter 8, "Behavioral Learning Theories," analyzes learning theories proposed by theorists who prefer to base their conclusions on observations of overt behavior and describes variations of programmed instructional techniques.

Chapter 9, "Information Processing Theory," analyzes ways in which humans encode, store, and retrieve information from memory.

Chapter 10, "Cognitive Learning Theories and Problem Solving," outlines concepts proposed by psychologists who have speculated about ways in which

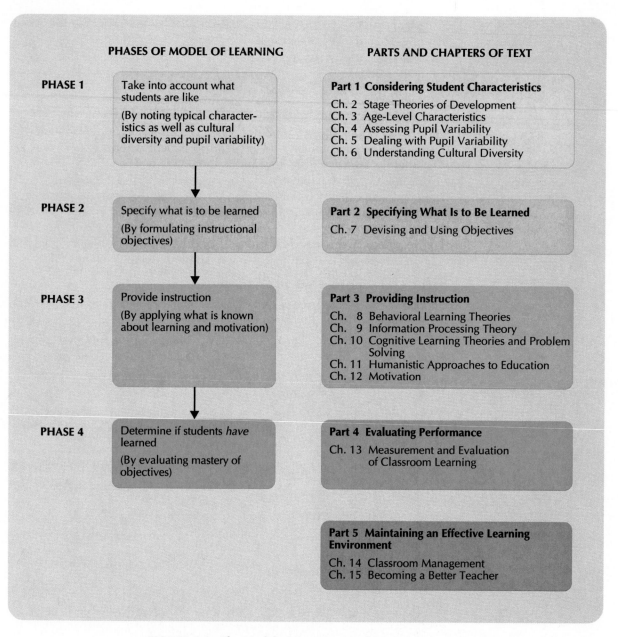

PHASES OF MODEL OF LEARNING

PARTS AND CHAPTERS OF TEXT

PHASE 1

Take into account what students are like

(By noting typical characteristics as well as cultural diversity and pupil variability)

Part 1 Considering Student Characteristics

Ch. 2 Stage Theories of Development
Ch. 3 Age-Level Characteristics
Ch. 4 Assessing Pupil Variability
Ch. 5 Dealing with Pupil Variability
Ch. 6 Understanding Cultural Diversity

PHASE 2

Specify what is to be learned

(By formulating instructional objectives)

Part 2 Specifying What Is to Be Learned

Ch. 7 Devising and Using Objectives

PHASE 3

Provide instruction

(By applying what is known about learning and motivation)

Part 3 Providing Instruction

Ch. 8 Behavioral Learning Theories
Ch. 9 Information Processing Theory
Ch. 10 Cognitive Learning Theories and Problem Solving
Ch. 11 Humanistic Approaches to Education
Ch. 12 Motivation

PHASE 4

Determine if students *have* learned

(By evaluating mastery of objectives)

Part 4 Evaluating Performance

Ch. 13 Measurement and Evaluation of Classroom Learning

Part 5 Maintaining an Effective Learning Environment

Ch. 14 Classroom Management
Ch. 15 Becoming a Better Teacher

FIGURE 1.1 The Model of Learning Used in Organizing This Book

humans solve problems and describes problem-solving techniques for different types of problems.

Chapter 11, "Humanistic Approaches to Education," discusses techniques of instruction intended to make teachers and pupils aware of feelings, interpersonal relationships, and values.

Chapter 12, "Motivation," examines several theories of motivation as background for developing a variety of ways to arouse and sustain student interest in learning.

Part 4 Evaluating Performance

Chapter 13, "Measurement and Evaluation of Classroom Learning," describes a variety of techniques for objectively and constructively determining whether instructional objectives have been met.

Part 5 Maintaining an Effective Learning Environment

Chapter 14, "Classroom Management," discusses approaches to classroom management and presents dozens of specific techniques for establishing and maintaining classroom control.

Chapter 15, "Becoming a Better Teacher," describes ways to cope with frustrations and provides suggestions for constantly improving your teaching effectiveness.

SPECIAL FEATURES OF THIS BOOK

Several distinctive features of this book merit comment since they are intended to be used in rather specialized ways. These features include Key Points, Suggestions for Teaching in Your Classroom, Handbook Headings, Questions and Suggestions for Becoming a Better Teacher, Applying Technology to Teaching, and Resources for Further Investigation. Each feature has been included for reasons explained below.

Key Points

At the beginning of each chapter, you will find a list of *Key Points*. The Key Points also appear within each chapter, printed in bold type in the margins. These points have been selected to help you learn and remember sections of each chapter that are considered to be of special significance to teachers. (They may be stressed on exams, but they were originally selected not to serve as the basis for test items, but because they are important.) If you were to try to learn everything in this book, you would be working against yourself because some of the information you might memorize would interfere with the acquisition of other information. To reduce forgetting due to such interference, you are asked to concentrate on only a few sections in each chapter. To grasp the nature of Key Points, turn to pages 38–39, which list points stressed under the major headings of Chapter 2. Then flip through the chapter to see how their appearance in the margins calls attention to significant sections of the text.

Suggestions for Teaching in Your Classroom

In most of the chapters of this book, you will find summaries of research that serve as the basis for related principles or conclusions. These sets of principles or conclusions, in turn, serve as the basis for *Suggestions for Teaching in Your Classroom*. Each suggestion is usually followed by a list of examples illustrating how it might be applied. In most cases examples are provided for both elementary and secondary grades since there usually are differences in the way a principle might be applied in dealing with younger and older pupils.

The principles, suggestions, and examples are intended to help you think about how you can apply psychology to teaching. The lists of Suggestions for Teaching in Your Classroom and the examples of some ways of applying principles are intended to help you compensate, at least partially, for lack of experience when you begin to teach. Since you will often want to find quick answers with a minimum of difficulty, applications of principles are first listed as sets of related ideas (which you can later refer to as reminders and as an "index" to detailed analyses of each point). Then each point is discussed and illustrated, in most cases by multiple examples. To permit you to find information relating to particular aspects of teaching, an index to the Suggestions for Teaching in Your Classroom is printed inside the back cover. To discover the nature of the Suggestions for Teaching in Your Classroom, turn to page 55. Read the list of suggestions, and then examine the following pages to become acquainted with the detailed suggestions and examples of applications.

Developing a Personal Handbook of Teaching

The Suggestions for Teaching in Your Classroom and the examples of applications are intended to help you prepare for your initial teaching experiences. It is impossible to supply for each point discussed information that will have direct relevance to all teachers. Therefore you should not expect to find under every list of suggestions an example that will be directly applicable to the grade level and subject you hope to teach. Most of the time you will need to devise your own specific applications of principles. To help you do this and to help reduce the pressure and tension of your student-teaching experience and your first years of professional teaching, you are urged to develop your own personal Handbook of Teaching. Since you may need to concentrate on learning Key Points in order to demonstrate understanding on exams during the course you are now taking, you may not have time to prepare a Handbook this quarter or semester. But after you have read this book as a text, you might go through it a second time for the purpose of developing a custom-designed Handbook. Record your ideas in a notebook, and leave space for ideas that occur to you during methods courses, during your student teaching, and during your first years as a full-time teacher. To allow room for expansion, you might purchase a three-ring binder so that pages can be added or dropped.

One way to organize your Handbook would be to revise and expand the lists of Suggestions for Teaching in Your Classroom presented in each chapter. If you write out your own version of these suggestions, devise your own examples of applications, and prepare an index, you will equip yourself with a custom-designed guidebook that should assist you in coping with many of the problems you will encounter when you first take over a classroom. To further help you organize your Handbook, frequent Handbook Headings are inserted in page margins opposite selected points. These headings are intended to serve as an outline you can use to amplify, supplement, and personalize the basic Suggestions for Teaching in Your Classroom provided in the text. You might print each heading under the appropriate suggestions for teaching recorded in your Handbook and then list any specific techniques you can remember or invent that relate to that aspect of teaching. On page 406, for instance, you will find "Handbook Heading: Ways to Make Learning Active." That heading is intended to stimulate you to jot down specific ways to motivate your pupils by working activity into lessons. To begin, you might search your memory for techniques used by your former teachers. Did your fifth-grade teacher, for instance, have a clever way of arranging for you and your classmates to move around as you studied? Describe the technique so you will remember to try it yourself. Did a high school teacher have an ingenious way of inducing you to work actively with others on group projects? Exactly how did she or he do it? After you exhaust your own recollections, ask roommates or classmates if they can remember any successful ways that *their* teachers made learning active. Next, look at the examples provided opposite the Handbook Heading. To grasp how you might proceed, turn to page 406 and examine the examples opposite "Handbook Heading: Ways to Make Learning Active." Which ones seem most appropriate for the grade level and subject you will be teaching? Jot them down. Do any of the examples suggest variations you can think of on your own? Write them down before you forget them. Finally, add ideas that you pick up in methods classes or during your student-teaching experience. If you see a film in a methods class that shows how a teacher makes learning active, describe it in your Handbook. If your master teacher uses a successful technique to permit students to move around as they learn, record it.

If you follow some or all of these suggestions for using the Handbook Headings, you will have a rich source of ideas to turn to when you discover that your students seem bored and listless because of inactivity and you find yourself wondering if there is anything you can do about it.

Becoming a Better Teacher

The Suggestions for Teaching in Your Classroom and the recommendation that you prepare a personal Handbook are intended to stimulate you to think about how you can apply what you learn. Such preparation for a teaching career may ease some of the trials and tribulations of your first few months in the classroom, but it will not eliminate problems. There are simply too many things to learn and to deal with at once. Furthermore, even if you have thought ahead about what you would like to do in a given situation, you may discover that, for one reason or another, it is extremely difficult or impossible to put your ideas into practice. Or you may become aware that you are so preoccupied with some aspects of teaching that you have slighted other facets of instruction.

For all these reasons, it will be to your advantage during the first months or years of your teaching career to make a systematic effort to evaluate selected aspects of your instructional technique. Otherwise, you may simply "do what comes naturally." Even with the guidance of this text, a personal Handbook, and other books on teaching, you will not be able to think of everything at once. To make it possible for you to analyze selected aspects of your teaching style over a period of time, questions and suggestions you might use to improve your teaching are listed in Chapter 15, "Becoming a Better Teacher."

You might use the questions and suggestions in "Becoming a Better Teacher" in two ways: (1) as troubleshooting aids when you are confronted with a specific, identifiable problem and (2) as a basis for systematic evaluations. To put the latter procedure into operation, you might make it a habit—at least during the first year of your teaching career—to take a few moments at the end of each school day to examine the questions for one chapter. If you feel that you might improve your teaching by concentrating on techniques highlighted by a particular question, plan a step-by-step campaign. The next day peruse the questions for the next chapter, and so on. If you follow this procedure for a few weeks, you should systematically evaluate all aspects of teaching discussed in this book. You will also know where to find information on different facets of teaching. Then, when you see the need to improve some phase of instruction, you will know exactly where to look for help, and you will have your own step-by-step plan for solving a particular problem.

Applying Technology to Teaching

As a teacher in the 1990s, you will want to be knowledgeable about the many ways educational technology—and computer technology in particular—can enhance your students' learning. For this reason, we have added a section called Applying Technology to Teaching to each of the learning theories chapters in Part 3. The suggestions in these sections can give you an idea of the many different ways that you can use technology in your own classroom teaching. You might wish to try some of the suggested software yourself to see how they function—and to help you develop your ability to select good software to meet the needs of your students and your own teaching goals.

Resources for Further Investigation

In the chapters that follow, you will find suggestions that cover many facets of teaching. You are likely to conclude, however, that information on particular aspects of teaching is not complete enough. Despite the book's attempt to provide at least partial solutions to the most common difficulties faced by teachers, you are bound, sooner or later, to become aware of problems that are not discussed in these pages. You may want additional data on some aspects of teaching, either while you are taking this course or after you are experienced enough to have time for a detailed look at some facet of education, psychology, or instruction. To allow for instances where you will need additional information, an annotated bibliography is provided at the end of each chapter. Resources for Further Investigation list articles and books you might consult for detailed information on many topics. Instructions for carrying out simple do-it-yourself studies are also included in the Resources for Further Investigation at the end of many chapters.

Resources for Further Investigation

Professional Journals

In order to gain some direct experience with the raw material of psychology—the building blocks that are eventually combined to establish a principle or theory—you might examine one or more of the professional journals in psychology. These journals consist primarily of reports of experiments. The following journals are likely to be found in a typical college library:

American Educational Research Journal

Behavioral Science

Child Development

Developmental Psychology

Educational and Psychological Measurement

Exceptional Child

Genetic Psychology Monographs

Harvard Educational Review

Journal of Abnormal and Social Psychology

Journal of Applied Behavior Analysis

Journal of Educational Psychology

Journal of Educational Research

Journal of Educational Sociology

Journal of Experimental Child Psychology

Journal of Experimental Education

Journal of Experimental Psychology

Journal of Teacher Education

Merrill-Palmer Quarterly of Behavior and Development

Psychological Monographs

Psychological Review

Psychology in the Schools

Society for Research in Child Development Monographs

To develop an awareness of the nature of research in psychology, examine recent issues of some of these journals. Then, select an article describing an experiment that intrigues you or appears to be relevant to your own interests, grade level, and subject. Finally, write an abstract (a brief summary of results) of the article, including the following information:

Author of article

Title of article

Journal in which article appears (including date, volume number, and page numbers)

Purpose (or description of problem)

Subjects

Procedure (or methods)

Treatment of data

Results

Conclusions

Are there any criticisms that you can make of the procedure or conclusions?

What inferences for your own teaching can you draw from this experiment?

Would you be willing to change your methods of teaching on the strength of this one article?

Journals of Abstracts and Reviews

Unless you are familiar with research in a particular aspect of educational psychology, you may find it difficult either to fit an individual study reported in a journal into a general framework or to relate it to other similar research. In most cases, it is prudent to find out what other experiments of a similar type have revealed about a particular point before making generalizations from the results of a single study. A variety of journals and reference works exist to assist you in doing this. The following journals consist of abstracts of articles that appear in the types of journals listed in the preceding section:

Child Development Abstracts and Bibliography

Exceptional Child Education Abstracts

Psychological Abstracts

Psyc SCAN

The journal *Contemporary Psychology* reviews new books in psychology, and the *Annual Review of Psychology* provides information reflected by the title—that is, a specialist in each of several areas of psychology reviews significant studies that have appeared during a given year.

The *Review of Educational Research* features articles that describe, relate, and analyze reports of studies on a particular theme.

To discover the nature of these journals and reference works, examine some of them and perhaps prepare a brief description of the most promising titles to save for future reference. Or select a topic of interest, search for reports of experiments, and summarize the conclusions you reach.

Journals That Describe Trends and Techniques

In addition to descriptions of actual experiments, "discussion" articles are published in some professional journals and in many teachers' magazines. Listed below are journals of this type.

Journals Consisting of General Discussions of Trends, Developments, and Techniques The following journals describe trends, developments, and techniques and also interpret research data. Some articles cite research studies; others offer interpretations of approaches to teaching without reference to specific data. Many of these journals also feature sections on tricks of the trade, and most provide book reviews.

> *Change in Higher Education*
>
> *Clearing House* (junior and senior high school teaching)
>
> *Contemporary Education*
>
> *Elementary School Journal*
>
> *Exceptional Children*
>
> *Journal of General Education*
>
> *Journal of Higher Education* (college and university teaching)
>
> *Junior College Journal*
>
> *Phi Delta Kappa*
>
> *Teachers College Record*
>
> *Theory into Practice*

Journals Consisting of Brief Commentaries on Trends, Developments, and Techniques The following journals consist of short articles (usually fewer than five pages each) on trends, developments, and techniques in education:

> *American Journal of Education*
>
> *Childhood Education*
>
> *Education*
>
> *Educational Forum*
>
> *Educational Leadership*
>
> *Educational Record* (college and university teaching)
>
> *Educational Technology* (computer-assisted instruction, behavior modification)
>
> *Electronic Learning*
>
> *High School Journal*
>
> *Journal of Education*

Note: *Education Digest* is made up of condensations of articles selected from the types of journals listed in this section and the preceding one.

Magazines for Teachers   The following publications provide articles, usually in magazine format, with emphasis on journalistic style, abundant illustrations, and colorful graphic design:

> *Instructor*
>
> *Learning*
>
> *NEA Today*
>
> *Psychology Today*

If you look through some recent issues of several of these journals, you will find typical trend-and-technique articles on psychology and education. For future reference, you might read an article that is relevant to your own interests, grade level, and subject and then write a synopsis of the author's arguments. If any of these arguments are pertinent to your own theorizing about teaching, briefly analyze your thoughts, perhaps by using the following outline:

> Author of article
>
> Name of article
>
> Journal in which article appeared (including date, volume number, and page numbers)
>
> Synopsis of arguments presented
>
> Your reaction to the arguments

Specialized Publications for Teachers

Almost every field of study in education has one or more journals devoted to reports of research, reviews of related experimental studies, discussions of teaching techniques, descriptions of tricks of the trade, and analyses of subject matter. The following list of journals may help you discover what is available in your area or areas of interest:

African Studies Journal	*Educational Theatre News*
Agricultural Education Magazine	*Elementary School Guidance and Counseling*
American Biology Teacher	*English Language Teaching Journal*
American Music Teacher	
American Speech	*English Studies*
American String Teacher	*Forecast* (home economics)
Arithmetic Teacher	*French Review*
Art Education	*Geography Teacher*
Business Education World	*Gifted Child Quarterly*
Communication Quarterly	*History Teacher*
Education and Training in Mental Retardation	*Industrial Arts and Vocational Education*

Instrumentalist

Journal of Industrial Teacher Education

Journal of Negro Education

Journal of Nursing Education

Journal of Reading

Journal of Research in Science Teaching

Journal of School Health

Journal of Special Education

Journal of Vocational Education Research

Language Arts

Marriage and Family Living

Mathematics Teacher

Music Educators Journal

Physical Educator

Physics Teacher

Reading Teacher

Scholastic Coach

School Arts

School Counselor

School Musician Director and Teacher

School Science and Mathematics

School Shop–Technical Directions

Science Education

Science Teacher

Swimming Technique

Teaching Exceptional Children

Tennis

Theatre World

Track Technique

To discover what is available, check titles that sound promising, spend some time in the periodicals section of your college library, and examine some recent issues. You might select an article you find interesting and write an abstract of it, together with your own interpretation. Or you might prepare a brief description of journals that impress you as worthy of attention. This list could serve as a source of information on what journals to consult after you begin your teaching career.

Educational Resources Information Center (ERIC)

As a number of journals listed on the preceding pages indicate, thousands of articles are published each year on every conceivable aspect of educational psychology and education. To assist psychologists and educators to discover what has been published on a specific topic, the Educational Resources Information Center was established by the U.S. Office of Education (now called the U.S. Department of Education). ERIC publishes two sources of information:

Current Index to Journals in Education—Annual Cumulation contains an index of articles in over three hundred education and education-oriented journals published in a given year. There are four sections in each volume: a Subject Index (which lists titles of articles organized under hundreds of subject headings), an Author Index, a Journal Contents Index (which lists the table of contents for each issue of journals published that year), and a Main Entry Section (which provides the title, author, journal reference, and a brief abstract of articles published in journals covered by the index).

Resources in Education lists curriculum guides, speeches, research reviews, convention papers, reports, and monographs not published in journals. The Document Résumé section presents descriptions of the documents arranged according to the ERIC classification scheme, together with information about where each can be obtained. There is also a Subject Index (in which titles of documents are listed according to the ERIC classification), an Author Index, an Institution Index (in which titles of articles are listed with reference to source), and a Publication Type Index. The documents cited in *Resources in Education* are available from the ERIC Document Reproduction Service in both microfiche and paper copy form.

You are urged to examine a recent issue of these publications to discover what is available in the ERIC network and how you might obtain information.

SUMMARY

1. Unsystematic observations of students may lead teachers to draw false conclusions because of limited cases, unrecognized or unusual factors, and a tendency to ignore contrary evidence.

2. Even though scientific evidence does not support the practice of grade retention, it remains popular among teachers and parents because of unsystematic observations about its effectiveness.

3. Scientifically gathered evidence is more trustworthy than casual observation because it involves sampling, control, objectivity, publication, and replication.

4. The scientific study of education is complicated by the limited focus of research, individual differences in perception and thinking, the inability of researchers to keep up with all published research, different interpretations of findings, and the ongoing accumulation of new knowledge.

5. Research on teaching and learning gives you a systematic, objective basis for making instructional decisions, but it cannot tell you how to handle every classroom situation. Many classroom decisions must be made on the spot. This contrast represents the science and art of teaching.

6. Those who argue that teaching is an art point to communication of emotions, to values, and to

flexibility as qualities that good teachers must possess but which are not easily taught.

7. Certain scholars contend that there is a scientific basis for the art of teaching that can be taught by drawing on established research findings.

8. Good teachers strike a balance between the art and science of teaching.

9. Reflective teachers constantly think about such issues as the worthwhileness of the goals they are trying to achieve, the types of teaching methods they use and how effective those methods are, and the extent to which their methods and goals are supported by scientific evidence.

KEY TERMS

teaching as an art   *(19)*
teaching as a science   *(20)*
reflective teaching   *(20)*

DISCUSSION QUESTIONS

1. Imagine that you are a second-grade teacher at the end of the school year. You have just finished telling your principal about a student who performed so poorly during the year that you question whether the student is adequately prepared for third grade. The principal suggests that the child should repeat second grade next year.

Given what you know about the research on retention, how would you respond to the principal's suggestion?

2. Think of or identify a popular instructional practice. Would you classify that practice as a fad or as the outgrowth of accumulated scientific knowledge? Why? How can you tell the difference between the two?

3. To play the role of teacher as artist effectively, you need to display enthusiasm and a sense of worthwhileness about the content you cover and the methods you use. At some point, however, you may be asked to teach a grade level or a subject for which you have little enthusiasm, or you may grow bored teaching the same grade level or subject in the same way year after year. How will you fulfill the role of teacher-artist if faced with these conditions?

4. The point was made in this chapter that good teachers strike a balance between the art and science of teaching. How do they do it? Are they born with the right type of personality? Are they the products of good teacher education programs? Or is some combination of these elements at work? If you believe that both factors play a role, which do you feel is more important?

5. To play the role of reflective teacher effectively, you need to set aside regular blocks of time to think about your actions and make new plans. Most teachers complain about having insufficient time to reflect and plan. What would you do to make more time available?

Part 1
CONSIDERING STUDENT CHARACTERISTICS

Chapter 2

STAGE THEORIES OF DEVELOPMENT

▶ Equilibration: tendency to organize schemes to allow better understanding of experiences

▶ Sensorimotor stage: schemes reflect sensory and motor experiences

▶ Preoperational stage: child forms many new schemes but does not think logically

▶ Perceptual centration, irreversibility, egocentrism: barriers to logical thought

▶ Egocentrism: assumption that others see things the same way

▶ Concrete operational stage: child is capable of mentally reversing actions but generalizes only from concrete experiences

▶ Formal operational stage: child is able to deal with abstractions, form hypotheses, engage in mental manipulations

▶ Adolescent egocentrism: one's thoughts and actions are as central to others as to oneself

▶ Instruction can accelerate development of schemes that have begun to form

▶ Vygotsky: cognitive development due to instruction in zone of proximal development

▶ Piaget's theory underestimates children's abilities

▶ Most adolescents are not formal operational thinkers

PIAGET, KOHLBERG, AND GILLIGAN: MORAL DEVELOPMENT

▶ Moral relativism: rules are flexible, intent important in determining guilt

▶ Moral realism: sacred rules, no exceptions, no allowance for intentions, consequences determine guilt

▶ Preconventional morality: avoid punishment, receive benefits in return

▶ Conventional morality: impress others, respect authority

▶ Postconventional morality: mutual agreements, consistent principles

▶ Moral education programs may produce modest acceleration in moral development

▶ Males and females may use different approaches to resolve real-life moral dilemmas

▶ Moral behavior depends on circumstances

In our discussion of theories of instruction and models of learning in Chapter 1, we pointed out that a logical first step for teachers, when planning instruction, is to take into account what students are like and how much they know. The term *entering behavior* is sometimes used to refer to the characteristics and knowledge that students possess at the beginning of a sequence of instruction. The types of behavior that students exhibit when they enter a learning situation are important for a teacher to know, and that is why this first part is devoted to descriptions of both typical and variant behavior.

Because the field of developmental psychology includes so many topics that have been studied intensively, separate courses are often given on infancy, early childhood, childhood, adolescence, and adulthood. If you have taken (or plan to take) one or more such courses, you will gain an understanding of the process of development and become familiar with the direction and significance of current research. The five chapters that make up this first part are intended to call your attention to aspects of human development that particularly concern teachers and to encourage you to make use of that knowledge.

For example, after you read these chapters, you should be able to answer the following questions:

What psychosocial stages of development described by Erik Erikson are significant at the preschool, elementary, and secondary school levels?

What are two key factors that contribute to an adolescent's sense of identity?

What cognitive stages of development described by Jean Piaget are significant at the preschool, elementary, and secondary school levels?

How does the moral reasoning of primary grade pupils differ from that of secondary grade students?

How does the rate of physical development influence the behavior of boys and girls?

What are some differences in the aptitudes and attitudes toward school of boys and girls?

What sorts of emotional disorders are most common in male and female secondary school students?

What is Public Law 94-142, and what significance does it have for teachers?

How do students' cultural background and social class affect their classroom behavior?

Human development is a difficult topic to discuss because, in addition to analyzing many different forms of behavior, one must trace the way each type of behavior changes as a child matures. Authors of books on development have adopted different strategies to cope with this problem. Some have described theories outlining stages in the emergence of particular forms of behavior. Others have written books that summarize significant types of behavior at successive age levels. Still others have written books made up of chapters devoted to specific types of behavior, noting age changes for every topic. Each approach has advantages and disadvantages.

Theories call attention to the overall sequence, continuity, and interrelatedness of aspects of development, but they typically account for only limited facets of behavior. Texts organized in terms of age levels make the reader aware of varied aspects of children's behavior at a given age but sometimes tend to obscure how particular types of behavior emerge and change. And although texts organized according to types of behavior do not have the limitation of the age-level approach, they may make it difficult for the reader to grasp the overall pattern of behavior at a particular stage of development.

In an effort to profit from the advantages and to minimize the disadvantages of each approach, Chapters 2 and 3 present discussions of development that combine all three. Chapter 2 focuses principally on Erik Erikson's psychosocial stages and Jean Piaget's cognitive stages. It also describes Piaget's ideas about moral development, Lawrence Kohlberg's extension of Piaget's work, and Carol Gilligan's criticism and modification of Kohlberg's theory. Chapter 3 describes age-level characteristics of pupils at five levels—preschool, primary and elementary grades, and junior high and high school. Discussion at each age level focuses on four types of behavior—physical, social, emotional, and cognitive. The information in these chapters will help you adapt teaching techniques to the pupils who are in the age range that you expect to teach. The first two chapters in this part describe patterns of behavior exhibited by typical children and adolescents. The following three chapters are devoted to student variability. Chapter 4 discusses the assessment of variability; Chapter 5 describes types of students who vary from their classmates to such an extent that they may require special kinds of education; and Chapter 6 describes the characteristics of students from different ethnic and social-class backgrounds.

ERIKSON: PSYCHOSOCIAL DEVELOPMENT

To better comprehend what they have learned and to impose at least a degree of order on related types of information, scientists propose theories. In a book on theories of development, Patricia Miller (1989) notes that an ideal theory has four characteristics: (1) It is logically consistent in that one part of the theory does not contradict another part; (2) It is not contradicted by existing research evidence; (3) It allows specific predictions about behavior that are verifiable through research; and (4) it integrates and makes sense of related research findings. While no current developmental theory meets all of these criteria, the views of Erikson (as well as those of Piaget) come closer than most. Another reason for studying Erickson's theory is that parts of it highlight the role teachers play in helping students develop a strong self-concept through their adjustment to the demands of school and society at large.

▶ Theories organize facts and guide research

Factors That Influenced Erikson

Erik Erikson was born in Germany of Danish parents. An indifferent student, he left high school without graduating and spent several years wandering around Europe and attending various art schools. At the age of twenty-five, he became friends with someone who later secured a job tutoring the children of an American woman who was being psychoanalyzed by Sigmund Freud. When some acquaintances of the woman asked if their children might also receive

Erik Erikson described how social and cultural factors influence the course of personality development. (Sarah Putnam/The Picture Cube)

instruction, the friend decided to start a school and asked Erikson to come to Vienna to assist him. Eventually, Erikson was introduced to Freud, who was impressed by the young man and invited him to prepare for a career as a psychoanalyst. Erikson completed his training just at the time Hitler came to power, and to escape from the tension building up in Europe, he decided to come to America. He taught at Harvard, Yale, and the University of California at Berkeley, did private counseling, and became interested in studying Native American tribes. He also did research on normal and abnormal children and served as a psychotherapist for soldiers during World War II. These experiences led Erikson to conclude that Freud's tendency to stay in Vienna and interact with only a small and very select group of individuals had prevented the founder of psychoanalysis from fully appreciating how social and cultural factors (for example, values, attitudes, beliefs, and customs) influence behavior, perception, and thinking. Erikson decided to formulate a theory of development based on psychoanalytic principles but taking into account such influences.

▶ Personality development based on epigenetic principle

Erikson bases his description of personality development on the **epigenetic principle.** In fetal development, certain organs of the body appear at certain specified times and eventually "combine" to form a child. Erikson hypothesizes that just as the parts of the body develop in interrelated ways in a human fetus, so the personality of an individual forms as the ego progresses through a series of interrelated stages. All these ego stages exist in some form from the very beginning, but each has a critical period of development.

▶ Personality grows out of successful resolution of dichotomies

In Erikson's view, personality development is a series of turning points or psychological crises, which he describes in terms of dichotomies of desirable qualities and dangers. Erikson does not mean to imply by this scheme that only positive qualities should emerge and that any manifestation of potentially dangerous traits is undesirable. He emphasizes that people are best able to adapt to their world when they possess both the positive and negative qualities of a particular stage, provided the positive quality is significantly stronger than the negative quality. Try to imagine, for example, the personality of an individual who was never mistrustful (stage 1) or who never felt guilt (stage 3). Only when the negative quality outweighs the positive for any given stage or when the outcome for most stages is negative do difficulties in development and adjustment arise (Hall, 1983).

As you read through the following brief descriptions, keep in mind that a positive resolution of the issue for each stage depends on how well the issue of the previous stage was resolved. An adolescent who at the end of the industry vs. inferiority stage strongly doubts her own capabilities and devalues the quality of her work, for example, will likely have a difficult time making the occupational commitments required for identity development (Marcia, 1991).

Stages of Psychosocial Development

The following designations, age ranges, and essential characteristics of the stages of personality development are proposed by Erikson in *Childhood and Society* (1963).[1]

Trust vs. Mistrust (Birth to 1 Year)   The basic psychosocial attitude to be learned by infants is that they can trust their world. Trust is fostered by "consistency, continuity, and sameness of experience" in the satisfaction of the infant's basic needs by the parents. If the needs of infants are met and if parents communicate genuine affection, children will think of their world as safe and dependable. Conversely, if care is inadequate, inconsistent, or negative, children will approach their world with fear and suspicion.

2 to 3 years: auton-
omy vs. shame and
doubt

Autonomy vs. Shame and Doubt (2 to 3 Years)   Just when children have learned to trust (or mistrust) their parents, they must exert a degree of independence. If toddlers are permitted and encouraged to do what they are capable of doing at their own pace and in their own way—but with judicious supervision by parents and teachers—they will develop a sense of autonomy. But if parents and teachers are impatient and do too many things for young children, two- and three-year-olds may doubt their ability to deal with the environment. Furthermore, adults should avoid shaming young children for unacceptable behavior, since shaming is likely to contribute to feelings of self-doubt.

4 to 5 years: initia-
tive vs. guilt

Initiative vs. Guilt (4 to 5 Years)   The ability to participate in many physical activities and to use language sets the stage for initiative, which "adds to autonomy the quality of undertaking, planning, and 'attacking' a task for the sake

1. All quotations under "Stages of Psychosocial Development" are drawn from Chapter 7 of *Childhood and Society*.

of being active and on the move." If four- and five-year-olds are given freedom to explore and experiment, and if parents and teachers take time to answer questions, tendencies toward initiative will be encouraged. Conversely, if children of this age are restricted and made to feel that their activities and questions are pointless or a nuisance, they will feel guilty about doing things on their own.

6 to 11 years: industry vs. inferiority

Industry vs. Inferiority (6 to 11 Years)   A child entering school is at a point in development when behavior is dominated by intellectual curiosity and performance. "He now learns to win recognition by producing things . . . he develops a sense of industry." The danger at this stage is that the child may experience feelings of inadequacy or inferiority. If the child is encouraged to make and do things well, helped to persevere, allowed to finish tasks, and praised for trying, industry results. If the child's efforts are unsuccessful or if they are derided or treated as bothersome, a feeling of inferiority results. Children who feel inferior may never learn to enjoy intellectual work and take pride in doing at least one kind of thing really well. At worst, they may believe they will never excel at anything.

12 to 18 years: identity vs. role confusion

Identity vs. Role Confusion (12 to 18 Years)   As young adults approach independence from parents and achieve physical maturity, they are concerned about what kind of persons they are becoming. The goal at this stage is development of ego identity, "the accrued confidence of sameness and continuity." The danger at this stage is role confusion, particularly doubt about sexual and occupational identity. If adolescents succeed (as reflected by the reactions of others) in integrating roles in different situations to the point of experiencing continuity in their perception of self, identity develops. If they are unable to establish a sense of stability in various aspects of their lives, role confusion results.

Intimacy vs. Isolation (Young Adulthood)   To experience satisfying development at this stage, the young adult needs to establish a close and committed intimate relationship with another person. Failure to do so will lead to a sense of isolation.

Generativity vs. Stagnation (Middle Age)   "Generativity . . . is primarily the concern of establishing and guiding the next generation." Erikson's use of the term *generativity* is purposely broad. It refers, of course, to having children and raising them. In addition, it refers to the productive and creative efforts in which adults take part that have a positive effect on younger generations (for example, teaching, doing medical research, supporting political and social policies that will benefit future generations). Those unable or unwilling to "establish" and "guide" the next generation become victims of stagnation and self-absorption.

Integrity vs. Despair (Old Age)   Integrity is "the acceptance of one's one and only life cycle as something that had to be and that, by necessity, permitted of no substitutions. . . . Despair expresses the feeling that the time is now short, too short for the attempt to start another life and to try out alternate roads to integrity."

Factors Affecting Identity

The most complex and misunderstood of Erikson's stages is identity vs. role confusion. Erikson has written more extensively about this stage than any other. His observations and those of researchers stimulated by his work (e.g., James Marcia, Alan Waterman, and Carol Gilligan) can be very instructive, not only to those who will be teaching adolescents but also to young adults who are in the process of establishing their own identities. Even if you do not plan to teach high school students, careful consideration of what Erikson and other psychologists have to say about identity may help you understand your own behavior better.

▶ Identity: acceptance of body, having goals, getting recognition

The terms *identity* and *identity crisis* have become so popularized that it is important to review Erikson's original meanings. Here is how he describes the concept of **identity:** "An optimal sense of identity . . . is experienced merely as a sense of psychosocial well-being. Its most obvious concomitants are a feeling

Identity, as Erikson defines it, involves acceptance of one's body, knowing where one is going, and recognition from those who count. A high school graduate who is pleased with his or her appearance, who has already decided on a college major, and who is admired by parents, relatives, and friends is likely to experience a sense of psychosocial well-being. (Bob Daemmrich)

of being at home in one's body, a sense of 'knowing where one is going' and an inner assuredness of anticipated recognition from those who count" (1968, p. 165).

The danger in adolescence is **role confusion:** having no clear conception of appropriate types of behavior that others will react to favorably. Erikson suggests that adolescence is a critical period in development because "new identifications are no longer characterized by the playfulness of childhood; . . . with dire urgency they force the young individual into choices and decisions which will, with increasing immediacy, lead to commitments 'for life' " (1968, p. 155).

▶ Role confusion: uncertainty as to what behaviors others will react to favorably

Clearly, then, the task of forming a stable identity and avoiding role confusion is a difficult one for adolescents, even under the best of circumstances. When social values begin to change, identity formation is made more difficult still. Beliefs about appropriate sex role behavior are one area in which such changes affect identity formation.

Changes in Sex Roles   Erikson believes that sex roles are particularly important in the development of identity because they establish a pattern for many types of behaviors. Until relatively recently (the early 1960s), there was little confusion about appropriate characteristics and activities for males and females in American society. Almost all adult males and females were expected to marry. Husband and wife would then take on well-defined and clearly established responsibilities: The man would function as the breadwinner, the woman would serve as the homemaker and child rearer. This certainty provided a clear code of behavior for those who had or were eager to develop those characteristics; but it created problems for those who did not, especially adolescent girls.

▶ Sex roles establish patterns for many behaviors

The typical female adolescent in the America of the 1950s did not formulate as clear a sense of identity as the typical male adolescent because she assumed that what she would become as an adult depended to a large extent on the man she would marry. The kind of job he secured after marriage and his success at that job would influence her conception of herself perhaps more than her own behavior (Douvan & Adelson, 1966).

▶ Traditionally, male identity linked to job, female identity linked to husband

Over the last thirty years, interpretations of appropriate behavior for men and women have changed dramatically. More than 60 percent of all mothers of school-age children now work outside the home. The high rate of divorce has led to a significant number of single-parent households. And in a growing number of families, both parents hold jobs. Several factors seem to be responsible for these trends: the need for increased family income to meet current lifestyles and future goals; a large increase in the number of jobs traditionally held by women (clerical workers, secretaries, telephone operators, teachers); increased opportunities for women in occupations that have been dominated by men; and a change in women's attitudes about the nature of the female sex role. A 1985 survey of women's attitudes found that 63 percent felt that combining marriage, career, and child rearing was the best alternative for a satisfying and interesting life (Borker, 1987).

▶ Female identity linked to job more now than in past

Because of the changing attitude toward the role of women in our society, the young woman of the 1990s is more likely to feel that her destiny is in her own hands than her mother did when she was the same age. The opportunity for self-fulfillment obviously opens up many other opportunities. But change in social values is a gradual process. There are still many people who hold traditional views of male and female roles and believe in traditional approaches to child rearing. The end product can be confusion and problems, especially for the adolescent who is trying to develop a clear sense of what it means to be a male or female.

Factors That Perpetuate Sex Roles Inge Broverman and several associates (1972) analyzed perceptions of "typical" masculine and feminine traits. There was considerable unanimity of opinion from respondents of both sexes, all age levels, and all types of backgrounds: Men were pictured as competent, rational, and assertive; women were thought of as warm and expressive. These sex role standards are remarkably robust and long-lived. David J. Bergen and John E. Williams (1991) replicated the Broverman et al. study in 1988 and found an almost identical pattern of responses despite the passage of sixteen years. John E. Williams and Deborah L. Best (1990) found similar perceptions in North and South America, Europe, Africa, Asia, and Australia.

What gives rise to these stereotypes is still an open question, although parenting behaviors are thought to be very influential. Parents, particularly fathers, emphasize achievement and exploration more for boys than for girls. Girls tend to be kept under closer supervision and are given more help in solving problems. As a consequence, they are much more likely than boys to ask for help—a tendency that is strengthened by the positive responses of adults. Boys, on the other hand, are often told directly or indirectly to handle things themselves. In the area of play, boys generally are given toys or are encouraged to participate in activities that involve exploration of the physical world (for example, baseball, blocks, construction toys, cars, and science kits); girls are encouraged to participate in activities that involve quiet play and imitation of interpersonal behavior (for example, doll play, dressing up, drawing, and painting) (Block, 1973; Carter, 1987; Fagot, 1978; Fagot & Leinbach, 1987). There are indications that adolescents come under increasing pressure by family members, peers, and teachers to engage in gender-appropriate behavior. One indication is a noticeable increase in academically related and socially related sex-typed behaviors. Girls, for instance, become less interested than boys in math and science but more interested in intimate interpersonal relationships (Crockett, 1991).

Social modeling (which we discuss in detail in Chapter 8) is another process that has long been suspected of contributing to the formation of sex role stereotypes. Analyses of television programs, for example, have shown that the ratio of male to female characters is about 70 to 30 (despite the fact that females outnumber males 52 percent to 48 percent in the real world), that females occupy

▶ American boys encouraged to be independent, active, exploratory; girls encouraged to be dependent, quiet

Boys who observe their fathers engaging in traditionally "feminine" activities (such as cooking) are likely to develop a flexible view of sex roles and be rated high in psychological androgyny. (Elizabeth Crews)

starring roles only about 30 percent of the time, that male characters are more often shown in high-status occupations, and that males are more likely to be shown as aggressive. Because of problems in defining and measuring sex role beliefs, there is no way to clearly determine the extent to which these factors contribute to sex role stereotypes (Durkin, 1985).

A major aspect of male-female sex role stereotypes is aggressive behavior. Contrary to earlier research findings, boys exhibit more physical *and* verbal aggression, although the difference is more pronounced for physical aggression. In addition, boys act more aggressively than girls following exposure to an aggressive model. Although gender differences in aggression decrease with age, researchers are not sure of the extent to which this narrowing is caused by social and/or hormonal factors (Hyde, 1986).

For those who believe sex role stereotyping is an obstacle to identity formation, one solution is to change the way in which parents raise their children. This is more difficult to accomplish than you might realize. Beverly Fagot (1978) found that parents of preschoolers are often unaware that they are responding differently to boys and girls. It is possible, then, that although contemporary parents may *think* they have rejected traditional conceptions of sex roles, they are still encouraging girls to be dependent and passive and boys to be independent and active.

We can look at the results of the studies cited above in both negative and positive lights. On the negative side, even though many young women of the 1990s believe they have unlimited career opportunities, they may still be socialized to prefer working with people and helping others. Furthermore, when girls display independent and competitive behaviors, they may be either deliberately or unconsciously discouraged by parents and teachers. On the positive side, greater sensitivity to and understanding of interpersonal relationships may help women in certain personal and professional situations.

Given the ways in which society maintains sex role stereotypes and the difficulties they create for some adolescents in establishing an identity, many researchers have suggested that children and adolescents should acquire a sex role that *combines* traditional masculine and feminine traits. This idea is called **psychological androgyny.**

Sex Typing and Psychological Androgyny   The findings reported in the previous section reveal the extent to which traditional conceptions of sex roles are ingrained in the minds of many Americans. But not all individuals react the same way, as indicated in studies by Sandra Bem (1975, 1976). Bem found that adults vary in the extent to which they can be classified as *sex typed* or as high in *psychological androgyny*. (*Androgyny* means possessing both male and female characteristics.) Sex-typed females (who endorse stereotyped conceptions of femininity) may refuse to nail two boards together because they feel it is a "masculine" rather than a "feminine" form of behavior. Sex-typed males may refuse to handle a baby or do household chores presumably because they feel that engaging in such behavior will make them appear less masculine. Only adults rated high in psychological androgyny appear able to move between masculine and feminine roles without difficulty or self-consciousness.

> Sex-typed individuals less flexible than those high in psychological androgyny

Because of this increased flexibility, proponents of androgyny argue that androgynous individuals are better adjusted than those who identify with traditional sex roles. Research findings reported by James Dusek (1987) seem to support this argument. In two studies, college students responded to a series of written questions designed to measure the first six stages of Erikson's theory. Androgynous students scored higher than sex-typed students for trust vs. mistrust, initiative vs. guilt, identity vs. role confusion, and intimacy vs. isolation. In terms of Erikson's theory, at least, these results suggest that androgynous individuals are better adjusted than sex-typed individuals.

How do you help students develop more flexible conceptions of sex roles? In general, you can encourage girls to be more competitive and achievement oriented, particularly in math and science (two areas in which women are seriously underrepresented). And you can encourage boys to be more sensitive to the feelings of others and to take part in other than traditional masculine activities without being self-conscious. The study by Fagot (1978) and analyses of research by Felicisima Serafica and Suzanna Rose (1982) and Carol A. Dwyer (1982) call attention to the extent to which sex-typed behavior is shaped by the responses of parents and teachers. Furthermore, observation of models has a significant impact on sex-typed behavior. A boy who watches his father unself-consciously care for an infant or wash the dishes is more likely to acquire a flexible view of sex roles than a boy whose father is a sex-typed male. And a girl who sees her mother go off to work is less inclined to picture women solely as mothers and homemakers.

The Significance of Occupational Choice   The occupation we choose influences other aspects of our lives perhaps more than any other single factor. Our job determines how we will spend a sizable proportion of our time; it determines how much money we earn; and our income, in turn, affects where and how we live. Moreover, the last two factors determine, to a considerable extent, the people we interact with socially. All these factors together influence the reactions of others, and these reactions lead us to develop perceptions of ourselves. The choice of a career, therefore, may be the biggest commitment of a person's life. But there are several factors that complicate the process of making an occupational choice in American society. One is that adolescents do not have many opportunities to observe and interact with working adults because they are required to be in school seven hours a day until they are at least sixteen years old. Second, the types of jobs most readily available to adolescents are minimum-wage, service-oriented jobs. Third, because of the sheer number of possible occupations (the Dictionary of Occupational Titles lists over 47,000) and the limited work experience of young people, most adolescents have little knowledge about which jobs they would enjoy and be able to do successfully, nor are they aware of the level of training required for a particular job. Fourth, because of sex role stereotyping, many adolescents exhibit relatively traditional sex-related occupational aspirations (e.g., elementary school teacher for girls, manager and administrator for boys) (Brown, 1982; Conger, 1991).

Dealing with Role Confusion   Confronted with the realization that the time has come to make a career choice, the young person seeking to avoid role confusion by making a firm vocational choice may feel overwhelmed and unable to act. Because of this, Erikson suggests that for many young people a **psychosocial moratorium** may be desirable. A psychosocial moratorium is a period marked by a delay of commitment. Such a postponement occurred in Erikson's own life: After leaving high school, Erikson spent several years wandering around Europe without making any firm decision about the sort of job he would seek. Under ideal circumstances, a psychosocial moratorium should be a period of adventure and exploration, having a positive, or at least neutral, impact on the individual and society.

In some cases, however, the young person may engage in defiant or destructive behavior. A young person who is unable to overcome role confusion—or to postpone choices leading to identity formation by engaging in a positive psychosocial moratorium—may attempt to resolve inner conflict by choosing what Erikson refers to as a **negative identity.**

> The loss of a sense of identity is often expressed in a scornful and snobbish hostility toward the roles offered as proper and desirable in one's family or immediate community. Any aspect of the required role, or all of it—be it masculinity or femininity, nationality or class membership—can become the main focus of the young person's acid disdain. (1968, pp. 172–173)

Occupational choice is a major commitment

Psychosocial moratorium delays commitment

Negative identity: rejection of accepted roles

Adolescents who are dissatisfied with themselves and unable to focus on constructive goals may fashion a negative identity by engaging in forms of behavior that their parents oppose. (Grant Le Duc/Monkmeyer Press)

For example, an adolescent boy whose parents have constantly stressed how important it is to do well in school may deliberately flunk out or quit school. Erikson explains such choices by suggesting that the young person finds it easier to "derive a sense of identity out of total identification with that which he is least supposed to be than to struggle for a feeling of reality in acceptable roles which are unattainable with his inner means" (1968, p. 176). If the young person who chooses a negative identity plays the role only long enough to gain greater self-insight, the experience may be positive. In some cases, however, the negative identity may be "confirmed" by the treatment the adolescent receives from those in authority. If forms of behavior adopted to express a negative identity bring the teenager into contact with excessively punitive parents, teachers, or law enforcement agencies, for example, the "young person may well put his energy into becoming exactly what the careless and fearful community expects him to be—and make a total job of it" (1968, p. 196).

As Erikson notes, one reason for the tendency to develop a negative identity is that the adolescent is capable of imagining many possibilities. The number of possible choices of groups, interests, and activities available to the contemporary American teenager may seem overwhelming to a young person who lacks a sense of identity. When confronted with so many choices, the adolescent may develop what Erikson refers to as a *historical perspective,* the fear that earlier events in one's life are irreversible and may limit the choices available.

Erikson's observations on identity and role confusion may help you understand several aspects of adolescent behavior. For instance, many high school students are probably bothered by the realization that they must make important decisions. They may also be confused about sex roles and reluctant to make a specific career choice. Keeping such realizations in mind, you might in some cases interpret their disinterest in class work as evidence that the students are engaging in a psychosocial moratorium and lack enthusiasm for school because of a sense of aimlessness about preparing for a specific career (or even just graduating). Moreover, some types of impertinent or disruptive behavior may be less likely to arouse you to counterattack if you allow for the possibility that those involved are acting out a negative identity.

Adolescent Identity Statuses   Erikson's observations on identity formation have been usefully extended by James Marcia's notion of *Identity Statuses* (1966, 1980, 1991). Identity statuses, of which there are four, are styles or processes "with which individuals handle the tasks of establishing, maintaining, and, if necessary, revising one's sense of personal identity" (Waterman, 1988, p. 193). Marcia developed this idea "as a device by means of which Erikson's theoretical notions about identity might be subjected to empirical study" (1980, p. 161).

Marcia established the four identity statuses after he had conducted semi-structured interviews with a selected sample of male youth. The interviewees were asked their thoughts about a career, their personal value system, their sexual attitudes, and their religious beliefs. Marcia proposed that the criteria for the attainment of a mature identity are based on two variables: crisis and commitment. "Crisis refers to times during adolescence when the individual seems to be actively involved in choosing among alternative occupations and beliefs. Commitment refers to the degree of personal investment the individual expresses in an occupation or belief " (1967, p. 119). After analyzing interview records with these two criteria in mind, Marcia established four identity statuses that vary in their degree of crisis and commitment: identity diffusion, moratorium, identity achievement, and foreclosure.

As you read the following brief descriptions of each identity type, please keep two points in mind. First, an identity status is not a once-and-for-all accomplishment. If an ego-shattering event (loss of a job, divorce) later occurs, identity achievement types, for example, may find themselves uncertain about old values and once again in crisis. Second, because identity is an amalgam of commitments from a number of different domains, only a small percentage (about 20 percent) of adolescents will experience a triumphant sense of having "put it all together." To cite just one example, an adolescent is more likely to have made a firm occupational choice but to be indecisive about sex role or religious values (Waterman, 1988).

Identity diffusion types have yet to experience a crisis because they have not given much serious thought to an occupation, sex roles, or values. Their positions on these issues are only casually held and are readily subject to change in response to positive or negative feedback. Identity diffusion types have little

| Identity diffusion types avoid thinking about jobs, roles, values

self-direction, are disorganized and impulsive, are low in self-esteem, are likely to feel alienated from their parents, and avoid getting involved either in school-work or interpersonal relationships.

Moratorium types have given a certain amount of thought to identity questions, but they have not come up with any satisfactory answers. They are aware that they are "in crisis" and wish to eventually form identity commitments. They are anxious, dissatisfied with school or college, change majors often, daydream a great deal, and engage in intense but short-lived relationships with others. They tend to have conflicting needs to conform and rebel, and may temporarily reject parental values. After a period of experimentation and restless searching, most moratorium types come to grips with themselves and take on characteristics of identity achievement types. (Notice that Marcia's use of *moratorium* stresses a state of crisis or an active exploring of alternative identity possibilities, while Erikson's use of *psychosocial moratorium* stresses a delay of commitment in order to create opportunities for role experimentation.)

Identity achievement types have made self-chosen commitments with respect to at least some aspects of their identity after considering and exploring distinctly different alternatives. They are reflective in their approach to decision-making, have high self-esteem, work effectively under stress, and are likely to form close interpersonal relationships. This status is usually the last to emerge developmentally and is most likely to figure into the domain of occupational choice.

Foreclosure types do not experience a crisis and may never suffer any doubts about occupational choice, sex roles, and values. The main reason for this lack of doubt about identity issues is that foreclosure types accept and endorse the values of their parents. Such individuals are likely to be closed-minded, authoritarian, low in anxiety, and to have difficulty solving problems under stress.

Although the percentage of individuals in each of the four categories changes over time (moratorium types were more numerous during the 1960s and 1970s than during the 1980s), the historical norm for Western societies is the foreclosure type (Scarr, Weinberg & Levine, 1986; Waterman, 1988). Gender differences are most apparent in the areas of political ideology, family/career priorities, and sexuality. With respect to political beliefs, males are more likely to exhibit a foreclosure process and females a diffusion process. With respect to family/career priorities and sexuality, males are likely to be foreclosed or diffuse, whereas females are likely to express an identity achievement or moratorium status (Archer, 1991).

A relevant question to ask about Marcia's identity statuses, particularly if you plan to teach in a foreign country or to instruct students with different cultural backgrounds, is whether these identity statuses occur only in the United States. The answer appears to be no. Researchers in such diverse countries as Korea, India, Nigeria, Japan, Denmark, and Holland report finding the same patterns (Scarr, Weinberg & Levine, 1986).

Marcia's description of identity statuses applies most directly to eighteen- to twenty-one-year-olds, but awareness of the various types may also help you

▶ Moratorium types suffer identity crises of various kinds

▶ Identity achievement types have made their own commitments

▶ Foreclosure types unquestioningly endorse parents' goals and values

understand aspects of high school students' behavior. Some adolescents who seek to establish a sense of identity, for instance, may experience little difficulty because they accept their parents' ideas regarding occupational choice, sex roles, and values. But other high school students may have a diffuse identity and try to distract themselves from thinking about values or about what they intend to do after graduation. Still others may be preoccupied with career and sexual identity problems to the point that they are openly dissatisfied. A few students may resolve identity conflicts before they leave high school, accomplishing in the adolescent years what many young people need another four years to achieve.

Criticisms of Erikson's Theory

Erikson's theory has been described as somewhat vague and difficult to test. As a result, researchers are not sure what the best way is to measure such complex qualities as initiative and integrity or which kinds of experiences should be studied in order to discover how people cope with and successfully resolve psychosocial conflicts (Ochse & Plug, 1986; Sigelman & Shaffer, 1991).

Although Erikson occasionally carried out research investigations, most of his conclusions are based on personal and subjective interpretations that have been only partly substantiated by controlled investigations of the type that are valued by American psychologists. As a result, there have been only limited checks on Erikson's tendency to generalize from limited experiences. Some of his observations on identity, for example, reflect his own indecision about occupational choice.

Some critics argue that Erikson's stages reflect the personality development of males more accurately than that of females. According to Carol Gilligan (1982, 1988), for example, Erikson's theory is a more accurate description of male psychosocial development than of female psychosocial development. In particular, she feels that the process and timing of identity formation are different for each gender. Marcia (1986) contends that, beginning in about fourth grade (the industry vs. inferiority stage), girls are as concerned with the nature of interpersonal relationships as they are with achievement, whereas boys focus mainly on achievement. And during adolescence, many young women seem to work through the crises of identity *and* intimacy simultaneously, whereas most young men follow the sequence described by Erikson—identity vs. role confusion, then intimacy vs. isolation (Gilligan, 1982; Ochse & Plug, 1986; Scarr, Weinberg & Levine, 1986).

A final criticism is that Erikson's early stages, those covering ages two through eleven, seem to stress the same basic qualities. Autonomy, initiative, and industry all emphasize the desirability of permitting and encouraging children to do things on their own. Doubt, guilt, and inferiority all focus on the need for parents and teachers to provide sympathetic support.

If you keep these reservations in mind, however, you are likely to discover that Erikson's observations (as well as the identity status types described by Marcia) will clarify important aspects of development. Suggestions you might refer to in order to take advantage of Erikson's observations are listed below. (These suggestions might also serve as the nucleus of a section to be inserted in your Handbook. Possible Handbook Headings are indicated in the margins.)

Suggestions for Teaching in Your Classroom

APPLYING ERIKSON'S THEORY

1. Keep in mind that certain types of behaviors and relationships may be of special significance at different age levels.

Handbook Heading:
Ways to Apply Erikson's Theory (Preschool and Kindergarten)

2. With younger preschool children, allow plenty of opportunities for free play and experimentation to encourage the development of autonomy, but provide guidance to reduce the possibility that the children will experience doubt. Also avoid shaming children for unacceptable behavior.

3. With older preschool children, encourage activities that permit the use of initiative and provide a sense of accomplishment. Avoid making children feel guilty about well-motivated but inconvenient (to you) questions or actions.

Handbook Heading:
Ways to Apply Erikson's Theory (Elementary Grades)

4. During the elementary school years, help children experience a sense of industry by presenting tasks that they can complete successfully. Arrange such tasks so that students will *know* they have been successful. Play down comparisons and encourage cooperation and self-competition to limit feelings of inferiority. Also try to help jealous children gain satisfaction from their own behavior. (Specific ways to accomplish these goals will be described in several later chapters.)

Handbook Heading:
Ways to Apply Erikson's Theory (Secondary Grades)

5. At the secondary school level, keep in mind the significance of each pupil's search for a sense of identity. The components of identity stressed by Erikson are acceptance of one's appearance, recognition from those who count, and knowing where one is going. Role confusion is most frequently caused by failure to formulate clear ideas about sex roles and by indecision about occupational choice.

The American school system, particularly at the high school level, has been described as a place where individual differences are either ignored or discouraged and where negative feedback greatly outweighs positive feedback (e.g., Boyer, 1983; Csikszentmihalyi & Larson, 1984; Friedenberg, 1963; Murphy, 1987). When John Murphy (1987), a professor of education at Brooklyn College, asked his students to recall positive learning experiences from high school, few were able to do so. But as "someone who counts" to your students, you can contribute to their sense of positive identity by recognizing them as individuals and praising them for their accomplishments. If you become aware that particular pupils lack recognition from peers because of abrasive qualities or ineptness, and if you have the time and opportunity, you might also attempt to encourage social skills. An excellent book to consult for this purpose is *Skill-Streaming the Adolescent: A Structured Learning Approach to Teaching Prosocial Skills* (Goldstein et al., 1980). This volume describes fifty specific skills that fall into five general categories: social skills, skills for dealing with feelings, skill alternatives to aggression, skills for dealing with stress, and planning skills. Each skill is taught by a four-step method:

1. Modeling (imitating those who use social skills effectively)

2. Role playing (gaining practice in social skills in simulated situations)

3. Performance feedback (improving techniques by noting their effectiveness or ineffectiveness)

4. Transfer of training (applying a technique that was learned in role-playing situations to everyday interactions with others).

Since the techniques are preplanned and structured, you will probably obtain the best results by following the procedures outlined in the book. But don't be afraid to experiment or make spontaneous changes.

You might be able to reduce identity problems resulting from indecisiveness about sex roles by having class discussions (e.g., in social science courses) centering on changes in attitudes regarding masculinity, femininity, and family responsibilities. Following the suggestions of Block (1973), you can encourage boys to become more sensitive to the needs of others and girls to be more achievement oriented. In addition, you can acquaint members of both sexes with the concept of psychological androgyny and make them aware of the advantages of possessing both "masculine" and "feminine" characteristics.

Working with your school counselor, you may in some cases be able to help students make decisions about occupational choice by providing them with information (gleaned from classroom performance and standardized test results) about intellectual capabilities, personality traits, interests, and values (Lambert & Mounce, 1991). Or you may be able to help students decide whether to apply for admission to a college instead of entering the job market just after graduation. There are many ways to enable students to work toward short-term goals, particularly in your classroom. These will be described in detail in Chapters 7 and 12, which deal with instructional objectives and motivation.

6. Remember, the aimlessness of some students may be evidence that they are engaging in a psychosocial moratorium. If possible, encourage such individuals to focus on short-term goals while they continue to search for long-term goals.

7. Try to be patient if you suspect that disruptive behavior on the part of a student may be due to the acting out of a negative identity. When you must control negative behavior in order to preserve a satisfactory learning environment for other students, try to do it in such a way that the troublemaker is not "confirmed" as a troublemaker. One way is to make clear that you do not hold

a grudge and that you have confidence in the student's ability to make positive contributions in class. (If possible, arrange opportunities for troublemakers to carry out assignments that will be positive and constructive.)

8. Remain aware that adolescents may exhibit characteristics of different identity status types. Some may drift aimlessly; others may be distressed because they realize they lack goals and values. A few high school students may have arrived at self-chosen commitments; others may have accepted the goals and values of their parents.

If you become aware that certain pupils seem depressed or bothered because they are unable to develop a satisfactory set of personal values, consult your school psychologist or counselor. In addition, you might use the techniques just summarized to try to help them experience at least a degree of identity achievement. You might also use the technique of *values clarification* (discussed in Chapter 11, in the section on affective goals) to help students become aware of attitudes they prize and wish to act on. Perhaps the main value of the identity status concept is that it calls attention to individual differences in the formation of identity. Foreclosure types will pose few, if any, classroom problems, so it is important for you as a teacher to keep in mind that foreclosure is not necessarily desirable for the individual student. Identity diffusion and moratorium types may be so bothered by role confusion that they are unwilling to carry out even simple assignments—unless you supply support and incentives.

PIAGET: COGNITIVE DEVELOPMENT

Factors That Influenced Piaget

Piaget was born in the small university town of Neuchatel, Switzerland, in 1896. His father was a professor of history who specialized in medieval literature, and young Jean was brought up in a scholarly atmosphere. His main boyhood interest was observation of animals in their natural habitat, an interest he pursued with considerable energy and sophistication. He published his first "professional" paper at the age of eleven. (He had seen an albino sparrow in a park and reported this in a nature magazine.)

When he entered school, Piaget concentrated on the biological sciences. A series of articles on shellfish so impressed the director of the natural history museum in Geneva that he offered fifteen-year-old Jean the post of curator of the mollusk collection. Since Piaget had not finished high school, he felt obliged to decline this offer. Piaget's fascination with the study of knowledge can be traced to a vacation with his godfather, a scholar specializing in philosophy who urged Jean to broaden his horizons and to study philosophy and logic.

Jean Piaget described how thinking develops from infancy through late adolescence. (Yves De Braine/Black Star)

After graduating from high school, Piaget entered the University of Neuchatel and earned undergraduate and graduate degrees in natural science; he was awarded the Ph.D. at the age of twenty-one. At that point he became intrigued with psychology. This he studied in Zurich, where he was introduced to Freudian theory and wrote a paper relating psychoanalysis to child psychology. From Zurich he went to Paris to study abnormal psychology. Shortly after his arrival, he obtained a position preparing a French version of some reasoning tests developed in England. As he recorded the responses of his subjects, Piaget found that he was much more intrigued with wrong answers than with correct ones. He became convinced that the thought processes of younger children are basically different from those of older children and adults. His lifelong fascination with biology and his interest in studying the nature of knowledge led him to speculate about the development of thinking in children.

In 1921 an appointment as director of research at the Jean Jacques Rousseau Institute in Geneva permitted Piaget to concentrate full time on the study of cognitive development. He engaged in active study at the Institute until 1975 and continued to analyze cognitive development in "retirement" until his death in 1980.

Basic Principles of Piaget's Theory

Piaget's conception of intellectual development reflects his basic interest in biology and knowledge. He postulates that human beings inherit two basic tendencies: **organization** (the tendency to systematize and combine processes into coherent general systems) and **adaptation** (the tendency to adjust to the environment). For Piaget, these tendencies govern both physiological functioning and mental functioning. Just as the biological process of digestion transforms food into a form that the body can use, so intellectual processes transform experiences into a form that the child can use in dealing with new situations. And just as biological processes must be kept in a state of balance (through homeostasis), intellectual processes seek a balance through the process of **equilibration** (a form of self-regulation that all individuals use to bring coherence and stability to their conception of the world).

| Organization: tendency to systematize processes

Organization   As we just stated, *organization* refers to the tendency of all individuals to systematize or combine processes into coherent (logically interrelated) systems. When we think of tulips and roses as subcategories of the more general category "flowers," instead of as two unrelated categories, we are using organization to aid our thinking process. This organizational capacity makes those thinking processes efficient and powerful, and allows for a better "fit" or adaptation of the individual to the environment.

| Scheme: organized pattern of behavior or thought

Schemes   These are organized patterns of behavior or thought that children formulate as they interact with their environment, parents, teachers, and agemates. **Schemes** can be behavioral (e.g., throwing a ball) or cognitive (e.g., realizing that there are many different kinds of balls). Whenever a child encounters a new experience that does not easily fit into an existing scheme, adaptation is necessary.

| Adaptation: tendency to adjust to environment

| Assimilation: new experience is fitted into existing scheme

| Accommodation: scheme is created or revised to fit new experience

Adaptation   This is the process of creating a good "fit" or match between one's conception of reality (one's schemes) and the real-life experiences one encounters. Adaptation, as described by Piaget, is accomplished by two subprocesses: **assimilation** and **accommodation**. A child may adapt either by interpreting an experience so that it *does* fit an existing scheme (assimilation) or by changing an existing scheme to incorporate the experience (accommodation). Imagine a six-year-old who goes to an aquarium for the first time and calls the minnows "little fish" and the whales "big fish." In both cases the child is assimilating—attempting to fit a new experience into an existing scheme (in this case, the conception that all animals that live in the water are fish). When her parents point out that even though whales live in the water they are mammals, not fish, the six-year-old begins to accommodate—to modify her existing scheme to fit the new experience she has encountered. Gradually (and it is important to realize that accommodations are made slowly, over repeated experiences), a new scheme forms that contains nonfish animals that live in the water.

Relationships Among Organization, Adaptation, and Schemes   In order to give you a basic understanding of Piaget's ideas, we have talked about them as distinct elements. But the concepts of organization, adaptation, and schemes are all related. In their drive to be organized, individuals try to have a place for everything (accommodation) so they can put everything in its place (assimilation). The product of organizing and adapting is the creation of new schemes that allow us to organize at a higher level and to adapt more effectively.

▶ Equilibration: tendency to organize schemes to allow better understanding of experiences

Equilibration, Disequilibrium, and Learning   Piaget believes that people are driven to organize their knowledge in order to achieve the best possible adaptation to their environment. Think of it as having a place for everything and having everything in its place. He calls this process *equilibration*. But what motivates people's drive toward equilibration? It is a state of *disequilibrium*, or a perceived discrepancy between an existing scheme and something new. In other words, when people encounter something that is inconsistent with or contradicts what they already know or believe, it produces a disequilibrium they are driven to eliminate (assuming they are sufficiently interested in the new experience to begin with). A student may wonder why, for example, tomatoes and cucumbers are referred to as fruits in a science text, since she had always referred to them as vegetables and had distinguished fruits from vegetables on the basis of sweetness. This discrepancy may cause the student to read the text carefully or to ask the teacher for further explanation. Gradually, the student reorganizes her thinking about the classification of fruits and vegetables in terms of edible plant roots, stems, leaves, and ovaries so that it is more consistent with the expert view. These processes are two sides of the learning coin: In order for equilibration to occur, disequilibrium must occur. Disequilibrium can occur spontaneously within an individual through maturation and experience, or it can be stimulated by someone else (such as a teacher).

Meaningful learning, then, occurs when people *create* new ideas, or knowledge (rules and hypotheses that explain things), from existing information (for example, facts, concepts, and procedures). To solve a problem, we have to search our memory for information that can be used to fashion a solution. Using information can mean experimenting, questioning, reflecting, discovering, inventing, and discussing. This process of creating knowledge in order to solve a problem and eliminate a disequilibrium is referred to by Piagetian psychologists and educators as **constructivism** (Blais, 1988; Brooks, 1990; Wheatley, 1991). It is a powerful notion that will reappear in other chapters (principally Chapters 10 and 12) and in other forms. (The discussion questions at the end of each chapter are intended to stimulate constructivist thinking.)

In *Horace's Compromise* (1985), a critical analysis of the American high school, Theodore Sizer provides a clear example of inducing constructivist thinking through the use of disequilibrating questions. He required his twelfth-grade history classes to read a passage that defined different social classes on the basis of how people behaved in regard to their own futures. According to this passage, an upper-class person postpones or sacrifices current satisfaction in order to achieve a distant goal, whereas a lower-class person lives for the present. This treatment of social class disturbed many of Sizer's students because it categorized and stereotyped people. They complained that it was unfair and un-American. Sizer then asked if the students didn't do the same thing by referring to their peers as jocks, freaks, nerds, and preppies. This led to a discussion of whether and how well labels help us understand, at a general level, the behavior of groups of people. The constructivist nature of this assignment can be seen in the following statement by Sizer: "Throughout this exercise, my role was that of questioner, never teller. The objective was to provoke the students to see an important idea in its complexity and to develop an understanding of it" (p. 119).

Stages of Cognitive Development

Organization and adaptation are what Piaget calls *invariant functions*. This means that these thought processes function the same way for infants, children, adolescents, and adults. Schemes, on the other hand, are not invariant. They undergo systematic change at particular points in time. As a result, there are real differences between the ways younger and older children think, and between the ways children and adults think. The schemes of infants and toddlers, for example, are sensory and motor in nature. They are often referred to as *habits* or *reflexes*. In early childhood, schemes gradually become more mental in nature; during this period they are called *concepts* or *categories*. Finally, by late adolescence or early adulthood, schemes are very complex and result in what we call *strategic* or *planful* behavior.

On the basis of his studies, Piaget concluded that schemes evolve through four stages. Although these stages reflect a generally continuous pattern of cognitive development, children do not suddenly "jump" from one stage to the next. Their cognitive development follows a definite sequence, but they may occasionally use a more advanced kind of thinking or revert to a more primitive form. The *rate* at which a particular child proceeds through these stages varies, but Piaget believes the *sequence* is the same in all children.

Piaget's four stages are described below. To help you grasp the sequence of these stages, Table 2.1 briefly outlines the range of ages to which they generally apply and their distinguishing characteristics.

▶ Sensorimotor stage: schemes reflect sensory and motor experiences

Sensorimotor Stage Infants and children up to the age of two years acquire understanding primarily through sensory impressions and motor activities. Therefore, Piaget calls this the *sensorimotor stage*. Because they are unable to move around much on their own during the first months of postnatal existence, infants develop schemes primarily by exploring their own bodies and senses. After they learn to walk and manipulate things, however, toddlers get into everything and build up a sizable repertoire of schemes involving external objects and situations.

An important cognitive development milestone, *object permanence*, occurs between the fourth and eighth months of this stage. Prior to this point, the phrase "out of sight, out of mind" is literally true. Infants treat objects that leave their field

TABLE 2.1 Stages of Cognitive Development		
Stage	**Age Range**	**Characteristics**
Sensorimotor	Birth to two years	Develops schemes primarily through sense and motor activities. Recognizes permanence of objects not seen.
Preoperational	Two to seven years	Gradually acquires ability to conserve and decenter, but not capable of operations and unable to mentally reverse actions.
Concrete operational	Seven to eleven years	Capable of operations, but solves problems by generalizing from concrete experiences. Not able to manipulate conditions mentally unless they have been experienced.
Formal operational	Eleven years and older	Able to deal with abstractions, form hypotheses, solve problems systematically, engage in mental manipulations.

of vision as if they no longer exist. When they drop an object from their hand or when an object at which they are looking is covered, for example, they do not search for it. During the same period, however, intentional search behaviors become increasingly apparent.

Most children under two are able to use schemes they have mastered to engage in mental, as well as physical, trial and error behavior. By age two, toddlers' schemes have become more mental in nature. You can see this in the way toddlers imitate the behavior of others. They imitate people they have not previously observed, they imitate the behavior of animals, and, most important, they imitate even when the model is no longer present (this is called *deferred imitation*). These types of imitative behaviors show the child's increasing ability to think in terms of symbols.

Preoperational Stage   The thinking of preschool children (roughly two to five years old) centers on mastery of symbols (such as words), which permits them to benefit much more from past experiences. Piaget believes that many symbols are derived from mental imitation and involve both visual images and bodily sensations (notice how the schemes of this stage incorporate and build on the schemes of the previous stage). Even though their thinking is much more sophisticated than that of one- and two-year-olds, preschool children are limited in their ability to use their new symbol-oriented schemes. From an adult perspective, their thinking and behavior are illogical. When Piaget uses the term *operation*, he means an action carried out through logical thinking. *Preoperational*, then, means prelogical. The main impediments to logical thinking that preschoolers have to overcome are *perceptual centration, irreversibility,* and *egocentrism*. You can see these impediments at work most clearly when children attempt to solve

▶ Preoperational stage: child forms many new schemes but does not think logically

▶ Perceptual centration, irreversibility, egocentrism: barriers to logical thought

One of Piaget's best-known experiments involves asking children to explain what happens when water is poured back and forth between containers of different sizes and shapes. The preoperational child is unable to consider more than one feature at a time and is unable to mentally reverse the action of pouring. He or she is likely to maintain, therefore, that a tall container holds more water than a squat container, even if the amount is the same. (Marcia Weinstein)

conservation problems, problems that test their ability to recognize that certain properties stay the same despite a change in appearance or position.

One of the best known conservation problems is conservation of continuous quantity. A child is taken to a quiet place by an experimenter, who then pours water (or juice, or beans, or whatever) into identical short glasses until the child agrees that each contains an equal amount. Then the water is poured from one of these glasses into a tall thin glass. At that point the child is asked, "Is there more water in this glass (the experimenter points to the tall thin glass) or this one?" Immediately after the child answers, the experimenter asks, "Why do you think so?" If the child's response is evasive or vague, the experimenter continues to probe until the underlying thought processes become clear.

In carrying out this experiment (and many others similar to it) with children of different ages, Piaget discovered that children below the age of six or so maintain that there is more water in the tall thin glass than in the short squat glass. Even though they agree at the beginning of the experiment that the water in the two identical glasses is equal, young children stoutly insist that after the water has been poured the taller glass contains more. When asked "Why do you think so?" many preschool children immediately and confidently reply, "Because it's taller." Children over the age of six or so, by contrast, are more likely to reply, "Well, it *looks* as if there's more water in this one because it's taller, but they're really the same."

One reason preoperational stage children have difficulty solving conservation problems (as well as other problems that require logical thinking) is **perceptual centration.** This is the very strong tendency to focus attention on only one characteristic of an object or aspect of a problem or event at a time. The young child focuses only on the height of the water in the two containers and ignores the differences in width and volume.

The second impediment to logical thinking is **irreversibility.** This means that young children cannot mentally pour the water from the tall thin glass back into the short squat one (thereby proving to themselves that the glasses contain the same amount of water). For the same reason, these youngsters do not understand the logic behind simple mathematical reversals ($4 + 5 = 9$; $9 - 5 = 4$).

Elementary school teachers who take into account Piaget's description of cognitive development may encourage their pupils to engage in small-group interactions. As children interact with each other they may not only learn from peers but also overcome the tendency to function as egocentric thinkers—convinced that everyone else sees things as they do. (Martha Cooper)

> Egocentrism: assumption that others see things the same way

The third major impediment is **egocentrism.** When applied to preschool children, *egocentric* does not mean selfish or conceited. It means that youngsters find it difficult, if not impossible, to take another person's point of view. In their conversations and in experimental situations in which they are asked to describe how something would look if viewed by someone else, preschool children reveal that they often have difficulty seeing things from another person's perspective (Piaget & Inhelder, 1956). They seem to assume that others see things the same way they see them. As a result, attempts to explain the logic behind conservation are usually met with quizzical looks and the insistence (some would mistakenly call it stubbornness) that the tall thin glass contains more water.

> Concrete operational stage: child is capable of mentally reversing actions but generalizes only from concrete experiences

Concrete Operational Stage   Through formal instruction, informal experiences, and maturation, children over the age of seven gradually become less influenced by perceptual centration, irreversibility, and egocentrism. Schemes are developing that allow a greater understanding of such logic-based tasks as conservation (matter is neither created nor destroyed but simply changes shape or form or position), class inclusion (constructing hierarchical relationships among related classes of items), and seriation (arranging items in a particular order). But operational thinking is limited to objects that are actually present or that children have experienced concretely and directly. For this reason, Piaget describes the stage from approximately seven to eleven years as that of *concrete operations.* The nature of the concrete operational stage can be illustrated by the child's mastery of different kinds of conservation.

By the age of seven most children are able to correctly explain that water poured from a short squat glass into a tall thin glass is still the same amount of water. Being able to solve the water-pouring problem, however, does not guarantee that a seven-year-old will be able to solve a similar problem involving two balls of clay. A child who has just explained why a tall glass of water contains the same amount as a short one may inconsistently maintain a few moments later that rolling one of two equal-sized balls of clay into an elongated shape causes it to become bigger. Children in the primary grades tend to react to each situation in terms of concrete experiences. The tendency to solve problems by generalizing from one situation to a similar but identical situation does not occur with any degree of consistency until the end of the elementary school years. Furthermore, if asked to deal with a hypothetical problem, the concrete operational child is likely to be stymied. Seven-year-olds are not likely to be able to solve abstract problems by engaging in mental explorations. They usually need to manipulate concrete objects physically or to recollect specific past experiences in order to explain things to themselves and others. If, for example, you told a student at the concrete operational stage to assume that a feather could break a piece of glass and then asked him whether the deduction "if one hits the glass with a feather, then the glass will break" is true or false, he would likely respond that it is false because in his experience feathers do not break glass (Overton & Byrnes, 1991).

▶ Formal operational
stage: child is able to
deal with abstrac-
tions, form hypothe-
ses, engage in mental
manipulations

Formal Operational Stage   When children *do* reach the point of being able to generalize and to engage in mental trial and error by thinking up hypotheses and testing them "in their heads," Piaget says they have reached the stage of *formal operations*. The term *formal* reflects the ability to respond to the *form* of a problem rather than its content, and to *form* hypotheses. For example, the formal operational thinker can read the analogies "5 is to 15 as 1 is to 3" and "penny is to dollar as year is to century" and realize that, despite the different content, the form of the two problems is identical (both analogies are based on ratios). In the same way, the formal thinker can understand and use complex language forms: proverbs ("strike while the iron is hot"), metaphor ("procrastination is the thief of time"), sarcasm, and satire.

We can see the nature of formal operational thinking and how it differs from concrete operational thinking by looking at a simplified version of Piaget's rod-bending experiment. Adolescents are given a basin filled with water, a set of metal rods of varying length, and a set of weights. The rods are attached to the edge of the basin and the weights to the ends of the rods. The subject's task is to figure out how much weight is required to bend a rod just enough to touch the water. Let's say that our hypothetical subject picks out the longest rod in the set (which is nine inches long), attaches it to the edge of the basin, and puts just enough weight on the end of it to get it to touch the water. This observation is then recorded. Successively shorter rods are selected and the same procedure is carried out. At some point the subject comes to the four-inch rod. This rod does not touch the water even when all of the weights have been attached to it. There are, however, three more rods, all of which are shorter than the last one tested. This is where the formal and concrete operators part company. The formal operational thinker reasons that if all of the available weights are not sufficient to bend the four-inch rod enough to touch the water, the same will be true of the remaining rods. In essence, the rest of the experiment is done mentally and symbolically. The concrete operational thinker, however, continues trying out each rod and recording each observation independent of the others. Although both subjects reach the same conclusions, the formal operator does so through a more powerful and efficient process.

But remember that new schemes develop gradually. Even though adolescents can sometimes deal with mental abstractions representing concrete objects, most twelve-year-olds solve problems haphazardly, using trial and error. It is not until the end of the high school years that adolescents are likely to attack a problem by forming hypotheses, mentally sorting out solutions, and systematically testing the most promising leads.

Some interpreters of Piaget (for example, Ginsburg & Opper, 1988) note that a significant aspect of formal thought is that it causes the adolescent to concentrate more on possibilities than on realities. This is the ability that Erikson and others (for example, Kalbaugh & Haviland, 1991) suggest is instrumental in the emergence of the identity crisis. At the point when older adolescents can become aware of all the factors that have to be considered in choosing a career and imagine what it might be like to be employed, some may feel so threatened and confused that they postpone the final choice. Yet the same capability can also help resolve the identity crisis because adolescents can reason about possibilities in a logical manner. An adolescent girl, for example, may consider working as a pediatrician, teacher, or child psychologist in an underprivileged environment because she has always enjoyed and sought out activities that allowed her to interact with children and has also been concerned with the effects of deprivation on development.

While mastery of formal thought equips the older adolescent with impressive intellectual skills, it may contribute to role confusion. It may also lead to a tendency for the burgeoning formal thinker to become preoccupied with abstract and theoretical matters. Herbert Ginsburg and Sylvia Opper interpret some of Piaget's observations on this point in the following way:

> In the intellectual sphere, the adolescent has a tendency to become involved in abstract and theoretical matters, constructing elaborate political theories or inventing complex philosophical doctrines. The adolescent may develop plans for the complete reorganization of society or indulge in metaphysical speculation. After discovering capabilities for abstract thought, he then proceeds to exercise them without restraint. Indeed, in the process of exploring these new abilities the adolescent sometimes loses touch with reality and feels that he can accomplish everything by thought alone. In the emotional sphere the adolescent now becomes capable of directing emotions at abstract ideals and not just toward people. Whereas earlier the adolescent could love his mother or hate a peer, now he can love freedom or hate exploitation. The adolescent has developed a new mode of life: the possible and the ideal captivate both mind and feeling. (1988, pp. 202–203)

David Elkind (1968) suggests that unrestrained theorizing about ideals without complete understanding of realities tends to make the young adolescent a militant rebel with little patience for parents or other adults who fail to find quick solutions to personal, social, and other problems. Only when the older adolescent begins to grasp the complexities of interpersonal relationships and of social and economic problems does more tempered understanding appear. Elkind also suggests that the egocentrism of early childhood reappears in a different form as **adolescent egocentrism.** This occurs when high school students turn their new powers of thought upon themselves and become introspective. The strong tendency to analyze self is projected upon others. This helps explain why adolescents are so self-conscious: They assume their thoughts and actions are as central to others as to themselves. The major difference between the egocentrism of childhood and that of adolescence is summed up in Elkind's observation: "The child is egocentric in the sense that he is unable to take another person's point of view. The adolescent, on the other hand, takes the other person's point of view to an extreme degree" (1968, p. 153).

▶ Adolescent egocentrism: one's thoughts and actions are as central to others as to oneself

Elkind believes that adolescent egocentrism also explains why the peer group becomes such a potent force in high school. He observes:

> Adolescent egocentrism . . . accounts, in part, for the power of the peer group during this period. The adolescent is so concerned with the reactions of others

toward him, particularly his peers, that he is willing to do many things which are opposed to all of his previous training and to his own best interests. At the same time, this egocentric impression that he is always on stage may help to account for the many and varied adolescent attention-getting maneuvers. (1968, p. 154)

Toward the end of adolescence, this form of exploitative egocentrism gradually declines. The young person comes to realize that other people are much more concerned with themselves and their problems than they are with him and his problems.

Accelerating Cognitive Development: Mission Impossible?

Piaget believed that cognitive development is caused by two general factors: heredity and environmental experience. *Heredity* establishes the basic nature of physical structures (such as the brain), the development of physical structures, the existence of reflexes (sucking, grasping, crying), and the tendency to organize experiences and adapt to the environment (through assimilation, accommodation, and equilibration). *Experience* refers to the variety of interactions we have with the world. These interactions can be classified in three ways: physical experiences, mental experiences, and social experiences. Picking up a bunch of rocks and estimating their size and weight is a physical experience. Arranging the rocks in sequence from smallest to largest or lightest to heaviest is a mental experience. (Piaget uses the term *logico-mathematical knowledge* because this type of knowledge is created from schemes based on logic and mathematics.) Watching other people behave, listening to other people's ideas, and discussing ideas with others are examples of social experience.

Piaget believed that the amount and quality of environmental experiences can alter the details of cognitive development for better or worse but cannot affect such basic tendencies as organization and adaptation, tendencies that are governed by heredity. Accordingly, he maintained that the rate of cognitive development cannot be accelerated through formal instruction. Many American psychologists are not willing to accept this conclusion at face value. Over the past twenty years, dozens of experiments have been conducted to see whether it is possible to teach preoperational stage children to understand and use concrete operational schemes or to teach students in the concrete operational stage to grasp formal operational reasoning.

The main conclusion of psychologists who have analyzed and evaluated this body of research is, unfortunately, one of uncertainty (see, for example, Case, 1975; Nagy & Griffiths, 1982; Slavin, 1988; Sprinthall & Sprinthall, 1987). Because of shortcomings in the way some studies were carried out and disagreements about what constitutes evidence of true concrete operational thinking or formal operational thinking, a decisive answer to this question is just not available. Still, something of value can be gleaned from the research on cognitive acceleration. Two recent analyses of this literature (Sigelman & Shaffer, 1991; Sprinthall &

Instruction can accelerate development of schemes that have begun to form

Sprinthall, 1987) concluded that children who are *in the process of developing the schemes* that will govern the next stage of cognitive functioning can, with good-quality instruction, be helped to refine those schemes a bit faster than would normally be the case. For example, the principle of conservation can be taught by using simple explanations and concrete materials, and by allowing children to manipulate the materials. This means that teachers should nurture the process of cognitive growth at any particular stage by presenting lessons in a form that is consistent with but slightly more advanced than the student's existing schemes. The objective here is to help the student assimilate and accommodate new and different experiences as efficiently as possible.

The finding that cognitive development can be accelerated if instruction is provided at the right time and in the right way is consistent with the ideas of Lev Vygotsky, a Russian psychologist and contemporary of Piaget who died prematurely from tuberculosis in 1934. Vygotsky emphasized more than Piaget the influence of social experience (of which teaching is a large part) on cognitive development. He maintained that the various things we learn, such as facts, concepts, rules, problem-solving skills, and attitudes, are strongly influenced by the kinds of social interactions that typify our culture. We can illustrate this point by paraphrasing an experiment described by Vygotsky (1934/1986). He gave two eight-year-olds of average ability problems that were a bit too difficult for them to solve on their own. (Although Vygotsky did not specify what types of problems they were, imagine that they were math problems.) He then tried to help the children solve the problems by giving them leading questions and hints. With this aid he found that one child was able to solve problems designed for twelve-year-olds whereas the other child could only reach a nine-year-old level.

Vygotsky referred to the difference between what a child can do on his or her own versus what can be accomplished with some assistance as the **zone of proximal development (ZPD).** The size of the first eight-year-old's zone is four whereas the second child has a zone of one. According to Vygotsky, students with wider zones are likely to experience greater cognitive development when instruction is pitched just above the lower limit of their ZPD than will students with narrower zones because they are in a better position to capitalize on the instruction. Instructional methods that are likely to help students traverse their ZPD include modeling, the use of rewards and punishments, feedback, cognitive structuring (using such devices as theories, categories, labels, and rules for helping students organize and understand ideas), and questioning (Gallimore & Tharp, 1990; Ratner, 1991). The first three techniques are discussed more fully in Chapter 8, cognitive structuring techniques are discussed in Chapter 9, and questioning is discussed in Chapter 10. As students approach the upper limit of their ZPD, their behavior becomes smoother, more internalized, and more automatized. Any assistance offered at this level is likely to be perceived as disruptive and irritating.

Vygotsky's notion of producing cognitive development by embedding instruction within a student's zone of proximal development is an attractive one

Vygotsky: cognitive development due to instruction in zone of proximal development and has many implications for instruction. In Chapter 10, for example, we describe how this notion was used to improve the reading comprehension skills of low-achieving seventh-graders. Whether or not it can be used to greatly accelerate students' passage through Piaget's stages remains to be seen.

Criticisms of Piaget's Theory

▶ Piaget's theory underestimates children's abilities

Among the thousand and more articles that have been published in response to Piaget's findings are many that offer critiques of his work. Some psychologists argue that Piaget underestimated children's abilities, not only because he imposed stringent criteria for inferring the presence of particular cognitive abilities, but also because the tasks he used were often complex and far removed from children's real-life experiences. The term *preoperational,* for instance, stresses what is absent rather than what is present. Within the last decade researchers have focused more on what preoperational children *can* do. Their results (summarized by Bryant, 1984; Gelman & Baillargeon, 1983) suggest that preschoolers' cognitive abilities are more advanced in some areas than Piaget's work suggested.

▶ Most adolescents are not formal operational thinkers

Other evidence suggests that Piaget may have overestimated the formal thinking capabilities of adolescents. Research summarized by Constance Kamii (1984) reveals that only 20 to 25 percent of college freshmen are able to consistently use formal operational reasoning. Epstein (1980) found that among a group of ninth-graders, 32 percent were just beginning the concrete operational stage, 43 percent were well within the concrete operational stage, 15 percent were just entering the formal operational stage, and only 9 percent were mature formal operators. In addition, Sprinthall and Sprinthall (1987) report that only 33 percent of a group of high school seniors could apply formal operational reasoning to scientific problem solving. Formal reasoning seems to be the exception, not the rule, throughout adolescence.

Questions have also been raised as to whether children from different cultures develop intellectually in the manner described by Piaget. The answer at this point is both yes and no. The sequence of stages appears to be universal, but the rate of development may vary from one culture to another (Dasen & Heron, 1981; Hughes & Noppe, 1991; Leadbeater, 1991). A sample of Oglala Sioux children, for example, was quite similar to the Swiss schoolchildren Piaget studied in their rate of cognitive development. In terms of performance on conservation, spatial relationship, class inclusion, and seriation tasks, all the four- and five-year-olds were preoperational, the six- and seven-year-olds were transitional, and the eight- and nine-year-olds were concrete operational (Voyat, 1983). The average Eskimo child acquires the spatial concept of horizontalness faster than the average West African child. But many West African children (around the age of twelve or thirteen) understand conservation of quantity, weight, and volume sooner than Eskimo children do (Dasen & Heron, 1981). Finally, there is some doubt that formal operational thinking occurs in every culture (Dasen & Heron, 1981; Leadbeater, 1991).

Now that you are familiar with Piaget's theory, you can formulate specific classroom applications. You might use the suggestions offered for the grade level you expect to teach as the basis for a section in your Handbook.

Suggestions for Teaching in Your Classroom

APPLYING PIAGET'S THEORY

General Guidelines

1. Focus on what children at each stage can do and avoid what they cannot meaningfully understand. This implication must be interpreted carefully, as recent research has shown that children at the preoperational and concrete operational levels can do more than Piaget believed. In general, however, it is safe to say that since preoperational stage children (preschoolers, kindergartners, most first- and some second-graders) can use language and other symbols to stand for objects, they should be given many opportunities to describe and explain things through the use of artwork, body movement, role play, musical performance, and speech. While the concepts of conservation, seriation, class inclusion, time, space, and number can be introduced, attempts at mastering them should probably be postponed until children are in the concrete operational stage. Concrete operational stage children (grades 3–5) can be given opportunities to master such mental processes as ordering, seriating, classifying, reversing, multiplying, dividing, subtracting, and adding by manipulating concrete objects or symbols. Exercises that involve theorizing, hypothesizing, or generalizing about abstract ideas should be avoided. Formal operational stage children (grades 6 through high school) can be given activities that require hypothetical-deductive reasoning, reflective thinking, analysis, synthesis, and evaluation.

2. Because individuals differ in their rates of intellectual growth, gear instructional materials and activities to each student's developmental level.

3. Because intellectual growth occurs when individuals attempt to eliminate a disequilibrium, instructional lessons and materials that introduce new concepts should provoke interest and curiosity and be moderately challenging in order to maximize assimilation and accommodation.

4. While information (facts, concepts, procedures) can be efficiently transmitted from teacher to student through direct instruction, knowledge (rules and hypotheses) is best created by each student through the mental and physical manipulation of information. Accordingly, lesson plans should also indicate opportunities for activity, manipulation, exploration, discussion, and application of information. Small-group science projects is one example of how this implication can be implemented.

5. Since a student's schemes at any given time are an outgrowth of earlier schemes, point out to students how new ideas relate to old ideas and allow the student a better understanding of something. Memorizing information for its own sake should be avoided.

6. Begin lessons with concrete objects or ideas and gradually shift explanations to a more abstract and general level.

Preschool and Elementary Grades [2]

1. Become thoroughly familiar with Piaget's theory so that you will be aware of how your students organize and synthesize ideas. You may gain extra insight if you analyze your own thinking, since you are likely to discover that in some situations you operate at a concrete rather than an abstract level.

2. If possible, assess the level and the type of thinking of each child in your class. Ask individual children to perform some of Piaget's experiments, and spend most of your time listening to each child explain her or his reactions.

3. Remember that learning through activity and direct experience is essential. Provide plenty of materials and opportunities for children to learn on their own.

4. Arrange situations to permit social interaction, so that children can learn from one another. Hearing others explain their views is a natural way for students to learn that not everyone sees things the same way. The placement of a few advanced thinkers with less mature thinkers is more likely to facilitate this process than is homogeneous grouping.

5. Plan learning experiences to take into account the level of thinking attained by an individual or group. Encourage children to classify things on the basis of a single attribute before you expose them to problems that involve relationships among two or more attributes. Ask many questions and give your students many opportunities to explain their interpretations of experiences so that you can remain aware of their level of thinking.

6. Keep in mind the possibility that pupils may be influenced by egocentric speech and thought. Allow for the possibility that each child may assume that everyone else has the same conception of a word he or she has. If confusion becomes apparent or if a child becomes impatient about failure to communicate, request an explanation in different terms. Or ask several children to explain their conception of an object or situation.

Secondary Grades [3]

1. Become well acquainted with the nature of concrete operational thinking and formal thought so that you can recognize when your students are resorting to either type or to a combination of the two.

2. These guidelines are adapted from Bryant (1984), Bybee and Sund (1982), Elkind (1989), Ginsburg and Opper (1988), and Wadsworth (1989).

3. Many of these suggestions are derived from points made in Chapter 7 of *Young Children's Thinking* (Almy, Chittenden & Miller, 1966).

2. To become aware of the type of thinking used by individual students, ask them to explain how they arrived at solutions to problems. Do this either as part of your classroom curriculum or in response to experimental situations similar to those devised by Piaget. (Sample problems are described in the Resources for Further Investigation section at the end of this chapter.)

3. Teach students how to solve problems more systematically. (Suggestions for doing this are provided in Chapters 9 and 10.)

4. Keep in mind that some high school students may be more interested in possibilities than in realities. If class discussions become unrealistically theoretical and hypothetical, call attention to facts and practical difficulties. If students are contemptuous of unsuccessful attempts by adults to solve school, local, national, and international problems, point out the complexity of many situations involving conflicts of interest, perhaps by summarizing arguments from both sides.

5. Allow for the possibility that younger adolescents may go through a period of egocentrism that will cause them to act as if they are always on stage and to be extremely concerned about the reactions of peers.

PIAGET, KOHLBERG, AND GILLIGAN: MORAL DEVELOPMENT

Piaget's Analysis of the Moral Judgment of the Child

Because he was intrigued by *all* aspects of children's thinking, Piaget became interested in moral development. He began his study of morality by observing how children played marbles. (He first took the trouble to learn the game himself, so that he would be able to understand the subtleties of the conception.) Piaget discovered that interpretations of rules followed by participants in marble games changed with age.

Age Changes in Interpretation of Rules   Four- to seven-year-olds just learning the game seemed to view rules as interesting examples of the social behavior of older children. They did not understand them but tried to go along with them. Seven- to ten-year-olds regarded rules as sacred pronouncements handed down by older children or adults. At about the age of eleven or twelve, children began to see rules as agreements reached by mutual consent. Piaget concluded that younger children see rules as absolute and external.

Even though children ranging from the age of four to about ten do not question rules, they may frequently break them because they do not understand them completely. After the age of eleven or so, children become increasingly capable of grasping why rules are necessary. At that point, Piaget concluded, they tend to lose interest in adult-imposed regulations and take delight in formulating their own variations of rules to fit a particular situation. Piaget illustrates this point by describing how a group of ten- and eleven-year-old boys prepared for a snowball fight (1962, p. 50). They divided themselves into teams, elected officers, decided on rules to govern the distances from which the snowballs could be thrown, and agreed on a system of punishments for those who violated the rules. Even though they spent a substantial amount of playtime engaging in such preliminary discussions, they seemed to thoroughly enjoy their newly discovered ability to make up rules to supplant those that had previously been imposed on them by their elders.

Reactions to Stories Involving Moral Decisions   The way children of different ages responded to rules so intrigued Piaget that he decided to use the interview method to obtain more systematic information about moral development. He made up pairs of stories and asked children of different ages to discuss them. Here is a typical pair of stories:

> There was a little boy called Julian. His father had gone out and Julian thought it would be fun to play with father's ink-pot. First he played with the pen, and then he made a little blot on the table cloth. A little boy who was called Augustus once noticed that his father's ink-pot was empty. One day that his father was away he thought of filling the ink-pot so as to help his father, and so that he should find it full when he came home. But while he was opening the ink-bottle he made a big blot on the table cloth. (1948, p. 118)

After reading these stories, Piaget asked, "Are these children equally guilty? Which of the two is naughtiest, and why?" As was the case with interpretations of rules, Piaget found that younger children reacted to these stories differently from older children. (We describe these differences below.) Piaget concluded from the way six-year-olds interpreted rules, and from the answers they gave when confronted with the pairs of stories, that their moral reasoning is quite different from that of twelve-year-olds.

Piaget refers to the moral thinking of children up to the age of ten or so as **morality of constraint,** but he also calls it *moral realism* or *heteronomous morality*. The thinking of children of eleven or older Piaget calls the **morality of cooperation.** He also occasionally used the term *moral relativism*. Piaget concluded that the two basic types of moral reasoning differ in several ways. We summarize these differences in Table 2.2.

To further clarify and illustrate some of the differences between the moralities of constraint and cooperation, we offer the following examples and explanations of types of thinking that characterize the thinking of moral realists (i.e., those who use the morality of constraint).

Moral realism: sacred rules, no exceptions, no allowance for intentions, consequences determine guilt

The Nature of the Morality of Constraint (or Moral Realism)   The younger child sees rules as *real*—ready-made and external. Because rules are imposed by outside authority, the child assumes they should always be obeyed the same way. The letter, not the spirit, of the law must be observed, and no exceptions are allowed. Reactions of younger and older children to a change in rules illustrate these characteristics of moral realism. Several elementary school children were

Moral realism: rules
are flexible, intent
important in deter-
mining guilt

TABLE 2.2 Morality of Constraint vs. Morality of Cooperation	
Morality of Constraint (Typical of Six-year-olds)	**Morality of Cooperation (Typical of Twelve-year-olds)**
Holds single, absolute moral perspective (behavior is right or wrong)	Is aware of different viewpoints regarding rules
Believes rules are unchangeable	Believes rules are flexible
Determines extent of guilt by amount of damage	Considers the wrongdoer's intentions when evaluating guilt
Defines moral wrongness in terms of what is forbidden or punished	Defines moral wrongness in terms of violation of spirit of cooperation
(Notice that these first four differences call attention to the tendency for children below the age of ten or so to think of rules as sacred pronouncements handed down by external authority.)	
Believes punishment should stress atonement and does not need to "fit the crime"	Believes punishment should involve either restitution or suffering the same fate as one's victim
Believes peer aggression should be punished by an external authority	Believes peer aggression should be punished by retaliatory behavior on the part of the victim*
Believes children should obey because rules are established by those in authority	Believes children should obey rules because of mutual concern for rights of others
(Notice how these last three differences call attention to the tendency for children above the age of ten or so to see rules as mutual agreements among equals.)	

* Beyond the age of twelve, adolescents increasingly affirm that reciprocal reactions, or "getting back," should be a response to good behavior, not bad.

Sources: Freely adapted from interpretations of Piaget (1932) by Kohlberg (1969) and Lickona (1976).

playing baseball in a vacant lot bordered by weeds. One excellent hitter decided to get some additional batting practice by deliberately hitting several foul balls in a row. Each time a ball was hit foul, however, the others took quite a bit of time to find it in the weeds. Accordingly, some of the older children proposed that anyone who hit two foul balls in a row was out. Most of the players agreed, but the youngest child in the group was so upset by this change in the official rules of baseball that he refused to play and went home in a huff. The moral realist thinks literally and in terms of absolute obedience—making no allowance for motives or intentions. The moral realist also equates the degree of guilt with the seriousness of the consequences. These characteristics of moral realism are illustrated by children's responses to the inkblot stories. Younger children interviewed by Piaget maintained that Augustus was more guilty than Julian because he had made a bigger blot. They took no account of the fact that Julian was misbehaving and that Augustus was trying to help his father.

Many aspects of these differences in the moral reasoning of younger and older children can be understood by taking into account Piaget's descriptions of cognitive development. The child of six who has not completely mastered **decentration**—the ability to think of more than one quality at a time—is therefore not inclined to weigh alternatives. Before the age of seven, a child who has not made the transition from egocentric to socialized speech finds it difficult to consider different points of view. And a child who has not moved from concrete operational to formal thought is unable to consider hypothetical situations and anticipate consequences. Because of the tendency to think of one thing at a time, the young child finds it difficult to comprehend situations in which a rule might be revised to allow for special circumstances. The same tendency leads the younger child to reason that a big inkblot, regardless of how it is caused, is worse than a small inkblot. In other words, the younger child concentrates on obvious physical properties and does not take into account nonobservable factors, such as intentions.

Kohlberg's Description of Moral Development

Just as James Marcia elaborated Erikson's concept of identity formation, Lawrence Kohlberg has elaborated Piaget's ideas on moral thinking.

Kohlberg's Use of Moral Dilemmas   As a graduate student at the University of Chicago in the 1950s, Lawrence Kohlberg became fascinated by Piaget's studies of moral development. He decided to expand on Piaget's original research by making up stories involving moral dilemmas that would be more appropriate for older children. Here is the story that is most often mentioned in discussions of his work:

> In Europe a woman was near death from cancer. One drug might save her, a form of radium that a druggist in the same town had recently discovered. The druggist was charging $2,000, ten times what the drug cost him to make. The sick woman's husband, Heinz, went to everyone he knew to borrow the money, but he could only get together about half of what it cost. He told the druggist that his wife was dying and asked him to sell it cheaper or let him pay later, but the druggist said "No." The husband got desperate and broke into the man's store to steal the drug for his wife. Should the husband have done that? Why? (Kohlberg, 1969, p. 376)

Kohlberg's Six Stages of Moral Reasoning   After analyzing the responses of ten- to sixteen-year-olds to this and similar moral dilemmas, Kohlberg (1963) eventually developed a description of six stages of moral reasoning. Be forewarned, however, that Kohlberg has revised some of his original stage designations, and that descriptions of the stages have been modified since he first proposed them. In different discussions of his stages, therefore, you may encounter varying descriptions. The outline presented in Table 2.3 is a composite summary of the sequence of moral development as it has been described by Kohlberg, but you should expect to find differences if you read other accounts of his theory.

Lawrence Kohlberg described how moral reasoning develops through six stages. (Harvard University News Office)

The scoring system Kohlberg developed to evaluate a given response to a moral dilemma is extremely complex. Furthermore, the responses of subjects are lengthy and may feature arguments about a particular decision. To help you understand a bit more about each Kohlberg stage, simplified examples of responses to a dilemma such as that faced by Heinz are noted below. For maximum clarity, only brief typical responses to the question "Why shouldn't you steal from a store?" are mentioned.

Stage 1 Punishment-obedience orientation. "You might get caught." (The physical consequences of an action determine goodness or badness.)

Stage 2 Instrumental relativist orientation. "You shouldn't steal something from a store, and the store owner shouldn't steal things that belong to you." (Obeying laws should involve an even exchange.)

Stage 3 Good boy–nice girl orientation. "Your parents will be proud of you if you are honest." (The right action is one that will impress others.)

Stage 4 Law and order orientation. "It's against the law, and if we don't obey laws our whole society might fall apart." (To maintain the social order, fixed rules must be obeyed.)

Stage 5 Social contract orientation. "Under certain circumstances laws may have to be disregarded—if a person's life depends on breaking a law, for instance." (Rules should involve mutual agreements; the rights of the individual should be protected.)

TABLE 2.3 Kohlberg's Stages of Moral Reasoning

Level 1 Preconventional Morality. (Typical of children up to the age of nine. Called *preconventional* because young children do not really understand the conventions or rules of a society.)

Stage 1 Punishment–Obedience Orientation. The physical consequences of an action determine goodness or badness. Those in authority have superior power and should be obeyed. Punishment should be avoided by staying out of trouble.

Stage 2 Instrumental Relativist Orientation. An action is judged to be right if it is instrumental in satisfying one's own needs or involves an even exchange. Obeying rules should bring some sort of benefit in return.

Level 2 Conventional Morality. (Typical of nine- to twenty-year-olds. Called *conventional* since most nine- to twenty-year-olds conform to the conventions of society because they *are* the rules of a society.)

Stage 3 Good Boy–Nice Girl Orientation. The right action is one that would be carried out by someone whose behavior is likely to please or impress others.

Stage 4 Law and Order Orientation. To maintain the social order, fixed rules must be established and obeyed. It is essential to respect authority.

Level 3 Postconventional Morality. (Usually reached only after the age of twenty and only by a small proportion of adults. Called *postconventional* because the moral principles that underlie the conventions of a society are understood.)

Stage 5 Social Contract Orientation. Rules needed to maintain the social order should be based not on blind obedience to authority, but on mutual agreement. At the same time, the rights of the individual should be protected.

Stage 6 Universal Ethical Principle Orientation. Moral decisions should be made in terms of self-chosen ethical principles. Once principles are chosen, they should be applied in consistent ways.*

---

* In an article published in 1978, several years after he originally described the six stages, Kohlberg indicated that he had concluded that the last stage is essentially a theoretical ideal and is rarely encountered in real life.

Source: Based on descriptions in Kohlberg (1969, 1976).

Stage 6 Universal ethical principle orientation. "You need to weigh all the factors and then try to make the most appropriate decision in a given situation. Sometimes it would be morally wrong *not* to steal." (Moral decisions should be based on consistent applications of self-chosen ethical principles.)

Similarities and Differences Between Piaget and Kohlberg   As you examined this list of stages and the examples of responses at each stage, you may have detected similarities between Piaget's and Kohlberg's descriptions of age changes in moral development. The first four of Kohlberg's stages are roughly equivalent to the moral realism described by Piaget. Kohlberg's preconventional and conventional moral thinkers and Piaget's moral realists all tend to think of rules as edicts handed down by external authority. The letter of the law is observed, and not much allowance is made for intentions or circumstances. The postconventional thinker of Kohlberg shares some similarities with the older children observed by Piaget: Rules are established by individuals who come to mutual agreement, and each moral decision is made by taking special circumstances into account.

While there are similarities in the conclusions drawn by Piaget and Kohlberg, there are important differences as well. Piaget believes that moral thinking changes as children mature. He does not, however, believe that the changes are clearly related to specific ages, nor are they considered to be sequential. Piaget maintains that the different types of moral thinking he describes often overlap and that a child might sometimes function as a moral realist, sometimes as a more mature moral decision-maker. Kohlberg (1969), by contrast, maintains that the order of the stages he has described is universal and fixed, and that a person moves through the stages in sequence. Not everyone reaches the top stages, but all individuals begin at Stage 1 and work their way upward.

Another difference concerns the acceleration of moral reasoning. Piaget believes that children in the preoperational and concrete operational stages cannot be helped to understand the logic behind moral relativism until the elements of formal operational schemes have begun to form. Kohlberg, on the other hand, believes that progress through his six stages can be accelerated with the proper type of instruction.

In some respects, there are greater similarities between Piaget's description of *cognitive* development and Kohlberg's description of *moral* development than between the two outlines of moral development. Piaget describes preoperational, concrete operational, and formal operational stages. Kohlberg describes preconventional, conventional, and postconventional levels. Even though he does not stress an orderly sequence of *moral* development, Piaget does believe that children go through the stages of *cognitive* development in a definite order. Both Piaget's formal operational stage and Kohlberg's postconventional level stress understanding and application of abstract principles and take into account unique circumstances in a given situation. A person cannot engage in postconventional moral reasoning, in fact, until formal thinking has been mastered.

Criticisms and Evaluations of Kohlberg's Theory

Is Kohlberg's contention that moral reasoning proceeds through a fixed universal sequence of stages accurate? Based on his analysis of research on moral development, Martin Hoffman (1980) feels that although Kohlberg's sequence of stages may not be true of every individual in every culture, it may provide a useful general description of how moral reasoning develops in American society. Carol Gilligan (1979), whose position we discuss in detail later on, has proposed two somewhat different sequences that reflect differences in male and female socialization.

What about Kohlberg's view that moral development can be accelerated through direct instruction? Is this another "mission impossible," as some critics contend? Research on this question has produced some limited but moderately positive results. Most of these studies have used a teaching method known as *direct discussion* or *dilemma discussion*. After reading a set of moral dilemmas (like the one about Heinz and the cancer drug) and identifying those issues that could help resolve the dilemma, students, under the teacher's guidance, discuss the different ways each of them chose to resolve the dilemma. This process can involve challenging one another's thinking, reexamining assumptions, building lines of argument, and responding to counterarguments.

Alan Lockwood (1979), after summarizing the findings of almost a dozen studies on acceleration of moral reasoning, concluded that the strongest effects (about half-a-stage increase in reasoning) occurred among individuals whose reasoning reflected Stages 2 and 3. The effect of the treatment varied considerably from one subject to another. Some individuals showed substantial increases in reasoning; others showed no change. A more recent and comprehensive review of research on this topic by Andre Schlaefli, James Rest, and Stephen Thoma (1985) revealed similar conclusions. The authors found that moral education programs produce modest positive effects. They also found that the strongest effects are obtained with adult subjects.

> Moral education programs may produce modest acceleration in moral development

Paul Vitz (1990) criticizes the use of moral dilemmas on the grounds that they are too far removed from the kinds of everyday social interactions in which children and adolescents engage. He prefers instead the use of narrative stories, be they fictional or real accounts of others, because they portray such basic moral values as honesty, compassion, fairness, and hard work in an understandable context.

Educational Implications of Kohlberg's Theory

In the 1970s, Kohlberg experimented with the use of discussion techniques to "teach" moral reasoning. An interesting outgrowth of that work (for example, see Blatt & Kohlberg, 1978) and his observations in 1969 of life on an Israeli kibbutz is the *just community,* an approach that brings students and teachers together to settle their own problems and make their own rules on a one-person, one-vote basis. (In one instance, students and teachers discussed how to handle immoral and illegal actions, such as the theft of stereo equipment from a camp where students had gone for an outing.) While the just community approach seems to have met with some success (for example, see Kohlberg, 1978; Power, 1981, 1985), it is useful only when a school system agrees to give students the time and power to make many of their own decisions about school rules and interpersonal relationships. It does not seem likely at present that many school boards would be willing to agree to those terms. Perhaps this is why the concept has been tried in only a few, relatively small alternative schools. Another problem with the just community has to do with the nature of participatory democracy. As soon as more than a few people become involved, participatory democracy becomes unwieldy. Piaget drew attention to this point when he described how a small group of ten-year-old boys spent as much time agreeing on rules to govern a snowball fight as they did actually playing. While rule making may be enjoyable when it is a novelty, those who have been involved in a participatory democracy for very long are likely to confess that they sometimes wish an external authority would simply tell them what the rules are so that they can go about their business.

Because of these potential weaknesses of the just community approach, teachers may find that other techniques of moral instruction based on Kohlberg's theory will be more workable. *Moral Reasoning* (1976), by Ronald Galbraith and Thomas Jones (subtitled "A Teaching Handbook for Adapting Kohlberg to the Classroom"), presents several realistic moral dilemmas. It also advises teachers how they might encourage students to write their own moral dilemmas. Both types of dilemmas can be used to stimulate thought and discussion. Richard Hersh, Diana Paolitto, and Joseph Reimer (1979) have developed techniques of moral education based on the observations of Piaget and Kohlberg that are more elaborate and sophisticated variations of the basic approach recommended by Hugh Hartshorne and Mark May in the 1930s. Hartshorne and May (1930a, p. 413) advised that teachers promote discussions of actual situations in detail so that children who found themselves in similar situations would recognize commonalities and be helped to choose a desirable course of action. Hersh, Paolitto, and Reimer recommend to teachers specific procedures for implementing what they refer to as developmental moral education. If for some reason these sources are not available but you occasionally wish to engage your students in a discussion of moral dilemmas, the daily newspaper is an excellent source of material. Biology teachers, for example, can point to stories of the conflicts produced by machines that keep comatose patients alive or by medical practices based on genetic engineering. Other science teachers might bring in articles that describe the moral dilemma produced by the debate over nuclear power versus fossil fuel. Civics or government teachers could use news items that reflect the dilemma that arises when freedom of speech conflicts with the need to curtail racism.

Gilligan's View of Identity and Moral Development

Carol Gilligan (1982, 1988) argues that Erikson's view of identity development and Kohlberg's view of moral development more accurately describe what occurs with adolescent males than with adolescent females. In her view, Erikson's and Kohlberg's ideas emphasize separation from parental authority and societal conventions. Instead of remaining loyal to adult authority, individuals as they mature shift their loyalty to abstract principles (for example, self-reliance, independence, justice, and fairness). This process of detachment allows adolescents to assume a more equal status with adults. It's almost as if adolescents are saying, "You have your life and I have mine; you don't intrude on mine and I won't intrude on yours." But, Gilligan argues, many adolescent females have a different primary concern. They care less about separation and independence and more

Carol Gilligan described how the personality and moral development of adolescent females differs from the personality and moral development of adolescent males. (Keith Carter)

about remaining loyal to others through expressions of caring, understanding, and sharing of experiences. Detachment for these female adolescents is a moral problem rather than a sought-after developmental milestone. The problem for them is how to become autonomous, while also being caring and connected.

Given this view, Gilligan feels that adolescent females are more likely to resolve Erikson's identity vs. role confusion and intimacy vs. isolation crises concurrently rather than consecutively. The results of at least one study (Ochse & Plug, 1986) support this view. With respect to Kohlberg's theory, Gilligan argues that because females are socialized to value more highly the qualities of understanding, helping, and cooperation with others than that of preserving individual rights, and because this orientation is reflected most strongly in Kohlberg's two conventional stages, females are more likely to be judged to be at a lower level of moral development than males.

Stephen Thoma (1986) offers a partial answer to Gilligan's criticism. After reviewing over fifty studies on gender differences in moral development, he drew three conclusions. First, the effect of gender on scores from the Defining Issues Test (the DIT is a device that uses responses to moral dilemmas to determine level of moral reasoning) was very small. Less than half of 1 percent of the differences in DIT scores was due to gender differences. Second, females almost always scored higher. This slight superiority for females appeared in every age group studied (junior high, high school, college, adults). Third, differences in DIT scores were strongly associated with differences in age and level of education. That is, individuals who were older and who had graduated from college were more likely to score at the postconventional level than those who were younger and who had less education. Thoma's findings suggest that females are just as likely as males to use justice and fairness concepts in their reasoning about *hypothetical* moral dilemmas.

But there is one aspect of Gilligan's criticism that cannot be answered by Thoma's analysis of existing research. She argues that when females are faced with their own real-life moral dilemmas (abortion, civil rights, environmental pollution), rather than hypothetical ones, they are more likely to favor a caring/helping/cooperation orientation than a justice/fairness/individual rights orientation. Perhaps the best approach that educators can take when they involve students in discussions of moral issues is to emphasize the utility of *both* orientations.

> Males and females may use different approaches to resolve real-life moral dilemmas

Does Moral Thinking Lead to Moral Behavior?

Piaget's description of cognitive development and Kohlberg's theory of moral development shed light on the results of an exhaustive series of studies of morality supervised by Hartshorne and May (1929, 1930a, 1930b). They observed thousands of children at different age levels reacting in situations that revealed their actual moral behavior. They also asked the children to respond to questions about hypothetical situations, to reveal how much they understood about right and wrong behavior. Elementary school children, for example, were allowed to correct their own papers or record their own scores on measures of athletic skill without being aware that accurate measures were being made independently by adult observers. The children were also asked what they *thought* was the right thing to do in similar situations. A comparison of the two sets of data made it possible to determine, among other things, whether children practiced what they preached. Hartshorne and May wanted information about these two aspects of moral development in order to determine whether the immoral behavior of young children was due to ignorance. What they discovered, however, was that many children who were able to describe right kinds of behavior in hypothetical situations indulged in wrong behavior in real-life situations.

One significant discovery of Hartshorne and May was that children react in specific, rather than consistent, ways to situations that call for moral judgment. Even a child who was rated as among the most honest in a group would behave in a dishonest way under certain circumstances. A boy who was an excellent student but an indifferent athlete, for example, would not cheat when asked to correct his own paper, but he *would* inflate scores on sports skills. A girl who was an excellent athlete but a terrible speller would alter dozens of misspelled words on a paper but be completely accurate in recording her physical performance.

> Moral behavior depends on circumstances

Another significant, and dismaying, discovery of Hartshorne and May was that children who went to Sunday school or who belonged to such organizations as the Boy Scouts or Girl Scouts were just as dishonest as children who were not exposed to the kind of moral instruction provided by such organizations. Hartshorne and May concluded that one explanation for the ineffectiveness of moral instruction in the 1920s was that too much stress was placed on having children memorize values such as the Ten Commandments or the Boy Scout oath and law. They suggested that many children who could recite "Thou shalt not steal" or who could unhesitatingly reel off "Trustworthy, loyal, helpful, friendly, courteous, kind, obedient, cheerful, thrifty, brave, clean, and reverent" either did not understand what they were saying or saw no connection between such elegant words and actual deeds. Hartshorne and May suggested that it would be more effective to invite children to discuss real-life moral situations as they occurred. Instead of having children chant "Honesty is the best policy," for example, they urged teachers to call attention to the positive consequences of honest acts. If a pupil in a school reported that he or she has found money belonging to someone else, the teacher might praise the child and ask everyone in the class to think about how relieved the person who had lost the money would be to get it back.

This suggestion has been echoed more recently by William Damon (1988) in *The Moral Child.* Damon argues that "children acquire moral values by actively participating in adult-child and child-child relationships that support, enhance, and guide their natural moral inclinations" (p. 118). A critical aspect of these relationships is that parents, teachers, and other adults must explain the reasons for requiring children to exhibit certain moral behaviors.

After reviewing research carried out in the forty-five years since Hartshorne and May published their findings, Thomas Lickona reported that "a huge and ever-expanding body of research . . . has replicated Hartshorne and May's basic finding: Variations in the situation produce variations in moral behavior" (1976, p. 15). Lickona further notes, though, that recent research supports another of Hartshorne and May's conclusions: Some children are more "integrated" (or consistent) than others in reacting to moral situations. It would appear to be a mistake, therefore, to assume that there is *no* consistency in moral thinking and behavior. If that hypothesis were endorsed, there would be little reason to assume that a child will develop any kind of personal code of ethics or that parents and teachers should try to promote the development of a strong conscience in children.

Piaget's description of cognitive development and Kohlberg's description of moral reasoning development help explain some of Hartshorne and May's conclusions. Elementary school children are in the concrete operational stage. They think in terms of actual experiences and treat situations that look different in different ways. Because many of these youngsters are also at Kohlberg's third stage (good boy–nice girl), their moral behavior is influenced by their eagerness to please or impress others. Thus, the inability of elementary grade children to comprehend and apply general principles in varied situations and their desire to do what they think will please or impress authority figures may explain, in part, the ineffectiveness of moral instruction that stresses the memorization of abstract principles.

Suggestions for Teaching in Your Classroom

ENCOURAGING MORAL DEVELOPMENT

Handbook Heading:
Ways to Encourage
Moral Development

1. Recognize that younger children will respond to moral conflicts differently from older children.
2. Try to take the perspective of students and stimulate their perspective-taking abilities.
3. Develop an awareness of moral issues by discussing a variety of real and hypothetical moral dilemmas and by using daily opportunities in the classroom to heighten moral awareness. (Moral education should be an integral part of the curriculum; it should not take place during "moral education period.")
4. Create a classroom atmosphere that will enhance open discussion. (For example, arrange face-to-face groupings, be an accepting model, foster listening and communication skills, and encourage student-to-student interaction.)

Specific suggestions for supervising classroom discussions offered by Hersh, Paolitto, and Reimer (1979) include the following:

1. Highlight the moral issue to be discussed. (Describe a specific real or hypothetical moral dilemma.)
2. Ask "Why?" questions. (After asking students what they would do if they were faced with the moral dilemma under discussion, ask them to explain why they would act that way.)
3. Complicate the circumstances. (After students have responded to the original dilemma, mention a factor that might complicate matters—for example, the involvement of a best friend in the dilemma.)
4. Use personal and naturalistic examples. (Invite students to put themselves in the position of individuals who are confronted by moral dilemmas described in newspapers or depicted on television.)

Before you use any techniques of moral education in your classes, it would be wise to check with your principal. In some communities, parents have insisted that they, not teachers, should take the responsibility for moral instruction.

Resources for Further Investigation

Erikson's Description of Development

Erik Erikson's books are of considerable significance in speculating about development and education. In the first six chapters of *Childhood and Society* (2d ed., 1963), he describes how studying Native Americans and observing patients in treatment led him to develop the Eight Ages of Man (described in Chapter 7 of *Childhood and Society*). In the final chapters of this book, Erikson analyzes the lives of Hitler and Maxim Gorky with reference to his conception of development. *Identity: Youth and Crisis* (1968) features a revised description of the eight stages of development, with emphasis on identity and role confusion. Erikson comments on many aspects of his work in an interview with Richard Evans, published under the title *Dialogue with Erik Erikson* (1967). And James Marcia reviews research on identity statuses in Chapter 5 (pp. 159–187) of the *Handbook of Adolescent Psychology* (1980), edited by Joseph Adelson.

Piaget's Theory of Cognitive Development

Jean Piaget has probably exerted more influence on theoretical discussions of development and on educational practices than any other contemporary psychologist. Of his own books, you might wish to consult *The Language and Thought of the Child* (1952a), *The Origins of Intelligence in Children* (1952b), and *The Psychology of the Child* (1969), the last of which was written in collaboration with Barbel Inhelder. H. E. Gruber and J. J. Voneche have edited *The Essential Piaget: An Interpretive Reference and Guide*, which Piaget describes in the foreword as "the best and most complete of all anthologies of my work." An inexpensive paperback that provides a biography of Piaget and an analysis of his work is *Piaget's Theory of Intellectual Development* (3d ed., 1988) by Herbert Ginsburg and Sylvia Opper. Other books about Piaget are *Piaget for Teachers* (1970) by Hans Furth, *Piaget's Theory of Cognitive and Affective Development* (4th ed., 1989) by Barry Wadsworth, *Understanding Piaget* (2d ed., 1980) by Mary Pulaski, and *Children and Adolescents: Interpretive Essays on Jean Piaget* (3d ed., 1981) by David Elkind.

Using Piaget's Interview Method to Assess Cognitive Development

Jean Piaget devised a series of simple experiments to gain insight into the thinking of children at different age levels. You can use similar experiments to determine the level of thinking of the pupils in your classes. If you carry out some of the following experiments with at least some of your pupils, you may be surprised by the amount of insight you acquire. You are almost sure to become aware of ways in which your pupils' thinking differs from yours. In addition, you may understand why some approaches to teaching are—or are not—appropriate with some or all of your students. It would be to your advantage to try out these experiments now, instead of waiting until you actually begin to teach. You should be able to carry out all the experiments for any age level in a single interview of not more than thirty minutes if you have familiarized yourself with the materials ahead of time.

It is not necessary to have a private testing room. You can interview your subject in a hall, a playground, or a school area that is not in a main traffic zone.

After you complete your experiments, you might record your results and conclusions and compare your findings with those of fellow students who interviewed different children.

The experiments described on the following pages can be carried out with easily obtainable objects. You should be able to get most of the items in just one trip to a shopping center or a department, drug, or variety store. After you obtain these materials, read the descriptions in the equipment sections of the experiments you will be carrying out. These explain how you can convert your acquisitions into full-fledged experimental apparatus. Place cards and the like in clasp envelopes, and store all your materials in a cardboard box of appropriate size. You will then be equipped with a test kit of your own devising.

If you carry out any of these experiments, record the name, age, grade, and sex of your subject, and try to record as much as you can of what the pupil does and says.

Piaget Experiment 1—Classification of Objects Approximate age and grade level: Five to seven years, kindergarten to second grade.

Purpose: To discover how the child classifies things. A child who does not grasp the concept of *class* will put together objects in a haphazard or unsystematic way. One who has partial understanding will group some similar objects but fail to group others. A child who understands the nature of classification will put together similar objects in a consistent way.

Equipment: Take some pieces of cardboard or some index cards, and draw six squares approximately 2 inches by 2 inches and six circles 2 inches in diameter. Cut along the lines, and then cut two of the squares along a diagonal line from one corner to the opposite (to form four triangles); then cut two of the circles in half. You will now have four squares, four triangles, four circles, and four semicircles. With paint, crayon, or colored pencil, color one of each shape in each of four colors.

Procedure: Place the pieces of cardboard in front of the child, and thoroughly mix them up so that they are in a random order. Then say: *Put together things that are alike—that are the same.*

Describe how the child proceeds (for example, confidently or tentatively) and what she or he does. When the child has finished, point to one group of pieces and ask: *How are these the same?* Record the child's answer.

Note: If you do not believe the child has used the same reasoning in making other groupings, ask for an explanation for each of these as well. Point to another group of pieces and ask: *How are these the same?* Record the child's answer. Point to still another group of pieces and ask: *How are these the same?* Record the child's answer.

Piaget Experiment 2—Conservation of Number

Approximate age and grade range: Five to seven years, kindergarten to second grade.

Purpose: To discover if the child grasps the fact that the number of objects in a row remains the same even if the distance between them is changed. Children of four or so will be unable to decenter and are likely to say that a longer row has more blocks—even though they can count the blocks in both rows. Older children will be able to understand that the number is constant, even when the appearance of the blocks is changed.

Equipment: Twenty blocks, poker chips, or the equivalent.

Procedure: Place the blocks (or whatever) in front of the child, and space out eight of them about an inch apart in a row. Place the remaining blocks in a pile close to the child. Then say: *Can you count the blocks? How many are there?* Point to the blocks you have arranged in a row. If the child can't count them accurately, give assistance. Then say: *Now take as many of these blocks as you need to make the same number.* Give assistance if necessary.

Describe how the child proceeds.

Next, take the blocks in the row nearest you and space them about 3 inches apart. Take the leftover blocks and place them in a row about 1 inch apart. Point to the longer row and say: *Let's say these are my blocks.* Point to the short row and say: *And these are your blocks. Do I have more blocks, or do you have more blocks, or do we have the same?* Record the child's response.

Then ask: *Why do you think so?* Record the child's response.

Finally, take the blocks that were spaced 3 inches apart and move them so that they are 1 inch apart, just below the other row. Then say: *Now, do you have more blocks, or do I have more blocks, or do we have the same?*

Note the child's response and reactions (e.g., surprise, confusion, and no outward appearance of being bothered).

Piaget Experiment 3—Conservation of Space

Approximate age and grade range: Five to seven years, kindergarten to second grade.

Purpose: To discover how the child handles a different situation involving conservation. A child who is able to handle the problem presented in Experiment 2 may encounter difficulty when confronted with the same basic problem presented in a different form. In solving the problem in Experiment 2, the child must grasp the fact that the number of blocks stays the same even though the space between them is changed. In this experiment the child must understand that four blocks placed on pieces of paper of equal size take up the same amount of space, even though they are arranged differently.

Equipment: Eight small blocks, poker chips, or the equivalent; two pieces of paper or cardboard at least $8^1/_2$ by 11 inches in size

Procedure: Place the two pieces of paper in front of the child and arrange the blocks in a pile to one side. Say: *Let's pretend these are fields owned by two farmers. They are exactly the same size, and both farmers have the same amount of space for their cows to graze in. One farmer decides to build a barn* (you might say "silo" if you use poker chips) *on his field, and we will make believe this is his barn.* (Take one of the blocks and place it near one corner of one piece of paper.) *The other farmer builds a barn on her field, too.* (Put a block on the other piece of paper in the same position as that on the first.) *Do they still have the same amount of space for their cows to graze in?* Record the child's response.

Then say: *Now let's suppose that both farmers make a lot of money and build three more barns. One farmer builds his barns this way* (place three blocks right next to the block already on one sheet of paper), *the other builds her barns this way* (place three blocks several inches apart at different places on the other piece of paper). *Do they still have the same amount of space for their cows to graze in, or does one farmer have more open land than the other?* Record the child's response.

Then ask: *Why do you think so?* Record the child's response.

Finally, take the blocks that were scattered, and place them together so that both sets of blocks are arranged in exactly the same way on each piece of paper. Then ask: *Now, does each farmer have the same amount of space for cows to graze in, or does one have more open land than the other?*

Note the child's response and reactions.

Piaget Experiment 4—Conservation of Continuous Quantity   Approximate age and grade range: Five to seven years, kindergarten to second grade.

Purpose: To discover if a child who can understand conservation of number can also grasp conservation of quantity. A child at the level of concrete operations will be unable to generalize from the block experiment and will solve the following problem only if she or he has had sufficient experience with liquids in glasses of different sizes.

Equipment: Two plastic or glass tumblers of the same size, one plastic or glass bowl or vase (or a tall thin tumbler).

Procedure: Fill one tumbler about two-thirds full of water, the other about one-third full. Put these down in front of the child and say: *Is there more water in this glass* (point to one) *or this one* (point to the other), *or are they the same?* Record the child's response.

Then pour water from the fuller glass into the emptier one until they are equal and ask: *What about now? Is there more water in this glass* (point to one) *or this glass* (point to the other), *or are they the same?* Record the child's response. (If the child says one has more water, invite him or her to pour liquid back and forth from one glass into the other until satisfied that they are the same.)

Next, pour water from one glass into the bowl (or vase) and ask: *Is there more water in this one* (point to the glass) *or this one* (point to the bowl or vase), *or do they contain the same amount of water?* Record the child's response.

Then ask: *Why do you think so?* Record the child's response.

Finally, pour the water from the bowl or vase back into the glass and ask: *Now is there more water in this glass* (point to one) *or this glass* (point to the other), *or are they the same?* Note the child's response and reactions.

Piaget Experiment 5—Conservation of Substance Approximate age and grade range: Five to seven years, kindergarten to second grade.

Purpose: To discover if a child understands that the amount of a substance remains the same even though its shape is changed. Children who are unable to decenter will be unable to grasp that the amount stays constant, since they will concentrate on only one quality. Older children will be able to allow for both qualities at once. They will be able to mentally reverse the action that changed the shape of the substance, which means they are capable of dealing with *operations*. However, if you ask them to deal with an abstract (not actually present) situation of a similar type, they may experience difficulty, indicating that they are at the level of *concrete* operations.

Equipment: A small amount of plasticene or clay.

Procedure: Take a piece of plasticene or clay and divide it as equally as possible. Roll the pieces into two balls and ask the child if he or she thinks the two are the same size. If the pupil says that one is bigger than the other, remove as much as necessary from the larger ball until you get agreement that they are identical. Then take one ball, roll it into a sausage shape, and ask: *Is there more clay here* (point to ball) *or here* (point to sausage), *or do they both have the same amount of clay?* Record the child's response.

Then ask: *Why do you think so?*

Then roll the sausage shape back into a ball and ask: *Is there more clay here* (point to one ball) *or here* (point to the other ball), *or are they the same?* Note the child's response and reactions.

Next, ask the child if the two balls are equal. If she or he says they are not, add or take away clay until the child agrees that they are the same. Then say: *Suppose I put these two pieces on two scales. Would this piece be heavier, or would this piece, or would they both be the same?* Record the child's response.

Then roll one ball into a sausage shape, and ask: *What would happen if I weighed these now? Would this one* (point to ball) *or this one* (point to sausage) *be heavier, or would one be as heavy as the other?* Record the child's response.

Then ask: *Why do you think so?* Record the child's response.

Piaget Experiment 6—Analyzing Aspects of Formal Thought (Solving a Problem) Approximate age and grade range: Twelve years and above, sixth grade and above.

Purpose: To discover how students attempt to solve a problem. Children at the level of concrete operations are able to solve problems if they have had actual experience with the kinds of objects and situations involved, but they are unable to handle new and unique situations. In addition, they are likely to approach a problem in a haphazard, unsystematic way. Students at the level of formal operations, on the other hand, can deal with combinations of ideas in a systematic way, propose and test hypotheses, and imagine what might happen in situations they have never before encountered.

Equipment: A piece of string about 6 feet long and three fishing weights, one small, one medium, and one large. (Any objects of different weights to which a string can be attached may be substituted for the fishing weights.)

Procedure: Take three pieces of string 18 inches long and attach one of the weights to the end of each. Pick up the string with the smallest weight and start it swinging, much like a pendulum, in both these ways: by holding the string at different places and letting the weight drop (when the string is held taut) from different positions, and by *pushing* the weight rather than simply letting it fall. Also, call attention to the fact that the strings are equal in length but the weights are different.

Then say: *There are four factors involved here: the length of the string, the difference in weight at the end of the string, the height from which the weight is released, and the force with which the weight is pushed. I want you to figure out which of these factors—or what combination of them—determines how fast the weight swings. Experiment with these pieces of string any way you like and, when you think you have it figured out, tell me what your solution is. Or, if you can, give me your solution without actually handling the strings.*

Describe how the student proceeds.

What solution does the student offer?

Once the solution is given, ask the student to prove it to you. If you detect an oversight, demonstrate the nature of the error and observe the student's reaction. (Note: The length of the string is the major determinant of the speed of the swing.)

Piaget Experiment 7—Analyzing Aspects of Formal Thought (Tendency to Theorize) Approximate age and grade range: Thirteen years and above, seventh grade and above.

Purpose: To gain insight into the tendency of students who have recently mastered formal thought to engage in hypothesizing, which may center more on possibilities than on realities, and to be somewhat unrestrained in dealing with abstract and theoretical matters.

Procedure: Ask students to respond to this question: *At the present time there are between six and eight million unemployed people in this country. If you had complete power to make laws and establish and finance programs in this country, how would you try to reduce unemployment? Tell me all the ideas you come up with as you think of them.* Record the student's response.

Piaget's Description of Moral Development

Piaget describes his observations on moral development in *The Moral Judgment of the Child* (1932). Thomas Lickona summarizes research investigations stimulated by Piaget's conclusions in "Research on Piaget's Theory of Moral Development" on pages 219–240 of *Moral Development and Behavior* (1976), an excellent compilation of articles on all aspects of morality, which he edited.

Kohlberg's Stages of Moral Development

If you would like to read Kohlberg's own account of the stages of moral development, examine "Moral Stages and Moralization: The Cognitive-Developmental Approach" in *Moral Development and Behavior* (1976), edited by Thomas Lickona. Kohlberg discusses "Revisions in the Theory and Practice of Moral Development" in *Moral Development: New Directions for Child Development* (no. 2, 1978), edited by W. Damon. Techniques for encouraging moral development by taking account of Kohlberg's stages are described in *Promoting Moral Growth* (1979) by Richard Hersh, Diana Paolitto, and Joseph Reimer.

Kohlberg's Just Community

To learn more about the nature of a just community and how it works in practice, read "The Just Community Approach to Moral Education in Theory and Practice" by Kohlberg and "Democratic Moral Education in the Large Public High School" by Clark Power. Both articles appear in *Moral Education: Theory and Application* (1985), edited by Marvin Berkowitz and Fritz Oser.

Gilligan's Analysis of Adolescent Development

If you would like to know more about the basis of Carol Gilligan's critique of Erikson's and Kohlberg's theories and her arguments for a broader view of adolescent development, start with her widely cited book *In a Different Voice: Psychological Theory and Women's Development* (1982). Briefer and more recent analyses of this issue are "Adolescent Development Reconsidered," a chapter in *Adolescent Social Behavior and Health* (1987), edited by C. E. Irwin, Jr., and "Exit-Voice Dilemmas in Adolescent Development," a chapter in *Mapping the Moral Domain: A Contribution of Women's Thinking to Psychological Theory and Education* (1988), edited by C. Gilligan, J. Ward, J. Taylor, and B. Bardige.

Hartshorne and May's Studies of Character

The series of studies on character development carried out by Hugh Hartshorne and Mark May have never been equaled in terms of ingenuity, thoroughness, or depth. Even though they were completed in the 1920s, the results of these studies are still well worth examining. The authors give detailed descriptions of how they developed and administered their various measures, as well as their results and conclusions, in a three-volume series published under the general title *Studies in the Nature of Character*. Volume 1, *Studies in Deceit* (1930), gives the background of the study and then provides a description of the methods and results of the studies of honesty. Volume 2, *Studies in Service and Self-Control* (1929), describes methods and conclusions regarding those types of behavior. Volume 3, *Studies in the Organization of Character* (1930), reports a follow-up study of interrelationships between the types of behavior reported in Volumes 1 and 2. (The final summary begins on page 382.)

SUMMARY

1. Theories organize and give meaning to facts and guide research. Developmental theories describe the sequence, continuity, and interrelatedness of aspects of development.

2. Erikson's theory of personality development is based on the epigenetic principle of biology. Just as certain parts of the fetus are formed at certain times and combine to produce a biologically whole individual at birth, certain aspects of personality develop at certain times and combine to form a psychologically whole individual.

3. Erikson's theory describes eight stages, from birth through old age. The stages that deal with the personality development of school-age children are initiative vs. guilt (four to five years), industry vs. inferiority (six to eleven years), and identity vs. role confusion (twelve to eighteen years).

4. Individuals with a strong sense of identity are comfortable with their physical selves, have a sense of purpose and direction, and know they will be recognized by others. Individuals with a poorly developed sense of identity are susceptible to role confusion.

5. Establishing a strong identity and avoiding role confusion are especially difficult for today's adolescents because of changing social values.

6. One solution to the conflict over appropriate sex role behavior is psychological androgyny.

7. When faced with making an occupational choice, some adolescents declare a psychosocial moratorium; others establish a negative identity.

8. Erikson's observations about identity were extended by Marcia, who described four identity statuses: identity diffusion, moratorium, identity achievement, and foreclosure.

9. Erikson's theory has been criticized for its heavy reliance on personal experience, for its inaccuracies in terms of female personality development, and for its failure to specify how individuals move from stage to stage.

10. Piaget believes that individuals inherit two basic intellectual tendencies: organization (the tendency to combine mental processes into more general systems) and adaptation (the tendency to adjust to the environment).

11. Adaptation occurs through the processes of assimilation (fitting an experience into an existing scheme) and accommodation (changing a scheme or creating a new one to incorporate a new experience).

12. A scheme is a mental framework that guides our thoughts and actions.

13. Equilibration is the process of trying to organize a system of schemes that allows us to adapt to current environmental conditions. Equilibration is produced by a state of disequilibrium.

14. On the basis of his studies, Piaget concluded that schemes evolve through four stages: sensorimotor (birth to two years), preoperational (two to seven years), concrete operational (seven to twelve years), and formal operational (twelve to eighteen years).

15. During the sensorimotor stage, the infant and toddler use senses and motor skills to explore and understand the environment.

16. In the preoperational stage, the child masters symbol systems but cannot manipulate symbols logically.

17. In the concrete operational stage, the child is capable of logical thinking, but only with ideas with which he or she has had firsthand experience.

18. During the formal operational stage, the individual is capable of hypothetical reasoning, dealing with abstractions, and engaging in mental manipulations.

19. Systematic instruction may have modest positive effects on the rate of cognitive development as long as the schemes that will govern the next stage have already begun to develop.

20. Piaget's theory has been criticized for underestimating children's abilities, for overestimating the capability of adolescents to engage in formal operational thinking, and for not addressing cultural differences.

21. Piaget identified two types of moral reasoning in children: morality of constraint (rules are inflexible and external) and morality of cooperation (rules are flexible and internal).

22. Kohlberg defined six stages in the development of moral reasoning: punishment-obedience, instrumental relativist, good boy–nice girl, law and order, social contract, and universal ethical principle.

23. Structured discussions based on moral dilemmas may have some positive effects on the rate of development of moral reasoning.

24. Carol Gilligan maintains that Erikson's theory of identity development and Kohlberg's theory of moral development more accurately describe male development than female development.

25. Studies show that children's moral behavior varies in different circumstances.

KEY TERMS

epigenetic principle   *(42)*
identity   *(45)*
role confusion   *(46)*
psychological androgyny   *(49)*
psychosocial moratorium   *(50)*
negative identity   *(50)*
identity diffusion type   *(52)*
moratorium type   *(53)*
identity achievement type   *(53)*
foreclosure type   *(53)*
organization   *(59)*
adaptation   *(59)*
equilibration   *(59)*
scheme   *(59)*
assimilation   *(59)*
accommodation   *(59)*
constructivism   *(60)*
conservation   *(63)*
perceptual centration   *(64)*
irreversibility   *(64)*
egocentrism   *(65)*
adolescent egocentrism   *(67)*

zone of proximal development (ZPD)   *(69)*
morality of constraint   *(74)*
morality of cooperation   *(74)*
decentration   *(76)*

DISCUSSION QUESTIONS

1. According to Erikson, the way in which personality develops among six- to eleven-year-old children depends on their attaining a sense of industry and avoiding a sense of inferiority. Suppose you were an elementary school teacher. What kinds of things would you do to help your students feel more capable and productive? What kinds of things would you avoid doing?

2. Between the ages of twelve and eighteen, personality development revolves around establishing an identity and avoiding role confusion. American high schools are often criticized for not helping adolescents resolve this conflict. Do you agree? Why? What do you think could be done to improve matters?

3. From Piaget's point of view, why is it wrong to think of children as "small adults"?

4. In response to reports that American schoolchildren do not score as well as many European and Asian schoolchildren on standardized achievement tests, some critics of American education argue that we should begin formal schooling earlier than age five and that it should focus on mastery of basic reading and computation skills. How would Piaget respond to this proposal?

5. How would you respond to a parent (or colleague) who argued that students have better things to do in class than discuss ways of resolving moral dilemmas?

Chapter 3
AGE-LEVEL CHARACTERISTICS

Key Points

PRESCHOOL AND KINDERGARTEN

▶ Large-muscle control better established than small-muscle control and eye-hand coordination

▶ Shift from parallel to cooperative play between 2 and 5 years

▶ Sex differences in toy preferences and play activities noticeable by kindergarten

▶ Young children stick to own language rules

PRIMARY GRADES

▶ Primary grade children have difficulty focusing on small print

▶ Accident rate peaks in 3d grade because of confidence in physical skills

▶ Rigid interpretation of rules in elementary grades

▶ To encourage industry, use praise, avoid criticism

ELEMENTARY GRADES

▶ Girls taller and heavier from 10 to 14 years

▶ After growth spurt, boys have greater strength and endurance

▶ Average age of puberty: girls, 11; boys, 14

▶ Peer group norms for behavior begin to replace adult norms

▶ Delinquents have few friends, are easily distracted, are not interested in schoolwork, lack basic skills

▶ Girls superior in verbal skills, math computation

▶ Boys superior in math reasoning, spatial abilities

▶ Sex differences in cognitive abilities getting smaller

▶ Impulsive thinkers look at big picture, reflective thinkers concentrate on details

JUNIOR HIGH

▶ Early-maturing boys likely to draw favorable responses

▶ Late-maturing boys may seek attention

▶ Late-maturing girls likely to be popular and care-free

▶ Discussion of controversial issues may be difficult because of strong desire to conform to peer norms

▶ Teen-agers experience different degrees of emotional turmoil

▶ Political thinking becomes more abstract, less authoritarian, more knowledgeable

HIGH SCHOOL

▶ Sexual activity among male, female teens due to different factors

▶ Adolescents likely to be confused about appropriateness of premarital sex

▶ Parents influence values, plans; peers influence immediate status

▶ Girls more likely than boys to experience anxiety about friendships

▶ Depression most common among females, teens from poor families

▶ Depression may be caused by negative set, learned helplessness, sense of loss

▶ Depression and unstable family situation place adolescents at risk for suicide

The theories described in Chapter 2 call attention to stages of psychosocial, cognitive, and moral development. While these types of behavior are important, they represent only a small part of the behavioral repertoire of a child or adolescent. In order to describe many aspects of development of potential significance to teachers, we must analyze types of behavior that are not directly related to the theories already discussed or to those (learning and information processing) to be discussed in Part 3. This chapter presents such an overview of types of behavior at different age and grade levels that are not directly related to any particular theory. In selecting points for emphasis, we used one basic criterion: Does this information about development have potential significance for teachers? In order to organize the points to be discussed, we have divided the developmental span into five levels, corresponding to common grade groupings in schools: preschool and kindergarten (three to six years), primary grades (1, 2, and 3; six to nine years), elementary grades (4, 5, and 6; nine to twelve years), junior high (7, 8, and 9; twelve to fifteen years), and senior high (10, 11, and 12; fifteen to eighteen years). Because the way grades are grouped varies, you may find yourself teaching in a school system where the arrangement described in this chapter is not followed. In that case, simply refer to the appropriate age-level designations, and, if necessary, concentrate on two levels rather than one. While you should concentrate on the descriptions of characteristics of pupils of the grade and age levels you expect to teach, you should also read the rest of the chapter with care. One reason for reading about characteristics of pupils at all levels is that even though you presently anticipate that you will teach a particular grade level, you may at some point teach younger or older pupils. Another reason is that you may gain awareness of continuities of development and come to realize how some aspects of the behavior of older children were influenced by earlier experiences. Finally, even though a particular type of behavior is discussed at a level where it is considered to be of special significance, it may be important at any age level. Techniques for encouraging students to become more sensitive to the feelings of others, to note just one example, are discussed in the section on the elementary grades, but the same techniques can be used at all grade levels.

Various types of behavior at each of the five levels are discussed under these headings: physical, social, emotional, and cognitive characteristics. Following each characteristic, implications for teachers are noted. To help you establish a general conception of what children are like at each level, brief summaries of the types of behavior stressed by the theorists discussed in the preceding chapter are listed in a table near the beginning of each section (Tables 3.1, 3.2, 3.3, 3.6, and 3.8).

PRESCHOOL AND KINDERGARTEN (THREE TO SIX YEARS)

Physical Characteristics: Preschool and Kindergarten

1. Preschool children are extremely active. They have good control of their bodies and enjoy activity for its own sake. Provide plenty of opportunities for the children to run, climb, and jump. Arrange these activities, as much as possible, so that they are under your control. If you follow a policy of complete freedom, you may discover that thirty improvising three- to five-year-olds can be a frightening thing. In your Handbook you might note some specific games and activities that you could use to achieve semicontrolled play.

Handbook Heading:
Active Games

2. Because of their inclination toward bursts of activity, kindergartners need frequent rest periods. They themselves often don't recognize

TABLE 3.1 Applying Stage Theories of Development to the Preschool and Kindergarten Years

Stage of psychosocial development: initiative vs. guilt. Pupils need opportunities for free play and experimentation, as well as experiences that give them a sense of accomplishment.

Stage of cognitive development: preoperational thought. Gradual acquisition of ability to conserve and center, but children not capable of operations and unable to mentally reverse actions.

Stage of moral development: morality of constraint, preconventional. Rules viewed as unchangeable edicts handed down by those in authority. Punishment-obedience orientation focuses on physical consequences rather than on intentions.

General factors to keep in mind: first experiences with school routine, interactions with more than a few peers. Preparation for initial academic experiences in group settings. Important to learn to follow directions, get along with others.

Handbook Heading:
Riot-Stopping Signals
and Activities

the need to slow down. Schedule quiet activities after strenuous ones. Have rest time. Realize that excitement may build up to a riot level if the attention of "catalytic agents" and their followers is not diverted. In your Handbook you might list some signals for calling a halt to a melee (for example, playing the opening chords of Beethoven's Fifth Symphony on the piano) or for diverting wild action

Young children are very active and possess good gross motor skills. (Crystal Images/Monkmeyer Press)

into more or less controlled activity (marching around the room to a brisk rendition of "The Stars and Stripes Forever").

3. Preschoolers' large muscles are more developed than those that control fingers and hands. Therefore, preschoolers may be quite clumsy at, or physically incapable of, such skills as tying shoes and buttoning coats. Avoid too many small-motor activities, such as pasting paper chains. Provide big brushes, crayons, and tools. In your Handbook you might note other activities or items of king-size equipment that would be appropriate for the children's level of muscular development.

Handbook Heading:
Allowing for Large-
Muscle Control

▶ Large-muscle control
better established
than small-muscle
control and eye-hand
coordination

4. Young children find it difficult to focus their eyes on small objects; therefore, their eye-hand coordination may be imperfect. If possible, minimize the necessity for the children to look at small things. (Incomplete eye development is the reason for large print in children's books.)

5. Although the children's bodies are flexible and resilient, the bones that protect the brain are still soft. Be extremely wary of blows to the head in games or fights between children. If you notice an activity involving such a blow, intervene immediately; warn the class that this is dangerous and explain why.

6. Although boys are bigger, girls are ahead of boys in practically all other areas of development, especially in fine motor skills, so don't be surprised if boys are clumsier at manipulating small objects. It may be desirable to avoid boy-girl comparisons or competition involving such skills.

Social Characteristics: Preschool and Kindergarten

1. Most children have one or two best friends, but these friendships may change rapidly. Preschoolers tend to be quite flexible socially; they are usually willing and able to play with most of the other children in the class. Favorite friends tend to be of the same sex, but many friendships between boys and girls develop. Youngsters are quite adept at figuring out which social and linguistic skills elicit responses from playmates. Typical gambits include inviting a peer to engage in rough-and-tumble play, offering an object to a playmate, offering to exchange objects with a playmate, sticking to the topic of a conversation, moving close to the person to whom one is speaking, and asking a question or giving a command (Guralnick, 1986). You might make it a habit to notice whether some children seem to lack the ability or confidence to join others. In some cases a child may prefer to be a loner or an observer rather than a participant. But if you sense that a child really wants to get to know others, you might provide some assistance.

2. Play groups tend to be small and not too highly organized; hence they change rapidly. You should not be concerned if children flit constantly from one activity to another. Such behavior is normal for this age group, although it may sometimes drive you wild. You might think about how much control you will want to exert over your pupils, particularly during free-play periods. At what

Handbook Heading:
How Much Control Is
Necessary?

During the early preschool years children tend to play beside, but not with, one another. As they approach kindergarten age, children engage more in forms of play that require cooperation. (K. B. Kaplan/The Picture Cube)

point is insistence on silence and sedentary activities justifiable? Should you insist that pupils stick with self-selected activities for a given period of time?

3. Younger children may play beside others; older ones, with others. Mildred Parten (1932) observed the free play of children in a nursery school and noted the types of social behavior they engaged in. Eventually, she was able to write quite precise descriptions of six types of behavior:

Unoccupied behavior. Children do not really play at all. They either stand around and look at others for a time or engage in aimless activities.

Solitary play. Children play alone with toys that are different from those used by other children within speaking distance of them. They make no attempt to interact with others.

Onlooker behavior. Children spend most of their time watching others. They may kibitz and make comments about the play of others, but they do not attempt to join in.

Parallel play. Children play *beside,* but not really with, other children. They use the same toys in close proximity to others but in an independent way.

Associative play. Children engage in rather disorganized play with other children. There is no assignment of activities or roles; individual children play in their own ways.

> ▶ Shift from parallel to cooperative play between 2 and 5 years

Cooperative play. Children engage in an organized form of play in which leadership and other roles are assigned. The members of the group may cooperate in creating some project, dramatize some situation, or engage in some sort of coordinated enterprise.

4. Play patterns also may vary as a function of social class and gender, as well as of age. Kenneth Rubin, Terence Maioni, and Margaret Hornung (1976) observed and classified the free play of preschoolers according to their level of social and cognitive participation. The four levels of social participation they observed (solitary, parallel, associative, and cooperative) were taken from the work of Parten described above. The four levels of cognitive participation they observed were taken from the work of Sara Smilansky (1968) (who based them on Piaget's work) and were as follows:

Functional play. Making simple repetitive muscle movements with or without objects.

Constructive play. Manipulating objects in order to construct or create something.

Dramatic play. Using an imaginary situation.

Games with rules. Using prearranged rules to play a game.

The Parten and Rubin et al. studies found that lower-class children engaged in more parallel and functional play than their middle-class peers, whereas middle-class children displayed more associative, cooperative, and constructive play. Girls engaged in more solitary- and parallel-constructive play but in less dramatic play than did the boys. Boys, on the other hand, engaged in more solitary-functional and associative dramatic play than did the girls.

The Parten and Rubin et al. studies call attention to the variety of play activities common to preschool children. This knowledge may help you determine if a child *prefers* solitary play or plays alone because of shyness or lack of skills for joining in associative or cooperative play.

5. Quarrels are frequent, but they tend to be of short duration and quickly forgotten. When thirty children are thrown together for the first time in a restricted environment, with a limited number of objects to be shared, disputes over property rights and similar matters are inevitable. Do not be surprised if you find that the majority of quarrels and aggressive acts involve two or more boys. Research has shown that males are more likely than females to behave aggressively. The gender difference in aggression is greatest among preschoolers and least noticeable among college students (Hyde, 1986). When possible, let the children settle these differences on their own, and intervene only if a quarrel gets out of hand. If you do have to intervene, you might try one of two tactics: Suggest that one or both children engage in another equally attractive activity, or impose a turn-taking rule. (Other methods of classroom control are discussed in Chapter 14.)

6. Awareness of sex roles and sex typing is evident. By the time they enter kindergarten, most children have developed awareness of sex differences

Sex differences in toy preferences and play activities noticeable by kindergarten

Handbook Heading: Encouraging Girls to Achieve, Boys to Be Sensitive

and of masculine and feminine roles (Wynn & Fletcher, 1987). This awareness shows up very clearly in the toys and activities that boys and girls prefer. Boys are more likely than girls to play outdoors, to engage in rough and tumble play, and to behave aggressively. Boys play with toy vehicles (cars, planes, and trucks, for example) and construction toys, and they engage in action games (such as football or soccer). Girls prefer art activities, doll play, and dancing (Carter, 1987). As we pointed out in Chapter 2, sex role differences are often reinforced by the way parents behave. Boys are encouraged to be active and independent, while girls are encouraged to be more docile and dependent. Peers may further reinforce these tendencies. A boy or girl may notice that other children are more willing to play when he or she selects a sex-appropriate toy.

Therefore, if you teach preschool children, you may have to guard against a tendency to respond too soon when little girls ask for help. If they *need* assistance, of course you should supply it; but if preschool girls can carry out tasks on their own, you should urge them to do so. You might also remind yourself that girls need to be encouraged to become more achievement oriented and boys to become more sensitive to the needs of others. Through such efforts, you may be able to help children resist some forms of sex typing and begin to acquire traits of psychological androgyny.

Emotional Characteristics: Preschool and Kindergarten

1. Kindergarten children tend to express their emotions freely and openly. Anger outbursts are frequent. It is probably desirable to let children at this age level express their feelings openly, at least within broad limits, so that they can recognize and face their emotions. In *Between Parent and Child* (1965) and *Teacher and Child* (1972), Haim Ginott offers some specific suggestions on how a parent or teacher can help children develop awareness of their feelings. His books may help you work out your own philosophy and techniques for dealing with emotional outbursts.

Suppose, for example, that a boy who was wildly waving his hand to be called on during share-and-tell time later knocks down a block tower made by a girl who monopolized sharing time with a spell-binding story of a kitten rescued by fire fighters. When you go over to break up the incipient fight, the boy angrily pushes you away. In such a situation, Ginott suggests you take the boy to a quiet corner and engage in a dialogue such as this:

You: It looks as if you are unhappy about something, Pete.
Boy: Yes, I am.
You: Are you angry about something that happened this morning?
Boy: Yes.
You: Tell me about it.
Boy: I wanted to tell the class about something at sharing time, and Mary talked for three hours, and you wouldn't let me say anything.
You: And that made you mad at Mary and at me?

Boy: Yes.

You: Well, I can understand why you are disappointed and angry. But Mary had an exciting story to tell, and we didn't have time for anyone else to tell what they had to say. You can be the very first one to share something tomorrow morning. Now how about doing an easel painting? You always do such interesting paintings.

Ginott suggests that when children are encouraged to analyze their own behavior, they are more likely to become aware of the causes of their feelings. This awareness, in turn, may help them learn to accept and control their feelings and to find more acceptable means of expressing them. But because these children are likely to be in Piaget's preoperational stage of intellectual development, bear in mind that this approach may not be successful with all of them. The egocentric orientation of four- to five-year-olds makes it difficult for them to reflect on the thoughts of self or others. (This point is spelled out in the context of other stages of interpersonal reasoning in Table 3.4, page 115.)

Handbook Heading:
Helping Pupils Understand Anger

Anger outbursts are more likely to occur when children are tired, hungry, and/or exposed to too much adult interference. If you take such conditions into account and try to alleviate them (by providing a nap or a snack, for example), temper tantrums may be minimized. However, by the time children enter the elementary grades, they should have begun learning to control anger themselves. In your Handbook you might jot down any techniques you have observed or can think of that will help children accomplish this goal. If some of the techniques described by Ginott strike you as especially promising guidelines, note these also.

2. Jealousy among classmates is likely to be fairly common at this age, since kindergarten children have much affection for the teacher and actively seek approval. When there are thirty individuals competing for the affection and attention of just one, some jealousy is inevitable. Try to spread your attention around as equitably as possible; and when you praise particular children, do it in a private or casual way. If one child is given lavish public recognition, it is only natural for the other children to feel resentful. Think back to how you felt about teachers' pets during your own school years. If you have observed or can think of other techniques for minimizing jealousy, jot them down in your Handbook.

Handbook Heading:
Ways to Avoid Playing Favorites

Cognitive Characteristics: Preschool and Kindergarten

1. Kindergartners are quite skillful with language. Most of them like to talk, especially in front of a group. Providing a "sharing time" gives children a natural opportunity for talking, but many will need help in becoming good listeners. Some sort of rotation scheme is usually necessary to divide talking opportunities between the gabby and silent extremes. You might provide activities or experiences for less confident children to talk about, such as a field trip, a book, or a film. In your Handbook you might note some comments to use if

Handbook Heading:
Handling Sharing

pupils start to share the wrong thing (such as a vivid account of a fight between their parents) or if they try to "one-up" classmates (for example, "Your cat may have had five kittens, but *our* cat had a *hundred* kittens"). For titillating topics, for instance, you might say, "There are some things that are private, and it's better not to talk about them to others."

2. Preschoolers may stick to their own rules in using language. One of the most intriguing aspects of early language development is the extent to which children stick to their own rules. This tendency is so strong that Roger Brown (1973) has concluded that efforts by parents and teachers to speed up acquisition of correct speech may not always be successful. Evidence to back up this conclusion is provided in an ingenious study by Jean Berko (1958). Berko found that if four-year-olds are shown pictures and told, for example, "Here is a goose, and here are two geese," and are then asked to complete the sentence "There are two _____," most will say "gooses." Further evidence of the degree to which children stick to their own view of language is provided by the following conversation (reported by Cazden, 1968), in which a mother attempts to supply subtle instruction:

▶ Young children stick to own language rules

Child: My teacher holded the baby rabbits and we patted them.
Mother: Did you say your teacher held the baby rabbits?
Child: Yes.
Mother: What did you say she did?
Child: She holded the baby rabbits and we patted them.
Mother: Did you say she held them tightly?
Child: No, she holded them loosely.

Given this strong tendency of children to use their own rules of grammar, you should probably limit any attempts at grammar instruction to modeling (as in the above exchange between mother and child). The possibility of getting youngsters to use adult forms of grammar would seem to be outweighed by the risk of inhibiting their spontaneous use of language. Direct and systematic instruction in grammar should be delayed until second or third grade.

Handbook Heading: Encouraging Competence

3. Competence is encouraged by interaction, interest, opportunities, urging, limits, admiration, and signs of affection. Studies of young children rated as highly competent (Ainsworth & Wittig, 1972; White & Watts, 1973) lead to the conclusion that those who desire to encourage preschoolers to make the most of their abilities should follow these guidelines:

1. Interact with the child often and in a variety of ways.

2. Show interest in what the child does and says.

3. Provide opportunities for the child to investigate and experience many things.

4. Permit and encourage the child to do many things independently.

5. Urge the child to try to achieve mature and skilled types of behavior.

6. Establish firm and consistent limits regarding unacceptable forms of behavior; explain the reasons for these as soon as the child is able to understand; listen to complaints if the child feels the restrictions are too confining; give additional reasons if the limits are still to be maintained as originally stated.

7. Show that the child's achievements are admired and appreciated.

8. Communicate love in a warm and sincere way.

Diana Baumrind's analysis (1971) of authoritative, authoritarian, and permissive child-rearing approaches shows why such techniques seem to lead to competence in children. Baumrind found that parents of competent children were **authoritative parents**. They had confidence in their abilities as parents and therefore provided a model of competence for their children to imitate. When they established limits and explained reasons for restrictions, they encouraged their children to set standards for themselves and to think about *why* certain procedures should be followed. And because the parents were warm and affectionate, their positive responses were valued by their children as rewards for mature behavior. **Authoritarian parents**, by contrast, made demands and wielded power, but their failure to take into account the child's point of view and their lack of warmth led to resentment and insecurity on the part of the child. Children of authoritarian parents may do as they are told, but they are likely to do so out of compliance or fear, not out of a desire to earn love or approval. Permissive parents, as defined by Baumrind, were disorganized, inconsistent, and lacked confidence. Their children were likely to imitate such behavior. Furthermore, such parents did not demand much of their children, nor did they discourage immature behavior.

You might refer to these observations on authoritative, authoritarian, and permissive approaches not only when you plan how to encourage competence but also when you think about the kind of classroom atmosphere you hope to establish.

PRIMARY GRADES (1, 2, AND 3; SIX TO NINE YEARS)

Physical Characteristics: Primary Grades

1. Primary grade children are still extremely active. Because they are frequently required to participate in sedentary pursuits, energy is often released in the form of nervous habits—for example, pencil chewing, fingernail biting, hair twirling, and general fidgeting. You will have to decide what noise and activity level should prevail during work periods. A few teachers insist on absolute quiet, but such a rule can make the children work so hard at remaining quiet that they cannot devote much effort to their lessons. The majority of teachers allow a certain amount of moving about and talking. Whatever you decide, be on the alert for the point of diminishing returns—whether from too much or too little restriction.

> **TABLE 3.2   Applying Stage Theories of Development to the Primary Grade Years**
>
> **Stage of psychosocial development:** industry vs. inferiority. Important to arrange for pupils to experience a sense of industry by presenting tasks they can complete successfully. Try to minimize and correct failures to prevent development of feelings of inferiority.
>
> **Stage of cognitive development:** in process of moving from preoperational to concrete operational stage. Gradual acquisition of ability to solve problems by generalizing from concrete experiences.
>
> **Stage of moral development:** morality of constraint, preconventional. Rules viewed as edicts handed down by authority. Focus on physical consequences; obeying rules should bring benefit in return.
>
> **General factors to keep in mind:** first experiences with school learning. Eager to learn to read and write, likely to be upset by lack of progress. Initial attitudes toward schooling are established. Initial roles in a group are formed, roles that may establish a lasting pattern (for example, leader, follower, loner, athlete, and underachiever).

Handbook Heading: Building Activity into Classwork

To minimize fidgeting, avoid situations in which your pupils must stay glued to their desks for long periods. Have frequent breaks and try to work activity into the lessons themselves. (For example, have children go up to the board, bring papers to your desk, or move their desks into different formations.) In your Handbook you might jot down other techniques for encouraging your pupils to be active while doing classwork.

2. Children at these grade levels still need rest periods; they become fatigued easily as a result of physical and mental exertion. Schedule quiet activities after strenuous ones (story time after recess, for example), and relaxing activities after periods of mental concentration (art after spelling or math).

3. Large-muscle control is still superior to fine coordination. Many children, especially boys, have difficulty manipulating a pencil. Try not to schedule too much writing at one time. If drill periods are too long, skill may deteriorate and the children may develop a negative attitude toward writing or toward school in general.

4. Many primary grade pupils may have difficulty focusing on small print or objects. Quite a few children may be far-sighted because of the shallow shape of the eye. Try not to require too much reading at one stretch. Be on the alert for signs of eye fatigue (rubbing the eyes or blinking). When preparing class handouts, be sure to print in large letters or use a primary grade typewriter. Until the lens of the eye can be easily focused, young children have trouble looking back and forth from near to far objects. Another vision problem encountered by preschool and primary grade children is amblyopia, or "lazy eye." In normal vision the muscles of the two eyes work together to fuse their two images into one. Until the eye muscles become coordinated, however, children may experience double vision. In their efforts to cope with this problem, children

▶ Primary grade children have difficulty focusing on small print

Because primary grade students cannot easily focus on small print and objects, they should read from books that have large print.
(1990 Frank Siteman/The Picture Cube)

may try to eliminate one image by closing one eye, tilting their heads, or blinking or rubbing their eyes. Treatment for amblyopia is aimed at strengthening the muscles of the weaker eye and may include covering the stronger eye with a patch, wearing glasses, eye exercises, or, in extreme cases, corrective surgery. In addition to being alert for signs of eye fatigue, therefore, you should watch for signs of amblyopia and let the parents know if you detect one or more signs of lazy eye in any of your pupils.

5. At this age children tend to be extreme in their physical activities. They have excellent control of their bodies and develop considerable confidence in their skills. As a result, they often underestimate the danger involved in their more daring exploits. The accident rate is at a peak in the third grade. You might check on school procedures for handling injuries, but also try to prevent reckless play. During recess, for example, encourage class participation in "wild" but essentially safe games (such as relay races involving stunts) to help the children get devil-may-care tendencies out of their systems. In your Handbook you might list other games to use for this purpose.

6. Bone growth is not yet complete; therefore, bones and ligaments can't stand heavy pressure. If you notice pupils indulging in strenuous tests of strength (punching each other on the arm until one person can't retaliate, for example), you might suggest that they switch to competition involving coordi-

Accident rate peaks in 3d grade because of confidence in physical skills

Handbook Heading: Safe but Strenuous Games

nated *skills.* During team games, rotate players in especially tiring positions (for example, the pitcher in baseball).

Social Characteristics: Primary Grades

The characteristics noted here are typical of both primary and elementary grade pupils and underlie the elementary-level characteristics described in the next section.

1. At this level children become somewhat more selective in their choice of friends and are likely to have a more or less permanent best friend. Among American children, friendships are typically same-sex relationships that are marked by mutual understanding, loyalty, cooperation, and sharing. Competition between friends should be discouraged as it can become intense and increase their dissatisfaction with each other. Although friends disagree with each other more often than with nonfriends, their conflicts are shorter, less heated, and less likely to lead to a dissolving of the friendship (Hartup, 1989).

You might use sociograms to gain some insight into friendships and then give tentative assistance to children who have difficulty in attracting friends. Also, be on the alert for feuds, which can develop beyond good-natured quarreling and teasing.

Sociometric techniques can reveal which playmates a shy child would like to get to know. To use sociometric techniques, ask each student to write down (or report orally) the name of the classmate she or he likes best. In some cases you may want to phrase the question more subtly; for example, "Write (or tell me) the name of someone you have fun with," or "Write (or tell me) the name of someone you would like to sit next to." Some advocates of sociometric techniques suggest that you request more than one choice. For most purposes, however, simply asking for the name of the best-liked classmate is probably most satisfactory, since the task of recording several choices can be complicated. Perhaps the best way to record responses is the *target diagram* (Northway, 1940) in Figure 3.1.

This diagram is largely self-explanatory. As you see, it focuses attention on the *stars* in the center and the *isolates* outside the circle. If an isolate seems content to be a loner, perhaps you should respect this preference. But when a child appears eager to join others yet seems unable to take the first step, you might subtly help by pairing him or her on some activity with the classmate she or he chose when asked to name the child liked best.

If you would like more information about the characteristics, strengths, and weaknesses of various sociometric techniques, see McConnell and Odum (1986). If you would like more information about how to obtain, interpret, and use sociometric techniques, see *Sociometry in the Classroom* by Norman E. Gronlund (1959).

2. Children during this age span often like organized games in small groups, but they may be overly concerned with rules or get carried away

Handbook Heading:
Using Sociometric
Techniques

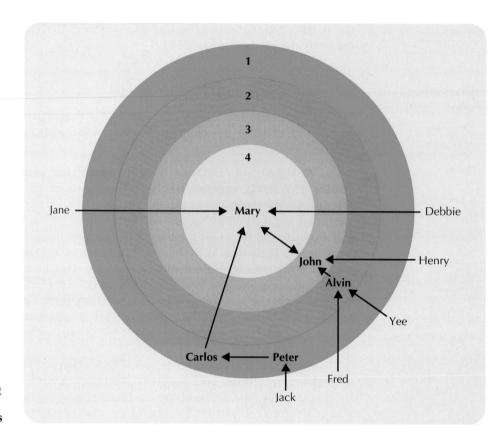

FIGURE 3.1   Target Diagram Showing Sociometric Choices

by team spirit. Keep in mind that, according to Piaget, children at this age practice the morality of constraint: They find it difficult to understand how and why
rules should be adjusted to special situations. When you divide a class into teams,
you may be amazed at the amount of rivalry that develops (and the noise level
generated). One way to reduce both the rivalry and the noise is to promote the
idea that games should be fun. Another technique is to rotate team membership
frequently. If you know any especially good—but not excessively competitive—team games, you might note them in your Handbook. You might also consult *Student Team Learning* (2d ed., 1988) by Robert Slavin for descriptions of
several team learning games that emphasize cooperation.

**3. Quarrels are still frequent. Words are used more often than physi-
cal aggression, but many boys (in particular) may indulge in punching,
wrestling, and shoving.** Occasional fights are to be expected, but if certain children, especially the same pair, seem to be involved in one long battle, you should
probably try to effect a truce. If you can discover the reason for the animosity,
that would be so much the better. But try to give children a chance to work out
their own solutions to disagreements, as social conflict is effective in spurring
cognitive growth (Smith, Johnson & Johnson, 1981; Tudge & Rogoff, 1989).

Rigid interpretation
of rules in elementary
grades

Handbook Heading:
Enjoyable Team Games

If you have observed or can think of some effective techniques for breaking up a fight or for arranging things so that a fight can have a reasonably satisfactory (noninjurious) conclusion, you might jot them down in your Handbook.

Emotional Characteristics: Primary Grades

1. Primary grade pupils are sensitive to criticism and ridicule and may have difficulty adjusting to failure. Young children need frequent praise and recognition. Because they tend to admire or even worship their teachers, they may be crushed by criticism. Provide positive reinforcement as frequently as possible, and reserve your negative reactions for nonacademic misbehavior. It is important that you scrupulously avoid sarcasm and ridicule. Remember that this is the stage of industry vs. inferiority. If you make a child feel inferior, you may prevent the development of industry.

> To encourage industry, use praise, avoid criticism

2. Most primary grade children are eager to please the teacher. They like to help, enjoy responsibility, and want to do well in their schoolwork. The time-honored technique for satisfying the urge to "help" is to assign jobs (eraser cleaner, wastebasket emptier, paper distributor, and the like) on a rotating basis. In your Handbook you might note other techniques for equal distribution of helping opportunities. (Do you remember, for example, any particular responsibilities you enjoyed as a pupil?)

3. Children of this age are becoming sensitive to the feelings of others. Unfortunately, this permits them to hurt others deeply by attacking a sensitive spot without realizing how devastating their attack really is. It sometimes happens

Most elementary school pupils eagerly strive to obtain "helping" jobs around the classroom. Accordingly, you may wish to arrange a rotating schedule for such jobs. (Geoffrey Biddle)

that teasing a particular child who has reacted to a gibe becomes a group pastime. Be on the alert for such situations. If you are able to make a private and personal appeal to the ringleaders, you may be able to prevent an escalation of the teasing, which may make a tremendous difference in the way the victim feels about school. (More specific comments on how to encourage sensitivity to the feelings of others will be noted in the discussion of emotional characteristics of elementary grade pupils.)

Cognitive Characteristics: Primary Grades

1. Generally speaking, primary grade pupils are extremely eager to learn. One of the best things about teaching in the primary grades is the built-in motivation of pupils. The teacher's problem is how to make the most of it. Suggestions for doing this will be offered in Part 3.

2. They like to talk and have much more facility in speech than in writing. Primary grade children are eager to recite—whether they know the right answer or not. The high school teacher may have difficulty stimulating voluntary class participation, but not the primary grade teacher. The problem here is more likely to be one of controlling participation so that children speak up only when called upon. Frequent reminders to take turns and to be good listeners are often necessary. And even if you are successful in this area, you may feel a bit unsettled to find that a pupil, after wildly waving a hand or pumping an arm to be recognized, supplies a hopelessly wrong answer. You may want to develop some phrases that gently and/or humorously indicate that an answer is erroneous or irrelevant. If you come up with some good ones, jot them down in your Handbook.

Handbook Heading:
Ways to Handle Wrong
Answers

3. Because of their literal interpretation of rules, primary grade children may tend to be tattletales. Sometimes telling the teacher that someone has broken a school or class rule is due to a child's level of moral development, sometimes it is due to jealousy or malice, and sometimes it is simply a way to get attention or curry favor. If a child calls your attention to the misbehavior of others and you respond by saying "Don't be a tattletale," the child may be hurt and confused. On the other hand, if you thank the child too enthusiastically and then proceed to punish the culprit, you may encourage most members of the class to begin to inform on each other. Perhaps the best policy is to tell an informant that you already are aware of the errant behavior and that you intend to do something about it. Then you might follow up by talking to the offending parties.

ELEMENTARY GRADES (4, 5, AND 6; NINE TO TWELVE YEARS)

Physical Characteristics: Elementary Grades

1. A growth spurt occurs in most girls and starts in early-maturing boys. On the average, girls between the ages of ten and fourteen are taller

> **TABLE 3.3   Applying Stage Theories of Development to the Elementary Grade Years**
>
> **Stage of psychosocial development:** industry vs. inferiority. Important to keep pupils constructively busy; try to play down comparisons between best and worst learners.
>
> **Stage of cognitive development:** concrete operational, beginning of formal operational. Toward the upper elementary grades some pupils may be able to deal with abstractions, but most will need to generalize from concrete experiences.
>
> **Stage of moral development:** transition from morality of constraint to morality of cooperation, preconventional to conventional. Shift to viewing rules as flexible mutual agreements, but "official" rules are obeyed out of respect for authority or to impress others.
>
> **General factors to keep in mind:** initial enthusiasm for learning may fade as the novelty wears off and as perfecting skills becomes more arduous. Differences in knowledge and skills of fastest and slowest learners become more noticeable. "Automatic" respect for teachers tends to diminish. Growth spurt and puberty lead to greater awareness of sex roles.

Girls taller and heavier from 10 to 14 years

and heavier than boys of the same age. Because girls mature more rapidly than boys, they experience their growth spurt about two years earlier. Some girls begin their spurt as early as nine and one-half years, but the average age is ten and a half (Dusek, 1987a).

J. M. Tanner (1972, p. 5) reports that until adolescence girls are equal to boys in strength but that girls between twelve and a half and thirteen and a half, on the average, have larger muscles than boys of the same age. After the growth spurt, however, the muscles in the average boy's body are larger, as are the heart and lungs. Furthermore, the body of the mature male has a greater capacity than that of the female for carrying oxygen to the blood and for neutralizing the chemical products of muscular exercise, such as lactic acid. Thus the average male has greater strength and endurance than the average female. A girl who is the star of a Little League team is likely to discover that she cannot compete with the best male athletes in high school. This realization might lead to lowered self-esteem—unless she values being the star of all-girl athletic teams.

After growth spurt, boys have greater strength and endurance

If you notice that pupils are upset about sudden growth (or lack of it), you might try to help them accept the situation by explaining that things will eventually even out. To reduce unhappiness that arises from conflicts between physical attributes and sex roles, you might try to persuade pupils that being male or female should not in itself determine what a person does.

Handbook Heading: Helping Pupils Adjust to the Growth Spurt

2. As children approach puberty, concern and curiosity about sex are almost universal, especially among girls. The average age of puberty for girls in the United States is eleven (Dusek, 1987a); the range is from eight to eighteen years. For boys the average age of puberty is fourteen years; the range is from ten to eighteen years. Since sexual maturation involves drastic biological and psychological adjustments, children are concerned and curious. It seems obvious that

Average age of puberty: girls, 11; boys 14

accurate, unemotional answers to questions about sex are desirable. However, for your own protection, you should find out about the sex education policy at your school. Many school districts have formal programs approved by community representatives and led by designated educators. Informal spur-of-the-moment class discussions may create more problems than they solve.

3. Fine motor coordination is quite good; therefore, the manipulation of small objects is easy and enjoyable for most children. Accordingly, arts and crafts and musical activities are popular. Encouraging active participation in drawing, painting, model making, ceramics, and so on is an excellent way to capitalize on the newly developed manipulative skills of students in the upper elementary grades. Ideally, such activities should center on originality and creativity. Copying, assembling prefabricated kits, filling in sections on paint-by-number pictures, and similar activities are less desirable. You might encourage children to play musical instruments by holding amateur hours or concerts or by inviting individual pupils to perform during music periods. In your Handbook you might note other activities that encourage pupils to use skills in creative ways.

Handbook Heading:
Encouraging Creative
Expression

Social Characteristics: Elementary Grades

See the description of primary grade social characteristics in the preceding section for characteristics that are common to both the primary and elementary grade levels.

1. The peer group becomes powerful and begins to replace adults as the major source of behavior standards and recognition of achievement. During the early school years, parents and teachers set standards of conduct, and most children try to live up to them. By the end of elementary school, however, children may be more eager to impress their friends than to please the teacher. Unfortunately, some children may try to impress their classmates by defying or ignoring the teacher.

▶ Peer group norms
for behavior begin to
replace adult norms

As peer groups become more important, children sometimes organize themselves into more or less exclusive all-boy and all-girl cliques. Generally speaking, these groups operate most actively outside of school. Occasionally, a battle between two groups may lead to trench warfare in class (involving, for example, the exchange of venomous notes). If this occurs, you may find it effective to place members of opposing factions on cooperative committees. Such committees will need close supervision, especially during the first few days, but this stratagem may enforce a truce.

Another characteristic of group behavior at the elementary level is the tendency to devise what amount to initiation rituals (for example, demonstrations of nerve such as shoplifting). In some cases, however, illegal activities simply stem from a desire to get back at authority for placing so many restrictions on behavior. If you encounter thefts in class or a chip-on-the-shoulder attitude, keep in mind the growing independence of children at this grade level and their need for understanding and limit setting rather than punishment.

2. Between the ages of six and twelve, the development of interpersonal reasoning leads to greater understanding of the feelings of others. Robert L. Selman (1980) has studied the development of **interpersonal reasoning** in children. Interpersonal reasoning is the ability to understand the relationship between motives and behavior among a group of people. The results of Selman's research are summarized in Table 3.4. The stages outlined there reveal that during the elementary school years children gradually grasp the fact that a person's overt actions or words do not always reflect inner feelings. They also come to comprehend that a person's reaction to a distressing situation can have many facets. Toward the end of the elementary school years—and increasingly during adolescence—children become capable of taking a somewhat detached and analytical view of their own behavior as well as the behavior of others.

Not surprisingly, a child's interpersonal sensitivity and maturity seem to have an impact on relationships with others. Selman compared the responses of seven- to twelve-year-old boys who were attending schools for children with learning and interpersonal problems with the responses of a matched group of boys attending regular schools. The boys attending special schools were below average for their age in understanding the feelings of others.

Selman believes that teachers and therapists might be able to aid children who are not as advanced in role-taking skills as their age-mates by helping them

---

TABLE 3.4   Stages of Interpersonal Reasoning Described by Selman

Stage 0: egocentric level (about ages 4 to 6). Children do not recognize that other persons may interpret the same social event or course of action differently from the way they do. They do not reflect on the thoughts of self or others. They can label the overtly expressed feelings of others but do not comprehend cause-and-effect relations of social actions.

Stage 1: social information role taking (about ages 6 to 8). Children are able to differentiate between their own interpretations of social interactions and the interpretations of others in limited ways. But they cannot simultaneously think of their own view and those of others.

Stage 2: self-reflective role taking (about ages 8 to 10). Interpersonal relations are interpreted in relation to specific situations whereby each person understands the expectations of the other in that particular context. Children are not yet able to view the two perspectives at once, however.

Stage 3: multiple role taking (about ages 10 to 12). Children become capable of taking a third-person view, which permits them to understand the expectations of themselves and of others in a variety of situations as if they were spectators.

Stage 4: social and conventional system taking (about ages 12 to 15+). Each individual involved in a relationship with another understands many of the subtleties of the interactions involved. In addition, a societal perspective begins to develop. That is, actions are judged by how they might influence *all* individuals, not just those who are immediately concerned.

Source: Adapted from discussions in Selman, 1980.

Between the ages of six and twelve children acquire greater sensitivity to the feelings of others. (Frank Siteman/Stock, Boston, Inc.)

become more sensitive to the feelings of others. If an eight-year-old boy is still functioning at the egocentric level, for example, he may fail to properly interpret the behavior of classmates and become a social isolate. Selman describes how one such boy was encouraged to think continually about the reasons behind his social actions and those of others and acquired sufficient social sensitivity to learn to get along with others.

Handbook Heading:
Ways to Promote Social
Sensitivity

Discussion techniques Selman recommends can be introduced in a natural rather than formal way. If you see a boy react with physical or verbal abuse when jostled by a playmate, for example, you might say, "You know, people don't always intentionally bump into others. Unless you are absolutely sure that someone has hurt you on purpose, it can be a lot pleasanter for all concerned if you don't make a big deal out of it."

A final point about fostering moral development relates to instruction or adult supervision, as contrasted with peer interactions. Piaget concluded that ten- to twelve-year-olds, who are in the process of overcoming the limitations of moral realism, seem to take delight in formulating their own rules. It appeared to Piaget that many children at this stage of moral development were so proud of their newly discovered ability to formulate rules that they preferred to ignore adult-imposed regulations and to substitute their own. Accordingly, after children reach the age of ten or so, there may be value in encouraging them to participate in rule making. They are not only more likely to understand and accept rules based on mutual agreements with peers; they may also be encouraged to move from conventional to postconventional moral thinking, as described by Kohlberg. (The

Handbook Heading:
Encouraging Participa-
tion in Rule Making

conventional level, you may recall, stresses obedience to external authority; the postconventional level stresses formulation of rules by mutual consent.) Two qualifications to this suggestion to encourage participation should be noted, however.

First of all, most children in the upper elementary grades are still concrete thinkers and may feel obliged to make up a separate rule for every contingency. A fifth-grade teacher encountered this problem when he asked his pupils to propose class rules. Within twenty minutes more than fifty rules had been proposed, and when the teacher ran out of blackboard space he had to call a halt. The major reason for this profusion of regulations was that a separate rule was suggested for variations of a particular type of behavior. For example, there was a rule "Don't run in the hall," followed by a rule "Don't run in the classroom," followed by a rule "Don't run on the way to the boys' room," and so on.

A second reason for exercising caution when encouraging children in the elementary grades to participate in making rules is that they may also wish to determine how rule breakers should be punished. When Piaget asked young children to propose punishments, he found that many of their choices were "astonishingly severe" (1948, p. 209). He offered this explanation for the harsh nature of child-determined punishments: "In these children's eyes, punishment consists, as a matter of course, in inflicting on the guilty party a pain that will smart enough to make them realize the gravity of their misdeed. Naturally, the fairest punishment will be the most severe" (p. 211). The same tendency for young children to propose severe punishments was observed by Urie Bronfenbrenner in Russian elementary schools. One of the techniques of character training used in the Soviet Union is to have school councils, made up of elected student representatives, determine if classmates have broken school rules and how guilty children should be punished. The punishments proposed by the children observed by Bronfenbrenner were often so severe that teachers had to intervene and suggest milder penalties (1970, pp. 66–68).

Emotional Characteristics: Elementary Grades

1. Disruptive family relationships, social rejection, and school failure may lead to delinquent behavior. G. R. Patterson, Barbara DeBarsyshe, and Elizabeth Ramsey (1989) marshal a wide array of evidence to support their belief that delinquent behavior is the result of a causal chain of events that originates in childhood with dysfunctional parent-child relationships. In their view, poor parent-child relationships lead to behavior problems, which lead to peer rejection and academic failure, which lead to identification with a deviant peer group, which results in delinquent behavior. Parents of such children administer harsh and inconsistent punishment, provide little positive reinforcement, and do little monitoring and supervising of each child's activities. Because these children have not learned to follow adult rules and regulations but have learned how to satisfy their needs through coercive behavior, they are rejected by their peers, are easily distracted from schoolwork, show little interest in the subjects they study, and do

▶ Delinquents have
few friends, are easily
distracted, are not in-
terested in school-
work, lack basic skills

not master many of the basic academic skills necessary for subsequent achievement. By late childhood or early adolescence, many of these children associate
with a deviant peer group that engages in delinquent behavior. If there is a bright
side to this picture, it is that only about half of all antisocial children become
adolescent delinquents, and only half to three-fourths of the adolescent delinquents become adult offenders. Attempts at short circuiting this chain of events
stand a greater chance of success if they begin early and are multifaceted. In addition to counseling and parent training, mastery of basic academic skills is
important.

   **2. About one elementary grade child out of ten is classified as having
a behavior disorder.** It is difficult to know precisely what percentage of elementary grade children develop a behavior disorder. Different surveys produce varying estimates because of differences in sampling procedures, differences in the
criteria used to classify children, and differences in the measures used to identify
the disorder. The figure reported in most surveys ranges from 6.5 percent to 15
percent, with 10 percent being a rough average. The specific disorders for which
children receive clinical services include hyperactivity, bed wetting, antisocial behavior, tics, excessive fears, eating disorders, and depression. Boys are more
likely to be referred for the first four disorders just mentioned; girls are more
likely to be referred for the last three (Kazdin, 1989; Tuma, 1989; Wicks-Nelson
& Israel, 1991).

   Surveys of juveniles (6–12 years of age) suggest that anywhere from 2 percent
to 5 percent suffer from major or minor forms of depression. Although these are
relatively small percentages, they are worth paying attention to for four reasons:
(1) Bouts of depression can last from several months to several years, (2) depression can lead to impaired social functioning and lowered classroom achievement,
(3) two-thirds of juveniles with a history of depression will probably experience
a recurrence during adolescence, and (4) depression and suicide are highly cor-
related in adolescence (Kovacs, 1989). For these reasons, unusual and repeated
episodes of crying, anxiety, unhappiness, and withdrawal should be reported to
the school counselor and the child's parents.

Cognitive Characteristics: Elementary Grades

▶ Girls superior in ver-
bal skills, math com-
putation

   **1. There are sex differences in specific abilities, although they are
decreasing in number and magnitude.** Early research on sex differences in
cognitive functioning found that during the elementary school years girls, on the
average, are superior in verbal fluency, spelling, reading, and mathematical computation. Boys, on the average, are superior in mathematical reasoning, in tasks
involving understanding of spatial relationships, and in solving insight problems
(Bee, 1978; Block, 1976; Maccoby & Jacklin, 1974).

▶ Boys superior in
math reasoning, spa-
tial abilities

   More recent research has confirmed these findings and added some interesting details to the picture. Sandra P. Marshall and Julie D. Smith (1987) examined
the mathematics performance of several thousand California schoolchildren who
took the *Surveys of Basic Skills* in both the third and sixth grades. Consistent with
the research findings of the 1970s, they reported that girls at both grade levels

significantly outscored the boys on computation problems. In addition, they found strong sex differences for certain types of errors. Boys were more likely to use the wrong rule in working a problem (for example, always subtracting the smaller number from the larger one in a subtraction problem regardless of whether the smaller number is in the minuend or the subtrahend; or switching from multiplication to addition midway through a multiplication problem). Girls were more likely to make an association error (such as misinterpreting the significance and meaning of a word in a word problem).

Alan Feingold (1988) analyzed the performance of eighth- through twelfth-grade students on eight subtests of the *Differential Aptitude Test* for the years 1947, 1962, 1972, and 1980. At every grade level and year, he found that the girls outscored the boys on tests of spelling, language, and clerical speed and accuracy. The boys, on the other hand, outscored the girls on the mechanical reasoning and space relations tests. The most interesting aspect of Feingold's analysis was the discovery that sex differences in cognitive abilities are decreasing. Between 1947 and 1980, the amount by which the girls outscored the boys, and vice versa, decreased at every grade level.

> Sex differences in cognitive abilities getting smaller

Marcia Linn and Janet Hyde (1991) take Feingold's conclusion one step further by concluding that significant differences between males and females no longer exist on measures of verbal ability, spatial visualization, and mathematics computation. Differences do remain, however, for the mathematics section of the Scholastic Aptitude Test, tests of mental rotation, and topics studied more by one sex than by the other (males still outscore females on tests of science knowledge, for example). This last finding suggests that gender differences in math and science are related to opportunity to learn.

Handbook Heading:
Encouraging Girls to Excel in Math and Science

2. Differences in cognitive style become apparent. In addition to sex differences in general and specific learning abilities, there are differences in **cognitive style** (see Table 3.5). Cognitive styles are tendencies or preferences to respond to a variety of intellectual tasks and problems in a particular fashion. Jerome Kagan (1964a, 1964b), for instance, found that some children seem to be characteristically *impulsive* whereas others are characteristically *reflective*. He notes that impulsive children have a fast conceptual tempo; they tend to come forth with the first answer they can think of and are concerned about giving quick responses. Reflective children, on the other hand, take time before they speak; they seem to prefer to evaluate alternative answers and to give correct, rather than quick, responses. Kagan discovered that when tests of reading and of inductive reasoning were administered in the first and second grades, impulsive pupils made more errors than reflective pupils. He also found that impulsiveness is a general trait; it appears early in a person's life and is consistently revealed in a great variety of situations.

> Impulsive thinkers look at big picture, reflective thinkers concentrate on details

Robert J. Sternberg (1990), whose ideas on intelligence we discuss in Chapter 4, has proposed an interesting theory of cognitive style that is roughly modeled on the different functions and forms of national governments. Sternberg's theory, which he calls a theory of mental self-government, proposes three functions (legislative, executive, judicial) and four forms (monarchic, hierarchical, oligarchic, anarchic) that can combine to produce twelve styles.

TABLE 3.5   Types of Cognitive Styles

Impulsive. Tendency to give first answer, to be eager to respond quickly.
Reflective. Tendency to think things over, to be deliberate and cautious in responding.

Analytic. Tendency to note details, preference for specifics.
Thematic. Tendency to respond to whole pattern, interest in "big picture."

Attentiveness to detail. Tendency to recognize and respond to many aspects of a situation.
One-track responding. Tendency to concentrate on only one aspect of a situation at a time.

Concentrated attention. Tendency to concentrate on a particular task or idea and to resist distractions or interruptions.
Distractibility. Tendency to be diverted from one task or idea when conflicting or different activities or ideas are present.

Resistance to change. Reluctance to accept unexpected or unconventional views or evidence.
Flexibility. High degree of adaptability to new, different, or unexpected points of view.

Conventionality. Tendency to seek or provide one right answer or a conventional answer.
Individuality. Tendency to respond in nonconventional, unexpected, or individual ways.

Listed above are pairs of terms that summarize essentially opposite types of thinking, perceiving, and reacting. They are based on descriptions of cognitive styles noted in this chapter's discussion of the work of Jerome Kagan (1964), Samuel Messick (1976), and J. P. Guilford (1967).

The *legislative* function deals with creating, formulating, imagining, and planning. Students who prefer this function like to create their own rules and do things in their own way. Activities they might particularly enjoy include designing experiments, writing stories, and organizing work groups. The *executive* function involves implementing what the legislative function creates. Students with an executive preference are comfortable following rules or guidelines. They would probably enjoy listening to lectures, preparing book reports, and working out the answers to clearly stated problems. The *judicial* function specializes in judging, evaluating, and comparing. Students with a judicial preference would probably gravitate toward such activities as comparing two literary characters, critiquing an article, or evaluating the effectiveness of a program.

Students who stick to a single way of doing things or who focus on accomplishing one goal at a time are exhibiting a preference for a *monarchic* style. This approach can be an asset when a task must be accomplished by a particular time. Students with a *hierarchic* style prefer instead to rank-order and pursue several goals. Such a student may assign different amounts of time to studying various school subjects but allocate more time overall to studying than to athletics or watching television. Students with an *oligarchic* style also pursue multiple goals,

Jerome Kagan found that some students are impulsive thinkers who tend to react quickly when asked a question. Other pupils are reflective thinkers who prefer to mull things over before answering. (Left: Susie Fitzhugh; right: Erika Stone)

but they give equal importance to each one. These students may spend as much time preparing for a quiz as for a major exam, or they may study each subject an equal amount of time. Students with an *anarchic* style might be called "free thinkers." They enjoy tasks and situations that are unstructured, they dislike and tend to ignore rules and regulations, and they like to try unique approaches to solving problems.

Sternberg emphasizes two points about cognitive styles that bear repeating. First, schools tend to be staffed by individuals who prefer the executive/hierarchic style. As a result, students with a similar style are likely to perform better and be more highly rewarded than students with other styles. Second, most individuals can use more than one style, although some are more flexible than others in shifting from one style to another.

Awareness of these varying styles of thinking may help you understand the need to recognize your own style (recall our discussion of the reflective teacher in Chapter 1) and to use different teaching methods and approaches so that all students are comfortable some of the time. An impulsive boy, for example, may disrupt a class discussion by blurting out the first thing that pops into his head, thereby upstaging the reflective types who are still in the process of formulating

Handbook Heading: Allowing for Differences in Cognitive Style

more searching answers. To minimize this possibility, you may want to have an informal rotation scheme for recitation or sometimes require that everyone sit and think about a question for two or three minutes before answering. To give the impulsive style its place in the sun, you might schedule speed drills or question-and-answer sessions covering previously learned basic material. To motivate students with a legislative style, have them describe what might have happened if a famous historical figure had acted differently than he or she did. For example, how might World War II have ended if President Harry Truman decided *not* to drop the atomic bomb on Japan? To motivate students with a judicial style, have them compare and contrast the literary characters Tom Sawyer (from the Mark Twain novel of the same name) and Holden Caulfield (from the J. D. Salinger novel *Catcher in the Rye*).

JUNIOR HIGH (GRADES 7, 8, AND 9; TWELVE TO FIFTEEN YEARS)

Physical Characteristics: Junior High

1. Most girls complete their growth spurt at the beginning of this period. A boy's growth spurt, however, is usually not completed before the eighth or ninth grade, and it may be precipitous. Some boys add as much as 6 inches and 25 pounds in a single year. The period of accelerated growth that may begin in the late elementary grades involves almost all pupils in junior high. The variation among individual students is tremendous. Some early-maturing, ninth-grade girls look as if they could *almost* be the mothers of some late-maturing, seventh-grade boys (Brooks-Gunn, 1987; Richards & Peterson, 1987).

TABLE 3.6   Applying Stage Theories of Development to the Junior High Years
Stage of psychosocial development: identity vs. role confusion. Growing independence leads to initial thoughts about identity. Greater concern about appearance and sex roles than about occupational choice.
Stage of cognitive development: beginning of formal operational thought. Increasing ability to engage in mental manipulations and test hypotheses.
Stage of moral development: transition to morality of cooperation, conventional. Increasing willingness to think of rules as flexible mutual agreements; "official" rules still likely to be obeyed out of respect for authority or to impress others.
General factors to keep in mind: growth spurt and puberty influence many aspects of behavior. Abrupt switch (for seventh-graders) from being oldest, biggest, most sophisticated pupils in elementary school to being youngest, smallest, least knowledgeable pupils in a large school. Peers begin to influence behavior more than parents. Acceptance by peers extremely important. Pupils who do poor schoolwork begin to feel bitter, resentful, and restless. Growing awareness of need to make personal value decisions regarding use of dress, premarital sex, and code of ethics.

Over a period of years, investigators at the University of California examined longitudinal data to determine the impact of early and later maturation on adolescents. Then, when the subjects were in their thirties, their adult behavior and adjustment was compared to the ratings made when they were in high school. The investigations are summarized in Table 3.7.

The characteristics noted in Table 3.7 cannot be interpreted too literally for several reasons. First of all, different groups of subjects were studied, and the types of behavior various investigators found typical of early and later maturers were not always consistent. Second, as indicated by the parenthetical notes regarding leadership in early-maturing adolescent males and confidence in later-maturing adolescent girls, the impact of the timing of puberty sometimes varied depending on social class. Third, comparatively small groups of subjects were studied. Such factors as attractiveness may thus have influenced some of the characteristics studied (for example, popularity). Finally, the subjects of these studies attended high school in the 1930s and 1940s. Changes in conceptions of sex roles and sexual behavior may have altered the significance of early and later maturation in the 1990s.

It does seem safe to conclude, however, that the behavior and development of individuals who mature substantially earlier or later than most of their peers may be influenced in significant and permanent ways. The exact nature of this influence may be difficult to predict, though, for reasons that become clear when

TABLE 3.7 The Impact of Early and Late Maturation

	Characteristics as Adolescents	Characteristics as Adults
Early-maturing boys	Self-confident, high in self-esteem, likely to be chosen as leaders (but leadership tendencies more likely in lower-class than middle-class boys)	Self-confident, responsible, cooperative, sociable. But also rigid, moralistic, humorless, conforming
Late-maturing boys	Energetic, bouncy, given to attention-getting behavior, not popular	Impulsive and assertive. But also insightful, perceptive, creatively playful, able to cope with new situations
Early-maturing girls	Not popular or likely to be leaders, indifferent in social situations, lacking in poise (but middle-class girls more confident than those from lower class)	Self-possessed, self-directed, able to cope, likely to score high in ratings of overall psychological health
Late-maturing girls	Confident, outgoing, assured, popular, likely to be chosen as leaders	Likely to experience difficulty adapting to stress, likely to score low in ratings of overall psychological health

Sources: H. E. Jones, 1946; M. C. Jones, 1957, 1965; P. H. Mussen & M. C. Jones, 1957; Peskin, 1967, 1973; Clausen, 1975; Livson & Peskin, 1980; Peterson & Taylor, 1980.

Early-maturing boys likely to draw favorable responses

Late-maturing boys may seek attention

Late-maturing girls likely to be popular and carefree

Handbook Heading: Helping Early and Late Maturers Cope

one attempts to interpret the data in Table 3.7. After reviewing research on early and later maturation, Norman Livson and Harvey Peskin (1980) speculated that the **early-maturing boy** is likely to draw favorable responses from adults (because of his adult appearance), which promotes confidence and poise (thus contributing to leadership and popularity with peers). The **late-maturing boy,** by contrast, may feel inferior and attempt to compensate for his physical and social frustration by engaging in bossy and attention-getting behavior. The very success of the early-maturing boy in high school, however, may cause him to develop an inflexible conception of himself, leading to problems when he must deal with new or negative situations later in life. The need for the late-maturing boy to cope with difficult adjustment situations in high school, on the other hand, may equip him to adapt to adversity and change later in life.

Livson and Peskin observe that the late-maturing boy is psychologically and socially out of step with peers, and the same applies to the **early-maturing girl.** The **late-maturing girl,** whose growth is less abrupt and whose size and appearance are likely to reflect the petiteness featured in stereotyped views of femininity, shares many of the characteristics (poise, popularity, leadership tendencies) of the early-maturing boy. The advantages enjoyed by the late-maturing girl are not permanent, however. Livson and Peskin report that "The stress-ridden early-maturing girl in adulthood has become clearly a more coping, self-possessed, and self-directed person than the late-maturing female in the cognitive and social as well as emotional sectors. . . . It is the late-maturing female, carefree and unchallenged in adolescence, who faces adversity maladroitly in adulthood" (1980, p. 72).

If late-maturing boys in your classes appear driven to seek attention or inclined to brood about their immaturity, you might try to give them extra opportunities to gain status and self-confidence by succeeding in schoolwork or other nonathletic activities. If you notice that early-maturing girls seem insecure, you might try to bolster their self-esteem by giving them extra attention and by recognizing their achievements.

2. Pubertal development is evident in practically all girls and in many boys. The sex organs (primary sexual characteristics) mature rapidly, and secondary sex characteristics appear: breast development, rounded hips, and the appearance of a waistline in girls; broadening of the shoulders and replacement of fat with muscle tissue in boys. In both sexes, pubic, axillary (armpit), facial, and body hair appear; the texture of the skin changes (often with temporary malfunctioning of the oil-producing glands, which leads to acne); and the voice changes. All these developments have a profound impact on the appearance, biological functioning, and psychological adjustment of the young person who is reaching puberty.

The remarks made earlier about sex education in the elementary grades apply even more directly to this age group. You should check on school policy and act accordingly. Girls, particularly, need accurate information, since the changes associated with menstruation may produce fear if the process is not understood.

3. There is likely to be a certain amount of adolescent awkwardness—probably due as much to self-consciousness as to sudden growth—and a great deal of concern about appearance. Both boys and girls take pains with their grooming. In order to prevent attempts at surreptitious grooming during class, some secondary school teachers establish a class routine of completion of schoolwork two minutes before the end of a period. Those last two minutes are free for grooming or social interaction.

4. Although this age period is marked by generally good health, the diet and sleeping habits of many junior high students are poor. Because of poor diet and insufficient sleep, many junior high pupils may exhibit a certain amount of listlessness. Frequent changes of pace and breaks for relaxation may alleviate drowsiness to a certain extent.

Social Characteristics: Junior High

1. The peer group becomes the general source of rules of behavior. Developing a code of behavior is a move toward adult independence and should be encouraged. In addition to forming their own rules for behavior in out-of-school situations, junior high students are often eager to participate in student government decisions. You are likely to get a favorable response if you invite the members of your class to participate in establishing class rules and routines.

Adolescents often find it reassuring to dress and behave like peers.
(Ulrike Welsch)

▶ Discussion of controversial issues may be difficult because of strong desire to conform to peer norms

2. The desire to conform reaches a peak during the junior high years. Adolescents find it reassuring to dress and behave like others, and they are likely to alter their own opinions to coincide with those of a group. When you encourage student participation in class discussions, you may need to be alert to the tendency for students at these grade levels to be reluctant to voice "minority" opinions. If you want them to think about controversial issues, it may be preferable to invite them to write their opinions anonymously rather than voice them in front of the rest of the class. In addition, you might use techniques of values clarification (to be discussed in Chapter 11) to encourage the formation of a set of *personal* values.

3. Students are greatly concerned about what others think of them. Both friendships and quarrels become more intense. You will have little or no control over most social interactions between students, but you may be able to function as a sympathetic listener at times. If you notice that a pupil suddenly seems depressed and preoccupied, you might ask if he or she would like to talk about whatever it is that is bothersome.

Emotional Characteristics: Junior High

1. Some, but not all, adolescents go through a period of "storm and stress." Starting with G. Stanley Hall, who wrote a pioneering two-volume text on adolescence in 1904, some theorists have described adolescence as a period of turmoil. Feelings of confusion, anxiety, and depression, extreme mood swings, and low levels of self-confidence were felt to be typical of this age group. Some of the reasons cited for this turbulence were rapid changes in height, weight, and body proportions; increases in hormone production; the task of identity formation; increased academic responsibilities; and the development of formal operational reasoning (Jackson & Bosma, 1990; Peterson, 1988; Susman, 1991).

Since the 1970s, however, a number of psychologists have questioned whether turmoil is universal during the teen years (for example, see Hill, 1987; Jackson & Bosma, 1990; Peterson, 1988). In one study (Offer & Offer, 1975) 79 percent of a group of middle-class adolescent boys were classified as falling into one of three categories: *continuous growth*, *surgent growth*, and *tumultuous growth*. Boys in the continuous growth group (23 percent of the sample) were easily able to cope with the various physiological, social, emotional, and cognitive changes they experienced. Boys in the surgent growth group (35 percent) alternated between difficult and easy periods, although in general they were reasonably well adjusted. Only 21 percent exhibited the type of chronic turmoil that marked early accounts of adolescent emotional development. (The remaining 21 percent could not be classified, although they were closest to the first two groups.)

▶ Teen-agers experience different degrees of emotional turmoil

Although the Offer and Offer study was limited to adolescent males, gender differences in psychological adjustment have been documented. Boys who exhibit problems during adolescence are more likely to have had similar problems in childhood, whereas girls are more likely to initially exhibit problems in adolescence. Achievement situations are more likely to produce anxiety responses in boys, whereas girls are more likely to become anxious in interpersonal situations. Finally, girls are more likely than boys to increasingly exhibit signs of depression (Peterson, 1988).

2. Crime rates are at a peak during the adolescent years, and vandalism may be a problem in certain schools. As noted under the emotional characteristics of elementary grade pupils, differences between delinquents and nondelinquents often become apparent before children leave the sixth grade. Boys who are rated as troublesome, difficult, and aggressive often become delinquent adolescents (Henggeler, 1989). Typically, the first illegal act is committed during the elementary school years, but both the rate and the seriousness of criminal acts increase during the secondary school years. In 1985, individuals between the ages of thirteen and twenty-one accounted for 35 percent of nontraffic offenses even though they represented only 14 percent of the population (Kennedy, 1991). In many communities, vandalism is a serious problem; rates appear to vary from one school to another. In an analysis of twelve inner-London schools, Michael Rutter and several associates (1979) found that the amount of damage to school property was significantly less in schools that had an academic emphasis, made available incentives and rewards, arranged good conditions for students, and provided opportunities for students to participate in decision making. You might be able to reduce tendencies toward vandalism if you emulate some of the characteristics of the schools and teachers described by Rutter and his colleagues.

Handbook Heading: Ways to Reduce Vandalism

Cognitive Characteristics: Junior High

1. This is a transition period between concrete operational and formal thought. Some pupils move through the stages of cognitive development outlined by Piaget more rapidly than others. But note that students who *sometimes* exhibit characteristics of formal thought do not *always* think that way. Accordingly, it would be wise to check on how completely your junior high students grasp abstract concepts. A simple way to obtain such information is to give a brief, ungraded, anonymous quiz after introducing a topic such as "Differences Between Capitalism and Communism." If you discover that many pupils explain concepts in concrete terms, use many concrete examples in class presentations.

2. This is a transition period between the moralities of constraint and cooperation. In discussions of school or class rules, or of laws or ethics, you may discover that strong differences of opinion will be voiced. Some students may think of all rules as sacred and unchangeable; others may understand that extenuating circumstances and intentions should be considered. Instead of introducing topics that are the equivalent of moral dilemmas by using whole-class discussion techniques, you may find it preferable to begin by asking students to write personal interpretations. Then you might refer to different points of view (without identifying those who expressed them) in structured small-group discussions. In small groups, more students can express opinions, and those who are shy about speaking in front of the entire class may be more inclined to participate. Encouraging the interchange of ideas between individuals may help pupils who think almost exclusively in terms of the morality of constraint to become more flexible about making moral judgments.

3. Between the ages of twelve and sixteen, political thinking becomes more abstract, liberal, and knowledgeable. Joseph Adelson (1972, 1986) used an interview approach to obtain information about the development of political thought during the adolescent years. At the start of the interviews, the subjects were requested to imagine that a thousand people ventured to an island in the Pacific for the purpose of establishing a new society. The respondents were then asked to explain how these people might establish a political order, devise a legal system, establish a balance among rights, responsibilities, personal liberty, and the common good, and deal with other problems of public policy.

The analysis of the interview responses showed no significant sex differences in understanding political concepts and no significant differences attributable to intelligence and social class, although brighter students were better able to deal with abstract ideas and upper-class students were less likely to be authoritarian. The most striking and consistent finding was the degree to which the political thinking of the adolescent changes in the years between twelve and sixteen. Adelson concluded that the most significant changes were (1) an increase in the ability to deal with such abstractions as freedom of speech, equal justice under law, and the concept of community, (2) a decline in authoritarian views, (3) an increase in the ability to imagine the consequences of current actions, and (4) an increase in political knowledge.

▶ Political thinking becomes more abstract, less authoritarian, more knowledgeable

Adolescents gradually become more knowledgeable about the workings of society and more capable of understanding abstract concepts. (Rick Falco/SIPA Press)

Increased ability to deal with abstractions is a function of the shift from concrete to formal operational thought. When thirteen-year-olds were asked, "What is the purpose of laws?" a typical answer was "So people don't steal or kill" (1972, p. 108). A fifteen- or sixteen-year-old, by contrast, was more likely to say, "To ensure safety and enforce the government" (p. 108). The young adolescent who thinks in concrete terms concentrates on individuals and finds it difficult to take society as a whole into account. When asked about the purpose of laws to require vaccination of children, for example, the twelve-year-old is likely to say it is to prevent sickness in the child who receives the treatment. The fifteen-year-old who has mastered aspects of formal thought is likely to take into account how it will protect the community at large. Concrete thinking causes the twelve-year-old to concentrate on the immediate present because he or she is unable to analyze the significance of past events or project ideas into the future. As Piaget noted in his discussion of moral realists, the younger child is not likely to take motives into account. When asked to explain why many prisoners are repeat offenders, for example, only older adolescents would mention such motives as having a grudge against society. Adelson and his colleagues found that when twelve-year-olds were asked how prisoners should be treated, many of them recommended that they be punished and taught a stern lesson. Adelson speculates that the tendency for younger adolescents to be punitive and authoritarian might be attributed to several factors: preoccupation with wickedness, the inability of the young adolescent to grasp the concept of rights, and the conviction that laws are immutable. But by fourteen and fifteen, the adolescents interviewed by Adelson were more likely to consider circumstances and individual rights and to recommend rehabilitation rather than punishment.

If you will be teaching courses in social studies, you may find this information useful in lesson planning. It may also help you understand why students may respond to discussions of political or other abstract matters in different ways.

HIGH SCHOOL (GRADES 10, 11, AND 12; SIXTEEN, SEVENTEEN, AND EIGHTEEN YEARS)

Physical Characteristics: High School

1. Most students reach physical maturity, and virtually all attain puberty. Although almost all girls reach their ultimate height, some boys may continue to grow even after graduation. Tremendous variation exists in height and weight and in rate of maturation. As noted earlier, late-maturing boys seem to have considerable difficulty adjusting to their slower rate of growth. There is still concern about appearance, although it may not be as strong as it was during the junior high years. Glandular changes leading to acne may be a source of worry and self-consciousness to some students. The most significant glandular change accompanying puberty is arousal of the sex drive.

2. Many adolescents become sexually active but experience confusion regarding sexual relationships. Recent surveys reveal that 78 percent of males

TABLE 3.8   Applying Stage Theories of Development to the High School Years
Stage of psychosocial development: identity vs. role confusion. Concern about sex roles and occupational choice. Different identity statuses become apparent.
Stage of cognitive development: formal thought. Increasing ability to engage in mental manipulations, understand abstractions, test hypotheses.
Stage of moral development: morality of cooperation, conventional. Increasing willingness to think of rules as mutual agreements and to allow for intentions and extenuating circumstances.
General factors to keep in mind: achievement of sexual maturity has a profound influence on many aspects of behavior. Peer group and reactions of friends extremely important. Concern about what will happen after graduation, particularly for students who do not intend to continue their education. Awareness of the significance of academic ability and importance of grades for certain career patterns. Need to make personal value decisions regarding use of drugs, premarital sex, and code of ethics.

and 63 percent of females have engaged in sexual intercourse at least once by age nineteen. The percentages for black, Hispanic, and white males are 92 percent, 78 percent, and 75 percent respectively. For black, Hispanic, and white females the percentages are 77 percent, 59 percent, and 61 percent, respectively (Irwin & Millstein, 1991). Comparable data for black and white males apparently do not exist at this point (Brooks-Gunn & Furstenberg, 1989). For a group of 1,100 adolescents, J. Richard Udrey (1990) found that initiation of sexual intercourse in white males was strongly related to hormone production and was only weakly related to the discouraging or encouraging efforts of parents, schools, friends, and the media. It was not unusual for adolescent males to experience a tenfold increase in testosterone levels over a period of six months. The initiation of sexual intercourse among white females, however, was more strongly associated with such social factors as grades in school and whether or not friends have engaged in sexual intercourse than with increases in hormone levels. For black females, the factors that best predicted onset of sexual intercourse were pubertal development and sexual intentions. The factors associated with initial sexual intercourse in black males could not be determined as most of them reported having had at least one sexual intercourse experience prior to the initial interview.

▶ Sexual activity among male, female teens due to different factors

In a discussion of the development of sexuality in adolescence, Patricia Y. Miller and William Simon (1980) point out that puberty, a biological event, causes adolescents to function as "self-motivated sexual actors," which is a social event. They comment that in technological societies "young people are defined as sexually mature while simultaneously being defined as socially and psychologically immature" (1980, p. 383). The result is that adolescents are pulled first one way and then another regarding sexual relationships. For example, many adolescents are motivated to engage in sexual intercourse for one or more of the following reasons: (1) as a sign that one person is truly in love with the other person,

Many adolescents may experience confusion about sexual relationships. They are expected to be interested in sex but at the same time attitudes toward sex are often imbued with strong moral overtones. (1991 John Curtis/D. Donne Bryant Stock)

Adolescents likely to be confused about appropriateness of premarital sex

(2) to keep the other person from breaking off the relationship, (3) curiosity, (4) peer pressure, (5) to affirm one's status as an adult (Gordon & Gilgun, 1987). These motives may be implicitly reinforced by adults when they openly provide adolescents with information about sexual drives, contraception, and pregnancy. But in the next breath, adolescents are admonished to avoid the very thing they are being informed about. It's a sort of "Do as I say but not as I do" message (Trost, 1990). Miller and Simon (1980) feel that adolescents may be further confused because "the sex education of the adolescent is empathically attached to moral education" (p. 392). Miller and Simon believe that this is the case because sex role expectations establish attitudes toward sexual morality. The traditional view of the "good girl," for example, is that she does not engage in premarital sex.

These findings illustrate the pressing need for sex education during the high school years. In particular, adolescents need to understand the distinction between sex and mature love. A major characteristic of mature love is that "the well-being of the other person is just a little bit more important than the well-being of the self" (Gordon & Gilgun, 1987, p. 180).

3. Increased sexual activity among adolescents has led to high rates of births outside of marriage and to sexually transmitted diseases. Recent surveys indicate that about 65 percent of all adolescent mothers (about 307,000 as of 1991) are unmarried and that the rate at which babies are born to unmarried adolescent females has quadrupled since 1960. Younger white females and black females are most likely to be unmarried at the birth of their child (Coates & van Widenfeldt, 1991). Some factors that predict adolescent pregnancy include race, having a mother who was pregnant as an adolescent, coming from a low-income family, coming from a one-parent family, and having low self-esteem (Coates &

van Widenfeldt, 1991; Stiffman et al., 1987). One factor contributing to the high rate of teenage pregnancies and births is the relatively low level of contraceptive use. Less than half of all adolescents regularly use some form of contraception (Conger, 1991).

The relatively high levels of sexual activity and low levels of regular contraception among adolescents are particularly worrisome as they put adolescents at risk for contracting sexually transmitted diseases (STDs). According to some experts, STDs among adolescents in the United States have reached epidemic proportions. The highest rates of STDs are found among younger adolescent females (fifteen years or younger) and inner-city minority youth. Over 60 percent of the STD cases reported annually occur among individuals under the age of twenty-five. And about 25 percent of the cases occur among individuals between the ages of fifteen and nineteen (Boyer & Hein, 1991). The worst of the STDs is, of course, acquired immune deficiency syndrome (AIDS) because there is no known cure. Although the number of AIDS cases among adolescents is currently low, it will rise in the future, potentially becoming a major problem. The percentage of adolescents who test positive for human immunodeficiency virus (HIV, the viral cause of AIDS) ranges from about 2 percent to 6 percent (Rotheram-Borus & Koopman, 1991). Because HIV has a long incubation period, AIDS symptoms may not show up for several years. Consequently, the proportion of today's teens who will be diagnosed with AIDS in their twenties will be more than the 2 percent to 6 percent figure just cited.

Social Characteristics: High School

1. Parents are likely to influence long-range plans; peers are likely to influence immediate status. A number of studies have attempted to compare the beliefs, attitudes, and values of parents and their children and also to compare the extent to which parent-peer and peer-peer opinions agree and conflict. Studies of values (reviewed by Feather, 1980), of political thinking (reviewed by Gallatin, 1980), of moral development (reviewed by M. L. Hoffman, 1980), and of occupational choice (reviewed by D. Rogers, 1972) lead to the conclusion that high school students are probably influenced in these areas of their lives more by parents than by peers. A visit to any high school, on the other hand, will reveal that in terms of dress, hair styles, interests, social relationships, and the like, the influence of peers is extremely potent. Not surprisingly, most conflicts between parents and their adolescent children are about such peer-influenced issues as personal appearance, friends, dating, hours, and eating habits (Hill, 1987). Erik Erikson (1968) saw this conflict between parental and peer values as related to the adolescent's search for identity: "To keep themselves together they temporarily overidentify with the heroes of cliques and crowds to the point of an apparently complete loss of individuality. . . . Young people can become remarkably clannish, intolerant, and cruel in their exclusion of others who are 'different,' in skin color or cultural background, in tastes and gifts, and often in entirely petty aspects of dress and gesture arbitrarily selected as the signs of an in-grouper or out-grouper" (p. 132). The hypothesis that parents and peers influence different aspects of adolescent behavior has been developed by C. V. Brittain (1968), who suggests that parents have a greater impact on decisions that have implications for the future (such as choice of a career), whereas peers influence decisions that involve current status and identity needs (such as choice of friends). The influence of parents appears to be greatest when there is mutual affection and respect between parent and child (Baumrind, 1991; Hill, 1987). It might be concluded, then, that parents are likely to influence the values, moral and political beliefs, and long-range plans of high school students. When adolescents seek to establish an immediate sense of identity or status, however, they are more likely to be influenced by peers.

Parents influence values, plans; peers influence immediate status

2. Girls seem to experience greater anxiety about friendships than boys. Factors that cause girls to become concerned about the reactions of others were summarized in the preceding chapter. Adolescent girls tend to seek intimacy in friendships (Coleman, 1980). Boys, on the other hand, often stress skills and interests when they form friendships, and their tendencies to be competitive and self-reliant may work against the formation of close relationships with male companions. Because they often wish to form an intimate relationship with another girl, female adolescents are more likely than boys to experience anxiety, jealousy, and conflicts regarding friendships with same-sex peers. You should not be surprised, therefore, if secondary school girls are much more preoccupied with positive and negative aspects of friendships than boys are.

Girls more likely than boys to experience anxiety about friendships

3. Many high school students are employed after school. Part-time employment among adolescents who attend school has increased in recent years and is more prevalent in the United States than in other industrialized countries. Between 1953 and 1983 the percentage of sixteen- and seventeen-year-old boys who attended school and worked part-time grew from 29 percent to 36 percent. The increase for girls was even more dramatic—a doubling from 18 percent to 36 percent. By 1987 the combined part-time employment figure for both sexes was 41 percent. According to self-report data, about 60 percent of high school sophomores and 75 percent of seniors engage in part-time employment to some degree. Sophomore boys who work average about fifteen hours a week; senior boys average about twenty-one hours a week. Sophomore and senior girls average about eleven and eighteen hours, respectively.

The pros and cons of after-school employment have been vigorously debated. On the positive side, it is thought to enhance self-discipline, a sense of responsibility, self-confidence, and attitudes toward work. On the negative side, part-time employment leaves less time for homework, participation in extracurricular activities, and the development of friendships; it may also lead to increased stress, lower grades, and lower career aspirations (Mortimer, 1991).

Emotional Characteristics: High School

1. Many psychiatric disorders either appear or become prominent during adolescence. Included among these are eating disorders, substance abuse, schizophrenia, depression, and suicide. Eating disorders are much more common in females than in males. *Anorexia nervosa* is an eating disorder characterized by a preoccupation with body weight and food, behavior directed toward losing weight, peculiar patterns of handling food, weight loss, intense fear of gaining weight, and a distorted perception of one's body. This disorder occurs predominantly in females (about 94 percent of the cases) and usually appears between the ages of fourteen and seventeen (Halmi, 1987). *Bulimia nervosa* is a disorder in which binge eating (uncontrolled, rapid eating of large quantities of food over a short period of time), followed by self-induced vomiting, is the predominant behavior. Binges are typically followed by feelings of guilt, depression, self-disgust, and fasting. Bulimia is a disorder that also appears predominantly in adolescent females (Halmi, 1987).

Overall *substance abuse* among adolescents has declined since 1980. Daily use of marijuana dropped from 11 percent of high school seniors to 5 percent between 1980 and 1984. Although sharp increases in cocaine use were reported between 1975 and 1985, usage rates declined throughout the rest of the 1980s. Approximately 5 percent of 1984 seniors reported drinking daily, and 39 percent admitted to having five or more drinks on one occasion within two weeks of being asked. Although cigarette smoking has declined slightly since 1975, the number of smokers increases with age. Among sixteen- and seventeen-year-olds, 31 percent of males and 26 percent of females smoked cigarettes at least weekly. Two-thirds of the males and more than half of the females exceeded half a pack a day (Conger, 1991; Horan & Strauss, 1987).

Although *schizophrenia* (a thinking disorder characterized by illogical and unrealistic thinking, delusions, and hallucinations) is relatively rare among adolescents, it is the most frequently occurring psychotic disorder and the number of cases diagnosed between the ages of twelve and eighteen is steadily increasing. In about half of the cases, behavioral abnormalities such as odd unpredictable behavior, social isolation, and rejection by peers were first noticeable in childhood (Conger, 1991; Rutter, 1990).

2. The most common type of emotional disorder during adolescence is depression. Estimates of depressed high school youth range from 7 percent to 28 percent depending on the level of depression being examined and the criterion used to measure depression. Individuals from low-income families are typically the most depressed. Depression in adolescents often precedes substance abuse (Petti & Larson, 1987). Prior to puberty, twice as many boys as girls exhibit depressive syndromes; after puberty the ratio is just the opposite (Rutter, 1990). Females may exhibit greater tendencies than males to feel depressed, but this does not mean that such reactions occur only in high school girls. Extreme feelings of depression are the most common reason for referring teen-agers of both sexes to psychiatric clinics.

▶ Depression most common among females, teens from poor families

Common symptoms of depression include self-deprecation, crying spells, and suicidal thoughts, threats, and attempts. Additional symptoms are moodiness, social isolation, fatigue, hypochondriasis, and difficulty in concentrating (Petti & Larson, 1987). High school students who experience such symptoms typically try to ward off their depression through restless activity or flight to or from others. They may also engage in problem behavior or delinquent acts carried out in ways

Many high school students, girls in particular, experience periods of depression. An invitation to talk for just a few moments with a sympathetic teacher might conceivably divert an extremely depressed adolescent from contemplating suicide.
(1990 Paul Rezendes/Positive Images)

that make it clear they are appealing for help. (A depressed fifteen-year-old boy may carry out an act of vandalism, for instance, at a time when a school authority or police officer is sure to observe the incident.) Adolescents over the age of seventeen who suffer from depression are likely to show little self-confidence and to feel worthless and discouraged. To combat such feelings they may join antiestablishment groups, manifest a "what's the use of it all?" attitude, or turn to sex and drugs. When it becomes sufficiently extreme, and when unfortunate experiences accumulate, depression may lead to suicide or attempted suicide.

▶ Depression may be caused by negative set, learned helplessness, sense of loss

A. T. Beck (1970) suggests that depression consists of a *cognitive set* made up of negative views of oneself, the world, and the future. M. E. P. Seligman (1975) has proposed that depression is caused by *learned helplessness,* which leads to feelings of having no control over one's life. Irving Weiner (1975) emphasizes that depression typically involves a *sense of loss* that may have many causes. Depression may stem from the abrupt end of a personal relationship through death, separation, or broken friendship. An individual may undergo a sharp drop in self-esteem as a result of failure or guilt. Or a person may experience a loss of bodily integrity following illness, incapacitation, or disfigurement.

Handbook Heading:
Helping Students Overcome Depression

Although many techniques exist for changing a negative self-concept to a positive view of self, one effective approach to minimizing depression is to help as many of your students as possible to experience success as they learn. Techniques to accomplish that goal are discussed in the next six chapters of this book.

3. If depression becomes severe, suicide may be contemplated. Suicide is now a major cause of death among adolescents and young adults. Among high school students only motor vehicle accidents claim more victims. The number of reported suicides among fifteen- to twenty-four-year-olds has increased by 300 percent for males and by 230 percent for females in the last thirty-five years. Fortunately, the youth suicide rate has begun to level off and perhaps even to decline. Between 1980 and 1985 the rate dropped from 12.3 per 100,000 individuals in the fifteen to twenty-four year range to 12.0 per 100,000 (Blumenthal & Kupfer, 1988; Garfinkle et al., 1988).

Suicide among the young seems to be associated with a variety of demographic and family variables. It occurs most frequently in the late fall and early winter and in the states of Alaska and Nevada. Many attempts are made on birthdays, holidays, anniversaries, and national events. For every Caucasian youth who commits suicide, about ten Native American youths do so. Southern states with large black populations, on the other hand, tend to have the lowest suicide rates. Individuals who commit suicide tend to come from families that have a history of alcohol and drug abuse; such individuals have often been placed outside the family for some period of time, and they often show symptoms of delinquency, aggression, or depression (Garfinkel et al., 1988; Strother, 1986).

Two or three times as many females as males *attempt* suicide, almost always by taking an overdose of drugs. But twice as many young males as females *complete* suicide, usually with a gun. Prior to age twelve, *completed suicides* are rare (.06 cases per million). Between the ages of twelve and sixteen, however, there is a hundredfold increase, and then an additional tenfold increase between the ages of sixteen and nineteen (76 cases per million) (Petti & Larson, 1987; Rutter, 1990).

The single most important signal of a youth at risk for suicide is depression. Along with the common symptoms noted earlier under point 2, signs of depression include poor appetite, weight loss, changes in sleeping patterns, difficulty in concentrating, academic problems, and poor self-concept. These symptoms take on added significance when accompanied by a family history of suicide or parents who commit abuse or use drugs and alcohol excessively (Strother, 1986).

▶ Depression and unstable family situation place adolescents at risk for suicide

If you notice that a student in one of your classes seems extremely depressed, take the trouble to ask if there is anything you can do to provide support. Your interest and sympathy may prevent a suicide attempt. In addition, don't hesitate to refer a seemingly depressed student to the school guidance counselor or the school psychologist. Their training and skills make them well equipped to diagnose and treat depression (Garfinkel et al., 1988; Strother, 1986). Finally, it is important to take seriously any threats or talk of suicide.

Cognitive Characteristics: High School

1. High school students become increasingly capable of engaging in formal thought, but they may not use this capability. As noted in the evaluation of Piaget's theory in the preceding chapter, it appears that formal thinking is not as universal or consistent as he originally thought it was. High school students are more likely than younger students to grasp relationships, mentally plan a course of action before proceeding, and test hypotheses systematically. Without supervision and guidance, however, they may not use such capabilities consistently. Accordingly, you might take advantage of opportunities to show students at these grade levels how they can function as formal thinkers. Call attention to relationships and to ways that previously acquired knowledge can be applied to new situations. Provide specific instruction in techniques of problem solving. (Ways you might do this will be discussed in Chapter 10.) Finally, make sure that your pupils understand abstract concepts by using the technique mentioned in the section on the junior high years: Give ungraded, anonymous quizzes to assess depth of understanding. If many pupils appear to be thinking at the concrete level, use concrete examples in your class presentations.

2. Keep in mind that novice formal thinkers may engage in unrestrained theorizing, be threatened by awareness of possibilities, and be subject to adolescent egocentrism. Suggestions for taking into account these various aspects of formal thinking were noted in Chapter 2. If students become unrealistically theoretical in class discussions, try to call attention to realities and to the complexity of most problems. If some students seem threatened by their newfound ability to imagine possibilities (in the form of future decisions and the various options that are open to young adults, for instance), urge them to concentrate on short-term goals and immediate decisions. And if younger adolescents act as if they are perpetually "on stage," be tolerant of their self-consciousness. Try to avoid class activities that force pupils to recite or perform in front of classmates.

Resources for Further Investigation

Comparing Real Students with Hypothetical Students

You can get a clear general picture of the types of students you will teach if you carry out one or more of these simple exercises:

1. Arrange to observe in a grade you eventually hope to teach. (All contacts with schools should be made directly or indirectly through your instructor.) Observe pupils in and out of the classroom and write down what you consider to be significant types of behavior.

2. If possible, interview one or more teachers of the grade level you hope to teach. Ask them to describe what they think are the most significant pupil characteristics at that grade level.

3. If possible, interview one or more pupils of the grade level you expect to teach. Ask them what they like and dislike about school, what they worry about, and what they wish teachers would do.

If you do have the opportunity to observe the behavior of students in and out of the classroom, compare your impressions with the age-level characteristics described in this chapter. You might also pick out the single characteristic that impresses you the most and speculate about what you might do—if anything—to allow for it when you begin to teach.

Time Sampling

Observing social behavior can be quite fascinating. If you would like to make a systematic record of some aspect of interactions between children, time sampling is easy and enjoyable. You could begin by using Parten's classifications of the social behavior of nursery school children. (For details of her descriptions and techniques, see her article "Social Participation Among Preschool Children," *Journal of Abnormal and Social Psychology, 27* (1932), 243–269.) Or select some form of behavior that interests you (elementary school playground interaction and high school between-class behavior are two possibilities). To develop your own list of categories, simply observe children of the age you have selected while they engage in a particular type of behavior and write down what they do. Eventually, you should be able to describe five or so categories that cover most aspects of their behavior. At that point, pick out a pupil to observe for ten seconds. At the end of that time, put a check mark in the appropriate column opposite the pupil's name. Then select another pupil, observe him or her for ten seconds, record the behavior, and so on. If you sample behavior on several different occasions, you will have a record of the types of behavior engaged in by different pupils. Parten's technique is just one of many types of time sampling. A summary of several variations of the basic technique is presented on pages 92–104 of Herbert F. Wright's "Observational Child Study," which is Chapter 3 in the *Handbook of Research Methods in Child Development* (1960), edited by Paul H. Mussen. Additional observational techniques are described by Gilbert R. Guerin and Arlee S. Maier in Chapter 4 of *Informal Assessment in Education* (1983). They describe the characteristics, strengths, and limitations of the chronology, frequency-recording, sequence-sample, trait-sample, event-recall, and rating-scale methods of observation.

Helping Girls and Boys Resist Sex Stereotypes

There are a number of publications for persons who would like to encourage young girls to overcome, at least partially, the stereotyped view of females presented in movies, TV shows and commercials, books, and magazines. Perhaps the best-known book of this type is *Free to Be You and Me* (1974) by Marlo Thomas and several associates. A similar publication is *What I Want to Be When I Grow Up* (1975) by Carol Burnett, George Mendoza, and Sheldon Secunda.

In *We've All Got Scars* (1983), Raphaela Best, a reading specialist for an affluent school district, describes how the school's "second curriculum" (sex role socialization) and "third curriculum" (self-taught sex education) affect interpersonal relationships and classroom achievement in six-, seven-, and eight-year-old boys and girls.

In the *Sex Equity Handbook for Schools* (1982), Myra Pollock Sadker and David Miller Sadker provide an overview of those aspects of education where sex equity is most needed (for example, instructional materials and teacher-student interactions), describe strategies and lesson plans for eliminating sex bias in the classroom, and provide a directory of sources of nonsexist instructional materials and classroom strategies.

For any prospective or practicing teacher interested in learning how to reduce his or her own gender bias, as well as the gender bias of others, *Building Gender Fairness in Schools* (1988) by Beverly Stitt is a useful resource. This book is made up of two parts. Part 1 contains a collection of six readings on various aspects of gender bias (for example, "Sexism in Education," "How Fair Is Your Language?" and "Confronting Sex Bias in Instructional Materials"). Part 2 contains a sequenced set of eleven instructional units, each of which presents a competency to be mastered by the pre-service or in-service teacher. The competencies become increasingly complex and difficult. Unit 1, for example, attempts to develop an awareness of the effects of gender bias. The goal of Unit 5 is to identify gender-fair curriculum materials. And the goal of Unit 11 is to conduct applied research to develop policies and programs to achieve gender fairness.

Impact of Puberty and the Growth Spurt

To appreciate the nature and magnitude of the changes that take place at the time of puberty, arrange to visit both a seventh-grade and a ninth-grade classroom. Observe the students not only in class but also in the halls and after school. Describe differences in physical appearance and in behavior between the seventh- and ninth-graders, paying particular attention to differences between boys and girls. You might also try to pick out the most and least mature children in a group and concentrate on their behavior in and out of the classroom. If you make an observation of this type, note your reactions and comment on the implications of differences you detect.

Early and Late Maturation

For a summary of research on early and late maturation, refer to "Perspectives on Adolescence from Longitudinal Research" by Norman Livson and Harvey Peskin in the *Handbook of Adolescent Psychology* (1980), edited by Joseph Adelson.

Biological and Physiological Aspects of Adolescence

For more complete information about biological changes at adolescence, consult *Growth at Adolescence* (2d ed., 1962) by J. M. Tanner. Condensed versions of the material in his book can be found in Chapter 3 of *Carmichael's Manual of Child Psychology* (3d ed., 1970), edited by Paul H. Mussen, and in Chapter 1 of *Twelve to Sixteen: Early Adolescence* (1972), edited by Jerome Kagan and Robert Coles.

Advanced treatments of this topic can be found in the *Handbook of Adolescent Psychology* (1987), edited by Vincent B. Van Hasselt and Michel Hersen. In particular, consult Chapter 3, "Biological Theoretical Models of Adolescent Development," and Chapter 7, "Pubertal Processes: Their Relevance for Developmental Research."

Emotional Characteristics of Adolescence

Useful, though advanced, information about the emotional aspects of adolescence can be gleaned from several chapters of the *Handbook of Adolescent Psychology* (1987), just mentioned. Chapter 9 covers adolescent sexuality; Chapter 16 discusses depression and suicide; and Chapter 17 discusses the causes and nature of substance abuse.

SUMMARY

1. Preschool and kindergarten children are quite active and enjoy physical activity. But incomplete muscle and motor development limits what they can accomplish on tasks that require fine motor skills, eye-hand coordination, and visual focusing.

2. The social behavior of preschool and kindergarten children is marked by rapidly changing friendships and play groups, a variety of types of play, short quarrels, and a growing awareness of sex roles.

3. Kindergartners openly display their emotions. Anger and jealousy are common.

4. Kindergartners like to talk and are reasonably skilled at using language. Preschoolers tend to apply their own rules of grammar.

5. Primary grade children exhibit many of the same physical characteristics as preschool and kindergarten children (high activity level, incomplete muscle and motor development, frequent periods of fatigue). Most accidents occur among third-graders because they overestimate their physical skills and underestimate the dangers in their activities.

6. Friendships are typically same-sex and are made on a more selective basis by primary grade children. Although quarrels among friends occur more frequently than among nonfriends and involve verbal arguments as well as punching, wrestling, and shoving, they are shorter and less intense.

7. Primary grade pupils are becoming more emotionally sensitive. As a result, they are more easily hurt by criticism, respond strongly to praise, and are more likely to hurt another child's feelings during a quarrel.

8. Primary grade pupils are eager to learn and like to speak up in class.

9. Elementary grade girls grow more quickly and begin puberty earlier than elementary grade boys. All children have developed sufficient fine motor coordination to enjoy arts and crafts and musical activities.

10. The social behavior of elementary grade children is increasingly influenced by peer group norms and the development of interpersonal reasoning.

11. Delinquency occurs more frequently among elementary grade children than at earlier ages, and is associated with dysfunctional parent-child relationships and academic failure. About 10 percent of elementary grade children exhibit a behavior disorder.

12. Although sex differences in cognitive abilities among elementary students have decreased over

the past forty years, they are still noticeable. Differences in cognitive style are also apparent.

13. In junior high, boys catch up with and begin to exceed girls in physical development. Almost all girls and many boys reach puberty. Diet and sleeping habits may change for the worse.

14. Because the peer group is the primary source for rules of acceptable behavior, conformity and concern about what peers think reaches a peak during the junior high years.

15. Although anxiety, worry, and concern about self-esteem, physical appearance, academic success, and acceptance by peers are prominent emotions among many adolescents, some cope with these emotions better than others. School vandalism peaks during the junior high years.

16. Junior high school marks a transition between concrete operational and formal operational thought and between moral realism and moral relativism.

17. Physical development during the high school years is marked by physical maturity for most students and by puberty for virtually all. Sexual activity increases.

18. The long-range goals, beliefs, and values of adolescents are likely to be influenced by parents, whereas immediate status is likely to be influenced by peers. Many teens have part-time, after-school employment.

19. Eating disorders, substance abuse, schizophrenia, depression, and suicide are prominent emotional disorders among adolescents. Depression is the most common emotional disorder during adolescence. Depression coupled with an unstable family situation places adolescents at risk for suicide.

20. Cognitively, high school students become increasingly capable of formal operational thought, although they may function at the concrete operational level a good deal of the time.

KEY TERMS

unoccupied behavior *(101)*
solitary play *(101)*
onlooker behavior *(101)*
parallel play *(101)*
associative play *(101)*
cooperative play *(102)*
functional play *(102)*
constructive play *(102)*
dramatic play *(102)*
games with rules *(102)*
authoritative parents *(106)*
authoritarian parents *(106)*
sociometric techniques *(109)*
interpersonal reasoning *(115)*
cognitive style *(119)*
early-maturing boy *(124)*
late-maturing boy *(124)*
early-maturing girl *(124)*
late-maturing girl *(124)*

DISCUSSION QUESTIONS

1. Given the physical, social, emotional, and cognitive characteristics of preschool and kindergarten children, what type of classroom atmosphere and instructional tactics would you use to foster learning and enjoyment of school?

2. The primary and elementary years correspond to Erikson's stage of industry vs. inferiority. The implication of this stage is that educators should do whatever is necessary to encourage a sense of industry and competence in each student. On a scale of 1 to 10, where 1 is the low end of the scale, how well do you think schools accomplish this goal? What is it that schools do (or not do) that prevented you from assigning them a 10?

3. During the junior high years the peer group becomes the general source for rules of behavior. Why? What advantages and disadvantages are associated with a situation in which the peer group establishes the norms for behavior?

4. Given the high rates of illegitimate births and sexually transmitted diseases among high school students, you could persuasively argue that adolescents should receive more sex education than they do. What are the advantages and disadvantages of providing this education in the school, instead of in the home?

Chapter 4

ASSESSING PUPIL VARIABILITY

▶ Criterion-referenced scores indicate degree of mastery of objectives

▶ Percentile rank: percentage of scores at or below a given point

▶ Standard deviation: degree of deviation from the mean of a distribution

▶ z score: how far a raw score is from the mean in standard deviation units

▶ T score: how far a raw score is from the mean in numerical terms

▶ Stanine score: pupil performance indicated with reference to a 9-point scale based on normal curve

THE NATURE AND MEASUREMENT OF INTELLIGENCE

▶ Intelligence test scores most closely related to school success

▶ Intelligence tests not good predictors of job success, marital happiness, life happiness

▶ Intelligence involves more than what intelligence tests measure

▶ IQ scores can change with experience, training

▶ IQ test items based on knowledge and situations thought to be common to most children

LEGAL CHALLENGES TO STANDARDIZED TESTING

▶ In the real world, test-based decisions sometimes harm children

▶ Conflicting opinions regarding bias in intelligence tests

▶ Overreliance on test scores can bar gifted and talented minority children from special programs

▶ Understanding the assessment process leads to nondiscriminatory testing

Sit back for a few minutes and think about some of your friends and classmates over the past twelve years. Make a list of their physical characteristics (height, weight, visual acuity, athletic skill, for example), social characteristics (outgoing, reserved, cooperative, sensitive to the needs of others, assertive), emotional characteristics (self-assured, optimistic, pessimistic, egotistical), and intellectual characteristics (methodical, creative, impulsive, good with numbers, terrible at organizing ideas). Now analyze your descriptions in terms of similarities and differences. In all likelihood, they point to many ways in which your friends and classmates have been alike, but to even more ways in which they have differed from one another. Indeed, although human beings share many important characteristics, they also differ from one another in significant ways (and we tend to notice the differences more readily than the similarities).

Now imagine yourself a few years from now, when your job as a teacher is to help every student learn as much as possible despite all the ways in which your students differ from one another. The variability among any group of students is one reason why teaching is both interesting and challenging. Richard Snow, who has written extensively about individual differences in education and how to deal with them, has summarized the problem as follows:

> Individual differences among students present a pervasive and profound problem to educators. At the outset of instruction in any topic, students of any age and in any culture will differ from one another in various intellectual and psychomotor abilities and skills, in both general and specialized prior knowledge, in interests and motives, and in personal styles of thought and work during learning. These differences, in turn, appear directly related to differences in the students' learning progress. (1986, p. 1029)

The significance of these observations on variability is that while it usually will be essential for you to plan lessons, assignments, and teaching techniques by taking into account *typical* characteristics, it will also be necessary for you to expect and make allowances for differences between pupils. Students vary not only in terms of all the characteristics described in Chapters 2 and 3 but also in terms of general and specific abilities to learn. The fact that some students learn more easily and successfully than others is one of the major problems you will need to deal with as a teacher.

THE MEANING OF VARIABILITY

Intraindividual varia-
tion: differences in a
person's behavior
over time and across
situations

When psychologists discuss variability, they often do so in terms of two broad categories. One category is called **intraindividual variation.** Since the prefix *intra* means within, the focus here is on how a given individual changes over time or acts differently in different situations. Can you recall, for example, any friends or classmates who gradually became more outgoing, or who excelled in algebra but struggled to write a coherent paragraph in English composition? A student's attention span, interest level, or motivation may change over time and tasks, because youngsters are sensitive to changes in such classroom variables as the subject matter, the pacing of instruction, the personality of the teacher, and the type of test being given. In Chapter 2 we pointed out how personality and thinking change with age and offered suggestions for teaching based on these differences. Likewise, in Chapter 3 we summarized physical, social, emotional, and intellectual changes (as well as similarities) as children progress from preschool through high school. In Chapters 8 through 12 we will mention intraindividual variability in learning and motivation.

Throughout their school years, students are interested in how they perform academically compared to classmates. (Bob Daemmrich/ The Image Works, Inc.)

Interindividual varia-
tion: differences be-
tween individuals at
a given point in time

The second category is called **interindividual variation.** Since the prefix *inter* means between, the focus here is on differences between individuals at any given point in time. Keep in mind that some ways in which students differ from each other are more important than others. The ones you want to pay special attention to are those that relate strongly to classroom achievement. What follows is a *sample* (in alphabetical order) of points of individual difference that, through extensive research, have been related to achievement:

age	learning strategies	problem solving
attention span	learning style	self-concept
attitudes	memory capacity	social class
cognitive style	motivation	social competence
ethnicity	perceptual skill	stage of cognitive
gender	personality	development
intelligence	prior knowledge	values
interest		

Most of the research on interindividual variation revolves around scholastic aptitude (another term for intelligence) and achievement, because large numbers of standardized tests have been constructed to measure these variables. These tests make it possible to identify both the range of variability among a group of students and the strengths and weaknesses of each student. Ideally, schools can use this information to select and place children in instructional programs that match their characteristics or to adjust programs to better meet individual needs.

Because standardized assessment of scholastic aptitude and achievement is such a popular practice in the United States (as well as in many other countries), this chapter focuses on the nature of standardized tests, how they are used to assess pupil variability, and how these test results can be employed in putting together effective instructional programs for "typical" students. The next two chapters describe techniques for dealing with the range of interindividual variability—intellectual, emotional, and cultural—that exists in the typical classroom and may in some cases require special kinds of instruction. As we will see, and as Richard Snow (1986) has pointed out, the use of standardized tests to assess variability and guide the subsequent placement of students into different instructional programs is truly a double-edged sword: It has the potential to harm students, as well as to help them.

STANDARDIZED TESTS

The Nature of Standardized Tests

▶ Standardized tests: item presented in standard fashion, results reported with reference to standards

The kinds of assessment instruments described in this chapter are typically referred to as **standardized tests,** although the term *published tests* is sometimes used. You have almost certainly taken several of these tests during your academic career, and so you are probably familiar with their appearance and general characteristics. They are called standardized tests because they contain a standard set of items that are presented to students in uniform fashion, the answers are evaluated according to precise scoring standards, and the scores are interpreted by comparing them to the scores obtained from a norm group. They are called published tests because they are prepared, distributed, and scored by publishing companies or independent test services. The more inclusive term *published tests* has been introduced also because the scores from some types of instruments (to be described later) are interpreted with reference to predetermined criteria rather than to the performance of a norm group.

Standardized tests are widely used in American schools to provide information about academic performance that cannot be obtained from teacher-made tests or grades. For example, students are often placed in special programs at least partly on the basis of how well they score on standardized achievement and aptitude tests. (We describe the use of standardized tests for this purpose in more detail in the next chapter.) In addition, it is not unusual these days for many school districts to use standardized achievement tests to compare the effectiveness of teachers and schools. The average scores for schools within a district and for districts within a region are often reported with much fanfare by local newspapers. Because most standardized achievement tests were not designed for this purpose (and for other reasons that will become clear as you learn about the concepts of reliability, validity, and norms in the next section), the use of standardized test scores to evaluate teachers, schools, and districts is strongly criticized by most measurement experts. On average, each school-age child takes 2 1/2 standardized tests per year. During the 1986–1987 school year, a total of 105 million such tests were administered to students in the United States (Green, 1991).

How Classroom Teachers Use Standardized Tests

The informal assessments you will devise for use in your classroom (a type we will cover in Chapter 13) will be custom designed to fit the texts and learning materials used by your students. Sometimes, however, you will want to obtain information about how well your students are performing compared with students in other classrooms. When a group of teachers was asked to indicate how they used standardized tests, diagnosis of students' strengths and weaknesses was mentioned most often—by 74 percent of the responding teachers. Assessment of academic growth came in second, having been mentioned by 66 percent of the responding teachers. And placement of students in the proper grade level or program, the third most popular use of tests, was mentioned by 65 percent of the sample (Mehrens & Lehmann, 1987).

> Most teachers use tests to diagnose students' strengths and weaknesses

When you read the test profiles that report how students in your classes have performed on standardized tests, you will get a general idea of some of your students' strengths and weaknesses. If certain pupils are weak in particular skill areas and you want to help them overcome those weaknesses, test results *may* give you *some* insights into possible ways to provide remedial instruction. If most of your students score below average in certain segments of the curriculum, you will know that you should devote more time and effort to presenting those topics and skills to the entire class. You can and should, of course, supplement what you learn from standardized test results with your own tests and observations in order to design potentially effective forms of remedial or advanced instruction.

In order to educate millions of American children who live in a complex and highly mobile society, it is essential to have them move through a reasonably standard basic curriculum. All the children who finish the sixth grade in several elementary schools in a large city, for instance, should have mastered the same basic learning tasks before they enter a common junior high or middle school. In addition, when a child moves to a different neighborhood within a city, or a different city within a state, or to a different part of the country, it is highly desirable to have some idea as to what the child knows about basic subjects. Standardized tests do an effective job of providing information about the mastery of general subject matter and skills.

> Standardized test scores are used to direct instruction and select students for programs

In addition to being used in planning instruction, standardized tests are used to select students for placement in certain types of school programs and for admission to college and graduate school. Tests of achievement and scholastic aptitude, for example, help schools identify and place students in classes for children with mental retardation, learning disabilities, or special gifts and talents.

Your college admissions committee took the grades you earned in high school into consideration when you applied for admission, but they also asked you to take a standardized test. That test allowed them to compare you with other applicants based on an academic achievement score that was not influenced by differences in grading standards among schools.

This brief description of standardized tests indicates that they can be used to determine student progress, identify academic strengths and weaknesses, evaluate the effectiveness of instruction, plan instructional and remedial programs, place students in specialized programs, and make comparisons of student performance independent of teacher evaluations of classroom performance.

Criteria for Evaluating Standardized Tests

Like most things, standardized tests vary in quality. To use test scores wisely, you need to be an informed consumer—to know what characteristics distinguish well-constructed from poorly constructed tests. Eight criteria are widely used to evaluate standardized tests: reliability, validity, normed excellence, examinee appropriateness, teaching feedback, usability, retest potential, and ethical propriety. Each of these criteria will be explained individually.

Reliability   A basic assumption that psychologists make about human characteristics (such as intelligence and achievement) is that they are relatively stable, at least over short periods of time. For most people this assumption seems to be true. Thus, you should be able to count on a test's results being consistent, just as you might count on a reliable worker doing a consistent job time after time. This stability in test performance is known as **reliability.** It is one of the most important characteristics of standardized tests and can be assessed in a number of ways.

To illustrate the importance of reliability, imagine that you have assigned each of your students to one of three reading groups on the basis of scores from the ABC Test of Reading Comprehension. One month later, you administer the ABC Test again and find that many of those who scored at the top initially (and were placed in the top reading group) now score in the middle or at the bottom. Conversely, many students who initially scored low now have average or above-average scores. What does that do to your confidence in making decisions based on scores from this test? If you want to be able to consistently differentiate among individuals, you need to use an instrument that performs consistently.

Psychologists who specialize in constructing standardized tests assess reliability in a variety of ways. One method is to administer the same test to the same people on two occasions and measure the extent to which the rankings change over time. This approach results in *test-retest reliability*. Another method is to administer two equivalent forms of a test to the same group of students at the same time. This approach results in *alternate-form reliability*. A third approach is to administer a single test to a group of students, create two scores by dividing the test in half, and measure the extent to which the rankings change from one half to the other. This method results in *split-half reliability* and measures the internal consistency of a test.

Regardless of which method is used to assess reliability, the goal is to create two rankings of scores and to see how similar the rankings are. This degree of consistency is expressed as a correlation coefficient (abbreviated with a lower-case *r*) that ranges from zero to one. Well-constructed standardized tests should have correlation coefficients of about .95 for split-half reliability, .90 for test-retest reliability, and .85 for alternate-form reliability (Kubiszyn & Borich, 1990). Bear in mind, however, that a particular test may not report all three forms of reliability and that reliabilities for subtests and for younger age groups (kindergarten through second grade) are likely to be lower than these overall figures.

Validity   A second important characteristic of a test is that it be an accurate measure of what it claims to measure. A reading comprehension test should measure just that—nothing more, nothing less. Whenever we speak of a test's accuracy, we are referring to its **validity.** Since most of the characteristics we are interested in knowing something about (such as arithmetic skills, spatial aptitude, intelligence, and knowledge of the American Civil War) are internal and, hence, not directly observable, tests are indirect measures of those attributes. Therefore, any test-based conclusions we may draw about how much of a characteristic a person possesses, or any predictions we might make about how well a person will perform in the future (on other types of tests, in a job, or in a specialized academic program, for example), are properly referred to as *inferences*. So, when one inquires about the validity of a test by asking, Does this test measure what it claims to measure? what one is really asking is, How accurate are the inferences that I wish to draw about the test taker? (See, for example, Messick, 1989.) The degree to which these inferences can be judged accurate, or valid, depends on the type and quality of the supporting evidence that one can muster. The kinds of evidence that underlie test-based inferences fall into one of three categories: content validity evidence, criterion-related validity evidence, and construct validity evidence.

Content validity evidence rests on a set of judgments about how well a test's items reflect the particular body of knowledge and skill (called a *domain* by measurement specialists) to which we want to infer. If a test on the American Civil War, for example, contained no items on the war's causes, its great battles, or the years it encompassed, some users might be hesitant to call someone who achieved a high score knowledgeable about this topic. Then again, other users might not be nearly so disturbed by these omissions (and the inference that would be drawn from the test score) if they considered such information to be relatively unimportant.

As we mentioned above, a basic reason for testing people is to predict how they will behave in the future. Many colleges, for example, require students to take the *American College Testing Program* (ACT) or the *Scholastic Aptitude Test* (SAT) and then use the results (along with other information) to predict each

Reliability: similarity between two rankings of test scores obtained from the same individual

Validity: how accurately a test measures what users want it to measure

Content validity: how well test items cover a type of learning

Predictive validity: how well a test score predicts later performance

prospective student's grade-point average at the end of the freshman year. All other things being equal, students with higher test scores are expected to have higher grade-point averages than students with lower test scores and thus stand a better chance of being admitted. This type of criterion-related validity evidence is called *predictive validity evidence.*

Construct validity evidence indicates how accurately a test measures a theoretical description of some internal attribute of a person. Such attributes, like intelligence, creativity, motivation, and anxiety, are called constructs by psychologists. To illustrate the nature of construct validity, we will use a hypothetical theory of intelligence called the ABC theory. This theory holds that highly intelligent individuals should have higher-than-average school grades now and in the future, demonstrate superior performance on tasks that involve abstract reasoning, and be able to distinguish worthwhile from nonworthwhile goals. They may or may not, however, be popular among their peers. If the ABC theory is accurate and if someone has done a good job of constructing an intelligence test based on this theory (the XYZ Intelligence Test), people's scores on the XYZ Test should vary in accordance with predictions derived from the ABC theory. We should see, for example, a strong positive relationship between IQ scores and grade-point average but no relationship between IQ scores and measures of popularity. As more and more of this type of evidence is supplied, we can feel increasingly confident in drawing the inference that the XYZ Intelligence Test is an accurate measure of the ABC theory of intelligence.

Construct validity: how accurately a test measures a particular attribute

Normed Excellence   For a test score to have any meaning, it has to be compared to some yardstick or measure of performance. Standardized tests use the performance of a norm group as the measure against which all other scores are compared. A **norm group** is a sample of individuals carefully chosen so as to reflect the larger population of students for whom the test is intended. In many cases, the larger population consists of all elementary school children or all high school children in the United States. The norm group must closely match the larger population it represents on such major demographic variables as age, sex, race, region of country, family income, and occupation of head of household. These variables are considered major because they are strongly associated with differences in school performance. If, for example, the U.S. Census Bureau reports that 38 percent of all Hispanic males between the ages of six and thirteen live in the southwestern region of the country, a good test constructor testing in the Southwest will try to put together a norm group that has the same percentage of six- to thirteen-year-old Hispanic males. As you might suspect, problems of score interpretation arise when the major demographic characteristics of individuals who take the test are not reflected in the norm group. Suppose you were trying to interpret the score of a fourteen-year-old African-American male on the EZ Test of Academic Achievement. If the oldest students in the norm group were twelve years of age and if African-American children were not part of the norm group, you would have no way of knowing if your student's score is below average, average, or above average, compared to the norm.

Meaningfulness of standardized test scores depends on representativeness of norm group

When high school seniors take exams such as the Scholastic Aptitude Test (or the equivalent) the results are reported in terms of norm-referenced scores. Each student's performance is compared to that of the sample of students who made up the standardization group when the test was devised. (Jim Harrison/Stock Boston, Inc.)

Examinee Appropriateness   Because developing a standardized test is a substantial undertaking that requires a considerable investment of money, time, and expertise, most tests of this type are designed for nationwide use. But the curriculum in school districts in different types of communities and in different sections of the country varies to a considerable extent. Therefore, it is important to estimate how appropriate a given test is for a particular group of pupils. When you are estimating the content validity of a test, you should pay attention not only to how well the questions measure what they are supposed to measure but also to whether they are appropriate in terms of level of difficulty and in relation to the vocabulary and characteristics of your students. For example, giving readiness tests to preschool and kindergarten children in order to determine whether they are ready to begin school or should be promoted to first grade has been heavily criticized on the basis of examinee appropriateness. A major problem with the use of tests for making admission and retention decisions in the early grades is their low reliability. Young children change physically, socially, emotionally, and intellectually so rapidly that many of them score very differently when retested six months later (Schultz, 1989).

> Formal testing of young children is inappropriate because of rapid developmental changes

Teaching Feedback   Most standardized tests are designed to be used all over the country, but in general the scores are used by particular teachers interested in individual pupils. An achievement test in reading will provide meaningful feedback only if the scores tell teachers something that can be used to improve instruction. If that is to happen, the scores should reveal significant things about pupil performance and be reasonably easy to interpret.

Usability   Most standardized tests are group tests designed to be given by one examiner to a class of students. (Some intelligence tests and a few performance tests that measure specialized aptitudes are individual tests given to one individual at a time.) Accordingly, the instructions and questions are typically printed in a test booklet, and the answers are recorded on a separate sheet that can be electronically processed. Sometimes special pencils must be used, and quite often students are given a specified number of minutes to work on each section. A test is usable if it provides clear instructions to the teacher (or other administrator) that can be put into practice without a great deal of difficulty or confusion, and if it does not force students to waste time dealing with the mechanics of recording answers. (Perhaps you can recall taking standardized tests that were so confusing you were not sure you recorded the correct answer even when you were certain you knew it.)

Retest Potential   Quite often it is desirable to obtain before-and-after information about student performance. But if students are tested before they study a unit and then tested again after instruction has taken place, an alternate form of the first exam should be available. Simply giving the same test over again would yield misleading information because students might remember specific questions and answers. Therefore, the availability of an equivalent but different form of a standardized test may be an important consideration.

Ethical Propriety   In the 1960s, when some school districts embarked on a veritable test-giving binge, attempts were sometimes made to measure not only achievement but various kinds of "adjustment" as well. Some of the items used to tap personality variables asked students to consider questions viewed as potentially harmful (such as "Do you love your mother more than your father?"). As a consequence, many school boards now insist that all tests be examined to determine if they contain questions that might be classified as offensive or likely to arouse feelings of confusion or guilt.

Types of Standardized Tests

The kinds of standardized tests you took most frequently during your elementary school years and perhaps during your secondary school years were **achievement tests,** designed to assess how much you had learned—or achieved—in basic school subjects. The very first standardized test you took was probably designed to evaluate aspects of reading performance. Then, at intervals of two years or so, you probably worked your way tensely and laboriously through *achievement batteries* designed to assess your performance in reading as well as

▶ Achievement tests measure how much has been learned about a subject

math, language, and perhaps other subjects. During your high school years, you may have taken one or more achievement batteries that evaluated more sophisticated understanding of the basic reading-writing-arithmetic skills, as well as course content in specific subjects. At some point during your elementary school years, you may also have been asked to take a **diagnostic test,** intended to reveal your strengths and weaknesses in basic subjects and perhaps in study skills as well. You may also have taken a *scholastic aptitude* test, intended to assess your general aptitude as a student rather than your actual knowledge of subject-area skills and content. **Aptitude tests** are intended to reveal potential maximum performance, or how well a pupil is capable of performing. Thus, your teachers may have discovered that your general aptitude for learning was higher than your achievement and urged you to make greater use of your potential.

> Diagnostic tests designed to identify specific strengths and weaknesses

> Aptitude tests provide estimates of potential ability

If one of your teachers felt that there was a substantial discrepancy between your scores on scholastic aptitude and achievement tests, or if you were ever considered for a special program of some sort, you may have been asked to take an *individual test of intelligence.* All the tests described up to this point have been *group* tests given to several students at the same time. Because group tests often make no provision for identifying and correcting students' misconceptions about how to respond to particular items, such tests are apt to contain some amount of what test specialists call measurement error. When more accuracy is desired, it is usually better to have a trained examiner give a test that has been designed for one pupil at a time. Many individual tests provide extensive explanations and illustrations of how to respond to items, allow the examiner to provide some degree of corrective feedback, and suggest ways of establishing a testing atmosphere in which the student will feel comfortable. Accordingly, the most highly

When maximum accuracy is desired—as when an estimate of intelligence is needed to determine eligibility for a special class—an individual test (such as the one shown here) is given by a trained examiner to one pupil at a time. (Bob Daemmrich)

regarded tests of intelligence (which will be described a bit later) are individual tests.

Depending on when and where you graduated from high school, you may have been asked to take a **competency test** a few months before the end of your senior year. Competency tests came into use in the mid-1970s, when it was discovered that many graduates of American high schools were unable to handle basic skills. In many school districts, therefore, students were asked to prove that they were competent in reading, writing, and arithmetic before they were awarded diplomas. It is almost certain that some time during your senior year of high school you took a test required by the admissions committee of the college you hoped to attend. You probably took either the *Scholastic Aptitude Test* (SAT) or the *American College Testing Program* (ACT) exam. If you decide to continue on to graduate school, you can expect to take the *Graduate Record Exam* (GRE). And depending on the state in which you choose to teach, you may be required to take the *National Teacher Examination* (NTE) in order to qualify for a teaching certificate.

Most of the exams just described are referred to as **norm-referenced tests** since performance is evaluated with reference to norms—the performance of others—established when the final form of the test was administered to the sample of students who made up the standardization group. After taking an achievement battery in the elementary grades, for example, you were probably told that you had performed as well on reading comprehension questions as 80 percent (or whatever) of all of the students who took the test. If you take the Graduate Record Exam, you will be told how far from the average score of 500 you are (in terms of a score to be described shortly). Thus, you will learn just where you stand in a distribution of scores arranged from lowest to highest. Recently, however, a *criterion-referenced* approach to reporting achievement scores has been developed. In the scoring of **criterion-referenced tests** an individual's performance, instead of being compared with the performance of other pupils, is evaluated with reference to mastery of specific objectives in various well-defined skill areas. Because of this feature, you may find criterion-referenced tests more useful than norm-referenced tests in determining who needs how much additional instruction in what areas (provided, of course, that the test's objectives closely match your own). The criterion-referenced approach is intended to reduce overtones of competition and emphasize mastery of objectives at a rate commensurate with students' abilities. (An approach to evaluation that stresses mastery of objectives will be detailed in Chapter 13, on classroom measurement.) A disadvantage of criterion-referenced tests is their lack of breadth; they usually cover a relatively small number of objectives. Norm-referenced achievement tests, on the other hand, usually cover a broader range of knowledge and skill.

Interpreting Standardized Test Scores

Scores on the most widely used standardized tests are typically reported on student profile forms that summarize and explain the results (see page 160 for an

---

Margin notes:

Competency tests determine if potential graduates possess basic skills

Norm-referenced scores compare one student with others

Criterion-referenced scores indicate degree of mastery of objectives

example of a test profile). While most profiles contain sufficient information to make it possible to interpret scores without additional background, you should know in advance about the kinds of scores you may encounter, particularly since you may be asked to explain scores to students as well as to their parents. The likelihood that parents would want information about standardized test scores increased in 1975, when Congress added a new part to the General Education Provisions Act entitled Privacy Rights of Parents and Students. The Privacy Rights amendment stipulates that all educational institutions must provide "parents of students access to all official records directly related to the students and an opportunity for a hearing to challenge such records on the grounds they are inaccurate, misleading, or otherwise inappropriate" (*Federal Register,* Jan. 6, 1975, p. 1028). This law was passed primarily to reduce the possibility that damaging statements about children recorded in cumulative folders might have negative repercussions, but it could lead to requests for detailed interpretation of test scores. Thus, in addition to explaining test scores to parents during parent conferences, you may be asked to supply such explanations "on demand." You should therefore know how to interpret standardized test scores, which can sometimes be misunderstood.

Grade Equivalent Scores The **grade equivalent score** is established by interpreting performance on tests in terms of grade levels. A student who makes a grade equivalent score of 4.7 on an achievement test, for example, got the same number of items right on this test as the average fourth-grader in the standardization group achieved by the seventh month of the school year. The grade equivalent score was once widely used at the elementary level, but because it may lead to misinterpretations, it is not as popular as it once was. One problem with grade equivalent scores is the tendency to misinterpret a score above a student's actual grade level as an indication that the student is capable of consistently working at that level. This kind of assumption might lead parents to agitate for an accelerated promotion. Such scores may show that a student did somewhat better on the test than the average student a grade or two above her or him, but they do not mean that the student tested has acquired knowledge of all the skills covered in the grade that would be skipped if demands for acceleration were granted.

Percentile Ranks Probably the most widely used score for standardized tests is the **percentile rank.** This score indicates the percentage of students who are at and below a given student's score. It provides specific information about relative position. Students earning a percentile rank of 87 did as well as or better than 87 percent of the students in the particular normative group being used. They did not get 87 percent of the questions right—unless by coincidence—and this is the point parents are most likely to misunderstand. Parents may have been brought up on the percentages grading system, in which 90 or above was A, 80 to 90 was B, and so on down the line. If you report that a son or daughter has a percentile rank of 50, some parents are horrorstruck or outraged, not understanding that the child's score on this test is average, not a failure. In such cases the best approach

▶ Percentile rank: percentage of scores at or below a given point

is to emphasize that the percentile rank tells the percentage of cases at or below the child's score. You might also talk in terms of a hypothetical group of 100; for example, a child with a percentile rank of 78 did as well as or better than 78 out of every 100 students who took the test.

Although the percentile rank gives simple and direct information on relative position, it has a major disadvantage: The difference in achievement between students clustered around the middle of the distribution is often considerably less than the difference between those at the extremes. The reason is that *most* scores are clustered around the middle of most distributions of large groups of students. The difference in raw score (number of items answered correctly) between students at percentile ranks 50 and 51 may be one point. But the difference in raw score between the student with a percentile rank of 98 and one ranked 97 may be ten or fifteen points because the best (and worst) students scatter toward the extremes. This quality of percentile ranks means that ranks on different tests cannot be averaged. To get around that difficulty, standard scores are often used.

Standard Scores   Standard scores are expressed in terms of a common unit—the **standard deviation.** This statistic indicates the degree to which scores in a group of tests (a distribution) differ from the average or mean. (The *mean* is the arithmetical average of a distribution and is calculated by adding all scores and dividing the total by the number of scores.) The standard deviation is most valuable when it can be related to the normal probability curve. Figure 4.1 shows a normal probability curve indicating the percentage of cases to be found within three standard deviations above and below the mean. The **normal curve** is a mathematical concept that depicts a hypothetical bell-shaped distribution of scores. Such a perfectly symmetrical distribution rarely, if ever, occurs in real life.

> Standard deviation: degree of deviation from the mean of a distribution

FIGURE 4.1 The Normal Probability Curve

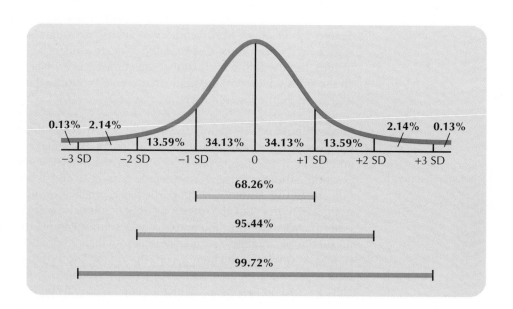

However, since many distributions of human characteristics and performance closely *resemble* the normal distribution, it is often assumed that such distributions are typical enough to be treated as "normal." Thus, information derived by mathematicians for the hypothetical normal distribution can be applied to the approximately normal distributions that are found when human attributes are measured. When very large numbers of pupils are asked to take tests designed by specialists who go to great lengths to cancel out the impact of selective factors, it may be appropriate to interpret their scores on such tests with reference to the normal curve.

For purposes of discussion, and for purposes of acquiring familiarity with test scores, it will be sufficient for you to know about two of the standard scores that are derived from standard deviations. One, called a **z score,** tells how far a given raw score is from the mean in standard deviation units. A z score of −1.5, for example, would mean that the pupil was one and one-half standard deviation units below the mean. Because some z scores (such as the one in the example just given) are negative and involve decimals, **T scores** are often used instead. T scores use a preselected mean (50) to get away from negative values.

> z score: how far a raw score is from the mean in standard deviation units

> T score: how far a raw score is from the mean in numerical terms

Most standardized tests that use T scores offer detailed explanations of how they should be interpreted either in the test booklet or on the student profile of scores. In fact, many test profiles adopt the form of a narrative report when explaining the meaning of all scores used. (See Figure 4.4, page 160.)

To grasp the relationship among z scores, T scores, and percentile ranks, examine Figure 4.2. The diagram shows each scale marked off below a normal

FIGURE 4.2 Relationship Among z Scores, T Scores, and Percentile Ranks

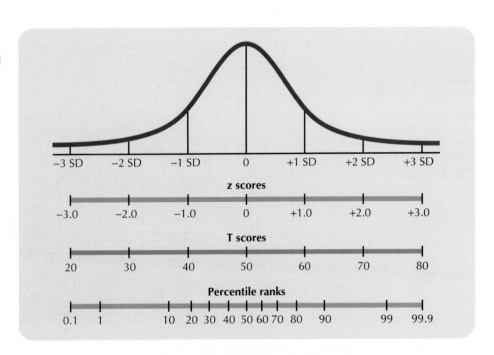

curve. It supplies information about the interrelationships of these various scores, provided that the distribution you are working with is essentially normal. In a normal distribution, for example, a z score of +1 is the same as a T score of 60 or a percentile rank of 84; a z score of –2 is the same as a T score of 30 or a percentile rank of about 2. (In addition, notice that the distance between the percentile ranks clustered around the middle is only a small fraction of the distance between the percentile ranks that are found at the ends of the distribution.)

Stanine Scores   During World War II, Air Force psychologists developed a statistic called the **stanine score** (an abbreviation of "standard nine-point scale"), reflecting the fact that it is a type of standard score and divides a population into nine groups. Each stanine is one-half of a standard deviation unit, as indicated in Figure 4.3.

Stanine scores were developed for use in wartime training programs, where efficiency was of paramount importance. The test specialists who devised the statistic developed a battery of several tests that, for instance, identified pilot candidates most likely to respond quickly and effectively to instruction. All of the candidates for pilot training who arrived at an Air Force base at a particular time would be given the battery of tests, and their performance would be reported in terms of stanines. If only a few pilots were needed at that particular moment during the war, only candidates in stanines 8 and 9 might be selected for training. If more pilots were needed, those in the next highest stanines might also be admitted to the training program. When stanines were first introduced on test profiles reporting the performance of public school children on standardized tests, they were often used to group students. (Students in stanines 1, 2, and 3 would be placed in one class, those in 4, 5, and 6 in another class, and so on.) For reasons to be described later in this chapter as well as in the next, grouping

FIGURE 4.3 Percentage of Cases in Each Stanine (with Standard Deviation Units Indicated)

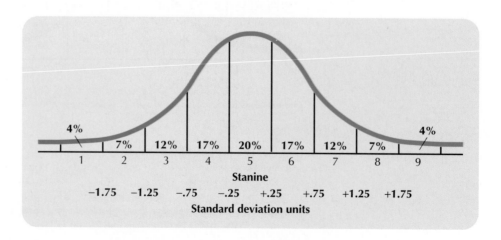

Stanine score: pupil performance indicated with reference to a 9-point scale based on normal curve

has become a highly controversial issue in American schools. Consequently, stanine scores are now used to indicate relative standing. They are easier to understand than z scores or T scores since any child or parent can understand that stanines represent a 9-point scale with 1 as the lowest, 5 as average, and 9 as the highest. Furthermore, unlike percentile ranks, stanine scores can be averaged. In those cases when it is desirable to have more precise information about relative standing, however, percentile ranks may be more useful, even though they cannot be averaged.

Percentile ranks and stanines are often used when local norms are prepared. As noted in our earlier description of how standardized tests are developed, the norms used to determine a student's level of performance are established by asking a representative sample of pupils to take the final form of the test. Inevitably, there will be differences between school systems (in texts used and the time during a school year or years when certain topics are covered, for instance). Accordingly, some test publishers report scores in terms of local, as well as national, norms. (Examine the test profile reproduced in Figure 4.4.) Each student's performance is thus compared not only with the performance of the members of the standardization group but also with the performance of all students in the same school system.

At the beginning of this chapter, we pointed out that the primary reason for administering standardized tests is to place students in instructional programs that best match their strengths and weaknesses. In instances where teachers fully understand the characteristic being measured, where reliable, valid, and well-normed tests are readily available, and where teachers know how to appropriately interpret test results, this strategy for dealing with individual differences can work quite well, particularly when it is supplemented with teacher observations and informal assessments. Effective remedial reading and math programs, for example, are based to a large extent on scores from diagnostic reading and math tests. But when the characteristic being measured and the nature of the test are poorly understood, inappropriate decisions and controversy often result. Nowhere are these negative outcomes more likely than in the assessment of intelligence. Since many instructional and placement decisions are based on intelligence test scores, it is important that you clearly understand this characteristic and how it is measured. Hence, this is the topic of the next section.

THE NATURE AND MEASUREMENT OF INTELLIGENCE

The Origin of Intelligence Testing

Our account of the origin of intelligence testing begins in the year 1904. In that year the Minister of Public Instruction for the Paris, France, school system appointed a commission of experts to study and recommend procedures for educating mentally retarded children. One member of the commission was a

FIGURE 4.4 Example of a Student Diagnostic Report (Based on Reading Yardsticks score report, Copyright © 1981. Reprinted with permission of the Publisher, THE RIVERSIDE PUBLISHING COMPANY, 8420 W. Bryn Mawr Avenue, Chicago IL, 60631. All rights reserved.)

STUDENT DIAGNOSTIC REPORT
THE RIVERSIDE PUBLISHING COMPANY

STUDENT RECORD FOR
RITA FINNEGAN

Test: READING YARDSTICKS
Level: 11 Date: 10/81 Form: 1 Norms: FALL
Sex: F Grade: 5 Process No: 000-1429-002
Building: KENNON MIDDLE System: KENNON
Teacher: MRS. ECKLAND

9-85002

Criterion-Referenced Interpretation

Performance on Objectives

* = DID NOT REACH MASTERY LEVEL OF 60 % AS SET BY SCHOOL DISTRICT

Part / Subtest / Objective	Number of Test Items	Number Attempted	Number Correct	Percent Correct by Student	Building Percent Correct
VOCABULARY					
SYNONYMS	10	9	8	90	51
ANTONYMS	10	10	10	100	55
MULTI-MEANING WORDS	10	10	10	100	82
PRONOUN REFERENTS	10	10	9	90	80
COMPREHENSION					
LITERAL READING COMPREHENSION	60	58	41	67	52
VISUALIZING	13	12	11	82	79
DETAILS	3	2	2	67	63
SEQUENCE	5	5	5	100	77
INTERPRETIVE READING COMPREHENSION	19	19	14	73	71
MAIN IDEA	5	5	4	80	61
DRAW CONCLUSIONS	5	5	3	60	54
CAUSE AND EFFECT	9	9	7	78	76
EVALUATIVE READING COMPREHENSION	14	14	8	*57	49
PREDICT OUTCOMES	5	5	3	60	52
FACT VS. OPINION	5	5	4	*50	53
CHARACTER TRAITS	4	4	2	*50	51
LANGUAGE COMPREHENSION	14	13	8	*56	62
SIMILES AND METAPHORS	3	3	2	67	59
IDIOMS	3	3	1	*33	42
PUNCTUATION, PERIOD, QUESTION MARK	4	4	4	*50	50
PUNCTUATION, QUOTATION MARKS	3	3	3	75	73
STRUCTURAL ANALYSIS					
PLURALS	55	45	35	64	64
POSSESSIVES	55	45	35	60	81
SYLLABICATION; NUMBER OF SYLLABLES	10	8	6	60	56
SYLLABICATION; WORD DIVISION	10	8	5	60	51
BASE WORDS	10	8	8	80	78
AFFIXES, WORD MEANING	10	6	6	60	65
CONTRACTIONS	10	7	5	50	53
STUDY SKILLS	55	49	38	68	66
REFERENCE MATERIAL	39	35	28	73	70
DICTIONARY; ALPHA ORDER, GUIDE WORDS	3	3	3	100	92
ALPHA ORDER, SECOND-FOURTH LETTERS	6	5	4	67	71
DICTIONARY; CHOOSING DEFINITIONS	5	3	3	60	58
PRONUNCIATION KEY	5	3	3	75	80
ENCYCLOPEDIA	3	3	2	67	62
CARD CATALOG	3	2	2	*50	50
PARTS OF BOOKS	5	5	5	100	77
CHOOSING REFERENCE SOURCES	5	4	4	80	85
MAPS	5	5	5	60	78
ORGANIZATIONAL STUDY SKILLS	16	14	10	63	61
TOPIC	4	3	3	75	74
TOPIC; SUBTOPICS	4	4	3	75	74
TOPIC; RELEVANT DETAILS	4	4	4	80	80
FOLLOWING DIRECTIONS	4	3	2	*50	75
TEST TOTAL	210	204	150	71	69

Norm-Referenced Interpretation

Scores / Profile

Subtest	RS	LCL PR	Below Average (1 – 10)	Average (25 – 50 – 75)	Above Average (99)
VOCABULARY	36	76	/////////////		
LITERAL READING COMPREHENSION	11	60	/////////////		
INTERPRETIVE READING COMPREHENSION	14	52	/////////////		
EVALUATIVE READING COMPREHENSION	8	53	/////////////		
LANGUAGE READING COMPREHENSION	8	24	/////////////		
WORD PARTS	35	49	/////////////		
REFERENCE MATERIAL STUDY SKILLS	28	50	/////////////		
ORGANIZATIONAL STUDY SKILLS	10	46	/////////////		

RITA'S ESTIMATED ITBS SCORES ARE AS FOLLOWS:

	OCTOBER 1981	MAY 1982	SEPTEMBER 1982
VOCABULARY			
GE	63	70	74
PR	76	76	76
NCE	65	65	65
SS	137	146	151
READING COMPREHENSION			
GE	51	57	61
PR	49	49	49
NCE	50	50	50
SS	124	130	136
WORK-STUDY SKILLS			
GE	52	58	62
PR	50	50	50
NCE	50	50	50
SS	124	131	137

* NOTE THAT IN ADDITION TO A DESCRIPTION OF WHERE SHE IS NOW, RITA'S PROJECTED GROWTH IS REPORTED FOR THE COMING YEAR.

Narrative Interpretation

HOW WELL IS RITA DOING IN READING? TO HELP ANSWER THIS QUESTION, RITA TOOK READING YARDSTICKS IN OCTOBER 1981. HER TEST RESULTS ARE SHOWN ON THE LEFT.

LET'S GO OVER THE RESULTS FOR RITA. WE START AT THE FAR LEFT, UNDER THE SECTION HEADED "CRITERION-REFERENCED INTERPRETATION." THE FIRST SUBTEST IN READING YARDSTICKS IS VOCABULARY. UNDER VOCABULARY, FOUR OBJECTIVES ARE MEASURED. THE FIRST OBJECTIVE IS SYNONYMS. RITA ATTEMPTED 9 OF 10 TEST EXERCISES UNDER SYNONYMS. SHE GOT 8 OF THEM CORRECT. HER PERCENT CORRECT IS 80. THIS COMPARES WITH THE BUILDING PERCENT CORRECT OF 51, WHICH HAS BASED ON 247 FIFTH GRADE STUDENTS WHO TOOK THE TEST WITH RITA. RITA'S PERCENT CORRECT IN SYNONYMS IS HIGHER THAN THE BUILDING PERCENT CORRECT. THIS MEANS THAT RITA MAY BE STRONGER IN SYNONYMS THAN OTHER FIFTH GRADE STUDENTS IN THE BUILDING. USING THIS APPROACH, WE CAN LOOK AT HOW RITA DID ON EACH OF THE READING OBJECTIVES.

HOW DID RITA DO COMPARED WITH OTHER STUDENTS? WE ALREADY HAVE SOME INFORMATION, BUT THE SECTION ON THE LEFT UNDER "NORM-REFERENCED INFORMATION" GIVES MORE. FOR EXAMPLE, RITA'S PERCENTILE RANK IN VOCABULARY IS 76. THIS MEANS THAT RITA SCORED HIGHER THAN 76 PERCENT OF THE FIFTH GRADE STUDENTS IN THE BUILDING. ON THE OTHER HAND, 24 PERCENT SCORED AS WELL OR BETTER. RITA SEEMS TO BE SOMEWHAT ABOVE AVERAGE IN VOCABULARY COMPARED TO OTHER FIFTH GRADE STUDENTS. LET'S SEE HOW RITA DID ON THE OTHER SUBTESTS. RITA WAS SOMEWHAT ABOVE AVERAGE IN LITERAL READING COMPREHENSION, ABOUT AVERAGE IN INTERPRETIVE READING COMPREHENSION, ABOUT AVERAGE IN EVALUATIVE READING COMPREHENSION, SOMEWHAT BELOW AVERAGE IN LANGUAGE, ABOUT AVERAGE IN WORD PARTS, AVERAGE IN REFERENCE MATERIAL STUDY SKILLS, AND ABOUT AVERAGE IN ORGANIZATIONAL STUDY SKILLS.

LET'S LOOK AT RITA'S HIGH AND LOW POINTS IN READING FOR DIAGNOSTIC PURPOSES. WE LOOK AT EACH PAIR OF TEST SCORES, TO SEE IF THERE IS BETTER THAN A 50 PERCENT CHANCE THAT THE OBSERVED DIFFERENCES BETWEEN THEM ARE RELIABLE ONES. RITA IS HIGHER IN VOCABULARY THAN IN WORD PARTS, IN LITERAL READING COMPREHENSION THAN IN LANGUAGE, AND IN WORD PARTS THAN ORGANIZATIONAL STUDY SKILLS.

RITA'S LEVEL OF PERFORMANCE ON THE IOWA TESTS OF BASIC SKILLS (ITBS) IS ESTIMATED ON THE LEFT, FOR VOCABULARY, READING COMPREHENSION, AND WORK-STUDY SKILLS. GRADE EQUIVALENTS (GE), NATIONAL PERCENTILE RANKS (PR), AND NORMAL CURVE EQUIVALENTS (NCE) ARE ESTIMATED FOR BOTH CURRENT STATUS AND PROJECTED FOR A YEAR FROM NOW. THE PROJECTED GROWTH IS AN AVERAGE GROWTH. SOME STUDENTS WILL GROW MORE AND SOME LESS. RITA CAN BE RETESTED IN MAY 1982 OR SEPTEMBER 1982 WITH THE ITBS OR YARDSTICKS AND HER ACTUAL SCORES COULD THEN BE COMPARED WITH THE PROJECTED GROWTH SCORES.

COULD RITA BENEFIT FROM SPECIAL HELP IN READING? ALL OF THE FIFTH GRADE STUDENTS WHO WERE TESTED WITH RITA HERE COMPARED WITH ONE ANOTHER ON EACH OF THE READING SUBTESTS. STUDENTS IN THE LOWER ONE-FOURTH OF THE GROUP ON ANY SUBTEST WOULD SEEM TO BENEFIT FROM SPECIAL HELP. IN THESE TERMS, RITA NEEDS HELP IN LANGUAGE.

LEGEND: RS = Raw Score (number of test items correct); SS = Standard Score; LCL PR = Local Percentile Rank; NAT SMP PR = National Sample Percentile Rank; GE = Grade Equivalent; NCE = Normal Curve Equivalent

French psychologist and expert on individual differences by the name of Alfred Binet.

One of the commission's recommendations was that children should be admitted to a school for the mentally retarded only after being given an educational and medical examination. Since the commission's recommendation did not specify the nature and extent of the educational examination, Binet and his commission colleague Theophile Simon proposed in 1905 a thirty-item scale of intelligence that attempted to measure the same mental processes that contribute to classroom achievement (processes like memory, attention, comprehension, discrimination, and reasoning). The logic behind the Binet-Simon scale stemmed from the work of Francis Galton, one of the first individuals to analyze measurement. Galton emphasized that a test consists of the *"sinking of shafts at critical points"* (1890, p. 373). Binet and Simon tried to select sample bits of behavior (critical points) that reflected mental ability.

This first test of intelligence was normed on a group of fifty nonretarded children who ranged from three to eleven years of age. Children suspected of mental retardation were given the test and their performance was compared with children from the norm group who were of the same chronological age. Those who performed significantly below their intellectually normal age-mates were judged incapable of profiting from normal classroom instruction and assigned to a school for the mentally retarded. Binet and Simon refined the 1905 scale in 1908 and again in 1911, the year Binet died.

The next significant development took place in 1916, when Lewis Terman of Stanford University published an extensive revision of Binet's 1911 test. This revision, which came to be known as the Stanford-Binet, proved to be extremely popular for three reasons. First, following the suggestion in 1912 of a German psychologist named William L. Stern, Terman expressed a child's level of performance as a global figure called an intelligence quotient (or IQ). Second, Terman's norm group included four hundred American children from a variety of backgrounds. They ranged from four years of age through nineteen years. Third, Terman provided clearer and more detailed instructions for administering the items than Binet had provided for the earlier versions. These additions and refinements made the Stanford-Binet a more reliable and useful instrument (Edwards, 1971; Seagoe, 1974).

We have provided this abbreviated history lesson to illustrate two important points. First, intelligence tests were originally devised to differentiate between children who could profit from normal classroom instruction and those who required special education. Thus, the items that Binet and Simon included in their scale related most closely to academic success. The Stanford-Binet has been revised several times since 1916, and many other similar tests have appeared (notably the intelligence scales devised by David Wechsler). Nevertheless, intelligence test items are still selected based on their relationship to school success. Trying to predict job success, marital bliss, happiness in life, or anything else on the basis of an IQ score is an attempt to make the test do something for which

▶ Intelligence test scores most closely related to school success

▶ Intelligence tests not good predictors of job success, marital happiness, life happiness

it was not designed. As some psychologists have pointed out, this type of test might better have been called a test of scholastic aptitude or school ability rather than a test of intelligence. The second point concerns Stern and Terman's use of the IQ as a quantitative summary of a child's performance. Binet, worried that educators would use a summary score as an excuse to ignore or get rid of disinterested or troublesome students, never endorsed this application. His intent "was to identify in order to help and improve, not to label in order to limit" (Gould, 1981, p. 152). A bit later we will describe the difference between an individually administered test (such as the Stanford-Binet or the Wechsler tests) and a group-administered test. We will also examine the legal challenges to standardized testing practices. And we will see that Binet's concern was well placed.

Now that you understand the context in which intelligence tests originated, we can turn to a more detailed consideration of what intelligence tests do and do not measure.

What Intelligence Tests Measure

In 1904, the British psychologist Charles Spearman noticed that children given a battery of intellectual tests (like the memory, reasoning, and comprehension tests used by Binet and Terman) showed a strong tendency to rank consistently from test to test: Children who scored high (or average or below average) on memory tests tended to score high (or average or below average) on reasoning and comprehension tests. Our use of the words *tendency* and *tended* indicates, of course, that the rankings were not identical. Some children scored well on some tests but performed more poorly on others. Spearman explained this pattern by saying that intelligence is made up of two types of factors: a general factor (abbreviated as g) that affected performance on all intellectual tests and a set of specific factors (abbreviated as s) that affected performance only on specific intellectual tests. Spearman ascribed to the g factor the tendency for score rankings to remain constant over tests. That the rankings varied somewhat from test to test, he said, resulted from individual differences in specific factors. Not surprisingly, Spearman's explanation is called the two-factor theory of intelligence.

When you examine such contemporary intelligence tests as the Stanford-Binet, the Wechsler Intelligence Scale for Children—Revised, or the Wechsler Adult Intelligence Scale—Revised, you will notice that the items in the various subtests differ greatly from one another. They may involve mental arithmetic, explaining the meanings of words, describing how two things are alike, indicating what part is missing from a pictured object, reproducing a pictured geometric design with blocks, or tracing a path through a maze. These varied items are included because, despite their apparent differences, they relate strongly to one another and to performance in the classroom. In other words, intelligence tests still reflect Binet's original goal and Spearman's two-factor theory. In practice, the examiner can combine the scores from each subtest into a global index (the IQ score), offer a prediction about the tested individual's degree of academic success for the next year or so, and make some judgments about specific strengths and weaknesses.

Other Views of Intelligence

> Intelligence involves more than what intelligence tests measure

However, as David Wechsler (1975) has persuasively pointed out, *intelligence is not simply the sum of one's tested abilities*. Wechsler defines intelligence as the global capacity of the individual to act purposefully, to think rationally, and to deal effectively with the environment. Given this definition, which is endorsed by many psychologists, an IQ score reflects just one facet of a person's global capacity—the ability to act purposefully, rationally, and effectively on academic tasks in a *classroom* environment. However, people display intelligent behavior in other settings (at work, home, and play, for example), and other characteristics contribute to intelligent behavior (such as persistence, realistic goal setting, the productive use of corrective feedback, creativity, and moral and aesthetic values). A true assessment of intelligence would take into account behavior related to these other settings and characteristics. That such an assessment would be highly subjective and take a great deal of time is one reason why current intelligence tests assess only a small sample of cognitive abilities. But if recent formulations of intelligence by psychologists Robert J. Sternberg (1988) and Howard Gardner (1983) become widely accepted, future intelligence tests may be broader in scope than those in use today. Even before such tests are devised, these theories serve a useful purpose by reminding us that intelligence is multifaceted and can be expressed in many ways.

Robert Sternberg's *triarchic theory of intelligence* has, as its name suggests, three main parts. Two of the three parts deal with thinking processes that we describe in Chapters 9 and 10 and so will not be described here. The third part, the contextual subtheory, focuses on an aspect of intelligence that has been and still is largely overlooked.

In describing the contextual subtheory, Sternberg argues that part of what makes an individual intelligent is the ability to achieve personal goals (for example, graduating from high school or college with honors, working for a particular company in a particular capacity, having a successful marriage). One way to accomplish personal goals is to understand and adapt to the values that govern behavior in a particular setting. For example, if most teachers in a particular school (or executives in a particular company) place a high value on conformity and cooperation, the person who persistently challenges authority, suggests new ideas without being asked, or operates without consulting others will, in all likelihood, receive fewer rewards than those who are more willing to conform and cooperate; and, according to Sternberg's theory, this person would be less intelligent. Where a mismatch exists and the individual cannot adapt to the values of the majority, the intelligent person explores ways to make the values of others more consistent with his or her own values and skills. An enterprising student may try to convince his or her teacher, for example, that short-answer questions are better measures of achievement than essay questions or that effort and classroom participation should count just as much toward a grade as test scores. Finally, where all attempts at adapting or attempting to change the views of others fail, the intelligent person seeks out a setting where his or her behaviors are more consistent with those of others. For instance, many gifted and talented students will seek out private alternative schools where their particular abilities are more highly prized.

Sternberg's basic point is that intelligence should be viewed as a broad characteristic of people that is evidenced not only by how well they answer a particular set of test questions but also by how well they function in different settings. The individual with average test scores who knows how to get people to do what he or she wants is, in this view, at least as intelligent as the person who scores at the 99th percentile of a science test.

Howard Gardner's conception of intelligence, like Sternberg's, is broader than currently popular conceptions. It is different from Sternberg's, however, in that it describes six separate types of intelligence. Accordingly, Gardner's work is referred to as the *theory of multiple intelligences.*

The intelligences described by Gardner are linguistic, logical-mathematical, spatial, musical, bodily-kinesthetic, and personal (both interpersonal and intrapersonal). Since these intelligences are presumed to be independent of one another, an individual would likely exhibit different levels of skill in each of these domains. One student, for example, may show evidence of becoming an outstanding trial lawyer, novelist, or journalist because his or her linguistic intelligence produces a facility for vividly describing, explaining, or persuading. Another student may be able to manipulate aspects of sound (such as pitch, rhythm, and timbre) to produce musical experiences that people find highly pleasing. And the student who is adept at understanding his or her own and others' feelings and how those feelings relate to behavior would be exhibiting high intrapersonal and interpersonal intelligence. Like Sternberg's work, Gardner's theory cautions us against focusing on the results of IQ tests to the exclusion of other worthwhile behaviors.

Gardner and his colleagues are now in the process of trying to validate the theory of multiple intelligences. In one program, called Arts PROPEL, junior and senior high school students in the Pittsburgh Public Schools were assessed for growth in the areas of music, creative writing, and the visual arts. In a second project, all students in an Indianapolis elementary school were exposed to special classes and enrichment activities designed to enhance the various intelligences. A third effort, called Project Spectrum, is aimed at preschool and kindergarten children. Spectrum classrooms are equipped with a variety of materials that invite children to use one or another intelligence. For example, household objects that can be taken apart and reassembled afford children the opportunity to exercise spatial intelligence. A preliminary assessment of Project Spectrum children provided partial support for Gardner's theory (Blythe & Gardner, 1990; Gardner & Hatch, 1989).

Limitations of Intelligence Tests

So where does that leave us in terms of trying to decide what intelligence tests do and do not measure? Four points seem to be in order. First, the appraisal of intelligence is limited by the fact that it cannot be measured directly. Our efforts are confined to measuring the overt manifestations (responses to test items) of what is ultimately based on brain function and experience. Second, as our summary of historical events and analysis of Wechsler's definition make clear, the intelligence we test is a sample of intellectual capabilities that relate to classroom achievement better than they relate to anything else. That is why, as we stated earlier, many psychologists prefer the terms *test of scholastic aptitude* or *test of school ability*. Third, no intelligence test score is an "absolute" measure. Many people—parents, especially—fail to grasp this fact. An IQ score is not a once-and-for-all judgment of how bright a person is. It is merely an estimate of how successful a child is in handling certain kinds of problems at a particular time on a particular test *as compared with other children of the same age*. Fourth, since IQ tests are designed to predict academic success, anything that enhances classroom performance (such as a wider range of factual information or more effective learning skills) will likely have a positive effect on intelligence test performance. In other words, IQ scores are not necessarily permanent. Research on the stability of IQ scores shows that while they do not change significantly for most people, they can change dramatically for given individuals, and changes are most likely to occur among individuals who were first tested as preschoolers (Brody & Brody, 1976). This last point is often used to support early intervention programs like Head Start and Follow-Through.

> ▶ IQ scores can change with experience, training

Given the constraints and qualifications we have just mentioned about interpreting IQ scores, you may be wondering whether the information they

These pictures record the changes in the appearance of a boy from the early elementary grades to the end of high school. If he had been tested with an individual intelligence test on the day each of these pictures was taken, it is likely that his IQ scores would have varied by a least several points. (Richard Hutchings)

provide is worth knowing. While every person must decide that for herself or himself, we believe that if you are fully aware of the nature and limitations of intelligence tests, they can be an effective tool for analyzing how individuals differ. Despite their shortcomings, they provide an objective, economical, and timely assessment of an individual's current level of intellectual functioning.

We mentioned earlier that Binet had wanted intelligence tests to be used to identify and help academically weak students. That goal is best accomplished when a trained examiner administers a well-designed test to one person at a time. In this way, the examiner can present test items clearly, correct misconceptions about how to respond, help the pupil maintain a high level of motivation, and note the test taker's emotional responses and problem-solving strategies. Since at some point in your teaching career you are likely to have one or more students taking an individual intelligence test, the next section briefly describes this type of instrument. The particular test we have chosen to describe is the Wechsler Intelligence Scale for Children—Revised, because it is one of the most frequently given individual intelligence tests.

Description of an Individual Intelligence Test

The Wechsler Intelligence Scale for Children—Revised (WISC-R, 1974) is one of three individual intelligence tests devised by David Wechsler that are currently in use. The other two are the Wechsler Preschool and Primary Scale of Intelligence (1967) and the Wechsler Adult Intelligence Scale—Revised (1981).

The WISC-R can be given to children from six through sixteen years of age. It is composed of twelve subtests equally divided between a verbal scale and a performance scale. The names of the subtests and the sequence in which they are given is as follows:

Verbal	**Performance**
1. Information	2. Picture Completion
3. Similarities	4. Picture Arrangement
5. Arithmetic	6. Block Design
7. Vocabulary	8. Object Assembly
9. Comprehension	10. Coding
11. Digit Span	12. Mazes

The WISC-R yields three summary scores: a verbal IQ, a performance IQ, and a full-scale IQ. The mean of the test is 100, and the standard deviation is 15. If you refer back to Figure 4.1 and do some arithmetic, you will realize that 99.72 percent of all IQ scores fall between 55 and 145 (these scores represent 3 standard deviations below the mean and 3 standard deviations above the mean, respectively).

For each subtest, a precise set of directions tells the examiner where to begin, how to present the items, what type of help or correction to offer, when to stop, and how to score the responses. In addition, examiners are trained to write down spontaneous comments the child may make and to note problem-solving strategies and unusual emotional reactions. This information is then interpreted to provide a picture of the child's intellectual strengths and weaknesses as well as a prediction about academic performance.

The items for each subtest range from easy to difficult in order to accommodate the six-to-sixteen-year age range and the full range of intellectual ability that can be seen at any age. Item 5 on the Similarities subtest, for example, asks the child to explain how the terms *apple* and *banana* are alike. By contrast, item 14 asks for an explanation of how the more abstract concepts of liberty and justice are alike.

▶ IQ test items based on knowledge and situations thought to be common to most children

Since those who construct intelligence tests are primarily interested in a general capacity, they want to avoid, as much as possible, measuring abilities that are largely the result of a particular set of home or school experiences. If they ask questions too directly related to a specific kind of home or curriculum, they will measure only how well children have responded to these experiences. Children who have not had these experiences may then be unfairly judged as lacking in scholastic aptitude. To avoid this sort of error, test makers try to base the questions on knowledge and situations common to practically all children. The degree to which they have met this challenge—elimination of biased test items—is currently a matter of heated debate. As we will see in the next section, it is an issue that sharply divides judges, psychologists, and educators.

LEGAL CHALLENGES TO STANDARDIZED TESTING

We have tried to point out in this chapter that standardized tests in general and intelligence tests in particular are specialized instruments for assessing how and by how much individuals differ from one another. In an ideal world every standardized test would have high reliability, high validity, and excellent norms; every person who had access to students' test scores would interpret them properly; and every decision based on test scores would result in a higher quality of education for the test taker. But, as you well know, we do not live in an ideal world. In the real world some tests are poorly designed and normed, experts disagree about how reliable and valid tests need to be in order to be useful, and educational decisions based on test scores sometimes harm children. Feeling unfairly discriminated against by the testing process, some parents have brought their grievances to court. In this section we will examine three court cases to illustrate how legal rulings have affected the assessment of pupil variability.

▶ In the real world, test-based decisions sometimes harm children

In 1979, the Florida state legislature passed a law stipulating that high school seniors would have to pass a competency test before they could be granted a diploma. When it became apparent that many more black students than white students were failing the test (about 20 percent versus 2 percent, respectively) and being denied diplomas, the law was challenged in a federal court. In *Debra P.* v. *Turlington* (1979) the judge concluded that the testing program was unconstitutional because it perpetuated the effects of past discrimination and because it was put into effect without an adequate phase-in period. He ruled that the test could not be used for four years so that students who had been in the schools prior to desegregation would have the opportunity to graduate. He expressed the opinion, though, that the test "had adequate content and construct validity and bore rational relation to state interest." He also ruled that the "plaintiffs failed to establish that the test was racially or ethnically biased."

A very different judicial ruling on the use of standardized tests came in the case of *Larry P.* v. *Riles* (1979). Until the late 1970s, students who had obvious difficulty coping with the standard curriculum in California public schools were given individual intelligence tests. If the score they earned fell within a designated range (and was consistent with other evidence), they were placed in special classes. Certain psychologists (Mercer, 1975, among others) and many minority-group leaders objected to the use of intelligence tests for that purpose and presented their case in federal court. In general, they claimed that the tests (Stanford-Binet and the WISC-R) were biased in favor of white, middle-class culture. One basis of their argument was the fact that black children represented 29 percent of the student population in Larry P.'s school district but constituted 66 percent of all students in classes for the educable mentally retarded. The judge in this case concluded that the standardized intelligence tests then used in California "are racially and culturally biased, have a discriminatory impact against black children, and have not been validated for the purpose of essentially permanent placement of blacks into educationally deadened, isolated, and stigmatizing classes for the so-called educable mentally retarded." He ruled that black students could not be placed in classes for the educable mentally retarded on the basis of an assessment that relied primarily on the results of an IQ test.

The third case we will consider, *PASE* v. *Hannon* (1980), contained many of the same elements as *Larry P.* v. *Riles* but produced a diametrically opposite ruling. The case was brought by Parents in Action for Special Education on behalf of "black children who have been or will be placed in special classes for the educable mentally handicapped in the Chicago school system." Judge John Grady, who presided over the case, examined each item on the two tests (the Stanford-Binet and the WISC-R) used to identify children for special classes in Chicago. On the basis of his analysis, only eight items on the WISC-R and one on the Stanford-Binet impressed him as being biased against black children. He therefore ruled, in opposition to the decision in the *Larry P.* case, that poor performance on the "biased" items was not sufficient to result in misclassification. (This informal approach to determining item bias is not accepted by most test experts, who favor statistical analysis of responses. [See Reynolds et al., 1984, pp. 252–254, for commentary on the *Larry P.* and *PASE* cases.])

▶ Conflicting opinions regarding bias in intelligence tests

The three cases just summarized illustrate the lack of agreement that exists among psychologists, lawyers, judges, and parents about using standardized test scores in educational decision making. It is difficult to evaluate the charge that standardized tests unfairly discriminate against certain groups. Substantial evidence has been offered to support arguments on both sides of the question. Jane Mercer, one of the most prolific critics of tests, has repeatedly offered data (1975, 1977) to support the view that most standardized tests are so biased against minority-group children that they should be declared illegal. Arthur Jensen, on

In recent years a number of critics have argued that most standardized tests are biased in favor of children from middle-class homes and biased against children from lower-class and/or minority group backgrounds. (Right: Owen Franken/Stock, Boston, Inc.; left: Ulrike Welsch)

the other hand, supplies evidence in *Bias in Mental Testing* (1980) to substantiate the view that the most highly regarded standardized tests are not biased with respect to any native-born English-speaking minority group in this country. He suggests that an unbiased test may be used in an unfair manner, and a biased test may be used in a fair way.

On the average, American children who come from upper- and middle-class homes perform better in school and on standardized tests than children who come from lower-class or minority-group homes. (Jensen summarizes research findings in this area in *Bias in Mental Testing.*) Some critics of tests argue that improperly used test scores perpetuate or increase such differences. Some cite the underrepresentation of minority-group students in programs for the gifted and talented as an example of how overreliance on a narrow range of test scores can harm students. Selection for gifted and talented programs is often based largely on classroom performance, standardized achievement test scores, and intelligence test scores. However, talented members of minorities often hold values about school and academic achievement that differ from the norm. Their classroom performance and test scores may suffer as a result, thereby making them ineligible for these programs (Whitmore, 1987). Consider Sioux children, for example. If they succeed in school, their Sioux peers think of them as lacking in independent thought, spontaneity, and creativity. Many Cherokee youngsters do not believe that success in school will have a positive impact on the quality of their lives on the reservation (Brantlinger & Guskin, 1985). Gifted and talented

▶ Overreliance on test scores can bar gifted and talented minority children from special programs

lower-class black children may not embrace such traditional middle-class values as deferring immediate gratification (as in "Study first, then go out and play"), accepting the importance of symbolic indicators of success (such as grades or test scores), and focusing on the future (as in "Learning geometry and trigonometry now will help you become an engineer later") (Frasier, 1987; Stronge, Lynch & Smith, 1987).

On the other hand, defenders of standardized tests (such as Jensen) maintain that tests can be used to help *reduce* differences in academic performance if they are interpreted properly. If a test accurately reveals that a pupil is below average in ability, for example, it is often wise to acknowledge that fact and arrange instructional experiences accordingly. If it is assumed that no differences in ability exist, teachers might be inclined to expose all pupils to the same sequences of educational experiences presented in the same way. In such a situation, more capable and better prepared students are likely to thrive and less capable students with inadequate backgrounds are likely to fall further and further behind. Busing, Head Start and Follow-Through programs, continuation schools, and equal opportunity and affirmative action regulations are all based on the premise that some American children are raised in learning environments that are less desirable than others and that such students need assistance if they are to compete against more favored age-mates.

The basic issue we have discussed in this section is whether relying on standardized test scores, particularly IQ scores, helps or harms students. You should recognize that this issue cannot be resolved to everyone's satisfaction. Every psychologist, teacher, parent, lawyer, or legislator must take his or her own position on the basis of available evidence. Our view is that standardized tests can benefit students if those who use the scores understand fully both the nature of the characteristic being measured and the nature of the test. Much of the criticism and controversy that has arisen over the use of standardized tests could perhaps have been avoided if the assessment principles proposed by Samuda, Kong, Cummins, Pascual-Leone, and Lewis (1989, p. 182) had been followed. They believe that nondiscriminatory assessment results from the application of the following five principles: (1) Use test scores to plan effective forms of instruction rather than as a basis for assigning students to existing programs. (2) Understand both the nature of the test being used and the student being tested. (3) Give students a comprehensive assessment that includes both standardized tests and informal measures. (4) Use the best data available to make decisions about students, regardless of whether the data reflects formal or informal assessment methods. (5) Assess a student's capacity to learn and develop in addition to his or her current knowledge and level of functioning.

▶ Understanding the assessment process leads to nondiscriminatory testing

Mid-Chapter Review

Several quite similar terms have been introduced in this chapter. To help you distinguish between them and clarify your understanding, they are summarized below.

Types of Variability

Intraindividual variation: the variability in a person's physical, social, emotional, and cognitive behavior over time and situations

Interindividual variation: the variability between different people's physical, social, emotional, and cognitive behavior at a given point in time

Criteria for Evaluating Tests

Reliability: the similarity between two rankings of test scores obtained from the same individual

Validity: how well a test appropriately measures what its users intend it to measure

Content validity: how well test items cover the content of a subject or type of learning

Predictive validity: how well a test score allows accurate predictions of later performance

Construct validity: how accurately a test measures a particular attribute

Types of Tests

Achievement test: indicates how much has been learned about a particular subject

Diagnostic test: identifies specific strengths or weaknesses in a learning skill

Aptitude test: estimates potential (how well a pupil is capable of performing) in specific or general abilities that can be applied to various tasks

Competency test: determines if a student has achieved basic reading, writing, and mathematical competencies

Norm-referenced test: indicates how well a student has performed compared to others

Criterion-referenced test: indicates how well a student has mastered a set of objectives

Types of Scores

Raw scores: number of points earned on a test

Percentile rank: percentage of cases at or below a given raw score

z score: how far a raw score is from the mean in standard deviation units

T score: how far a raw score is from the mean in numerical terms

Stanine score: pupil performance indicated with reference to a 9-point scale derived from the normal curve

Intelligence Testing

The first practical test of intelligence was devised by Alfred Binet in 1905 to distinguish mentally retarded from normal students.

Current intelligence tests continue to predict academic success better than such outcomes as job success or marital happiness because they are based on Binet's purpose for mental testing.

Continued

Other views of intelligence, such as those of David Wechsler, Robert Sternberg, and Howard Gardner, are broader in scope than Binet's and Spearman's views.

The question of whether intelligence tests are racially and culturally biased has been debated, with no resolution, by psychologists, lawyers, and judges.

Much of the controversy about standardized tests unfairly discriminating against one group or another may be eliminated if test users understand the assessment process and use test scores to formulate effective forms of instruction.

Suggestions for Teaching in Your Classroom

USING STANDARDIZED TESTS

Handbook Heading:
Using Standardized
Tests

1. Before giving a standardized test, emphasize that students should do their best and give them suggestions for taking such tests.

2. Examine the test booklet and answer sheet in advance so that you are familiar with the test.

3. Do your best to minimize distractions and interruptions during the testing period.

4. Follow the instructions for administration with scrupulous care.

5. Emphasize that you cannot answer questions during the test.

6. Be cautious when interpreting scores, and always give the pupil the benefit of the doubt.

7. Do your best to control the impact of negative expectations.

8. If student folders contain individual intelligence test scores, ask for an interpretation by the psychometrist who administered the test (or ask an equally knowledgeable person).

9. Be prepared to offer parents clear and accurate information about their children's test scores.

1. Before giving a standardized test, emphasize that students should do their best and give suggestions for taking such tests.

For maximum usefulness, scores on standardized tests should be as accurate a representation of actual ability as possible. Accordingly, the day before a standardized test is scheduled, tell your students that they should do their best. Emphasize that the scores will be used to help them improve their school performance and that they should concentrate on answering questions as well as they can without feeling that they are competing against others. You may be able to partly reduce the anxiety and tension that are almost inevitable under formal testing conditions by giving some test-taking hints in advance. Norman E. Gronlund notes the following skills that might be stressed (depending on the type of test and the grade level of the student):

Handbook Heading:
Explaining Test-Taking
Skills

1. Listening to or reading directions carefully.
2. Listening to or reading test items carefully.
3. Setting a pace that will allow time to complete the test.
4. Bypassing difficult items and returning to them later.
5. Making informed guesses rather than omitting items.
6. Eliminating as many alternatives as possible on multiple-choice items before guessing.
7. Following directions carefully in marking the answer sheet (tell students to darken the entire space, for example).
8. Checking to be sure the item number and answer number match when marking an answer.
9. Checking to be sure the appropriate response was marked on the answer sheet.
10. Going back and checking the answers if time permits. (1985b, p. 332)

2. Examine the test booklet and answer sheet in advance so that you are familiar with the test.

Ideally you might take the test yourself so that you become thoroughly familiar with what your students will be doing. If there are any aspects of recording scores that are especially tricky, you might mention these when you give your test-taking skills presentation or at the time you hand out examination booklets and answer sheets.

3. Do your best to minimize distractions and interruptions during the testing period.

You probably know from personal experience how annoying and unnerving it is to be interrupted while taking an important test. To minimize such distractions, you might put a "Testing in Progress" sign on the door, and perhaps ask that the bell system be disconnected. If not all pupils in the school take tests the same day, you might ask teachers of other classes to request their pupils to be quiet in hallways and to move away from the building during recess periods.

4. Follow instructions for administration with scrupulous care.

For maximum accuracy, standardized tests should be given in standard fashion. Therefore, you should examine the instructions for administering the test ahead of time and read specific instructions to pupils exactly as written. You should also be completely faithful to instructions for handing out materials, timing tests, and collecting answer sheets promptly.

5. Emphasize that you cannot answer questions during the test.

After reading instructions, emphasize that you will be unable to answer questions once testing has begun. Stress that any questions about how to proceed must be asked before test booklets are opened.

6. Be cautious when interpreting scores, and always give the pupil the benefit of the doubt.

Handbook Heading:
Interpreting Test Scores

The profiles or reports you will receive a few weeks after a test has been administered will contain information that is potentially beneficial to you and to your pupils. If misused or misinterpreted, however, the information is potentially harmful. Misinterpretations of scores could lead to complaints by parents. As you examine the scores, therefore, concentrate on ways you can make positive use of the results. Look for areas of weakness in pupil performance that need special attention. At the same time, do your best to avoid forming negative expectations. Chances are that the overall test scores will often reinforce your own impressions of the general abilities of pupils. You can't help forming such impressions, and they can work to the advantage of students. If a student has had trouble with almost every assignment and classroom test you have given, it is often the case that test scores will reflect that level of performance. If such a pupil scores higher than expected, though, you might ask yourself if your expectations for that pupil have been too low and make a resolution to give extra help and encouragement, using the test scores to provide direction.

If a pupil's test scores are lower than you expected them to be, examine them to discover areas of weakness, but guard against thinking "Well, I guess he had me fooled. He's not as sharp as I thought he was. Maybe I had better lower grades a notch on the next report card." There are many reasons why a student may not do well on a test (for example, anxiety, fatigue, coming down with an illness, worrying about some home or school interpersonal situation), and scores may not be an accurate reflection of current capability. Thus, whenever there is a discrepancy between test scores and observed classroom performance, always assume that the more favorable impression is the one to use as an indication of general capability. Try to use indications of below-average performance in constructive ways to help students overcome inadequacies.

7. Do your best to control the impact of negative expectations.

As you peruse student test scores, do your best to resist the temptation to label or categorize pupils, particularly those who have a consistent pattern of low scores. Instead of succumbing to thoughts that such students are incapable of learning, you might make an effort to concentrate on the idea that they need extra encouragement and individualized attention. Use the information on test profiles to help them overcome their learning difficulties, not to justify fatalistically ignoring their problems. (Specific techniques for guarding against the tendency to communicate negative expectations will be described in Chapter 13, "Measurement and Evaluation of Classroom Learning.")

8. If student folders contain individual intelligence test scores, ask for an interpretation by the psychometrist who administered the test (or ask an equally knowledgeable person).

As noted in the discussion of court cases involving use of IQ scores, you should be extremely careful about how you interpret scores on tests such as the Stanford-Binet or WISC-R. Such scores are not likely to be found in the folders of more than a few of your students; but when they *are* included, ask for an interpretation by a qualified person, particularly if the parents ask for an explanation.

9. Be prepared to offer parents clear and accurate information about their children's test scores.

For a variety of reasons, misconceptions about the nature of standardized tests are common. As a result, many parents do not fully understand what their children's scores mean. Parent-teacher conferences are probably the best time to correct misconceptions and provide some basic information about the meaning of standardized test scores. In an unobtrusive place on your desk you might keep a brief list of points to cover as you converse with each parent. In one way or another, you should mention the following general points.

Test scores should be treated as *estimates* of whatever was measured (achievement, for example). There are two reasons for representing test scores in this fashion. First, tests do not (indeed, they cannot) assess everything that students know or that makes up a particular capability. Standardized achievement tests, for example, tend to cover a relatively broad range of knowledge but do not assess any one topic in great depth. Therefore, students may know more than their scores suggest. Second, all tests contain some degree of error because of such factors as vaguely worded items, confusing directions, and low motivation on the day the test is administered.

Test scores reflect a student's *current* level of performance. Because of changes in such characteristics as interests, motives, and cognitive skills, test scores can change, sometimes dramatically. The younger the student and the longer the interval between testings (on the same test), the greater the likelihood that a test score will change significantly.

What a test score means depends on the nature of the test. If an intelligence or scholastic aptitude test was taken by your students, point out that such tests measure the current status of those cognitive skills that most closely relate to academic success. Also mention that IQ scores are judged to be below average, average, or above average on the basis of how they compare to the scores of a norm group. You might use personal wealth as an analogy to illustrate this last point. Whether someone is considered poor, financially comfortable, or wealthy depends on how much money everyone else in that person's reference group possesses. A net worth of $100,000 is considered wealthy in some circles but barely adequate in others. If you are discussing achievement test scores, make sure you understand the difference between diagnostic tests, norm-referenced tests, and criterion-referenced tests. Scores from a diagnostic achievement test can be used to discuss a student's strengths and weaknesses in such skills as reading, math, and spelling. Scores from a norm-referenced achievement test can be used to discuss general strengths and weaknesses in one or more content areas. For achievement tests that provide multiple sets of norms, start your interpretation at the most local level (school norms, ideally) since they are likely to be the most meaningful to parents, and then move to a more broad-based interpretation (district, state, or national norms). Scores from a criterion-refer-enced achievement test can be used to discuss how well a student has mastered the objectives on which the test is based. If there is a close correspondence between the test's objectives and those of the teacher, the test score can be used as an indicator of how much the student has learned in class.

The instructional decisions you make in the classroom will be *guided* but not dictated by the test scores. Many parents fear that if their child obtains a low score on a test, he or she will be labeled a slow learner by the teacher and will receive less attention than higher-scoring students. This is a good opportunity to lay such a fear to rest, in two ways. First, note that test scores are but *one* source of information about students. You will also take into account how well they perform on classroom tests, homework assignments, and special projects, as well as in classroom discussions. Second, emphasize that you are committed to using test scores not to classify students but to help them learn (and think of Alfred Binet as you say this).

Resources for Further Investigation

Taking an Intelligence Test

If you wonder what it is like to take an individual test of intelligence, you might check on the possibility that a course in individual testing needs subjects for practice purposes. (In most courses of this type, each student is required to give several tests under practice conditions.) Look in a class schedule for a course in psychology or education designated as Individual Testing, Practicum in Testing, or something similar. Contact the instructor and ask whether he or she wants subjects. If you do find yourself acting as a guinea pig, jot down your reactions to the test immediately after you take it. Would you feel comfortable having the score used to determine whether you are admitted to some program or qualify for a promotion? Did the test seem to provide an adequate sample of your intelligence? Were the kinds of questions appropriate for your conception of intelligence? Write down comments on the implications of your reactions.

References for Evaluating Standardized Tests

To obtain the information necessary for evaluating standardized tests, examine the *Ninth Mental Measurements Yearbook* (1985), edited by James V. Mitchell, Jr.; the *Tenth Mental Measurements Yearbook* (1989), edited by Jane Close Conoley and Jack J. Kramer; and *Test Critiques* (Vols. I–VIII) (1984–1991), edited by Daniel J. Keyser and Richard C. Sweetland. You may have to check earlier editions of *Mental Measurements Yearbook* and *Test Critiques* for information on a specific test since there are far too many tests available for either publication to review in a single edition.

Technical Aspects of Testing

For more information about standardized tests and scores, consult one or more of these books: *Essentials of Psychological Testing* (5th ed., 1990) by Lee J. Cronbach, *Psychological Testing* (6th ed., 1990) by Anne Anastasi, *Measurement and Evaluation in Teaching* (5th ed., 1985) by Norman Gronlund and Robert L. Lynn, and *Essentials of Educational Measurement* (5th ed., 1991) by Robert L. Ebel and David A. Frisbie.

SUMMARY

1. Two types of pupil variability can be observed: intraindividual and interindividual. Intraindividual variability refers to differences in an individual's behavior over time and across situations. Interindividual variability refers to the differences between individuals at a given point in time.

2. Most of the research on interindividual variation revolves around scholastic aptitude, achievement, and their assessment with standardized tests.

3. Standardized tests are used primarily to assess students' strengths and weaknesses and to select students for specialized programs.

4. One of the most important characteristics of a standardized test is its reliability—the similarity between two rankings of test scores obtained from the same individuals.

5. Another important characteristic of standardized tests is validity. A valid test accurately measures what its users intend it to measure.

6. A third important characteristic of a standardized test is its norm group—a sample of students specially chosen and tested so as to reflect the population of students for whom the test is intended. The norm group's performance becomes the standard against which scores are compared.

7. Standardized achievement tests measure how much has been learned about a particular subject.

8. Diagnostic tests identify specific strengths and weaknesses in basic learning skills.

9. Aptitude tests estimate students' potential in specific or general abilities that can be applied to various tasks.

10. Competency tests are given to determine if high school students have learned basic reading, writing, and mathematical skills.

11. Norm-referenced tests compare all scores to the performance of a norm group.

12. Criterion-referenced tests judge scores in terms of mastery of a set of objectives.

13. Percentile rank indicates the percentage of scores that are at or below a person's score.

14. A z score indicates how far in standard deviation units a raw score is from the mean.

15. A T score indicates in whole positive numbers how far a raw score is from the mean.

16. A stanine score indicates in which of nine normal-curve segments a person's performance falls.

17. One of the most widely used and poorly understood standardized tests is the intelligence or IQ test.

18. The first practical test of intelligence was devised by Alfred Binet to identify students who would be best served in a special education program.

19. Because of their focus on academic success, intelligence tests are not good predictors of anything else, such as job success, marital happiness, and life satisfaction.

20. Intelligence, broadly defined, is the global capacity of the individual to act purposefully, think rationally, and deal effectively with the environment.

21. The intelligence that we test is but a sample of intellectual skills—those that closely relate to classroom achievement.

22. As a person's intellectual skills improve with experience and/or training, the individual's IQ score may improve.

23. In the 1970s and 1980s legal questions arose over the effects of competency tests and intelligence tests. Judges have ruled inconsistently as to whether these tests unfairly discriminate against minorities.

KEY TERMS

intraindividual variation   *(144)*
interindividual variation   *(145)*
standardized tests   *(146)*
reliability   *(148)*
validity   *(149)*
norm group   *(150)*
achievement test   *(152)*
diagnostic test   *(153)*
aptitude test   *(153)*
competency test   *(154)*
norm-referenced test   *(154)*
criterion-referenced test   *(154)*
grade equivalent score   *(155)*
percentile rank   *(155)*
standard deviation   *(156)*
normal curve   *(156)*
z score   *(157)*
T score   *(157)*
stanine score   *(158)*

DISCUSSION QUESTIONS

1. If you are like most people, you took a variety of standardized tests throughout your elementary and high school years. The results of those tests were probably used to help determine what you would be taught and how. Do you think that those tests adequately reflected what you had learned and were capable of learning and, therefore, were always used in your best interest? What can you do to increase the chances that test scores will be used to help *your* students fulfill their potential?

2. Think about norm-referenced tests and criterion-referenced tests. Which do you think you prefer? Why? Can you describe a set of circumstances in which a norm-referenced test would

be clearly preferable to a criterion-referenced test, and vice versa?

3. If you had to tell parents about the results of a standardized test, which type of score could you explain most clearly: raw score, percentile rank, z score, T score, or stanine score? Which do you think would be most informative for parents? for you as a teacher? If you do not understand best the one that you think most informative, what can you do about it?

4. Imagine that you are sitting in the faculty lounge listening to a colleague describe one of her students. Your colleague points out that this student has a C+ average and received an IQ score of 92 (low average) on a recently administered test. She concludes that since the student is working up to his ability level, he should not be encouraged to set higher goals since that would only lead to frustration. Your colleague then asks for your opinion. How do you respond?

Chapter 5

DEALING WITH PUPIL VARIABILITY

Key Points

ABILITY GROUPING

▶ Between-class ability grouping: classes of students with similar intelligence, achievement test scores

▶ No research support for between-class ability grouping

▶ Joplin Plan and within-class ability grouping for math produce moderate increases in learning

▶ Between-class ability grouping negatively influences teaching goals and methods

▶ Joplin Plan and within-class ability grouping may allow for better-quality instruction

THE EDUCATION FOR ALL HANDICAPPED CHILDREN ACT (PL 94-142)

▶ IEP must include objectives, services to be provided, criteria for determining achievement

▶ Handicapped students must be educated in least restrictive environment

▶ Mainstreaming: policy of placing handicapped pupils in regular classes

▶ Due process provisions intended to protect rights of pupil

▶ Tests used to determine placement must be valid, administered in native language

▶ Mainstreaming seems to produce modest improvements in learning

▶ PL 94-142 amended to provide services to preschool and post–high school individuals with handicaps

▶ Learning disabled, speech impaired, mentally retarded, emotionally disturbed students most likely to be served under PL 94-142

▶ Speech impaired, learning disabled, visually handicapped, other health impaired students most likely to attend regular classes

▶ Interdisciplinary assessment team determines if pupil needs special services

▶ Classroom teacher, parents, several specialists prepare IEP

STUDENTS WITH MENTAL RETARDATION

▶ Mildly retarded students may frustrate easily, lack confidence and self-esteem

▶ Mildly retarded students tend to oversimplify, have difficulty generalizing

▶ Give mildly retarded students specific assignments that can be completed quickly

STUDENTS WITH LEARNING DISABILITIES

▶ Learning disabilities: disorders in basic processes that lead to learning problems not due to other causes

▶ Increased number of learning disabled students due to faulty assessment procedures, poor-quality tests

▶ Help learning disabled students learn to reduce distractions, attend, perceive

STUDENTS WITH EMOTIONAL DISTURBANCE

▶ Emotional disturbance: poor relationships, inappropriate behavior, depression, fears

▶ Term *behavior disorders* calls attention to behavior that needs to be changed

▶ Pupils with behavior disorders tend to be either aggressive or withdrawn

▶ Foster interpersonal contact among withdrawn students

▶ Use techniques to forestall aggressive or antisocial behavior

GIFTED AND TALENTED STUDENTS

▶ Gifted and talented students show high performance on wide range of tasks

▶ Inconsistency often exists among definition, identification, and teaching of gifted students

▶ Minorities underrepresented in gifted classes because of overreliance on test scores

▶ Gifted and talented students generally show average physical, social, emotional development

▶ Some rapid learners convergent thinkers, others divergent thinkers

If you have had the opportunity to observe or work in an elementary or secondary classroom recently, you know that today's teacher can expect to have a wide variety of students who differ in abilities, talents, and backgrounds. The reasons for such diversity include compulsory attendance laws, patterns of immigration, and laws that govern which students can and cannot be placed in special classes, not to mention normal variations in physical, social, emotional, and cognitive development. The task of guiding each member of a diverse group of students toward high levels of learning is one of teaching's major challenges. We hope to help you meet this challenge by making you aware in this chapter of different ways of dealing with pupil variability.

HISTORICAL DEVELOPMENTS IN DEALING WITH VARIABILITY

Prior to the turn of the century, dealing with pupil variability was an issue few educators had to face. Most communities were fairly small, and students in a given school tended to come from similar ethnic and economic backgrounds. In addition, lower-class families often viewed a child's labor as more important than a complete, formal education, and many states had not yet enacted compulsory attendance laws. As a result, many lower-class children did not attend school regularly or at all. In 1900, for example, only 8.5 percent of eligible students attended high school (Boyer, 1983), and these students were almost entirely from the upper and middle classes (Gutek, 1988). In comparison with today's schools, then, earlier student populations were considerably less diverse.

By 1920 this picture had changed, largely because of three developments. First, by 1918 all states had passed compulsory attendance laws. Second, child labor laws had been enacted by many states, as well as by Congress in 1916, to eliminate the hiring of children and adolescents in mines and factories. Third, large numbers of immigrant children arrived in the United States from 1901 through 1920. During those years 14.5 million individuals, mostly from eastern and southern Europe, arrived on U.S. shores (Morris, 1961). The result was a vast increase in the number and diversity of children attending elementary and high school.

Educators initially dealt with this growth in pupil variability by forming age-graded classrooms. All students of a particular age were grouped together each year to master a certain portion of the school's curriculum. The main assumptions behind this approach were that teachers could be more effective in helping students learn and that students would have more positive attitudes toward themselves and school when classrooms were more *homogeneous* than *heterogeneous* (Oakes, 1985; Peltier, 1991). Whether or not these assumptions were well founded (an issue we will address shortly), they were (and still are) so widely held by educators that two additional approaches to creating even more homogeneous groups were eventually implemented—ability grouping and special class placement.

Ability grouping involved the use of standardized mental ability or achievement tests to create groups of students who were considered very similar to each other in learning ability. In a limited sense, this approach was made possible by the pioneering work of Alfred Binet and Lewis Terman. It was, however, the work of one of Terman's graduate students, Arthur Otis, and a group of U.S. Army psychologists led by Robert Yerkes that made possible the mass use of standardized tests. The United States' entry into World War I in 1917 made it necessary to efficiently test the mental ability of large numbers of recruits to make appropriate decisions about selection, placement, and classification. Building on Otis's attempt to create a group-administered version of the Stanford-Binet, Yerkes and his colleagues produced two of the first group-administered, paper-and-pencil tests of intelligence: the Army Scale Alpha (a verbal scale for English-speaking and literate recruits) and the Army Scale Beta (a nonverbal scale for non-English-speaking and illiterate recruits). In the years after World War I, group-administered intelligence and achievement tests were quickly developed to serve the needs of business and education (Matarazzo, 1972).

The use of standardized mental ability tests for selection and placement in education received another boost from the success of testing programs in the armed forces during World War II (for example, stanines were used to select candidates for pilot training). Primary schools of the 1950s often assigned children on the basis of standardized test scores to fast, average, or slow ability groups, and they remained in those groups through the elementary grades. High schools placed students into different tracks geared toward post–high school goals such as college, secretarial work, or vocational school.

For more or less normal children, age-grading and ability testing were seen as workable approaches to creating more homogeneous classes. But compulsory attendance laws also brought to school many children with more severe mental and physical disabilities. These students were deemed incapable of profiting from any type of normal classroom instruction and so were assigned to special schools. Unfortunately, and as Alfred Binet feared, labeling a student as mentally retarded or physically disabled often resulted in a vastly inferior education. Early in this century, special schools served as convenient dumping grounds for all kinds of children who could not adapt to the regular classroom (Ysseldyke & Algozzine, 1990).

This chapter describes and evaluates current versions of these two approaches to dealing with pupil variability. We first look at ability grouping, which nowadays takes several forms and is still used to reduce the normal range of variability in cognitive ability and achievement that one finds in the typical classroom. We then detail the varied types and degrees of special class placement for children whose intellectual, social, emotional, or physical development falls outside (above as well as below) the range of normal variation. In discussing this approach we pay particular attention to Public Law 94-142, which was enacted to counter past excesses of special class placement and to encourage the placement of children with disabilities in regular classes to the greatest extent possible.

ABILITY GROUPING

Types of Ability Groups

Four approaches to ability grouping are popular among educators today: *between-class ability grouping, regrouping,* the *Joplin Plan,* and *within-class grouping*. Given their widespread use, you may be able to recall a few classes in which one or another of these techniques was used. If not, you will no doubt encounter at least one of them during your first year of teaching.

Between-class ability grouping: classes of students with similar intelligence, achievement test scores

Between-Class Ability Grouping   The goal of **between-class ability grouping** is that each class should be made up of students who are homogeneous in standardized intelligence or achievement test scores. Three levels of classes are usually formed—high, average, and low—although some schools use four levels. Students in one ability group typically have little or no contact with students in others during the school day. Although each group covers the same subjects, a higher group does so in greater depth and breadth than lower groups. At the high school level this approach is often called *tracking*. Instead of labeling the groups as having high, average, and low ability, they are usually referred to as college preparatory, business/secretarial, vocational/technical, and general. The rationale behind between-class ability grouping is that it improves the teacher's efficiency and effectiveness, since the level and pace of instruction can match the intellectual characteristics of the learners. Low achievers, for example, can have the individual attention, slow pace, repetition, and review that they require, and high achievers can be given more autonomy as well as more difficult tasks.

Regrouping   The groups formed under a **regrouping** plan are more flexible in assignments and are narrower in scope than between-class groups. Students of the same age, ability, and grade but from different classrooms come together for instruction in a specific subject, usually reading or mathematics. If a student begins to significantly outperform the other members of the group, a change of group assignment is easier since it involves just that particular subject. Regrouping has two major disadvantages, however. First, it requires a certain degree of planning and cooperation among the teachers involved. They must agree, for example, to schedule reading and arithmetic during the same periods. Second, many teachers are uncomfortable working with children whom they see only once a day for an hour or so.

Joplin Plan   The **Joplin Plan** is a variation of regrouping. The main difference is that the regroupings take place *across* grade levels. For example, all third-, fourth-, and fifth-graders whose grade-equivalent scores in reading are 4.6 (fourth grade, sixth month) would come together for reading instruction. The same would be done for mathematics. The Joplin Plan has the same advantages and disadvantages as simple regrouping.

Within-Class Ability Grouping   The most popular form of ability grouping, occurring in almost all elementary school classes, **within-class ability grouping** involves dividing a single class of students into two or three groups for reading and math instruction. Like regrouping and the Joplin Plan, it has the advantages of being flexible in terms of group assignments and restricted to one or two subjects. In addition, it eliminates the need for cooperative scheduling. One disadvantage of this approach is that the teacher needs to be skilled at keeping the other students in the class productively occupied while working with a particular group.

In ability grouping, students are selected and placed in homogeneous groups with other students who are considered to have very similar learning abilities.
(Don and Pat Valenti/Tony Stone Worldwide)

Prevalence of Ability Grouping

In a national survey of middle and junior high schools (grades five through nine), about 23 percent of the respondents reported using between-class ability grouping for all subjects. This practice occurred more frequently in schools that had large enrollments of black and Hispanic students. An additional 45 percent of the responding schools used some form of regrouping for certain subjects (reading, English, mathematics, and science, for example). Although the percentage of fifth through eighth grades using between-class grouping stayed constant, a steady increase in the use of regrouping was noted (40 percent, 44 percent, 47 percent, and 50 percent for grades five through eight, respectively).

The percentage of *students* who experienced some form of ability grouping increased from about 70 percent of fifth-graders to 80 percent of sixth-graders, to 85 percent of seventh- and eighth-graders. And the proportion of students who were in between-class programs increased from 12 percent of fifth-graders to about 25 percent of sixth- through eighth-graders (Braddock, 1990).

Evaluations of Ability Grouping

Because ability grouping has been practiced in one form or another for several decades and occurs in virtually all school districts, its effects have been intensively studied. Robert E. Slavin (1987, 1990a) and Margaret M. Dawson (1987) have reviewed and analyzed dozens of studies on ability grouping at the elementary and secondary levels. Their main findings are as follows:

No research support
for between-class
ability grouping

1. There is no support for between-class ability grouping. Students assigned to homogeneous classes performed no better and no worse than comparable

students in heterogeneous classes. This finding was obtained for high, average, and low ability students, thereby failing to support the often-made argument that between-class ability grouping benefits high achievers.

2. Regrouping for reading or mathematics can be effective if the instructional pace and level of the text match the student's actual achievement level rather than the student's nominal grade level. In other words, a fifth-grader who scores at the fourth-grade level on a reading test should be reading out of a fourth-grade reading book.

3. The Joplin Plan yields moderate to strong positive effects compared with instruction in heterogeneous classes.

4. Within-class ability grouping in mathematics in grades three through six produced moderately positive results compared with instruction in heterogeneous classes. Low achievers appeared to benefit the most from this arrangement. Because within-class ability grouping for reading is an almost universal practice at every grade level, researchers have not had the opportunity to compare its effectiveness with whole-class reading instruction. Nevertheless, it would be reasonable to expect pretty much the same results for reading as were found for mathematics.

5. Students in homogeneously grouped classes scored the same as students in heterogeneously grouped classes on measures of self-esteem.

6. Students in high ability classes had more positive attitudes about school and their educational aspirations than did students in low ability classrooms.

7. Teachers of high ability groups had different goals and used more effective instructional practices than did teachers of low ability groups. For high ability classes teachers stressed critical thinking, self-direction, creativity, and active participation. For low ability classes teachers stressed working quietly, following rules, and getting along with classmates. This finding was echoed by the personal experiences of Stanford University education professor Larry Cuban (1990). A one-time social studies teacher in inner-city high schools, Cuban taught an eleventh-grade U.S. history class for the first semester of the 1988–1989 school year in order to see what had changed about classroom teaching in twenty years. One practice that had not changed and that Cuban did not approve of was between-class ability grouping. As he put it, "Grouping practices that label students as low achievers or slow learners and that place them in separate classes influenced how I taught and how the students in my class performed" (p. 481). Specifically, Cuban found that the learning process was defined as coming up with the right answer in order to pass quizzes and tests as opposed to learning how to reason. Marjorie Wuthrick (1990) also noted that middle school teachers altered the nature and pacing of their reading instruction as a function of the level of the reading group.

Joplin Plan and within-class ability grouping for math produce moderate increases in learning

Between-class ability grouping negatively influences teaching goals and methods

To Group, or Not to Group?

These findings suggest three courses of action. The first course is to discontinue the use of between-class ability groups. The findings presented above clearly show that the assumptions upon which this practice is based are false. Students do not learn more or feel more positively about themselves and school when they are grouped with students of similar ability for the entire day. The fact that almost 25 percent of the nation's middle schools continue to use this form of ability grouping is testament to the powerful influence of out-of-date beliefs on educational practices. You may recall that we made the same point in Chapter 1 during our discussion of Doyle's (1989) attempts to change people's beliefs about the utility of grade retention. You will have to learn, and help others to learn as well, that beliefs must be modified or eliminated when the weight of evidence goes against them.

The second course of action is to use only those forms of ability grouping that produce positive results: within-class grouping and the Joplin Plan, especially for reading and mathematics. We don't know at present why these forms of ability grouping work. It is *assumed* that the increase in class homogeneity allows for more appropriate and potent forms of instruction (for example, greater flexibility in moving students into and out of a particular group, greater availability of high-achieving role models, and greater effort by the teacher to bring lower-achieving groups up to the level of higher-achieving groups). If this assumption is correct, within-class ability grouping and the Joplin Plan must be carried out in such a way that homogeneous groups are guaranteed to result. The best way to achieve similarity in cognitive ability among students is to group them on the basis of past classroom performance, standardized achievement test scores, or both. The least desirable (but most frequently used) approach is to base the assignments solely on IQ scores.

> Joplin Plan and within-class ability grouping may allow for better-quality instruction

The third course of action is to dispense with all forms of ability grouping and use a variety of organizational and instructional techniques that will allow you to cope with a heterogeneous class, or to use these same techniques in conjunction with the Joplin Plan or within-class grouping. One suggestion is to make sure that at least two-thirds of the students in a class are of average and above-average ability. Another suggestion is to use with all students instructional techniques that are associated with high achievement. These would include clear presentations, a high level of enthusiasm, reinforcing students for correct responses, providing sufficient time for students to formulate answers to questions, prompting correct responses, providing detailed feedback about the accuracy of responses, and requiring a high level of work and effort. A third suggestion is to emphasize a mastery approach to learning (which we describe in detail in Chapter 13). A fourth suggestion is to organize students into small, heterogeneous learning groups. This technique, known as cooperative learning, is discussed in more detail in Chapter 12. A final suggestion is to periodically use such individual forms of instruction as worksheets, workbooks, and, increasingly, computer-assisted instruction (which we describe in Chapter 8).

The discussion in this chapter has thus far focused on students whose intellectual, social, emotional, and physical characteristics fall within a range that is considered normal. But for reasons detailed in the next two sections, teachers are also required at times to deal with students having some degree of mental, emotional, or physical disability.

Until recently, pupils with disabilities often were placed in special classes or schools on the assumption that they needed special forms of education provided by specially trained teachers. However, many of the criticisms and arguments marshaled against ability grouping came to be applied as well to special classes for students with disabilities. In addition, the elimination of racially segregated schools by the U.S. Supreme Court in the case of *Brown* v. *Board of Education* established a precedent for providing students with disabilities an equal opportunity for a free and appropriate education (Ornstein & Levine, 1993). As a result, influential members of Congress were persuaded in the early 1970s that it was time for the federal government to take steps to correct the perceived inequities and deficiencies in our educational system. The result was a landmark piece of legislation called Public Law 94-142.

THE EDUCATION FOR ALL HANDICAPPED CHILDREN ACT (PL 94-142)

In November of 1975 Congress approved Public Law 94-142, the Education for All Handicapped Children Act. This legislation was intended "to assure the free, appropriate public education of all handicapped children." PL 94-142 stipulated that by 1978 all states wishing to receive federal funds would be required to put into effect the various provisions of the act.

Provisions of Public Law 94-142

Individual Education Programs   One of the key provisions of PL 94-142 is the development of an **individualized education program (IEP)** for each child identified as having a handicapping condition. The IEP must include the following elements:

▶ IEP must include objectives, services to be provided, criteria for determining achievement

(a)   A statement of the child's present levels of educational performance;

(b)   A statement of annual goals, including short-term instructional objectives;

(c)   A statement of the specific special education and related services to be provided to the child, and the extent to which the child will be able to participate in regular educational programs;

(d)   The projected dates for initiation of services and the anticipated duration of the services; and

(e)   Appropriate objective criteria and evaluation procedures and schedules for determining, on at least an annual basis, whether short-term objectives are being achieved. (*Federal Register,* August 23, 1977, p. 42491)

The IEP is to be planned by the pupil's classroom teacher in collaboration with a person qualified in special education, one or both of the pupil's parents, the pupil (when appropriate), and other individuals at the discretion of the parents or school. (An example of an IEP is depicted on page 199.)

Least Restrictive Environment   Another key provision of PL 94-142 is that educational services must be provided to children in the **least restrictive environment.** That is, each state must establish policies and procedures to ensure that a child with disabilities is placed in the least restrictive educational setting that his or her disability will allow.

> Handicapped students must be educated in least restrictive environment

All handicapped students, including those in public or private institutions or other care facilities, are educated with children who are not handicapped, and that special classes, separate schooling, or other removal of handicapped children from the regular education environment occurs only when the nature or severity of the handicap is such that an education in regular classes with the use of supplementary aids and services cannot be achieved satisfactorily. (Section 612-5)

> Mainstreaming: policy of placing handicapped pupils in regular classes

The least restrictive environment provision establishes a basic policy that is often referred to as **mainstreaming,** since as many children with disabilities as possible are to enter the mainstream of education by attending regular classes with nondisabled pupils. Thus, an evaluation is made for each pupil included under PL 94-142 to determine the feasibility of at least part-time instruction in a regular class.

Other Provisions   Other provisions of PL 94-142 allow for **due process**—legal procedures and safeguards intended to protect the rights of the pupil. Due process elements include the right of the parents to examine all of their child's school records, prior notice to parents of any change in identification or placement, and parental consent before a student is evaluated or placed.

> Due process provisions intended to protect rights of pupil

A provision referred to as *protection in evaluation procedures* includes the following regulations:

> Tests used to determine placement must be valid, administered in native language

1. A "full and individual evaluation" of a student must be made prior to initial placement in a special educational program.

2. All tests used must have been validated for the specific purpose for which they are used.

3. Tests must be administered in the pupil's native language.

4. When tests are administered to students who have impaired sensory, manual, or speaking skills, the results must reflect aptitude or achievement rather than the impairment.

5. No single procedure (such as an IQ score) is to be the sole criterion on which special education placement is determined.

6. Evaluations for placement in special classes are to be made by a multidisciplinary team, including at least one teacher or other specialist with "knowledge in the area of suspected disability."

The least restrictive environment provision of the Education for All Handicapped Children Act (PL 94–142) has led to mainstreaming—*the policy that handicapped children should attend regular classes to the maximum extent possible.* (Will McIntyre/ Photo Researchers, Inc.)

If you teach in an area with a large concentration of students having limited English proficiency (children of Hispanic origin whose families have recently immigrated to the United States, for example), you may find long delays between referral and assessment of a child suspected of having a disability, as well as deviations from some of the protection in evaluation procedures. The reason is a shortage of both bilingual psychologists and tests that include a representative sample of ethnic minorities in their norms. Few tests are directed toward South American, Central American, Mexican, Cuban, or Puerto Rican children, for instance. When such tests are used to assess Spanish-speaking children, they are simply translated from English into Spanish. Because standardized tests are designed to reflect cultural experiences common to the United States, and because English words and phrases may not mean quite the same thing when translated into Spanish, these tests may not be measuring what they were developed to measure. In other words, they may not be valid. The results of such assessments should therefore be interpreted very cautiously (Nuttall, 1987; Wilen & Sweeting, 1986).

Given the substantial body of evidence demonstrating the propensity of children to observe and imitate more competent children (see, for example, Schunk, 1987), it was assumed that students with disabilities would learn more by interacting with nondisabled students than by attending homogeneous classes. It has been difficult to validate the mainstreaming assumption, however, because of the scarcity of experimental evidence. What limited data do exist suggest that exposure to and involvement with nondisabled children produce small improvements in academic and social behaviors (Guralnick, 1987). Susan Ohanian (1990), a longtime teacher, reinforces this conclusion with accounts of several mildly

▶ Mainstreaming seems to produce modest improvements in learning

retarded students who were placed in her classes. For some, the experience was modestly productive, but for others it was largely a wasted effort. Even for those students who seemed to profit, growth was very uneven. One student, for example, managed to learn quite a bit about dinosaurs and was able to narrate the class production of "The Frog Prince" but, at twelve years of age, could not reliably add or subtract, couldn't tell time, and couldn't pass a spelling test of three-letter rhyming words. On the basis of the experimental and first-person evidence, two conclusions seem warranted. One is that mainstreaming may not be an appropriate course of action for every child with a disability. The second is that for students who are mainstreamed, IEPs should be written so as to better reflect what a given student probably can and cannot accomplish.

Recent Changes in PL 94-142

Since 1975, PL 94-142 has been amended several times. The two most recent revisions were passed in 1986 (PL 99-457) and 1990 (PL 101-476). PL 99-457, the Handicapped Children's Protection Act, requires all states that apply for funds under PL 94-142 to provide to disabled children ages three through five the same educational services as are provided to school-age children with disabilities. In addition, Congress has made available to states funds for an early intervention program. Infants and toddlers (birth through two years of age) who show delays in development or who are judged to be at risk for developmental delays are eligible for this program. As with PL 94-142, infants, toddlers, and preschoolers must be given multidisciplinary assessments and individualized programs (called an individualized family service plan) by their school system (Ysseldyke & Algozzine, 1990).

▶ PL 94-142 amended to provide services to preschool and post–high school individuals with handicaps

Whereas the main focus of PL 99-457 was to extend educational services downward to infants, toddlers, and preschoolers with disabilities, PL 101-476, the Individuals with Disabilities Education Act, was primarily intended to help individuals with disabilities make the transition from school to post-school activities. The legislation provides for transition services (such as assessments or individualized programs) that help students move into such post-school activities as college, vocational training, employment, and independent living. Because of this added feature, IEPs must now include an annual statement of needed transition services. PL 101-476 also provides for the purchase of any commercially available or customized technological device that is used to increase, maintain, or improve the functional capabilities of students with disabilities. In recognition of the special needs of an increasingly diverse society, this legislation also recommends that the federal government recruit minority members into the special education profession. Although PL 101-476 contains several other features, the last one we will mention becomes apparent when we compare its title with those of PL 94-142 and PL 99-457. It substitutes the term *disability* for *handicap* in order to remind people that individuals with disabilities can do many things (Council for Exceptional Children, 1991).

Taking into account the various developments that led to the passage of PL 94-142, you can readily understand why the law was enacted. While all the provisions are well intended, few of them are easy to put into practice. Accordingly, you will be curious about what PL 94-142 means to a regular classroom teacher.

What PL 94-142 Means to Regular Classroom Teachers

By the time you begin your teaching career, PL 94-142 will have been in effect for more than twenty years. Each state was required to have established laws and policies for implementing the various provisions by 1978. Thus, the trial and error process that inevitably follows a radical departure from previous routine will have taken place by the time you enter a classroom. The first guiding principle to follow, therefore, is *Find out what the local ground rules are.* You will probably be told during orientation meetings about the ways PL 94-142 is being put into effect in your state and local school district. But if such a presentation is not given or is incomplete, it would be wise to ask about guidelines you should follow. Your second guiding principle, then, should be *When in doubt, ask.*

The degree to which you will actually be involved with PL 94-142 decisions and pupils will depend on several factors. If you teach in the primary grades of an inner-city school, for instance, you will be much more aware of PL 94-142 than if you teach advanced college-preparatory classes in a high school located in an affluent suburb. Children who come from disadvantaged minority-group backgrounds are more likely (for reasons to be described later in this chapter) to be classified as having disabilities under the law than those from upper-class white backgrounds. Teachers in the lower grades are almost always the first school personnel to observe signs of disabilities and to make initial referrals. In addition, there are more likely to be children deemed to have disabilities under PL 94-142 in classes where pupils are grouped primarily or exclusively by age than in classes for pupils who have undergone a process of selection (for example, college-preparatory seniors taking advanced chemistry). And because most secondary schools have vocational and college-preparatory programs, some high school teachers are more likely than others to have a larger proportion of students with disabilities. A teacher of home economics or industrial arts, for example, may be asked to teach a disproportionate number of students who have experienced difficulties with the academic curriculum.

Another set of factors that may contribute to the degree of your involvement with children with disabilities will be a result of how your local school system has chosen to resolve two somewhat conflicting demands: restrictions against ability grouping, and current insistence on upholding academic standards and avoiding inflated grades. As noted in the evaluation of reactions against ability grouping, as well as in comments on the mainstreaming provisions of PL 94-142, court rulings at the state and federal levels have had a chilling effect on the use of tracking systems (particularly at the elementary grade levels) and the assignment of students to special education classes on a full-time basis (Valente, 1987). At the same time, there is a renewed emphasis on realistic grading because of evidence that contemporary American schoolchildren perform less well on achievement tests than did their predecessors. (It is argued that inflated grades given by teachers of the 1970s contributed substantially to the decline in scores on achievement tests.) As a result of these two trends, you are likely to be asked to teach in a single classroom students who will vary substantially in academic ability *and* to evaluate their performance stringently. "Automatic promotion" is likely to be discouraged, and various measures will be used to evaluate achievement. As a result, parents of pupils in the elementary grades (in particular) may be alarmed if they discover that their children are receiving low grades or earning low scores on achievement tests. If they are assertive—and aware of PL 94-142—they may insist that their children be considered for special educational services.

With these general considerations as background, consider some questions you may be asking yourself about the impact of PL 94-142 as you approach your first teaching job.

What Kinds of Disabling Conditions Are Included Under PL 94-142?   According to the U.S. Department of Education, during the 1989–1990 academic year 4.68 million children from birth through age twenty-one (about 6.9 percent of the total number of individuals in this age group) received special education services under the Individuals with Disabilities Education Act (the amended successor to PL 94-142). Most of these children (4.02 million) were between the ages of six and seventeen.

The Department of Education recognizes eleven categories of students with disabilities. Many states use the same categories. Others use fewer, more inclusive, classification schemes. Commonly used categories are listed below, together with brief definitions of each type; but you should be prepared to find other categories and terms used in various reports, articles, and books.

> *Deafness.* Absence of hearing in both ears. Or a hearing disability that prevents understanding of speech with or without a hearing aid.
>
> *Hardness of hearing.* Significant difficulty in understanding speech, even when equipped with a hearing aid.
>
> *Blindness.* Visual acuity of 20/200 or less in the better eye with correction, or visual acuity of more than 20/200 if the widest diameter of the field of vision subtends an angle no greater than 20 degrees. As you probably know, 20/20 vision means that a person with "perfect" sight can see print of a given size at 20 feet. Visual acuity of 20/200 means that the person sees at 20 feet what an individual with "perfect" vision sees at 200 feet. The field-of-vision aspect of blindness means that the individual views things as if looking through a tunnel.
>
> *Visual impairments.* Visual acuity between 20/70 and 20/200 in the better eye after correction.
>
> *Speech impairments.* A disorder such as stuttering, impaired articulation, or a language or voice impairment that adversely affects educational performance.

Physical and health impairments. Conditions such as orthopedic handicaps, cerebral palsy, epilepsy, heart disease, or diabetes.

Mental retardation. Subaverage general intellectual functioning as indicated by abnormally low scores on intelligence tests, as well as by deficits in adaptive behavior—that is, how well a person functions in social environments. (A more precise definition of mental retardation will be provided later in this chapter.)

Learning disabilities. Disorders in basic psychological processes that lead to learning problems not traceable to physical disabilities or mental retardation. (A more complete definition of learning disabilities will be presented later in this chapter.)

Emotional disturbance. Personal and social problems exhibited in an extreme degree over a period of time that adversely affect the ability to learn and get along with others. (A more complete definition of emotional disturbance will be presented later in this chapter.)

▶ Learning disabled, speech impaired, mentally retarded, emotionally disturbed students most likely to be served under PL 94-142

Percentages of each type of student who received special educational services during the school year 1989–1990 are indicated in Table 5.1.

As you can see, the most common types of children with disabilities receiving services were those classified as learning disabled, speech impaired, mentally retarded, and emotionally disturbed.

TABLE 5.1   Students Receiving Special Education Services: 1989–1990

Disabling Condition	Percentage of Total School Enrollment[1]	Percentage of Students with Disabilities Served
Specific learning disabilities	5.01	48.5
Speech or language impairments	2.59	22.9
Mental retardation	1.38	13.3
Serious emotional disturbance	0.96	9.0
Multiple disabilities	0.18	2.1
Hearing impairments	0.14	1.4
Orthopedic impairments	0.12	1.1
Other health impairments	0.11	1.2
Visual impairments	0.06	0.5
Deaf-blindness	0.00	0.0
Total	10.55	100.0

1. Percentages are based on disabled children aged 6–21 as a percentage of total school enrollment for kindergarten through twelfth grade.
Source: U.S. Department of Education, "To Assure the Free Appropriate Public Education of All Children with Disabilities." *Thirteenth Annual Report to Congress on the Implementation of the Individuals with Disabilities Education Act* (Washington, D.C.: U.S. Department of Education, 1991).

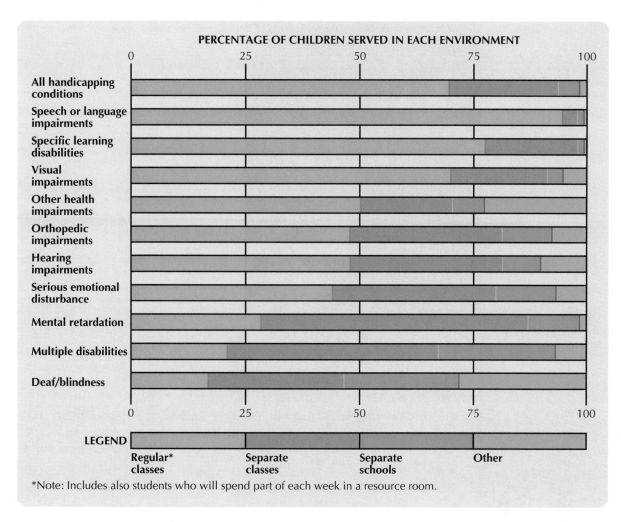

FIGURE 5.1   Environments in Which 6- to 21-Year-Old Children with Disabilities Were Served During the School Year 1988–1989 (U.S. Department of Education, "To Assure the Free Appropriate Public Education of All Children with Disabilities," *Thirteenth Annual Report to Congress on the Implementation of the Individuals with Disabilities Education Act* (Washington, D.C.: U.S. Department of Education, 1991).)

Which Types of Students Are Most Likely to Attend Regular Classes?   Figure 5.1 supplies information about the percentages of students with specific disabling conditions served in regular classes, separate classes, separate schools, and other educational environments.

As you can see, those students most likely to spend most or part of each day in a regular classroom are classified as speech or language impaired, learning disabled, visually handicapped, and other health impaired. Those students least

▶ Speech impaired, learning disabled, visually handicapped, other health impaired students most likely to attend regular classes

Under PL 94–142, students with disabling conditions are entitled to receive specialized services, such as speech therapy. (Nathan Benn/Stock, Boston, Inc.)

likely to attend regular classes are classified as seriously emotionally disturbed, mentally retarded, multiply disabled, and deaf/blind.

What Help Will Regular Classroom Teachers Receive from Specialists?   Depending on the size, policies, and financial resources of the school system in which you teach, you might work with one or more of the following specialists in meeting the provisions of PL 94-142:

Special education teachers, trained and certified to teach children with one or more specific disabilities, often in self-contained (separate) classrooms.

Resource room teachers, who instruct students with disabilities in special resource rooms for part of a school day.

Itinerant teachers, who travel from school to school in a district and usually provide short-term (for example, one day a week) instruction.

Consultation teachers, who consult with regular classroom teachers and offer suggestions for instructing pupils with disabilities.

Clinical teachers, who provide instruction or therapy of various kinds in separate clinics or, alternatively, use clinical teaching techniques. Clinical teaching techniques may center on methods derived from various forms of psychotherapy or be based on the premise that instruction should be arranged to match pupil strengths and weaknesses.

Guidance counselors, who often function as coordinators for assessment and IEP teams, supervise comprehensive testing programs, and advise students about personal, academic, or vocational problems.

School psychologists, who administer and evaluate tests, sometimes provide psychotherapy, and consult with teachers and parents who are concerned about pupil problem behavior.

Occupational therapists, who assist handicapped students with disabilities to develop self-help skills such as feeding or dressing, as well as motor and perceptual skills such as writing or distinguishing between shapes.

Physical therapists, who help pupils with disabilities develop or recover physical strength and endurance.

Speech-language pathologists, who make assessments and provide therapy for pupils with speech and/or language impairments.

Audiologists, who administer hearing tests and recommend ways pupils might correct or compensate for hearing impairments.

What Are the Regular Classroom Teacher's Responsibilities Under PL 94-142?   Regular classroom teachers may be involved in activities required directly or indirectly by PL 94-142 in four possible ways: referral, assessment, planning of an individual education program, and implementation and evaluation of the IEP.

Referral. The first step leading to the provision of services under PL 94-142 is referral—someone comes to the conclusion that a child differs from the norm to the point that special instruction may be required. If a child has a physical disability, the parents may explain the extent and severity of the disability to school authorities when the child is enrolled. In some cases, a written statement from a physician or licensed eye or ear specialist may be required. For some disabilities, however, the initial referral is likely to come from a regular classroom teacher. Learning disabilities, emotional disturbance, and mild mental retardation may not become apparent until after a child has actually been exposed to normal school conditions for a period of months or years.

Once you decide that a student's behavior differs sufficiently from that of other students to raise the possibility of special services or perhaps special class placement, you will need to collect data to support your referral. In general, you should have information about the student's current educational status (this would include attendance records, scores from tests and quizzes, and evaluation of homework assignments), how the student has responded to various instructional strategies, and any information provided to you by the parents (Kubiszyn & Borich, 1990; Langone, 1990).

Because you will be inexperienced, because referral is an important first step, and because classifying a pupil as eligible for special education under PL 94-142 is a significant (and often costly) decision, you are almost certain to be given advice and assistance about how to handle a possible referral. In any event, if a referral is seen as appropriate by the person or persons delegated to process referrals, the next step is assessment.

Assessment. The initial assessment procedures, which must be approved by parents, are usually carried out by school psychologists who are certified to ad-

One of the provisions of PL 94–142 stipulates that an individualized education program must be prepared by specialists in the education of exceptional children, the classroom teacher, and perhaps the parents when a handicapped child is mainstreamed. (Richard Hutchings)

▶ Interdisciplinary assessment team determines if pupil needs special services

minister tests. As noted earlier, typically several tests are given. For example, one group of school psychologists reported that an average of eleven tests were given before a student was classified as learning disabled (Thurlow & Ysseldyke, 1979). If the initial conclusions of the school psychologist support the teacher's perception that the student needs special services, the **interdisciplinary assessment team** required under PL 94-142 will be formed. Depending on the type of personnel available and the nature of a child's disabling condition, an interdisciplinary team may consist of several of the following specialists: school psychologist, guidance counselor, classroom teacher, school social worker, learning disability specialist, speech therapist, physician, psychiatrist. Since a classroom teacher is sometimes asked to be a member of this team, you may serve in this capacity. In all likelihood, you will be asked to describe the referred child's intellectual, social, emotional, and physical performance. You should be prepared to provide such information as the quality of the child's homework and his or her test scores, ability to understand and use language, ability to perform various motor functions, alertness at different times of the day, and interpersonal relationships with classmates (Kubiszyn & Borich, 1990; Langone, 1990). If the team decides that the student *does* qualify for special services, the next step is preparation of the individualized education program.

▶ Classroom teacher, parents, several specialists prepare IEP

Preparation of the IEP. At least some, if not all, of the members of the assessment team work with the teacher (and the parents) in preparing the IEP. The necessary components of an IEP were described earlier, and they are illustrated in Figure 5.2.

FIGURE 5.2 Example of an Individualized Education Program (IEP)

INDIVIDUAL EDUCATIONAL PLAN ___11/11/92___
DATE

STUDENT: Last Name _____ First _____ Middle _____ Grade Level _5.3_ Birthdate/Age _8-4-81_

School of Attendance _____ Home School _____

School Address _____ School Telephone Number _____

Child Study Team Members

Case Manager	_LD Teacher_
Homeroom	_Parents_
Name _Facilitator_ Title	Name Title
Name _Speech_ Title	Name Title
Name Title	Name Title

Summary of Assessment results

IDENTIFIED STUDENT NEEDS: _Reading from last half of_
DISTAR II – present performance level

LONG TERM GOALS: _To improve reading achievement level_
by at least one year's gain. To improve math
achievement to grade level. To improve
language skills by one year's gain.
_+_

SHORT TERM GOALS: _Master grade level vocabulary and reading_
skills. Master math skills in basic curriculum.
Master spelling words from Level 3 list. Complete
units 1–9 from grade level curriculum.

MAINSTREAM MODIFICATIONS _____

White Copy - Cumulative Folder   Golden Rod - Case Manager
Pink Copy - Special Teacher   Yellow Copy - Parent

Description of Services to be Provided

Type of Service	Teacher	Starting Date	Amt. of time per day	OBJECTIVES AND CRITERIA FOR ATTAINMENT
Level III	_LD teacher_	_11-11-92_	_2½ hrs._	Reading: will know all vocabulary through the "Honeycomb" level. Will master skills as presented through Distar II. will know 123 sound-symbols presented in "Second Way to Reading." Math: will pass all tests at Basic 4 level. Spelling: 5 words each week from Level 3 list. Language: will complete Units 1–9 of the 4th grade language program. will also complete supplemental units from Language Step by step.

Mainstream Classes	Teacher	Starting Date	Amt. of time per day	OBJECTIVES AND CRITERIA FOR ATTAINMENT
SCD			_.514_ _3½ hrs._	Out of seat behavior: sit attentively and listen during mainstream class discussions. A simple management plan will be implemented if the does not meet this expectation. Mainstream modifications of Social Studies: will keep a folder in which he expresses through drawing the topics his class will cover. Modified district social studies curriculum. No formal testing will be made. An oral results test taken and oral questions will be asked.

The following equipment, and other changes in personnel, transportation, curriculum, methods, and educational services will be made:
Distar II Reading Program Spelling Level 3 "Sound
Way to Reading "Program Vocabulary tapes

Substantiation of least restrictive alternatives: _The planning team has deter-_
mined   academic needs are best met
with direct SCD support in reading, math, language
and spelling.

ANTICIPATED LENGTH OF PLAN _1 yr._   The next periodic review will be held: _May 1992_
                                                                          DATE/TIME/PLACE

☑ I approve this program placement and the above IEP
☐ I do not approve this placement and/or the IEP
☐ I request a conciliation conference

_____
PARENT/GUARDIAN

Form 2011

_____
Principal or Designee

Implementation of the IEP. Depending on the nature and severity of the handicap, the student may spend part or all of the school day in a regular classroom or be placed in a separate class or school. If the pupil stays in a regular classroom, the teacher will be expected to put into practice the various instructional techniques listed in the IEP. One or more of the specialists listed earlier may give assistance by providing part-time instruction or treatment and/or by supplying specific advice. The classroom teacher may also be expected to determine if the listed objectives are being met and to furnish evidence of attainment. Various techniques of instruction, as well as approaches to evaluation that stress pupil mastery of individualized assignments, will be discussed in several of the chapters that follow. Specific techniques that you might use when instructing exceptional students most likely to be placed in regular classrooms, including some who qualify under the provisions of PL 94-142, will be summarized later in this chapter.

Because the IEP is planned by a multidisciplinary team, you will be given direction and support when providing regular class instruction for pupils who have a disabling condition as defined under PL 94-142. Thus, you will not be expected to start from scratch or to handle planning and instructional responsibilities entirely by yourself.

The types of atypical students you will sometimes be expected to teach in your classroom will vary. Some will be special education students who are being mainstreamed for a certain part of the school day. Others, while different from typical students in some noticeable respect, will not qualify for special education services under PL 94-142. The remainder of this chapter describes atypical pupils from both categories and techniques for teaching them. Of the disabling conditions covered by PL 94-142, the ones that occur most frequently are specific learning disabilities, speech or language impairments, mental retardation, and emotional disturbance (as indicated earlier, in Table 5.1). Mentally retarded, learning disabled, and emotionally disturbed students often require special forms of instruction, and we will focus on these categories. In addition, though not mentioned in PL 94-142, students who are gifted and talented require special forms of instruction, as we will also discuss.

STUDENTS WITH MENTAL RETARDATION

The Classification of Children with Mental Retardation

As noted in Chapter 4 and at the beginning of this chapter, there has been a trend away from the rigid use of classification schemes in American education. Nevertheless, it is sometimes essential, as Nicholas Hobbs (1975) pointed out in *The Futures of Children,* to classify children who differ in significant ways from the norm in order to plan and finance special education for them. The need for classifying children with mental retardation has been recognized by the American Association on Mental Deficiency (AAMD), which proposed this definition: "Mental retardation refers to significantly subaverage intellectual functioning existing concurrently with defects in adaptive behavior and manifested during the developmental period" (Grossman, 1977, 1983). The AAMD applies the term **mental retardation** to individuals having IQ scores of 67 and below, and classifies those with IQ scores within that range into the following categories:

Mild retardation—IQ score between 67 and 52

Moderate retardation—IQ score between 51 and 36

Severe retardation—IQ score between 35 and 20

Profound retardation—IQ score of 19 and below

Owing to the legal challenges to IQ testing and special class placement as well as to the trend toward mainstreaming, students classified as mildly retarded who were once separated are more likely now to be placed in regular classes. You probably will not encounter a great many mainstreamed children classified as moderately or severely retarded, because of the specialized forms of care and instruction they need. You may, however, be asked to teach for at least part of the day one or more higher-scoring mildly retarded children.

Characteristics of Children with Mild Retardation[1]

Students who have below-average IQ scores follow the same general developmental pattern as their peers with higher IQ scores, but they differ in the rate and degree of development. Accordingly, pupils with low IQ scores may possess characteristics typical of pupils with average IQ scores who are younger than they are. One general characteristic of such students, therefore, is that they often appear immature compared with their age-mates. Immature pupils are likely to experience frustration frequently when they find they are unable to do things their classmates can do, and many mildly retarded students tend to have a low tolerance for frustration. It helps to remember that a mildly retarded child generally needs to expend effort to cope with situations that more favored peers take in stride. Related to frustration proneness is a tendency toward self-devaluation. When students with retardation become aware that they are having difficulty

> Mildly retarded students may frustrate easily, lack confidence and self-esteem

---

1. Many of the points in this section are based on a discussion of characteristics of mentally retarded children in *Introduction to Special Education* (2d ed., 1990) by James E. Ysseldyke and Bob Algozzine, and in *Educating Exceptional Children* (6th ed., 1989) by Samuel Kirk and James J. Gallagher.

For the sake of emphasis, many of the characteristics and teaching techniques described in this section refer to children who might barely qualify for mainstreaming (as opposed to special class placement). Most of the students with retardation you are likely to have in your classes will exhibit less extreme variations of the following traits. The basic teaching techniques that are recommended, though, should be effective with all pupils who learn less rapidly than most of their classmates.

doing what classmates do with ease, they are likely to doubt their own abilities and suffer from lack of confidence and low self-esteem.

The intellectual characteristics of mildly retarded children include tendencies to oversimplify concepts, the inability to generalize, short memory and attention span, the inclination to concentrate on only one aspect of a learning situation and to ignore incidentals, the inability to formulate learning strategies that fit particular situations, and delayed language development. Several of these characteristics can be understood more completely if they are related to Piaget's description of cognitive development. The mildly retarded students in secondary schools may never move beyond the level of concrete operations. Younger children with retardation will tend to classify things in terms of a single feature. Older ones may be able to deal with concrete situations but find it difficult to grasp abstractions, generalize from one situation to another, or state and test hypotheses.

Now that you are familiar with some characteristics of mildly retarded pupils, it is time to discuss techniques of teaching. The following suggestions take into account the characteristics just described, as well as points made by Samuel Kirk and James J. Gallagher (1989, pp. 168–172) and by James E. Ysseldyke and Bob Algozzine (1990, pp. 185–186, 399–408).

Mildly retarded students tend to oversimplify, have difficulty generalizing

Suggestions for Teaching in Your Classroom

INSTRUCTING STUDENTS WITH MILD RETARDATION

1. As much as possible, try to avoid placing mildly retarded students in situations that are likely to lead to frustration. When, despite your efforts, such students indicate that they are close to their limit of frustration tolerance, encourage them to engage in relaxing change-of-pace pursuits or in physical activities.

2. Do everything possible to encourage a sense of self-esteem.

3. Present learning tasks that contain a small number of elements, at least some of which are familiar to the pupil.

4. Give a series of brief lessons that can be completed in short periods of time instead of comprehensive assignments that require sustained concentration and effort.

5. Build overlearning into lessons. Keep going back over material previously learned, but make drill as interesting and enjoyable as possible.

6. Try to arrange what is to be learned into a series of small steps, each of which leads to immediate feedback.

7. Devise and use record-keeping techniques that make it clear that assignments have been completed successfully and that progress is taking place.

1. As much as possible, try to avoid placing mildly retarded students in situations that are likely to lead to frustration. When, despite your efforts, such students indicate that they are close to their limit of frustration tolerance, encourage them to engage in relaxing change-of-pace pursuits or in physical activities.

Handbook Heading: Helping Mildly Retarded Pupils Deal with Frustration

Since children with retardation are more likely to experience frustration than their more capable peers, it is desirable to try to minimize the frequency of such experiences in the classroom. Probably the most effective way to do this is to give mildly retarded pupils individual assignments so that they are not placed in situations where their work is compared with that of others. No matter how hard you try, though, you will not be able to eliminate frustrating experiences, partly because you will have to schedule some all-class activities and partly because even individual assignments may be difficult for a mildly retarded child to handle. If you happen to notice that such a pupil appears to be getting more and more bothered by inability to complete a task, you might try to divert attention to a less demanding form of activity or have the pupil engage in physical exercise of some kind.

Examples

Have a primary grade pupil who is having trouble with arithmetic problems do some artwork or run to the end of the playground.

Have a secondary grade pupil who is frustrated by inability to complete an assignment take a note to the office.

2. Do everything possible to encourage a sense of self-esteem.

Handbook Heading: Combating the Tendency to Communicate Low Expectations

Children with mild retardation are prone to devalue themselves because they are aware that they are less capable than their classmates at doing many things. One way to combat this tendency toward self-devaluation is to make a point of showing that you have positive feelings about less capable students. If you indicate that you have positive feelings about an individual, that person is likely to acquire similar feelings about himself or herself.

Jere Brophy and Thomas Good (1974) report that many teachers, usually without realizing it, tend to communicate low expectations to students of low ability. Following is a list of some of the ways in which teachers tend to cause mildly retarded students to think of themselves as less capable than classmates. An antidote for combating the tendency described follows each point.

Tendency: Wait less time for mildly retarded pupils to answer.

Antidote: Make it clear that you will allow plenty of time for the pupil to come up with an answer.

Tendency: Respond to a wrong answer supplied by a mildly retarded student by giving the correct answer or by calling on another student.

Antidote: Repeat the question, give a clue, ask a different question.

Tendency: Praise mildly retarded students less frequently.

Antidote: Remind yourself to give frequent personal attention to such students.

Tendency: Expect and demand less from mildly retarded students.

Antidote: Remember how the self-fulfilling prophecy may shape aspirations and esteem. Try to convey to mildly retarded pupils the expectation that they can learn.

Perhaps the best overall strategy to use in building self-esteem is to help children with retardation successfully complete learning tasks. Suggestions 3 through 7 offer ideas you might use.

3. Present learning tasks that contain a small number of elements, at least some of which are familiar to the pupil.

Handbook Heading:
Giving Mildly Retarded
Students Simple Assignments

Since students with retardation tend to oversimplify concepts, try to provide learning tasks that contain only a few elements, at least some of which have been previously learned.

Examples

Give mildly retarded primary grade students books that tell a simple story and that contain words the pupil has recently learned.

Ask secondary school social studies students with mild retardation to prepare a report on the work of a single police officer, as opposed to preparing an analysis of law enforcement agencies (which might be an appropriate topic for the best student in the class).

4. Give a series of brief lessons that can be completed in short periods of time instead of comprehensive assignments that require sustained concentration and effort.

▶ Give mildly retarded
students specific as-
signments that can be
completed quickly

Students with retardation tend to have a short attention span. If they are asked to concentrate on demanding tasks that lead to a delayed payoff, they are likely to become distracted or discouraged. Therefore, it is better to give a series of short assignments that produce immediate feedback than to use any sort of contract approach or the equivalent where the student is expected to engage in self-directed effort leading to a remote goal.

Examples

With mildly retarded elementary school pupils, make frequent use of curriculum materials that consist of a series of short, quickly graded tasks that call attention to progress.

Ask secondary school English students to read a series of short stories instead of a novel.

5. Build overlearning into lessons. Keep going back over material previously learned, but make drill as interesting and enjoyable as possible.

Mildly retarded children have a short memory span and find it difficult to place what is learned in their long-term storage system. Explanations for this include their tendency to oversimplify concepts and their limited ability to generalize. A person with high intelligence is able to grasp the structure of a field of study and comprehend relationships. Both of these abilities make memorizing simpler and forgetting less likely. The child with mild retardation, by contrast, tends to learn one isolated thing at a time. This is essentially what is meant by rote memorization, and it is unfortunate that many individuals with mild retardation can learn only by repeatedly going over specific items again and again. When teaching such pupils, it is often necessary, therefore, to engage in what amounts to drill; but you might do your best to avoid making this drill seem pointless or tedious.

Handbook Heading:
Using Overlearning
with Mildly Retarded
Students

Examples

Have mildly retarded primary grade students form a group and practice the same ten spelling words every day for a week. Then include the same words in lists presented during following weeks. To give such sessions a bit of variety, use different games, such as "spelling baseball," or have children pick out cards containing a word to be spelled.

In a secondary school home economics class, have students bake a series of cakes by following recipes that are essentially the same but produce a variety of desserts.

Children with mild retardation are more likely to respond to instruction if they are presented with simple learning tasks and provided with immediate feedback. (Paul Conklin)

6. Try to arrange what is to be learned into a series of small steps, each of which leads to immediate feedback.

Students who lack confidence, tend to think of one thing at a time, are unable to generalize, and have a short memory and attention span usually respond quite positively to programmed instruction and linear forms of computer-assisted instruction (to be described more completely in Chapter 8). Linear computer programs offer a systematic step-by-step procedure that emphasizes only one specific idea per step, or frame. They also offer immediate feedback. These characteristics closely fit the needs of mildly retarded children. You might look for computer programs in the subject or subjects you teach or develop your own materials, perhaps in the form of a workbook of some kind.

Examples

In the primary grades, use programmed readers and look for computer programs in spelling and arithmetic.

At the secondary level, distribute a list of questions on a chapter, and urge mildly retarded students to be especially conscientious about completing brief answers to one question at a time.

Handbook Heading:
Giving Mildly Retarded
Students Proof of Progress

7. Devise and use record-keeping techniques that make it clear that assignments have been completed successfully and that progress is taking place.

Students who are experiencing difficulties in learning are especially in need of tangible proof of progress. When, for instance, they correctly fill in blanks in a programmed workbook and discover that their answers are correct, they are encouraged to go on to the next question. You might use the same basic approach in more general ways by having students with retardation keep records of progress. (This technique might be used with *all* students in a class, not just mildly retarded ones.)

Examples

Make individual charts for primary grade pupils. As they successfully complete assignments, have them color in marked-off sections; or paste on gold stars or the equivalent; or trace the movement of animal figures, rockets, or whatever, toward a destination.

At the secondary level, make up a chart showing which scores on a series of tasks are to be recorded. Then encourage students to record each score as the work is completed.

At any grade level, use a mastery approach: Establish criteria. Present lessons. Measure achievement. Provide remedial instruction if necessary. Measure achievement again. Record successful completion of each unit and total points as they are accumulated. (Mastery learning is explained in detail in Chapter 12.)

STUDENTS WITH LEARNING DISABILITIES

By far the greatest number of students who qualify for special education under PL 94-142 are those classified as learning disabled. According to U.S. Department of Education figures, the number of students identified as learning disabled increased from 969,423 in 1977–1978 to 1,926,097 in 1986–1987. In 1978 learning disabled students accounted for about 29 percent of the handicapped population. By 1982 that estimate had grown to about 40 percent (Lovitt, 1989). These figures lead to two questions: What are the characteristics of students with **learning disabilities?** And why have the numbers of students classified as learning disabled increased so dramatically during the last few years?

Characteristics of Students with Learning Disabilities

In the early 1960s groups of concerned parents called attention to a problem in American education: A significant number of pupils in public schools were experiencing difficulties in learning but were not eligible for special classes or remedial instruction programs. These children were not mentally retarded, deaf, blind, or otherwise handicapped, but they were unable to respond to aspects of the curriculum presented in regular classrooms. In 1963 parents of such children formed the Association for Children with Learning Disabilities to call attention to the scope of these problems not traceable to any specific cause. Their efforts were rewarded in 1968, when the National Advisory Committee on the Handicapped of the U.S. Office of Education developed a definition of specific learning disabilities, which was utilized by Congress the following year in the Learning Disability Act of 1969. That definition was revised and inserted in PL 94-142. It stresses the following basic points (Lerner, 1989):

> Learning disabilities: disorders in basic processes that lead to learning problems not due to other causes

1. The individual has a *disorder in one or more of the basic psychological processes.* (These processes refer to intrinsic prerequisite abilities such as memory, auditory perception, visual perception, and oral language.)
2. The individual has *difficulty in learning,* specifically in the areas of speaking, listening, writing, reading (word recognition skills and comprehension), and mathematics (calculation and reasoning).
3. The problem is *not primarily due to other causes,* such as visual or hearing impairments, motor handicapped, mental retardation, emotional disturbance, or economic, environmental, or cultural disadvantage.
4. A *severe discrepancy exists between the student's apparent potential for learning and low level of achievement.* (p. 7)

You should be aware, however, that other definitions of learning disabilities are preferred by many specialists in the field. A widely used definition was proposed by the National Joint Committee on Learning Disabilities (NJCLD) in 1981 (Hammill et al., 1981). The NJCLD definition states:

> Learning disabilities is a generic term that refers to a heterogeneous group of disorders manifested by significant difficulties in the acquisition and use of

Learning disabilities often result from perceptual problems which are analyzed through use of specialized tests. Several tests are usually administered in order to identify a pupil as learning disabled under PL 94–142. (Hank Morgan)

listening, speaking, reading, writing, reasoning, or mathematical abilities. These disorders are intrinsic to the individual and presumed to be due to central nervous system dysfunction. Even though a learning disability may occur concomitantly with other handicapping conditions (e.g., sensory impairment, mental retardation, social and emotional disturbance) or environmental influences (e.g., cultural differences, or inappropriate instruction, psycholinguistic factors), it is not the direct result of those conditions or influences.

Important concepts in the NJCLD definition (summarized by Lerner, 1989) include the following:

1. *Learning disabilities are a heterogeneous group of disorders.* (Individuals with learning disabilities exhibit many kinds of problems. Some may struggle with an individual subject or skill like mathematics, reading comprehension, listening, and writing. Some may be seriously deficient in more than one of these areas. And some students may exhibit poor socialization skills in addition to academic deficits.)
2. *The problem is intrinsic to the individual.* (Learning disabilities are due to factors within the person rather than to external factors, such as the environment or the educational system.)
3. *The problem is thought to be related to a central nervous system dysfunction.* (There is recognition of the biological basis of the problem.)
4. *Learning disabilities may occur along with other handicapping conditions.* (There is recognition that individuals can have several problems at the same time, such as learning disabilities and emotional disorders.) (p. 8)

The complexity of the PL 94-142 and NJCLD definitions and the fact that they are somewhat different indicate that it may often be difficult to make a diagnosis. The provision that the individual exhibit a disorder in one or more of the basic psychological processes, for instance, is likely to be a problem because there is no consensus as to which processes should be measured and few valid and reliable instruments exist with which to measure them. Excluding students whose primary disability is emotional or environmental in nature is difficult because the criteria for identifying emotional disturbance or cultural disadvantage are somewhat imprecise. Finally, satisfying the achievement-ability discrepancy criterion may be a problem because there are differences of opinion about how best to determine ability levels and how to determine when a discrepancy is severe (Chalfant, 1989; Lovitt, 1989).

Reasons for the Increased Number of Pupils Classified as Learning Disabled

When the number of students classified as learning disabled almost doubled in six years, many people wondered if this increase was due, at least in part, to mislabeling. Evidence presented by Lorrie Shepard, Mary Lee Smith, and Carol Vojir (1983) suggests that mislabeling did, and probably still does, play a significant role. These researchers randomly selected for analysis the records of 790 Colorado schoolchildren classified as learning disabled. Their findings can be summarized as follows:

1. Psychological assessments were often either incomplete or based on poor-quality tests. For example, 40 percent of the students were either missing an IQ test or an achievement test or had been given achievement tests that lacked normative data (recall from Chapter 4 that normed excellence is one of the characteristics of a well-constructed standardized test).

2. The ability-achievement discrepancy that is so critical to the definition of learning disability may be a function as much of the particular tests used as of a basic cognitive deficiency of the child. In 12 percent of the cases, children took two IQ tests and two math achievement tests. Only 5 percent of those who had two math scores showed significant discrepancies between IQ and both tests. In 15 percent of the cases, children took two reading achievement tests. Only 27 percent of those who had two reading scores showed significant discrepancies between IQ and both reading tests.

3. Until about fourth grade, the average learning disabled student scored at or slightly below grade level at the time of classification.

4. The researchers judged 57 percent of the children, on the basis of the information in their files, to be suffering from other problems (such as mild retardation, emotional disturbance, hearing impairment, and minor behavioral problems). In other words, Shepard, Smith, and Vojir judged only about 43 percent of the sample to have been properly classified.

Increased number of learning disabled students due to faulty assessment procedures, poor-quality tests

Shepard, Smith, and Vojir have offered several possible reasons for such massive mislabeling:

1. The desire to provide remedial and support services to students who would not otherwise receive them because they did not qualify for any other handicapping category under PL 94-142.

2. A lack of understanding about the definition of learning disability and its relevant diagnostic indicators.

3. Administrative pressures to find and serve all handicapped pupils in order to maintain the viability of special education programs.

4. Pressure from parents to secure remedial services for their failing children.

Note that Shepard and her colleagues found that some children labeled as learning disabled seemed to better fit the categories of mental retardation or emotional disturbance. As a potential member of an interdisciplinary assessment team, you should carefully compare the classification criteria of the two categories we have covered so far with criteria for the next category, emotional disturbance. By doing so, you may in the future be able to help others avoid this type of mislabeling.

Suggestions for Teaching in Your Classroom

INSTRUCTING PUPILS WITH LEARNING DISABILITIES

1. If an IEP has been prepared for a pupil with a learning disability, make sure you understand what instructional materials are to be used, how to implement the plan, and how and when to evaluate progress.

2. If a pupil has a learning disability but is not officially identified as learning disabled, prepare your own version of an IEP.

3. Refer to the suggestions for teaching students with mild retardation, presented earlier in this chapter.

4. Seek ways to help learning disabled pupils compensate for weaknesses in psychological processes as they improve achievement in specific subject areas.

5. Use systematic procedures for helping students use psychological processes more effectively.

---

1. If an IEP has been prepared for a pupil with a learning disability, make sure you understand what instructional materials are to be used, how to implement the plan, and how and when to evaluate progress.

Many pupils with learning disabilities will be identified as such under PL 94-142. Accordingly, an IEP may have been prepared by a multidisciplinary team assigned to that task. If you are a member of that team, make sure you understand how you are expected to implement and evaluate the listed objectives. If you "inherit" the plan from a teacher you are replacing, make it a point to ask someone who prepared the IEP what you are expected to do.

2. If a pupil has a learning disability but is not officially identified as learning disabled, prepare your own version of an IEP.

As noted in the preceding chapter, the number of pupils identified as having learning disabilities has increased dramatically in the last few years. Even so, less than 5 percent of the school population is included under the learning disability category of PL 94-142. There are bound to be many students, therefore, who manifest discrepancies between ability and achievement but whose discrepancies are not severe enough to satisfy the criteria specified in the law. If you notice that certain students in your classes seem to be having difficulty with particular aspects of the curriculum, despite signs of being capable learners in other ways, you might try to function as a one-person multidisciplinary team. Evaluate oral and written class work and examine test profiles in the student's cumulative folder in an effort to detect areas of weakness. Observe the student in informal "test" situations and see if you notice sources of potential difficulty (for example, problems in attention or perception). Then prepare a modest, exploratory version of an IEP by drawing up a set of objectives with the pupil and outlining a plan of attack for achieving them. (Detailed instructions for preparing instructional objectives will be presented in the next chapter.)

Handbook Heading:
Preparing Your Own
Versions of IEPs

Before actually preparing the IEP, you might analyze both psychological processes and subject matter skills. Can you detect weakness in the way the pupil attends to stimuli, or perceives them? Does the student seem to have problems memorizing and remembering what has been learned? What happens just after you give a desk assignment? Does the student dawdle, procrastinate, and become distracted by even the slightest disturbance? Next, try to determine precisely which areas of the curriculum cause the greatest difficulty. Profiles recording a pupil's performance on many achievement tests include detailed information about strengths and weaknesses, as noted in the preceding chapter. If the student is having difficulty with one or more of the basic subject areas, look for special remedial materials. There is a lively competition among publishers to provide coordinated sets of materials in all the basic skills, and if you check a school or curriculum library, you will discover what is available locally. If several sets of similar materials are available, you might ask a curriculum consultant, special education coordinator, or experienced teacher for advice about the best one to use.

After you have made some inferences about psychological processes that are ineffective and curriculum areas that need special attention, you can sit down with the student and prepare an IEP, complete with specified goals, dates for achievement of those goals, and evaluation procedures to be used. (Many suggestions for setting up such learning contracts will be described in Chapter 8.)

  3. Refer to the suggestions for teaching students with mild retardation, presented earlier in this chapter.

As noted in the preceding chapter, it is often difficult to determine whether learning problems are due to mild retardation or to learning disabilities. For purposes of classifying a child for special services under PL 94-142, it may be essential for an assessment team to make a distinction between the two conditions. For purposes of teaching, no distinction needs to be made and many of the techniques for teaching mildly retarded pupils, outlined earlier in this chapter, also are effective methods of instruction with the learning disabled. Learning disabled pupils may be even more likely than those with mild retardation to experience frustration because of their inability to do certain kinds of school assignments. They may lack self-esteem because they realize that they are unable to finish assignments that seem simple to classmates. Accordingly, they are likely to need to experience success with assignments that are within their capability. The basic procedure of presenting short lessons that provide both immediate positive feedback and tangible evidence of progress works well with both mildly retarded and learning disabled students. Many sets of published materials prepared for use with the learning disabled are designed to be used in just such a way. In addition to using techniques recommended by the authors of published materials, you can also devise classroom techniques on your own by following the suggestions for teaching students with mild retardation, outlined starting on page 202.

  4. Seek ways to help learning disabled pupils compensate for weaknesses in psychological processes as they improve achievement in specific subject areas.

Because many publishers have prepared sets of materials for use with learning disabled students, you should be able to find instructional aids that consist of series of lessons graded in difficulty. Such sets of materials are almost invariably accompanied by a detailed teacher's manual that will provide guidelines for you to follow. But even though you will be given direction about ways to present subject matter, you may not be given suggestions about how to arrange the learning environment. With a little ingenuity, you can set up the learning situation so that at least some of the problems caused by inadequacies in psychological processes can be compensated for.

Examples

Help learning disabled students learn to reduce distractions, attend, perceive

For students who are easily distracted, place their desks in a corner facing a blank wall or behind a partition. Instruct each pupil to place only the materials being used on top of the desk or within sight.

Handbook Heading:
Arranging the Class-
room Environment to
Facilitate Learning

For students who seem unable to attend to important stimuli such as significant sections of a text page, show them how to underline or outline in an
effort to distinguish between important and unimportant material. Or suggest
that they use a marker under each line as they read so that they can evaluate
one sentence at a time.

For students who have a short attention span, give brief assignments and divide complex material into smaller segments.

For students who have difficulty memorizing and/or understanding information, teach them such simple memory improvement devices as the first letter
mnemonic, the acrostic, and the method of loci and such comprehension-
aiding devices as summarizing and self-questioning. (All of these techniques
are described in Chapter 9.)

For students with low self-esteem, have them tutor either a low-achieving
classmate in a subject that is not affected by their disability or a younger student in a lower grade. As we point out in the next chapter, learning disabled
students can fill the role of tutor as effectively as non–learning disabled students and typically experience increases in self-esteem and achievement as
a result of doing so.

For students who have difficulty printing or writing legibly, cut out stencils
so that the pupils can begin by tracing the form of a letter within a pattern.
Then have the pupils print the letter without using the stencil.

5. Use systematic procedures for helping students use psychological processes
more effectively.

The techniques just described (as well as many others summarized in *Learning
Disabilities* [6th edition, 1993] by Janet Lerner, and in *Introduction to Learning
Disabilities* [1989] by Thomas C. Lovitt) are simple techniques that can be used in
a variety of situations as subject matter is being studied. As noted earlier, some
specialists in the education of learning disabled pupils have developed comprehensive techniques for working with pupils who suffer from inadequacies in
psychological processes. Refer to the book by Lerner, or ask an experienced
teacher or special education consultant for information about where to obtain
and how to use such comprehensive procedures.

STUDENTS WITH EMOTIONAL DISTURBANCE

Estimates of Emotional Disturbance

In its 1989 Report to Congress on the implementation of PL 94-142, the U.S.
Department of Education noted that 374,730 students were classified as emotionally disturbed. This figure accounts for approximately 9 percent of all schoolchil-

dren classified as handicapped and 1 percent of the general school-age population. Not everyone agrees, however, that these figures accurately reflect the scope of the problem. Other estimates range from 0.5 percent to 20 percent (Kirk & Gallagher, 1989). F. W. Wood and R. H. Zabel (1978) offer an explanation for these differences between estimates and classifications by suggesting that most identification procedures ask teachers to rate children in their classes at a particular point in time. Some identification procedures, however, stress recurrent problems. It seems possible, therefore, that while perhaps one out of five students attending public schools may sometimes exhibit emotional problems, only two or three out of one hundred will display severe, persistent problems.

Definitions of Emotional Disturbance

Other reasons why estimates of **emotional disturbance** vary are the lack of any clear descriptions of such forms of behavior and different interpretations of the descriptions that do exist. Only *seriously emotionally disturbed* children are mentioned in PL 94-142, for instance, and the term is defined in this way:

> Emotional disturbance: poor relationships, inappropriate behavior, depression, fears

(i)   The term means a condition exhibiting one or more of the following characteristics over a long period of time and to a marked degree, which adversely affects educational performance:

  (A)   An inability to learn which cannot be explained by intellectual, sensory, and health factors;

  (B)   An inability to build or maintain satisfactory interpersonal relationships with peers and teachers;

  (C)   Inappropriate types of behavior or feelings under normal circumstances;

  (D)   A general pervasive mood of unhappiness or depression; or

  (E)   A tendency to develop physical symptoms or fears associated with personal or school problems.

(ii)   The term includes children who are schizophrenic or autistic. The term does not include children who are socially maladjusted unless it is determined that they are seriously emotionally disturbed. (*Federal Register,* August 23, 1977, p. 42478)

James E. Ysseldyke and Bob Algozzine (1990, pp. 175–176) point out the difficulties involved in distinguishing between emotionally disturbed and normal students due to the inclusion of such vague terms in the definition as *satisfactory interpersonal relationships, a general pervasive mood,* and *inappropriate types of behavior or feelings under normal circumstances.* Such behaviors are difficult to measure objectively and can often be observed in normal individuals. Since long-term observation of behavior is often critical in making a correct diagnosis of emotional disturbance, you can aid the interdisciplinary assessment team in this task by keeping a behavioral log of a child you suspect suffers from this disorder.

Ysseldyke and Algozzine also call attention to confusion resulting from the use of the terms *emotionally disturbed, socially maladjusted,* and *behavior disor-*

Behavior disorders tend to be either aggressive or withdrawn. Withdrawal reactions are more likely to lead to severe problems since they do not provide release of tension (which often occurs with aggresive reactions). (Bob Daemmrich/Stock, Boston, Inc.)

▶ Term *behavior disorders* calls attention to behavior that needs to be changed

ders. They trace *emotionally disturbed* to the influence of Sigmund Freud and note that this term is favored by psychotherapists who endorse the view that the causes of maladjustment need to be considered. The term *socially maladjusted* was frequently used from the 1940s through the 1960s, perhaps as a result of the determination of educators of that period to teach the "whole child." During these years, social adjustment was often considered to be as significant as academic progress. Then starting in the 1960s, the term **behavior disorders** came into wide use due to the influence of psychologists who applied behavioral learning theory principles to education and psychotherapy. Those who favor this term argue that it calls attention to the actual behavior that is disordered and needs to be changed. While there are subtle differences between the terms *emotionally disturbed* and *behavior disorder,* they are essentially interchangeable and you can probably assume that those who use them are referring to children who share similar characteristics. Because of the nature of bureaucracies, however, it may be necessary for anyone hoping to obtain special assistance for a child with what many contemporary psychologists would call a behavior disorder to refer to that child as *seriously emotionally disturbed* since that is the label used in PL 94-142.

Several classifications of emotional disturbance (or behavior disorders) have been made (see, for example, Achenbach & Edelbrock, 1983; Quay, 1986; Wicks-Nelson & Israel, 1991). Most psychologists who have attempted to classify such forms of behavior describe two basic patterns: externalizing and internalizing. Externalizing pupils are often aggressive, uncooperative, restless, and negativistic. They tend to lie and steal, to defy teachers, and to be hostile to authority figures. Sometimes they are cruel and malicious. Internalizing pupils, by contrast, are typically shy, timid, anxious, and fearful. They are often depressed, and lack

▶ Pupils with behavior disorders tend to be either aggressive or withdrawn

self-confidence. Teachers tend to be more aware of pupils who display aggressive disorders because their behavior often stimulates or forces reactions. The withdrawn student, however, may be more likely to develop serious emotional problems. (In Chapter 3 we mentioned that suicide, depression, and schizophrenia are the most common types of severe psychological disturbance during the adolescent years. All of these are withdrawal rather than aggressive reactions.) It seems that those who wrote the definition of serious emotional disturbance that is included in PL 94-142 wanted to stress the potential dangers of withdrawal reactions since such forms of behavior are repeatedly mentioned.

When you obtain your first teaching position, you will probably be informed of procedures for requesting help in identifying students with serious emotional disturbances. If you become aware that one of your pupils is displaying either aggressive or withdrawal behavior severe enough to cause serious problems, your first step might be to make a referral and ask for an evaluation by a competent counselor or psychologist. If the pupil does qualify as seriously disturbed under the provisions of PL 94-142, you will be assisted in developing an IEP. It is likely that a guidance counselor or school psychologist will give you specific suggestions and perhaps also work with the student in individual counseling sessions. In addition to whatever help you may receive from the guidance counselor or school psychologist, you might want to try the suggestions for teaching that follow.

If the emotionally disturbed pupil's behavior becomes extreme, placement in a separate class or special school might be arranged. (Information charted earlier in Figure 5.1 indicates that more than half of emotionally disturbed students under PL 94-142 attend separate classes or schools.) Of course, many students who are classified as emotionally disturbed do not require separate classes or schools, at least not for the entire day. Under the provisions of PL 94-142, these students will be mainstreamed for a certain part of the day.

Suggestions for Teaching in Your Classroom

INSTRUCTING EMOTIONALLY DISTURBED STUDENTS [2]

Instructing the Withdrawn Student

1. Design the classroom environment and formulate lesson plans to encourage social interaction and cooperation.

2. Most of these suggestions were derived from points made in Chapters 7 and 10 of *Strategies for Managing Behavior Problems in the Classroom* (2d ed., 1989) by Mary Margaret Kerr and C. Michael Nelson.

2. Prompt and reinforce appropriate social interactions.

3. Train other students to initiate social interaction.

Instructing the Aggressive Student

4. Design the classroom environment to reduce the probability of disruptive behavior.

5. Reinforce appropriate behavior and, if necessary, punish inappropriate behavior.

6. Use group contingency-management techniques.

---

1. Design the classroom environment and formulate lesson plans to encourage social interaction and cooperation.

Students whose emotional disturbance manifests itself as social withdrawal may stay away from others on purpose (perhaps because they find social contacts threatening) or they may find that others stay away from them (perhaps because they have poorly developed social skills). Regardless of the cause, the classroom environment and your instructional activities can be designed to foster appropriate interpersonal contact.

> ▶ Foster interpersonal contact among withdrawn students

Handbook Heading: Activities and Materials That Encourage Cooperation

Examples

Preschool and primary grade teachers should urge withdrawn children toward toys and materials that encourage cooperative play and away from those that foster isolated play. Examples of the first category are checkers, dolls and doll houses, sand piles, card games, dress-up games, cars and trucks, kitchen play equipment, puppets, and balls. Examples of the second category are beads, crayons, puzzles, modeling clay, chalkboard, and books.

Elementary grade teachers can use the toys and materials just mentioned as well as organized games and sports with a reduced focus on individual performance. Candidates here include soccer, variations of "it" (such as tag), and kickball or softball modified such that everyone on the team gets a turn to kick or bat before the team plays in the field.

Elementary and junior high teachers can use one or more of several team-oriented learning activities. See *Cooperative Learning: Theory, Research, and Practice* (1990b) by Robert Slavin for details on using such activities as Student Teams–Achievement Divisions, Jigsaw, and Team Accelerated Instruction. Team Accelerated Instruction, for example, was designed for use in elementary and middle school mathematics classes. The first step is to form four- or five-member groups that reflect the makeup of the entire class (with respect to gender, ability level, ethnic background, and so on). Each member of the group works individually on problems at his or her own level of understanding. Teammates then check each other's work against answer sheets.

Team scores are based on the average number of units completed each week by the team members and on the accuracy of the work. Attractive rewards can be given to each team when a predetermined amount of work is completed at a predetermined level of quality.

2. Prompt and reinforce appropriate social interactions.

Prompting and positive reinforcement are basic learning principles that are discussed at length in Chapter 8. Essentially, a prompt is a stimulus that draws out a desired response, and positive reinforcement involves giving the student a positive reinforcer (which is something the student wants) immediately after a desired behavior. The aim is to get the student to behave that way again. Typical reinforcers include verbal praise, stickers (with pictures of gold stars and smiley faces, for instance), and small prizes (such as a pencil with the child's name engraved on it).

Example

Set up a cooperative task or activity: "Marc, I would like you to help Carol and Jane paint the scenery for next week's play. You can paint the trees and flowers, Carol will paint the grass, and Jane will do the people." After several minutes, say something like, "That's good work. I am really pleased at how well the three of you are working together." Similar comments can be made at intervals as the interaction continues.

3. Train other students to initiate social interaction.

In all likelihood, you will have too many classroom responsibilities to spend a great deal of time working directly with a withdrawn child. It may be possible, however, using the steps below, to train other students to initiate contact with withdrawn students.

Example

1. Choose a student who interacts freely and well, who can follow your instructions, and who can concentrate on the training task for at least ten minutes.

Handbook Heading:
Getting Students to Initiate Interaction with a Withdrawn Child

2. Explain that the goal is to get the withdrawn child to work or play with the helping student, but that the helper should expect rejection, particularly at first. Role-play the actions of a withdrawn child so the helper understands what you mean by rejection. Emphasize the importance of making periodic attempts at interaction.

3. Instruct the helper to suggest games or activities that appeal to the withdrawn student.

4. Reinforce the helper's attempts to interact with the withdrawn child.

4. Design the classroom environment to reduce the probability of disruptive behavior.

Use techniques to forestall aggressive or antisocial behavior

The best way to deal with aggressive or antisocial behavior is to nip it in the bud. This strategy has at least three related benefits. One benefit of fewer disruptions is that you can better accomplish what you had planned for the day. The second benefit is that you are likely to be in a more positive frame of mind than if you spend half the day acting as a referee. Finally, because of fewer disruptions and a more positive attitude, you may be less inclined to resort to physical punishment (which, as we point out in Chapter 8, often produces undesirable side effects).

Examples

Through careful observation, determine which students do and do not get along with the aggressive student. Seat the former next to the aggressive student and the latter some distance away.

With student input, formulate rules for classroom behavior and penalties for infractions of rules. Remind all students of the penalties, particularly when a disruptive incident seems about to occur, and consistently apply the penalties when the rules are broken.

Place valued objects and materials out of reach when they are not needed or in use.

Minimize frustration with learning for the aggressive student by using some of the same techniques you would use for a mildly retarded child: Break tasks down into small, easy-to-manage pieces, provide clear directions, reinforce correct responses.

5. Reinforce appropriate behavior and, if necessary, punish inappropriate behavior.

In suggestion 2 we described the use of positive reinforcement to encourage desired behavior. Reinforcement has the dual effect of teaching the aggressive student which behavior is appropriate and reducing the frequency of inappropriate behavior as it is replaced by desired behavior. Disruptive behavior will still occur, however. Three effective techniques for suppressing it while reinforcing desired behaviors are contingency contracts, token economies and fines, and time-out. Each of these techniques is described in Chapter 8 of this book.

6. Use group contingency-management techniques.

Up to now we have suggested methods focusing on the aggressive student. In addition, you may want to reward the entire class when the aggressive student behaves appropriately for a certain period of time. Such rewards—which may be free time, special classroom events, or certain privileges—should make the aggressive student the hero and foster better peer relationships.

Mid-Chapter Review

Ability Grouping

Ability grouping was devised early in this century as a means of increasing the efficiency and effectiveness of normal classroom instruction.

The most popular approaches to ability grouping today are *between-class ability grouping, regrouping,* the *Joplin Plan,* and *within-class ability grouping.*

There is no support in the research literature for the practice of between-class ability grouping. Regrouping has received only limited support. And the Joplin Plan as well as within-class ability grouping have been documented as producing positive effects in comparison to instruction in heterogeneous classes.

Mental ability tests, which form the basis of most ability groupings, have been heavily criticized in recent years for unfairly discriminating against minority-group children.

Key Provisions of PL 94-142

Spurred by reports revealing deficiencies in educational services for handicapped children, Congress in 1975 enacted PL 94-142, the Education for All Handicapped Children Act, to reduce the negative impact of educating handicapped children in separate classes and schools.

1. An *individualized education program* (IEP) shall be prepared for each child identified as handicapped under the law. The IEP must include a statement of objectives, a description of the services to be provided, and an explanation of the criteria to be used for determining achievement of objectives.

2. All handicapped pupils shall be placed in the *least restrictive environment,* which leads to *mainstreaming,* or the policy of having handicapped pupils attend regular classes to the maximum extent possible.

3. The legal and civil rights of each handicapped child shall be protected by *due process* procedures.

4. There shall be *protection in evaluation procedures* to ensure that tests used to determine placement are valid and are administered in the pupil's native language.

5. Two recent revisions of PL 94-142 are PL 99-457 and PL 101-476. PL 99-457, the Handicapped Children's Protection Act, extends the basic provisions of PL 94-142 to preschoolers and encourages early intervention programs for infants and toddlers. PL 101-476, the Individuals with Disabilities Education Act, provides services to help adolescents with disabilities make the transition from high school to work, higher education, or independent living.

What PL 94-142 Means to Regular Classroom Teachers

The types of students most likely to receive services under PL 94-142 are classified (in order of frequency) as learning disabled, speech impaired, mentally retarded, and emotionally disturbed.

The types of students most likely to spend most or all of the school day in regular classes are classified (in order of frequency) as speech or language impaired, learning disabled, and visually handicapped.

An *interdisciplinary assessment team* must be formed to determine if a pupil qualifies for services under PL 94-142.

The IEP is prepared by members of the interdisciplinary assessment team, the classroom teacher, and the parents of the pupil.

Students with Mental Retardation

Mentally retarded students exhibit significantly subaverage intellectual functioning (IQ score below 68) and defects in adaptive behavior during the development period.

Mentally retarded students are likely to exhibit a low tolerance for frustration, low levels of confidence and self-esteem, a tendency to oversimplify, and difficulty in understanding and generalizing from abstract ideas.

Students with Learning Disabilities

More pupils are classified as learning disabled under PL 94-142 than as having any other type of handicap. Learning disabilities are defined in various ways and are difficult to assess. Key factors in all definitions stress that learning disabilities involve disorders in basic processes (such as perceptual functions) that lead to learning problems not due to other causes (such as mental retardation).

In recent years the number of pupils classified as learning disabled has increased. This increase seems to be largely due to mislabeling, which is caused by faulty assessment procedures, poor-quality tests, and various pressures to provide remedial and support services to low-achieving students.

Students with Emotional Disturbance

Students who exhibit poor relationships with others, or engage in inappropriate behavior, or who are abnormally depressed or fearful may be classified as *emotionally disturbed* under PL 94-142. Many psychologists use the term *behavior disorder,* which calls attention to the behavior that needs to be changed, in preference to the term *emotionally disturbed.*

Pupils with behavior disorders tend to be either *aggressive* (exhibiting negative and hostile behavior) or *withdrawn* (manifesting depression and lack of confidence).

GIFTED AND TALENTED STUDENTS

Students who learn at a significantly faster rate than their peers or who possess superior talent in one or more areas also need to be taught in special ways if they are to make the most of their abilities. Unlike mentally retarded, learning disabled, and emotionally disturbed children, however, students with superior capabilities are not covered by PL 94-142. Instead, the federal government provides technical assistance to states and local school districts in establishing programs for superior students. Although most states have such programs, some experts in special education (for example, Horowitz & O'Brien, 1986) feel that they are not given the resources they need to adequately meet the needs of all gifted and talented students. The suggestions for teaching that follow a bit later reflect this situation. All of them are inexpensive to implement and require few additional personnel.

A recent definition of the term **gifted and talented** was part of a bill passed by Congress in 1988:

> The term *gifted and talented children and youth* means children and youth who give evidence of high performance capability in areas such as intellectual, creative, artistic, or leadership capacity, or in specific academic fields, and who require services or activities not ordinarily provided by the school in order to fully develop such capabilities. (Title IV–H.R.5, 1988, pp. 227–228)

Identifying Gifted and Talented Students

The AAMD classification of mental retardation refers to specific IQ scores in establishing the upper and lower limits of various categories. But it is not possible to be that specific about the test scores of atypically bright students. From the 1920s through the 1950s an IQ score of 140 was commonly accepted for classifying children as gifted. Beginning in the early 1960s, however, this dividing line was increasingly criticized. A number of psychologists (such as Getzels & Jackson, 1962) called attention to the fact that many children who deserved to be classified as gifted did not earn IQ scores of 140 or above, primarily because the tests used to measure IQ seemed to discriminate against divergent thinkers.

Because of these criticisms, most states have eliminated mention of a specific IQ score from their definition of gifted students. A 1985 survey (Cassidy & Johnson, 1986) found only four states that use some sort of numerical cutoff score. While this is seen as a step in the right direction, critical weaknesses in the identification of gifted and talented children remain. The main problem is a lack of correspondence among the definition of giftedness adopted by a school district (which is usually modeled after the just-mentioned federal definition), the methods used to identify gifted pupils, and the type of instruction given to them. Robert D. Hoge (1988), for example, has argued that giftedness is usually defined by school boards in terms of one or more of the following characteristics: superior performance on a standardized intelligence test, superior performance on a standardized achievement test, superior performance on tests of specific aptitudes, evidence of creativity, or a high level of motivation. The actual identification of gifted children, however, is usually made on the basis of an IQ score and/or teacher nominations. To compound the problem even further, the teachers of gifted and talented pupils, working from the school district's definition, emphasize such things as independent work, the exercise of creativity, and

Gifted and talented students show high performance on wide range of tasks

Inconsistency often exists among definition, identification, and teaching of gifted students

leadership. As we saw in Chapter 4, since IQ tests are not designed to measure such qualities as motivation, creativity, and leadership, relying on them as the only or the major index of giftedness produces at least two problems: Errors of placement (and nonplacement) occur, and students are exposed to forms of instruction for which they may not be prepared.

The issue of nonplacement is particularly acute for minority-group members of color. As we mentioned in Chapter 4, blacks, Hispanics, and Native Americans are greatly underrepresented in gifted and talented programs. Similar observations have been made about gifted students with a learning disability (see, for example, Suter & Wolf, 1987; Pendarvis, Howley & Howley, 1990). A major reason why these groups are underrepresented (to repeat the point made in Chapter 4 as well as in the preceding paragraph) is overreliance on a narrow range of standardized tests as indicators of giftedness. Other characteristics that might be taken into account in deciding on placement are creativity, wide-ranging interests, leadership, communication skills, critical-thinking ability, and task persistence (Frasier, 1991).

> Minorities underrepresented in gifted classes because of overreliance on test scores

Several reasons may explain the stress on achievement and mental ability as indicators of giftedness at the expense of the characteristics just mentioned. One is the historical emphasis on IQ. Another is educators' unfamiliarity with ways of measuring human characteristics other than by standardized tests. A third reason is a general ignorance of characteristics that are more highly valued by the minority culture than by the majority culture. Members of many Native American tribes, for example, place as much value on a child's knowledge of tribal traditions, storytelling ability, and artistic ability as they do on problem-solving ability and scientific reasoning (Tonemah, 1987). A child's giftedness may therefore be evident in such "unmeasurable" skills.

Other methods of identifying gifted and talented children (whether from a minority or from the majority) include nominations from peers, community leaders, and the students themselves (in the form of biographical statements). Checklist and rating scales exist that include such characteristics as logical reasoning skills, interpersonal communication skills, ability to improvise with commonplace materials, use of expressive speech, and use of humor. Other types of standardized tests are also relevant, such as the Torrance Tests of Creative Thinking, the Raven Standard Progressive Matrices (a nonverbal test of inductive reasoning), and the Watson-Glaser Test of Critical Thinking (Baldwin, 1991; Frasier, 1987).

Characteristics of Gifted and Talented Students

> Gifted and talented students generally show average physical, social, emotional development

Gifted and talented individuals are often thought of as being significantly different from their age-mates. In some respects they are different, but in other respects they are not. Despite the popular conception of gifted children as physically inferior, socially inept, and emotionally underdeveloped, the evidence provides a different picture. On average, such students are physically, socially, and emotionally indistinguishable from the general student population. Some are healthy and well-coordinated, others are not; some are extremely popular and well-liked, others are not; some are well-adjusted, others are not (Piechowski, 1991; Ysseldyke & Algozzine, 1990).

Cognitively and academically, however, gifted and talented students are often noticeably different. Gifted students are quick to understand abstract concepts and to organize them into complex, efficient schemes. Hence they can understand and manipulate such abstract concepts as symbiosis, probability, and conservation. In addition, gifted students are quick to generalize their knowledge to new but related tasks and settings.

Some gifted students think in orthodox ways. Given some information and a problem, they excel at coming up with the one correct answer. In terms of J. P. Guilford's (1967) description of intellectual operations, such students might be classified as extremely competent *convergent* thinkers. When teachers are asked to nominate the most capable students in their classes, they tend to choose children of this type. They are likely to become successful doctors, lawyers, professors, and business people, but they are not likely to make original contributions in their fields. Other gifted learners do *not* respond to instruction in expected ways. Instead, they often respond to questions and problems in unorthodox or unsettling ways, and perhaps give the impression that they are

| Some rapid learners convergent thinkers, others divergent thinkers

When planning instructional experiences for gifted and talented students, it may help to make a distinction between convergent *and* divergent *types. Albert Einstein, for example, was regarded as incapable of learning by most of his teachers. He may have given that impression because of his unorthodox approach to many things. This photo, for instance, shows him recording a formula at a conference of scientists. He never explained what it meant and his colleagues were unable to figure out its significance.* (UPI/Bettman Newsphotos)

uncooperative or disruptive. Many pupils of this type might be classified as brilliant *divergent* thinkers.

Gifted and talented students do not necessarily excel in all academic areas. They usually perform very well on measures of reading, social studies, and science, but their performance on mathematics tests are only at or slightly above grade level (Ysseldyke & Algozzine, 1990).

Accelerated Instruction: Pros and Cons

Gifted and talented students, whether convergent thinkers or divergent thinkers, constantly challenge a teacher's skill, ingenuity, and classroom resources. While trying to teach the class as a whole, the teacher is faced with the need to provide more and more interesting and challenging materials and ideas to the gifted student. Accelerated instruction is often suggested as a solution to this problem. For many people, the phrase *accelerated instruction* means allowing the student to skip one or more grades, which often happens. But there are at least three other ways of accomplishing the same goal. The curriculum can be compressed, allowing gifted and talented students to complete the work for more than one grade during the regular school year; the school year can be extended by the use of summer sessions; and students can take college courses while still in high school.

Whether or not gifted and talented children should be accelerated through the grades has been hotly debated for decades. Those who support the practice offer the following arguments:

1. In the case of grade skipping, the challenge of working with older, equally bright students on complex tasks keeps gifted students from becoming bored with school.

2. Schoolwork that matches the student's abilities produces more positive attitudes toward learning and subject matter.

3. By completing their education sooner, gifted and talented individuals can begin contributing to their chosen occupations sooner. (Benbow, 1991; Kulik & Kulik, 1984)

Those who oppose accelerated instruction make the following points:

1. A gifted and talented child may be able to handle the intellectual demands of acceleration but may have trouble with the social and emotional demands.

2. It is difficult to predict whether acceleration will benefit or create problems for a given student.

3. Less talented students of the same age lose the positive role model that a gifted student provides.

4. Acceleration produces an undesirable sense of elitism among gifted students. (Kulik & Kulik, 1984)

The research findings on accelerated instruction shed light on some, but not all, of these issues. A review of research by James A. Kulik and Chen-Lin Kulik (1984) found that gifted and talented pupils who were accelerated into higher grades performed as well as their talented older grade-mates on standardized achievement tests. In addition, the test scores of accelerated students were almost one grade level higher than the scores of nonaccelerated gifted age-mates. The Kuliks also reviewed research on acceleration's effect on nonintellectual outcomes—for example, attitudes toward school and school subjects, popularity, and adjustment. Because few studies have looked at these outcomes and because the results varied considerably from one study to another, the Kuliks drew no conclusions.

Once gifted and talented students reach adolescence, an alternative to accelerated instruction may be available. Many school districts contain either public or private high schools in which the average level of ability is higher than is the case in a general high school. In addition, many states sponsor high-ability high schools, particularly in mathematics and science. Recent findings do not support this approach, however. Herbert W. Marsh (1991) analyzed the effect of higher-ability and lower-ability high schools on the performance of more than 14,000 students during their sophomore year, senior year, and two years after high school graduation. He found that "on average, equally able students attending higher-ability high schools were likely to select less demanding coursework and to have lower academic self-concepts, lower GPAs, lower educational aspirations, and lower occupational aspirations in both their sophomore and senior years of high school" (p. 470).

Suggestions for Teaching in Your Classroom

INSTRUCTING GIFTED AND TALENTED STUDENTS

1. Provide horizontal or vertical enrichment.
2. Consult with gifted and talented students regarding individual study projects, perhaps involving a learning contract.
3. Encourage supplementary reading and writing.
4. Foster the development of creative hobbies and interests.
5. Check into the possibility of correspondence courses or tutoring.
6. Perhaps experiment with having gifted students act as tutors.

1. Provide horizontal or vertical enrichment.

Most discussions of enrichment techniques distinguish between horizontal and vertical enrichment. **Horizontal enrichment** consists of giving a rapid learner who has finished an assignment before the rest of the class more material at the same general level of difficulty. **Vertical enrichment** involves giving more advanced work of the same general type. Take a math period as an example. Assume that you have started the class on a workbook assignment in math. About the time you get your pencil sharpened and turn around to start giving individual help, you bump into a girl with an IQ score of 146 who has come up to announce that she has finished and to ask what you would like her to do next. One reaction is to say, "Go back to your seat and do the next five pages of problems." If these problems are at the same level of difficulty, that's horizontal enrichment. If the forest of waving hands signaling the need for special help induces panic, a vertical enrichment assignment may be forthcoming: "Why don't you read the next chapter and see how well you can handle the problems we are going to take up next month."

These examples emphasize the pitfalls of literal horizontal or vertical enrichment. If you assign the fast workers more of the same, it won't take them long to figure out that there is little point in making much of an effort. This can ruin motivation, destroy the ability to concentrate, and squelch interest. On the other hand, if you urge gifted students to take off on their own, what will happen when you reach next month's problems? The more often you resort to vertical enrichment assignments that simply anticipate what is to come, the bigger the problem becomes. Before long you are rummaging around the storeroom for next year's text. And that can *really* lead to a mess when the clear innocent voice pipes up to announce to the teacher of the next higher grade that she's already finished the standard text that Mr. or Ms. So-and-So gave to her.

To avoid such unpleasantness, use some discretion in applying horizontal and vertical enrichment. Don't let an assignment of more of the same seem like a punishment. If the skill in question is not likely to be improved substantially by more repetition (for example, problems in addition), find some related exercises of equivalent difficulty (perhaps a book of math "puzzlers"). In reading classes, permit superior pupils to read several other books at the same level of difficulty, instead of stultifying them with an additional dose of primer material. In high school classes, keep on hand some optional extra assignments for the fast workers.

If you choose to give an assignment at a more advanced level, take care not to anticipate what is to be covered in ensuing semesters and years. Try to obtain curriculum materials that will supplement, not duplicate, the standard curriculum. A series of books from a different publisher is the most logical source of such materials, and most school districts have consultants who can help you obtain what you need. In any event, it pays to do some planning. Trying to take care of enrichment problems by tossing spur-of-the-moment instructions over your shoulder as you dash off to provide remedial help for less talented students is ineffective at best and, at worst, potentially disastrous.

2. Consult with gifted and talented students regarding individual study projects, perhaps involving a learning contract.

Handbook Heading:
Individual Study for the
Gifted and Talented

One of the most effective ways to provide enrichment when straight horizontal or vertical techniques fail to fill the gap is by assigning individual study projects. These assignments should probably be related to some part of the curriculum. If you are studying Mexico, for example, a gifted pupil could devote free time to a special report on some aspect of Mexican life that intrigues her or him.

To provide another variation of the individual study project, you could ask the gifted student to act as a research specialist and report on questions that puzzle the class. An incident in a third-grade classroom illustrates this technique. A child asked about sponges and triggered a whole series of related questions that the teacher couldn't answer. There happened to be a boy with an IQ score of 150 in this class, and he agreed to spend his reading period with the encyclopedia and to give a report on sponges the next day.

Still another individual study project is the creation of an open-ended, personal yearbook. Any time a gifted pupil finishes the assigned work, he or she might be allowed to write stories or do drawings for such a journal. When possible, though, unobtrusive projects are preferable. Perhaps you can recall a teacher who rewarded the fast workers by letting them work on a mural (or the equivalent) covering the side board. If you were an average student, you can probably attest that the sight of the class "brains" having the time of their lives was not conducive to diligent effort on the part of the have-nots sweating away at their workbooks. Reward assignments should probably be restricted to individual work on unostentatious projects.

Another way to set up independent study projects is to use the contract approach (to be described more completely in Chapters 8 and 14). Consult with pupils on an individual basis and agree on a personal assignment that is to be completed by a certain date. One point to keep in mind about a contract approach is that this technique may be one of the best ways to accommodate the characteristics of gifted and talented students. If highly capable students are urged to really come to grips with a topic, seek out relationships, organize ideas, and apply them, they are likely to gain maximum benefit from their learning efforts. Another point to remember, though, is that even very bright pupils may not be able to absorb, organize, and apply abstract concepts until they become formal thinkers. Up until sixth grade or so, it may be more preferable to ask bright pupils to carry out a series of brief assignments than to attempt a comprehensive independent project.

3. Encourage supplementary reading and writing.

A common enough complaint about modern American education is that pupils don't do enough reading and writing. At any grade level, an excellent enrichment goal is to try to remedy relative illiteracy. Encourage the capable students to spend extra time reading and writing. A logical method of combining both skills

Gifted students should be encouraged and helped by their teachers to develop creative hobbies and to pursue interests in particular subjects. (Loren Santow/ Tony Stone Worldwide)

is the preparation of book reports. It is perhaps less threatening to call them book *reviews* and emphasize that you are interested in personal reaction, not in a precis or abstract. Some specialists in the education of the gifted have suggested that such students be urged to read biographies and autobiographies. Their line of reasoning is that potential leaders might be inspired to emulate the exploits of a famous person. Even if such inspiration does not result, you could recommend life stories simply because they are usually interesting.

4. Foster the development of creative hobbies and interests.

Handbook Heading:
Urging Gifted Students
to Develop Creative
Hobbies and Interests

At the elementary level, a gifted student might devote spare class time to the intensive development of a hobby. If the pupil has an interest in poetry or rocks or butterflies, encouragement from you may lead to future specialization.

At the secondary level, pupils who are gifted in your particular subject might be urged to spend time writing a paper for an essay contest, building a science fair project, or sewing a dress or making a piece of furniture to be entered in the county fair. A related point is that you should help high school seniors who are talented in your field to apply for scholarships. Some schools—and teachers—place winners each year, basically because they take the trouble to assist logical candidates.

5. Check into the possibility of correspondence courses or tutoring.

In small school districts, one or two brilliant children are occasionally found to have IQ scores several dozen points higher than those of other above-average pupils. One way to provide for them is tutorial instruction. In some cases, this is given by a principal or a teacher with released time. Because of the expense, however, the solution is more likely to be a correspondence course. A combination of these two techniques, called the Sponsor-Correspondent Plan, has met with a good deal of success. It establishes a liaison between a brilliant pupil and someone with training and experience in the area of that pupil's greatest interest. Often the person who serves as a sponsor is a retired expert in the field.

Suppose a brilliant boy in a small high school is fascinated by inorganic chemistry. Because of his intellect and his single-minded drive, he learns more about the subject than is known by his teacher—who also teaches three other subjects. The teacher asks a university or professional organization if it knows of, say, a retired inorganic chemist who might enjoy assisting a young enthusiast. If such a person is found, the sponsor and the pupil correspond with each other and, as often as circumstances permit, have personal conferences. Highly successful experiences with this technique have been reported. If you find yourself teaching in a small school and are bedeviled by an incipient Einstein, it could be your salvation.

6. Perhaps experiment with having gifted students act as tutors.

Depending on the grade, subject, and personalities of those involved, gifted pupils might be asked to act occasionally as tutors, lab assistants, or the equivalent. Some bright students will welcome such opportunities and are capable of providing instruction in such a way that their peers do not feel self-conscious or humiliated. Others, however, may resent being asked to spend school time helping classmates and/or may lack skills in interpersonal relationships. If you do decide to ask a gifted student to function as a tutor, therefore, it would be wise to proceed tentatively and cautiously.

Resources for Further Investigation

Ability Grouping

Additional discussions of the merits and effects of ability grouping can be found in *Handicapping the Handicapped* (1986, pp. 16–23) by Hugh Mehan, Alma Hertweck, and J. Lee Meihls, and in *Classroom Composition and Pupil Achievement* (1986) by Yehezkel Dar and Nura Resh. An alternative to ability grouping, *mixed ability teaching,* is discussed by Margaret I. Reid, Louise R. Clunies-Ross, Brian Goacher, and Carol Vile in *Mixed Ability Teaching: Problems and Possibilities* (1981) and by John Evans in *Teaching in Transition: The Challenge of Mixed Ability Grouping* (1985). Legal aspects of ability grouping are discussed by Joseph Bryson and Charles Bentley in *Ability Grouping of Public School Students* (1980).

Texts on the Education of Exceptional Children

The following books provide general coverage of the education of exceptional children: *Educating Exceptional Children* (7th ed., 1993) by Samuel A. Kirk and James J. Gallagher, *Introduction to Special Education* (2d ed., 1990) by James E. Ysseldyke and Bob Algozzine, and *Educating Special Learners* (3d ed., 1989) by G. P. Cartwright, C. A. Cartwright, and M. E. Ward.

Books with Emphasis on Teaching Techniques

For information about teaching techniques that can be used with various types of exceptional pupils, consult one or more of the following: *Structured Experiences for Integration of Handicapped Children* (1983) by Karen Anderson and A. Milliren; *Educating Young Handicapped Children: A Developmental Approach* (2d ed., 1983), edited by S. Gray Garwood; and *Teaching Students with Learning and Behavior Problems* (2d ed., 1989) by Deborah Deutsch Smith. The Smith book is divided into three parts. Part One describes general teaching and classroom skills that all teachers of special students should possess. Part Two presents techniques for managing disruptive behavior and teaching appropriate social skills. And Part Three describes techniques for improving reading, writing, mathematics, and study skills.

Teaching Students with Mental Retardation

Specialized techniques for teaching the mentally retarded can be applied, in many cases, to teaching mildly retarded pupils in regular classrooms. The following books provide suggestions: *Educating Mentally Retarded Persons in the Mainstream* (1980), edited by Jay Gottlieb; and *Intelligence, Mental Retardation, and the Culturally Different Child: A Practitioner's Guide* (1984) by John L. Manni and David W. Winikur.

Learning Disabilities

The following books provide information about the diagnosis and remediation of learning disabilities: *Educating the Learning Disabled* (1982) by E. Siegel and R. Gold, *Learning Disabilities* (6th ed., 1993) by Janet Lerner, *Teaching Students with Learning Problems* (2d ed., 1985) by Cecil D. Mercer and Ann R. Mercer, and *Developmental and Academic Learning Disabilities* (1984) by S. Kirk and J. Chalfant.

Teaching Gifted and Talented Learners

These books describe various techniques to use in instructing gifted and talented learners: *Handbook of Instructional Resources and References for Teaching the*

Gifted (1980) by F. Karnes and E. Collins, *Curriculum Development for the Gifted* (1982) by C. Marker, and *Teaching the Gifted Child* (3d ed., 1988) by James Gallagher.

SUMMARY

1. Two early attempts at dealing with pupil variability were ability grouping and special class placement. Ability grouping sorted normal students into separate classes according to mental ability test scores, whereas special class placement was used to separate normal students from those with mental and physical disabilities.

2. The four currently popular approaches to ability grouping are between-class ability grouping, regrouping, the Joplin Plan, and within-class ability grouping.

3. There is no research support for between-class ability grouping and limited support for regrouping. Moderately positive results have been found for the Joplin Plan as well as within-class ability grouping.

4. Ability grouping, particularly between-class ability grouping, and the IQ tests used to assign students to groups have been criticized as unfairly discriminating against minority groups.

5. The Education for All Handicapped Children Act (Public Law 94-142) was enacted in 1975 to ensure that students with handicapping conditions receive the same free and appropriate education as nonhandicapped students.

6. Major provisions of PL 94-142 include the development of an individualized education program, due process, protection in evaluation procedures, and the least restrictive environment (also known as mainstreaming).

7. The Handicapped Children's Protection Act (PL 99-457) extends the basic provisions of PL 94-142 to preschoolers and provides funds to states that wish to initiate early intervention programs aimed at infants and toddlers.

8. The Individuals with Disabilities Education Act (PL 101-476) provides services to help adolescents with disabilities make the transition from high school to work, higher education, or independent living.

9. Students who are speech or language impaired, learning disabled, or visually handicapped are most likely to attend regular classes.

10. The regular classroom teacher's responsibilities under PL 94-142 may include participation in referral, assessment, preparation of the IEP, and implementation of the IEP.

11. Children with mild mental retardation are likely to be mainstreamed for some part of the school day and week. They are likely to have a low tolerance for frustration, to lack confidence and self-esteem, to oversimplify matters, and to have difficulty generalizing from one situation to another.

12. Students with learning disabilities have a disorder in one or more basic psychological processes, which leads to learning problems not attributable to other causes.

13. Recent evidence suggests that many children are mislabeled as learning disabled because of inappropriate assessment procedures and poor-quality tests.

14. The true number of emotionally disturbed schoolchildren is unknown because of variation in identification procedures, vague definitions of emotional disturbance, and differences in interpretation of definitions.

15. Most classifications of disturbed behavior focus on aggressive behavior or withdrawn behavior.

16. Gifted and talented students are highly capable in performing tasks that require intellectual, creative, artistic, or leadership ability.

17. Minorities are underrepresented in gifted and talented classes because standardized test scores are emphasized at the expense of other indices such as creativity, leadership, communication skill, critical-thinking ability, and persistence.

KEY TERMS

between-class ability grouping *(184)*
regrouping *(184)*
Joplin Plan *(184)*
within-class ability grouping *(184)*
individualized education program (IEP) *(188)*
least restrictive environment *(189)*
mainstreaming *(189)*
due process *(189)*
interdisciplinary assessment team *(198)*
mental retardation *(201)*
learning disabilities *(207)*
emotional disturbance *(214)*
behavior disorders *(215)*
gifted and talented *(222)*
horizontal enrichment *(227)*
vertical enrichment *(227)*

DISCUSSION QUESTIONS

1. You yourself probably experienced ability grouping, in one form or another, at the elementary and secondary levels. Try to recall the ability grouping used in your schools. Think about whether it might have been between-class grouping, regrouping, the Joplin Plan, or within-class grouping. Could you tell which group you were in? Did you have feelings about being in that group? How did you feel about classmates who were in other groups? Do you think this practice aided or hindered your educational progress? Why? Given your own experiences as a student and what you have learned from this chapter, would you advocate or employ some form of ability grouping for your own students someday?

2. Many regular classroom teachers say that while they agree with the philosophy behind PL 94-142, they feel that their training has not adequately prepared them for meeting the needs of students with disabling conditions. Would you say the same about your teacher education program? Why? If you feel that your training is not adequately equipping you to teach mentally retarded, learning disabled, and emotionally disturbed students, what might you do to prepare yourself better?

3. Relatively little money is spent on programs for the gifted and talented compared to the amounts made available for the disabled. Defenders of this arrangement sometimes argue that since money for educational programs is always short, and since gifted students have a built-in advantage rather than a disability, we *should* invest most of our resources in programs and services for the disabled. Do you agree or disagree? Explain why.

Chapter 6
UNDERSTANDING CULTURAL DIVERSITY

MULTICULTURAL EDUCATION PROGRAMS

▷ Multicultural education can be approached in different ways

▷ Peer tutoring improves achievement, interpersonal relationships, attitudes toward subjects

▷ Cooperative learning: students work together in small groups

▷ Cooperative learning fosters better understanding among ethnically diverse students

▷ Mastery learning: all students can master the curriculum

▷ Minority children score lower on tests, drop out of school sooner

▷ Minority drop-out rate due to alienation, differences in values, poverty

BILINGUAL EDUCATION PROGRAMS

▷ Two main approaches to bilingual education: transition, maintenance

▷ Transition programs focus on rapid shift to English proficiency

▷ Maintenance programs focus on maintaining native-language competence

▷ Bilingual education programs produce moderate learning gains

In the introduction to Chapter 2, we pointed out that if your instructional plans are to be effective, they need to take into account what your students are like. (The term *entering behavior* was used to refer to the characteristics students bring with them to class.) In Chapters 2 and 3 we described students in terms of their age-related differences in psychosocial, cognitive, and moral development, and how students typically are similar to and different from one another in terms of physical, social, emotional, and cognitive characteristics. In Chapter 4 we discussed individual differences in intelligence, and in

Chapter 5 we described several categories of exceptionality. Now, in this chapter, we turn to another important way that students differ—cultural background.

Culture is a term that is used to describe how a group of people perceives the world; formulates beliefs; evaluates objects, ideas, and experiences; and behaves. It can be thought of as a blueprint that guides the ways in which individuals within a group do such important things as communicate with others (both verbally and nonverbally), handle time and space, express emotions, and approach work and play. The concept of culture typically includes ethnic status but can also encompass religious beliefs and socioeconomic status (Gollnick & Chinn, 1990).

Different groups of people will, of course, vary in their beliefs, attitudes, values, and behavior patterns because of differences in cultural norms. (By *norms* we mean the perceptions, beliefs, and behaviors that characterize most members of a group.) People who were raised with mainstream American values, for example, find acceptable the practice of adults gently patting children on the head but find unacceptable the practice of two boys holding hands. Most Vietnamese, on the other hand, disapprove of the former but not the latter (Sadker & Sadker, 1991).

To provide the appropriate classroom and school conditions that will help your students from different cultural backgrounds to master a common curriculum, you must come to understand and take into account your students' differing cultural backgrounds. For example, a culturally aware teacher will emphasize the way in which American society has been enriched by the contributions of many different ethnic groups (and place special emphasis on those ethnic groups to which the students belong), will not schedule a major exam or field trip for a day when certain students are likely to be out of school in observance of a religious holiday, and will not consider a newly arrived Asian student to be evasive just because he or she does not maintain direct eye contact while being questioned.

The approach to teaching and learning that we will describe in this chapter, one that seeks to foster an understanding of and mutual respect for the values, beliefs, and practices of different cultural groups, is typically referred to as **multicultural education.** In the next section we will examine some of the main reasons behind the rise in cultural pluralism and multicultural education.

THE RISE OF MULTICULTURALISM

From Melting Pot to Cultural Pluralism

More than most other countries, the United States is made up of numerous ethnic groups of widely diverse histories, cultural backgrounds, and values. In addition to the hundreds of thousands of African-Americans who came to the United States as slaves, the United States was peopled by many waves of immigrants, mostly from Europe but also from Asia and Latin America. Throughout the eighteenth

TABLE 6.1   Immigrants to the United States

Immigration Totals by Decade			
Years	*Number*	*Years*	*Number*
1820–1830	151,824	1911–1920	5,735,811
1831–1840	599,125	1921–1930	4,107,209
1841–1850	1,713,251	1931–1940	528,431
1851–1860	2,598,214	1941–1950	1,035,039
1861–1870	2,314,824	1951–1960	2,515,479
1871–1880	2,812,191	1961–1970	3,321,677
1881–1890	5,246,613	1971–1980	4,493,000
1891–1900	3,687,546	1981–1990 (projected)	8,500,000
1901–1910	8,795,386	Total	58,155,620

Source: *U.S. Bureau of the Census,* Historical Statistics of the United States, Colonial Times to 1970 (1975); *U.S. Bureau of the Census.* Statistical Abstract of the United States, 1988 (1987).

and nineteenth centuries, the United States needed large numbers of people to settle its western frontier, build its railroads, harvest its natural resources, and work in its growing factories. As Table 6.1 indicates, between 1820 and 1920 approximately 33 million people immigrated to the United States.

Throughout this period, the basic view of American society toward immigrants was that they should divest themselves of their old customs, views, allegiances, and rivalries as soon as possible and adopt English as their primary language along with mainstream American ideals, values, and customs. This assimilation of diverse ethnic groups into one national mainstream was known as the **melting pot,** a term and viewpoint that were popularized in a 1909 play by Israel Zangwill called *The Melting Pot.* The main institution responsible for bringing about this assimilation was the public school (Levine & Havighurst, 1992).

The notion of America as a great melting pot was generally accepted until the social unrest of the late 1960s and early 1970s. As an outgrowth of urban riots and the civil rights movement, minority ethnic groups argued not only for bilingual education programs in public schools, but also for ethnic studies. It might be said that many American citizens realized that they did not wish to fit the white Anglo-Saxon Protestant mold of a "traditional American" and began to express a desire to be Americans who have different characteristics. Michael Novak (1971) has referred to this movement as the "rise of the unmeltable ethnics." Since the early 1970s factors such as discrimination, the desire to maintain culturally specific ideas and practices, and continued immigration from different parts of the world have served to maintain, if not accelerate, this trend toward cultural diversity (or *cultural pluralism,* to use the preferred term).

The Changing Face of the United States

Given recent changes in birth rates and immigration patterns and population projections for the next 30 to 50 years, one could argue that the decline of the melting pot philosophy and the rise of cultural pluralism and multicultural education will only accelerate in the years ahead. Consider, for example, the following statistics.

Between 1981 and 1986, 89 percent of legal immigrants to the United States came from non-European countries. Most of these immigrants came from Asia (principally the Philippine Islands, Korea, and China) and the Americas (principally Mexico and Cuba) and settled in the major cities of California, New York, Texas, and Florida. Estimates are that in the ten-year period 1981–1990, almost 9 million legal immigrants arrived in the United States. If this estimate proves accurate, it will virtually match the all-time immigration record of 1901–1910. Immigrant mothers bore 10 percent of all babies born in the United States in 1986. Native-born women in 1986 averaged 67.5 births per 1,000, while foreign-born women averaged 98.9 per 1,000 (Banks, 1991; Bennett, 1990; Kellogg, 1988).

▶ U.S. becoming more culturally diverse because of changes in immigration, birth rates

Between 1982 and 2020 the number of white non-Hispanic-American children from birth through age seventeen is expected to decline by 13 percent whereas the number of Hispanic-American children is expected to triple, increasing from 5.9 million in 1982 to 18.6 million in 2020. At that point, one child out of every four through age seventeen will be of Hispanic-American origin. The population of African-American youth under age eighteen is expected to grow

Multicultural education programs have become more widespread because changing immigration patterns and birth rates have made the United States a more culturally diverse nation. (Bob Daemmrich/ Tony Stone Worldwide)

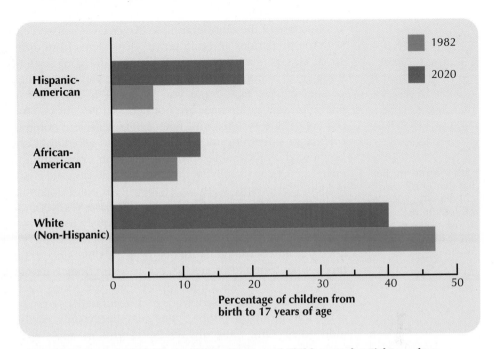

FIGURE 6.1   Projected Change in Percentage of Children under Eighteen from Three Ethnic Groups Between 1982 and 2020 (Source: Adapted from Pallas, Natriello & McDill, 1989.)

from 9.3 million in 1982 to 11.9 million in 2020, an increase of 28 percent. By 2020, African-American youth should account for approximately 16 percent of the school-age population (see Figure 6.1). And by the year 2050, Asians are expected to increase their representation in the general population from 1.6 percent to 10 percent. In general, the proportion of white school-age children is projected to decline from 73 percent in 1982 to 55 percent in 2020 (Pallas, Natriello & McDill, 1989). As these figures make clear, the United States is rapidly on its way to becoming an even more ethically diverse nation than ever before.

TAKING ACCOUNT OF YOUR STUDENTS' CULTURAL DIFFERENCES

▶ Culture: how a group of people perceive, believe, think, behave

As we pointed out in the opening paragraphs of this chapter, culture refers to the way in which a group of people perceives, thinks about, and interacts with the world. It is a way of giving meaning to experiences. As Donna M. Gollnick and Philip C. Chinn (1990) put it, "Culture gives us a certain lifestyle that is peculiarly our own. It becomes so peculiar to us that someone from a different culture can easily identify us as Americans" (p. 7). Two significant factors that most readily distinguish one culture from another are ethnicity and social class.

Because of the demographic changes we discussed earlier, becoming familiar with the similarities and differences of students from different ethnic groups and social classes is a necessity. But for you and your students to benefit from your knowledge of cultural diversity, it must be viewed in the proper perspective. The perspective we encourage you to adopt is a twofold one. First, you should recognize that differences are not necessarily deficits. Students who subscribe to different value systems and who exhibit different communication patterns, time orientations, learning modes, motives, and aspirations should not automatically be viewed as incapable students. Looking upon ethnic and social class differences as deficits usually stems from an attitude called *ethnocentrism.* This is the tendency of people to think of their own culture as superior to the culture of other groups. You may be able to moderate your ethnocentric tendencies and motivate your students to learn by consciously using instructional tactics that are congruent with the different cultural backgrounds of your students. It is also advisable to encourage students to be flexible since there will undoubtedly be times when your approach is not to everybody's liking. Second, note that in characterizing various ethnic groups we use terms such as *many, some,* and *probably.* While our descriptions may accurately portray some general tendencies of a large group of people, they may apply only partly or not at all to given individuals. One must always be careful in applying general knowledge to particular cases. The Mexican-American high school student who vehemently opposes abortion, for example, may do so more because of his or her Roman Catholic faith than because of cultural values concerning family relationships (Chinn & Plata, 1987/1988).

Ethnocentrism: Belief that one's own culture is superior to other cultures

The Effect of Ethnicity on Learning

An **ethnic group** is a collection of people who identify with one another on the basis of one or more of the following characteristics: country from which one's ancestors came, race, religion, language, values, political interests, economic interests, and behavior patterns (Banks, 1991; Gollnick & Chinn, 1990). Viewed separately, the ethnic groups in the United States, particularly those of color, are numerical minorities; collectively, however, they constitute a significant portion of American society (Banks, 1991). Most Americans identify with some ethnic group (for example, Irish-Americans, German-Americans, Italian-Americans, African-Americans, Chinese-Americans, and Hispanic-Americans, to name but a few). As a teacher you need to know how your students' ethnicity can affect student-teacher relationships. Christine Bennett (1990) identified five aspects of ethnicity that are potential sources of student-student and student-teacher misunderstanding: verbal communication, nonverbal communication, orientation modes, social value patterns, and intellectual modes.

Problems with verbal communication can occur in a number of ways. Children for whom English is a second language may not hear or accurately discriminate between certain speech sounds. Many African-American students are perceived as uneducated or less intelligent for no other reason than that they speak nonstandard English. Classroom discussions may not go as planned if teachers have students who do not understand or find confining the mainstream convention of "you-take-a-turn-then-somebody-else-takes-a-turn." Because of differences in cultural experiences, some students may be very reluctant to speak or perform in public whereas others may prefer exchanges that resemble a free-for-all shouting match. Some Native American children, for example, prefer to work on ideas and skills in private. A public performance is given only after an acceptable degree of mastery is attained (Bennett, 1990; Vasquez, 1990). This last practice is not as unique to Native American culture as it might seem at first glance. Music lessons and practices are typically done in private, and public performances are not given until a piece or program is mastered.

▶ Ethnic group members differ in verbal and nonverbal communication patterns

A form of nonverbal communication that is highly valued by mainstream American culture is direct eye contact. Most people are taught to look directly at the person to whom they are speaking, as this behavior signifies honesty on the part of the speaker and interest on the part of the listener. Among certain Native American and Asian cultures, however, averting one's eyes is a sign of deference to and respect for the other person. Thus, an Asian or Native American student who looks down or away when being questioned about something is not necessarily trying to hide guilt or ignorance or to communicate disinterest (Bennett, 1990).

Mainstream American culture is very time oriented. People who know how to organize their time and work efficiently are praised and rewarded. We teach our children to value such statements as "Time is money" and "Never put off until tomorrow what you can accomplish today." Nowhere is this time orientation more evident than in our schools. Classes begin and end at a specified time regardless of whether one is interested in starting a project, pursuing a discussion, or finishing an experiment. But for students whose ethnic cultures are not so time-bound (Hispanic-Americans and Native Americans, for example), such a rigid approach to learning may be upsetting. Indeed, it may also be upsetting to some students who reflect the mainstream culture (Bennett, 1990).

▶ Ethnic group members may hold different values

Two values that lie at the heart of mainstream American society are competition ("Competition brings out the best in people") and rugged individualism ("People's accomplishments should reflect their own efforts"). Since schools tend to reflect mainstream beliefs, many classroom activities are competitive and done on one's own for one's personal benefit. Mexican-American students, however, are more likely to have been taught to value cooperative relationships and family loyalty. These students may thus prefer group projects; they may also respond more positively to praise that emphasizes family pride rather than individual glory (Bennett, 1990; Vasquez, 1990). You might want to make a note to refer back to this point when you read Chapter 12 ("Motivation"). In that chapter we review research that supports the superiority of cooperative learning over competitive arrangements for a variety of achievement, attitude, and interpersonal relationship outcomes.

Finally, ethnic groups may differ in terms of the value they place on different types of knowledge and the learning modes they prefer. Some groups may place a higher value on spiritual knowledge than on scientific knowledge; others may be more attracted to practical knowledge than to theoretical knowledge. Students who have adopted mainstream American values tend to favor a learning mode that is based on logical analysis of the written word. Other cultures (African-American, Native American, and rural white, for example) favor an aural/oral mode. Christine Bennett (1990) found that many African-American and Mexican-American eighth-graders in Texas could better understand their United States history text if they listened to a tape of the text while they read it. Many white students, by contrast, preferred to read the text without listening to the tape. In the Appalachian mountain states of the American Southeast, many traditional folk songs were never written down but were passed orally from one person to another. And it has been said that some African-Americans, because of socialization patterns, have a person-centered approach to learning. Not only do they prefer working with other people, but they prefer tasks that are set in the context of people dealing with one another. For example, they might prefer learning math concepts by reading about or listening to descriptions of people buying, trading, or borrowing things. In addition, some researchers have found that many Native Americans prefer deductively oriented rather than inductively oriented lessons. That is, they perform better when lessons begin with an overview and proceed to an examination of the parts, as opposed to an approach that stresses the details first and then draws general conclusions (Bennett, 1990; Vasquez, 1990).

> Ethnic group members may favor different learning modes

Emily Comstock DiMartino (1989), a teacher educator at Baruch College of the City University of New York, provides an illuminating example of how other people's cultural practices can differ markedly from those of mainstream America. She spent a month in the small (3,000-inhabitant) rural Sicilian town of Licodia Eubea. One difference she noticed was the primacy of the family. Children were expected to attend all adult family gatherings, which typically included aunts, uncles, and cousins, even if it meant a school assignment would go uncompleted. A second difference concerned attitudes toward time. One was simply not expected to be somewhere or other at a particular time. If, for example, children returned to the house from play an hour later than expected, no one noticed or said anything. Similarly, promptness at school and church was not insisted upon. A third difference concerned sex role variations. In one family, a bicycle had to be shared by a sister (who was older) and a brother. The sister was allowed to use the bike only when the brother was not using it, and then only after securing his permission. In another family, a younger sister was expected to make her older brother's bed every morning as well as her own, clean up the kitchen, and start dinner. The final difference noted by DiMartino was one that she called *being* versus *becoming*. Most Americans in her view are always trying to improve some aspect of themselves—from the way they look to their basic nature. Licodians, on the other hand, are more apt to accept themselves and others as they are. If someone is overweight or self-centered or a good speaker, that characteristic is seen as part of the person's nature and he or she is simply accepted as such.

The Effect of Social Class on Learning

In the previous section we pointed out how ethnic background can influence a student's values and behavior. The social class from which a student comes plays an influential role as well. **Social class** is an indicator of an individual's or family's relative standing in society. It is determined by such factors as annual income, occupation, amount of education, place of residence, types of organizations to which family members belong, manner of dress, and material possessions. The first three factors are used by the federal government to determine the closely related concept of socioeconomic status. The influence of social class is such that the members of working-class Hispanic-American and Irish-American families may have more in common than the members of an upper-middle-class Hispanic-American family and those of a working-class Hispanic-American family (Gollnick & Chinn, 1990).

Because of the severe and long-lasting historic pattern of unfair discrimination experienced by ethnic groups of color in the United States, many members of these groups have fewer years of education, a less prestigious occupation, and a lower income than the average white person. Significantly more African-American, Hispanic-American, and Native American adolescents drop out of high school than do whites, thereby shortening their years of education. And because they have less education, people of color are more likely to be unemployed or working in such low-paying occupations as office clerk, private house cleaner, and manual laborer. In 1986, the median income of African-American and Hispanic-American families was $17,604 and $19,995, respectively, as compared to a median income of $30,809 for white families. In the mid-1980s, moreover, 31 percent of all African-American families, 27.5 percent of all Native American families, and 27 percent of all Hispanic-American families lived below the poverty line (about $11,200 for a family of four) as compared to 9.4 percent of all white families (see Figure 6.2). These factors place many ethnic families of color either in the working class (consisting of so-called blue-collar workers) or in what is called the underclass (Gollnick & Chinn, 1990).

> Many ethnic families of color earn less than white families

Many lower-class students are also, at least potentially, at a disadvantage when it comes to classroom performance. For clarification of this point, consider the following review of some of the major factors that may have an adverse effect on the academic performance of low-income students.

> Lower-class children experience inferior health care

1. Many low-income Americans do not receive satisfactory health care. As a consequence, there is a greater incidence of premature births, birth defects, and infant mortality among lower-class children, as compared to middle-class children (as consistently revealed by National Institutes of Health statistics). Since poor children do not receive medical or dental care regularly, accurate statistics on general health are difficult to compile. It seems reasonable to assume, however, that the infant mortality rate, in particular, reflects a trend that probably continues in later years. In other words, lower-class children probably continue to suffer from untreated illnesses at a rate that may be at least twice that of middle-class children.

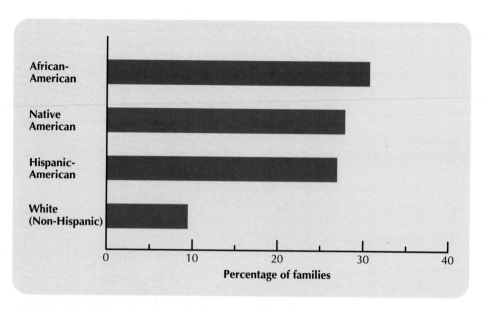

FIGURE 6.2   Percentage of Families Living Below Poverty Level in the Mid-1980s
(Source: Adapted from Pallas, Natriello & McDill, 1989.)

The lasting impact on disadvantaged children of inadequate prenatal care, prematurity, birth complications, and insufficient or absent treatment during the first months of postnatal existence was revealed in a study carried out by E. E. Werner, J. M. Bierman, and F. E. French (1971). These researchers studied the development of all 670 children born on the Hawaiian island of Kauai in 1955. Each newborn infant was rated on a scale reflecting severity of prenatal and birth complications. Later, the researchers made periodic assessments of physical health, intelligence, social maturity, and environmental variables. Werner and her colleagues found that most children from middle- and upper-income homes who were judged to have had a poor start because of prenatal or birth complications seemed to have overcome their early handicaps by the time they entered school. On intelligence tests, for instance, they scored only slightly below children from similar backgrounds who were judged to have had uneventful prenatal and birth experiences. By contrast, children from lower economic backgrounds who had experienced difficulties at the beginning of their lives seemed to remain at a disadvantage. They scored from 19 to 37 points lower on IQ tests than did children from similar backgrounds who were judged to have had normal prenatal and birth experiences. Based on this finding, as well as on other analyses of their data, Werner and her associates concluded that the single most important variable leading to retardation or aberrations in development among disadvantaged children is the poor environment in which they mature. This conclusion is supported by other research summarized by Arnold Sameroff and Michael J. Chandler (1975, pp. 205–210).

In comparison to students from middle- and upper-class families, students from lower-class families are more likely to receive inadequate health care, be raised by one parent, be less skilled in the use of language, have fewer experiences, be less motivated to do well in school, and have lower career aspirations. (1991 Peter Morgan/ Matrix.)

2. Disadvantaged students are more likely than middle-class students to grow up in one-parent families (the father usually being the missing parent). While some studies have shown that the presence of only one parent may be a major factor contributing to low achievement, other studies have failed to confirm this finding (Levine & Havighurst, 1992).

3. Many lower-class parents use forms of child care that work against their children's success in school. Upon observing mother-child interactions in lower-class homes, Robert D. Hess and Virginia Shipman (1965) found that the mothers were often inattentive and unresponsive to the child, used impoverished language, tended to lack self-confidence, were disorganized in the way they ran their homes, and quite frequently functioned at the preoperational stage of cognitive development. These aspects of child care are essentially the opposite of those that Diana Baumrind (1971) found were used by parents of highly competent children.

4. Both lower-class and middle-class children are adept at the language of ordinary conversation. Such interchanges are grammatically simple, utilize stereotyped expressions, do not communicate ideas or emotions precisely, and make heavy use of gesture and inflection to transmit meaning. This form of language is sometimes referred to as "public" or "restricted" language. On the other hand, lower-class children are much less proficient than middle-class children in their use of the "formal" or "elaborated" language of the classroom. Elaborated language is more precise in conveying meaning; it is also a more effective tool for

▶ Lower-class children more proficient with everyday language than with language of classroom

organizing experiences because it includes the bases for associations among ideas (Levine & Havighurst, 1992).

5. Disadvantaged children typically have not been exposed to a wide variety of experiences. The parents of middle-class children in the United States frequently function as teachers, although *tutors* would be a more appropriate word, since instruction is often given to one child at a time. Every time they talk to their children, answer questions, take them on trips, and buy books or educational toys, middle-class parents provide knowledge and experiences that accumulate to make school learning familiar and easy. A child who does not receive such continuous tutoring in the home is clearly at a disadvantage when placed in competitive academic situations (Levine & Havighurst, 1992).

▶ Disadvantaged children often lack motivation, academic skills

6. Disadvantaged pupils may not be strongly motivated to do well in school, and they may not be knowledgeable about techniques for becoming successful in school. Middle-class parents who have benefited in a variety of ways from education serve as effective and enthusiastic advocates of schooling. Because doing well in school paid off for them, they are eager to persuade their children to do well academically in order to achieve similar or greater benefits. They also serve as positive role models. By contrast, lower-class parents who did not do well may describe school in negative terms and perhaps blame teachers for their failure in classrooms as well as for their difficulties later in life. If the parents were inept students, they are also unable to tell their children about how to study for exams, meet requirements, select courses, or acquire the general all-around academic know-how that middle-class parents pass on to their offspring (Levine & Havighurst, 1992).

▶ Lower-class adolescents often have lower career aspirations

7. Lower-class adolescents typically have low career aspirations. The impact of social class on career choice was revealed by a comprehensive study (J. K. Little, 1967) of all the graduating seniors in Wisconsin's public and private high schools. At the time of graduation, the students were asked to note the occupations they hoped to enter. Their choices were later compared with the jobs they actually attained. Students in the lower third of their graduating class in socioeconomic status had significantly lower aspirations than those in the middle and upper thirds. In addition, the later actual job attainments of the lower-class students were closer to their expectations.

A lower-class student who has had a history of failure in school is understandably reluctant to risk further failure by working toward a remote, difficult-to-achieve vocational goal. Furthermore, parents may not offer much encouragement. R. L. Simpson (1962) found that high school students, regardless of social class, were likely to seek higher education and higher-level careers if their parents urged them to, but they were unlikely to do so if their parents were neutral or negative about preparation for a career. Lower-class parents who had dropped out of school and were later unable to find satisfying jobs—or any jobs at all—are less likely to urge their children to go to college than are middle-class parents who have discovered firsthand the employment value of a college degree.

8. In addition to having a low level of aspiration and a low need for achievement, disadvantaged pupils may feel role confusion and have poor self-esteem. As Erik Erikson has stressed, two key components of identity are acceptance by those who count and knowing where one is going. A disadvantaged adolescent who has no definite career plans after leaving school (with or without a diploma) is more likely to experience role confusion than a sense of identity achievement. If such an adolescent is unable to find a job (a common occurrence, given that the unemployment rate for minority-group youth is typically several times greater than the average rate for that age group), low self-esteem may contribute to the formation of a negative identity.

Using the following list of points as a framework, you will readily be able to draw up a list of general guidelines for teaching disadvantaged students.

Suggestions for Teaching in Your Classroom

INSTRUCTING DISADVANTAGED STUDENTS

1. Be alert to the potential dangers of labeling. Concentrate on individuals while guarding against the impact of stereotyping.

2. Allow for the possibility that disadvantaged students may have inadequate diets and may not receive adequate medical attention.

3. Remain aware that disadvantaged students may not be familiar with many things that you take for granted. Try to supply experiences that such students may have missed.

4. Use every possible means for motivating disadvantaged students to do well in school.

5. Give specific assignments, arrange for abundant practice, supply immediate feedback, and stress overlearning.

6. In the secondary grades, introduce topics in a concrete way; then have students develop their own learning materials, make observations, engage in role playing, and be active as they learn.

---

1. Be alert to the potential dangers of labeling. Concentrate on individuals while guarding against the impact of stereotyping.

Under certain circumstances, the potential dangers of labeling noted in the preceding chapter may lead to unfortunate consequences. The negative impact of labels can be minimized, however, if pupils are placed in categories primarily for the purpose of improving instruction or securing services. Instead of thinking that a disadvantaged student is beyond help, for example, you might ask yourself, "What kinds of disadvantages does this pupil need to overcome?" and also "What kinds of strengths does this student have?" By asking these questions, you concentrate on *individuals,* which is the surest way to avoid succumbing to the perils of stereotyping. It is reported that Samuel Johnson, the famous English literary figure, was once asked, "Are men more intelligent than women?" He replied, "Which man? Which woman?" If you think in the same way, you can avoid the error of assigning to individuals characteristics that are sometimes attributed to a group. For example, instead of searching for evidence to determine if African-Americans, on the average, exhibit more or less of a certain characteristic than whites, on the average, you should simply concentrate on the unique individual characteristics of a particular black or white student.

2. Allow for the possibility that disadvantaged students may have inadequate diets and may not receive adequate medical attention.

As you seek explanations for why disadvantaged students may have learning difficulties, some of the first factors to be considered are diet and health. A pupil who is malnourished or has a debilitating illness or an undetected physical handicap of some sort (for example, nearsightedness) cannot be expected to function as an effective learner. If you suspect that a student needs medical attention, you might inquire about possible aid from governmental agencies or charitable organizations. (This is a situation in which labeling may work to the advantage of a pupil. Only after an individual has been classified as coming from a poverty-level family or the equivalent are certain kinds of aid made available.)

3. Remain aware that disadvantaged students may not be familiar with many things that you take for granted. Try to supply experiences that such students may have missed.

Many disadvantaged students have led extremely restricted lives. They may have had no experience with the everyday objects or situations presented in books or featured in instructional material. A prudent teacher will find out what such pupils know and do not know. If inner-city primary grade children have never taken a drive through a rural area, they may have difficulty reading a simple story about farm life. In a situation such as this, it would be beneficial to try to arrange a field trip through rural areas or at least to show a film or film strip about country life to familiarize disadvantaged children with what more favored pupils already know. Regardless of the grade level you teach, you might make it a practice to ask disadvantaged pupils if they have had any personal experience with objects and situations mentioned in books and lessons. If they have not, try to supply familiarity with such experiences in either direct or pictorial form.

4. Use every possible means for motivating disadvantaged students to do well in school.

Perhaps the major reason some disadvantaged pupils do poorly in school is not lack of ability but lack of interest in learning. A number of circumstances may conspire to prevent such students from acquiring a desire to do well in school: lack of encouragement from parents, the absence of role models in the form of parents and siblings who have benefited from schooling, a level of aspiration set low to avoid possible failure, and lack of success leading to a low need for achievement. One of the major tasks facing the teacher of disadvantaged pupils is to arouse and sustain interest in learning. Techniques for doing so will be described in detail in Chapter 12.

5. Give specific assignments, arrange for abundant practice, supply immediate feedback, and stress overlearning.

Handbook Heading: Using Productive Techniques of Teaching

Several evaluations of teaching techniques that have proven effective with disadvantaged primary grade pupils have been published (see, among others, Soar, 1973; Stallings & Kaskowitz, 1974). Based on his review of these evaluations, Barak Rosenshine (1976) offers the following conclusions regarding techniques that did and did not lead to improved performance as measured by standardized tests:

Most Productive	**Least Productive**
Pupils study texts, complete workbook exercises, or respond to direct questions asked by the teacher.	Pupils engage in self-selected learning (as in open education approaches), participate in learning games.
Pupils work individually at their desks completing workbook exercises at their own pace but under direct supervision of the teacher.	Pupils given free study time, allowed to socialize with classmates as they study, not provided with close supervision.
Pupils work on specific exercises in small groups.	Pupils work alone (and without close teacher supervision).
Teacher makes almost all decisions about what will be learned.	Students often allowed to choose what they will learn.
Teacher asks direct questions that have specific answers.	Teacher asks general questions or invites pupils to comment on or suggest related ideas.
Students asked to give many answers, required to guess if they aren't sure of the right answer, are given immediate feedback for every answer.	Teacher asks open-ended questions, does not require direct answers; feedback is vague or absent.

Jere E. Brophy and Carolyn M. Evertson (1976) made detailed observations of teachers who were consistently effective as instructors of disadvantaged second- and third-graders. Many of their findings corroborate the conclusions of Rosenshine. That is, the effective teachers they observed used a structured approach, made specific assignments, arranged for pupils to get plenty of practice working with basic texts and workbooks, and gave immediate feedback. Brophy and Evertson also describe some interesting subtleties in the techniques used by effective teachers of the disadvantaged. Quite often, for instance, such teachers had to "patiently and doggedly [work] to get responses" (p. 79) during class recitation periods. Upper- and middle-class pupils observed by Brophy and Evertson typically had to be kept under control during such periods. They were so eager to prove that they had come up with the right answer more quickly than classmates that they often threatened to disrupt the lesson. Lower-class pupils, by contrast, often were reluctant to answer and exhibited anxiety about being called on for fear of not being able to supply the right answer. In their efforts to overcome students' fear of failure, teachers in lower-class schools moved at a slow pace, gave extra time for pupils to think before speaking, and encouraged *any* kind of answer, even if it was wrong. If a wrong answer *was* supplied, the teacher either gave hints so that the student could correct the error or else matter-of-factly provided the correct response and went on to another question. Brophy and Evertson also stressed that it seems to be especially important for teachers of the disadvantaged to allow for closely supervised practice immediately after a new skill is demonstrated or a new idea is introduced. If disadvantaged pupils do not get off to a good start with a new skill, they are likely to practice errors during unsupervised study periods. Lack of a rich background experience and of self-confidence is likely to limit self-correcting tendencies. A related point emphasized by Brophy and Evertson is that teachers of the disadvantaged appear to be more effective when they *overteach* and ask pupils to *overlearn* rather than the opposite.

Although all of the research findings just summarized were based on observations of primary grade pupils and teachers, the same basic techniques may be effective with disadvantaged students of any age.

Examples

Use curriculum materials that feature repeated, brief, and easily graded exercises.

Instead of having pupils study individually just before exams, have them study together in groups of two to five.

Make recitation periods as relaxed as possible. If pupils still act afraid to speak up for fear of appearing ignorant, have them write out answers, perhaps in the form of formative quizzes. Insist that they at least take a stab at answering every question, and point out that a "wrong" answer often gives clues as to what is missing or misunderstood.

To encourage students to overlearn without becoming bored or turned off by repetition, first have them study material individually but under your close supervision, and then have them study together in small groups. In both types of study sessions, try to provide a series of short, interesting, varied exercises with clear terminal behavior.

If students demonstrate on a quiz that they seem to have mastered a particular unit, give them a slightly different quiz a week later to make sure the material or skill has been retained.

6. In the secondary grades, introduce topics in a concrete way; then have students develop their own learning materials, make observations, engage in role playing, and be active as they learn.

Techniques for teaching disadvantaged secondary school students have been developed and practiced by Hilda Taba and Deborah Elkins, who explain their approach in *Teaching Strategies for the Culturally Disadvantaged* (1966). The basic guidelines for instructional strategies recommended by Taba and Elkins include continual diagnosis to discover gaps in knowledge and areas in need of attention and the simultaneous pursuit of objectives in six areas: (1) knowledge, thinking, attitudes, and skills; (2) providing for heterogeneity; (3) pacing learning by providing "bite-size" chunks arranged in hierarchical fashion; (4) extensive use of dramatization, play making, and role playing; and (6) providing experiences in observing and interviewing.

The implementation of these guidelines can be illustrated by a unit called "Human Hands." The unit was introduced at a concrete level. Students were asked to trace their hands, and the tracings were used first as a basis for discussing the beauty and similarity of hands and then as a stimulus for writing on the topic "Important Things My Hands Can Do." The descriptions provided were analyzed and tallied on the board under different categories to encourage awareness of concepts. The final list of categories was reproduced and added to the written theme as the beginning of an individual notebook for each pupil. Then the teacher read a story, and students were asked to discuss how hands were used by the characters; afterward, the original categories were revised and expanded. For homework, the students were asked to observe an adult for thirty minutes and to write down everything the person did with his or her hands. These reports were discussed, tallied, categorized, and added to the notebooks; then each student summed up general observations on hands in a short paragraph, which was later reproduced in a booklet and distributed to members of the class. Next, help-wanted ads in newspapers were analyzed to illustrate how hands are used in many different occupations. Magazines were distributed, and students were asked to cut out pictures of hands; newspaper articles on hands were also collected. All of these were used in group discussion and as the basis for written exercises to be added to the notebooks.

The same general techniques were used for units on "Walls in Our Life" and "Aspirations." The purpose of the latter topic was to build understanding of goals and encourage the development of realistic aspirations. It featured interviews with parents and other adults, the dramatization of original plays, and role playing (some students acted as employers, others as job seekers).

Teaching Strategies for the Culturally Disadvantaged offers detailed suggestions for setting up and carrying out social studies units for secondary school students, although the basic methods described could be adapted for use with almost any grade level or subject. It is one of the most practical how-to-do-it books on teaching secondary school students from disadvantaged backgrounds, and it is highly recommended.

MULTICULTURAL EDUCATION PROGRAMS

Earlier in this chapter you were introduced to some basic concepts that underlie multicultural education and to some reasons for its current popularity. In the next section we will give you some idea of what it might be like to teach from a multicultural perspective by describing the basic goals, assumptions, and characteristics of such programs. You might be interested to know that the concept of multicultural education has been around for some time. Many of the elements that constitute contemporary programs were devised sixty to seventy years ago as part of a then-current emphasis on international education (Gollnick & Chinn, 1990).

Assumptions and Goals

The various suggestions that are made by proponents of multicultural education (for example, Banks, 1991; Bennett, 1990; Gollnick & Chinn, 1990; Lynch, 1986; Ramsey, 1987) stem from several assumptions. The most frequently mentioned are as follows:

1. The culture of the United States has been formed to a great extent by the contributions of many different cultural groups.

2. People must possess a degree of self- and group-esteem in order to productively interact with members of other cultures.

3. Learning of the achievements of one's own cultural group will enhance self- and group-esteem.

4. Interaction among members of culturally diverse groups is beneficial for the health and continued development of American society.

5. Cultural values and experiences predispose children to think and behave in particular ways. When these values and experiences are understood, accepted as worthwhile, incorporated into instructional lessons, and rewarded by the teacher, the students involved will perform better academically than they otherwise would.

In order for children to understand and appreciate different cultural values and experiences, those values and experiences have to be integrated into the curriculum and rewarded by the teacher. (Bernsau/The Image Works, Inc.)

These assumptions have given rise to several goals that proponents of multicultural education believe educators should strive to attain. Some of the most frequently mentioned are as follows:

1. Help students understand how the past and present experiences of various ethnic groups, including their own, have had or are having a significant impact on American society in order to promote self-acceptance and respect for the diverse ways in which other people live.

2. Help students understand how various historical events and artistic creations were influenced and perceived by various cultural groups in order to reduce ethnocentrism and foster productive relationships among members of those groups.

3. Help students combat such harmful stereotypes as African-Americans are violent, southern whites are racially prejudiced, Jews are stingy, Asian-Americans excel at math and science, and Hispanic-Americans are hot-tempered.

4. Help teachers develop the attitudes, expectations, instructional practices, disciplinary policies and practices, and classroom climate that give *all* students a sense of being valued and accepted.

5. Help students master basic reading, writing, and computation skills by embedding them in a personally meaningful (that is, ethnically related) context.

Advocates of multicultural education believe that ethnic minority students learn more effectively when some of the learning materials and assignments contain ethnically related content. (Jeff Dunn/Stock, Boston, Inc.)

Intended Audience

In theory, multicultural programs are applicable to every student, since every student represents an identifiable cultural or ethnic group. In practice, the programs are directed primarily at members of ethnic minority groups. Some of these groups have been a part of American society for generations; others have arrived more recently. The former category takes in Native Americans, African-Americans, and Mexican-Americans whose ancestors became citizens as a consequence of the Mexican-American War (1846–1848). The latter category currently includes people whose families immigrated from Puerto Rico (although since Puerto Rico is an American commonwealth, all Puerto Ricans are U.S. citizens), Cuba, Mexico, China, Japan, Korea, the Philippine Islands, Cambodia, Laos, Vietnam, Thailand, El Salvador, Nicaragua, and Guatemala (Gutek, 1988; Kellogg, 1988).

Basic Approaches and Concepts

▸ Multicultural education can be approached in different ways

Approaches   James A. Banks (1991), a noted authority on multicultural education, describes four approaches to multicultural education. Most multicultural programs, particularly those in the primary grades, adopt what he calls the *contributions approach*. Under this approach, ethnic historical figures whose values and behaviors are consistent with American mainstream culture (for example, Booker T. Washington, Sacajawea) are studied whereas individuals who have challenged the dominant view (such as W.E.B. DuBois, Geronimo) are ignored. A second approach, which incorporates the first, is called the *additive approach*. Here, an instructional unit composed of concepts, themes, points of view, and individual accomplishments is simply added to the curriculum. The perspective from which they are viewed, however, tends to be that of the mainstream. Moving one step further produces what Banks calls the *transformation approach*. This approach assumes that there is no one valid way of understanding people, events, concepts, and themes. Rather, there are multiple views, each of which has something of value to offer. Because this approach requires the concrete operational schemes described in Chapter 2, it is typically introduced at the junior high school level. Finally, there is the *social action approach*. It incorporates all of the components of the previous approaches and adds the requirement that students make decisions and take actions concerning a concept, issue, or problem being studied.

Concepts   Regardless of which approach you use, Banks suggests that multicultural units and lessons be organized around a set of key concepts that incorporate a range of facts, generalizations, and subject-matter disciplines. These concepts can be used to analyze a particular ethnic group or to compare and contrast groups. The following set of key concepts and associated questions illustrates what Banks had in mind.

> *Identity:* To what extent is the group aware of its ethnic identity, and how does it express that identity?

> *Culture:* What ethnic elements (for example, values, customs, perspectives) are present in the group's culture today? How is the group's culture reflected in its music, literature, and art?

The contributions approach to multicultural education, which is commonly found in the primary grades, focuses on the contributions made by prominent individuals from different ethnic backgrounds to mainstream culture. (Ulrike Welsch)

Immigration: From what country or countries did this group originate? When and in what numbers did this group immigrate to the United States?

Ethnic community: To what extent are members of the group concentrated within particular geographic regions?

Racism and discrimination: In what ways has this group been subjected to racism and discrimination?

Communication: To what extent and why do members of the group encounter problems when communicating with other ethnic groups?

Self-concept: How have the group's societal experiences affected the self-concepts of its members?

Power: What is the group's social, political, and economic status? To what extent does the group exercise power within the community? Within the larger society?

Acculturation: To what extent has the group influenced and been influenced by the mainstream society?

For each key concept one would formulate a set of high-level, intermediate-level, and low-level generalizations, a set of cognitive and affective objectives (the nature of which are described in Chapter 7), and a set of activities. Generalizations are summaries of facts that can be verified with empirical data. The difference between high-, intermediate-, and low-level generalizations is their range of applicability. Banks uses the concept of *social protest* by Mexican-Americans to illustrate the different levels of generalization and an activity that might be used with each one.

Low-level generalization: Mexican-Americans have resisted Anglo discrimination since Anglo-Americans conquered and occupied the Southwest.

Activity: Have students prepare an oral report that describes Chicano involvement in strikes and unions between 1900 and 1940.

Intermediate-level generalization: Throughout their experiences in the United States, ethnic minorities have resisted discrimination in various ways.

Activity: Have students summarize and generalize how Mexican-Americans have resisted Anglo discrimination in past and present American society.

High-level generalization: When individuals and groups are victims of discrimination, they tend to protest against their situation in various ways.

Activity: Have students research the goals, tactics, and strategies used by various Mexican-American civil rights groups, and write several generalizations about the activities of these groups.

Instructional Tactics

The three instructional tactics that are recommended most often by proponents of multicultural education are peer tutoring, cooperative learning, and mastery learning. While each of these techniques can be used with any group of students

Peer tutoring is an effective method for fostering positive interactions between students of different cultural backgrounds as well as for improving achievement. (Kenneth Murray/ Photo Researchers, Inc.)

and for most any purpose, they are particularly well suited to the goals of multicultural education.

Peer Tutoring   As its name implies, **peer tutoring** involves the teaching of one student by another. The students may be similar in age or separated by one or more years. (The latter arrangement is usually referred to as cross-age tutoring.) The theoretical basis of peer tutoring comes from Piaget's notions about cognitive development. Recall from our discussion of Piaget in Chapter 2 that cognitive growth depended on the presence of a disequilibrating stimulus that the learner was motivated to eliminate. When children with different cognitive schemes (because of differences in age, knowledge, or cultural background) are forced to interact with one another, cognitive conflict results. Growth occurs when children try to resolve this conflict (through assimilation and accommodation) by comparing and contrasting each other's views. The presumed benefits of peer tutoring include improved communication skills, increased awareness of the perspectives of others, an increased ability to analyze ideas and provide feedback to others, higher levels of achievement, and a more positive attitude toward the subject being studied (Foot, Shute & Morgan, 1990). This technique—as well as the one we discuss next, cooperative learning—is likely to be particularly effective with Hispanic-American and Native American students, as their cultural backgrounds place a high value on cooperation and mentoring (Sadker & Sadker, 1991).

An early review of peer tutoring research (Cohen, Kulik & Kulik, 1982) found that tutored students outscored nontutored students on classroom examinations by a fairly substantial margin in forty-five of fifty-two studies. The average student who was tutored scored at the 66th percentile, whereas the average nontutored student scored at the 50th percentile. Tutored students also demonstrated more positive attitudes toward the subject matter than nontutored students. While the students who provided the tutoring did not benefit quite as much as the students who received it, they still scored higher on classroom tests than their nontutoring peers.

> Peer tutoring improves achievement, interpersonal relationships, attitudes toward subjects

Strong support for peer tutoring has been provided by subsequent studies involving a variety of students and yielding many different outcomes. In particular, peer tutoring has been shown to increase the arithmetic skills of low-socioeconomic-status, low-achieving elementary school students (Fantuzzo, Polite & Grayson, 1990); the self-esteem and achievement of learning disabled students (Beirne-Smith, 1991; Byrd, 1990); and the arithmetic accuracy, self-concept, attitude toward mathematics, and social interactions between tutor and tutee of behaviorally disordered students (Franca et al., 1990). Two conditions seem to account for the success of peer tutoring. One is the presence of an explicit set of guidelines that informs the tutor and tutee of their respective roles and responsibilities. The other condition is fulfilled when the tutor is held accountable for the performance of the tutee (Fantuzzo et al., 1989).

Cooperative Learning   Closely related to peer tutoring is the tactic of cooperative learning. The general idea behind **cooperative learning** is that by working in small heterogeneous groups (of four or five students total) and by helping one another master the various aspects of a particular task, students will be more motivated to learn, will learn more than if they had to work independently, and will forge stronger interpersonal relationships (Slavin, 1990b, 1991).

> Cooperative learning: students work together in small groups

There are several forms of cooperative learning, one of which is Student Team Learning. Student Team Learning techniques are built on the concepts of

Students from different cultural backgrounds who learn in small cooperative groups are more likely to make friends with one another than are culturally different studetnts who do not interact with one another. (Diane Graham-Henry/Tony Stone Worldwide)

team reward, individual accountability, and equal opportunities for success. *Team reward* means that teams are not in competition with each other for limited rewards. All of the teams, some of them, or none of them may earn whatever rewards are made available depending on how well the team's performance matches a predetermined standard. *Individual accountability* means that each member of the team must perform at a certain level (on a quiz, for example) in order for the team's effort to be judged successful. It is not permissible for one team member's above-average performance to compensate for another team member's below-average performance. Finally, *equal opportunities for success* allow students of all ability levels to contribute to their team's success by improving on their own past performances (Slavin, 1991).

Robert E. Slavin (1990b, 1991), a leading exponent of cooperative learning, reports that forty-one of sixty-seven studies found significantly greater incidence of achievement in cooperative as opposed to noncooperative arrangements. The results for the Student Team Learning programs have been the most consistently positive. Of particular relevance to this chapter are the findings that students who cooperate in learning are more apt to list as friends peers from different ethnic groups and are better able to take the perspective of a classmate than are students who do not work in cooperative groups.

Although cooperative learning is a generally effective instructional tactic, it is likely to be particularly useful with Hispanic-American and Native American students. Children from both cultures often come from extended families that emphasize cooperation and sharing. Thus, they may be more prepared than other individuals to work productively as part of a group by carrying out their own responsibilities as well as helping others do the same (Sadker & Sadker, 1991; Soldier, 1989). We will have more to say about cooperative learning in Chapter 12.

Mastery Learning   The third instructional tactic, **mastery learning,** deserves mention here as well because it is an approach to teaching and learning that assumes most students can master the curriculum if certain conditions are established. These conditions are (a) sufficient aptitude to learn a particular task, (b) sufficient ability to understand instruction, (c) the willingness to persevere until a certain level of mastery is attained, (d) being allowed however much time is necessary to attain mastery, and (e) being provided good-quality instruction. Mastery learning proponents assume that all of these conditions can be created if they are not already present. Aptitude, for example, is seen as being partly determined by how well prerequisite knowledge and skills have been learned. And perseverance can be strengthened by the deft use of creative teaching methods and various forms of reward for successful performance. The basic mastery learning approach is to clearly specify what is to be learned, organize the content into a sequence of relatively short units, use a variety of instructional methods and materials, allow students to progress through the material at their own rate, monitor student progress in order to identify budding problems and

Marginal notes:

▶ Cooperative learning fosters better understanding among ethnically diverse students

▶ Mastery learning: all students can master the curriculum

provide corrective feedback, and allow students to relearn and retest on each unit until mastery is attained (Block, Efthim & Burns, 1989). We describe mastery learning in more detail in Chapter 13.

Like the research on peer tutoring and cooperative learning, the research on mastery learning has generally been positive. On the basis of a comprehensive review of this literature, Chen-Lin Kulik, James Kulik, and Robert Bangert-Drowns (1990) concluded that mastery learning programs produce moderately strong effects on achievement. The average student in a mastery learning class scored at the 70th percentile on a classroom examination, whereas the average student in a conventional class scored at the 50th percentile. The positive effect of mastery learning was slightly more pronounced for lower-ability students. As compared to students in conventional classes, those in mastery classes had more positive feelings about the subjects they studied and the way in which they were taught.

A Rationale for Multicultural Education

Some people seem to believe that multicultural education programs represent a rejection of basic American values and that this opposition to traditional values is the only rationale behind such programs. We feel this belief is mistaken on both counts. We see multicultural programs as being consistent with basic American values (such as tolerance of differences and equality of opportunity) and consider them to be justified in several ways.

One argument in favor of multicultural programs is that they foster teaching practices that are effective in general as well as for members of a particular group. For example, expressing an interest in a student through occasional touching and smiling and allowing the child to tutor a younger student are practices likely to benefit most students, not just those of Hispanic-American origin.

A second argument in favor of multicultural education is that all students may profit from understanding different cultural values. For example, the respect for elders that characterizes Native American and Asian-American cultures is likely to become increasingly desirable as the percentage of elderly Americans increases over the years. Similarly, learning the Native American value of living in harmony with nature may come to be essential as we run out of natural resources and attempt to alleviate environmental pollution (Triandis, 1986).

A third argument in support of multicultural education programs is that the United States is becoming an increasingly multicultural society (because of the immigration and birth rate trends mentioned earlier) and students thus need to understand and know how to work with people of cultures different from their own.

And last but not least, multicultural programs can encourage student motivation and learning. These programs demonstrate respect for a child's culture and teach about the contributions that the student's group has made to American society. Proponents argue that these features both personalize education and make it more meaningful. Conversely, when children perceive disrespect for their cultural background, the result can be disastrous. Consider the following comment by a New York City student:

> I came upon a world unknown to me, a language I did not understand, and a school administration which made ugly faces at me every time I spoke Spanish. Many teachers referred to us as animals. Believe me, maintaining a half-decent image of yourself wasn't an easy thing. . . . I had enough strength of character to withstand the many school personnel who tried to destroy my motivation. But many of my classmates didn't make it. (First, 1988, p. 210)

Statistical evidence of the need for multicultural programs can be seen in the disappointing academic performance of a significant number of minority-group students. Compared to white high school sophomores and seniors, African-American, Hispanic-American, and Native American students score lower on standardized tests of vocabulary, reading, writing, mathematics, and science (Levine & Havighurst, 1989). These differences appear early. Recent results from the National Assessment of Educational Progress reveal that the reading and writing skills of African-American and Hispanic-American children are substantially below those of white children as early as third grade (Pallas, Natriello & McDill, 1989).

Given these achievement differences, it should come as no surprise that there are parallel differences in school dropout rates. Whereas 14.3 percent of whites drop out of school before graduation, 24.7 percent of African-Americans, 39.9 percent of Hispanic-Americans, and 42 percent of Native Americans do so (Bennett, 1990).

▶ Minority children score lower on tests, drop out of school sooner

Investigations into the reasons for which minority students leave school prematurely have found that individual factors, school environment factors, social class factors, and economic factors may all play a role. Compared to white students who stay in school, minority dropouts have lower levels of motivation, lower self-esteem, and weaker academic skills; they are also more impulsive. In addition, dropouts nearly always report a sense of alienation from school because of low teacher expectations, expressions of racial or ethnic group prejudice from teachers and students, and unfair discrimination. Students required to repeat grades (recall our discussion of this topic in Chapter 1) are among the most likely to drop out of school. Differences in social class values can also contribute to low levels of achievement and a subsequent early exit from school. Two middle-class values, order and discipline, fit nicely with the expectations and activities of schools. The lower-class values of avoiding trouble with authorities, developing physical prowess, and establishing independence from external control, on the other hand, are not likely to be as productive in achieving school success (Tidwell, 1989). Finally, minority students who do poorly in school and leave early typically come from the poorest households. In 1984, the poverty rate for white children was 16.4 percent, whereas 38.7 percent of Hispanic-American children and 46.2 percent of African-American children were living in poverty (Pallas, Natriello & McDill, 1989). Multicultural theorists believe that the inclusion of ethnically related content and activities in the curriculum will make classroom

▶ Minority drop-out rate due to alienation, differences in values, poverty

assignments more meaningful and will help minority students master basic reading, writing, computational, and reasoning skills (Banks, 1991; Vasquez, 1990).

Mid-Chapter Review

Understanding Cultural Diversity	**Culture:** the particular way in which a group of people perceives the world, the beliefs and values to which they subscribe, and the behavior patterns they exhibit in different situations.
	Multicultural education: an approach to teaching and learning that incorporates the cultural background of students.
Taking Account of Cultural Differences	**Ethnic group:** a collection of people who identify with one another on the basis of ancestral country of origin, religion, language, values, interests, and behavior patterns. Differences among ethnic groups in communication patterns, time orientation, social values, and learning modes are potential sources of classroom misunderstanding.
	Social class: a group's position in society as determined by income, occupation, and education. Many ethnic group members belong to the lower social classes.
The Nature of Multicultural Education	Multicultural education programs are based on assumptions about relationships among cultural background, self-esteem, motivation, and learning.
	Multicultural education programs may stress the contributions of famous ethnic minority individuals to the mainstream culture; multicultural concepts, themes, and points of view; and the need to take actions concerning multicultural issues.
	Multicultural education programs should include such key concepts as ethnic identity, culture, ethnic community, racism, communication, self-concept, power, and acculturation.
	Peer tutoring, cooperative learning, and mastery learning are three instructional tactics that are particularly well-suited to multicultural education.
The Need for Multicultural Education	Multicultural education has become an important part of education because of changes in immigration patterns and birth rates, concern about low levels of achievement among ethnic minority groups, and discrimination against ethnic minority groups.

Trends toward ethnic awareness mean that you may find yourself teaching in a system that has authorized some form of multicultural education. If the program is well established, you should be given instructions about how to work cultural and ethnic studies into the curriculum. Be aware, though, that people in some areas hold strong feelings against bilingual and multicultural education. If a formal program is absent and you want to incorporate some multicultural activities on your own, it would be wise to find out about prevailing attitudes in your school district first. If you discover that you have the green light in your school, you might institute a limited program intended to make pupils more familiar with the cultural backgrounds of their classmates. This limited approach is recommended by some experts. Nicholas Appleton (1983), for example, feels that multicultural education should be seen as a long-term process that will produce gradual awareness rather than rapid, dramatic changes in students' perceptions and behaviors. Accordingly, he sees nothing wrong with teachers starting off by supplementing their existing curriculum with small multicultural units. The following Suggestions for Teaching should help you get started.

Suggestions for Teaching in Your Classroom

PROMOTING MULTICULTURAL UNDERSTANDING

1. Help make students aware of the contributions that specific ethnic groups have made to the development of the United States and the world.

2. Assign projects and activities that allow students to demonstrate culture-specific knowledge and skills.

3. Encourage students to identify with representatives of their ethnic group who have achieved success.

4. At the secondary level, involve students in activities that explore cultural differences in perceptions, beliefs, and values.

---

1. Help make students aware of the contributions that specific ethnic groups have made to the development of the United States and the world.

Handbook Heading: Ways to Promote Awareness of Contributions of Ethnic Minorities

The first principle suggested by Nicholas Appleton (1983) for implementing a multicultural education program is that each student should examine his or her own ethnic background before examining the backgrounds of others. Appleton's rationale is that racism in the United States has had a negative impact on the self-concepts of ethnic minority children. Since self-concept is related to achievement, it is important to help students develop positive attitudes about their ethnic heritage. One suggestion for accomplishing this goal is to invite family members of students (and other local residents) of different ethnic backgrounds to the classroom. Ask them to describe the values subscribed to by members of their group and to explain how those values have contributed to life in the United States and to the world in general.

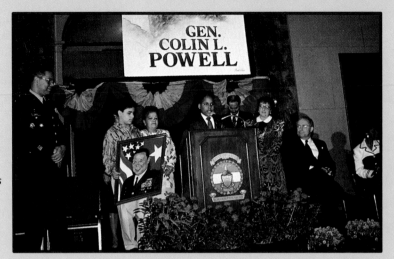

One way to help minority group students develop a need for achievement is to encourage them to identify with representatives of their ethnic group who achieved success in various fields of endeavor. (R. Maiman/ SYGMA)

2. Assign projects and activities that allow students to demonstrate culture-specific knowledge and skills.

You might encourage pupils from similar ethnic and religious backgrounds to get together at designated periods and prepare presentations for the rest of the class. Ask them to illustrate and explain the art, music, beliefs, and ceremonies of their particular group. On special holidays honored by different groups, the entire class can take part in the celebration, perhaps including the preparation of appropriate decorations and food.

3. Encourage students to identify with representatives of their ethnic group who have achieved success.

Erikson has called attention to the role confusion experienced by many minority-group Americans. He has also concluded that one of the most important factors leading to a sense of identity is occupational choice. You might help minority-group pupils avoid role confusion and develop a sense of identity if you can acquaint them with the accomplishments of eminent and successful people who share their ethnic background. Models might practice in the professions, business, education, or the arts. Identifying with prominent people can help youngsters develop a sense of their group's identity as successful Americans. Once that identity is achieved, individuals can freely cherish the language and culture of their heritage without risking role confusion.

4. At the secondary level, involve students in activities that explore cultural differences in perceptions, beliefs, and values.

A point made by several scholars of cultural pluralism (for example, Appleton, 1983; Banks, 1991), and one certainly worth keeping in mind, is that a well-conceived multicultural education program cannot, and should not, avoid or minimize the issue of cultural conflict. There are at least two reasons for helping students examine this issue. One is that conflict has been a constant and salient aspect of relationships among cultural groups. A second is that cultural conflicts often produce changes that benefit all members of a society (a prime example being the civil rights boycotts, marches, and demonstrations of the 1960s).

Cultural conflicts arise from differences in perceptions, beliefs, and values. American culture, for example, places great value on self-reliance. Americans generally respect and praise individuals who, through their own initiative, persistence, and ingenuity, achieve substantial personal goals; and they tend to look down on individuals who are dependent on others for their welfare. Consequently, American parents who are financially dependent upon their children, even though the children may be prosperous enough to support them, would probably feel ashamed enough to hide the fact. The same situation in China, on the other hand, would likely elicit a different reaction because of different values about self-reliance and family responsibilities. Chinese parents who were unable to provide for themselves in their old age but had children successful enough to support them might well brag about it to others (Appleton, 1983).

Handbook Heading: Ways to Help Students Explore Conflicts Between Cultures

One technique for exploring cultural conflict is to have students search through newspapers and news magazines for articles that describe clashes. Ask them to try to identify the source of the conflict and how it might be positively resolved. Another technique is to involve students in games that simulate group conflict. Class members can, for example, play the role of city council members who represent the interests of diverse ethnic groups and who have been ordered by the federal government to integrate their school system (Appleton, 1983). In the Resources for Further Investigation we indicate where you can find and learn more about simulations of cultural conflict. Both the use of simulations as well as the discussion of newspaper articles will probably work best at the high school level, because adolescents are better able than younger students to understand the abstract concepts involved in these activities.

BILINGUAL EDUCATION

As we mentioned earlier, almost 1 million legal immigrants a year for the ten-year period from 1981 to 1990 were estimated to have arrived in the United States. Not surprisingly, many of the school-age children of these families have either limited or no English proficiency. To address this need, the federal government provides financial support for the establishment of bilingual education programs. Because language is viewed as an important part of a group's culture, many school districts integrate bilingual education with multicultural education. In this section we will examine the nature and effectiveness of bilingual education programs.

Before we consider various approaches to bilingual education, we would like to make a few introductory comments about bilingual education that you should be aware of as a teacher. First, bilingual programs have become an emotionally charged and politicized topic. Educators, parents, and legislators have strong opinions regarding the time and resources that should be devoted to helping students master native language skills and whether such programs should include cultural awareness goals. Some individuals favor moving students into all-English classes as quickly as possible; others believe that students should have a firm grasp of their native language *and* English before attempting to make the transition to regular classes. While research on this issue is helpful because it informs us about what *is,* it cannot tell us what we *should do* about what we know. Second, some language-minority students may suffer from problems that bilingual education alone cannot solve. If (as noted earlier) parents do not model the types of behaviors valued by schools or encourage their children to exhibit such behaviors, learning difficulties often result. Finally, you should realize that no one approach to bilingual education is likely to be equally effective for all language-minority students. What works well for some lower-class Puerto Rican children may not work well for middle-class Cuban children, and vice versa.

Historical Developments

In the introduction to this chapter we described a turn-of-the-century view of the United States as a great melting pot. Immigrants were expected to leave behind their old allegiances, languages, customs, and views and to adopt English as their primary language as well as American values and ideals. To help immigrant schoolchildren make this linguistic and cultural transition as quickly as possible, many communities established bilingual schools. After World War I, however, public financing of bilingual schools was abruptly withdrawn, partly because of increasing nationalism and isolationism. Foreign languages were classified as electives to be studied in a superficial way only by students preparing for college. Most students were given intensive instruction only in English (Bennett, 1990).

This situation remained essentially unchanged until 1965. In that year Congress provided funds for the creation of bilingual education programs for lower-class students with limited English skills through Title VII of the Elementary and Secondary Education Act. Additional funds were authorized in 1968 with the passage of the Bilingual Education Act. The impetus for providing bilingual education programs to a wider audience came from the U.S. Supreme Court in 1974 in the case of *Lau* v. *Nicholls.* The Court ruled that *all* non- and limited-English-speaking children were entitled to some sort of appropriate language instruction in order to preserve their constitutional right to equal educational opportunities. In the same year Congress revised the Bilingual Education Act, creating a greater range of programs for a larger number of children. Since 1974, the federal government has provided hundreds of millions of dollars to states and local school districts in support of programs aimed at improving English language proficiency. The federal government currently sponsors bilingual programs for more than 70 Asian, Indo-European, and Native American languages, with Hispanics being the single largest group served (Gollnick & Chinn, 1990; Levine & Havighurst, 1989; Scarcella, 1990).

Goals and Approaches

Two main approaches to bilingual education: transition, maintenance

Most bilingual education programs have a common long-term goal but differ in their approach to that goal. The goal is to help minority language students acquire as efficiently as possible the English skills they will need to succeed in school and society. The approaches to that goal fall into one of two categories: *transition* or *maintenance.*

Transition programs focus on rapid shift to English proficiency

Programs that have a transition approach teach students wholly (in the case of non-English proficient students) or partly (in the case of limited-English proficient students) in their native language so as not to retard their academic progress, but only until they can function adequately in English. At that point, they are placed in regular classes where all of the instruction is in English. To make the transition time as brief as possible, some programs add an ESL (English as a Second Language) component. Supporters of this approach point out that much of what occurs in classrooms takes the form of verbal directions, descriptions, and explanations, question-and-answer sessions, and references to abstract ideas. The ability to speak a common language allows individuals to feel part of a larger group. Most current programs are transitional in nature, possibly because this was the goal espoused by such early legislation as the Bilingual Education Act of 1968 (Bowman, 1989; Hakuta & Garcia, 1989).

Maintenance programs focus on maintaining native-language competence

Programs that have a maintenance approach try to maintain or improve the students' native-language skills prior to instruction in English. Supporters of maintenance programs point to the results of psychological and linguistic studies which suggest that a strong native-language foundation supports the subsequent

Awareness of the limitations of knowledge of just one language (as well as of the problems faced by school children reared in non-English-speaking homes) has led to expansion of bilingual education. (Ulrike Welsch)

learning of both English and subject-matter knowledge. In addition, many proponents of multicultural education favor a maintenance approach because they see language as an important part of a group's cultural heritage (Hakuta & Garcia, 1989; Hakuta & Gould, 1987).

In addition to programs whose goal is exclusively or predominantly English acquisition, there are programs that combine cultural awareness goals with language acquisition goals and that are directed at a wider audience. Daniel U. Levine and Robert J. Havighurst (1989) describe a five-part classification scheme proposed by Josué González, a former director of the U.S. Office of Bilingual Education, that encompasses all of these programs. The five types are as follows:

1. *Transitional bilingual:* Students are taught wholly or partly in their native language only until they can function adequately in English.

2. *Bilingual maintenance:* In addition to helping students become fluent in English, efforts are made to help students maintain or improve their native-language skills.

3. *Bilingual/bicultural maintenance:* In addition to helping students become fluent in English and their native language, efforts are made to teach students about their cultural background.

4. *Bilingual/bicultural restorationist:* Students are helped to become fluent in English and in a native language that has been lost through assimilation. Aspects of the students' lost culture are taught as well.

5. *Bilingual/bicultural culturally pluralistic:* All students in the program, regardless of their ethnic and linguistic backgrounds, learn to function in two languages and to appreciate one another's cultural background.

Teaching Methods

Robin Scarcella (1990) describes three methods of bilingual instruction that are currently in use. The preferred method is the three-part *Preview/Review* technique. The teacher summarizes the main points of the lesson in the students' primary language, presents the lesson in English, and then concludes with a review of the main points in the students' primary language. An alternative but less frequently used method is the *Alternate Language Method.* A lesson is presented in the students' native language one day and is repeated in English the next day. A third technique that is used but considered less effective than either of the first two is the *Concurrent Method.* Small amounts of a lesson are given in the primary language, followed immediately by a translation. The problem with this method is that students tend to pay attention only to those portions of the lesson that are spoken in their native language.

Research Findings

In comparison to immersion (English-only) programs, how successful have bilingual education programs been in helping non-English-speaking students

▶ Bilingual education programs produce moderate learning gains

learn English and other subjects? After analyzing twenty-three studies, Anne C. Willig (1985) concluded that participation in bilingual education programs produced small to moderate gains on tests of reading, language skills, mathematics, and total achievement when measured by tests in English. When measured by tests administered in the student's native language, however, participation in bilingual education led to significantly better performance on tests of listening comprehension, reading, writing, total language, mathematics, social studies, and attitudes toward school and self.

Resources for Further Investigation

Multicultural Education: Theory and Practice

James A. Banks offers a comprehensive examination of multicultural education in *Teaching Strategies for Ethnic Studies* (5th ed., 1991). Part I discusses goals for multicultural programs, key concepts, and planning a multicultural curriculum. Parts II through V provide background information about twelve ethnic groups and strategies for teaching about each group. Part VI provides an example of a multicultural unit and an evaluation strategy. The book concludes with such useful appendices as a list of videotapes and films on U.S. ethnic groups, a bibliography of books about women of color, and a chronology of key events concerning ethnic groups in U.S. history.

Another practical book is *Comprehensive Multicultural Education: Theory and Practice* (2d ed., 1990) by Christine I. Bennett. The first part of this book (Chapters 1 to 3) presents the case for multicultural education. Part Two (Chapters 4 to 6) describes culturally based individual differences that affect teaching and learning. Part Three (Chapters 7 and 8) presents a model for multicultural education, guidelines for instruction, and a set of twenty-two illustrative lessons. The lessons include statements of goals and objectives, a description of the instructional sequence, a list of needed materials, and a means for evaluating how well the objectives were met.

Teaching and Learning in a Diverse World: Multicultural Education for Young Children (1987) by Patricia G. Ramsey describes how to construct a multicultural education program for children as young as three or four years of age.

Ethnic Minority Groups

American Indian Leaders: Studies in Diversity (1980), edited by R. David Edmunds, contains chapters on twelve Native American leaders from the mid-1700s to the present. For information about how to obtain books, films, and reports about African-Americans, Asian-Americans, Hispanic-Americans, and Native Americans, consult *Guide to Multicultural Resources* (1989), edited by Charles A.

Taylor. *Sourcebook of Hispanic Culture in the United States* (1982), edited by David W. Foster, contains several chapters on the history, anthropology, sociology, literature, and art of Hispanic-American groups living in the United States. Angela L. Carrasquillo provides a comprehensive discussion of Hispanic-American children and youth in the United States in *Hispanic Children and Youth in the United States: A Resource Guide* (1991). Chapter 12 provides the names and addresses as well as brief descriptions of fifteen Hispanic advocacy groups. For information about various aspects of development among African-American adolescents, see *Black Adolescence: Current Issues and Annotated Bibliography* (1990), by the Consortium for Research on Black Adolescence.

Bilingual Education

Deborah Sauve provides a compilation of computer-assisted instruction programs in bilingual education, English as a Second Language, and second-language instructional settings in *Guide to Microcomputer Courseware for Bilingual Education* (revised and expanded, 1985). Each entry provides the name of the program; the producer's name, address, and telephone number; the type of computer needed; the type of instructional techniques used; the content area; the grade level or proficiency level of the program; and a brief abstract.

    Bilingual Education: Issues and Strategies (1990), edited by Amado Padilla, Halford Fairchild, and Concepcion Valadez, contains sixteen chapters that discuss various aspects of research on bilingual education, program design and evaluation, and classroom strategies. Finally, *Bilingual and ESL Classrooms: Teaching in Multicultural Contexts* (1985), by Carlos Ovando and Virginia Collier, covers the special characteristics of students in bilingual and ESL classes, the development and nature of bilingual and ESL programs, the nature of language and culture, and methods for teaching various subjects.

SUMMARY

1. Culture refers to the perceptions, emotions, beliefs, ideas, experiences, and behavior patterns that a group of people have in common.

2. Beginning in the 1960s, the notion of the United States as a cultural melting pot became less popular and the concept of cultural diversity, or cultural pluralism, increased in popularity. As the latter became more widely accepted, calls were made for the establishment of multicultural education programs in American public schools.

3. Two important factors that distinguish one culture from another are ethnicity and social class.

4. People of the same ethnic group typically share the following characteristics: ancestral country or origin, race, religion, values, political interests, economic interests, and behavior patterns.

5. Ethnic differences in communication patterns and preferences, time orientation, values, and thinking styles can lead to misunderstandings among students and between students and teachers.

6. Social class indicates an individual's or family's relative position in society in terms of such factors as income, occupation, level of education, place of residence, and material possessions.

7. Disadvantaged students often receive irregular health care, experience child-care practices that do not effectively prepare them for school, are not exposed to a wide variety of experiences, are not motivated to do well in school, and have low career aspirations.

8. Multicultural education programs assume that minority students will learn more and have a stronger self-concept if teachers understand, accept, and reward the thinking and behavior patterns characteristic of the student's culture.

9. Peer tutoring, cooperative learning, and mastery learning are three generally effective instructional tactics that are particularly well suited to multicultural education programs.

10. Calls for multicultural education were stimulated by changing immigration and birth rate patterns, low levels of school achievement by many ethnic minority children, and students' need to work productively with members of other cultures.

11. Most bilingual education programs reflect either a transition goal or a maintenance goal. Transition programs teach students in their native language only until they speak and understand English well enough to be placed in a regular classroom. Maintenance programs try to maintain or improve students' native-language skills prior to instruction in English.

KEY TERMS

culture *(236)*
multicultural education *(236)*
melting pot *(237)*
ethnic group *(240)*
social class *(243)*
peer tutoring *(257)*
cooperative learning *(258)*
mastery learning *(259)*

DISCUSSION QUESTIONS

1. Culture refers to the way in which a group of people views the world; formulates beliefs; evaluates objects, ideas, and experiences; and behaves. Ethnocentrism often causes people to view the cultural beliefs and practices of others as deficits. How can you use the concept of constructivism (mentioned in Chapters 1, 2 and 10) to help students overcome any ethnocentrism they may have and understand the beliefs and practices of other cultures?

2. The school dropout rate for African-American, Hispanic-American, and Native American students is two to three times the rate for white students. A likely contributing factor is the sense of alienation from school that grows out of low teacher expectations, expressions of racial or ethnic group prejudice, and unfair discrimination. What steps might you take to reduce or eliminate this sense of alienation in students?

3. How have your experiences with members of ethnic or racial minority groups been similar or different from what you have heard and read about those groups?

4. On pages 254–255 we briefly describe four approaches to multicultural education: contributions, additive, transformation, and social action. What advantages and disadvantages do you see for each approach? Which approach would you use? Why?

5. On pages 255–256 we describe a set of key concepts proposed by James A. Banks around which multicultural lessons and units can be organized. Why are these concepts so important that Banks labeled them *key* concepts?

Chapter 7

Devising and Using Objectives

Part 2
SPECIFYING
WHAT IS TO BE
LEARNED

Chapter 7
DEVISING AND USING OBJECTIVES

EVALUATIONS OF THE EFFECTIVENESS OF OBJECTIVES

▶ Objectives work best when students are aware of them

▶ General objectives lead to more incidental learning than specific objectives

▶ Arranging objectives in strict hierarchical order does not seem to be essential

▶ Most test questions stress knowledge, ignore higher levels of cognitive taxonomy

SUGGESTIONS FOR TEACHING IN YOUR CLASSROOM

▶ Before devising objectives, examine curriculum materials, find out about tests

▶ Check on availability of appropriate lists of objectives

▶ Use taxonomies to make survey of what students should be able to do

▶ Use specific learning-outcome descriptions to arrange learning experiences

In Chapter 1, theories of instruction or models of learning were mentioned. The purpose of such theories or models is to provide a basic strategy of instruction that consists of four phases:

1. Take into account what students are like and how much they know.

2. Specify what is to be learned.

3. Provide instruction to help students achieve specified objectives by taking advantage of what has been discovered about learning, cognitive strategies, and motivation.

4. Determine if students have achieved specified objectives.

The preceding part was devoted to descriptions of what students are like and how they differ. It is now time to consider ways to specify what is to be learned.

REASONS FOR THINKING ABOUT OBJECTIVES

To grasp why this chapter on objectives appears before chapters on learning, motivation, and evaluation, imagine that it is your first day in your own classroom. If you plan to teach in the elementary grades, you will observe (probably with mixed feelings of excitement, curiosity, and a bit of anxiety) the arrival of the twenty-five or so children who will be spending up to five hours a day in your room for the next nine months. If you expect to teach at the secondary level, you will experience the same feelings as you observe the arrival of the first of (typically) five batches of students whose destiny has been linked to yours by a computer and/or an administrator. They will size you up probably even more keenly than you will sort out your first impressions of them. If you remember some of the things you read in Chapters 2 and 3 of this book, you will be familiar with at least some of the characteristics of the pupils who will seat themselves in front of you. If you recall the emphasis on variability stressed in Chapters 4, 5, and 6, you may detect, even on the basis of extremely brief first impressions, noticeable differences between students. You might find yourself thinking, "I'll bet she's going to be a sharp student" or "That boy looks so scared and unhappy about being back in school I wonder if he has learning problems?" or "Juan will probably enjoy the cooperative learning projects I have planned since he is such an outgoing and friendly boy."

After the bell rings and you conclude that all your charges are present, you will close the door, walk to the front of the room, and introduce yourself. You will either call roll or otherwise check that all students are present or accounted for. You will probably need to make some announcements; then you will explain classroom routine and pass out books and materials. Eventually, though, the moment of truth will arrive: You are going to have to start teaching. When that climactic moment comes, you had better convey the impression that you know what you are doing and make clear to your students exactly what you want them to do. This chapter on objectives is intended to help you achieve both of those goals not only the first day but *every* day in the classroom.

Your reactions at this point may be "Well, sure, of course I'm going to have planned what I'm going to do the first day and at least for the next few days after that." The plans you make for presenting lessons, though, are likely to be much more effective if you take into account the values of stating instructional objectives in specific terms. Furthermore, the specific objectives you devise are more likely to be effective if you start at the *end* of an instructional sequence rather than just taking a stab at formulating a beginning. To grasp that point, suppose that you follow the common practice of many teachers and prepare lesson plans by examining texts and other curriculum materials in order to devise an instructional sequence. Probably your first inclination is to concentrate on what is going to happen tomorrow and to put off thinking about what is going to happen two

Educators who advocate use of instructional objectives point out that it makes sense to concentrate at the very beginning on what you will want your students to do at the end of a unit of study. (Susie Fitzhugh)

weeks or a month ahead when the time comes to evaluate what students have learned. You might reason that there is no point in thinking about tests until it is time to prepare tests. Quite a few teachers operate in such a one-thing-at-a-time way, and you are probably familiar with the results—disorganized lessons, lectures, and assignments, followed by exams that may not have much to do with what you think you were supposed to have learned. You can avoid falling into that common trap by concentrating at the very beginning on what you want your students to be able to do at the end of a unit of study. If you decide in advance what you desire your students to achieve, you can prepare lessons that logically lead to a particular result and also use evaluation techniques efficiently designed to determine if achievement has occurred.

To help you grasp why and how specific objectives can be used to make teaching and testing effective, a history of various approaches to and arguments for goals and objectives will be presented as background for the specific suggestions that follow.

GOALS LISTED BY EDUCATIONAL LEADERS

Most discussions of what children should learn in school take the form of lists of general goals of education. And from time to time, such lists have been proposed by educational leaders or government officials who have been invited to Washington to participate in what are referred to as White House Conferences on Education.

The most recent discussion of education goals by government officials occurred at the University of Virginia in September 1989. At the invitation of

President George Bush, members of his cabinet and the nation's governors attended what was called an Education Summit to propose a set of national education goals. After several months of discussion they concluded that the following six goals should be achieved by the year 2000:

1. All children will be ready to learn when they start school.
2. At least 90 percent of all students will graduate from high school.
3. At the end of the fourth, eighth, and twelfth grades, students will demonstrate their competency in such basic subjects as English, mathematics, science, history, and geography. In addition, students will acquire the thinking skills that will allow them to become responsible citizens, independent learners, and productive workers.
4. U.S. students will be ranked first in the world in science and mathematics achievement.
5. All adults will be sufficiently literate, knowledgeable, and skilled to compete in a global economy and behave as responsible citizens.
6. All schools will be free of drugs and violence and will offer an environment conducive to learning.

This list clearly mentions skills, attitudes, and interests that are desirable, if not essential, for someone who hopes to live successfully and happily in America. Unfortunately, these statements do not provide very useful guidelines for teachers charged with the responsibility for achieving them. Precisely how, for example, are you supposed to make students independent learners and responsible citizens?

TAXONOMIES OF OBJECTIVES

Awareness of the vagueness of such goals stimulated a group of psychologists who specialized in testing to seek a better way to describe educational objectives. They reasoned that group tests used to measure school achievement could be made more effective and accurate if they were based on a school curriculum derived from a systematic list of objectives. The fact that psychologists interested in testing took the lead in describing specific objectives is related to the point made a bit earlier that you should start at the end rather than just jumping in at the beginning. It makes more sense to decide in advance what is important enough to be tested rather than simply teaching an assortment of information and skills and then discovering in hit-or-miss fashion how much has been achieved. After experimenting with various ways to prepare lists of objectives that would be more useful to teachers than vaguely worded sets of goals, the test specialists

> Taxonomy: categories arranged in hierarchical order

decided to develop taxonomies of educational objectives. A **taxonomy** is a classification scheme with categories arranged in hierarchical order. Because goals of education are extremely diverse (take another look at those listed by the Education Summit participants), the decision was made to prepare taxonomies in three *domains:* cognitive, affective, and psychomotor. The taxonomy for the

cognitive domain stresses knowledge and intellectual skills; the taxonomy for the **affective domain** concentrates on attitudes and values; and that for the **psychomotor domain** focuses on physical abilities and skills.

Taxonomy for the Cognitive Domain

The taxonomy for the cognitive domain was prepared by Benjamin S. Bloom and several associates (1956). It consists of six hierarchically ordered levels of instructional outcomes: knowledge, comprehension, application, analysis, synthesis, and evaluation. The taxonomy is described as a hierarchy because it was reasoned that comprehension relies on prior mastery of knowledge or facts, application depends on comprehension of relevant ideas, and so on through the remaining levels. An abridged outline of the taxonomy for the cognitive domain appears below.

▶ Cognitive taxonomy: knowledge, comprehension, application, analysis, synthesis, evaluation

Taxonomy of Educational Objectives: Cognitive Domain

1.00 *Knowledge.* Remembering previously learned information.

    1.10 *Knowledge of specifics.*

        1.11 *Knowledge of terminology.* What terms and symbols will your students need to know? (for example, verbs, nouns, +, −, H_2SO_4).

        1.12 *Knowledge of specific facts.* What specific facts will your students need to know? (for example, names of the states, chief exports of Brazil, and the properties of H_2SO_4).

The taxonomy of objectives for the cognitive domain calls attention to the point that knowledge *and* comprehension *must occur before* application *can take place.* (Ulrike Welsch)

1.20 *Knowledge of ways and means of dealing with specifics.*

    1.21 *Knowledge of conventions.* What sets of rules will your students need to know? (for example, rules of etiquette, rules of punctuation).

    1.22 *Knowledge of trends and sequences.* What awareness of trends and sequences will your students need to have? (for example, nature of evolution and changes in attitudes about the role of women in American society).

    1.23 *Knowledge of classifications and categories.* What classifications and category schemes will your students need to know? (for example, types of literature, types of business ownership, and types of government).

    1.24 *Knowledge of criteria.* What sets of criteria will your students need to be able to apply? (for example, factors to consider in judging the nutritional value of a meal or the qualities of a work of art).

    1.25 *Knowledge of methodology.* What sorts of methodology will your students need to master? (for example, ways to solve problems in math and how to set up an experiment in chemistry).

1.30 *Knowledge of the universals and abstractions in a field.*

    1.31 *Knowledge of principles and generalizations.* What general principles will your students need to know? (for example, laws of heredity and laws of motion).

    1.32 *Knowledge of theories and structure.* What general theories will your students need to know? (for example, nature of free enterprise system, theory of evolution).

2.00 *Comprehension.* Grasping the meaning of information.

    2.10 *Translation.* Ability to put communication into another form (for example, stating problems in own words, reading a musical score, translating words and phrases from a foreign language, interpreting a diagram, and grasping the meaning of a political cartoon).

    2.20 *Interpretation.* Ability to reorder ideas and comprehend interrelationships (for example, giving own interpretation of a novel or a poem, gathering data from a variety of sources, and preparing an organized report).

    2.30 *Extrapolation.* Ability to go beyond given data (for example, theorizing about what might happen if . . . , drawing conclusions from given sets of data, and predicting trends).

3.00 *Application.* Applying knowledge to actual situations (for example, taking principles learned in math and applying them to laying out a baseball diamond, and applying principles of civil liberties to current events).

4.00 *Analysis.* Breaking down objects or ideas into simpler parts and seeing how the parts relate and are organized (for example, discussing how democracy and communism differ and detecting logical fallacies in an argument).

5.00 *Synthesis.* Rearranging component ideas into a new whole (for example, planning a program or panel discussion and writing a comprehensive term paper).

6.00 *Evaluation.* Making judgments based on internal evidence or external criteria (for example, evaluating a work of art, editing a term paper, and detecting inconsistencies in the speech of a politician).

Taxonomy for the Affective Domain

Taxonomy of affective objectives stresses attitudes and values

In addition to arranging instructional experiences to help students achieve cognitive objectives, virtually all teachers are interested in encouraging the development of attitudes and values. To clarify the nature of such objectives, a taxonomy for the affective domain was prepared (Krathwohl, Bloom & Masia, 1964). Affective objectives are more difficult to define, evaluate, or encourage than cognitive objectives because they are often demonstrated in subtle or indirect ways. Furthermore, certain aspects of value development are sometimes considered to be more the responsibility of parents than of teachers. Finally, because values and attitudes involve a significant element of personal choice, they are often expressed more clearly out of school than in the classroom. The complete taxonomy for the affective domain stresses out-of-school values as much as, if not more than, in-school values. The following abridgment concentrates on the kinds of affective objectives you are most likely to be concerned with as a teacher. You will probably recognize, though, that there is not much you can do to substantially influence the kinds of objectives described in the higher levels of the taxonomy since they represent a crystallization of values formed by experiences over an extended period of time. (*Values clarification,* a technique for encouraging the development of a value system, will be described in Chapter 11.)

Taxonomy of Educational Objectives: Affective Domain

1.0 *Receiving (attending).* Willingness to receive or attend.

    1.1 *Awareness.* Being aware of distinctive features (for example, listening attentively and concentrating on distinctive features of a complex stimulus).

    1.2 *Willingness to receive.* Showing a willingness to consider various interpretations and the opinions of others (for example, listening to discussions of controversial issues with an open mind and respecting the rights of others).

    1.3 *Controlled or selected attention.* Actively attending to experiences or presentations of the ideas of others (for example, willingly participating in class discussions and reading articles that present both sides of a controversial issue).

2.0 *Responding.* Active participation indicating positive response or acceptance of an idea or policy.

The taxonomy of objectives for the affective domain emphasizes that receiving *(attending) and* responding *typically precede* valuing—where a person expresses support for a particular point of view. (Billy E. Barnes/Stock, Boston, Inc.)

2.1 *Acquiescence in responding.* Exhibiting acceptance of expectations and responsibilities (for example, completing homework assignments and obeying school rules).

2.2 *Willingness to respond.* Voluntarily or willingly choosing to respond (for example, willingly participating in class discussion and voluntarily completing optional assignments).

2.3 *Satisfaction in response.* Experiencing a sense of satisfaction or enjoyment by responding in a particular way (for example, showing enjoyment when working on a self-selected project and enthusiastically participating in group activities).

3.0 *Valuing.* Expressing a belief or attitude about the value or worth of something.

3.1 *Acceptance of value.* Endorsing a basic proposition or assumption (for example, endorsing the concept of democratic forms of government and accepting the idea that good health habits are important).

3.2 *Preference for a value.* Expressing willingness to be identified with a value (for example, expressing support for a particular point of view and defending an opinion questioned by another student).

3.3 *Commitment.* Expressing a strongly held value or conviction (for example, participating in a campaign to clean up the playground and volunteering to serve on a school committee formed to raise funds for homeless people in your community).

4.0 *Organization.* Organizing various values into an internalized system.

4.1 *Conceptualization of a value.* Understanding how a value relates to values already held (for example, recognizing the need to seek a balance between economic growth and conservation of natural resources).

4.2 *Organization of a value system.* Bringing several, possibly disparate, values together into a consistent system (for example, recognizing own abilities, limitations, and values and developing realistic aspirations).

5.0 *Characterization by a value or value complex.* The value system becomes a way of life.

    5.1 *Generalized set.* Exhibiting a predisposition to act in certain ways (for example, a person's lifestyle influences reactions to many different kinds of situations).

Taxonomy for the Psychomotor Domain

Cognitive and affective objectives are important at all grade levels, but so are psychomotor objectives. Regardless of the grade level or subject you teach, at some point you are likely to want to help your students acquire physical skills of various kinds. In the primary grades, for example, you will want your pupils to learn how to print legibly. And in many subjects in junior and senior high school, psychomotor skills (for example, driving a car, playing a violin, adjusting a microscope, manipulating an electric typewriter, operating a power saw, throwing a pot, swinging a golf club) may be essential. Recognition of the importance of physical skills prompted Elizabeth Simpson (1972) to prepare a taxonomy for the psychomotor domain. An abridged version of the taxonomy follows.

Psychomotor taxonomy outlines steps that lead to skilled performance

Taxonomy of Educational Objectives: Psychomotor Domain

1.0 *Perception.* Using sense organs to obtain cues needed to guide motor activity.

    1.1 *Sensory stimulation.* Interpreting a sensory stimulus (for example, listening to the sounds made by violin strings before tuning them).

    1.2 *Cue selection.* Identifying relevant cues and associating them with appropriate behavior (for example, recognizing sounds that indicate malfunctioning of equipment).

    1.3 *Translation.* Relating sensory cues to performing a motor act (for example, relating musical tempo and rhythm to dance forms).

2.0 *Set.* Being ready to perform a particular action.

    2.1 *Mental set.* Being mentally ready to perform (for example, knowing the steps to follow in order to replace a muffler).

    2.2 *Physical set.* Being physically ready to perform in terms of body position, posture, focusing of visual and auditory attention (for example, having instrument ready to play and watching conductor at start of a musical performance).

    2.3 *Emotional set.* Being willing and eager to perform (for example, exhibiting eagerness to use a sewing machine to make a garment).

3.0 *Guided response.* Performing under guidance of a model.

    3.1 *Imitation.* Copying the performance of someone else (for example, swinging a tennis racket just after observing an expert demonstrate a stroke).

3.2 *Trial and error.* Trying various responses until the correct one is selected (for example, experimenting with various ways to use a saw with a particular type of material).

4.0 *Mechanism.* Being able to perform a task habitually with some degree of confidence and proficiency (for example, demonstrating the ability to get first serve in service area 70 percent of the time).

5.0 *Complex or overt response.* Performing a task with a high degree of proficiency and skill (for example, typing all kinds of business letters and forms quickly with no errors).

6.0 *Adaptation.* Using previously learned skills to perform new but related tasks (for example, using skills developed while learning how to operate an electric typewriter or word processor).

7.0 *Origination.* Creating new performances after having developed skills (for example, creating a new form of modern dance).

The hierarchically arranged lists of objectives you have just examined clearly provide more tangible descriptions of objectives than the goals listed by the participants in the Education Summit. Although they were devised to aid educators charged with developing comprehensive curricula, they can be used by classroom teachers in a variety of ways that will be described later in this chapter. Before turning to applications and uses of objectives, however, we shall describe yet another approach to stating educational goals. As part of a comprehensive program to assess the performance of public school students in this country, sets of objectives have been devised for basic subjects taught in American schools.

A basic instructional technique for helping students master psycho-motor objectives is to demonstrate a skill and then give guidance as students try out the skill. (Bob Daemmrich/ Tony Stone Worldwide)

NATIONAL ASSESSMENT OBJECTIVES

In the 1960s the amount of public money spent on education exceeded $30 billion per year. By 1986–1987 that amount had increased to over $160 billion. By 1998 total expenditures are predicted to be about $200 billion (Ornstein & Levine, 1989, p. 275; Sadker & Sadker, 1991, p. 389). When legislators, taxpayers, and educators realized how quickly educational expenditures were increasing, they quite naturally began to wonder whether the investment was paying dividends. Many individuals were convinced that education was not all that it might be, but these opinions were based on impressions. There was no trustworthy way to determine what students were actually learning—or not learning—in American schools. For this reason, the Education Commission of the States was formed in 1964 for the purpose of initiating what came to be called the **National Assessment of Educational Progress.**

The purpose of National Assessment is to provide information about the knowledge, understanding, skills, and attitudes that American children acquire in the public schools. Toward this end, the decision was made to test periodically thousands of individuals at four age levels—nine, thirteen, seventeen, and twenty-six through thirty-five—in ten learning areas: art, career and occupational development, citizenship, literature, mathematics, music, reading, science, social studies, and writing.

Groups of teachers, scholars, educators, and laymen drew up lists of educational goals and objectives for each of the ten areas. Then specialists in each subject area prepared examinations to measure how well these objectives were being achieved. Finally, a rotating schedule for administering the tests was developed, and the examinations were given to representative samples of individuals.

The results are reported in terms of geographic region, size of community, type of community, age, sex, race, and socioeducational background. (No data on specific students, school districts, cities, or states are provided.) The information gives data on general trends (for example, big cities and small towns are low in science and writing) and specific questions (only 20 percent of the seventeen-year-olds tested knew that in human females the egg is released an average of fourteen days after menstruation begins). Figure 7.1 shows a page from a National Assessment test of ability to recognize literary works and characters.

Major objectives for several of the current measurement areas are listed here. Sub-objectives for one section of each list are also supplied. These lists indicate the kinds of objectives experienced educators feel should be stressed by teachers of various subjects and also the kind of information supplied in National Assessment reports. If you would like more complete information about any of the lists, including all the sub-objectives for different grade levels, you can obtain booklets from National Assessment at the address supplied at the end of this chapter. The objectives lists are occasionally revised. Subsequent lists of objectives may thus differ from those summarized here. You are urged to examine all the lists, even though they do not relate to subjects you expect to teach because they illustrate different ways to describe objectives.

▶ National Assessment provides lists of objectives, results of periodic evaluations of knowledge, attitudes, skills

FIGURE 7.1   Page from the *National Assessment of Educational Progress* "Recognizing Literary Works and Characters" (From the National Assessment of Educational Progress, a project carried out under a grant from the National Institute of Education and administered by the Education Commission of the United States.)

Exercise R308

Ages 13, 17, Adult
Objective IA

Many people or animals that we read about in books become so well-known that we can name them just from a picture. Above is a picture of a man who appears in a story.

What is the name of the <u>man</u> in the picture?

Write your answer on the line provided.

Sherlock Holmes

	Age 13	Age 17	Adult
Acceptable responses	57.2%	78.5%	75.6%
Unacceptable responses	7.2	4.7	3.2
I don't know.	34.8	15.7	19.9
No response	.8	1.1	1.4

Citizenship and Social Studies Objectives

I. Demonstrates skills necessary to acquire information.

II. Demonstrates skills necessary to use information.

III. Demonstrates an understanding of individual development and the skills necessary to communicate with others.

IV. Demonstrates an understanding of and interest in the ways human beings organize, adapt to, and change their environments.

V. Demonstrates an understanding of and interest in the development of the United States.
   A. Understands the principles and purposes of the United States.
   B. Understands the organization and operation of the governments in the United States.
   C. Understands political decision making in the United States.
   D. Understands the electoral process in the United States.
   E. Understands the basis and organization of the legal system in the United States.
   F. Knows rights of individuals in the United States.
   G. Recognizes civil and criminal judicial systems in the United States.
   H. Has a commitment to support justice and rights of all individuals.
   I. Understands economics in the United States.
   J. Understands major social changes that have occurred in American society.
   K. Has a commitment to participating in community service and civic improvement.

Mathematics Objectives

I. Mathematical knowledge.

II. Mathematical skill.
   A. How well can students perform computations, including computations with whole numbers, integers, fractions, decimals, percents, ratios, and proportions?
   B. How well can students make measurements?
   C. How well can students read graphs and tables?
   D. How well can students perform geometric manipulations such as constructions and spatial visualizations?
   E. How well can students perform algebraic manipulations?
   F. How well can students estimate the answers to computations and measurements?

III. Mathematical understanding.

IV. Mathematical application.

Music Objectives

I. Performs a piece of music.

II. Reads standard musical notation.

III. Listens to music with understanding.

IV. Is knowledgeable about some musical instruments, some of the terminology of music, methods of performance and forms, some of the standard literature of music, and some aspects of the history of music.
   A. Knows the meanings of common musical terms used in connection with the performance of music, and identifies musical instruments and performing ensembles in illustrations.

    B. Knows standard pieces of music by title, composer, or brief descriptions of the music, or identifies literary-pictorial materials associated with the music from its inception.

    C. Knows prominent composers and performers by name and chief accomplishment.

    D. Knows something of the history of music.

V. Knows about the musical resources of the community and seeks musical experiences by performing music.

VI. Makes judgments about music, and acknowledges the value and personal worth of music.

Reading and Literature Objectives

I. Values reading and literature.

II. Comprehends written works.

III. Responds to written works in interpretive and evaluative ways.

    A. Extends understanding of written works through interpretation.

      1. Demonstrates an awareness of the emotional impact of written works.

      2. Applies personal experiences to written works.

      3. Applies knowledge of other works or fields of study.

      4. Analyzes written works.

IV. Applies study skills in reading.

Science Objectives

I. Knows the fundamental aspects of science.

II. Understands and applies the fundamental aspects of science in a wide range of problem situations.

III. Appreciates the knowledge and processes of science, the consequences and limitations of science, and the personal and social relevance of science and technology in our society.

    A. Appreciates facts and simple concepts, laws (principles), and conceptual schemes. Appreciates science as a dynamic body of knowledge.

    B. Appreciates inquiry skills as fundamental tools for solving problems.

    C. Appreciates the scientific enterprise. Has one's value system affected by his or her understanding of the scientific enterprise. Appreciates the need for, and value of, the activities and products of science.

The Education Summit goals, the taxonomies of objectives, and the National Assessment sets of objectives illustrate quite different ways to analyze what pupils should learn in schools. All three approaches, however, call attention to these points:

1. The need to consider cognitive, affective, and psychomotor factors.

2. The need to take into account acquisition of immediate knowledge, traits, and skills, as well as the long-term impact of learning.

The Education Summit participants agreed, for example, that students should achieve a minimum level of competence in basic subjects but that they should also become independent learners, responsible citizens, and productive workers. The three taxonomies stress that lower-level knowledge, habits, and skills should be acquired as background for more comprehensive and higher-level attributes such as analysis, synthesis, and evaluation; that a set of values should be acquired; and that something original should be created. National Assessment sets of objectives typically include acquisition of specific information and skills, as well as applications to out-of-school situations.

WAYS TO STATE AND USE OBJECTIVES

Many psychologists have offered suggestions for use of objectives, but the following discussion is limited to recommendations made by two of the most influential writers on the subject: Robert F. Mager and Norman E. Gronlund.

Mager's Recommendations for Use of Specific Objectives

With the publication of a provocative and unorthodox little treatise titled *Preparing Instructional Objectives* (1962, 1984), Mager sparked considerable interest in

Students who have not been provided with clearly stated instructional objectives may lack motivation to learn. (Bob Daemmerich)

the use of objectives. The revised second edition of this book (1984) opens with the following statement:

> Once you decide to teach someone something, several kinds of activity are indicated if your instruction is to be successful. For one thing, you must assure yourself that there is a need for the instruction, making certain that (1) your students don't already know what you intend to teach and (2) instruction is the best means for bringing about a desired change. For another, you must clearly specify the outcomes or objectives you intend your instruction to accomplish. You must select and arrange learning experiences for your students in accordance with principles of learning and must evaluate student performance according to the objectives originally selected. In other words, first you decide where you want to go, then you create and administer the means of getting there, and then you arrange to find out whether you arrived. (p. 1)

As you undoubtedly recognized, this is a description of the model of instruction that is being used as the organizational frame of reference for this book, and Mager was one of several psychologists who were given credit in Chapter 1 for suggesting the model.

Having described his model of instruction, Mager then emphasizes the importance of objectives, pointing out that "You cannot concern yourself with the problem of selecting the most efficient route to your destination [of having students exhibit knowledge or perform a skill] until you know what your destination is" (p. 1). Having described how important it is to state objectives at the beginning of a unit of study, Mager then offers these suggestions for writing **specific objectives** of instruction:

> Mager: state specific objectives that identify act, define conditions, state criteria

1. Describe what you want learners to be doing when demonstrating achievement, and indicate how you will know they are doing it.

2. In your description, identify and name the behavioral act that indicates achievement, define the conditions under which the behavior is to occur, and state the criterion of acceptable performance.

3. Write a separate objective for each learning performance.

   Here are some examples of the types of objectives Mager recommends:

   Correctly solves at least seven addition problems consisting of three two-digit numbers within a period of three minutes.

   Correctly answers at least four of the five questions on the last page of story booklet 16 in the Reading Comprehension series of booklets.

   Given pictures of ten trees, correctly identifies at least eight as either deciduous or evergreen.

   Correctly spells at least 90 percent of the words on the list handed out last week.

   Given an electric typewriter, sets it up to type a business letter (according to the specifications provided on page 352 of the text) within two minutes.

(Note that the criterion of acceptable performance can be stated as a time limit, a minimum number of correct responses, or a proportion of correct responses.)

Mager's proposals were widely endorsed immediately after the publication of *Preparing Instructional Objectives,* but in time it became apparent that the very specific kinds of objectives he recommended were most useful in situations where students were asked to acquire knowledge of factual information or learn simple skills. Norman E. Gronlund concluded that a different type of objective was more appropriate for more complex and advanced kinds of learning.

Gronlund's Recommendations for Use of General Objectives

Gronlund (1991) has developed a two-step procedure for writing a more general type of objective. He suggests that teachers follow this procedure:

> ▶ Gronlund: state general objective, list sample of specific learning outcomes

1. Examine what is to be learned with reference to lists of objectives such as those included in the three taxonomies and in National Assessment booklets. Use such lists to formulate **general objectives** of instruction that describe types of behavior students should exhibit in order to demonstrate that they have learned.

2. Under each general instructional objective, list up to five *specific learning outcomes* that begin with an *action verb* and indicate specific, observable responses. These sets of specific learning outcomes should provide a representative sample of what pupils should be able to do when they have achieved the general objective.

If you were teaching an educational psychology course and you wanted to write a Gronlund-type objective that reflected an understanding of the four stages of Piaget's theory of cognitive development, it might look like this:

1. The student will understand the characteristics of Piaget's four stages of cognitive development.
   1.1 Describes in his or her own words the type of thinking in which pupils at each stage can and cannot engage.
   1.2 Predicts behaviors of pupils of different ages.
   1.3 Explains why certain teaching techniques would or would not be successful with pupils of different ages.

On the other hand, if you wanted to cover the same outcome with a list of Mager-type objectives, it might look like this:

1. Given a list of the names of each of Piaget's four stages of cognitive development, the student, within twenty minutes, will describe in his or her own words two problems that pupils at each stage should and should not be able to solve.

2. Given a videotape of kindergarten pupils presented with a conservation-of-volume problem, the student will predict the response of 90 percent of the pupils.

3. Given a videotape of fifth-grade pupils presented with a class inclusion problem, the student will predict the response of 90 percent of the pupils.

4. Given eight descriptions of instructional lessons, two at each of Piaget's four stages, the student will be able to explain in each case why the lesson would or would not succeed.

Gronlund recommends that you begin with general objectives for several reasons. One reason is that most learning activities are too complex to be described in terms of a specific objective for every learning outcome, as proposed by Mager. A second reason is that the types of objectives recommended by Mager may tend to cause both instructors and pupils to concentrate on memorizing facts and mastery of simple skills. As indicated in the taxonomies presented earlier, these types of behaviors are at the lowest levels of the taxonomies of objectives. A third reason is that specific objectives result in long cumbersome lists that restrict the flexibility of the teacher. Gronlund argues, for example, that the performance criteria should be kept separate from the objective in order to vary the standards as needed without having to rewrite the objective. This feature is useful if the same behavior is to be evaluated several times over the course of a unit of instruction, with successively higher levels of performance required. A fourth and final reason is that general objectives help keep you aware that the main target of your instructional efforts is the general outcome (such as compre-hension, application, or analysis), not the more specific objectives. The latter provide just a *sample* of the types of behaviors that signify the general outcome. A different sample could just as easily be used.

To illustrate the differences between general objectives and specific outcomes, Gronlund has prepared lists of phrases and verbs that can be used in writing each type of objective for each of the levels of all three taxonomies of educational objectives. These lists can be found in Chapter 4 of Gronlund's *How to Write and Use Instructional Objectives* (4th ed., 1991) and in Appendix E of his *Measurement and Evaluation in Teaching* (6th ed., 1990). The lists in Tables 7.1, 7.2, and 7.3 are abridged and paraphrased versions of those devised by Gronlund.

Using General Objectives and Specific Outcomes

To illustrate how you might take advantage of the information just summarized, we now provide a few examples of the use of objectives and specific outcomes at different grade levels and with different subjects.

Third-Grade Mathematics   To begin, you might examine the National Assess-ment objectives for mathematics, noting that four basic objectives are listed: knowledge, skill, understanding, and application. Next, you might refer to the taxonomy for the cognitive domain and peruse the various descriptions under the

TABLE 7.1 Taxonomy for the Cognitive Domain: Objectives and Outcomes		
Level of Taxonomy	**General Objectives**	**Specific-Outcome Action Verbs**
Knowledge	Knows terms Knows specific facts Knows rules Knows trends and sequences Knows classifications and categories Knows methods and procedures	Defines, names, states, identifies, describes, outlines, reproduces
Comprehension	Translates communications Interprets relationships Understands facts	Paraphrases, converts, explains, predicts, generalizes, infers
Application	Applies principles	Uses, solves, constructs, prepares, demonstrates
Analysis	Analyzes organization and relationships Recognizes unstated assumptions	Discriminates, outlines, diagrams, differentiates, infers, subdivides
Synthesis	Produces new arrangements	Designs, organizes, rearranges, compiles, modifies, creates
Evaluation	Judges on basis of external criteria Judges on basis of evidence	Appraises, compares, contrasts, discriminates, criticizes, justifies
Example: (Comprehension)	Understands the meaning of a constitutional democracy	Paraphrases the contents of a country's constitution Explains the functions of various branches of government Gives an example of a constitutional democracy Explains how to convert a dictatorship into a constitutional democracy

headings of knowledge, comprehension, and application. (Since third-graders are concrete operational thinkers, you reason that the analysis, synthesis, and evaluation objectives are too advanced to be appropriate.) Using the knowledge heading of the taxonomy as a guide, you might ask yourself what terms, symbols, and rules your students need to know and what methods they need to know how to use. Next, you refer to Mager's suggestions for preparing objectives to see if his approach would be appropriate. You conclude that his recommendations might be very useful in arranging short classroom exercises. You devise a page of addition and subtraction problems and plan to hand them out the next day with the announcement that anyone who gets more than eight out of ten correct will earn a passing grade. You also announce that similar exercises will be handed out every day and that those who get a passing grade on four in a row will not have to complete the exercise scheduled for Friday.

Next, you refer to the lists of objectives and outcomes derived from Gronlund's description, paying particular attention to the knowledge category of the

▶ Mager-style objectives useful in arranging classroom exercises

	TABLE 7.2 Taxonomy for the Affective Domain: Objectives and Outcomes	
Level of Taxonomy	**General Objectives**	**Specific-Outcome Action Verbs**
Receiving (Attending)	Shows awareness of distinctive features Shows willingness to receive Indicates attention	Describes, identifies, selects, points to
Responding	Accepts need for regulations and responsibilities Chooses to respond in acceptable ways Shows interest in responding	Complies, tells, performs
Valuing	Endorses propositions Shows preference for values Expresses commitment to values	Explains, justifies, shares, initiates
Organization	Understands relationships between values Develops a value system	Explains, defends, organizes
Value Complex	Acts in ways consistent with values	Displays, practices, performs
Example: (Valuing)	Shows concern for the welfare of the less fortunate	Reads reports on causes of homelessness Attends local government hearings on proposed policies toward poor and homeless Joins organizations that serve the less fortunate Donates money to organizations that serve the less fortunate Lobbies politicians to support building of low-cost housing

▶ Gronlund-type objectives lead to comprehensive coverage of a skill or topic

taxonomy for the cognitive domain. You decide that "Knows methods and procedures" is especially important, so you write it down, followed by these specific outcomes (which you devise after referring to the complete list of specific-outcome action verbs):

1. Identifies plus and minus signs in problems.

2. Describes how to add and subtract numbers.

3. Demonstrates ability to add and subtract numbers.

4. Shows ability to take sets of numbers supplied and arrange them to be added or subtracted by self or others.

5. Explains how to use knowledge of addition and subtraction to handle situations outside of school (for example, deciding if enough money has been saved to buy three different objects of known value).

Sixth-Grade Music   Even though you don't know a great deal about musical performance and had only a brief unit on music in an education course, you

TABLE 7.3 Taxonomy for the Psychomotor Domain: Objectives and Outcomes

Level of Taxonomy	General Objectives	Specific-Outcome Action Verbs
Perception (Attending)	Recognizes significant cues Relates cues to actions	Chooses, detects, identifies, differentiates, demonstrates
Set	Displays mental readiness to perform Displays physical readiness to perform Displays emotional readiness to perform	Begins, proceeds, starts, volunteers, shows, demonstrates
Guided Response	Imitates a response Experiments with responses	Assembles, fixes, manipulates
Mechanism	Performs task habitually	Assembles, fixes, manipulates
Complex Response	Performs with confidence and proficiency	Assembles, fixes, manipulates, mends
Adaptation	Adapts skills to fit situation	Alters, varies, revises
Organization	Creates new performance	Originates, composes, constructs, devises
Example: (Adaptation)	Adjusts tennis game to counteract opponent's style	Changes racquet grip to impart different spin Alters stance to better return opponent's serve Rushes net more often than usual

suddenly discover that you are supposed to present a unit on musical knowledge to your sixth-grade class. You examine the National Assessment music objectives and are delighted to discover that the preliminary work has already been done for you by experts. You decide that a logical first objective is "Is knowledgeable about some musical instruments," and you refer to the list of objectives and specific outcomes relating to knowledge in the taxonomy for the cognitive domain to devise these specific outcomes:

1. Names the instruments of an orchestra when pictures of each are displayed.
2. Identifies the instruments of an orchestra when each is played on a recording.
3. States differences between the instruments of an orchestra and those of a band.
4. Differentiates between recordings played by an orchestra and a band.

Eighth-Grade Literature You begin by examining the National Assessment objectives for reading and literature, noting the basic objectives: values, comprehends, responds, and applies. Next you examine the taxonomy for the cognitive domain as well as that for the affective domain, since both types of objectives are included in the National Assessment list. You conclude that the comprehension, application, analysis, synthesis, and evaluation levels from the cognitive domain may all be appropriate, at least to some extent. The receiving, responding, and valuing levels of the affective domain also seem worth examining. A brief look at Mager's recommendations leads you to conclude that his approach is not appropriate for your classes, so you concentrate on the lists of general objectives and specific outcomes for the levels of the taxonomies you have selected. Since *values* was the first objective listed by the National Assessment committee, you peruse the outline for the affective domain and record the general objective "Values well-written short stories." Under that statement you list these specific outcomes:

1. Selects a well-written short story from a book containing stories of varying quality.
2. Identifies well-written and poorly written short stories.
3. Explains why a short story identified as good is superior to one identified as poorly written.
4. Tells classmates why a particular short story is good.
5. Justifies preference for a favorite short story.

High School Social Studies   You begin by examining the National Assessment objectives for your subject and are impressed by those listed under "Demonstrates skills necessary to use information," particularly the sub-objective regarding detection of errors and unwarranted generalizations. You turn to the outline of the taxonomy for the cognitive domain and concentrate on the analysis, synthesis, and evaluation levels. Using the lists of objectives and outcomes as a guide, you select the general objective "Judges on basis of evidence," and list these specific outcomes:

1. Identifies limitations of evidence given in an article to justify statement.
2. Distinguishes between evidence and opinions.
3. Relates evidence to conclusions.
4. Detects conclusions based on insufficient or irrelevant evidence.
5. Explains why it is not always possible to determine the direction of cause and effect relationships.
6. Criticizes statements made by public figures that cannot be backed up by evidence.

High School Physical Education   Since you are about to introduce archery as an activity for the first time, you turn directly to the taxonomy for the psychomotor domain. You realize that most of your students have never had a bow in their hands, so you decide to concentrate on the first two levels (perception and set) the first day. You jot down the general objective "Relates cues to actions" and list these specific outcomes:

1. Detects balance point of bow.
2. Differentiates between feel of moderate and extreme string pressure.

If you are asked to present a unit on citizenship to an elementary school class, you might start by referring to the list of objectives prepared by the National Assessment committee on citizenship. (Bachmann/Stock, Boston, Inc.)

3. Identifies correct placement of arrow in bow and above hand.
4. Chooses proper stance to achieve good balance.

MULTIPLE VALUES OF OBJECTIVES

The brief examples just provided give only a sketchy idea of the usefulness of objectives since they illustrate only selected aspects of a few limited teaching units. Even so, they are sufficient to reveal the potential of objectives. If you follow the procedures just illustrated in systematic and comprehensive ways as you prepare lessons, you will not only develop firsthand appreciation of the values of objectives, but you and your students will also be likely to benefit in a variety of ways. To get maximum value from objectives, it would be to your advantage to follow this procedure.

First, examine the texts and curriculum materials you will be asked to use. Then, look over the curriculum outlines and lesson plan instructions that may have been supplied by your supervisors. Next, note your own general ideas about what should be included in lessons and assignments. At that point, peruse the appropriate National Assessment lists for your grade and subject to get some initial leads about how to state objectives. (If one or more of the brief lists presented earlier in this chapter are relevant, you might write to National Assessment headquarters and order the complete objectives booklets.) In addition, look through teachers' journals for your grade level or subject area. Quite often individuals or groups present lists of objectives they have devised through a process of trial and error. If you are unable to find lists in journals but still desire at least some direction, write to one or more of the organizations that specialize in providing objectives for teachers. (Names and addresses are supplied in the Resources for Further Investigation section at the end of this chapter.)

After you have found helpful lists of objectives and/or developed your own, systematically go through all three taxonomies of objectives and begin to develop a master set of instructional goals. Make it a point to include objectives from all three taxonomies (if appropriate) as well as at least some objectives from higher levels (depending on the stage of cognitive development of your pupils). Then refer to the suggestions offered by Mager and Gronlund, and begin to experiment with various ways to actually write objectives.

Regardless of how much assistance you get from other sources, you and your students will benefit if you make an effort to devise lists of objectives that are custom-designed for use in your classroom. That statement is based on the following assumptions:

1. You are more likely to arrange learning experiences in a logical and comprehensive order if you devise sets of objectives than if you operate on a one-thing-at-a-time basis.

2. You will provide yourself with leads for developing specific classroom activities and perhaps get clues you can use in remedial instruction. The description of objectives for third-grade math, for instance, illustrates how taking the trouble to list specific outcomes not only provides ideas for class exercises but also might give you information about sources of learning problems. Asking students to explain *how* they add and subtract, for example, might reveal reasons why some pupils are unable to solve problems consistently. The description of objectives for eighth-grade literature illustrates how an apparently elusive goal such as encouraging appreciation of good literature might be made quite tangible and attainable.

3. You will give yourself guidelines for doing an effective job of evaluation. For instance, if you ask students to *supply* answers (for example, to name or define), you know in advance that you should use short-answer questions or the equivalent. If you ask them to *identify* or *differentiate,* you know you can logically use multiple-choice questions. If you ask them to *perform* in some way (for example, to demonstrate), you know that you should develop ways to evaluate performance. Quite often you will discover that *what* you should evaluate also has been specified by your objectives. Take the music unit for the sixth-grade class. To evaluate achievement in that unit, all you would need to do is follow the objectives in order. That is, first ask students to write down the various instruments of an orchestra as you hold up pictures. Then ask them to identify the instruments when you play a recording. Next, ask them to explain the differences between instruments used in an orchestra and a band. Finally, play band and orchestra recordings and ask them to differentiate between the two.

4. You will help your students become more effective strategic learners. As we point out in Chapter 9, a strategic learner is one who analyzes the factors that bear on a particular task, formulates a plan for mastering the task, and skillfully implements the plan. One important factor that affects performance, and that therefore needs to be accounted for in developing a learning plan, is the nature of the expected outcome. By telling students that they will have to supply or identify answers for this or that content, or that they will have to exhibit a particular type of performance, you are providing them with information that is critical to the formulation of an effective learning plan. The alternative is to leave the situation so vague that students are forced to guess about what and how to study. Inevitably, some of them will guess wrong.

In addition to reasoning about potential values of objectives, however, you should take into account the available research on their effectiveness. A brief analysis of such research will now be provided.

> Using objectives can lead to improved planning, instruction, evaluation

EVALUATIONS OF THE EFFECTIVENESS OF OBJECTIVES

The publication of the various taxonomies and of books by Mager, Gronlund, and others led to widespread use of objectives in American schools and colleges. To determine if objectives were as useful as enthusiasts claimed or implied they were, many psychologists compared the achievement of students who had and had not been provided with specific instructional goals. The results of such research proved to be inconclusive. In one review of over fifty studies, for example, the authors (Duchastel & Merrill, 1973) noted: "A number of studies have shown facilitative effects. However, an equal number of studies have failed to demonstrate any significant difference" (p. 54). The authors concluded that since "objectives sometimes help and are almost never harmful . . . one might as well make them available to students" (p. 63). It is probably safe to assume that the supporters of objectives were less than pleased with this conclusion.

The reason why early studies on the effectiveness of objectives produced such inconsistent results was that the researchers were not asking quite the right question. For example, four variables that work in combination with objectives are individual differences (in ability or motivation, for instance), variations in the subject matter under study, variations in the type of objective provided, and variations in the outcome that is measured (which might be recall, recognition, comprehension, or problem solving). When researchers simply ask whether students who receive objectives will learn more than students who do not, they are assuming such variables to be of little or no importance. It would be nice if the world were that simple. But it is not—particularly when classroom learning is the phenomenon under study. More consistent and useful results ensued when researchers began asking more pointed questions, such as, For what type of learner will objectives work best? What types of things are learned with different types of objectives? For what types of subjects will objectives produce the best

Mager recommends that teachers use objectives that identify the behavioral act that indicates achievement, define the conditions under which the behavior is to occur, and state the criterion of acceptable performance. (Bob Daemmrich)

results? Later reviews (for example, Faw & Waller, 1976; Klauer, 1984; Melton, 1978) were able to draw the following conclusions:

> Objectives work best when students are aware of them

1. Objectives seem to work best when students are aware of them, treat them as directions to learn specific sections of material, and feel they will aid learning.

2. Objectives seem to work best when they are clearly written and the learning task is neither too difficult nor too easy.

3. Students of average ability seem to profit more from being given objectives than do students of higher or lower ability.

4. Objectives lead to an improvement in intentional learning (what is stressed as important) but to a decline in incidental learning (not emphasized by the teacher). General objectives of the type recommended by Gronlund seem to lead to more incidental learning than do specific objectives of the type recommended by Mager.

This last point might be clarified by reference to the Key Points in this book. The Key Points function as a type of instructional objective in that they call your attention to sections of the text that are considered to be particularly important and are likely to be stressed on examinations. If you were to be given an announced exam on the Key Points for this chapter and another unannounced exam immediately after on the other parts of this chapter, you would almost certainly earn a higher score on the Key Points test. The use of Key Points as objectives directs your attention to important parts of the text but also tends to cause you to pay less attention to other potentially significant sections of chapters. An antidote to this tendency is to pay particular attention to the Key Points, but don't skip over other parts of a chapter because you might miss information that could clarify your understanding of the Key Points and/or be useful to you later. Despite that suggestion, you are still virtually certain to engage in more intentional than incidental learning. If the Key Points (or some other form of objectives) were omitted, however, you might be even worse off. Realizing that you will be unable to learn everything in every chapter of this book, you might waste valuable study time procrastinating about which parts of the text you should concentrate on when preparing for exams. Furthermore, you might feel as if you had been "tricked" into doing too much incidental learning that didn't lead to a payoff. (Perhaps you have found yourself preoccupied with this bitter thought as you left an examination room: "Rats. I wasted all that time learning a lot of junk I never used answering questions.") Incidental learning is an advantage when discussing education in abstract terms. But it may be an unrealistic expectation when dealing with real learning situations involving exams. It does appear, however, that using objectives similar to the type recommended by Gronlund leads to more incidental learning than using specific objectives such as those recommended by Mager (Klauer, 1984). Thus, you may be able to encourage at least some incidental learning by stating general objectives followed by a sample of specific outcomes.

▶ General objectives lead to more incidental learning than specific objectives

A final observation on evaluations of the effectiveness of objectives relates to the kinds of outcomes that are typically stressed by researchers. Most of the research investigations upon which the conclusions summarized earlier were based concentrated on pupil achievement as the measure of the impact of objectives. Researchers often fail to take into account less easily measured factors such as positive pupil response to explicit directions, the teacher's feelings of confidence and satisfaction when presenting well-organized lessons, or the ease and efficiency with which evaluations can be made. When these not-so-easy-to-prove factors are added to evidence from the better-designed studies, it seems reasonable to say that there are definite advantages to using objectives.

A final aspect of objectives that has been studied by a number of psychologists centers on arranging what is to be learned in strict hierarchical order. The various taxonomies were based on the assumption that learning experiences ideally should be systematically arranged so that lower-level skills are acquired as background for advanced skills. Evaluations of efforts to use the taxonomies to develop highly systematic hierarchies of learning experiences lead to the conclusion that it is rarely possible to use them exactly as published to plan a completely consistent overall curriculum (Furst, 1981). It appears, therefore, that while there are some benefits to be gained by analyzing sequences of things to be learned, you should not attempt to devise a perfectly ordered set of objectives, with each item in a series preparing the way for the next. You are likely to find that it doesn't work and you may get discouraged about using objectives.

▶ Arranging objectives in strict hierarchical order does not seem to be essential

At the same time, you should habitually make it a point to analyze the kinds of abilities represented by each of the levels in the various taxonomies, particularly the taxonomy for the cognitive domain. Benjamin S. Bloom, organizer and driving force of the team that prepared the first taxonomy, recently made this observation about how it has been used (or not used):

> After the sale of over one million copies of the *Taxonomy of Educational Objectives—Cognitive Domain* [Bloom et al., 1956] and over a quarter of a century of use of this domain in preservice and in-service teacher training, it is estimated that over 90% of test questions that U.S. public school students are *now* expected to answer deal with little more than information. Our instructional material, our classroom teaching methods, and our testing methods rarely rise above the lowest category of the Taxonomy—knowledge. (1984, p. 13)

▶ Most test questions stress knowledge, ignore higher levels of cognitive taxonomy

Now that you are familiar with the types of objectives, various recommendations for using them, and evaluations of their effectiveness, it is time to turn to specific applications. The following Suggestions for Teaching in Your Classroom summarize and reinforce points already discussed.

Mid-Chapter Review

Characteristics of Taxonomies of Objectives

Taxonomy: classification scheme of categories arranged in hierarchical order

Cognitive taxonomy: objectives stressing knowledge, comprehension, application, synthesis, evaluation

Affective taxonomy: objectives stressing attitudes and values

Psychomotor taxonomy: objectives stressing skills

Nature of National Assessment

National Assessment program involves comprehensive, periodic analyses of knowledge, attitudes, and skills

National Assessment publications provide lists of objectives and reports of results of periodic testing programs

Uses of Objectives

Objectives help teachers plan lessons so that students learn efficiently

Mager: use specific objectives by identifying behavioral act that indicates achievement, defining conditions, stating criteria

Specific objectives are useful in arranging classroom exercises but tend to discourage incidental learning

Gronlund: examine what is to be learned, state general objectives, list sample of specific learning outcomes

General objectives with specific outcomes lead to comprehensive coverage, improve planning and instruction, make evaluation simple and efficient

Arranging objectives or learning experiences in strict hierarchical order does not seem to be essential

Referring to taxonomies may be desirable when planning evaluation procedures to make sure higher-level skills are not ignored

Suggestions for Teaching in Your Classroom

USING INSTRUCTIONAL OBJECTIVES

1. Look over texts, curriculum guides, and report cards (for the elementary grades); ask about achievement and competency tests; and think about your own goals to get a general picture of what you want your students to achieve.

2. Check to see if appropriate and useful lists of objectives for your subject and grade level have been developed by others.

3. Examine the taxonomies of objectives for the three domains, and make a preliminary outline of objectives and activities.

4. Refer to the listings of objectives and specific outcomes in Tables 7.1, 7.2, and 7.3, and begin to write sets of objectives.
   a. Describe a general objective in brief terms.
   b. Under that general objective, list from three to five specific outcomes that begin with an action verb. Try to write specific outcomes that reflect a representative sample of what a student should do when demonstrating achievement of the objective.

5. Examine your lists of objectives to determine how they might be converted into specific classroom learning exercises and/or examination questions.

6. Examine your lesson plans to determine if you should occasionally use specific objectives that include a statement of the criterion of acceptable performance.

7. Develop your own variations of the types of instructional objectives described in this and other books.

8. Keep in mind that measurement and evaluation of classroom learning must accurately reflect your learning objectives.

---

1. Look over texts, curriculum guides, and report cards (for the elementary grades); ask about achievement and competency tests; and think about your own goals to get a general picture of what you want your students to achieve.

At the beginning of this chapter the point was made that you will not be able to determine at the end of a report period or year whether your students have achieved specific objectives unless you describe those objectives before you start. Perhaps the most logical way to begin to formulate objectives is to institute a survey of general goals and progressively refine them until you have devised specific objectives and learning outcomes. First of all, it would be wise to find out what others have already decided you should do. Most of the texts you will be asked to use probably will have been selected by state and/or local committees. It is quite likely that you will be asked to follow curriculum guides developed for use in your school system. At the elementary level, the kinds of report cards you will be expected to fill out and/or the kinds of points you will be expected to

The first step in using instructional objectives is to look over texts, curriculum guides, and perhaps inquire about standardized tests your pupils will be asked to take, to get a general picture of what you want your students to achieve. (Richard Hutchings 1992)

▶ Before devising objectives, examine curriculum materials, find out about tests

stress in parent conferences often will indicate what your students will be expected to achieve. It would also be prudent to find out whether your students will be asked to take achievement or competency tests. At present in American education there is quite a bit of stress on measuring student competency in basic skills. Even though it is usually unwise and ineffective to try to "teach to a test," it does make sense to stress the kinds of abilities that are measured by tests used to evaluate student (and perhaps teacher) achievement. If you will be teaching high school English, for example, and you discover that students in your school will not graduate unless they pass a competency test that includes questions designed to measure their ability to write clearly and accurately, it would be sensible to treat that skill as an important objective. Finally, you might note some of your own general goals that are not directly related to texts, curriculum guides, or examinations.

In developing a "starter" list of objectives, you might include items such as these:

Knows important information covered in required text.

Understands information stressed in curriculum guide.

Demonstrates proficiency in subjects listed on report card.

Demonstrates proficiency in types of skills measured by achievement and competency exams.

Applies at least some of the things learned in class to out-of-class situations.

Works diligently and cooperatively in the classroom.

Even if such a list of objectives may be a bit vague, it represents an attempt to develop a general conception of what you want your students to achieve by the last day of class.

2. Check to see if appropriate and useful lists of objectives for your subject and grade level have been developed by others.

After you have outlined the general objectives you want your students to achieve in your particular school and classroom, it makes sense to check on the availability of objectives prepared by experienced educators. It may be well worth the trouble to obtain appropriate National Assessment booklets, for example. You should also ask experienced teachers or supervisors in your school if they know of lists of objectives that have proven to be useful. In addition, peruse recent issues of teachers' journals for articles on objectives. If you are unable to find any sets of goals that provide helpful leads, you might write to the organizations that serve as clearing-houses for objectives (whose addresses are supplied in the Resources for Further Investigation section later in this chapter).

3. Examine the taxonomies of objectives for the three domains, and make a preliminary outline of objectives and activities.

The taxonomies of objectives for the cognitive, affective, and psychomotor domains can be used as all-purpose guides for translating general goals into specific objectives and classroom practices. After you have made your general survey of what you want your students to achieve, for example, you might systematically work your way through the taxonomy for the cognitive domain and jot down brief answers to the following questions:

What sorts of terms and symbols will my students need to know?

What specific facts will they need to know?

What sets of rules will they need to know?

What awareness of trends and sequences will they need to have?

What classifications and categories will they benefit from knowing?

What sets of criteria will they need to be able to apply?

What methods will they need to master?

What general principles will they benefit from knowing?

What theories will they benefit from knowing?

What sorts of translations will they need to perform?

What sorts of interpretations will they need to make?

What sorts of extrapolations will they need to make?

What sorts of applications should they be able to make?

What kinds of analyses will they need to make?

What kinds of syntheses should they be able to make?

What kinds of evaluations should they be able to make?

A similar procedure might be followed for the various categories in the affective and psychomotor domains. The purpose of carrying out this sort of survey would be to get a more complete idea of the kinds of things your students should be able to achieve by the last day of class. It will probably be impossible for you to list all items for an entire year or report period with reference to such sets of questions, but if you follow this procedure for at least the first teaching unit you expect to present, you should end up with an outline of information that can be converted into more specific objectives and learning outcomes. Then you could repeat the procedure for the next teaching unit, and so on. In preparing such lists, remember to take into account the cognitive abilities of your students so that you do not waste time speculating about higher levels of a taxonomy if these are not appropriate. If you will be teaching students in the upper elementary grades or beyond, though, pay *special* attention to the higher-level categories. Devising lists of objectives under analysis, synthesis, and evaluation categories may be more difficult than devising lists under the knowledge category, but higher-level skills are too often omitted (as noted by Bloom) when examinations are prepared. (One of the major advantages of objectives, you are reminded, is that they can be used to make evaluations more systematic and effective.)

Having written down lists of things your students should achieve, it is now time to convert them into objectives and specific learning outcomes.

4. Refer to the listings of objectives and specific outcomes in Tables 7.1, 7.2, and 7.3, and begin to write sets of objectives.
   a. Describe a general objective in brief terms.
   b. Under that general objective, list from three to five specific outcomes that begin with an action verb. Try to write specific outcomes that reflect a representative sample of what a student should do when demonstrating achievement of the objective.

Since selected examples of objectives for different grade levels and subject areas were given earlier, and since it is impossible to provide further examples for all subjects at all grades, the following examples are based on material in this chapter. The general objectives and specific outcomes are written so that they can be applied to almost any subject matter. The examples in parentheses refer to points covered in this chapter. Thus, the examples serve to review what has been covered, permit you to test your knowledge, and help you prepare for exams.

Examples

Knows essential terms

1. Defines essential terms (for example, *taxonomy, cognitive, affective, psychomotor, domain,* and *transfer*)

2. Illustrates understanding of terms when presented with sets of examples (for example, match the terms *goals, general objectives, specific outcomes,* with an example of each)

3. Distinguishes between similar terms (for example, explain difference between *specific objectives* and *general objectives*)

4. Discriminates between terms (for example, note differences between *goals, objectives,* and *specific outcomes*)

Knows methods and procedures

1. Describes how to use knowledge of procedures (for example, tell where to look for information about hierarchies and lists of objectives)

2. States steps to follow when using a given procedure (for example, describe how to use Mager-style objectives and Gronlund-style objectives)

3. States procedure to follow when provided with problems (for example, describe how to proceed when instructed to teach math in third grade, music in sixth grade, and so forth)

Interprets ideas and concepts to display comprehension

1. Interprets general ideas in specific terms (for example, provide examples of general objectives and specific outcomes for teaching a given subject)

In order for students to gain maximum benefit from classification schemes such as the periodic table of the elements they need to know terms as well as methods and procedures. Referring to the taxonomy of objectives for the cognitive domain will help you make sure they acquire necessary background information before attempting advanced problem solving. (Lawrence Migdale/Stock, Boston, Inc.)

2. Converts suggestions described for one situation to another (for example, take example for teaching a sixth-grade unit on music and apply it to teaching a ninth-grade unit on art appreciation)

3. Explains how to adapt given procedures to special circumstances (for example, describe how to use Mager-style objectives when teaching typing)

Applies principles to hypothetical or actual situations

1. Uses principles to develop procedures (for example, explain how to prepare objectives for a unit on general science)

2. Solves a problem by applying principles (for example, develop useful objectives for a required teaching unit)

3. Demonstrates ability to apply principles (for example, develop a set of Gronlund-style objectives for a unit you expect to teach)

Analyzes organization and relationships

1. Outlines nature of relationships in a given set of data (for example, explain hierarchical arrangement of taxonomies)

2. Discriminates between parts of an organized whole (for example, note differences between lower and higher levels of taxonomies)

3. Differentiates between organizational schemes (for example, explain differences between the taxonomies for the cognitive, affective, and psychomotor domains)

Produces new arrangements

1. Compiles given ideas into a new arrangement (for example, draw up a list of general objectives for your particular grade level and subject)

2. Combines separate sets of ideas into a new pattern (for example, tell how you might use techniques recommended by both Mager and Gronlund in the same teaching unit)

3. Creates custom-designed approach by modifying original description (for example, take examples given in this chapter and modify them so that they fit your own teaching situation)

Judges on basis of criteria or evidence

1. Criticizes misuse of a given technique (for example, specify when Mager-style objectives are not appropriate)

2. Discriminates between proper and improper applications (for example, make judgments about whether the cognitive level of students is likely to permit them to engage in analysis, synthesis, and evaluation)

3. Detects inconsistencies in applications (for example, note when specific outcomes are not defined in terms of action verbs)

4. Evaluates criticisms (for example, evaluate the conclusions of research on the effectiveness of use of objectives)

The sets of objectives just illustrated are arranged in a hierarchical order that parallels the arrangement of the taxonomy for the cognitive domain. While it would be important to make sure that objectives centering on knowledge were mastered first, the results of research noted earlier lead to the conclusion that it is not necessarily an advantage to arrange higher levels of the taxonomy in order. For instance, rather than try to devise a perfectly ordered step-by-step sequence, you might ask students to demonstrate their ability to analyze or evaluate before you ask them to make applications, if that seems a more logical or convenient way to proceed.

Handbook Heading:
Using the Taxonomy of
Affective Objectives

After you have prepared sets of objectives for the cognitive domain, examine the affective and psychomotor taxonomies to determine if there are attitudes and skills you will want your students to acquire along with subject matter. The first level in the taxonomy of affective objectives, for instance, is *receiving* or *attending,* which includes showing willingness to receive and indicating attention. Suppose you conclude that many of your pupils need to pay closer attention to class demonstrations. You might devise an objective such as this:

Observes attentively

1. Puts away distracting material when a demonstration is announced
2. Observes demonstration with alertness
3. Follows instructions for following up on demonstration accurately
4. Describes procedure accurately after having seen a demonstration
5. Answers questions about how to proceed after having seen a demonstration
6. Correctly carries out a procedure shown in a demonstration

Or suppose you want to try to encourage your students to develop an appreciation for the values of science. You might devise an objective such as this:

Appreciates the values of scientific methods and discoveries

1. Describes the characteristics of scientific methods
2. Distinguishes between scientific and nonscientific conclusions
3. Explains why conclusions based on scientific evidence are more trustworthy than conclusions based on hunches or opinions
4. Identifies scientific conclusions by referring to trustworthy evidence

Or suppose you would like your students to become more considerate of others. You might devise an objective similar to this one:

Appreciates the rights and feelings of others

1. Explains how one person's actions may be irritating or distracting to others

2. Invites others to indicate if certain actions are bothersome or distracting

3. Lists kinds of behavior of others that are bothersome or irritating

4. Keeps a record of own behavior that might be bothersome to others

5. Describes specific actions that might be taken to show greater consideration for others

Handbook Heading:
Using the Taxonomy of
Psychomotor Objectives

Suppose you notice that your students seem to be having trouble with the sequence of steps in carrying out some activity. You might devise an objective similar to this one:

Knows sequence of steps in a procedure

1. Describes correct sequence of steps

2. Explains how to carry out each step

3. Shows how to carry out each step

4. Combines all steps in correct order with confidence

Other objectives derived from the taxonomies for the affective and psychomotor domains might be written by referring to Tables 7.2 and 7.3.

5. Examine your lists of objectives to determine how they might be converted into specific classroom learning exercises and/or examination questions.

As you looked over the various examples of objectives provided earlier and in the preceding suggestions, you may have noticed that many of them give specific leads for arranging classroom learning experiences and for devising exams. The objective "Knows terms," for example, could be converted into this announcement to your students:

▸ Use specific
learning-outcome
descriptions to
arrange learning
experiences

"Here is a list of the most important terms in the next chapter of the text. As you read the chapter, write down the definition of each term. I will give you my definitions after you finish, and we can discuss differences between yours and mine. You will be asked to define five terms selected from this list on the exam scheduled for Friday."

Or "Here is a list of ten terms and twenty examples. Write down the correct term next to each example. A test item just like this one will be included on the next exam."

Or "These three terms are very similar. Read pages 75–79 of the text and carefully describe the differences between the terms that are explained on those pages. You will be asked to explain these differences on the next exam, so if you aren't sure about what you have written, ask me to look over your descriptions."

These examples illustrate that when you take the trouble to describe specific learning outcomes, you not only give yourself instructions on ways to present lessons but you also pretty much determine in advance how you will evaluate achievement.

You undoubtedly recognized as you read the suggestions just offered that the basic procedure outlined so far is based on Gronlund's recommendations for using objectives. His approach is quite versatile and has many advantages, but you should also consider other alternatives.

6. Examine your lesson plans to determine if you should occasionally use specific objectives that include a statement of the criterion of acceptable performance.

As noted in the discussion of Mager's recommendations and in the section on evaluations of objectives, too much stress on specific objectives tends to cause teachers to concentrate on knowledge and simple skills and to discourage incidental learning. Even so, there are times when you may find it desirable to describe precisely what you want your students to do and specify the criterion for acceptable performance.

Examples

In order to "pass" this unit you will need to spell correctly at least eighteen of these twenty words on the quiz to be given on Friday.

By the end of this month you should be able to type a 240-word selection in less than six minutes with no errors.

After you watch this film, you should be able to list five basic kinds of crops and give an example of each within three minutes.

In order to earn an A in this course, you will need to answer correctly at least twenty of twenty-five questions on each of five exams.

After you take notes on this lecture, you will be asked to list four types of trees and give an example of each. If you correctly supply all four types and examples, you will not have to take a quiz at the end of the period.

7. Develop your own variations of the types of instructional objectives described in this and other books.

The top levels of the various taxonomies stress creating something new, or at least modifying things to fit particular situations. As a result of reading this chapter, therefore, it would be fitting for you to devise your own variations of the techniques described. Here are a few variations you might consider as examples of ways you might modify the basic suggestions that have been supplied. They all stress objectives, but in different ways than those already described.

Here are some ways you might use objectives to help your pupils study texts and respond selectively to lectures and assignments:

Before distributing a new text to the class, go through it and underline all terms that some students may not understand. List and define these terms; then give an informal quiz to determine if students have learned them.

Invite students to list all terms that they are not sure about as they read or listen. Suggest that they look up such terms in a dictionary or encyclopedia. Perhaps invite discussion of different interpretations of the same terms and decide on an "official" definition that will be used in class discussions or on exams.

Go through each chapter in a text and list Key Points under major headings. If you plan to use these as the basis for exam questions, inform students of that fact.

Look over lecture notes and select the most important points. List these on the board before you begin to lecture.

Say to your students, "There may seem to be an overwhelming amount of factual information in this book. Here are the facts that I want you to concentrate on when you prepare for exams." Then hand out an organized list of these facts.

You might state objectives for a unit of study in ways such as these:

The basic goal of this unit is to help you learn to appreciate and enjoy poetry. When you have finished it you should be able to
1. distinguish between superior and inferior poetry.
2. give reasons for classifying a poem as superior or inferior.
3. explain why you like some poems better than others.
4. find books and magazines that contain poems you are likely to enjoy.

The primary objective of this unit is to help you comprehend and apply the laws of thermodynamics. To earn a passing grade on this unit you will be asked to
1. state the first and second laws of thermodynamics in the same basic terminology used in the text. (Slight alterations will be permitted, provided they do not change the meaning of the law.)
2. rewrite these laws in your own words.
3. predict what will happen in various energy-producing situations.
4. explain how any energy system works.

At the end of this unit on use of the table saw, you will be expected to
1. state five safety rules to observe every time you use the saw.
2. set up the saw for crosscutting and ripping.

3. use the dado head to cut half-lap joints, tongue-and-groove joints, and box joints.

The two examples below suggest how you can call attention to the advantages of developing knowledge of classifications and categories:

"There are so many different kinds of birds it's hard to identify them without some classification scheme. Here is a scheme devised by a famous ornithologist."

"Here are pictures of ten trees. Pick out the ones that are deciduous. Then, see if you can find other ways to call attention to similarities and differences."

The following approaches might encourage students to use criteria and external and internal standards when making judgments:

"We're going to look at some slides of different buildings. Before you see them, though, let's list some things that make a building well designed or poorly designed."

"There are usually several different brands of any food product. What are some factors to consider when making a choice?"

"We all buy clothes from time to time. Let's discuss factors you might consider before you make your next purchase."

"I'm going to project some slides of different sets of dining room furniture. I'd like you to pick out the set you like the most and describe why you like it. What features of the set make it seem more attractive to you than the other sets? Then next week we will take a field trip to a large furniture store, and you can make a detailed examination of different dining room sets and use what you learn today to select the furniture you would like best."

"I'm going to play two different recordings of the same musical composition. Listen very carefully. Choose the one you prefer and then write down why you think it is better than the other."

These ways can help you to focus on just one of the key verbs in the taxonomy for the cognitive domain and use it to develop a teaching exercise:

"Here is an excerpt from a recent speech by the President. *Translate* it into your own words."

Ask students to write their own brief summary of a chapter, their *interpretation* of a poem, or the meaning of a short story. Then arrange students in small groups to compare how they interpreted others' information.

Show a political cartoon from a newspaper and ask students to give their *interpretation* of what the artist intended to convey.

"As you read the next two chapters, I want you to draw up your own *analysis* of what is covered. Try to pick out points that are important and organize them into an outline."

"Here are copies of three different newspaper reports of the same event. I'd like you to prepare a *synthesis* of the points made and write your own composite interpretation of what occurred."

"Your political science assignment this week is to watch the presidential candidates debate on television this Wednesday and *evaluate* the arguments of each candidate. On Thursday morning we will divide into small groups to compare our evaluations, and then we will have a class election to find out which candidate 'won.'"

8. Keep in mind that measurement and evaluation of classroom learning must accurately reflect your learning objectives.

In the opening to this chapter we pointed out that there are three related benefits to writing objectives: (1) It helps you identify in advance a body of knowledge and skill that students must learn; (2) it helps you prepare lessons that directly relate to the objectives, and (3) it helps you identify the content of your exams. By teaching for one thing but testing for something else (a common flaw, unfortunately), you do yourself and your students a great disservice. As we will point out in Chapter 9, forcing students to guess at the content of an exam makes it more difficult for them to be strategic learners.

As you write objectives, note how you intend to evaluate students' mastery of them and use these notes when you prepare your assessment procedure. We will describe this process in more detail in Chapter 13. Finally, keep in mind the variability and diversity of your students when developing objectives. For example, write objectives that are consistent with your students' stage of cognitive development, that reinforce an understanding of and respect for cultural diversity, and that allow students to capitalize on cultural characteristics.

Resources for Further Investigation

Taxonomy of Educational Objectives: Cognitive Domain

This chapter presents an abridged outline of the taxonomy developed by Benjamin S. Bloom and several associates in *Taxonomy of Educational Objectives, Handbook I: Cognitive Domain* (1956). To better understand the taxonomy and to gain insight into coordinating objectives and evaluation, examine Bloom's book—particularly Chapter 1, "The Nature and Development of the Taxonomy," and Chapter 2, "Educational Objectives and Curriculum Development." The remainder of the book consists of definitions of the general and specific classifications, followed by illustrations and exam questions.

Taxonomy of Educational Objectives: Affective Domain

To become more familiar with the possible values of the *Taxonomy of Educational Objectives: Affective Domain* (1964), refer to the complete list and explanation of objectives in this book by David B. Krathwohl, Benjamin S. Bloom, and Bertram B. Masia.

Taxonomy of Educational Objectives: Psychomotor Domain

The Psychomotor Domain (1972) by Elizabeth J. Simpson gives a complete description of the taxonomy for the psychomotor domain noted in this chapter. A different *Taxonomy of the Psychomotor Domain* (1972) has been developed by A. J. Harrow.

Mager and Gronlund on Objectives

If you would like to read Robert Mager's complete description of his recommendations for writing specific objectives, peruse his brief paperback *Preparing Instructional Objectives* (Rev. 2d ed., 1984). Norman Gronlund explains his approach to using objectives in *How to Write and Use Instructional Objectives* (4th ed., 1991) and in *Measurement and Evaluation in Teaching* (6th ed., 1990).

Where to Seek Information About Objective-Item Pools

Collections of instructional objectives and related test items may be obtained from the following sources:

Institute for Educational
Research
1400 West Maple Ave.
Downer's Grove, Illinois 60515

Instructional Objectives
Exchange
Box 24095
Los Angeles, California 90024

Objectives and Items CO-OP
School of Education
University of Massachusetts
Amherst, Massachusetts 01002

Westinghouse Learning Corp.
P.O. Box 30
Iowa City, Iowa 52240

National Assessment Publications

National Assessment objectives booklets and publications that report the results of recent assessments are described in the NAEP publications catalogue, which can be obtained free of charge by writing to:

National Assessment of Educational Progress
P.O. Box 6710
Princeton, New Jersey 08541-6710

SUMMARY

1. Early attempts at specifying the outcomes of education focused on general goals that meant different things to different people.

2. The vagueness of such goals stimulated psychologists to formulate taxonomies of specific, clearly stated objectives in each of three domains: cognitive, affective, and psychomotor.

3. The taxonomy for the cognitive domain that was prepared by Benjamin Bloom and several associates is composed of six levels: knowledge, comprehension, application, analysis, synthesis, and evaluation.

4. The taxonomy for the affective domain that was prepared by David Krathwohl and several associates is composed of five levels: receiving, responding, valuing, organization, and characterization by a value or value complex.

5. The taxonomy for the psychomotor domain that was prepared by Elizabeth Simpson is composed of seven levels: perception, set, guided response, mechanism, complex or overt response, adaptation, and origination.

6. The National Assessment of Educational Progress was begun in 1964 to determine how well individuals of various ages have mastered cognitive, affective, and psychomotor objectives. These lists indicate the kinds of objectives experienced educators feel should be stressed by teachers of various subjects.

7. Robert Mager states that well-written objectives should specify what behaviors the learner will exhibit to indicate mastery, the conditions under which the behavior will be exhibited, and the criterion of acceptable performance.

8. Norman Gronlund believes that complex and advanced kinds of learning do not lend themselves to Mager-type objectives. Complex outcomes are so broad in scope that it is impractical to ask students to demonstrate everything they have learned. Instead, Gronlund suggests that teachers first state a general objective and then specify a sample of related specific outcomes.

9. Formulating objectives helps you plan a logical sequence of instruction, provides you with ideas for classroom activities and remedial instruction, and helps you specify tests that will determine if learning has occurred.

10. Objectives work best when students are aware of them and understand their intent, when they are clearly written, when they are provided to average students for tasks of average difficulty, and when intentional learning is measured.

11. Incidental learning occurs more often with Gronlund-type objectives than with Mager-type objectives.

12. Most teachers use test questions that measure knowledge-level objectives, largely ignoring higher-level outcomes.

KEY TERMS

taxonomy *(278)*
cognitive domain *(279)*
affective domain *(279)*
psychomotor domain *(279)*
National Assessment of Educational
Progress *(285)*
specific objectives *(290)*
general objectives *(291)*

DISCUSSION QUESTIONS

1. Based on the content of this chapter and your own experiences as a student, do you agree that writing objectives and providing them to stu-

dents is a worthwhile expenditure of a teacher's time and effort? If so, then what steps will you take to ensure that, unlike many teachers today, you will make writing objectives a standard part of your professional behavior?

2. One criticism of writing objectives is that it limits the artistic side of teaching. That is, objectives lock teachers into a predetermined plan of instruction and eliminate the ability to pursue unplanned topics or interests. Can you respond to this criticism by recalling a teacher who provided you and your classmates with objectives but was still enthusiastic, flexible, spontaneous, and inventive?

3. Although, for the sake of clarity and simplicity, textbooks discuss objectives in terms of separate domains, many educational outcomes are in reality a combination of cognitive, affective, and psychomotor elements. Can you describe a few instructional outcomes that incorporate objectives from two or three domains (such as playing a piece of music "with feeling")?

4. As Benjamin Bloom has pointed out, over 90 percent of the test questions teachers write reflect the lowest level of the cognitive taxonomy. How can you avoid doing the same thing?

Part 3
PROVIDING INSTRUCTION

Chapter 8

BEHAVIORAL LEARNING THEORIES

EDUCATIONAL APPLICATIONS OF OPERANT CONDITIONING PRINCIPLES

▶ Programmed instruction: arrange material in small steps, reinforce correct responses

▶ Linear programs provide one path; branching programs have multiple paths

▶ CAI works best for elementary grade students, especially low achievers

▶ CAI not meant to replace teachers

▶ Behavior modification: shape behavior by ignoring undesirable responses, reinforcing desirable responses

▶ Premack principle: required work first, then chosen reward

▶ Token economy is a flexible reinforcement system

▶ Contingency contracting: reinforcement supplied after student completes mutually agreed-upon assignment

▶ Time-out works best with disruptive, aggressive children

▶ Punishment is likely to be ineffective because of temporary impact, side effects

SOCIAL LEARNING THEORY

▶ Observational learning occurs when one person imitates another

▶ People learn to inhibit or make responses by observing others

▶ Processes of observational learning: attention, retention, production, motivation

▶ Imitation is strengthened through direct reinforcement, vicarious reinforcement, self-reinforcement

▶ Persistence, self-confidence, cognitive skills can be learned by observing models

SUGGESTIONS FOR TEACHING IN YOUR CLASSROOM

▶ Delayed feedback can be as effective as immediate feedback

▶ Reinforcement menu: student-selected enjoyable activities

Now that you are familiar with characteristics of students at different ages, with pupil variability, and with a variety of ways to specify what is to be learned, it is time to turn to the third phase in the model of learning. This third step in the sequence of instruction, helping students achieve specified objectives, is the aspect of the model of learning that will demand most of your attention when you begin to teach. You will improve your teaching effectiveness if you frequently think about student characteristics and prepare instructional objectives, but most of your time in the classroom will be devoted to instruction or supervision of student activities. If you will be teaching in the elementary grades, you will need to find ways to keep your students constructively occupied for up to five hours each day. If you will be teaching in the secondary grades you will need to arrange instructional activities for periods ranging from forty minutes to several hours.

THE ORGANIZATION OF CHAPTERS IN PART THREE

The various types of objectives described in the preceding chapter call attention to *what* you will be doing. The five chapters that make up this part give you scientifically based ideas about *how* you might do it. Part three consists of four chapters on learning and one on motivation. To understand why, think for a moment about what you will be doing when you begin to teach. If you obtain a position in an elementary school you will be responsible for teaching some, or perhaps all, of the following subjects: reading, writing, arithmetic, science, social studies, citizenship, arts and crafts, music, and physical education. If you are heading for a position in a secondary school you will specialize in advanced instruction of one or more of the subjects just listed or in courses in vocational education. Now, think for a moment about what you will be doing. At the elementary school level you will ask your pupils to read texts (once they *have* learned to read), complete exercises in workbooks, watch demonstrations, practice skills, participate in group work, engage in class discussions, work on individual and group projects, and prepare for and take exams. At the secondary school level you will carry out more advanced and sophisticated variations of the activities just listed. In addition, you may sometimes present lectures similar to those you are currently so familiar with in college courses. In certain cases, you may ask pupils to spend a good proportion of class time completing experiments or the equivalent (as in a chemistry course) or creating products (as in home economics, business, or shop courses).

This brief outline of what you will be doing as a teacher calls attention to the fact that you will be primarily concerned with helping students learn. That is why this part begins with four chapters on learning. You will also need to try to keep your students constructively busy for up to five hours a day. That is why this section ends with a chapter on motivation. Since learning is such a basic activity, psychologists have been interested in studying how animals and humans change their behavior as a result of experience from the time the first psychology departments were established in American and European universities. Different psychologists have approached the study of learning with different theoretical orientations, however, and they have used different methods of study. As a result, there are varied, sometimes conflicting, opinions about how teachers should arrange learning activities in classrooms. Such differences of opinion are not necessarily a disadvantage since contrasting views of learning provide a variety of ideas about ways to teach different kinds of subject matter.

The first chapter on learning, for instance, is devoted to *behavioral* learning theories. Behavioral theories were proposed by psychologists who argue that the

The first four chapters in this section devoted to Phase Three of the model of instruction are concerned with aspects of learning because your primary concern as a teacher will be helping students learn.
(Elizabeth Crews)

only scientific way to study learning is to base all conclusions on observations of how overt behavior is influenced by forces in the external environment. Principles of such theories, to note just one application, can be used to make the learning of factual material extremely efficient. The second chapter on learning is devoted to *information processing.* As the name implies, psychologists who specialize in this area of study are curious about how humans encode, store, and retrieve information. Many of the principles proposed by information processing theorists can be used to make comprehension and memorization more efficient and to help students recall and apply what they have memorized. Information processing takes a cognitive approach to learning. The third learning chapter outlines other cognitive learning theories and focuses especially on the nature of *problem solving.* While recent theorizing and research on the process of problem solving draws heavily from information processing, theories of how this process should be taught reflect widely different points of view. Some psychologists argue that students learn problem-solving skills most effectively when they have the opportunity to experiment and discover solutions to problems. Other psychologists argue that direct step-by-step instruction in the use of problem-solving skills produces better problem solvers than a discovery approach. Following the chapter on cognitive learning theories and problem solving, *humanistic* approaches to education are briefly discussed. Humanistic teaching concentrates on the affective (or emotional) side of learning. Many humanistic education techniques center on the establishment of a warm, positive classroom atmosphere; others are intended to encourage students to examine attitudes, values, and feelings.

Each of the chapters on learning includes some discussion of ways to keep students constructively occupied. But arousing and sustaining interest in learning is such a basic problem for almost all teachers that it merits extensive coverage. Accordingly, a separate chapter on *motivation* follows the four on learning.

Now that you are familiar with the organization of the chapters in part three, we are ready to examine the nature of behavioral theories of learning.

All psychologists who endorse the behavioral view share the belief that those who study learning should base their conclusions on observations of how the overt behavior of organisms is influenced by factors in the external environment. They differ, however, in how they study learning and the types of learning they analyze. You may have noticed that this chapter is titled "Behavioral Learning Theories"—in the plural. That title emphasizes that there is no single behavioral view of learning, but several different ones. Three of these theories, *classical conditioning, operant conditioning,* and *social learning,* will be summarized in this chapter. Differences between these three interpretations of the behavioral view will become clear as early experiments by leading exponents of each variation are discussed. Original experiments are described to give some historical perspective and to illustrate basic principles in simplified form.

CLASSICAL CONDITIONING

The Russian scientist Ivan Pavlov is certain to be mentioned in any history of psychology, but he began his career in a different field of study. During the late 1800s and early 1900s he specialized in research on the physiology of digestion, work that earned him a Nobel Prize in 1904. As part of his research on digestion, Pavlov set out to measure the degree to which dogs salivated while eating. A dog, placed in a harness so that it could not move about, was given a measured amount of food and the resulting saliva was collected by means of a surgical incision on the underside of the dog's mouth (see Figure 8.1). One day Pavlov noticed an intriguing aspect of the dog's behavior. It began to salivate at the *sight* of food or even the individual who brought it. Pavlov decided to study this phenomenon systematically. He set up a carefully controlled situation in which a bell was sounded just before the dog was presented with a small amount of food. After several pairings of bell and food, the bell alone aroused salivation.

▶ Pavlovian conditioning: reflexive response associated with new stimulus

Pavlov called the food an *unconditioned stimulus* (abbreviated UCS)—because it naturally elicits salivation in hungry organisms—and the salivation an *unconditioned response* (UCR)—since it was a naturally occurring reflex. The new stimulus (the bell) he called a *conditioned stimulus* (CS) because it was a previously neutral stimulus that did not elicit salivation. The response to the bell was labeled a *conditioned response* (CR). The complete sequence of events Pavlov studied can be diagrammed this way:

$$\text{CS (bell)} \longrightarrow \begin{array}{l} \text{UCS (food)} \longrightarrow \text{UCR (salivation)} \\ \longrightarrow \text{UCS (food)} \longrightarrow \text{UCR (salivation)} \\ \text{CS (bell)} \longrightarrow \text{CR (salivation)} \end{array}$$

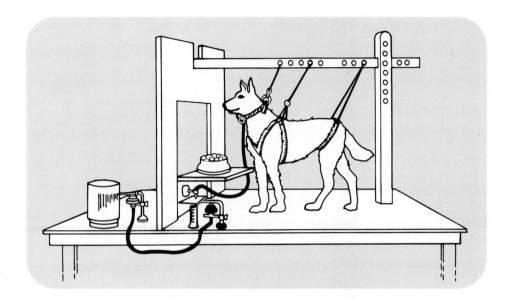

**FIGURE 8.1
Pavlov's Apparatus
for Studying Condi-
tioning**

▶ Conditioning princi-
ples: reinforcement,
extinction, general-
ization, discrimina-
tion

In Pavlov's view, the CR was learned because of repeated *reinforcement,* which in this case means following the CS by the UCS and UCR at appropriate time intervals. If the food was not resupplied from time to time, the response would begin to disappear or *extinguish.* Pavlov also pointed out that a dog who learned to salivate to the sound of a bell would salivate to similar sounds, such as a buzzer or whistle. He called this tendency *stimulus generalization.* Such generalized responses could be overcome by supplying reinforcement after the bell was rung but never after a whistle was sounded. When this occurred, he said, *discrimination* had taken place.

The kind of learning described by Pavlov—in which a naturally occurring involuntary response becomes associated with a previously neutral stimulus—is often called **classical conditioning** because it is based on classic experiments that were excellent examples of scientific methodology. While Pavlov's experiments were ingenious and thought provoking, theorists interested in learning soon realized that classical conditioning applies only to essentially involuntary reflex actions (such as salivation or fear). Such reactions are not very common types of behavior. Accordingly, experimenters sought other ways to analyze associations between stimuli and responses. The psychologist who did this most successfully was B. F. Skinner.

OPERANT CONDITIONING

In a survey of psychology department heads conducted in 1967 (Myers, 1970, p. 1045), B. F. Skinner was chosen as the most influential American psychologist of the twentieth century. Skinner was accorded this honor because he put together

FIGURE 8.2   A Rat in a Skinner Box
The rat's behavior is reinforced with a food pellet when it presses the bar under conditions preselected by the experimenter. The rat does not respond in a reflexive manner, as is the case with Pavlovian conditioning, but engages in self-selected behavior. In the process of exploring the Skinner box, for instance, the rat is almost certain to touch the bar. When that occurs, the experimenter supplies a food pellet and bar-pressing behavior is reinforced. Eventually, the rat may be reinforced only when a particular sequence of actions (for example, pressing the bar five times in succession) is performed. (Richard Wood/The Picture Cube)

a theory that not only successfully combines many different ideas but also serves as the basis for a variety of applications to human behavior. Skinner's theory emphasizes **operant conditioning,** a type of learning that is significantly different from that supplied by Pavlov. In operant conditioning, a voluntary response is strengthened when it is reinforced.

The Skinner Box

Most of the experiments on which principles of operant conditioning are based involved an ingenious apparatus invented by Skinner and appropriately referred to as a Skinner box. A Skinner box (see Figure 8.2) is a small enclosure that contains only a bar (or lever) and a small tray. Outside the box is a hopper holding a supply of food pellets that are dropped into the tray when the bar is pressed under certain conditions.

A hungry rat is placed in the box, and when—in the course of exploring its new environment—it approaches and then presses the bar, it is rewarded with a food pellet. Then food pellets are supplied under some conditions when the bar is pushed down (for example, when a tone is sounded) but not under others. The rat would learn this and the rate of pressing would drop noticeably when the tone was not sounded.

All the basic principles of Pavlovian conditioning are found in this experiment. The rat learned to press the bar more frequently when this behavior was *reinforced* by a food pellet. If it was not reinforced, *extinction* occurred. For a while the rat *generalized* and pushed the bar at the same rate whether a tone was sounded or not. Eventually, after selective reinforcement had been repeated often enough, it *discriminated* and pushed the bar more frequently when the tone was sounded.

The Skinner box's prominent role in operant conditioning experiments reflects Skinner's view of psychology as a natural science. One important assumption that underlies all natural sciences is that natural phenomena (such as weather patterns, earthquakes, sunspots, and human behavior) may appear on the surface to be random but really operate according to set laws. That is, forces in the environment cause such events to occur. What psychology needed, in Skinner's view, was the means by which a researcher could control the environment to observe the law-bound and hence predictable influence of environmental factors on behavior. All sciences operate pretty much in this fashion. The meteorologist, for example, tries to create and control weather conditions in a laboratory to study the effects of temperature, humidity, and air flow on various weather phenomena such as tornadoes and drought.

A second assumption underlying Skinner's work is that a science develops most effectively by studying some phenomenon at its most simple, fundamental level. What is learned at this level can then be used to understand more complex processes. In the case of behavior, the most fundamental elements are the stimulus situation, the response, and the consequences (positive, negative, or neutral) that follow the response. The Skinner box, then, allows researchers to study, in a controlled, precise, and objective fashion, the most basic aspects of learning.

Differences Between Operant and Classical Conditioning

Although the Skinner box experiment seems similar to Pavlov's work with dogs, Skinner has pointed out important differences, notably in regard to the source of the behavior. In Pavlov's experiment the dog was essentially passive, and its response (salivation) had to be *elicited* by the experimenter. By contrast, Skinner's rats *emitted* behavior in an essentially spontaneous way. And since the rats "operated" the bar, Skinner's kind of conditioning is called *operant*. (Some

▶ Operant conditioning: voluntary response influenced by consequences that follow

psychologists use the term *instrumental* since the behavior is instrumental in bringing about the reinforcement.)

Another way of comparing operant and classical conditioning is in terms of the elements of the learning process each one emphasizes. Classical conditioning repeatedly pairs two stimuli (CS followed by UCS) close together in time. This pairing leads the organism to respond to one stimulus (the CS) in the same way it naturally responds to the other stimulus (the UCS). The emphasis here is on the association that forms between an earlier occurring stimulus (often called an antecedent stimulus) and a response. For example, most young children react to sudden, loud noises by attempting to avoid or withdraw from the situation. Operant conditioning, on the other hand, emphasizes the relationship between a response and how that response is treated by the environment. The nature of the antecedent stimulus is not always taken into account. The reason for this occasional disregard is that in many everyday situations several stimuli operate simultaneously, making it difficult or impossible to know precisely what triggered a particular behavior. For example, we may eat lunch at noon because that is when we are hungry *and* because that is when we can socialize with others as we eat. In sum, classical conditioning emphasizes the relationship between antecedent stimuli and responses whereas operant conditioning emphasizes the relationship between responses and their consequences.

Basic Principles of Operant Conditioning

The basic idea behind operant conditioning is really quite simple: All behaviors are accompanied by certain consequences, and these consequences strongly influence (some might say determine) whether or not these behaviors are repeated and at what level of intensity. This section describes the nature of different types of consequences and several related principles that can be applied to aspects of human learning.

In general, the consequences that follow behavior are either positive or negative. Depending on conditions that we will discuss shortly, these consequences either increase (strengthen) or decrease (weaken) the likelihood that the preceding behavior will recur under the same or similar circumstances. When consequences strengthen a preceding behavior, the term *reinforcement* is used. There are positive and negative forms of reinforcement. When consequences weaken a preceding behavior, the terms *punishment* and *extinction* are used. There are two forms of punishment, type I and type II.

Positive Reinforcement   Although the term *positive reinforcement* may be unfamiliar to you, the idea behind it probably is not. If you can recall spending more time studying for a certain subject because of a compliment from the teacher or a high grade on an examination, you have experienced positive reinforcement. Specifically, **positive reinforcement** involves strengthening behavior—that is, increasing and maintaining the probability that a particular behavior will be repeated—by presenting a positive stimulus (for example, praise, candy, money, the opportunity for free play) immediately after the desired behavior has oc-

▶ Positive reinforcement: strengthen desired behavior by presenting a positive stimulus after the behavior occurs

Students are likely to be eager to learn if they receive evidence that they have successfully completed a project or task. Such evidence might take the form of awards, a record booklet that makes it possible to chart progress, and praise from the teacher and one's peers. (John S. Abbott)

curred. This positive stimulus is the *positive reinforcer*. What makes a positive reinforcer different from a reward is that the former strengthens the preceding behavior. Thus, two students who rarely study may be given the same amount of money for studying one hour every day after school. If, in the first case, there is no effect on amount of study in the future, the money is considered a reward. If, in the second case, the student continues to study for an hour each day, the money is considered a positive reinforcer.

Negative Reinforcement   People often confuse negative reinforcement with positive reinforcement or with punishment (a third type of consequence that we will take up next); so a careful consideration of similarities and differences is critical. The goal of positive reinforcement is to increase the strength of a desired behavior by supplying a positive stimulus. The student is motivated to learn new behaviors in order to obtain the positive reinforcer. The goal of **negative reinforcement** is the same—to *increase* the strength of a desired behavior. The method, however, is different. Instead of supplying a positive stimulus, *one removes an aversive (meaning unpleasant or unwanted) stimulus whenever a target behavior is exhibited*. The student is now motivated to learn new behaviors so as to escape or avoid the aversive stimulus.

▶ Negative reinforcement: strengthen desired behavior by removing a negative stimulus after the behavior occurs

In laboratory studies, animals in a Skinner box have been taught to jump over a barrier, push on a panel, step on a pedal, or press a lever to escape or avoid mild doses of electric shock or other intense stimulation (Keller, 1954). In everyday life, negative reinforcement occurs quite frequently. Examples include the child who picks up his clothes or toys to stop his parents' nagging, the driver who obeys speed limits to avoid getting a ticket, and the person who abuses alcohol or drugs to escape from stressful life situations (Nye, 1979). Later in the chapter we will describe how educators use negative reinforcement. We will also discuss its desirability relative to positive reinforcement.

Punishment   So far, we have talked about behavioral consequences that serve to strengthen and maintain *desired* behaviors. We will now discuss three consequences that reduce the likelihood of *undesired* behaviors being repeated. The first is **punishment** (also called type I punishment). Punishment is defined by operant psychologists as the presentation of an aversive stimulus that weakens, suppresses, or eliminates undesired behavior. Scolding, paddling, ridiculing, or making a student write five hundred times "I will not chew gum in class" are all examples of punishment if, *and only if,* the student ceases the undesired behavior.

> Punishment: weaken undesired behavior by presenting a negative stimulus after the behavior occurs

Many people confuse negative reinforcement with punishment. Both involve the use of an aversive stimulus, but the effect of the aversive stimulus on behavior is what matters. Remember that negative reinforcement strengthens a desired behavior, whereas punishment works against an undesired behavior.

Time-Out   A consequence that is considered to be a different form of punishment (and so is called type II punishment) is **time-out.** Like type I punishment, time-out decreases the frequency of or eliminates undesired behavior. However, instead of presenting an aversive or negative stimulus, time-out *temporarily removes the opportunity to receive positive reinforcement.* Thus, a student who frequently disrupts classroom routine to get attention may be sent to sit in an empty room for five minutes. Many consider time-out to be type II punishment because removal from a reinforcing environment (as well as the angry tone of voice and facial expression that normally go with it) is usually looked upon as an aversive consequence by the individual being removed. Other sorts of type II punishment include an athlete who is suspended from competition and a child who temporarily loses certain privileges.

> Time-out: weaken undesired behavior by temporarily removing positive reinforcement

Extinction   A third consequence that weakens undesired behavior is **extinction.** Extinction occurs when a previously reinforced behavior decreases in frequency, and eventually ceases altogether, because reinforcement is withheld. Examples of extinction include a mother ignoring a whining child, a teacher ignoring a student who spontaneously answers a question without waiting to be called on, and a counselor ignoring a client's self-deprecating remarks. As we shall see later, both extinction and time-out are most effective when combined with other consequences such as positive reinforcement.

> Extinction: weaken undesired behavior by ignoring it

To help yourself define and remember the distinguishing characteristics of positive reinforcement, negative reinforcement, punishment, and extinction, study Table 8.1.

Spontaneous Recovery   Extinction is sometimes a slow and difficult means of decreasing the frequency of undesired behavior when used alone, because "extinguished" behaviors occasionally reappear without having been reinforced

> Spontaneous recovery: extinguished behaviors may reappear spontaneously

TABLE 8.1	Conditions That Define Reinforcement, Punishment, and Extinction			
Type of Stimulus +	**Environmental Action** +	**Effect on Behavior** =	**Result**
Positive	Present	Strengthen	Positive reinforcement
Negative	Withdraw	Strengthen	Negative reinforcement
Negative	Present	Weaken	Punishment I
Positive	Withdraw	Weaken	Punishment II
Positive	Withhold	Weaken	Extinction

(an occurrence known as **spontaneous recovery**). Under normal circumstances, however, the time between spontaneous recoveries lengthens and the intensity of the recurring behavior becomes progressively weaker. If the behavior undergoing extinction is not terribly disruptive, and if the teacher (or parent, counselor, or supervisor) is willing to persevere, these episodes can sometimes be tolerated on the way to more complete extinction.

Generalization   When an individual learns to make a particular response to a particular stimulus and then makes the same or a similar response in a slightly different situation, **generalization** has occurred. Pigeons in a Skinner box that have been reinforced for pecking at a red spot will also peck at other spots that differ somewhat in hue (for example, orange or yellow), shape, and size. The less similar the new stimulus is to the original, however, the weaker the response. Eventually, with increased variation, the new stimulus grows so different in appearance from the original that the response rarely occurs.

> Generalization: responding in similar ways to similar stimuli

Whether or not generalization is desirable depends, of course, on the circumstances. It is highly pleasing to parents and teachers to see students who were positively reinforced for using effective study skills in history use those same skills in chemistry, social studies, algebra, and so on. On the other hand, it is disappointing to see students ignore or question a teacher's every request and direction because they have been reinforced for responding that way to their parents at home.

Discrimination   When inappropriate generalizations occur, as in the above example, they can be essentially extinguished through discrimination training. Quite simply, **discrimination** involves learning to notice the unique aspects of seemingly similar situations (for example, that teachers are not parents, although both are adults) and to respond differently to each situation. This process can be encouraged by reinforcing only the desired behaviors (for instance, attention,

> Discrimination: responding in different ways to similar stimuli

obedience, and cooperation) and withholding reinforcement following undesired behaviors (such as inattention or disobedience) when they occur in the teacher's presence. In the terminology of operant conditioning, behavior comes to be controlled by discriminative stimuli. Thus, driving a car is a reasonably safe activity in our society because all drivers learn to make the same unique response to green, amber, and red traffic lights (most of the time, at any rate).

Shaping   Up to now, the descriptions and illustrations of basic operant conditioning principles have not distinguished relatively simple behaviors that people and animals enact spontaneously in final form from more complex behaviors that rarely occur spontaneously in finished form. A bit of reflection, however, should enable you to realize that many of the behaviors human beings learn (such as playing a sport or writing a term paper) are complex and are acquired gradually. The one principle that best explains how complex responses are learned is **shaping.**

Some of the experiments on shaping conducted by Skinner were carried out with pigeons placed in an apparatus similar to the original Skinner box. Instead of a bar to be pushed, the pigeon shared quarters with a disk to be pecked (since pigeons spontaneously peck a great deal). By manipulating the presentation of a positive reinforcer in specific ways, Skinner trained his pigeons to, among other things, peck out tunes on a toy xylophone and play a game similar to table tennis. The pigeon-musicians acquired their skill by pecking first one key, then two, then three, and then four in sequence. At first, pecking one key was reinforced with food. Eventually, the pigeons received food only when all four bars on the xylophone were pecked in the correct sequence. (If you would like to attempt roughly similar feats with a pet dog or cat, read Skinner's article "How to Teach Animals" in the December 1951 issue of *Scientific American,* pp. 26–29.)

The basic principle of learning in shaping is to reinforce actions that move progressively closer to the desired *terminal behavior* (to use Skinner's term). Actions that do not represent closer approximations of the terminal behavior are ignored. The key to success is to take one step at a time. The movements must be gradual enough so that the person or animal becomes aware that each step in the sequence is essential.

▶ Complex behaviors are shaped by reinforcing closer approximations to terminal behavior

At least three factors can undermine the effectiveness of shaping. First, supplying too much positive reinforcement for early, crude responses may reduce the learner's willingness to attempt a more complex response. Second, expecting too much progress too soon (by making the next step in the sequence too "large") may decrease the likelihood of an appropriate response. If this results in a long period of nonreinforcement, what has been learned up to that point may be extinguished. Expecting a student to work industriously on a homework assignment for ninety minutes just after you have shaped forty-five minutes of appropriate homework behavior is probably too big a jump. If it is, the student may revert to his or her original level of performance owing to the lack of reinforcement. Third, delaying reinforcement of the terminal behavior allows time for additional, unrelated behaviors to occur. When the reinforcement eventually occurs, it may strengthen one or more of the more recent behaviors rather than the terminal behavior. For example, a teacher may shape a student to study each subject for several hours per week (a tactic that has been proved effective) but may not give weekly grades. If the student then stays up half the night cramming for the next day's midterm exam, a high grade may reinforce the cramming more than the distributed studying. The solution in this case would be to schedule more frequent exams to allow for more immediate reinforcement (Nye, 1979).

Schedules of Reinforcement   If you have been reading this section on basic principles carefully, you may have begun to wonder if the use of operant conditioning principles, particularly positive reinforcement, requires you to be present every time a desired response happens. If so, you might have some justifiable reservations about the practicality of this theory. The answer is yes, up to a point, but after that, no. As we have pointed out, when you are trying to get a new behavior established, especially if it is a complex behavior that requires shaping, learning proceeds best when every desired response is positively reinforced and every undesired response is ignored. This is known as a *continuous reinforcement* schedule.

Once the behavior has been learned, however, positive reinforcement can be employed on a noncontinuous or intermittent basis to perpetuate it. There are four basic *intermittent reinforcement* schedules: fixed interval (FI), variable interval (VI), fixed ratio (FR), and variable ratio (VR). Each schedule produces a different pattern of behavior.

The two interval schedules govern the delivery of reinforcement according to the passage of time. When that interval of time is fixed, as in a **fixed interval schedule,** a learner is reinforced for the first desired response that occurs after a predetermined amount of time has elapsed (for example, five minutes, one hour, or seven days). Once the response has occurred and been reinforced, the next interval begins. Any desired responses that are made during an interval are ignored. If the pattern of behavior that is usually produced by a fixed interval schedule were to be graphed on paper, it would be scallop shaped. That means the reinforced behavior occurs at a lower level during the early part of the interval and gradually rises as the time for reinforcement draws closer. Once the reinforcer is delivered, the relevant behavior declines in frequency and gradually rises toward the end of that next interval. Fixed interval schedules of reinforcement occur in education when teachers schedule exams or projects at regular intervals. The grade or score is considered to be a reinforcer. As you are certainly aware, it is not unusual to see little studying or progress occur during the early part of the interval. However, several days before an exam or due date, the pace quickens considerably.

If you would like to see a more consistent pattern of behavior, you might consider using a **variable interval schedule** of reinforcement. With this schedule, the length of time between reinforcements is essentially random but averages out to a predetermined interval. Thus, four successive reinforcements may occur

▶ Fixed interval schedules: reinforce after regular time intervals

▶ Variable interval schedules: reinforce after random time intervals

at the following intervals: one week, four weeks, two weeks, five weeks. The average interval is three weeks. Teachers who give surprise quizzes or who call on students to answer oral questions on the average of once every third day are invoking a variable interval schedule.

Fixed ratio schedules: reinforce after a set number of responses

A **fixed ratio schedule** provides reinforcement whenever a predetermined number of responses are made. A rat in a Skinner box may be reinforced with a food pellet whenever it presses a lever fifty times. A factory worker may earn twenty dollars each time he or she assembles five electronic circuit boards. A teacher may reinforce a student with praise for every ten arithmetic problems correctly completed. Fixed ratio schedules tend to produce high response rates since the faster the learner responds, the sooner the reinforcement is delivered. However, a relatively brief period of no or few responses occurs immediately after the reinforcer is delivered. The larger the ratio (meaning the number of responses required for a reinforcement), the longer the pause. If this response pattern were graphed on paper, it would look something like a set of stairs.

Variable ratio schedules: reinforce after a different number of responses each time

A **variable ratio schedule,** like a variable interval schedule, tends to eliminate these irregularities, thereby producing a more consistent response rate. This is accomplished by reinforcing after a different number of responses from one time to the next according to a predetermined average. If you decided to use a variable ratio 15 schedule, you might reinforce a desired behavior after 12, 7, 23, and 18 occurrences, respectively (that is, after the 12th, 19th, 42nd, and 60th desired behaviors). Because the occurrence of reinforcement is so unpredictable, learners tend to respond fairly rapidly for long periods of time. If you need proof, just watch people play the slot machines in Las Vegas. Variable ratio schedules also help to explain why scientists continue to work on the same problem (such as cancer research) for many years. Every once in a while (sometimes a great while) a scientist will obtain results that provide a better understanding of the nature of the problem. When that will occur is, of course, unpredictable. It may be the next experiment, or it may not occur for another thirty experiments. Out of such reinforcement schedules arise Nobel Prize winners!

EDUCATIONAL APPLICATIONS OF OPERANT CONDITIONING PRINCIPLES

By arranging conditions and supplying reinforcement according to the principles just described, Skinner succeeded in shaping the behavior of rats and pigeons in quite amazing ways, as pigeons playing ping-pong and the xylophone attest. Because he was so successful in getting animals to learn new forms of behavior, he concluded that similar techniques could be used to shape human behavior. He wrote a novel, *Walden Two* (1948), in which he described a utopian community based on principles of operant conditioning. The child-rearing specialists at Walden Two use the same methods that Skinner employed on animals to strengthen desirable traits (such as perseverance) and to eliminate undesirable traits (such as jealousy). The leader of Walden Two, who speaks for Skinner, defends this practice by arguing that highly successful and creative people get that way not because of inherited tendencies but because of a fortunate series of reinforcements. Instead of just hoping that such traits as perseverance and self-control will be reinforced, the scientific child rearers of Walden Two *arrange* situations to make sure that this happens. Psychologists impressed by Skinner's writings have used techniques similar to those of the fictional child rearers of Walden Two to shape many different kinds of human behavior (see, for example, Craighead, Kazden & Mahoney, 1981).

About the time Skinner was working on *Walden Two,* his daughter was a student in public school. When he asked her what the class had done each day and examined the books and assignments she brought home, Skinner became increasingly appalled about the kind of education his child was receiving. He concluded that traditional teaching techniques were terribly confused and inefficient and also primarily negative, in the sense that most children study to avoid negative consequences. It appeared to Skinner, for example, that his daughter studied most diligently to avoid being embarrassed or punished or to avoid a low grade. When he analyzed teacher-pupil behavior with reference to principles of operant conditioning, he was especially bothered by the fact that there was almost always a substantial interval between the point at which pupils answered questions and the point at which they received feedback as to whether their responses were correct or incorrect. Skinner realized that it was physically impossible for a teacher responsible for a class of thirty to respond to more than a few students at a time, but he was still bothered by this situation. Finally, he noticed that lessons and workbooks were often poorly organized and did not seem to lead students to any specific goal. Skinner became convinced that if the principles of operant conditioning were systematically applied to education, all these limitations could be either reduced or eliminated.

In the intervening forty-five years, little has changed, according to Skinner. In an article written in 1984 titled "The Shame of American Education," Skinner makes the following assertion:

> I claim that the school system of any large American city could be so redesigned, at little or no additional cost, that students would come to school and apply themselves to their work with a minimum of punitive coercion and, with very rare exceptions, learn to read with reasonable ease, express themselves well in speech and writing, and solve a fair range of mathematical problems. (p. 984)

Skinner's claim is based on four prescriptions related to operant conditioning: (1) Be clear about what is to be taught; (2) teach first things first; (3) allow students to learn at their own rate; and (4) program the subject matter. The primary means by which this group of goals would be accomplished are programmed instruction and teaching machines (that is, computer-assisted instruction). The next few sections will describe the nature of these applications and assess the extent to which they improve classroom learning. In addition, we will discuss behavior modification, a general application of operant conditioning principles.

B. F. Skinner's theory of operant conditioning maintains that the positive, neutral, or negative consequences that follow behavior strongly influence whether that behavior will be learned. (Chris J. Johnson/Stock, Boston, Inc.)

Programmed Instruction

The key idea behind Skinner's approach to teaching is that learning should be *shaped.* Programs of stimuli and consequences should be designed to lead students step by step to a predetermined end result. In the mid-1950s Skinner turned this shaping approach into an innovation called programmed instruction.

Programmed instruction can be described as specially designed written material that presents small amounts of written information to the student in a predetermined sequence, provides prompts to draw out the desired written response, calls for the response to be repeated in several ways in order to produce mastery, immediately reinforces correct responses, and allows the student to work through the program at his or her own pace.

According to Skinner (1968, 1986), when programmed materials are well designed and appropriately used, they produce the following effects:

1. Reinforcement for the right answer is immediate.

2. The teacher can monitor each student's progress more closely.

3. Each student learns at his or her own rate, completing as many problems as possible within the allotted time.

4. Motivation stays high because of the high success level designed into the program.

5. Students can easily stop and begin at almost any point.

6. Learning a complex repertoire of knowledge proceeds efficiently.

When programmed materials were first made commercially available during the mid-1950s, they were designed to be presented to students in one of two ways: in book form or incorporated into mechanical teaching machines. The earliest teaching machines were simple mechanical devices. A program was inserted in the machine and the first statement or question was "framed" in a viewing window. (That is why the individual steps of a program are referred to as **frames.**) The student printed an answer on a designated line, then moved a knob that pulled a transparent cover over what had been written (to prevent erasing a wrong answer). At the same time, information appeared in the opening, revealing whether or not the response was correct. After checking the correctness of the response, the student turned another knob, which presented the next frame, and so on.

Developing a Program The first step in developing a program is to define precisely what is to be learned (the terminal behavior). Then, facts, concepts, and principles must be arranged in a sequence designed to lead the student to the desired end result. This requires first making the steps (the knowledge needed to go from frame to frame) small enough so that reinforcement occurs with optimal frequency, then putting them in the proper order and arranging them so that students will be adequately prepared for each frame, or numbered problem, when they reach it.

> Programmed instruction: arrange material in small steps, reinforce correct responses

In arranging the sequence of steps, programmers may use a **linear program,** which tries to ensure that every response will be correct, since there is only one path to the terminal behavior. Or they may use a **branching program,** in which there is less concern that all responses be right. If students give a wrong answer, the program provides a branching set of questions to enable them to master the troublesome point. Another type of branching program provides students with a more complete explanation of the misunderstood material and then urges them to go back and study the original explanations more carefully.

> Linear programs provide one path; branching programs have multiple paths

Skinner prefers the linear approach because it requires students to supply their own responses and because it makes the most of reinforcement. Other psychologists favor branching programs because students are able to advance in larger steps and because the program can "talk back" to them and thus come closer to approximating a human tutor.

In composing a program, the writer strives to progressively reduce the degree of *prompt*, or the number of *cues* necessary to elicit the correct answer. In the language of programming, the prompt is *vanished*. But in reducing cues, it is important to remember Skinner's experiments with pigeons and not go too far too fast.

Computer-Assisted Instruction

The mechanical teaching machines devised by Skinner have been almost totally supplanted by the computer, particularly the microcomputer, because computers can do everything the machine could do and more. Nevertheless, we would do well to remember that a teaching machine—be it mechanical or electronic—is only as good as the instructional program that runs it (the "software" in today's computer terminology).[1]

With this caveat in mind, we can now turn to a consideration of the effectiveness of **computer-assisted instruction** (CAI).

Do Computers Aid Learning?   The answer to this question, like the answers to most of the questions posed in this book, is that it depends—in this case, largely on the nature of the learner. In a review of CAI research done in actual classrooms in grades one through six, Kulik, Kulik, and Bangert-Drowns (1985) found a fairly substantial advantage for CAI. The typical CAI-taught student scored at the 68th percentile on a classroom examination, whereas the average student in a conventionally taught class scored at the 50th percentile. CAI-taught students also scored higher than conventionally taught students when retested some weeks later. And low-aptitude students benefited more from CAI than did high-aptitude students. These results were obtained with a rather modest amount of input. In the typical study, students received a total of about 26 hours of CAI: 15 minutes a day, 4 days a week, for 26 weeks.

> CAI works best for elementary grade students, especially low achievers

In a companion review of CAI research done in actual classrooms in grades seven through twelve, Bangert-Drowns, Kulik, and Kulik (1985) again found an advantage for CAI, although not as large as was the case for primary and elementary grade students. At this level the difference between CAI-taught and conventionally taught students on examination scores was about ten percentile ranks. Once again, low-aptitude students gained more from CAI than did high-aptitude students.

These findings suggest that CAI, when properly designed, can effectively supplement a teacher's attempts to present, explain, apply, and reinforce knowledge and skills. The relatively high degree of structure inherent in CAI seems to be particularly helpful to low-achieving and younger students. These findings also reaffirm what was suggested in Chapter 1's section on "Teaching as an Art and a Science": that whenever you as a teacher apply any psychological principle in your classroom, you will need to ask, For whom is this instructional technique likely to be beneficial? With what materials? For what outcome? Whether CAI ever becomes more than a moderately effective supplement to classroom instruction will depend largely on the quality of the software. While predicting future developments is a risky business, you would probably do well to expect advances in software quality to be gradual.

A Cautionary Note   The history of education is filled with innovative practices of which great things were expected. In the past thirty years programmed instruction, instructional objectives, discovery learning, and mastery learning, to name a few examples, were expected to greatly enhance student motivation and

---

1. In case you have never quite understood the terms *hardware* and *software* when used with reference to computers, *hardware* refers to the machine and electronic devices and *software* to the program, language, or instructions used in the machine.

Computer-assisted in-struction can effectively supplement conven-tional classroom teach-ing, particularly for ele-mentary grade students.
(Bob Daemmrich/The Image Works, Inc.)

produce substantial gains in achievement for all students in all subject areas. As you may already know, such gains did not occur. Indeed, they couldn't have occurred. The expectations people had for each of those innovations were simply unrealistic. It now appears as if this pattern is being repeated with computer-as-sisted instruction. Between the advertising claims made by various computer manufacturers and the promises made by proponents of CAI, one could get the impression that the goals of universally high levels of motivation and achieve-ment are within our grasp. Perhaps so, but we would urge you for two reasons to take a cue from history and be cautious, if not skeptical, of such claims.

First, there is still much that we do not know about the circumstances under which CAI is most effective. Take, for example, the issue of student versus computer control of the instructional process. We still know relatively little about whether the student or the computer should initiate help. Leaving this decision to the student may enhance one's sense of self-control or it may frustrate the student who is reluctant to ask for help. Another example concerns the use of color, animation, and sound effects. While these features may produce learning gains over the short-term, we do not know if they will depress students' interest in tasks that do not possess such features (Lepper & Chabay, 1985; Lepper & Gurtner, 1989).

Second, there is much the computer cannot capture in its attempt to play teacher. As we noted in Chapter 1, and as Larry Cuban (1986) points out in a provocative book about the relationship between teachers and machines, suc-cessful teaching often depends on the ability of a live teacher to establish a positive emotional climate (by communicating interest, excitement, expectations, and caring), to monitor student actions and reactions (by "reading" their verbal

▶ CAI not meant to re-place teachers

and nonverbal communications), and to orchestrate the sequence and pace of instructional events (by making additions, deletions, and modifications in lesson plans). To the degree that students spend large chunks of their school day working at computer consoles that cannot adequately perform these functions, they may find learning less enjoyable, and teachers may find teaching less satisfying.

Behavior Modification

Behavior modification: shape behavior by ignoring undesirable responses, reinforcing desirable responses

Though applied in many ways, the term **behavior modification** basically refers to the use of operant conditioning techniques to—as the phrase indicates—modify behavior. Since those who use such techniques attempt to manage behavior by making rewards contingent upon certain actions, the term *contingency management* is also sometimes used.

After Skinner and his followers had perfected techniques of operant conditioning in modifying the behavior of animals, they concluded that similar techniques could be used with humans. We will briefly discuss several techniques in this section that teachers may use to strengthen or weaken specific behaviors. Techniques applied in education to strengthen behaviors include shaping, token economies, and contingency contracts. Techniques that aim to weaken behaviors include extinction and punishment.

Shaping   An explanation of shaping was provided earlier in the chapter (pp. 332–333). You may want to take a few minutes now to review those few paragraphs. Most attempts at shaping important classroom behaviors should include at least the following steps (Walker & Shea, 1991):

1. Select the target behavior.
2. Obtain reliable baseline data (that is, determine how often the target behavior occurs in the normal course of events).
3. Select potent reinforcers.
4. Reinforce successive approximations of the target behavior each time they occur.
5. Reinforce the newly established target behavior each time it occurs.
6. Reinforce the target behavior on a variable reinforcement schedule (pp. 58–86).

To illustrate how shaping might be used, imagine that you are a third-grade teacher (or a high school teacher) with a chronic problem: One of your students rarely completes more than a small percentage of the arithmetic (or algebra) problems on the worksheets you distribute in class, even though you know the student possesses the necessary skills.

To begin, you decide that a reasonable goal would be for the student to complete at least 85 percent of the problems on a given worksheet. Next, you review the student's work for the past several weeks and determine that, on average, only 25 percent of the problems per worksheet are being completed. Your third step is to select positive reinforcers that you know or suspect will work. Reinforcers come in a variety of forms. Most elementary school teachers typically use such things as stickers, verbal praise, smiles, hugs, and classroom privileges (for example, feed the gerbil, clean the erasers). Occasionally, a teacher might hand out small pieces of candy like M&M's.

High school teachers can use letter or numerical grades, public forms of recognition (such as displaying high-quality work in the classroom or awarding certificates for achievement, effort, citizenship, and the like), material incentives (such as discarded classroom materials, board games, computer games, and books, so long as school policy and your financial resources allow it), and, of course, privately given verbal praise. Since some adolescents get embarrassed at being singled out for attention, display the work of or give awards to several students at the same time (Emmer et al., 1989).

One popular shaping technique that has stood the test of time involves having students first list favorite activities on a card. Then they are told that they will be able to indulge in one of those activities for a stated period of time after they have completed a set of instructional objectives. This technique is sometimes called the **Premack principle** after the psychologist, David Premack (1959), who first proposed it. It is also called *Grandma's rule,* since it is a variation of a technique that grandmothers have used for hundreds of years ("Finish your peas and you can have dessert").

> **Premack principle: required work first, then chosen reward**

Once you have decided on a sequence of objectives and a method of reinforcement, you are ready to shape the target behavior. For example, you can start by reinforcing the student for completing five problems (25 percent) each day for several consecutive days. Then you reinforce the student for completing five problems and starting a sixth. Then you reinforce the student for six completed problems, and so on. Once the student consistently completes at least 85 percent of the problems, you provide reinforcement after every fifth worksheet on the average (a variable ratio schedule).

Although you control the classroom environment while students are in school, this accounts for only about half of their waking hours. Accordingly, parents might supplement your efforts at shaping behavior. Establishing what is called a home-based reinforcement program is quite simple. Once the parents and student have been informed about and agree to participate in the program, the teacher will typically send home a brief note or form on a regular basis (daily, weekly, etc.) indicating whether the student exhibited the desired behaviors. For example, in response to the items "Was prepared for class" and "Handed in homework," the teacher would circle "yes" or "no." In response to a homework grade or test grade, the teacher would circle the appropriate letter or percent correct designation. The parents are then responsible for providing the appropriate reinforcement or punishment (temporary loss of a privilege, for example). This procedure has been successful in both reducing disruptive classroom behavior and increasing academic performance (longer time on tasks and higher test scores, for example). Some studies suggest that it may not be necessary to target both areas, as improved academic performance often results in decreased disruptiveness (Kelley & Carper, 1988).

Token Economies   A second technique used to strengthen behavior in the classroom, the **token economy,** was introduced first with people who had been hospitalized for emotional disturbances and then in special education classes. A token is something that has little or no inherent value but can be used to "purchase" things that do have inherent value. In society, money is our most ubiquitous token. Its value lies not in what it is made of but in what it can purchase—a car, a house, or a college education. By the same token (if you will excuse the pun), students can accumulate check marks, gold stars, or happy faces and "cash them in" at some later date for any of the reinforcers already mentioned.

One reason for the advent of the token economy approach was the limited flexibility of more commonly used reinforcers. Candies and cookies, for instance, tend to lose their reinforcing value fairly quickly when supplied continuously. It is not always convenient to award free time or the opportunity to engage in a highly preferred activity immediately after a desired response. And social rewards may or may not be sufficiently reinforcing for some individuals. Tokens, however, can always be given immediately after a desirable behavior, can be awarded according to one of the four schedules mentioned earlier, and can be redeemed for reinforcers that have high reinforcing value.

> Token economy is a flexible reinforcement system

Token economies are effective in reducing such disruptive classroom behaviors as talking out of turn, being out of one's seat, fighting, and being off task. They are also effective in improving academic performance in a variety of subject areas. Token economies have been used successfully with individual students, groups of students, entire classrooms, and even entire schools. Some studies have shown that awarding tokens for group efforts is at least as effective and possibly more effective than awarding them to individuals. Accordingly, this technique can be easily used in conjunction with the previously mentioned cooperative learning technique (McLaughlin & Williams, 1988; Shook et al., 1990).

Contingency Contracting   A third technique teachers use to strengthen behavior is **contingency contracting.** A contingency contract is simply a more formal method of specifying desirable behaviors and consequent reinforcement. The contract, which can be written or verbal, is an agreement worked out by two people (teacher and student, parent and child, counselor and client) in which one person (student, child, client) agrees to behave in a mutually acceptable way, and the other person (teacher, parent, counselor) agrees to provide a mutually acceptable form of reinforcement. For example, a student may contract to sit quietly and work on an arithmetic assignment for thirty minutes. When the student is done, the teacher may reinforce the child with ten minutes of free time, a token, or a small toy. Contracts can be drawn up with all members of a class

> Contingency contracting: reinforcement supplied after student completes mutually agreed-upon assignment

individually, with selected individual class members, or with the class as a whole. As with most contracts, provisions can be made for renegotiating the terms. Moreover, the technique is flexible enough to incorporate the previously discussed techniques of token economies and shaping. It is possible, for example, to draw up a contract that provides tokens for successive approximations to some target behavior.

Extinction, Time-Out, and Response Cost   The primary goal of behavior modification is to strengthen desired behaviors. Toward that end, techniques such as shaping, token economies, and contingency contracts are likely to be very useful. There will be times, however, when you have to weaken or eliminate undesired behaviors because they interfere with instruction and learning. For these occasions, you might consider some form of extinction. The most straightforward approach is to simply ignore the undesired response. If a pupil bids for your attention by clowning around, for instance, you may discourage repetition of that sort of behavior by ignoring it. It is possible, however, that classmates will not ignore the behavior but laugh at it. Such response-strengthening reactions from classmates will likely counteract your lack of reinforcement. Accordingly, you need to observe what happens when you try to extinguish behavior by not responding.

If other students are reinforcing a youngster's undesired behavior, you may want to apply the time-out procedure briefly discussed earlier (p. 330). Suppose a physically active third-grade boy seems unable to keep himself from shoving classmates during recess. If verbal requests, reminders, or warnings fail to limit shoving, the boy can be required to take a five-minute time-out period immediately after he shoves a classmate. He must sit alone in the classroom for that period of time while the rest of the class remains out on the playground. Time-out appears to be most effective when it is used with aggressive, group-oriented children who want the attention of the teacher and their peers (Walker & Shea, 1991). The rules for the procedure should be clearly explained, and after being sentenced to time-out (which should last no more than five minutes) a child should be given reinforcement for positive forms of behavior—for example, "Thank you for collecting all the playground balls so nicely, Tommy."

▶ Time-out works best with disruptive, aggressive children

A third technique that is another form of type II punishment, and can be used with a token economy, is **response cost.** With this procedure, a certain amount of positive reinforcement (for example, 5 percent of previously earned tokens) is withdrawn every time a child makes an undesired response. Anyone who has been caught exceeding the speed limit and been fined at least fifty dollars can probably attest to the power of response cost as a modifier of behavior.

Punishment   Punishment is one of the most popular behavior modification techniques, particularly when it takes the form of corporal punishment. It is also one of the most controversial. At the present time, corporal punishment has been banned by only twelve state legislatures. That number will undoubtedly grow

The time-out procedure recommended by behavior modification enthusiasts involves weakening an undesirable form of behavior (such as shoving on the playground) by temporarily removing positive reinforcement (by having the culprit remain in a corner of the classroom for five minutes while the rest of the class continues to enjoy another activity). (Bob Daemmrich/The Image Works, Inc.)

over the years since many states are considering legislation that would abolish the practice (Ryan & Cooper, 1992). The remaining thirty-eight states either explicitly permit schools to physically punish students or are silent on the matter. In states that allow corporal punishment, local school districts may regulate, but not prohibit, its use. Where states have not addressed the issue, local districts may regulate its use or ban it altogether. It has been estimated that over one million children are spanked or paddled each year, and ten thousand of these students receive injuries that require medical attention (Ornstein & Levine, 1993). Corporal punishment occurs in virtually every region of the country, in communities of every size, and at every grade level; it is administered by the majority of principals of either sex, and it is applied to male students more often than to female students (Rose, 1984).

One of the reasons that corporal punishment is controversial springs from a difference of opinion about the relationship between punishment and discipline. Many people feel that discipline—meaning the willingness to behave consistently in desired ways—is best developed through fear of punishment. The alternative point of view holds that discipline is the result of internal controls and is best learned through approaches that enhance self-esteem and encourage cooperation (Hyman & D'Alessandro, 1984).

A second source of controversy about corporal punishment is the extent and nature of the relevant research. There is a general lack of research-based evidence outside of the psychological laboratory that speaks directly to the effectiveness of punishment as a modifier of classroom behavior. What supportive evidence there is tends to come from isolated anecdotes and case histories (Rose, 1984). On the other hand, considerable laboratory evidence, collected from human and animal subjects, suggests that corporal punishment is likely to be ineffective in modifying behavior. The following reasons are typically cited.

▶ Punishment is likely to be ineffective because of temporary impact, side effects

1. Mild punishment (which is the kind usually applied) does not permanently eliminate undesirable behaviors. At best, it suppresses them temporarily.

2. Punished behaviors may continue to occur when the punisher is not present.

3. Punishment may actually increase the strength of undesirable behavior. Many teachers assume that a public reprimand is aversive. But for some students, teacher and peer attention, regardless of the form it takes, is a positive reinforcer and thus tends to increase behaviors the teacher seeks to eliminate.

4. Punishment may produce undesirable emotional side effects. Just as a shocked rat comes to fear a Skinner box, punished children may perceive the teacher and the school as objects to fear and avoid. The result is truancy, tardiness, and high levels of anxiety, all of which impair ability to learn.

5. Punishers model a type of behavior (physical aggression) that they do not want students to exhibit.

6. To be effective, punishment must often be severe and must occur immediately after an undesirable response. Legal and ethical restrictions do not allow severe punishment.

Should You Use Behavior Modification?   This may seem a strange question to ask given the number of pages we have just spent covering behavior modification methods. Obviously, we feel that the results of decades of research on these techniques justify their use by teachers. Nevertheless, there are criticisms of behavior modification that are not adequately addressed by research findings and that you should carefully consider.

One criticism is that many students, including those in the primary grades, will eventually catch on to the fact that they get reinforced only when they do what the teacher wants them to do. Some may resent this and misbehave out of spite. Others may weigh the amount of effort required to earn a favorable comment or a privilege and decide the reinforcer isn't worth the trouble. Still others may develop a "What's in it for me?" attitude. That is, some students may come to think of learning as something they do only to earn an immediate reinforcer. The potential danger of using behavior modification over an extended period of time is that learning may come to an abrupt halt when no one is around to supply reinforcement. (This point is addressed by the next theory to be examined, social learning theory.)

A second major criticism is that behavior modification methods, because of their potential power, may lend themselves to inappropriate or even unethical uses. For example, teachers may shape students to be quiet and obedient because it makes their job easier, even though such behaviors do not always produce optimum conditions for learning.

In response to these criticisms, Skinner and other behavioral scientists argue that if we do not systematically use what we know about the effects of stimuli and consequences on behavior, we will leave things to chance. In an uncontrolled situation some fortunate individuals will have a favorable chain of experiences that will equip them with desirable attitudes and skills; but others will suffer an unfortunate series of experiences that will lead to difficulties and disappointment. In a controlled situation it may be possible to arrange experiences so that almost everyone acquires desirable traits and abilities. What behavioral psychologists seem to be saying is that educators could be accused of being unethical for not making use of an effective learning tool. The challenge, of course, is to use it wisely.

Despite the popularity of operant conditioning among many American psychologists, a number of researchers, beginning in the 1940s, were eager to study types of human behavior that could not be readily explained in terms of principles of operant conditioning. They shared the desire of Skinner and his followers to study behavior as objectively as possible, but they wanted to analyze human behavior in social settings—to see how children acquire acceptable forms of social behavior (or become socialized). Together, they contributed to the development of what came to be called social learning theory—the third and last behavioral theory to be discussed in this chapter.

SOCIAL LEARNING THEORY

In essence, **social learning theory** attributes changes in behavior to observation and imitation. In one of the earliest reports of research and speculations of this type, Neal E. Miller and John Dollard introduced the key ideas reflected by the title of their book: *Social Learning and Imitation* (1941).

> Observational learning occurs when one person imitates another

Miller and Dollard pointed out that it is not always essential for children to have their own spontaneous actions reinforced in order to acquire a new pattern of behavior (as Skinner was maintaining). They suggested that reinforcement and learning can occur in children when their behavior *matches* that of another person. A boy might be praised by his mother, for example, when imitating some form of desirable behavior he had seen displayed by an older brother. Albert Bandura and Richard Walters agreed with Miller and Dollard about the significance of imitation, but in *Social Learning and Personality Development* (1963) they argued that merely *observing* another person might be sufficient to lead to a learned response (which explains why social learning is also called **observational learning**). They pointed out that reinforcement is not always necessary. Eventually, Bandura emerged as the acknowledged spokesman for the social learning theory point of view, and he presented what is generally considered to be the definitive exposition of this theory in *Social Foundations of Thought and Action* (1986). In the sections that follow we will discuss some of the main features of Bandura's social learning theory and examine some of the research it has spawned. The first feature we will describe is the various effects that occur when people observe and imitate a model's behavior: inhibition, disinhibition, facilitation, and true observational learning. Following this we will describe the four processes that underlie observational learning: attention, retention, production, and motivation.

Types of Observational Learning Effects

Inhibition   In many instances we learn *not* to do something that we already know how to do because a model we are observing refrains from behaving, is punished for behaving, or does something different from what we intended to do. Consider the following example: A ten-year-old is taken to her first symphony concert by her parents. After the first movement of Beethoven's fifth symphony she is about to applaud but notices that her parents are sitting quietly with their hands in their laps. She does the same.

Disinhibition   On occasion we learn to exhibit a behavior—one that is usually disapproved of by most people—because a model does the same without being punished. For example, a student attends his school's final football game of the season. As time expires, thousands of students run onto the field and begin tearing up pieces of turf to take home as a souvenir. Noticing that the police do nothing, the student joins in.

> People learn to inhibit or make responses by observing others

Facilitation   This effect occurs whenever we are prompted to do something that we do not ordinarily do because of insufficient motivation rather than social disapproval. For example, a college student attends a lecture on reforming the American education system. Impressed by the lecturer's enthusiasm and ideas, the student vigorously applauds at the end of the presentation. As several members of the audience stand and applaud, so does the student.

Observational Learning   This effect occurs when we learn a *new* behavior pattern by watching and imitating the performance of someone else. A teen-age girl learning how to hit a top-spin forehand in tennis by watching her instructor do the same is an example of observational learning. The four processes that make this form of learning possible are discussed next.

Processes in Observational Learning

Attention   Clearly, if learning is *observational*, paying attention to a model's behavior is a critical first step. If an individual chooses not to observe a model or observes in a half-hearted fashion, little can be expected in terms of retention, production, and motivation with regard to the modeled behavior. What factors, then, affect the willingness of a child to observe and mimic the behavior of a model? The most important factor seems to be the degree of similarity between the model and the observer. On the basis of an extensive review and analysis of previous research, Dale Schunk (1987) drew the following conclusions about the effect of observer-model similarity on observational learning:

1. When children are concerned about the appropriateness of a behavior, or when they have self-doubts about their capabilities, they are more likely to model a peer than an older child or adult.

2. Age similarity seems less important for the learning of skills, rules, and novel responses than competence of the model. When children question the competence of peers, they tend to model the behavior of adults.

3. Children learn academic skills from models of either sex, but they are more apt to perform behaviors displayed by models who they believe are good examples of their sex role.

4. Children who have a negative self-concept, or who have had learning problems in the past, are more likely to imitate a peer who exhibits some initial learning difficulties and overcomes them (a coping model) than a peer who performs flawlessly (a mastery model). Improvements in self-concept and achievement are more likely to occur in response to coping models than to master models.

Retention   Once we have noticed a model's behavior with the intention of imitating it, we must encode that behavior in memory. Encoding may encompass just the observed behaviors or it may also include an explanation of why, how, and when something is done. In the case of behavior, the encoding may be visual (that is, mental pictures) and/or verbal. In the case of behavioral rules, the encoding will likely be in terms of verbal propositions. The benefit of encoding behavioral rules is the ability to generalize the response. Modeled behaviors may be unitary, terminal behaviors (for example, working on a problem until it is solved) or they may be components of a complex behavior (such as striking a golf ball with a golf club). Once the behavior has been modeled, the observer should have several opportunities to engage in overt and/or covert rehearsal.

▶ Processes of observational learning: attention, retention, production, motivation

Production   Bandura divides production into (a) selecting and organizing the response elements, and (b) refining the response on the basis of informative feedback. The smooth operation of the production process is based on the assumption that the necessary response elements have been previously acquired (for example, gripping a golf club, addressing the ball, executing the swing, following through).

Motivation   Like Skinner, Bandura acknowledges the motivational value of reinforcement and incorporates it into his theory. Unlike Skinner, however, he thinks of reinforcement in broader terms. As a result, Bandura talks about direct reinforcement, vicarious reinforcement, and self-reinforcement.

As part of observational learning, *direct reinforcement* occurs when an individual watches a model perform, imitates that behavior, and is reinforced (or punished) by the model or some other individual. A primary grade pupil, for example, may be told by the teacher to observe how a fellow pupil cleans up his or her desk at the end of the day. If that behavior is imitated, the teacher will praise the child. **Vicarious reinforcement** refers to a situation where the observer anticipates receiving a reward for behaving in a given way, because someone else has been so rewarded. A pupil who observes that a classmate is praised by the teacher for completing an assignment promptly may strive to work quickly and diligently on the next assignment in anticipation of receiving similar praise. **Self-reinforcement** refers to a situation where the individual strives to meet personal standards and does not depend on or care about the reactions of others. A high school student may strive to become as good a typist as a classmate not in order to gain teacher approval but primarily because of a desire to prove to herself or himself that such a skill can be mastered and so make the skill more pleasurable and valuable.

▶ Imitation is strengthened through direct reinforcement, vicarious reinforcement, self-reinforcement

Research on Social Learning Theory

The essential principles of social learning theory as described by Bandura can be illustrated by a series of three classic experiments he carried out in the 1960s. In the first experiment (Bandura, Ross & Ross, 1961), a child was seated at a table and encouraged to play with a toy. The model sat at a nearby table and either played quietly with Tinker Toys for ten minutes or played with the Tinker Toys for a minute and then played aggressively with an inflatable clown "Bobo" doll for several minutes, punching, kicking, and sitting on it and hitting it with a hammer. After one or the other of these modeled behaviors, each child was allowed to become engrossed with an attractive toy and then told he or she couldn't play with it any longer, a condition assumed to produce mild frustration. Each child was then led to another room containing a variety of toys including those the model had played with. Children who did not observe a model, as well as those who observed a nonaggressive model, displayed little aggression. By contrast, children exposed to the aggressive model behaved with considerably more aggression toward the Bobo doll and other toys.

The second study (Bandura, Ross & Ross, 1963a) obtained similar results in response to viewing a film of either an adult or an adult dressed as a cartoon character engaging in aggressive behavior. The third study (Bandura, Ross & Ross, 1963b) attempted to determine how rewarding the model for aggressive behavior would affect children's imitative behavior. In general, children were more aggressive after they saw an aggressive model positively rewarded than when the model was punished. These studies, as you may have realized, illustrate the disinhibition effect described earlier.

These three studies stimulated hundreds of other investigations of the same type, particularly because of the implication that viewing aggressive behavior in a film or television program would lead to violence. Reviews of this research, such as those by Parke and Slaby (1983) and T.H.A. van der Voort (1986), have found that despite sometimes conflicting results, quite a bit of evidence suggests that exposure to repeated scenes of violence *does* engender violent behavior.

In addition to modeled aggression, social learning theorists have investigated a variety of academically related behaviors. Among these are modeled persistence, self-confidence, and arithmetic skills. Zimmerman and Blotner (1979), for example, had first- and second-grade children watch a model work for fifteen minutes at separating two interlocked rings and then succeed. Children in this group worked considerably longer at solving a similar puzzle than children who watched a model work for only thirty seconds at separating the rings, regardless of whether or not the thirty-second model was successful. In a follow-up study, Zimmerman and Ringle (1981) found that a model's persistence and statements of confidence in being able to solve a wire-puzzle problem increased first- and second-grade children's degree of persistence on both a wire puzzle and a word puzzle.

The main implication of these two studies is that, to the degree that academic success depends on persistent effort and self-confidence, students who have seen these behaviors modeled are likely to be more successful than students who have not. As important as persistence and self-confidence are, however, at some point they have to be supplemented by effective cognitive skills. This raises at least two basic questions: Can cognitive skills be learned through modeling? And will such modeling improve achievement? A study by Dale Schunk (1981) provides an answer. Schunk arranged for nine-, ten-, and eleven-year-old children who had done poorly in arithmetic to receive one of two types of instruction. Children in the modeling condition received written materials that explained how to solve long-division problems and observed an adult model. While solving a series of problems, the model verbalized the underlying cognitive operations (such as estimating the quotient and multiplying the quotient by the divisor). The children then practiced what they had observed, with the researchers providing corrective modeling for any operations the youngsters failed to grasp. Children in the nonmodeling condition received the same written materials, which they studied on their own. When comprehension problems arose, these children were told to review the relevant section of the written instructions. In comparison to pretest scores, both treatments enhanced persistence, self-confidence, and accuracy of performance. The modeling condition, however, produced greater gains in accuracy than the nonmodeling condition. (For additional examples of how modeling aids achievement, see Schunk [1991, pp. 108–112].)

▶ Persistence, self-confidence, cognitive skills can be learned by observing models

Evaluation of the Effectiveness of Social Learning Theory

It is not possible to evaluate the effectiveness of social learning theory as precisely as it is to evaluate the other two behavioral learning theories discussed in this chapter. A response such as salivation or pecking often can be traced quite directly to particular stimulating conditions. Many forms of imitative behavior, by

When teaching students a potentially dangerous skill, it is particularly important to remember the principles of observational learning noted by Bandura. First, make sure everyone is paying close attention as you demonstrate. Then, determine if retention has occurred by having each student give a "dry run" demonstration. Next, have students reproduce the correct procedures themselves. Finally, provide reinforcement for correct perform- ance. (Will and Deni McIntyre/Photo Researchers, Inc.)

contrast, cannot be attributed to a specific experience or observation. Other factors that have been shown to play a role include the nature of the television program being watched, the characteristics of the individual child (some children are inherently more aggressive than others), the child's family, the child's neighborhood, and the reactions of others who are watching the program with the child (van der Voort, 1986). This is the main reason research on the impact of televised violence has led to inconclusive results. It is not possible to prove, except in a few cases of direct imitation, that a particular act of aggressive behavior was caused by a particular television program or series of programs. Even if a child imitates a particular act of behavior under controlled conditions, the imitative response may have been influenced by observations made outside of the experimental situation.

The classic experiments of Bandura involving the Bobo doll have been criticized, for example, because such dolls were *designed* to be hit, kicked, and knocked over. Many of the subjects of his experiments may have observed Bobo dolls being hit (in television commercials, for instance) before they watched the model in the experimental situations. As Bandura himself has stressed, the behavior of models must be encoded in a person's memory before it will have an impact on behavior. When information is encoded in one's memory, though (as we shall see in the next chapter), it is typically associated with already stored information. Thus, the observation of a "new" kind of behavior is very likely to be incorporated with already-stored information from observations of previous experiences of the same type. If you were asked to try to trace the source of a particular aspect of your own behavior, for instance, you might be able to report that it was probably due to imitation but be unable to specify the particular individuals or events that served as models. In most cases you might conclude that there were multiple models from whom you "abstracted" specific variations to add to previously imitated behavior.

Perhaps the safest conclusion to draw about the effectiveness of observational learning, therefore, is that it undeniably influences behavior in many ways even though it may not be possible to trace causes with precision.

Now that you are familiar with behavioral learning theories, it is time to examine Suggestions for Teaching derived from the experimental findings and principles that have just been discussed. First, though, you may find it helpful to peruse the mid-chapter review presented below.

Mid-Chapter Review

Types of Behavioral Learning Theories

Classical conditioning (Pavlov): reflexive response associated with a new stimulus (original experiment: salivation in dogs)

Operant conditioning (Skinner): voluntary response strengthened by reinforcement (original experiment: rats in Skinner box)

Social learning theory (Bandura): ways in which observation and imitation of a model lead to learned behavior (original experiment: imitation of aggression by young children)

Basic Principles of Operant Conditioning

Positive reinforcement: response strengthened when followed by a positive consequence

Negative reinforcement: response strengthened when disagreeable stimulus removed

Punishment: response weakened when followed by a disagreeable stimulus

Time-out: response weakened when positive reinforcement is temporarily removed

Extinction: response weakened when it is ignored

Generalization: tendency for a conditioned response to be aroused by any stimulus similar to the original stimulus coupled with reinforcement

Discrimination: ability to distinguish between similar stimuli when one is reinforced, other is not

Shaping: movements in direction of preselected terminal behavior strengthened by reinforcement

Schedules of Reinforcement

Fixed interval: supply reinforcement after preselected intervals of time (leads to bursts of responses as end of interval approaches)

Variable interval: supply reinforcement after intervals of various lengths that correspond to a preselected average (leads to steady rate of response, limits extinction)

Fixed ratio: supply reinforcement after preselected number of responses (leads to series of rapid responses)

Variable ratio: supply reinforcement after different numbers of responses that correspond to a predetermined average (leads to high and steady rate of response, limits extinction)

Applications of Operant Conditioning

Programmed instruction: arrange material to be learned in small, sequential steps; provide feedback regarding correctness of responses

Linear program: single sequence of frames presented to all students

Branching program: main sequence of frames supplemented by shorter remedial sequences of frames to correct misunderstandings

Computer-assisted instruction: present programs through use of computers

Behavior modification: use of operant conditioning principles to shape desired classroom behaviors

Premack principle: strengthen desired behavior by using student's preferred behaviors as reinforcers

Social Learning Theory Processes

For observational learning to be effective, students should attend to significant features of the model's behavior, retain what they observe, produce the activity, experience satisfaction or reinforcement

Suggestions for Teaching in Your Classroom

APPLYING BEHAVIORAL THEORIES IN THE CLASSROOM

1. Remain aware that behavior is the result of particular conditions.
2. Use reinforcement to strengthen behavior you want to encourage.
   a. Do your best to give feedback frequently, specifically, and quickly.
   b. When immediate feedback is not possible, use delayed feedback.
   c. Use several kinds of reinforcers so that each retains its effectiveness.
3. Use awareness of extinction to combat forgetting and to reduce the frequency of undesirable forms of behavior.

4. Be alert for generalization. When it occurs, use reinforcement (or lack of it) and explanations to bring about discrimination.

5. Take advantage of knowing about the impact of different reinforcement schedules to encourage persistent and permanent learning.
   a. When students first attempt a new kind of learning, supply frequent reinforcement. Then supply rewards less often.
   b. If you want to encourage periodic spurts of activity, use a fixed interval schedule of reinforcement.

6. Use programmed approaches to teaching by describing terminal behavior, organizing what is to be learned, and providing feedback.
   a. Describe the terminal behavior. That is, follow the procedures described in Chapter 6 to list exactly what you want students to learn after they have completed a given unit of study.
   b. If appropriate, arrange the material to be learned into a series of steps or an outline of points.
   c. Provide feedback so that correct responses will be reinforced and students will become aware of and correct errors.

7. When students must struggle to concentrate on material that is not intrinsically interesting, use special forms of reinforcement to motivate them to persevere.
   a. Select, with student assistance, a variety of reinforcers.
   b. Establish, in consultation with individual students, an initial contract of work to be performed to earn a particular reward.
   c. Once the initial reward is earned, establish a series of short contracts leading to frequent, immediate rewards.

8. To reduce the tendency for pupils to engage in undesirable forms of behavior, first try withholding reinforcement and calling attention to rewards that will follow completion of a task. If that does not work, consider the possibility of taking away a privilege or resorting to punishment.

9. Remember the basic processes of observational learning and make effective use of observation and imitation.

---

1. Remain aware that behavior is the result of particular conditions.

Skinner and his followers believe that it should be possible to specify the conditions leading to any act of behavior if observations are made systematically. That is why they argue that you have two choices: Either shape behavior systematically, or do it in a haphazard way. But this argument does not take into account the fact that in a classroom (as contrasted with a Skinner box) many causes of behavior may not be observable or traceable. Furthermore, it is clearly impossible for a classroom teacher to handle teaching routine and also minutely observe and analyze the behavior of thirty pupils. You might as well accept the fact, therefore, that quite often you are going to be a haphazard shaper of behavior. Nevertheless, there will be times when you and your pupils may benefit if you say to yourself, "Now, there *have* to be some causes for that behavior. Can I figure out what they are and do something about changing things for the better? Am I doing something that is leading to types of behavior that are making life difficult for some or all of us in the room?" When engaging in such speculations, keep in mind that reinforcement strengthens behavior. And check to see if you are inadvertently rewarding pupils for misbehavior (by calling attention to them, for example, or failing to reinforce those who engage in desirable forms of behavior).

Examples

If you become aware that it takes a long time for your students to settle down at the beginning of a period and that you are reacting by addressing critical remarks specifically to those who dawdle the longest, ignore the dawdlers, and respond positively to those who are ready to get to work.

Let's say that you have given students thirty minutes to finish an assignment. To your dismay, few of them get to work until almost the end of the period, and you find that you have to do a lot of nagging to hold down gossip and horseplay. When you later analyze why this happened, you conclude that you actually encouraged the time-killing behavior because of the way you set up the lesson. The next time you give a similar assignment, tell the students that as soon as they complete it, they can have class time to work on homework, a term project, or the equivalent and that you will be available to give help or advice to those who want it.

2. Use reinforcement to strengthen behavior you want to encourage.

Four basic principles of conditioning are reinforcement, extinction, generalization, and discrimination. Awareness of each of these can be of value when you arrange learning experiences, but the most important and significant is reinforcement. Several techniques of teaching can be derived from knowledge of the impact of rewards on behavior.

a. Do your best to give feedback frequently, specifically, and quickly.

Although frequent, clear, and timely feedback is generally useful in helping students learn efficiently, this form of reinforcement is particularly important when the material is complex and the student is unsure of the correctness of his or her response. Accordingly, if a student misspells a word, uses the wrong procedure in solving a mathematics problem, uses the wrong technique in performing calisthenics, or misinterprets the theme of a novel, you should call attention to the error as quickly as possible, point out the correct response, and

One of the basic principles of instruction derived from operant conditioning experiments is that teachers should provide elementary grade students with immediate reinforcement for correct responses. (Jeffrey W. Myers/Stock, Boston, Inc.)

explain why it is superior to the response made by the student (Bangert-Drowns, Kulik & Kulik, 1991; Kulik & Kulik, 1988).

Examples

Handbook Heading:
Ways to Supply Specific and Immediate Feedback

After giving a problem, go over the correct answer immediately.

Have pupils team up and give each other feedback.

Have some pupils go to the board while others work at their desks.

Give a problem, and have those at their desks compare their answers to the one at the board that you identify as correct.

Meet with students in small groups so that you can give each pupil more individual feedback.

When you assign reading or give a lecture or demonstration, present a short self-corrected quiz or an informal question-and-answer session immediately afterward.

In your Handbook, you might note other techniques that you could use to supply specific and immediate reinforcement for correct responses.

b. When immediate feedback is not possible, use delayed feedback.

Although quick knowledge of correctness is desirable in many types of learning, some tasks are so lengthy or complex that a proper evaluation precludes immediate feedback. Nevertheless, you should not feel that supplying corrections of student work several days after it was completed will necessarily be ineffective. Students sometimes continue to think about their responses to essay questions or the content of term papers and come up with their own "corrections" in the interval between responding and receiving feedback. Because of this mental activity, delayed feedback may be "fresher" than you realize.

> Delayed feedback can be as effective as immediate feedback

Examples

Handbook Heading:
Ways to Supply
Delayed Feedback

Hand back and discuss all exams. Even though students may have written their answers a week or more earlier, they will still be getting feedback when they look at the answer they wrote as you discuss it.

On written work, correct spelling and grammatical errors (if you can), and make brief favorable comments when a section is particularly well phrased or when an important point is emphasized. Make general favorable comments—if deserved—at the end of the paper.

Before handing back a term paper, essay exam, or the equivalent, you might ask students to jot down additional points they thought of after they completed the work. Or you might announce, "If you realized after you completed your work that you had made a mistake, make a note of it and mention how you would correct it if you were to do the assignment over again now. Then we can see if your evaluation agrees with mine." If you try out this idea, you might make some sort of allowance (perhaps in the form of bonus points) for corrections made by students before they examine your corrections.

If you can think of other ways to supply delayed feedback, note them in your Handbook.

c. Use several kinds of reinforcers so that each retains its effectiveness.

In many learning situations the correct answer to a problem serves as the reinforcer. In other situations, however, the reinforcer will take the form of a comment or a smile from you, a mark or a grade or some other symbol of achievement, or the chance to engage in a desired activity. Some enthusiasts for behavior modification urge teachers to try to shape their own praising behavior by first making a record of the number of favorable comments, smiles, and so on, emitted before behavior control is instituted (called the baseline period by behavior modification specialists) and then engaging in a systematic effort to increase the frequency of each type of reinforcement.[2] It seems possible, however, that if you are too methodical about supplying reinforcement, students might think that you are insincere. If you try to increase your praising ratio from

2. If this idea sounds appealing to you, you will find instructions and sample forms to use on pages 485–590 of *Teaching: A Course in Applied Psychology* (1971) by Becker, Englemann, and Thomas.

ten to twenty per period, for example, you might have to work extra hard at projecting enthusiasm and genuine appreciation. On the other hand, if you do not pay any attention to how you dispense reinforcement you may be inefficient or actually work against yourself. Perhaps the best policy is to think frequently about how and when you use different types of reinforcement, but not to the point of keeping a tally of techniques.

Examples

When a student gives a correct answer, makes a good point in class discussion, or does something helpful, say things like: "Good." "That's right." "Terrific." "Great." "Very interesting point." "I hadn't thought of that." "I really appreciated what you did." "That was a big help." (If you believe in being prepared, you might list in your Handbook similar statements to use as verbal reinforcers. In addition to making such comments, smile and show that you are sincere.)

Walk over to stand near and smile encouragingly at a pupil who seems to be working industriously.

With younger pupils give a pat on the back after an especially good achievement.

Encourage students to keep a private chart of their achievements and to record their progress, perhaps with colored ink, gold stars, or the like. (Before you dismiss gold stars or the equivalent as infantile or silly, glance through several issues of a local newspaper and count the number of pictures or articles reporting awards that have been made. If the most improved junior varsity football player is given a 2-foot-high trophy, for example, why shouldn't a math student get a similar—if less impressive—symbol of achievement?)

Announce in advance how many points a particular assignment will count toward a final grade. Award bonus points for work completed ahead of time or for extra work.

3. Use awareness of extinction to combat forgetting and to reduce the frequency of undesirable forms of behavior.

When dealing with nonacademic forms of behavior, you will sometimes want to use knowledge of extinction to reduce the frequency of minor misconduct. The basic rule is to consistently ignore behavior that you would prefer to have weakened or to disappear. It is not always possible or desirable to do so, of course. Sometimes your lack of response will be offset by positive responses from students, and some students may get the idea that they can exhibit normally prohibited behaviors if peers who do the same receive no negative consequences.

Examples

> If a student experiments with knocking his books off his desk in an effort to arouse a response, pay no attention and continue with the lesson.
>
> If a student says something transparently provocative in class discussion, don't comment, and immediately call on someone else.

4. Be alert for generalization. When it occurs, use reinforcement (or lack of it) and explanations to bring about discrimination.

Regardless of the grade level or subject you teach, your students will tend to apply what they learn in one situation to what they perceive to be similar situations. Sometimes this is desirable. In other cases, however, it will cause problems. When you become aware that pupils are generalizing in ways that lead to errors or misconceptions, encourage them to discriminate by using selective reinforcement or by calling their attention to differences.

Examples

> When a kindergartner says, "I saw two gooses," explain that even though it seems like the logical way to say it, the word for more than one goose is *geese*.
>
> If a high school language student conjugates an irregular verb by applying rules for regular verbs, point out that the verb is irregular and should simply be memorized.

5. Take advantage of knowing about the impact of different reinforcement schedules to encourage persistent and permanent learning.
   a. When students first attempt a new kind of learning, supply frequent reinforcement. Then supply rewards less often.

Keep in mind the impact of different schedules of reinforcement by taking into account Skinner's experiments with rats and pigeons. When Skinner wanted to encourage rats and pigeons to learn bar pressing and disk pecking, he first reinforced every response. While this was the most efficient way to train the animals initially, the behavior extinguished rapidly as soon as reinforcement stopped. After the animals had learned the basic skill, they were more likely to continue to respond at a steady rate when put on a fixed ratio, variable ratio, or variable interval schedule of reinforcement. You can use the same techniques of reinforcement in your classroom.

Examples

Handbook Heading:
Ways to Use Schedules
of Reinforcement

> When introducing new material, give a point for every correct response. Then specify that a point can be earned only if five questions are answered correctly.

When students first try a new skill or type of learning, praise almost any genuine attempt, even though it may be inept. Then as they become more skillful, reserve your praise only for especially good performances.

Avoid a set pattern of commenting on student work.

Make favorable remarks at unpredictable intervals.

If students in physical education catch on that the instructor walks methodically up and down checking to see if everyone is doing calisthenics, they may do their pushups (or whatever) only when they know they are being watched. To encourage steady exercise, it would be better to follow an unpredictable pattern when observing this kind of behavior.

If you can think of other ways to use fixed ratio or variable interval schedules of reinforcement, note them in your Handbook.

b. If you want to encourage periodic spurts of activity, use a fixed interval schedule of reinforcement.

Occasionally, you will want to encourage students to engage in spurts of activity, since steady output might be too demanding or fatiguing. In such cases, supply reinforcement at specified periods of time.

Examples

Schedule a quiz every Wednesday.

When students are engaging in strenuous or concentrated activity, circulate and provide praise and encouragement by following a set pattern that will bring you in contact with each student at predictable intervals.

6. Use programmed approaches to teaching by describing terminal behavior, organizing what is to be learned, and providing feedback.

Skinner taught pigeons to peck tunes on a xylophone and to play table tennis by reinforcing a series of approximations to the desired terminal behavior. His success in doing this led him to propose that programmed instruction, based on the same principles and techniques, should become the basic form of instruction used in schools. It is highly unlikely that you will be able to use an all-programmed approach in your classroom. It is almost certain, however, that some of the lessons you present will be more effective if you take account of some of Skinner's suggestions.

Regardless of the grade level or subject you teach, there are likely to be some types of knowledge that can be specifically defined. In order to learn how to read, primary grade pupils need to master letters and words. In order to learn how to spell and do mathematics, elementary grade students need to memorize combinations of letters and numbers. In order to comprehend discussions of most subjects, junior high students need to acquire understanding of facts and

Handbook Heading:
Describing Terminal
Behavior

principles. And in order to learn a foreign language, high school students need to memorize thousands of words and verb forms. Whenever you want to help students master information of this type, consider using the following procedure.

a. Describe the terminal behavior. That is, follow the procedures described in Chapter 7 to list exactly what you want students to learn after they have completed a given unit of study.

Examples

List all the mathematical concepts to be learned during a report period or year.

Pick out fifty frequently misspelled words.

Select ten or so facts or principles that you consider to be the key points in a chapter or text.

b. If appropriate, arrange the material to be learned into a series of steps or an outline of points.

In some cases, there will be no logical way to organize the points you have listed. It rarely makes any difference, for example, how a list of spelling words is arranged. Most of the time, though, you can help your students master material by arranging ideas in sequence or by organizing points so that one emerges from or is related to others. Use of the various taxonomies outlined in the preceding chapter should help you do this.

Examples

Select a series of readers for use in the primary grades. Choose a series where the words learned in the first book make it simpler to read those in later books.

Have language students use a conversational approach so that they can grasp sentence structure as they memorize vocabulary and verb forms.

In a science class, group related facts and concepts and present them as separate units.

Before giving a lecture or demonstration or showing a film, hand out a sheet of paper listing in organized form the points that will be covered, leaving space under each for student notes.

c. Provide feedback so that correct responses will be reinforced and students will become aware of and correct errors.

Since the key principle of operant conditioning is reinforcement, it is essential to provide feedback to strengthen correct responses and inform students when their

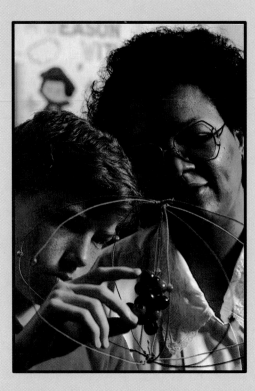

According to research, the effectiveness of feedback is greatest when learner confidence is high but the answer is incorrect because the learner is most likely to use the feedback to satisfy curiosity about why the answer was wrong.
(Charles Gupton/Tony Stone Worldwide)

responses are incorrect. Therefore, you should follow the procedures noted under Suggestion 2 to supply frequent, specific, and prompt feedback. In addition, use techniques such as those listed below.

Examples

Immediately after students read a chapter in a text, give them an informal quiz on the key points you listed. Then have them pair off, exchange quizzes, and correct and discuss them.

As soon as you complete a lecture or demonstration, ask individual students to volunteer to read to the rest of the class what they wrote about the points they were told to look for. Indicate whether the answer is correct; and if it is incorrect or incomplete, ask (in a relaxed and nonthreatening way) for additional comments. Urge students to amend and revise their notes as they listen to the responses.

7. When students must struggle to concentrate on material that is not intrinsically interesting, use special forms of reinforcement to motivate them to persevere.

In discussing uses of reinforcement, the stress has been on providing feedback or taking advantage of your knowledge of the impact of different schedules of reinforcement. You can also use reinforcement to motivate students to complete difficult tasks. In order to master almost any skill or subject, a certain amount of tedious and disagreeable effort is usually necessary. Hardly any students shout with joy, for example, when they are requested to learn spelling words, practice addition or multiplication, memorize chemical symbols, do calisthenics, and so on. Furthermore, some students—for a variety of reasons—may have an extraordinarily difficult time concentrating on almost anything. Accordingly, you may sometimes find it essential to use techniques of behavior modification to help students stick to a task. If and when that time comes, you might follow these procedures.

Handbook Heading:
Ways to Encourage Perseverance

a. Select, with student assistance, a variety of reinforcers.

A behavior modification approach to motivation appears to work most successfully when students are aware of and eager to earn a payoff. Because students react differently to rewards and because any reward is likely to lose effectiveness if used to excess, it is desirable to list several kinds of rewards and permit students to choose. Some behavior modification enthusiasts (for example, Homme & Tosti, 1971) even recommend that you make up a *reinforcement menu* for each pupil. If you allow your students to prepare individual reinforcement menus themselves, they should be instructed to list school activities they really enjoy doing. It would be wise, however, to stress that entrees on anyone's menu must be approved by you in order to make sure that they will not conflict with school regulations or interfere with the rights of others. A student's reward menu might consist of activities such as these: Read a book of one's choice, work on an art or craft project, use earphones to listen to a tape or record, explore a general interest corner, go to the library, view a videotape in another room, or work on homework for another class. A reinforcement menu can be used in conjunction with Grandma's rule (the Premack principle). Set up learning situations, particularly those that are not intrinsically appealing, by telling students that as soon as they finish their broccoli (for example, doing a series of multiplication problems) they can have a chocolate sundae (an item from their reinforcement menu).

▶ Reinforcement menu: student-selected enjoyable activities

b. Establish, in consultation with individual students, an initial contract of work to be performed in order to earn a particular reward.

Once you have established a list of payoffs, you might consult with students (on an individual basis, if possible) to establish a certain amount of work that must be completed in order to obtain a reward selected from the menu. (Refer to Mager's suggestions for preparing specific objectives for guidelines.) The first contract should not be too demanding, to ensure that the student will earn the reward.

Examples

Successfully spell at least seven out of ten words on a list of previously mis-spelled words.

Correctly complete twenty addition problems made up of two-digit numbers.

Outline twenty pages in the text, and correctly answer at least seven out of ten questions based on the key points.

    c. Once the initial reward is earned, establish a series of short contracts leading to frequent, immediate rewards.

The results of many operant conditioning experiments lead to the conclusion that the frequency of reinforcement is of greater significance than the amount of reinforcement. Therefore, having students work on a series of brief contracts leading to frequent payoffs provided immediately after the task is completed is preferable to having them work toward a delayed, king-size award.

Examples

Ask students to learn how to spell a list of fifty tough words by rewarding themselves after they have mastered batches of five or ten.

Have students accumulate points toward a final grade by completing an exam or project every week, instead of scheduling one or two comprehensive exams and a blockbuster term paper.

8. To reduce the tendency of pupils to engage in undesirable forms of behavior, first try withholding reinforcement and calling attention to rewards that will follow completion of a task. If that does not work, consider the possibility of taking away a privilege or resorting to punishment.

Students often engage in types of behavior that are disruptive in one way or another. Theoretically, such behavior will tend to extinguish if it is not reinforced. Therefore, as noted in Suggestion 3, your first reaction might be to ignore it. Unfortunately, however, you will not be the only reinforcing agent in the classroom. As noted earlier, you may ignore a wisecrack, but classmates sitting around the culprit may respond enthusiastically and strengthen the tendency to wisecrack. Furthermore, in some cases you simply cannot ignore behavior. If a pupil is on the verge of destroying school property or injuring a classmate, you must respond immediately.

Handbook Heading: Ways to Use Behavior Modification to Maintain Control

You may need to follow a sequence something like this when confronted by undesirable but relatively minor misbehavior, such as two boys fooling around when assigned to work together on a chemistry experiment.

First, ignore the behavior.

Second, remind the class that those who finish the experiment early earn five bonus points and will be allowed to see a film.

Third, approach the boys and tell them (privately and nicely) that they are disturbing others and making life difficult for themselves because if they do not complete the experiment in the allotted time, they will have to make it up at some other time.

Fourth, resort to punishment by informing the boys (in a firm but not nasty way) that they must leave the classroom immediately and report to the vice principal to be assigned to a study hall for the rest of the class period. Tell them they will have to complete the experiment when the rest of the class has free experiment time.

Finish by pointing out that once the work is made up, they will be all caught up and in a good position to do above-average work the rest of the period.

This sequence is based on studies (for example, Hall et al., 1971) leading to the conclusion that punishment is most effective when it occurs immediately after a response, cannot be avoided, is as intense as seems necessary, and provides the individual with an alternative and desirable response.

Constructive classroom control will be discussed more completely in Chapter 13, but in this outline of applications of behavioral theory it is appropriate to call attention once again to a few undesirable by-products of punishment. Even though punishment may be effective in inhibiting student behavior, there is the risk that the individual will come to associate the anxiety, shame, and anger aroused by the act with the punisher and the situation. A student may come to fear and hate a teacher, a classroom, a subject of study, or the whole idea of school, particularly if punishment is excessively harsh, protracted, or embarrassing. This may be especially true if the punishment is perceived as unfair or if there is no escape from it.

You are reminded that behavioral psychologists make a distinction between punishment and negative reinforcement. Skinner describes punishment as the use of an aversive stimulus intended to inhibit the response that preceded it. Negative reinforcement, on the other hand, is designed to strengthen an escape response. The sequence outlined above ended with punishment—the boys were required to endure the aversive consequences of being banished to a study hall. Instead of resorting to punishment in a situation, suppose you say, "If you don't stop that fooling around and finish that experiment, I'll give you both an F for this unit." That would be an application of negative reinforcement because if the boys responded as planned they would do the experiment not to gain a reward but to avoid negative consequences.

Negative reinforcement is sometimes effective, but it may be risky because it is not always possible to predict the kind of escape behavior that will be used. In this case, your intention would be that the boys would try to escape the low grade by working diligently on the experiment. If the boys resented the threat, though, or were fooling around because they did not know how to get started on the experiment, they might literally escape from the whole situation by not coming to class for several days. Thus it is preferable to use positive reinforcement and stress the rewards that will follow desired activities.

9. Remember the basic processes of observational learning and make effective use of observation and imitation.

Students learn many skills and forms of classroom behavior by observing and imitating others. You can enhance learning of skills and promote desirable kinds of behavior if you take into account the four basic processes of observational learning: attention, retention, production, and motivation. If you plan to demonstrate the correct way to perform some skill or process, first make sure you have the attention of everyone in the class. (Techniques for securing attention will be discussed in the analysis of information processing in Chapter 8.) Then, after explaining what you are going to do (perhaps noting particular points students should look for), demonstrate. Immediately after you demonstrate, have all the students in the class try out the new skill to foster retention. Or, for complex skills, have them write down the steps to follow before they try the activity on their own. Finally, arrange for all the students to get feedback and experience satisfaction and/or reinforcement immediately after they imitate your behavior by proving to themselves that they can carry out the activity on their own.

Examples

Show primary grade pupils how to solve multiplication problems by first placing a large, colorful poster on a bulletin board with a diagram of the process. Explain the diagram and then demonstrate how to solve some simple problems. As soon as you finish, hand out a worksheet containing several simple problems similar to those you just demonstrated.

Have students work on the problems for a specified period of time, and then secure their attention once again and demonstrate on the board the correct procedure for solving each problem. Have students correct their own papers as you demonstrate, point out that they now know how to do multiplication problems, and praise them for learning the skill so rapidly.

In a high school business class, follow a similar procedure when showing students how to set up a word processor to type a form letter. Make sure everyone is paying attention. Demonstrate the correct procedure. Have students write down the steps they should follow in order to imitate your actions. Have them study the steps before setting up their own word processor. Have them reproduce the letter. Provide reinforcement to supplement their own satisfaction in having completed the task successfully.

Select low-achieving students who have mastered a skill to demonstrate the skill to other low-achieving students.

Pair a socially competent student with a less socially competent classmate to work on a task.

A final point to remember about observational learning is that, in the lower grades particularly, you will be an admired model your students will be inclined to imitate. If you are well-organized and businesslike, but also thoughtful and considerate, your pupils may act that way themselves.

Applying Technology to Teaching

USING COMPUTERS IN YOUR CLASSROOM

We mentioned earlier that under the right conditions computers can effectively supplement classroom instruction. If you are now thinking that you might like to use computers in your own classroom, there are a few additional things you need to know before you get started. You should know something about the types of programs that exist, their general quality, and how you can identify the best available programs.

Uses of Computers

Perhaps the most general distinction that can be made about the use of computers in schools is *learning about computers* versus *learning with computers*. The first approach, used primarily at the high school level, emphasizes two things: understanding how computers work, and learning how to use the various computer languages, such as BASIC, PASCAL, and LOGO, that control its functions (for example, to teach, analyze and display data, or process words). The second approach is what we refer to as computer-assisted instruction (CAI), whereby students use the computer and instructional programs to master typical school subject matter, like English, science, and arithmetic. CAI is typically found at the elementary level (Hassett, 1984) and relies on one or more of the following types of programs: drill and practice, tutorial, and problem solving.

Drill and Practice Programs   These programs provide students with opportunities to practice knowledge and skills that were presented earlier by the teacher or by a textbook. The computer presents, for example, an arithmetic problem or a question about English vocabulary or a spelling exercise; the student types an answer; and the computer checks the accuracy of the response, provides feedback, and then presents the next item. Some programs keep track of how many errors a student makes, provide help when a student gets stuck, and adjust the difficulty level of the problems or questions to the proficiency level of the student. Some drill and practice programs are designed to look like arcade games. For example, an arithmetic program requires you to type in the correct answer to a multiplication problem in order to save your space station from being destroyed by a meteor (Doll, 1987; Willis, Hovey & Hovey, 1987). Because these programs can be produced relatively easily and quickly, they dominate the marketplace. The Educational Products Information Exchange (EPIE), a nonprofit organization that classifies and evaluates computer programs, estimates that drill and practice programs constitute almost 50 percent of the educational programs that are on the market (Hassett, 1984). As we shall see shortly, drill and practice programs can be valuable adjuncts to the curriculum, particularly if they are well designed. They can also be so poorly designed as to be little more than expensive "electronic workbooks."

Tutorial Programs   These programs go one step beyond drill and practice in that they attempt to teach new material (for example, facts, definitions, concepts). Tutorial programs may be written in either a linear or a branching format. When a branching format is chosen, the program writer has to anticipate where incorrect responses are likely to be made and provide remedial frames. Tutorial programs can be enhanced by combining them with video disks. In addition to text and graphics, this arrangement can provide still and moving pictures that can be replayed as needed. Since tutorial programs are more complex, they take longer to develop (one hour of tutorial instruction often requires several thousand hours of development time on the part of a computer programmer, teaching methods specialist, and content area specialist) and are more expensive to develop than simple linear programs. As a result, there are relatively few tutorial programs available.

Some tutorial programs are referred to as *dialogue programs* because they mimic the instructional interchange that often occurs between student and teacher. For example, a program in reading instruction would begin with the computer examining a student's file to determine current reading level and displaying appropriate reading exercises. The student reads the material, is presented with a set of questions, and types responses on the keyboard. The computer evaluates the responses and displays the results of the evaluation. If the student's responses are correct, the computer provides more difficult passages and questions. If the responses are incorrect, less difficult exercises are presented (Doll, 1987; Willis, Hovey & Hovey, 1987).

Problem-Solving Programs   Problem-solving programs come in a variety of forms. Some might be viewed as elaborated tutorials. They teach new material and then provide opportunities for the learner to apply what has been learned. A second type requires the student to use existing knowledge, perhaps in a new way, to discover the solution to a problem. Some problem-solving programs are embedded in a game format. Games are basically contests based on skills and/or chance that are played according to rules. Mapping skills, strategy formulation, record keeping, and deductive reasoning are some of the skills called upon by game-type problem-solving programs. The last type of problem-solving program that we will discuss are simulations. In simulations, students must work out the solution to a problem that is embedded in a real-life context. For example, one simulation gives students experience in designing and managing a city. Once the city is built, they have to deal with such tasks as managing the budget, providing services, and dealing with pollution and traffic problems. They can ask the computer to give them budget information, poll results, maps, and a variety of statistics. Simulations are particularly useful when students are denied first-hand experience because of factors like cost (for example, diagnose and repair a malfunctioning car), danger (for example, operate a nuclear reactor), and time constraints (for example, recreate a Civil War battle) (Doll, 1987; Neill & Neill, 1990; Willis, Hovey & Hovey, 1987).

Program Quality

If you like to think in terms of analogies, you might consider the program to be the brain of CAI. The program is the one component that allows the computer to "come to life" and fulfill its potential. It is more important than how much information the computer can store, how many disk drives it has, how many columns of characters it can display on its screen, and so on. Thus, one should pay particular attention to the quality of available programs in deciding which computers to buy, or whether one should be purchased at all. This is doubly important since most opinions of program quality are strongly negative (for example, Hassett, 1984; Komoski, 1984; Walker, 1983). Consider, for instance, the following statement by James Hassett (1984):

> One advantage of presenting material on a computer rather than through a text-book or an overhead projector is that a computer can ask questions as it goes along. In theory, this means that instruction can be tailored to each student's knowledge and abilities in a way that will increase motivation, attention, and learning. In practice, much of the available software is poorly developed and deadly dull. (p. 24)

Hassett (1984) also notes that out of more than seven thousand educational programs, the Educational Products Information Exchange (EPIE) judged only about 25 percent as meeting minimum technical and instructional standards. Further, only 3 to 4 percent were judged to be excellent in quality.

Why are good programs in such short supply? Largely because their development requires a set of capabilities that are difficult to find in one person or among a small group of people. In general, an educational software developer should be familiar with computer languages, learning theory, instructional techniques, and principles of instructional development. "The best teachers, as a consequence, frequently are not the best software writers, and vice versa" (Kindel & Benoit, 1984).

The importance of integrating learning principles into the design of instructional programs has been discussed by Julie Vargas (1986). She finds that poor-quality programs often overlook such basic operant conditioning principles as offering maximum opportunities for active responding, providing immediate feedback, and shaping behavior. Some drill and practice programs, for example, incorporate into their lessons a variety of attention-getting features (such as familiar tunes, trains that puff across the screen, and animal characters that gesture or make facial expressions) in an attempt to keep the student interested and motivated. But the more often these features are used, the more time students spend watching them rather than practicing skills. As a result, it takes longer for students to make basic cognitive skills automatic (such as adding or multiplying numbers or recognizing and spelling words). Even worse, the student may become distracted altogether from the goal of the drill if the motivational features are too numerous and compelling. In other instances, tutorials and simulations often violate the principles of shaping. Instead of breaking a lesson into small, easy-to-handle steps, providing prompts, and requiring mastery of each step before moving on to more complex responses, they typically throw students into a situation that requires learning by trial and error.

A basic principle of instructional development that authors of poor-quality programs frequently ignore (deliberately or otherwise) is the field test. Even though a program may have been revised several times by its author and reviewed by a panel of experts, its effectiveness as instructional material is still essentially unknown. The best way to identify and eliminate problems of step size, clarity, sequencing, feedback, attention getting, motivation, and so on, is to try the program out on a representative group of students. The principle of conducting a field test strikes people as so obviously necessary that they just assume it is a standard part of instructional software development. Unfortunately, this assumption is unfounded. EPIE researchers found that creators of 50 percent of a group of 163 popular programs skipped this step (Hassett, 1984).

To help you evaluate the quality of instructional software you may one day want to use in your classroom, an eight-point checklist devised by Julie Vargas is presented in Table 8.2.

Identifying High-Quality Programs

If and when you find yourself in a position to employ computer-assisted instruction, take the time and effort to identify well-designed programs. Four publica-

---

TABLE 8.2 Eight Points to Consider When Choosing a CAI Program

1. Does the software require a high frequency of responding (as opposed to screens of material to read)? For tutorials and drills, how many problems does a student actually do in a 10-minute session?

2. Is the responding relevant to your goals? (Do students do what they are to learn?)

3. Do students have to respond to the critical parts of the problems?

4. Is most of the screen content necessary for the response, or does the program assume that students will learn content without having to respond overtly to it?

5. Does the screen ask students to discriminate between at least two possible responses?

6. Can students see their progress as they work with the program from day to day or session to session?

7. Are students mostly successful going through the program (as opposed to becoming frustrated)? Do they enjoy using the program?

8. For series, or lessons to be used repeatedly: Does the program adjust according to the performance level or progress of the student?

Source: From "Instructional Design Flaws in Computer-Assisted Instruction" by J. S. Vargas, 1986, *Phi Delta Kappan, 67*, p. 744. Copyright 1986 by Phi Delta Kappa. Adapted by permission.

tions can help you in this effort. *Only the Best: Preschool-Grade 12* by Shirley Boes Neill and George W. Neill is an annual guide to educational software that has been judged to be of high quality by two or more educational organizations. *T.E.S.S. The Educational Software Selector* is a comprehensive guide to educational software that is published by the Educational Products Information Exchange Institute, a nonprofit organization. This volume contains over 7,700 descriptions of programs in more than one hundred subject areas. While the descriptions are brief, each contains upwards of fourteen pieces of relevant information. Hundreds of these summaries include a rating based on the evaluations of trained analysts. Detailed reports of these evaluated programs can be found in EPIE's periodical, *MICROgram*. In addition, volume 17, number 3 (1990) of another EPIE publication, *EPIEgram*, describes the twelve criteria used by EPIE analysts to evaluate the quality of educational software. *Software Reports,* which is published by Trade Service Corporation, 10096 Torreyana Road, San Diego, CA 92121, provides program evaluations in twenty subject areas that cover every grade level. Each review includes a summary of the program's features, a description of the program, a graded evaluation, and comments made by the evaluator.

Resources for Further Investigation

B. F. Skinner on B. F. Skinner

In three highly readable volumes, B. F. Skinner describes his interests, aspirations, triumphs, and failures; the people and events that led him into psychology; and the forces that led him to devise operant conditioning. *Particulars of My Life* (1976) covers the period from early childhood through the early postcollege years. Skinner describes his ill-fated aspiration as a college student to be a writer and his eventual interest in psychology. In *The Shaping of a Behaviorist* (1979) Skinner chronicles his years as a graduate student at Harvard University, his first faculty position at the University of Minnesota, and his subsequent position as chairman of the psychology department of Indiana University. *A Matter of Consequences* (1983) picks up with Skinner's invitation from Harvard to join its psychology faculty just after World War II.

B. F. Skinner and Operant Conditioning

A highly readable summary and critical analysis of Skinner's brand of operant conditioning can be found in Robert D. Nye's (1979) *What Is B. F. Skinner Really Saying?* According to Nye, "Two major thoughts accompanied the writing of this book: a growing sense of the importance of Skinner's work and the awareness that his ideas are often misjudged." Accordingly, Nye attempts to provide "a clear, concise picture of what Skinner has said in various writings . . . so that individuals can decide for themselves whether or not the Skinnerian approach has value." In nine well-written chapters, Nye provides a brief biography of Skinner, describes the basic concepts of operant conditioning, analyzes the misunderstandings that have arisen about operant conditioning, and compares operant conditioning with such alternative theoretical systems as Sigmund Freud's psychoanalysis and Carl Rogers' humanism.

The Technology of Teaching

The Technology of Teaching (1968) is B. F. Skinner's most concise and application-oriented discussion of operant conditioning techniques related to pedagogy. There are several sections of this book you might want to sample. For an overview of programmed learning and teaching machines, see Chapter 3. In Chapter 5, "Why Teachers Fail," Skinner describes what he perceives to be common mistakes made by many teachers. In Chapter 8, "The Creative Student," he discusses determinism and the issue of personal freedom. If you read any of these chapters, or another of your choice, you might record your reactions to general or specific arguments in the book.

Skinner's Utopia

In *Walden Two* (1948) B. F. Skinner describes his conception of a utopia based on the application of science to human behavior. To get the full impact of the novel and of Skinner's ideas, you should read the entire book. (As a matter of fact, it may be hard to put down once you begin it.) However, if you cannot read the whole thing at this time, Chapters 12 through 17—in which the approach to child rearing and education at Walden Two is described—may be of special interest to you as a future teacher. Read from page 95 to page 148 to get a good sample of life in Skinner's utopia. Then record your reactions, perhaps including an opinion as to whether you might like to join a society based on the ideas of Walden Two. You might also take a stab at sketching out a utopia of your own—perhaps you will be able to improve on Skinner's version.

Behavior Modification

If the possibilities of behavior modification seem attractive, you may wish to examine issues of the journals *Behavior Modification, Behavior Research and Therapy, Child Behavior Therapy,* and the *Journal of Applied Behavior Analysis.* If you browse through the education and psychology sections of your college bookstore, you are likely to find a number of books on behavior modification. Or you might look for these titles in the library: *Classroom Management for Elementary Teachers* (2d ed., 1989) by Carolyn Evertson, Edmund Emmer, Barbara Clements, Julie Sanford, and Murray Worsham; *Classroom Management for Sec-*

ondary Teachers (2d ed., 1989) by Edmund Emmer, Carolyn Evertson, Julie Sanford, Barbara Clements, and Murray Worsham; *Achieving Educational Excellence: Using Behavioral Strategies* (1986) by Beth Sulzer-Azaroff and G. Roy Mayer; and *Making It Till Friday: A Guide to Successful Classroom Management* (3d ed., 1988) by James P. Long, Virginia H. Frye, and Elizabeth W. Long. And, as the title suggests, *Beyond Behavior Modification: A Cognitive-Behavioral Approach to Behavior Management in the School* (2d ed., 1991) by J. S. Kaplan goes beyond the typical behavior modification book. It includes chapters on assessing the classroom and school environment and teaching students how to use self-management, social, and stress-management skills.

SUMMARY

1. Behavioral theories of learning focus on ways in which the responses that people learn to make are influenced by the stimuli that precede and/or follow those responses.

2. An early behavioral theory, classical conditioning, was devised by Ivan Pavlov. This theory explains how animals and human beings learn to respond to a new, introduced stimulus in the same way they respond to some naturally occurring stimulus, such as food.

3. Four basic learning principles that derive from Pavlov's work are reinforcement, extinction, generalization, and discrimination.

4. A second behavioral theory, operant conditioning, was devised by B. F. Skinner. This theory explains how animals and people learn new behaviors as a result of the consequences that follow a response.

5. Basic learning principles that derive from Skinner's work are positive reinforcement, negative reinforcement, punishment, time-out, extinction, spontaneous recovery, generalization, and discrimination.

6. Complex behaviors can be learned by reinforcing closer approximations to the final behavior and ignoring nonapproximate behaviors, a process called shaping.

7. Once a new behavior is well established, it can be maintained at that level by supplying reinforcement on an intermittent schedule. The four basic schedules are fixed interval, variable interval, fixed ratio, and variable ratio.

8. One of the first educational applications of operant conditioning principles was programmed instruction. Programmed instruction involves presenting written material in small steps according to a predetermined sequence, prompting the correct response, and presenting positive reinforcement in the form of knowledge of results.

9. Linear programs, the type favored by Skinner, contain only one sequence of frames leading to the terminal behavior. They use extremely small steps and heavy prompting, since they make no provision for incorrect responses.

10. Branching programs use larger steps and less prompting. If an incorrect response to a frame occurs, the learner is routed through a "branch"—a remedial set of frames—before proceeding further.

11. A second application of operant conditioning principles is computer-assisted instruction (CAI), which involves presenting programmed materials on a computer screen.

12. The main types of CAI programs are drill and practice, tutorial, and problem solving.

13. The most important part of CAI is the program. Independent evaluations of CAI programs have found that only 3 to 4 percent are of excellent quality.

14. Computer-assisted instruction can be an effective supplement to regular classroom instruction, particularly for low-achieving students.

15. A third application of operant conditioning principles is behavior modification. The goal of behavior modification is to help students learn desirable behaviors by ignoring or punishing undesired behaviors and reinforcing desired ones. Techniques for achieving this goal include shaping, token economies, contingency contracts, extinction, and punishment.

16. A third behavioral theory, social learning theory, was devised largely by Albert Bandura. This theory explains how individuals learn by observing a model (who may or may not be reinforced for the behavior involved) and imitating the model's behavior.

17. The processes involved in social learning (also called observational learning) are attention, retention, production, and motivation (reinforcement). The reinforcement can come from someone else (direct), from anticipating that one will be treated as the model was (vicarious), or from meeting personal standards (self-reinforcement).

18. Research suggests that many social behaviors, such as aggression, may be learned by imitation of a model. Many academic-related behaviors, such as persistence, self-confidence, and cognitive skills, can also be learned by observing and imitating a model.

KEY TERMS

classical conditioning *(325)*
operant conditioning *(326)*
positive reinforcement *(328)*
negative reinforcement *(329)*
punishment *(330)*
time-out *(330)*
extinction *(330)*
spontaneous recovery *(330)*
generalization *(331)*
discrimination *(331)*
shaping *(332)*
fixed interval schedule *(333)*
variable interval schedule *(333)*
fixed ratio schedule *(334)*

variable ratio schedule *(334)*
programmed instruction *(336)*
frames *(337)*
linear program *(337)*
branching program *(337)*
computer-assisted instruction *(338)*
behavior modification *(340)*
Premack principle *(341)*
token economy *(342)*
contingency contracting *(342)*
response cost *(343)*
social learning theory *(346)*
observational learning *(346)*
vicarious reinforcement *(349)*
self-reinforcement *(349)*

DISCUSSION QUESTIONS

1. The theory of operant conditioning holds that we learn to respond or not respond to certain stimuli because our responses are followed by positive or negative consequences. How many of your own behaviors can you explain in this fashion? Why, for example, are you reading this book and answering these questions?

2. Many educators have a negative attitude about operant conditioning because they feel it presents a cold, dehumanizing picture of human learning. That is, because it portrays learning as governed by the consequences that follow responses, it ignores the role of such things as free will, motives, and creativity. Did you feel this way as you read through the chapter? Do you think positive attributes of operant conditioning balance out possible negative aspects of the theory?

3. Skinner has argued that society too frequently uses aversive means to shape desired behavior (particularly punishment) rather than the more effective positive reinforcement. As you think about how your behavior has been shaped by your parents, teachers, friends, supervisors at work, law enforcement officials, and so on, would you agree or disagree with Skinner's observation? Can you think of some possible reasons why we tend to use punishment more frequently than positive reinforcement?

4. Although computers and computer-assisted instruction have become widespread in public school classrooms, the number of well-designed instructional programs is disappointingly low. One way to encourage the development of better-quality programs is to be an informed consumer. How can you keep yourself, colleagues, and parents informed about instructional programs that do or do not deserve consumer support? Are there any other things you can do or think of to encourage the development of effective programs?

5. Can you recall a teacher who you admired so much that you imitated some aspects of his or her behavior (if not immediately, then some time later)? What was it about this teacher that caused you to behave in the same way? How might you have the same effect on your students?

Chapter 9

INFORMATION PROCESSING THEORY

HELPING STUDENTS BECOME STRATEGIC LEARNERS

▶ Strategy: plan to achieve a long-term goal

▶ Tactic: specific technique that helps achieve long-term goal

▶ Rote rehearsal not a very effective memory tactic

▶ Acronym: word made from first letters of items to be learned

▶ Acrostic: sentence made up of words derived from first letters of items to be learned

▶ Pegword: associate memory pegs with items to be learned

▶ Loci method: visualize items to be learned stored in specific locations

▶ Keyword method: visually link pronunciation of foreign word to English translation

▶ Mnemonic devices organize, provide retrieval cues, can be acquired

▶ Taking notes and reviewing notes aid retention and comprehension

▶ Learning strategy components: metacognition, analysis, planning, implementation, monitoring, modification

SUGGESTIONS FOR TEACHING IN YOUR CLASSROOM

▶ Unpredictable changes in environment usually command attention

▶ Attention span can be increased with practice

▶ Distributed practice: short study periods at frequent intervals

▶ Serial position effect: tendency to remember items at beginning and end of a long list

▶ Concrete analogies can make abstract information meaningful

In discussing the organization of Part Three, we distinguished between behavioral and cognitive theories. We noted that behavioral theories, especially operant conditioning, emphasize the role of external factors in learning. Behavioral psychologists focus on the nature of a stimulus to which a student is exposed, the response that the student makes, and the consequences that follow the response. They see no reason to speculate about what takes place in the student's mind before and after a response. The extensive Suggestions for Teaching in Your Classroom presented at the end of the chapter on behavioral

377

learning theories serve as evidence that conclusions and principles based on analyses of external stimuli, observable responses, and observable consequences can be of considerable value to teachers.

Cognitive psychologists, however, are convinced that it is possible to study nonobservable behavior, such as thought processes, in a scientific manner. Some cognitive psychologists focus on meaningful learning and problem solving; their work is discussed in the next chapter. Many cognitive psychologists are especially interested in an area of study known as **information processing theory,** which seeks to understand how people acquire new information, how they store information and recall it from memory, and how what they already know guides and determines what and how they will learn.

Bits and pieces of information processing theory and research first trickled into the psychological literature during the mid-1950s. That trickle soon became a flood. Today, information processing theory is a major force in the psychology of learning and can be of great value to teachers in enhancing student learning. Given the prominence of this view of learning, it will be useful to spend a little time tracing its roots.

THE ORIGINS OF INFORMATION PROCESSING THEORY

Whenever a particular point of view attains rapid prominence in a field of study, it is usually due, at least in part, to a growing disenchantment with the current view of things. In psychology during the 1950s and 1960s, the current view seemed taken up with studying the conditions under which rats learned to run mazes or people learned lists of nonsense syllables (consonant-vowel-consonant arrangements of three letters each). Many psychologists came to believe that such an approach would not help explain how people learn to perform more complex tasks. At least three factors contributed to this disenchantment.

The first was the experience of many psychologists who were asked during World War II to help train large numbers of individuals in the use, maintenance, and repair of complex equipment and weapons. As psychologists studied how an aircraft pilot divided his attention among a plane's controls, instructions from a radio, detecting blips on a radar screen, interpreting various instrument readings, and deciding when to fire on an enemy, they began to think of human beings as complex information transmitters, receivers, and decision makers (Miller, 1983).

A second factor was the influence of communications research on psychologists during and after World War II. Engineers working on communication systems (telephone, telegraph, radio) were interested in such things as how many messages could pass through a system in a given period, whether two messages could be communicated simultaneously with no loss of information, and how stimuli could be converted from one form into another. Psychologists began to use these concepts as metaphors for human thought (Miller, 1983; Siegler, 1983).

The third factor behind the rise of information processing theory was the development of computers and the field of computer science. The operation of computers suggested to psychologists that a human being might also be seen as a symbol-manipulating system. The main parts of the system are the memory stores where information is held and the processes that govern how information is coded, stored, retrieved, and manipulated (Miller, 1983).

In sum, information processing theory became a popular approach to the study of learning because the concepts and questions it adopted from other fields provided psychologists with a framework for investigating the role of a variable that behaviorism had ignored—the nature of the learner. Instead of being viewed as relatively passive organisms that respond in fairly predictable ways to environmental stimuli, learners were now seen as highly active interpreters and manipulators of environmental stimuli. The stage was set for psychology to study learning from a broader and more complicated perspective—namely, as an *interaction* between the learner and the environment.

THE INFORMATION PROCESSING VIEW OF LEARNING

> Information processing: how humans attend to, recognize, transform, store, retrieve information

Information processing theory rests on a set of assumptions of which three are worth noting. First, information is processed in steps or stages. The major steps typically include attending to a stimulus, recognizing it, transforming it into some type of mental representation, comparing it with information already stored in memory, assigning meaning to it, and acting on it in some fashion (Miller, 1983). At an early processing stage, human beings encode information (represent it in thought) in somewhat superficial ways (as when they represent visual and auditory stimuli as true-to-life pictures and sounds) and at later stages in more meaningful ways (as when they grasp the gist of an idea or its relationship to other ideas). Second, there are limits on how much information can be processed at each stage. Although the absolute amount of information human beings can learn appears to be limitless, it must be acquired gradually. Third, the human information processing system is interactive. Information already stored in memory influences and is influenced by perception and attention. We see what our prior experiences direct us to see, and, in turn, what we see affects what we know.

Thus, according to the information processing view, learning results from an interaction between an environmental stimulus (the *information* that is to be learned) and a learner (the one who *processes,* or transforms, the information). What an information processing psychologist wants to know, for instance, is what goes on in a student's mind as a teacher demonstrates how to calculate the area of a triangle or while the student reads twenty pages of a social studies text or responds to test questions.

To deal effectively with such questions we must specify more clearly what we mean by the terms *learner* and *environmental stimulus.* One useful approach has been suggested by John Bransford (1979). He describes four general factors that interact with one another to affect the learning process. The first two concern the learner; the last two concern the task environment.

1. The first factor, *learner characteristics,* pertains to the broad, fairly stable attributes that a learner brings to a task—attributes like prior knowledge, attitudes, motives, and cognitive style. Some students may know quite a bit about a subject being studied while others may know very little. Some may show a strong interest in a topic while others would rather study something else. Some may approach tasks impulsively and superficially while others may tackle the same tasks in a deliberate, analytical style.

2. The second factor, *learner activities,* concerns the kind of mental operations learners employ when presented with a task. Students may underline key points while they read, take notes during a lecture, rehearse information, or generate visual images of things they want to remember. Which of these activities students engage in, and to what extent, depends largely on the last two factors.

3. Factor three involves the *nature of the learning material.* The vast majority of classroom materials that students learn from are written and linguistic in nature. Written materials may be long or short, filled with concrete ideas or abstract ones, and organized logically or illogically, to name just a few possibilities.

4. The fourth factor, *nature of the criterion,* deals with the manner in which the learner is expected to demonstrate his or her competence. Typically, students take written exams, although they may also be asked to give an oral presentation (for example, to make a speech or participate in a debate) or to produce a complex motor response (such as typing fifty words per minute). An exam can ask students to recall or recognize information, to apply knowledge, or to demonstrate any of several other forms of knowledge. Each outcome places different demands on a learner.

When learning is viewed this way, as an interaction among the above four factors, we are less apt to classify students with such simplistic and useless labels as "lazy" or "slow." Some students may not perform well because they lack or have an inadequate understanding of prerequisite knowledge. Other students may lack useful study skills. Still others may perform very well on tests that measure verbatim knowledge but poorly on tests that require analysis and synthesis of different ideas.

The first two factors—learner characteristics and learner activities—tend to be the focal point of information processing theory and research. Unlike operant conditioning theory or social learning theory, information processing is not associated with a particular individual or a single theoretical formulation. Rather, it encompasses a large number of research studies in such areas as perception, attention, memory, comprehension, and problem solving.

A great many studies have looked at the various information processing decisions that different types of learners make when confronted with a learning task. As you read this book, for example, numerous other stimuli may compete for your attention. Will you close the book because someone just turned on the television, or because you feel drowsy, or because you were just invited out for pizza? Assuming you decide to read, do you underline key points, take notes, organize your notes into a topical outline, think of analogies for abstract ideas, or imagine yourself applying educational psychology principles in your own classroom?

We believe that this is one chapter you ought to read very carefully, because the information processing decisions you make affect when you learn, how much you learn, how well you learn—indeed, whether you learn at all. To give you an appreciation of the information processing approach to learning and how it can help teachers and students do their jobs, the next section describes several basic cognitive processes and their role in how people store and retrieve information. The section following that describes research on selected learning tactics and discusses the nature of strategic learning.

A MODEL OF INFORMATION PROCESSING

A popular approach to summarizing and illustrating ways that we process information is to construct diagrams called *flow charts.* Figure 9.1 presents a simplified version of a flow chart, derived from the work of several theorists (for

FIGURE 9.1   An Information Processing Model of Learning

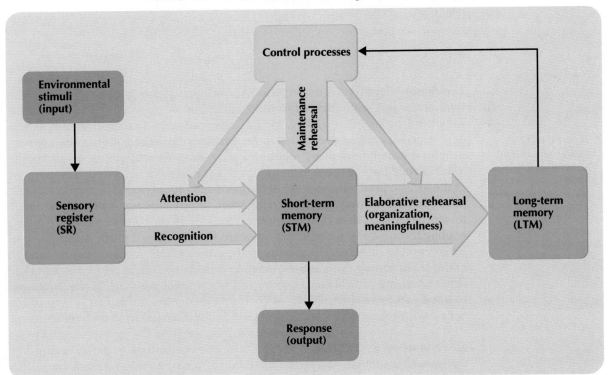

example, Atkinson & Shiffrin, 1968; Norman & Rumelhart, 1970). The various boxes in Figure 9.1 depict what are often referred to as memory stores and control processes.

The information processing model of learning identifies three *memory stores,* called the sensory register (SR), short-term memory (STM), and long-term memory (LTM). Each store varies as to how much information it can hold and for how long. (Our use of the term *memory stores* is not meant to suggest specific locations in the brain where information is held; it is simply a metaphorical device for classifying different memory phenomena.)

The *control processes* govern both the manner in which information is encoded and its flow between memory stores. These processes include *recognition, attention, maintenance rehearsal,* and *elaborative rehearsal* (also called *elaborative encoding*). Elaborative rehearsal is a general label that includes a variety of organizational and meaning-enhancing encoding techniques. As described below, each control process is associated primarily with a particular memory store. The control processes play a key role in the information processing system for two reasons. First, they determine the quantity and quality of information that the learner stores in and retrieves from memory. Second, though, it is the learner who decides whether, when, and how to employ them. That the control processes are under our direct, conscious control will take on added importance when we discuss educational applications a bit later. Before we get to applications, however, we need to make you more familiar with the three memory stores and the control processes specifically associated with each of them.

The Sensory Register and Its Control Processes

The Sensory Register   A description of how human learners process information typically begins with environmental stimuli. Our sense receptors are constantly stimulated by visual, auditory, tactile, olfactory, and gustatory stimuli. These experiences are initially recorded in the **sensory register** (SR), the first memory store. It is called the sensory register because the information it stores is thought to be encoded in the same form in which it is originally perceived. The purpose of the SR is to hold information just long enough (about one to three seconds) for us to decide if we want to attend to it further. Information not selectively attended to and recognized decays or disappears from the system. At the moment you are reading these words, for example, you are being exposed to the appearance of letters printed on paper, to sounds in the place where you are reading, and to many other stimuli. The sensory register might be compared to an unending series of instant-camera snapshots or videotape segments, each lasting from one to three seconds before fading away. If you recognize and attend to one of the snapshots, though, it will be "processed" and transferred to short-term memory.

The Nature of Recognition   The process of **recognition** involves noting key features of a stimulus and relating them to already stored information. This

> Sensory register: stimuli held briefly for possible processing

> Recognition: noting key features and relating them to stored information

process is interactive in that it depends partly on information extracted from the stimulus itself and partly on information stored in long-term memory. The ability to recognize a dog, for example, involves noticing those physical features of the animal that give it "dogness" (for example, height, length, number of feet, type of coat) and combining the results of that analysis with relevant information from LTM (such as that dogs are household pets, are walked on a leash by their owners, are used to guard property). To the degree that an object's defining features are ambiguous (as when observing a dog from a great distance) or a learner lacks relevant prior knowledge (as many culturally disadvantaged students do), recognition and more meaningful processing will suffer. Recognition of words and sentences during reading, for example, can be aided by such factors as clear printing, knowledge of spelling patterns, knowledge of letter sounds, and the frequency with which words appear in natural language. The important point to remember is that recognition and meaningful processing of information is most effective when we make use of all available sources of information (Klatzky, 1980, p. 64).

One implication of this work to be discussed in more detail in this and other chapters is that, according to the information processing view, primary and elementary grade students need more structured learning tasks than junior high or high school students. Because of their limited store of knowledge in long-term memory and narrow ability to logically relate what they do know to the task at hand, younger students should be provided with clear, complete, explicit directions and learning materials (see, for example, Doyle, 1983).

The Impact of Attention The environment usually provides us with more information than we can deal with at one time. From the multitude of sights, sounds, smells, and other stimuli impinging on us at a given moment, only a fraction are noticed and recorded in the sensory register. At this point, yet another reduction typically occurs. We may process only one-third of the already-selected information recorded in the SR. We continually focus on one thing at the expense of something else. This selective focusing on a portion of the information currently stored in the sensory register is what we call **attention.**

> Attention: focusing on a portion of currently available information

> Information in long-term memory influences what we attend to

As with any human characteristic, there are individual differences in attention. Some people can concentrate on a task while they are surrounded by a variety of sights and sounds. Others need to isolate themselves in a private study area. Still others have difficulty attending under any conditions. What explains these differences? Again, information from long-term memory plays an influential role. According to Ulric Neisser (1976), "perceivers pick up only what they have schemata for, and willy-nilly ignore the rest" (p. 79). In other words, we choose what we will see (or hear) by *anticipating* the information it will provide. Students daydream, doodle, and write letters rather than listen to a lecture because they anticipate hearing little of value. Moreover, these anticipatory schemata are likely to have long-lasting effects. If someone asked you now to read a book about English grammar, you might recall having been bored by diagramming sentences and memorizing grammatical rules in elementary school. If that were the case, you might not read the grammar text very carefully. A basic challenge for teachers is to convince students that a learning task will be useful, enjoyable, informative, and meaningful. Later in this chapter we present some ideas as to how this might be accomplished.

Short-Term Memory and Its Control Processes

Short-Term Memory   Once information has been attended to, it is transferred to **short-term memory** (STM), the second memory store. Short-term memory can hold about seven unrelated bits of information for approximately twenty seconds. While this brief time span may seem surprising, it can be easily demonstrated. Imagine that you look up and dial an unfamiliar phone number, and you receive a busy signal. If you are then distracted by something or someone else for fifteen to twenty seconds, chances are you will forget the number. Short-term memory is often referred to as "working memory," since it holds information we are currently aware of at any given moment.

The following analogy also may help you grasp the nature of short-term memory. Visualize your STM as a filing cabinet with a capacity of seven pictures that will hold their image for about twenty seconds. As new items are placed in the file, either they are incorporated into one of the existing pictures or they push out one that was previously encoded.

Rehearsal   A severe limitation of short-term memory, as you can see, is how quickly information disappears or is forgotten in the absence of further processing. This problem can be dealt with through *rehearsal*. Most people think of rehearsal as repeating something to oneself over and over either silently or out loud. The usual purpose for such behavior is to memorize information for later use, although occasionally we simply want to hold information in short-term memory for immediate use (for example, to redial a phone number after getting a busy signal). Rehearsal can serve both purposes, but not in the same way. Accordingly, cognitive psychologists have found it necessary and useful to distinguish between two types of rehearsal: maintenance and elaborative.

Maintenance rehearsal (also called *rote rehearsal* or *repetition*) has a mechanical quality. Its only purpose is to use mental and verbal repetition to hold information in short-term memory for some immediate purpose. While this is a useful and often-used capability (as in the telephone example), it has no effect on long-term memory storage.

Elaborative rehearsal (also called *elaborative encoding*), on the other hand, consciously relates new information to knowledge already stored in long-term memory. In this way it facilitates both the transfer of information to long-term memory and its maintenance in short-term memory. For example, if you wanted to learn the lines for a part in a play, you might try to relate the dialogue and behavior of your character to similar personal experiences you remember. As you strive to memorize the lines and actions, your mental "elaborations" will help you store your part in long-term memory so that you can retrieve it later. Elaborative

▶ Short-term memory: about seven bits of information held for about twenty seconds

▶ Maintenance rehearsal: hold information for immediate use

▶ Elaborative rehearsal: use stored information to aid learning

rehearsal, whereby information from long-term memory is used in learning new information, is the rule rather than the exception. Mature learners don't often employ maintenance rehearsal by itself. The decision to use one or the other, however, depends on the demands you expect the environment to make on you. If you will need to remember things for future use, use elaborative rehearsal; if you want to keep something in consciousness just for the moment, use rote rehearsal.

When discussing rehearsal processes, it is important to keep in mind that younger children may not behave in the same way as more mature learners. Kindergarten pupils rarely engage in spontaneous rehearsal. By the age of seven, however, children do typically use simple rehearsal strategies. When presented with a list of items, the average seven-year-old rehearses each word by itself, several times. From the age of ten, rehearsal becomes more like that of an adult. Several items may be grouped together and rehearsed as a set.

So far, we have explained the effect of elaborative rehearsal in terms of relating new information to information already stored in long-term memory. That's fine as a very general explanation. But to be more precise, we need to point out that elaborative rehearsal is based on *organization* (as in the above example, where several items are grouped together on some basis and rehearsed as a set) and *meaningfulness* (as in the earlier example, where lines in a play are related to similar personal experiences).

Organization   Quite often the information we want to learn is complex and interrelated. We can simplify the task by organizing several separate chunks of information into a few "clumps" of information, particularly when each part of a clump helps us remember other parts. The value of organizing material was illustrated by an experiment (Bower et al., 1969) in which two groups of subjects were asked to learn a list of words, but under different conditions. One group was given the entire list in a random order for four trials. The second group was given the list arranged under different headings (see Figure 9.2). The subjects in this group were urged to concentrate on learning items listed under the headings designated Level 1 and Level 2 during trial one, Levels 1, 2, and 3 during trial two, and Levels 1, 2, 3, and 4 during trials three and four. After trial four the second group recalled almost twice as many words as the first. The organized material was much easier to learn not only because there were fewer chunks to memorize but also because each item in a group served as a cue for the other items. When you decide to store pertinent material from this chapter in your long-term memory in preparation for an exam, you will find the job much easier if you organize what you are studying. To learn the various parts of the information processing model under discussion, for instance, you might group the ideas being described under the various headings used in this chapter (as we do in the *Study Guide*).

> ▶ Organizing material reduces number of chunks, provides recall cues

Meaningfulness   In a review of research on meaningful learning, Ronald E. Johnson (1975) concludes that "meaningfulness is potentially the most powerful

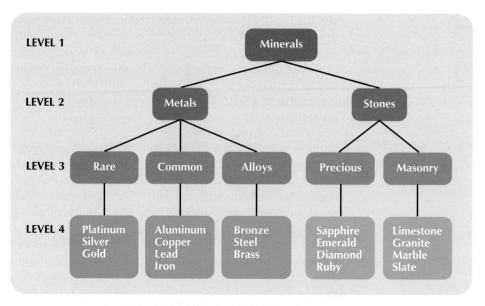

FIGURE 9.2   Superordinate-Subordinate Arrangement of Words (From G.H. Bower, M.C. Clark, A.M. Lesgold, and D. Winzenz, "Hierarchical Retrieval Schemes in Recall of Categorized Word Lists," *Journal of Verbal Learning and Verbal Behavior,* 1969, 8, 323–343. Copyright 1969 by Academic Press. Reproduced by permission of the publisher and the authors.)

▶ Meaningfulness effective because new information is associated with stored knowledge

variable for explaining the learning of complex verbal discourse" (pp. 425–426). In defining meaningfulness, Johnson notes: "Learning may be said to be meaningful to the extent that the new learning task can be related to the existing cognitive structure of the learner, i.e., the residual of his earlier learnings" (p. 427). This observation stresses the point that memories are more likely to be retained in long-term storage if they can be related to what is familiar—or already remembered. Another way of stressing the same idea is to say that a new idea associated with an old one is likely to be remembered. Johnson emphasizes that the degree of meaningfulness depends on the "associational background of the learner" (p. 427). The use of the word *associational* calls attention to the significance of connecting what is to be learned with what the learner already knows. In making associations, it is desirable to relate ideas to a variety of other ideas and experiences by noting points of similarity, since superficial similarities are not likely to lead to encoding. The questions that we pose to you at the end of each chapter, for example, are designed to foster meaningful encoding by getting you to relate text information with relevant prior experience. This brief description of meaningfulness and its role in learning contains a strong implication for teaching in culturally diverse classrooms. You can foster meaningful learning for students from other cultures by pointing out similarities between ideas presented in class and students' culture-specific knowledge. For example, you might point out that September 16th has the same significance to people of Mexican origin as July 4th has to U.S. citizens since that date commemorates Mexico's revolution against and independence from Spain.

Long-Term Memory

▶ Long-term memory: permanent storehouse of unlimited capacity

So far, we have discussed two memory stores—the sensory register and short-term memory. We have also referred, in a general way, to **long-term memory** (LTM). This third memory store is perhaps the most interesting. On the basis of neurological, experimental, and clinical evidence, most cognitive psychologists believe that the storage capacity of long-term memory is unlimited and contains a permanent record of everything an individual has learned, although some doubt exists about the latter point (see, for example, Loftus & Loftus, 1980).

The neurological evidence comes from the work of Wilder Penfield (1969), a Canadian neurosurgeon who operated on over one thousand patients who experienced epileptic seizures. To determine the source of the seizures, Penfield electrically stimulated various parts of the brain's surface. During this procedure many patients reported vivid images of long-dormant events from their past. It was as if a neurological videotape had been turned on.

The experimental evidence, while less dramatic, is just as interesting. In a typical memory study (such as Tulving & Pearlstone, 1966), subjects receive a list of nouns to learn. After giving subjects ample opportunity to recall as many of the words as possible, the researchers provide retrieval cues—for instance, category labels such as "clothing," "food," or "animals." In many cases, cued subjects quickly recall additional items. Experiments on how well people recognize previously seen pictures have produced some startling findings. Thirty-six hours after viewing over 2,500 pictures, a group of college students correctly identified an average of about 2,250 or 90 percent (Standing, Conezio & Haber, 1970). In fact, it has been estimated that if one million pictures could be shown, recognition memory would be 90 percent or better (Standing, 1973).

Finally, psychiatrists and psychotherapists have reported many case histories of individuals who have been helped to recall seemingly forgotten events through hypnosis and other techniques (Erdelyi & Goldberg, 1979).

How Information Is Organized in Long-Term Memory As we have seen, long-term memory plays an influential role throughout the information processing system. The interests, attitudes, skills, and knowledge of the world that reside there influence what we perceive, how we interpret our perceptions, and whether we process information for short-term or long-term storage. In most instances, retrieving information from long-term memory is extremely rapid and accurate, like finding a book in a well-run library. Accordingly, we can conclude that information in long-term memory must be organized. The nature of this organization is a key area in the study of memory. The insights it provides help illuminate the encoding and retrieval processes associated with long-term memory.

Many cognitive psychologists believe that our store of knowledge in long-term memory is organized in terms of **schemata** (which is plural for *schema*

Long-term memory storage and meaningfulness can be enhanced by relating what is to be learned to what is familiar to the student.
(Bob Daemmrich/Stock, Boston, Inc.)

▶ Information in long-term memory organized as schemata

and is related in meaning to Piaget's *scheme*). Richard C. Anderson (1984) defines a schema as an abstract structure of information. It is abstract because it summarizes information about many different cases or examples of something, and it is structured because it represents how its own informational components are interrelated. Schemata give us expectations about objects and events (dogs bark, birds fly, students listen to their teachers and study industriously). When our schemata are well formed and a specific event is consistent with our expectation, comprehension occurs. When schemata are poorly structured or absent, learning is slow and uncertain. The following example should make this notion of schemata more understandable. For most everyone raised in the United States, the word *classroom* typically calls to mind a scene that includes certain people (teacher, students), objects (desks, chalkboard, books, pencils), rules (attend to the teacher's instructions, stay in the classroom unless given permission to leave), and events (reading, listening, writing, talking, drawing). This is a generalized representation, and some classrooms may contain fewer or more of the above characteristics. However, as long as students and teachers share the same basic classroom schema, each will generally know what to expect and how to behave in any given classroom. It is when people do not possess an appropriate schema that comprehension, memory, and behavior problems arise.

This notion was first investigated during the early 1930s by Sir Frederick Bartlett (1932), an English psychologist. In one experiment, Bartlett had subjects read and recall a brief story entitled "The War of the Ghosts" that was based on North American Indian folklore. Since Bartlett's subjects had little knowledge of Indian culture, they had difficulty accurately recalling the story, omitting certain details and distorting others. The distortions were particularly interesting because they reflected an attempt to interpret the story in terms of the logic and beliefs of Western culture. The conclusion that Bartlett drew from this and similar studies was that remembering is not simply a matter of retrieving a true-to-life record of information. People often remember their *interpretations* or *constructions* of something read, seen, or heard. In addition, when they experience crucial gaps in memory, people tend to fill in these blanks with logical reconstructions of what they think must have been. People then report these reconstructions as memories of actual events (di Sibio, 1982).

For those who would argue that Bartlett's findings were simply the result of an atypical reading passage, similar ones have been reported more recently with other kinds of reading materials. Mary di Sibio (1982) cites one study in which some subjects read the sentence "The secretary circled the dates," whereas others read "The proofreader circled the dates." Those who read the first sentence were more likely to recall it when given the word *calendar* as a cue than when given the word *manuscript;* the reverse was true for those who read the second sentence. The explanation for this effect is that in the process of comprehending the sentence information, subjects make inferences about its meaning and store that in memory as well. These inferences are presumably based on some prior knowledge of how things happen in the world—namely, that secretaries circle dates on a calendar while proofreaders circle dates on a manuscript. Thus, retrieval is most effective when cues match particular stored inferences.

Another study cited by di Sibio (1982) illustrates how prior knowledge may come into play during recall and lead subjects to guess at what they learned based on their schema. The typical result when this happens is distorted recall. In this study, two groups of college subjects read the same biographical passage. One group was told that the passage was about a fictitious dictator named Gerald Martin. The other group was told that the passage was about Adolph Hitler. Subjects were tested either five minutes after reading or after one week. They were asked to distinguish sentences taken from the passage ("old" sentences) from sentences that never actually appeared but were consistent with the topic ("new" sentences). Subjects in both groups could accurately distinguish "old" from "new" sentences after the five-minute delay. After one week, however, subjects who read the Adolph Hitler passage were far more likely to mistakenly recognize a new sentence such as "He hated the Jews particularly and so persecuted them."

These experiments vividly demonstrate the importance of providing students with relevant background knowledge and helping them use it to understand and accurately remember new information. Sometimes it is better to back up and build a solid basis for subsequent learning than to spend all of your teaching time on the materials to be learned.

The discussion up to this point has focused on a general explanation of how people attend to, encode, store, and retrieve information. In a word, we have described some of the major aspects of *thinking*. During the last twenty years, researchers have inquired into how much knowledge individuals have about their own thought processes and what significance this knowledge has for learning. The term that was coined to refer to how much we know of our own thought processes is *metacognition*. As we will see, it plays a very important role in learning.

METACOGNITION

The Nature and Importance of Metacognition

The notion of metacognition was proposed by developmental psychologist John Flavell (1976) to explain why children of different ages deal with learning tasks in different ways. For example, when seven-year-olds are taught how to use both a less effective technique (simple repetition) to remember pairs of nouns and a more effective technique (imagining the members of each pair doing something together), most of them will use the less effective technique when given a new set of pairs to learn. Most ten-year-olds, however, will opt to use the more effective method (Kail, 1984). The explanation for this finding is that the seven-year-old has not had enough learning experiences to recognize that some problem-solving methods are better than others. To the younger child, one means is as good as another. This lack of metacognitive knowledge makes true strategic learning impossible for young children.

One way to grasp the essence of metacognition is to contrast it with cognition. The term *cognition* is used to describe the ways in which information is processed—that is, the ways it is attended to, recognized, encoded, stored in memory for various lengths of time, retrieved from storage, and used for one purpose or another. **Metacognition** refers to our knowledge about those operations and how they might best be used to achieve a learning goal. As Flavell has put it,

> I am engaging in metacognition . . . if I notice that I am having more trouble learning A than B; if it strikes me that I should double-check C before accepting it as a fact; if it occurs to me that I had better scrutinize each and every alternative in any multiple-choice type task situation before deciding which is the best one; if I become aware that I am not sure what the experimenter really wants me to do; if I sense that I had better make a note of D because I may forget it; if I think to ask someone about E to see if I have it right. Such examples could be multiplied endlessly. (1976, p. 232)

Metacognition: knowledge of how we think

Metacognition is obviously a very broad concept. It covers everything an individual can know that relates to how information is processed. To get a better grasp of this concept, you may want to use the three-part classification scheme proposed by Flavell (1987): knowledge of person variables, task variables, and strategy variables. An example of knowledge of person variables is that one is good at learning verbal material but poor at learning mathematical material. Another example is knowing that information not rehearsed or encoded is quickly forgotten. An example of knowledge of task variables is that reading passages with long sentences and unfamiliar words are usually harder to understand than reading passages that are more simply written. An example of knowledge of strategy variables is knowing that one should skim through a text passage before reading it to determine its length and difficulty level.

Recent research indicates significant differences in what younger and older children know about metacognition. What follows is a discussion of some of these differences.

Age Trends in Metacognition

Two recent reviews of research on metacognition (Duell, 1986; Kail, 1984) reviewed studies of ways students of different ages use memorization techniques and how well they understand what they are doing. They came to the following conclusions:

1. In terms of diagnosing task difficulty, most six-year-olds know that more familiar items are easier to remember than less familiar items and that a small set of items is easier to recall than a large set of items. What does not develop until a child is about nine years of age, however, is awareness that the amount of information one can recall immediately after studying it is limited. Consequently, children through the third grade usually overestimate how much they can store in and retrieve from short-term memory.

2. Similar findings have been obtained for reading tasks. Most second-graders know that interest, familiarity, and story length influence comprehension and recall. However, they are relatively unaware of the effect of how ideas are sequenced, of the introductory and summary qualities of first and last paragraphs, and of the relationship between reading goals and tactics. Sixth-graders, by contrast, are much more aware of the effects of these variables on comprehension and recall. Partly because of these differences in metacognitive knowledge, young children tend to treat reading as a task of decoding symbols rather than of constructing and comprehending meaning. Recent research has clearly shown that children's metacognitive awareness about reading is positively related to performance on a variety of reading tasks.

3. Most children know very little about the role their own capabilities play in learning. For example, not until about nine years of age do most children realize that the amount of information they can recall immediately after studying is limited. Consequently, children through the third grade usually overestimate how much they can store in and retrieve from short-term memory. One likely reason for this developmental difference is that younger children base their prediction on irrelevant personal characteristics (such as "I just think I'm pretty smart"), whereas older children focus more on relevant task characteristics.

4. There are clear developmental differences in how well students understand the need to tailor learning tactics to task demands. For example, four- and six-year-old children in one study cited by Kail (1984) did not alter how much time they spent studying a set of pictures when they were told that a recognition test would follow either three minutes later, one day later, or one week later. Eight-year-olds did use that information to allocate less or more study time to the

task. In another study, children of various ages were trained to use interactive visual imagery to learn a list of concrete noun pairs. When given a similar task and left on their own, most of those below ten years of age reverted to the less effective technique of rote rehearsal.

5. In terms of monitoring the progress of learning, most children younger than seven or eight are not very proficient at determining when they know something well enough to pass a memory test. Also, most first-graders typically don't know what they don't know. When given multiple opportunities to study and recall a lengthy set of pictures, six-year-olds chose to study pictures they had previously seen and recalled as well as ones they hadn't. Thus, they wasted time studying things they already knew. Third-graders, by contrast, focused on previously unseen pictures.

The general conclusion that emerges from these findings is that the youngest school-age children have only limited knowledge of how their cognitive processes work and when to use them. Consequently, primary grade children do not systematically analyze learning tasks, formulate plans for learning, use appropriate techniques of enhancing memory and comprehension, or monitor their progress, because they do not (some would say cannot) understand the benefits of doing these things. But as children develop and gain more experience with increasingly complex academic tasks, they acquire a greater awareness of metacognitive knowledge and its relationship to classroom learning. In this process, teachers can assist their students and guide them toward maximum use of their metacognitive knowledge. To help you understand how, the next section discusses learning tactics and strategies.

> Insight into one's learning processes improves with age

HELPING STUDENTS BECOME STRATEGIC LEARNERS

With some effort and planning, the teacher can make logically organized and relevant lessons. However, this is only half the battle, since students must then attend to the information, encode it into long-term memory, and retrieve it when needed. Getting students to use the attention, encoding, and retrieval processes discussed in the previous section is not always easy. The sad fact is that most children and adults are inefficient learners (as evidenced, for example, by Annis & Annis, 1979; Selmes, 1987; Brown, Campione & Day, 1981; Covington, 1985; Simpson, 1984). Their attempts at encoding rarely go beyond rote rehearsal (for example, rereading a textbook chapter), simple organizational schemes (outlining), and various cuing devices (underlining or highlighting). When the nature of the learning task changes, few students think about changing their encoding techniques accordingly.

One reason for this state of affairs is that students are rarely taught how to make the most of their cognitive capabilities. This is surprising, not to mention disappointing, since it is widely recognized that the amount of independent learning expected of students increases consistently from elementary school through high school and into college. Perhaps we rely too much on subject matter instruction (such as lecturing or computer-assisted instruction) at the expense of teaching students *how* to learn (Rohwer, 1984). The rest of this chapter will try to convince you that it need not be this way, at least for your students. The rise of information processing theory has led researchers to study how cognitive processes can be taught to and used by students as learning tactics and strategies.

The Nature of Learning Tactics and Strategies

The distinction between tactics and strategy, while relatively new to the psychology of learning, has been part of military training for thousands of years. In a military context, *strategy* refers to the accomplishment of general, long-term objectives by *planning* a course of action and placing forces in the most advantageous position *prior to* actual engagement with the enemy. *Tactics,* on the other hand, refer to the accomplishment of specific and more immediate objectives by *arranging* and *directing* forces *in action.*

Strategy: plan to achieve a long-term goal

Tactic: specific technique that helps achieve long-term goal

A **learning strategy,** then, can be described as a general *plan* someone formulates for determining how best to achieve an overall academic goal *before* dealing with the learning task itself. A **learning tactic** is a specific *technique* one uses in the service of the strategy *while* confronted with the task. Perhaps the most important thing to understand about these two concepts is that tactics must be chosen so as to be consistent with the goals of a strategy. If you had to recall verbatim the preamble to the U.S. Constitution, for example, would you use a learning tactic that would help you understand the gist of each stanza or one that would allow for accurate and complete recall? It is surprising how often students fail to consider this point.

Using Learning Tactics Effectively

A fairly lengthy list of learning tactics could be generated by looking through several how-to-study books (for example, Bragstad & Stumpf, 1987; Devine, 1987; Pauk, 1984) and how-to-remember books (for example, Kellett, 1980; Lorayne & Lucas, 1974). Your list would likely reflect influences of both recent information processing theory (for instance, visual imagery and organization) and more traditional methods (such as rote rehearsal, notetaking, and outlining). While many of these tactics are potentially useful, the how-to books in which they are discussed usually do not tell you how to use them as part of a broad strategy. Thus, you may not realize at first that not all tactics are equally suited to the same purpose.

One approach that you might find useful is to place tactics in one of two categories based on each tactic's intended primary purpose. One category, called *memory-directed tactics,* contains techniques that help produce accurate storage and retrieval of information. Examples of memory-directed tactics include simple rehearsal and any of several types of mnemonic devices (which we will explain shortly). The second category, called *comprehension-directed tactics,* contains techniques that aid in understanding the meaning of ideas and their interrelationships. Examples of this category include notetaking and certain forms of question asking (Levin, 1982).

There are numerous learning tactics, but we cannot discuss them all because of space limitations. Instead, we have chosen to briefly discuss a few that are either very popular with students or have been shown to be reasonably effective. The first two, rehearsal and mnemonic devices, are memory-directed tactics. Both can take several forms and are used by students of almost every age. The last two, notetaking and questioning, are comprehension-directed tactics and are used frequently by students from the upper elementary grades through college.

Rehearsal   The simplest form of rehearsal involves repeating the name of a single piece of information (for example, the date of a historic event or the capital of a state) several times either silently or out loud, and then doing the same thing with the next item to be remembered. It is not a particularly effective tactic for accurate long-term storage and retrieval because it does not produce distinct encoding or good retrieval cues (although, as discussed earlier, it is a useful tactic for purposes of short-term memory). However, rote rehearsal is one of the earliest tactics to appear during childhood and is used by most everyone on occasion. According to research reviewed by Robert Kail (1984), most five- and six-year-olds do not rehearse at all. Seven-year-olds sometimes use the simplest form of rehearsal. By eight years of age, instead of rehearsing single pieces of information one at a time, youngsters start to rehearse several items together as a set. A slightly more advanced version, called *cumulative rehearsal,* involves rehearsing a small set of items for several repetitions, dropping the item at the top of the list and adding a new one, giving the set several repetitions, dropping the item at the head of the set and adding a new one, rehearsing the set, and so on. By early adolescence, rehearsal reflects the learner's growing awareness of the organizational properties of information. When given a list of randomly arranged words from familiar categories, thirteen-year-olds will group items by category to form rehearsal sets. This version of rehearsal is likely to be the most effective because of the implicit association between the category members and the more general category label. If, at the time of recall, the learner is given the category label or can generate it spontaneously, the probability of accurately recalling the category members increases significantly.

> Rote rehearsal not a very effective memory tactic

Mnemonic Devices   A **mnemonic device** is a memory-directed tactic that helps a learner transform or organize information to enhance its retrievability. Such devices can be used to learn and remember individual items of information (a name, a fact, a date), sets of information (a list of names, a list of vocabulary definitions, a sequence of events), and ideas expressed in text. They range from simple, easy-to-learn techniques to somewhat complex systems that require a fair amount of practice. Since they incorporate visual and verbal forms of elaborative encoding, their effectiveness is due to the same factors that make imagery and category clustering successful—organization and meaningfulness.

Although mnemonic devices have been described and practiced for over two thousand years, they were rarely made the object of scientific study until the 1960s (see Yates, 1966, for a detailed discussion of the history of mnemonics). Since that time, however, mnemonics have been frequently and intensively studied by researchers. In recent years, there have been several reviews of mnemonics research (for example, Bellezza, 1981; Higbee, 1979; Pressley, Levin & Delaney, 1982; Snowman, 1986). In the next few pages, we briefly discuss six mnemonic devices: rhymes, acronyms, acrostics, pegwords, the loci method, and the keyword method.

Rhymes, acronyms, and acrostics. Most students learn a few time-honored *rhyme* mnemonics during their elementary school years. The spelling rule "*i* before *e* except after *c*" and the calendar rule "thirty days hath September, April, June, and November" are but two examples.

A second class of mnemonics is the *acronym* or first-letter mnemonic. With this technique, you take the first letter from each of a set of items to be learned and make up a word (it doesn't have to be a real word). For example, take the first letter from each of the Great Lakes—Huron, Ontario, Michigan, Erie, Superior. Combined, they form the word *HOMES.* In this case, you can add imagery by visualizing five homes on the shore of a lake. Another often-cited example is the acronym *ROYGBIV* (pronounced *roy-gee-biv*), which stands for the spectrum of visible light—red, orange, yellow, green, blue, indigo, violet. Surveys of mnemonic use among college students have found the acronym technique to be very well known and widely used. It appears to be most effective for recalling a short set of items, particularly abstract items, in serial order. It is hard to say just how useful the acronym can be, since researchers rarely train subjects long enough to allow them to become highly proficient in its use.

If an acronym is not feasible, you can construct an *acrostic,* or sentence mnemonic. Simply make up a sentence such that each word begins with the first letter of each item to be learned. Thus, *ROYGBIV* becomes "Richard of York Gave Battle in Vain." To learn and remember the nine planets, the sentence "Men Very Easily Make Jugs Serve Useful New Purposes" works quite well. A variation of the acrostic is to embed information to be learned in a meaningful sentence. For instance, when trying to decide whether the port or starboard side of a ship is left or right, just remember one of the following sentences: "The ship *left port*" or "The *star boarder* is always *right*." The acrostic is most useful for recalling abstract items of information. It can be used by students of all ages but seems to be most effective for those who might otherwise rely on rote rehearsal, such as primary grade children, low-ability children, or children from lower socioeconomic classes.

The pegword method. This mnemonic is particularly useful for learning lists of items. As the name implies, the idea is to link up or associate the list items with memory pegs. The pegs, previously learned associations based on rhyme, are one-bun, two-shoe, three-tree, four-door, five-hive, six-sticks, seven-heaven, eight-gate, nine-line, and ten-hen. Once the pegs have been learned, you make up an interacting image consisting of the first list item and the first peg. If the first

Acronym: word made from first letters of items to be learned

Acrostic: sentence made up of words derived from first letters of items to be learned

Pegword: associate memory pegs with items to be learned

item on your errand list is to buy house paint, you might imagine a bun floating in a can of paint. If your next errand is to buy roses at the florist, think of a bouquet of red roses growing out of a shoe. Two advantages of the pegword mnemonic are that a list can be accessed at any point by remembering the relevant number rhyme and recall may proceed just as easily forward or backward. Because this technique incorporates visual imagery, it is most effective with concrete items. It has been proved effective with children, military personnel, and graduate students for a variety of recall measures. It can be used to learn most anything that can be arranged in lists (including the ten commandments, according to one study).

The loci method. The oldest known mnemonic, the method of loci (pronounced *low-sigh* and meaning "places"), is also one of the most popular. The loci method is similar to the pegword mnemonic in that the loci, or places, serve as memory pegs. Commonly used loci are rooms in a house, buildings on a campus, or stores on a street. In practice, the first task is to form a set of memory locations that constitute a natural series, are numbered, are highly familiar, and can be easily imagined. Second, images of the things you want to remember (for example, objects, events, or ideas) should be generated and placed in each location as you mentally walk from one location to another. Within each location there should be particular pieces of furniture (chair, table, piano) or architectural features (fireplace, mantel, archway, lobby) on, in, or under which one or more images can be placed. Finally, when you want to recall, simply retrace your steps through each location, retrieve each image from where it was originally placed, and decode each image into a written or spoken message. The loci method is an effective memory-directed tactic for children, college students, and the elderly. When combined with an outlining tactic, it can be used to recall ideas from prose. It is effective for both free recall and serial recall.

> Loci method: visualize items to be learned stored in specific locations

Students who study a foreign language can make good use of many mnemonic devices, particularly the keyword method. (Paul Conklin)

FIGURE 9.3 Illustration of the Keyword Method

(From R. C. Atkinson, "Mnemonotechnics in Second-Language Learning," *American Psychologist*, 1975, *30*(8) 821–828. Copyright 1975 by the American Psychological Association. Reproduced by permission of the publisher.)

PATO — pot — DUCK

▶ Keyword method: visually link pronunciation of foreign word to English translation

The keyword method. The last mnemonic to be discussed is also the newest to be devised. Called the *keyword method,* it first appeared in 1975 as a means for learning foreign language vocabulary (Atkinson, 1975; Atkinson & Raugh, 1975; Raugh & Atkinson, 1975). The technique is fairly simple and involves two steps. First, isolate some part of the foreign word that, when spoken, sounds like a real English word. This is the keyword. Second, form an interacting visual image between the keyword and the English translation of the foreign word. Thus, the foreign word becomes associated to the keyword by an acoustic link and the keyword becomes associated to the English translation by an imagery link. As an example, take the Spanish word *pato* (pronounced *pot-o*), which means "duck" in English. The keyword in this case is *pot.* The next step, generating a visual image combining pot and duck, can be satisfied by imagining a duck with a pot over its head, as in Figure 9.3. The keyword mnemonic has proved effective in one form or another with preschoolers, elementary school children, adolescents, and college students. For children who cannot spontaneously generate visual images (preschool through fourth grade), two variations have been devised. In one, children are given the keyword and a picture that incorporates the keyword and the English translation. The other variation uses sentences instead of pictures. The sentence variation can also be used to remember abstract material. The keyword is a very flexible mnemonic. Besides foreign language vocabulary, it facilitates the recall of cities and their products, states and their capitals, medical definitions, and famous people's accomplishments.

Why mnemonic devices are effective. Mnemonic devices work so well because they enhance the encodability and retrievability of information. First, they

▶ Mnemonic devices organize, provide retrieval cues, can be acquired

provide a context (such as acronyms, sentences, mental walks) in which apparently unrelated items can be organized. Second, the meaningfulness of material to be learned is enhanced through associations with more familiar, meaningful information (for example, memory pegs or loci). Third, they provide distinctive retrieval cues that must be encoded with the material to be learned. Fourth, they force the learner to be an active participant in the learning process (Morris, 1977).

Despite the demonstrated effectiveness of mnemonic devices, many people argue against teaching them to students. They feel that students should learn the skills of critical thinking and problem solving rather than ways to reliably recall isolated bits of verbatim information. We feel this view is shortsighted for two reasons. First, it ignores the fact that effective problem-solving depends on ready access to a well-organized and meaningful knowledge base. Second, it focuses only on the "little idea" that mnemonic usage aids verbatim recall of bits of information. The "big idea" is that students come to realize that the ability to learn and remember large amounts of information is an acquired capability. Too often students (and adults) assume that an effective memory is innate and requires high intelligence. Once they realize that learning is a skill, students may be more inclined to learn how to use other tactics and how to formulate broad-based strategies.

Self-Questioning   Since students are expected to demonstrate much of what they know by answering written test questions, self-questioning can be a valuable learning tactic. The key to using questions profitably is to recognize that different types of questions make different cognitive demands. Some questions require little more than verbatim recall or recognition of simple facts and details. If an exam is to stress factual recall, then it may be helpful to generate such questions while studying. Other questions, however, assess comprehension, application, or synthesis of main ideas or other high-level information. Since many teachers favor higher-level test questions, we will focus on self-questioning as an aid to comprehension.

Much of the research on self-questioning addresses two basic questions: Can students as young as those in fourth grade be trained to write comprehension questions about the content of a reading passage? And does writing such questions lead to better comprehension of the passage in comparison to students who do not write questions? The answer to both questions is yes—if certain conditions are present. According to a survey of self-questioning research by Bernice Wong (1985), the following five conditions help determine how useful self-questioning will be as a comprehension-directed learning tactic.

1. *The amount of prior knowledge the questioner has about the topic of the passage:* The more one knows about a topic, the easier it is to formulate questions that reflect factual knowledge, comprehension of main ideas, similarities and differences among different ideas, and so on.

2. *The amount of metacognitive knowledge the questioner has compiled:* Before effective self-questioning is possible, a student has to be aware of, for example, the types of questions that could be asked (such as, questions dealing with knowledge level, comprehension level, or application level) and the reasons for asking them.

3. *The clarity of instructions:* Students should be given clear and detailed instructions in how to write good questions of a particular type.

4. *The amount of practice allowed the student:* Students should be given enough practice in writing questions to develop high proficiency.

5. *The length of each practice session:* Each practice session should be long enough for all students to comfortably read the passage and think of good questions. Giving students twenty minutes to read a 1,400-word passage and write six comprehension questions is likely to produce poorly framed questions.

Notetaking   When you take notes on the contents of a reading passage or a lecture, depending on your objectives, your notes may be lengthy or brief, a verbatim reproduction of the text, or a paraphrase. The information you write down may be limited strictly to the passage content, or it may be integrated with relevant prior knowledge. And you may plan to use your notes to enhance accurate recall or to help with comprehension (Cook & Mayer, 1983).

> Taking notes and reviewing notes aid retention and comprehension

As a learning tactic, notetaking comes with good news and bad. The good news is that notetaking can benefit a student in two ways. First, the process of taking notes while listening to a lecture or reading a text leads to better retention and comprehension of the noted information than just listening or reading does. Second, reviewing notes produces additional chances to recall and comprehend the noted material. The bad news is that we know very little at the present time about the specific conditions that make notetaking an effective tactic. As a result, we have no definitive answers to questions like the following: Should notes be extensive or brief? Does it make any difference whether notes are verbatim statements or paraphrases? Should a notetaker concentrate on recording facts and details, or should more general ideas be the focus? Should notes be reorganized (in outline form, for example) and then used as a basis for review, or should they be left in their original form? Is it best to review notes shortly after they have been taken or just before an exam? How long should a review session be? Is notetaking likely to be a useful tactic for every student?

The main reason we have no definitive answers to these and other questions is a shortage of relevant research. For the time being, the best we can say is that the process of taking and reviewing notes is likely to benefit most students and should be encouraged (Kiewra, 1985, 1988).

One conclusion we would like you to draw from this section is that learning tactics should not be taught as isolated techniques, particularly to high school students. If they are taught that way, most students probably will not keep using them for very long; nor will they recognize that as the situation changes, so should the tactic. Therefore, as we implied at the start of this section, students should be taught how to use tactics as part of a broader learning strategy.

Using Learning Strategies Effectively

The Components of a Learning Strategy   As noted, a learning strategy is a plan for accomplishing a learning goal. It consists of six components: metacognition, analysis, planning, implementation of the plan, monitoring progress, and modification. To give you a better idea of how to formulate a learning strategy of your own, here is a detailed description of each of these components (Snowman, 1986, 1987):

Learning strategy components: meta-cognition, analysis, planning, implementation, monitoring, modification

1. *Metacognition:* In the absence of some minimal awareness of how we think and how our thought processes affect our academic performance, a strategic approach to learning is simply not possible. We need to know, at the very least, that effective learning requires an analysis of the learning situation, formulation of a learning plan, skillful implementation of appropriate tactics, periodic monitoring of our progress, and modification of things that go wrong. In addition, we need to know why each of the above steps is necessary, when each step should be carried out, and how well prepared we are to perform each step. Without this knowledge, students who are taught one or more of the learning tactics mentioned earlier do not keep up their use for very long, nor do they apply the tactics to relevant tasks.

2. *Analysis:* Any workable plan must be based on relevant information. By using the four learning factors that were described at the beginning of the chapter (p. 380), the strategic learner can generate this information by playing the role of an investigative journalist and asking questions that pertain to what, when, where, why, who, and how. In this way the learner can identify important aspects of the material to be learned (what, when, where), understand the nature of the criterion (why), recognize relevant personal learner characteristics (who), and identify potentially useful learning activities or tactics (how). The importance of identifying these factors and understanding their role in strategy use was illustrated by Susan Nolen (1988). She found two factors that predicted continued use of such learning tactics as self-questioning, notetaking, and paraphrasing among a group of eighth-graders. One factor was the knowledge that certain tactics (such as the ones just mentioned) are more effective than other tactics (such as role rehearsal). The second factor was an intrinsic desire to do one's best on the task at hand.

3. *Planning:* Assuming that satisfactory answers can be gained from the preceding analysis, the strategic learner would formulate a learning plan by hypothesizing something like the following: "I know something about the material to be learned (I have to read and comprehend five chapters of my music appreciation text within the next three weeks), the nature of the criterion (I will have to compare and contrast the musical structure of symphonies that were written by Beethoven, Schubert, and Brahms), my strengths and weaknesses as a learner (I am

good at tasks that involve the identification of similarities and differences, but I have difficulty concentrating for long periods of time), and the nature of various learning activities (skimming is a good way to get a general sense of the structure of a chapter; mnemonic devices make memorizing important details easier and more reliable; notetaking and self-questioning are more effective ways to enhance comprehension than simple rereading). Based on this knowledge, I should divide each chapter into several smaller units that will take no longer than thirty minutes to read, take notes as I read, answer self-generated compare-and-contrast questions, use the loci mnemonic to memorize details, and repeat this sequence several times over the course of each week."

4. *Implementation of the plan:* Once the learner has formulated a plan, each of its elements must be implemented—*skillfully.* A careful analysis and a well-conceived plan will not work if tactics are carried out badly. On the other hand, of course, a poorly executed plan may not be entirely attributable to a learner's tactical skill deficiencies. Part of the problem may be a general lack of knowledge about what conditions make for effective use of tactics (as is the case with notetaking).

5. *Monitoring progress:* Once the learning process is under way, the strategic learner assesses how well the chosen tactics are working. Possible monitoring techniques include writing out a summary, giving an oral presentation, working practice problems, and answering questions.

6. *Modification:* If the monitoring assessment is positive, the learner may decide no changes are needed. If, however, attempts to memorize or understand the learning material seem to be producing unsatisfactory results, the learner will need to reevaluate and modify the analysis. This, in turn, will cause changes in both the plan and the implementation.

There are two points we would like to emphasize about the nature of a learning strategy. The first is that learning conditions constantly change. Subject matters have different types of information and structures, teachers use different instructional methods and have different styles, exams differ in the kinds of demands they make, and the interests, motives, and capabilities of students change over time. Accordingly, strategies must be *formulated* or constructed anew as one moves from task to task rather than *selected* from a bank of previously formulated strategies. The true strategist, in other words, is very mentally active. The second point is that the concept of learning strategy is obviously complex and requires a certain level of intellectual maturity. Thus, you may be tempted to conclude that although *you* could do it, learning to be strategic is beyond the reach of most elementary and high school students. Research evidence suggests otherwise, however. A study of high school students in Scotland, for example, found that some students are sensitive to contextual differences among school tasks and vary their approach to studying accordingly (Selmes, 1987). Furthermore, as we are about to show, research in the United States suggests that elementary grade youngsters can be trained to use many of the strategy components mentioned above.

Students can formulate strategic learning plans that identify and analyze the important aspects of a task. Then, they can tailor these plans to their own strengths and weaknesses as learners. (Rick Friedman/Black Star)

Research on Learning Strategy Training   An ambitious project to teach third- and fifth-grade children how, when, and why to use various elements of a reading comprehension strategy was evaluated on two occasions by Scott Paris and his associates (Paris, Cross & Lipson, 1984; Paris & Oka, 1986). Over the course of an academic year, several hundred third- and fifth-grade children participated either in a supplemental reading comprehension training program called Informed Strategies for Learning (ISL) or in a control condition.

The basic purposes of the ISL program were to increase the students' metacognitive awareness of reading strategies, convince them that reading strategies are useful skills, and teach them how to use strategic skills to improve reading comprehension. The entire package of instructional materials included four main units, each of which contained five modules. The goals of the units were, respectively, (a) planning and preparing to read, (b) identifying meaning, (c) reasoning about text content, and (d) monitoring comprehension. Each of the modules within a unit dealt with a particular aspect of that unit's goal. To make the point of each module clear, a concrete metaphor was developed and presented as a bulletin board display. For example, the module on task evaluation used the metaphor "Be a Reading Detective" to point out the importance of analyzing such comprehension clues as passage topic, length, and difficulty. Each module was presented over three lessons and included the following activities: Introduce the metaphor; describe the strategic skill; explain and demonstrate how to use the skill; provide opportunities to practice using the skill; provide corrective feedback; initiate discussions of thoughts and feelings about how, when, and why to use the skill; and encourage independent use of the skill.

The major findings from this program are mostly positive:

1. As measured by a twenty-item test, ISL children showed a much greater awareness than control group children of why one should use strategic reading skills, when such skills should be used, how to use them, and what benefits to expect from them.

2. Fifth-grade ISL children showed more metacognitive awareness than third-grade ISL children.

3. Third-grade and fifth-grade ISL children scored higher on two different measures of reading comprehension than third-grade and fifth-grade control group children.

4. Children's comprehension strategies, metacognitive knowledge, and motivation were all significantly related to achievement.

5. ISL did not improve self-perception about reading or perceived self-competence.

Another study of strategy training aimed at improving reading comprehension is the *reciprocal teaching* (RT) program of Annemarie Palincsar and Ann Brown (1984). As the title of this program indicates, the students learn certain comprehension skills by demonstrating them to each other. Palincsar and Brown trained a small group of seventh-graders whose reading comprehension scores were at least two years below grade level to use the techniques of summarizing, self-questioning, clarifying, and predicting to improve their reading comprehension. These four methods were chosen because they can be used by students to improve *and* monitor comprehension.

During the early training sessions the teacher explained and demonstrated the four methods while reading various passages. The students were then given gradually increasing responsibility for demonstrating these techniques to their peers, with the teacher supplying prompts and corrective feedback as needed. Eventually, each student was expected to offer a good summary of a passage, pose questions about important ideas, clarify ambiguous words or phrases, and predict upcoming events, all to be done with little or no intervention by the teacher. (This approach to strategy instruction, by the way, is based on the zone of proximal development concept that we first mentioned in Chapter 2.)

This program was evaluated in terms of two general questions. First, did the RT students improve in their ability to summarize, question, clarify, and predict? The answer to this question was yes. Early in the program, students produced overly detailed summaries and many unclear questions. But in later sessions, concise summaries and questions dealing explicitly with main ideas were the rule. For example, questions on main ideas increased from 54 percent to 70 percent. In addition, the questions were increasingly stated in paraphrase form rather than as verbatim statements from the passage.

Second, did the RT students improve their reading comprehension scores? Again the answer was yes. By the end of the study, RT-trained students were scoring as well as a group of average readers on tests of comprehension (about

75 percent correct for both groups) and much better than a group taught how to locate information that might show up in a test question (75 percent correct versus 45 percent correct). Most impressively, these levels of performance held up for at least eight weeks after the study ended (no measures were taken after that point) and generalized to tests of social studies and science (20 percent correct prior to training versus 60 percent correct after training).

The message of strategy-training programs like Informed Strategies for Learning and reciprocal teaching is that knowledge of the learning process and the conditions that affect it should be as much a part of the curriculum as learning to read, write, and compute. Proponents have argued persuasively that mastery of traditional basic skills is influenced by the nontraditional but more basic skills of strategic reasoning (see, for example, Bracey, 1983). Accordingly, children should gradually be made aware of the general relationship between cognitive means and academic ends, the potential range of application of various learning tactics, how to determine if learning is proceeding as planned, and what to do if it is not.

Mid-Chapter Review

The Nature of Information Processing Theory

Information processing theory: study of the ways people acquire, store, recall, and use information

A Model of Information Processing

A popular model of information processing visualizes three memory stores and a set of processes that determine whether and how stimuli undergo further processing:

Sensory register (SR): first memory store; hold stimuli briefly (about one to three seconds) in original form for possible future processing

Recognition: noting key features of a stimulus and relating them to already-stored information

Attention: selective focusing on a portion of the information currently stored in the sensory register

Short-term memory (STM): second memory store, also called working memory; holds about seven bits of information for about twenty seconds (or longer if maintenance rehearsal is used)

Maintenance rehearsal: using mental and verbal repetition to hold information in STM for immediate use

Elaborative rehearsal: encoding new information in long-term memory by consciously relating it to already-stored knowledge

Organization: grouping what is to be learned into fewer chunks in ways that provide retrieval cues

Meaningfulness: relating a new learning task to an existing cognitive structure (previously learned information)

Long-term memory (LTM): third memory store; permanent storehouse of information, which is thought to have an essentially unlimited capacity

Schema: abstract representations of ideas and experiences that are stored in LTM and make comprehension possible

Metacognition

Metacognition: knowledge of how we process information under a variety of conditions and with what effects

Helping Students Become Strategic Learners

Learning strategy: a plan for accomplishing a general learning goal, consisting of six elements: metacognition, analysis, planning, implementation of plan, monitoring of progress, and, if necessary, modification

Learning tactic: a specific technique, consistent with a person's overall learning strategy, that is used in mastering a learning task

Memory-directed tactics: tactics (such as rehearsal and mnemonic devices) whose primary purpose is to ensure accurate storage and retrieval of information

Comprehension-directed tactics: tactics (such as notetaking and self-questioning) whose primary purpose is to ensure comprehension of ideas and their interrelationships

Mnemonic devices: memory-directed tactics that transform or organize information, thereby making it more retrievable; popular types include rhymes, acronyms, acrostics, the pegword method, the loci method, and the keyword method

Suggestions for Teaching in Your Classroom

HELPING YOUR STUDENTS BECOME EFFICIENT INFORMATION PROCESSORS

1. Develop and use a variety of techniques to attract and hold attention, and give your students opportunities to practice and refine their skills in maintaining attention.
   a. Be aware of what will capture your students' attention.
   b. To maintain attention, emphasize the possible utility of learning new ideas.
   c. Teach students how to increase their span of attention.

2. Point out and encourage students to recognize that certain bits of information are important and can be related to what is already known.

3. Use appropriate rehearsal techniques, including an emphasis on meaning and chunking.

4. Organize what you ask your pupils to learn, and urge older students to organize material on their own.

5. As much as possible, stress meaningfulness.

6. Demonstrate a variety of learning tactics and allow students to practice them.
   a. Teach students how to use various forms of rehearsal and mnemonic devices.
   b. Teach students how to formulate comprehension questions.
   c. Teach students how to take notes.

7. Encourage students to think about the various conditions that affect *how* they learn and remember.

8. Each time you prepare an assignment, think about learning strategies that you and your students might use.

---

1. Develop and use a variety of techniques to attract and hold attention, and give your students opportunities to practice and refine their skills in maintaining attention.
   a. Be aware of what will capture your students' attention.

Handbook Heading:
Techniques for Capturing Attention

You can help your students learn more effectively if you keep in mind how the sensory register works. As the first memory store in the information processing system, the SR holds sensory information (sights, sounds, smells, and the like) just long enough for the learner to attend selectively to whatever will receive additional encoding. Attention to first impressions is influenced by characteristics of the information itself and by the learners' related past experiences. Learners are more likely to attend to things they expect to find interesting or meaningful.

▶ Unpredictable changes in environment usually command attention

Almost all students at one time or another have difficulty concentrating on a task. Remember that human beings are sensitive to abrupt, sudden changes in their environment. Thus, anything that stands out, breaks a rhythm, or is unpredictable is almost certain to command a student's attention.

Examples

Print key words or ideas in extra-large letters on the board.

Use colored chalk to emphasize important points written on the board.

Give students colored marking pens and urge them to underline key words or phrases in any learning materials that will not need to be used later by other students.

When you come to a particularly important part of a lesson, say, "Now really concentrate on this. It's especially important." Then present the idea with intensity and emphasis.

When lecturing about or discussing a particular historical figure, dress and act the part (if you are uninhibited and/or a former member of a dramatic club).

To call attention to information or procedures, it is often a good idea to use unusual, novel, or appealing stimuli. (N. Rowan/The Image Works, Inc.)

Start off a lesson with unexpected remarks, such as "Imagine that you have just inherited a million dollars and. . . ."

b. To maintain attention, emphasize the possible utility of learning new ideas.

Handbook Heading:
Techniques for Maintaining Attention

While it is possible to overdo attempts at making the curriculum relevant, it never hurts to think of possible ways of relating school learning to the present and future lives of students. When students realize that the basic purpose of school is to help them adapt to their environment, they are more apt to pay close attention to what it is you are trying to do.

Example

Teach basic skills—such as arithmetic computation, arithmetic reasoning, spelling, writing, and reading—as part of class projects that relate to students' natural interests (for example, keeping records of money for newspaper deliveries; measuring rainfall, temperature, and wind speed; writing letters to local television stations to express opinions on or request information about television shows).

c. Teach students how to increase their span of attention.

▶ Attention span can be increased with practice

Remember that paying attention is a skill that many students have not had an opportunity to refine. Give your students plenty of opportunities to practice and improve their ability to maintain attention.

Examples

Institute games that depend on maintaining attention, such as "Simon Says," keeping track of an object hidden under one of several boxes (the old shell game), or determining whether two pictures are identical or different. At first, positively reinforce students for all correct responses. Then reinforce only for improvements in performance. Remind students that their success is a direct result of how well they pay attention.

Read a short magazine or newspaper story and ask students to report who, what, where, when, and why.

Whisper a message to one student and have her or him repeat it to another, who in turn, repeats it to another, and so on down the line. The last child to hear the message then repeats it aloud and compares it with the original message you whispered.

2. Point out and encourage students to recognize that certain bits of information are important and can be related to what is already known.

Attention is one control process for the sensory register; the other is recognition. Sometimes the two processes can be used together to induce students to focus on important parts of material to be learned. Sometimes you can urge your students to recognize key features or familiar relationships on their own.

Examples

When teaching letter or object recognition to primary graders, have them trace the letter or object with their index finger while saying the name of each item aloud.

When teaching word recognition, display words in bright colors and in different-sized letters.

Have students practice grouping numbers, letters, or classroom items according to some shared feature, such as odd numbers, multiples of five, letters with circles, or things made of wood.

Say, "This math problem is very similar to one you solved last week. Does anyone recognize something familiar about this problem?"

Say, "In this chapter the same basic point is made in several different ways. As you read, try to recognize and write down as many variations on that basic theme as you can."

3. Use appropriate rehearsal techniques, including an emphasis on meaning and chunking.

One of the basic ways that information is encoded in long-term memory is through elaborative rehearsal. Only rarely do we learn something at first glance. Most of the time we have to elaboratively rehearse something several times in order to remember it. Without knowledge of learning strategies, or in the absence of proper guidance by a teacher, however, many students resort to "thoughtless" rehearsal. They simply repeat words over and over again without attempting to search for meaning or relate what they are saying to what they already know. A story is told of an elementary school boy who persisted in saying, "I have went." After correcting him a dozen times, his teacher finally exploded and sentenced him to write "I have gone" a hundred times after school. As the student reached the ninetieth repetition late that afternoon, the teacher left the room on an errand. When she returned, she discovered that the hapless pupil had finished his task and departed. On the board were a hundred progressively sloppier "I have gone's," together with this note: "Dear teacher, I have wrote 'I have gone' a hundred times and I have went home."

The moral of this tale is, of course, that repetition does little good unless students are helped to *understand* their errors. This story also points up the futility of requiring an excessive number of repetitions. It is usually more effective to ask error makers to do something the correct way a few times and *think about it* than to force them to do it a hundred times, which will be so tedious and distasteful that they will almost certainly think about something else. For example, it is much better for a girl who can't remember how to spell *principal* to write the word five times and make use of a mnemonic device by thinking to herself, "The principal is a pal," than to write it a hundred times and think that her teacher is a louse.

The power of chunking information into meaningful units was demonstrated in a study conducted with a single college student of average memory ability and intelligence (Ericson, Chase & Faloon, 1980). Over twenty months he was able to improve his memory for digits from seven to almost eighty. Being a track and field buff, he categorized three- and four-digit groups as running times for imaginary races. Thus, 3492 became "3 minutes and 49.2 seconds, near world record time." Number groups that could not be encoded as running times were encoded as ages. These two chunking techniques accounted for almost 90 percent of his associations.

Handbook Heading:
Ways to Use Chunking
to Facilitate Learning

▶ Distributed practice: short study periods at frequent intervals

▶ Serial position effect: tendency to remember items at beginning and end of a long list

The main purpose of chunking is to enhance learning by breaking tasks into small, easy-to-manage pieces. To a large degree, students can learn to do this for themselves if you show them how chunking works. In addition, you can help by not requiring students to learn more than they can reasonably handle at one time. If you have a list of fifty spelling words to be learned, it is far better to present ten words a day, five days in a row, during short study periods than to give all fifty at once. This method of presentation is called **distributed practice.** In distributed practice, it is usually necessary to divide the material into small parts, which—because of the serial-position effect—seems to be the best way for students to learn and retain unrelated material (for example, spelling words). The **serial position effect** refers to people's tendency to learn and remember the words at the beginning and end of a list more easily than those in the middle. By using short lists, then, you in effect eliminate the hard-to-memorize middle ground. A description of the positive effect of distributed practice on classroom learning and an explanation of why educators do not make greater use of it have been offered by Frank Dempster (1988).

Distributed practice may not be desirable for all learning tasks, however. If you ask pupils to learn roles in a play, short rehearsals might not be effective because students may have a difficult time grasping the entire plot. If you allow enough rehearsal time to run through a whole act, on the other hand, your students will be able to relate one speech to another and comprehend the overall structure of the play. When students learn by way of a few rather long study periods, spaced infrequently, psychologists call it **massed practice.**

You might also tell your students about the relative merits of distributed versus massed practice. Robert Bjork (1979) has pointed out that most students not only are unaware of the benefits of distributed study periods but go to considerable lengths to block or mass the study time devoted to a particular subject.

The above suggestions about teaching chunking are likely to be most effective with children who are around ten years of age. Between the ages of five and seven, children rarely engage in spontaneous rehearsal. Between seven and ten, rehearsal strategies are very primitive, with each term rehearsed separately. But, around ten years of age, items may be grouped together and rehearsed as a set, making chunking possible.

4. Organize what you ask your pupils to learn, and urge older students to organize material on their own.

Handbook Heading:
Organizing Information
into Related Categories

Simply grouping items is appropriate when dealing with "illogical" information such as the order of the letters of the alphabet or telephone numbers. But most information you will ask your students to learn will make sense in one way or another. At least some items in most sets of information will be related to other items, and you will find it desirable to call attention to interrelationships. The experiment described earlier, in which one group of students was given a single long list of items to learn and another group was presented the same items in logically ordered groups, illustrates the value of organization. By placing related items in groups, you reduce the number of chunks to be learned and also make it possible for students to benefit from cues supplied by the interrelationships between items in any given set. And by placing items in logical order, you help students grasp how information at the beginning of a chapter or lesson makes it easier to learn information that is presented later.

Examples

If students are to learn how to identify trees, birds, rocks, or the equivalent, group items that are related (for example, deciduous and evergreen trees). Call attention to distinctive features and to organizational schemes that have been developed.

Print an outline of a chapter on the board, or give students a duplicated outline, and have them record notes under the various headings.

To help students encode information, teach them how to group objects and ideas according to some shared feature. (Ralf-Finn Hestoft/SABA)

Whenever you give a lecture or demonstration, print an outline on the board. Call attention to the sequence of topics and demonstrate how various points emerge from or are related to other points.

5. As much as possible, stress meaningfulness.

Handbook Heading:
Ways to Stress Meaningfulness

Much of the information you will ask students to learn will be logical and meaningful. Even students at the college level, however, often treat information that makes sense as if it were nonsensical. Instead of using what they already know to encode new information, many students resort to rote memorization, which is not only tedious but also ineffective. So when you present material to be learned, emphasize the logic behind it and urge students to look for meaning on their own.

Concrete analogies can make abstract information meaningful

Concrete analogies offer one effective way to add meaning to material. Consider someone who has no knowledge of basic physics but is trying to understand a passage about the flow of electricity through metal. For this person, statements about crystalline lattice arrays, free-floating electrons, and the effects of impurities will mean very little. However, such abstract ideas can be explained in more familiar terms. You might compare the molecular structure of a metal bar to a tinker toy arrangement, for example, or liken the effect of impurities to placing a book in the middle of a row of falling dominoes. Such analogies increase recall and comprehension (Royer & Cable, 1975, 1976).

Examples

Give students opportunities to express ideas in their own words and to relate new knowledge to previous learning.

When you explain or demonstrate, express complex and abstract ideas several different ways. Be sure to provide plenty of examples.

Construct essay tests and homework assignments that emphasize comprehension and application. Give credit for thoughtful answers even though they do not exactly match the answer you would have given.

For topics that are somewhat controversial (for example, nuclear energy, genetic engineering, pesticide use), require students to present both pro and con arguments.

6. Demonstrate a variety of learning tactics and allow students to practice them.
   a. Teach students how to use various forms of rehearsal and mnemonic devices.

Handbook Heading:
Ways to Teach Memory
Tactics

At least two reasons recommend the teaching of rehearsal. One is that maintenance rehearsal is a useful tactic for keeping a relatively small amount of information active in short-term memory. Second, it is one of a few tactics that young children can learn to use. If you do decide to teach rehearsal, we have two suggestions. First, remind young children that rehearsal is something that learners consciously decide to do when they want to remember things. Second, remind students to rehearse no more than seven items (or chunks) at a time.

Upper elementary grade students (fourth, fifth, and sixth graders) can be taught advanced forms of maintenance rehearsal, such as cumulative rehearsal, and forms of elaborative rehearsal, such as rehearsing sets of items that form homogeneous categories. As with younger students, provide several opportunities each week to practice these skills.

As you prepare class presentations or encounter bits of information that students seem to have difficulty learning, ask yourself if a mnemonic device would be useful. You might write up a list of the devices discussed earlier and refer to it often. Part of the value of mnemonic devices is that they make learning easier. They are also fun to make up and use. Moreover, rhymes, acronyms, and acrostics can be constructed rather quickly. You might consider setting aside about thirty minutes two or three times a week to teach mnemonics. First, explain how rhyme, acronym, and acrostic mnemonics work, and then provide examples of each. For younger children use short, simple rhymes like "Columbus crossed the ocean blue in fourteen hundred ninety-two." For older students, the rhymes can be longer and more complex. The following rhyme is often used as a way to remember the value of pi from one to twenty decimal places:

Pie.

I wish I could reproduce pi.

Eureka cried the great inventor,

Christmas pudding Christmas pie

Is the problem's very center.

If you count the number of letters in each word, you come up with the answer—3.14159265358979323846.

Acrostics can be used to remember particularly difficult spelling words. The word *arithmetic* can be spelled by taking the first letter from each word of the following sentence: A Rat in the House May Eat the Ice Cream.

Once students understand how the mnemonic is supposed to work, have them construct mnemonics to learn various facts and concepts. You might offer a prize for the most ingenious mnemonic.

The pegword and loci mnemonics are particularly suited for learning long lists of items in serial order. For both, the first step involves learning a set of memory pegs. Because the pegs rhyme with the ordinal position they represent (for example, one-bun, two-shoe), they are fairly easy to learn. Familiar places are used as the pegs for the loci method and therefore will vary from person to person. As with rhymes, acronyms, and acrostics, explain how the pegword and loci mnemonics work and provide a demonstration. Once students have memorized the pegs or locations, allow them to practice with short lists of concrete nouns, abstract nouns, and mixed lists. Gradually lengthen the lists to ten, fifteen, and twenty or more items and introduce material from the curriculum. This may include the names of elements that make up the periodic table from lightest to heaviest, the names of bones in the human body, the names of various traffic signs, and the like. When the class exhibits skill in memorizing lists of items, you might encourage them to list ideas from a reading passage or speech and learn them with either mnemonic.

The keyword method should be used whenever pairs of items have to be learned. Learning a foreign language vocabulary, abstract or technical terminology, the accomplishments of people, and states and their capitals are tasks ideally suited to the keyword mnemonic. Because the keyword technique uses imagery, one of the first things you will have to do is explain what an image is and provide students with sufficient practice in generating images. Then, help students generate appropriate keywords. Keywords are known words that sound like or are some part of the word to be learned. Adapting the keyword method to learning two-part facts, like states and their capitals, is a little different in that it involves generating two keywords (see, for example, Levin et al., 1980). To learn the association Maryland-Annapolis, for instance, the student would need a keyword for Maryland, such as *marry,* and a keyword for Annapolis, such as *apple.* The two keywords are then embedded in an interacting visual image. Imagine, if you will, two apples being married. For Springfield, Illinois, imagine a field of springs making a lot of noise.

b. Teach students how to formulate comprehension questions.

Handbook Heading:
Ways to Teach Comprehension Tactics

We concluded earlier that self-questioning could be an effective comprehension tactic if students were trained to write good comprehension questions and given opportunities to practice the technique. We suggest you try the following instructional sequence:

1. Discuss the purpose of student-generated questions.

2. Point out the differences between knowledge-level questions and comprehension-level questions. An excellent discussion of this distinction can be found in the *Taxonomy of Educational Objectives, Handbook I: Cognitive Domain* (Bloom et al., 1956).

3. Provide students with a sample paragraph and several comprehension questions. Again, good examples of comprehension questions and guidelines for writing your own can be found in the *Taxonomy*.

4. Hand out paragraphs from which students can practice constructing questions.

5. Provide corrective feedback.

6. Give students short passages from which to practice.

7. Provide corrective feedback (Andre & Anderson, 1978–1979).

c. Teach students how to take notes.

Despite the limitations of research on notetaking, mentioned earlier, three suggestions should lead to more effective notetaking. First, provide students with clear, detailed objectives for every reading assignment. The objectives should indicate what parts of the assignment to focus on and how that material should be processed (whether memorized verbatim, reorganized and paraphrased, or integrated with earlier reading assignments). Second, inform students that notetaking is an effective comprehension tactic when used appropriately. Think, for example, about a reading passage that is long and for which test items will demand analysis and synthesis of broad concepts (as in "Compare and contrast the economic, social, and political causes of World War I with those of World War II"). Tell students to concentrate on identifying main ideas and supporting details, paraphrase this information, and record similarities and differences. Third, provide students with practice and corrective feedback in answering questions that are similar to those on the criterion test.

7. Encourage students to think about the various conditions that affect *how* they learn and remember.

Although awareness of the factors that affect comprehension and recall develops with age and experience, classroom performance may be improved by helping students understand the role of different variables in learning. One approach is to use the four factors described by John Bransford (p. 380). In this way, you can attempt to increase awareness of how personal characteristics, learning tactics, learning materials, and criteria tasks like tests, projects, and performances affect classroom learning.

The very youngest students (through third grade) should be told periodically that such cognitive behaviors as describing, recalling, guessing, and understanding mean different things, produce different results, and vary in how well they fit a task's demands.

For older elementary students, explain the learning process more simply, focusing on the circumstances in which different learning tactics are likely to be useful. Then, have students keep a diary or log in which they note when they use learning tactics, which ones, and with what success. Look for cases where good performance corresponds to frequent reported use of tactics, and positively reinforce those individuals. Encourage greater use of tactics among students whose performance and reported use of them is below average.

While this same technique can be used with high school and college students, they should also be made aware of the other elements that make up strategic learning. Discuss the meaning of and necessity for analyzing a learning task, developing a learning plan, using appropriate tactics, monitoring the effectiveness of the plan, and implementing whatever corrective measures might be called for.

8. Each time you prepare an assignment, think about learning strategies that you and your students might use.

Handbook Heading:
Ways to Teach Learning
Strategies

As noted in our earlier discussion of age trends in metacognition, virtually all elementary school pupils and many high school students will not be able to devise and use their own coordinated set of learning strategies. Accordingly, you should devise such strategies for them, explain how the strategies work, and urge them to use these techniques on their own. With high school students, you might consider giving a "How to Study" lecture at the beginning of a report period to provide your students with general information about learning strategies. Even if you do give such an orientation, however, it would still be wise to give specific instructions as each assignment is made. In devising learning strategies, follow the procedure that was described earlier in this chapter: analyze, plan, implement, monitor, modify. When you analyze, though, take into account not only the material to be learned and the nature of the tests you will give but also the cognitive characteristics of the learners.

Examples

To help elementary school pupils prepare for a spelling test to be administered on a district-wide basis, begin by analyzing the nature of the task and the cognitive abilities of your pupils. Select mnemonic devices likely to lead to effective encoding. Divide the words students will be tested on into short lists. Schedule several brief study sessions each day, and follow each session with a nonmemorization activity. Have students pair off and test each other.

Use flash cards, and encourage your students to make and use their own. Occasionally, have some students go to the board and write out words you dictate at a rapid pace. Give frequent practice quizzes. Have each pupil prepare a list of "Words I Know" and "Words I Don't Know." For words they don't know, suggest new mnemonic devices and arrange for plenty of rehearsal.

In a secondary grade class, analyze each text chapter and decide what kind of exam you intend to use to evaluate your students' understanding. Perhaps draw up a list of key points, print these on the board, and announce that they will be emphasized on exam questions. Explain what kinds of test questions you intend to ask, and give some suggestions on the best ways to study in order to be able to answer such questions. Announce the date of the exam well in advance. Schedule supervised study sessions during class periods. Give your students specific suggestions about learning strategies that they might use during each study session. At least a week or so before the exam give a practice quiz featuring questions similar to those that will be on the exam, and have students note points they know and don't know. Tell them to concentrate on material that is incompletely learned and recommend trouble-shooting learning strategies. Give a follow-up quiz and repeat the monitor-modify procedure.

Applying Technology to Teaching

USING TECHNOLOGY TO AID INFORMATION PROCESSING

Computer-based instructional technology can help students learn *how* to think in addition to helping them learn *what* to think. Accordingly, we now want to suggest a few ways in which computers can be used to help students improve their information processing skills.

The first way in which computer-based learning aids students' information processing is by creating a different relationship between teacher and students. There are two types of changes that typically occur. First, the role of the teacher changes. Instead of being a dispenser of information and directions (a task now done by the computer), the teacher becomes more of a facilitator and guide (Collins, 1991). Second, the teacher's focus of instruction shifts. Because the teacher is no longer primarily responsible for presenting information and providing feedback, he or she has more time to help students acquire and improve learning and problem-solving skills.

A second way in which computers can make students better information processors is through programs that teach learning tactics. For example, a program called *Mind-Step 1* teaches students from sixth grade to college how to create and use mnemonic devices. *Mind-Step 2* extends the lessons in *Mind-Step 1* with analysis and memorization of poetry and text, developing good listening habits, and remembering visual information. *Fundamentals of Outlining* is a tutorial program that teaches students correct outlining form and how to recognize and write titles, main topics, subtopics, details, and subpoints. *Mystery Master Murder by Dozen* is a deductive reasoning game that encourages the development of notetaking skills. And *Plan Ahead* is a tutorial that teaches students how to schedule their own time (EPIE Institute, 1986).

A third way in which computers can help students is through programs that prompt them to think about how various ideas and pieces of information are interrelated. You may recall that we discussed this thought process earlier in the chapter, in the sections on elaborative encoding and schema formation. Another phrase commonly used is *mental model building*. A popular computer program that seems to foster this process is *HyperCard*. HyperCard is an information management program that was created for the Apple Macintosh computer. It can be used to store and retrieve text, charts, and pictures about any subject. The basic unit of information in HyperCard is called a *card*. Cards can contain any type of verbal, graphic, or pictorial information. A collection of cards that is organized around a common theme is called a *stack*. Ready-made stacks can be purchased for hundreds of subjects or they can be custom-made by the learner. The aspect of stacks that would seem to foster schema formation is that any card can be connected to any other card. Thus, cards in a stack can be sorted into subsets according to some common characteristic. To use a simple example: If you had several dozen names in a stack called "business associates," you could sort them by state, area code, gender, occupation, interests, position within their company, and so on. (See Kozma, 1991, for a general discussion of this type of program.)

The computer can also be used to help students forge links between a symbolic form of representation, such as a graph, and its real-world counterpart. Many seventh- and eighth-grade students, for example, do not understand certain graphic representations. When asked to draw a graph depicting how fast a bicyclist travels uphill, downhill, and on flat stretches, their products represented the hills and valleys rather than the bicyclist's speed. That is, they drew an ascending line to represent the bicyclist's speed going uphill without realizing that such a line represented the downhill portion of the journey since it indicated increasing speed. In effect, they were drawing pictures that represented the exact opposite of what they were asked to represent. This graph interpretation skill was significantly improved by having students work with computers that were connected to a variety of sensors (temperature probes, microphones, and motion sensors, for example). As the student applied a source of energy to one of the sensors—heating up and allowing to cool down a beaker of water, for example—a corresponding graphic representation was instantly created on the computer's screen (Kozma, 1991).

Resources for Further Investigation

The Nature of Information Processing Theory

For more on how information processing theory relates to teaching and learning, read Chapter 1 of *Cognitive Classroom Learning* (1986), edited by Gary D. Phye and Thomas Andre. Titled "Cognition, Learning, and Education," the chapter compares information processing with behavioral learning theory, describes the nature of memory stores and control processes, and discusses the value of an information processing perspective for educational practice.

Another source of information is Chapter 2 of *The Cognitive Psychology of Learning* (1985) by Ellen D. Gagné. This chapter, in addition to describing the characteristics of memory stores and control processes, covers the research methods that are used by information processing psychologists, how cognitive theories are developed, and how teachers can use an information processing perspective in planning instruction.

Memory Structures and Processes

Henry C. Ellis and R. Reed Hunt provide detailed analyses of the sensory register, recognition, attention, short-term memory, elaborative rehearsal, long-term memory, and retrieval in the fourth edition of *Fundamentals of Human Memory and Cognition* (1989).

Mark Grabe describes how knowledge of attentional processes can enhance instructional practices in Chapter 3 of *Cognitive Classroom Learning* (1986). Raymond W. Kulhavy, Neil H. Schwartz, and Sarah Peterson do the same for encoding processes in Chapter 5 of the same book.

Metacognition

Orpha K. Duell provides a summary of research on metacognition in Chapter 8 of Phye and Andre's *Cognitive Classroom Learning* (1986). Bonnie B. Armbruster, Catharine H. Echols, and Ann L. Brown discuss metacognition's role in reading in volume 84 of *The Volta Review* (1982).

Learning Tactics and Strategies

One of the most popular (and useful) memory improvement books available is *The Memory Book* (1974) by Harry Lorayne and Jerry Lucas. In Chapter 2 of their book, Lorayne and Lucas explain why and how you should think up ridiculous associations; in Chapter 4 they offer suggestions for using substitute words; techniques for learning foreign and English vocabulary are explained in Chapter 7; ways to remember names and faces are described in Chapter 8.

Bernice Bragstad and Sharyn Stumpf (1987) offer practical advice and instructional materials for teachers of study skills in *A Guidebook for Teaching Study Skills and Motivation* (2d ed.). Each chapter contains a brief introduction to its main concept, a set of learning experiences designed to stimulate students' interest and proficiency in that topic (for example, time management, storing and retrieving information, notetaking), a set of exercises or tips that can be reproduced for student use, and a list of suggestions for determining whether the students have mastered the chapter's objectives.

M. D. Gall, Joyce Gall, Dennis Jacobsen, and Terry Bullock (1990) outline why it is important to teach students study skills, summarize underlying theories of information processing and motivation, and describe how a school or district can implement a study skills program in *Tools for Learning: A Guide to Teaching Study Skills*.

In Part C of *Teaching Reading, Writing, and Study Strategies* (3d ed., 1983), H. Alan Robinson describes patterns of writing (text structures) and associated comprehension tactics for four major content areas: science, social studies, English, and mathematics.

Individual Differences in Memory

One of the most striking accounts of supernormal memory is provided by Alexander Luria in *The Mind of a Mnemonist: A Little Book About a Vast Memory* (1968). Luria describes his experiments and experiences over a period of almost thirty years with the man he refers to as S. What made S. remarkable was his apparent photographic memory, allowing him to recall nonsense material he had not seen for fifteen years. Additional articles about people with unusually proficient memory capability can be found in *Memory Observed* (1982), edited by Ulric Neisser.

Robert Kail describes memory differences among normal children, as well as differences between normal and retarded children, in *The Development of Memory in Children* (1984). Also briefly discussed is the phenomenon of the idiot savant—an individual who is below average on all measures of ability except one, in which he or she far surpasses almost all other individuals. Kail discusses one such individual whose knowledge of the calendar was essentially perfect between the years 1 and 40400, despite having an IQ score in the 60–70 range.

Mnemonic instruction with various special education populations is discussed by James E. Turnure and John F. Lane (Chapter 15) and by Margo A. Mastropieri, Thomas E. Scruggs, and Joel R. Levin (Chapter 16) in *Imagery and Related Mnemonic Processes* (1987), edited by Mark A. McDaniel and Michael Pressley.

SUMMARY

1. Information processing theory attempts to explain how individuals acquire, store, recall, and use information.

2. Information processing theory arose in part because psychologists were dissatisfied with behavioral learning theory's omission of the mental activities of the learner.

3. From an information processing perspective, learning can be seen as an interaction among characteristics of the learner, mental activities in which the learner engages, the nature of the learning material, and the nature of the criterion.

4. A popular model of information processing is composed of three memory stores and a set of control processes that determine the flow of information from one memory store to another. The memory stores are the sensory register, short-term memory, and long-term memory. The control processes are recognition, attention, maintenance rehearsal, elaborative rehearsal, and retrieval.

5. The sensory register holds information in its original form for two or three seconds, during which time we may recognize and attend to it further.

6. Recognition involves noticing key features of a stimulus and integrating those features with relevant information from long-term memory.

7. Attention is a selective focusing on a portion of the information in the sensory register. Information from long-term memory influences what we focus on.

8. Short-term memory holds about seven bits of information for about twenty seconds (in the absence of rehearsal). It is often called working memory because it contains information we are conscious of.

9. Information can be held in short-term memory indefinitely through the use of maintenance rehearsal, which is rote repetition of information.

10. Information is transferred from short-term memory to long-term memory by linking the new information to related information in long-term memory. This process is called elaborative rehearsal.

11. Elaborative rehearsal is based partly on organization. This involves grouping together, or chunking, items of information that share some important characteristic.

12. Elaborative rehearsal is also based on meaningfulness. Meaningfulness exists when new information can be related to the current cognitive structures (schemata) of the learner.

13. Long-term memory is thought to be an unlimited storehouse of information from which nothing is ever lost.

14. Many psychologists believe the information in long-term memory is organized in the form of schemata. A schema has been defined as a generalized abstract structure of information. When schemata are absent or crudely formed, learning and recall problems occur.

15. Metacognition refers to any knowledge an individual has about how humans think and the circumstances that affect thinking.

16. Metacognitive knowledge increases gradually with experience. This helps explain why junior high and high school students are more flexible and effective learners than primary grade students.

17. A learning strategy is a general plan that specifies the resources one will use and how one will use them to achieve a learning goal.

18. A learning tactic is a specific technique one uses to help achieve an academic goal when confronted with a task.

19. Learning tactics can be classified as memory directed or comprehension directed. The former are used when accurate storage and retrieval of information are important. The latter are used when comprehension of ideas is important.

20. Two types of memory-directed tactics are rehearsal and mnemonic devices. Since most forms of rehearsal involve little or no encoding of information, they are not very effective memory tactics. Because mnemonic devices organize information and provide built-in retrieval cues, they are effective memory tactics.

21. Popular mnemonic devices include rhymes, acronyms, acrostics, the pegword method, the loci method, and the keyword method.

22. Two effective comprehension tactics are self-questioning and notetaking.

23. The components of a learning strategy are metacognition, analysis, planning, implementation, monitoring, and modifying.

KEY TERMS

information processing theory *(378)*
sensory register *(382)*
recognition *(382)*
attention *(383)*

short-term memory *(384)*
maintenance rehearsal *(384)*
elaborative rehearsal *(384)*
long-term memory *(387)*
schemata *(387)*
metacognition *(390)*
learning strategy *(393)*
learning tactic *(393)*
mnemonic device *(394)*
distributed practice *(409)*
serial position effect *(409)*
massed practice *(410)*

DISCUSSION QUESTIONS

1. Can you think of any personal, everyday experiences that illustrate the nature of one or more of the three memory stores? Have you recently, for instance, retrieved a long-dormant memory because of a chance encounter with an associated word, sound, or smell?

2. Information processing psychologists have expressed disappointment that the results of their research on memory stores and processes, learning tactics, and learning strategies have not been widely implemented by teachers. Is this complaint consistent with your experience? Can you recall any instances when you were taught how to use a variety of learning tactics to formulate different strategies? How about out of school? Did you acquire any such skills without the help of a classroom teacher?

3. Many teachers have said that they would like to teach their students more about the nature and use of learning processes, but that they don't have time because of the amount of subject material they must cover. What can you do as a teacher to avoid this pitfall?

4. A major problem in training students to use learning strategies and tactics is getting the youngsters to spend the time and effort required to master these skills. Suppose some students expressed their disinterest, saying their own methods would be just as effective (although you know full well they would not be). How would you convince them otherwise?

Chapter 10

COGNITIVE LEARNING THEORIES AND PROBLEM SOLVING

▶ Solve simpler version of problem first, then transfer process to harder problem

▶ Break complex problems into manageable parts

▶ Work backward when goal is clear but beginning state is not

▶ Analogous problems must be very similar to target problem

▶ Evaluate solutions to well-structured problems by estimating or checking

SUGGESTIONS FOR TEACHING IN YOUR CLASSROOM

▶ Students are poor problem solvers because of too much TV, lack of reinforcement, lack of critical attitude

▶ Comprehension of subject matter critical to problem solving

TRANSFER OF LEARNING

▶ Early view of transfer based on degree of similarity between two tasks

▶ Positive transfer: previous learning makes later learning easier

▶ Negative transfer: previous learning interferes with later learning

▶ Specific transfer due to specific similarities between two tasks

▶ General transfer due to use of same cognitive strategies

▶ Low-road transfer: previously learned skill automatically applied to similar current task

▶ High-road transfer: formulate rule from one task and apply to related task

▶ Low-road and high-road transfer produced by varied practice at applying skills, rules, memory retrieval cues

When you begin to teach, you may devote a substantial amount of class time to having pupils learn information discovered by others. But acquiring a storehouse of facts, concepts, and principles is only part of what constitutes an appropriate education. Students must also learn how to *find*, *evaluate*, and *use* what they need to know to accomplish whatever goals they set for themselves. In other words, students need to learn how to be effective problem solvers. One justification for teaching problem-solving skills *in addition* to ensuring mastery of factual information is that life in the United States (and other technologically oriented countries) is marked by speedy change. New products, services, and social conventions are rapidly introduced and integrated into our lifestyles. Microcomputers, videocassette recorders, microwave ovens, anticancer drugs, and in vitro fertilization, to name just a few examples, are relatively recent innovations that significantly affect the lives of many people.

But change, particularly rapid change, can be viewed as a mixed blessing. On the one hand, new products and services such as those mentioned can make life more convenient, efficient, and enjoyable. On the other hand, they can make life more complicated and problematic. Factory automation, for example, promises increased efficiency and productivity (which contribute to our standard of living), but it also threatens the job security of thousands of workers. Advances in medical care promise healthier and longer lives, but they introduce a host of moral, ethical, legal, and economic problems.

The educational implication that flows from these observations is clear: If we are to benefit from our ability to produce rapid and sometimes dramatic change, our schools need to invest more time, money, and effort in teaching students how to be effective problem solvers. As Lauren Resnick, a past president of the American Educational Research Association, has argued,

> We need to identify and closely examine the aspects of education that are most likely to produce ability to adapt in the face of transitions and breakdowns. Rather than training people for particular jobs—a task better left to revised forms of on-the-job training—school should focus its efforts on preparing people to be good *adaptive learners,* so that they can perform effectively when situations are unpredictable and task demands change. (1987, p. 18)

Resnick's argument, which echoes many others, is not without some justification. According to estimates made by the Carnegie Foundation, big business spends up to $100 billion a year on corporate classrooms that try to develop the thinking skills corporate management feels the schools have failed to teach (Ruggiero, 1988).

Good problem solvers share two general characteristics: a well-organized, meaningful fund of knowledge and a systematic set of problem-solving skills. Historically, cognitive learning theories have been particularly useful sources of ideas for imparting both. In this chapter, then, we examine the issue of meaningful learning from three cognitive perspectives: that of Jerome S. Bruner; that of constructivism, a contemporary view closely related to Bruner's; and that of David P. Ausubel. We then go on to describe the nature of the problem-solving process and what you can do to help your students become better problem solvers. We conclude by describing the circumstances under which learned capabilities are applied to new tasks, a process known as transfer of learning.

THE NATURE OF MEANINGFUL LEARNING

For as long as there have been schools, educators have wrestled with the questions "What should students learn?" and "How should they learn it?" The

The essence of the approach to teaching advocated by Bruner is that students should be encouraged to make their own discoveries.
(Richard Kalvar/Magnum)

debates that have occurred both in the past and at present over these two questions are usually not framed in either/or terms. Most people agree that learning should in some degree encompass problem-solving skills, creativity, basic intellectual skills (such as reading, writing, and computation), and knowledge of basic subject matter (such as history, geography, or science), and that students should pursue their own natural interests and self-discovery of facts and problem-solving procedures as well as memorize a predetermined body of knowledge. Whatever differences exist among theorists are a matter of emphasis. The emphasis favored by psychologist Jerome Bruner is twofold: Students should understand the structure of a body of knowledge rather than memorize names, dates, places, rules, formulas, and so on, as isolated fragments; and they should learn how to discover what they need to know.

Bruner: The Importance of Structure and Discovery

Bruner's interest in meaningful learning and the discovery approach began with his studies on perception (1951) and thinking (Bruner, Goodnow & Austin, 1956). His interest in finding ways to apply to education what he had discovered about these two areas drew impetus from his directorship of the Woods Hole Conference on Education. This conference was called in 1959 to find ways to improve science education in the public schools (at the time Russia had recently demonstrated its superiority in space technology). In *The Process of Education* (1960), Bruner summarized his perception of the main points brought out in the conference. This book, now viewed as a classic statement on education, triggered an interest in school learning in general, which Bruner discussed in *Toward a Theory of Instruction* (1966) and *The Relevance of Education* (1971).

Structure   One of the major points emphasized in *The Process of Education* is
that teachers should assist students in grasping the structure of a field of study.
Understanding the **structure** of a subject means understanding its basic or
fundamental ideas and how they relate to one another. Ideas that are truly
fundamental share a number of characteristics: They can be simply represented
as a diagram, picture, verbal statement, or formula (as in Einstein's formula for
relativity, $E = mc^2$); they can be represented in more than one sensory modality;
and they are applicable to a wide range of new problems. The operant conditioning principle of reinforcement is an example of a fundamental idea. It is simple
to understand and to state; it can be expressed as a simple verbal proposition or
illustrated on film; and it helps explain the learning of habits, verbal skills,
attitudes, motor skills, and behavior in home, work, play, and school settings.
Good versus evil is another fundamental idea that appears repeatedly in varied
forms in religion, literature, art, and philosophy. Bruner suggests that when
students are helped to grasp the structure of a field of study, they are more likely
to remember what they learn, comprehend principles that can be applied in a
variety of situations, and be prepared for mastering more complex knowledge.
As we will see a bit later in this chapter, understanding structure is critical to
effective problem solving and transfer of learning.

▶ Bruner: students
should learn structure
of a field of study

Spiral Curriculum   Closely related to the issue of understanding structure is the
question of when children are old enough to grasp the meaning of fundamental
ideas. Bruner's response, detailed in *The Relevance of Education,* is that if you
take into account the nature of children's thought, then "any subject can be taught
to any child in some honest form . . ." (1971, p. 52). Since this statement has been
widely quoted, and often misunderstood, a little elaboration is in order. Like
Piaget, Bruner believed that children of different ages represent the world to
themselves in fundamentally different ways. Toddlers and preschoolers think of
the world primarily in terms of the actions that can be performed on it. Bruner
calls this the *enactive* mode of representation. Throughout much of childhood,
ideas are represented primarily in terms of pictures or images. This form of
representation is called *iconic*. Finally, in late childhood and early adolescence,
ideas tend to be represented in terms of verbal propositions, mathematical
formulas, logical symbols, and the like (although the enactive and iconic modes
are equally available). Not surprisingly, Bruner terms this form of representation
symbolic. Bruner argues that even young children can grasp the essence of basic
ideas—albeit in a simplified, intuitive fashion—provided the presentation is
geared to the child's predominant mode of representation. In later years, as a
child's thinking becomes more mature, these same ideas can be reintroduced
with more complexity. Bruner refers to this practice of introducing something
early in simple form and then again later in more complex form as the **spiral
curriculum.**

▶ Spiral curriculum:
reteach same idea in
more complex form
over time

Discovery Learning   Another point stressed by Bruner is that too much school
learning takes the form of step-by-step study of verbal or numerical statements or
formulas that students can reproduce on cue but are unable to use outside the

classroom. When students are presented with such highly structured materials as linear computer-assisted instruction programs, Bruner argues, they become too dependent on others. Furthermore, they are likely to think of learning as something done only to earn a reward.

Instead of using techniques that feature preselected and prearranged materials, Bruner believes teachers should confront children with problems and help them seek solutions either independently or by engaging in group discussion. True learning, says Bruner, involves "figuring out how to use what you already know in order to go beyond what you already think" (1983, p. 183). Like Piaget, Bruner argues that conceptions that children arrive at on their own are usually more meaningful than those proposed by others, and that students do not need to be rewarded when they seek to make sense of things that puzzle them. Bruner maintains, in addition, that when children are given a substantial amount of practice in finding their own solutions to problems, they not only develop problem-solving skills but also acquire confidence in their own learning abilities as well as a propensity to function later in life as problem solvers. They learn *how* to learn *as* they learn.

This approach to education is sometimes called **discovery learning** (or *discovery teaching* if you prefer to look at it from the instructor's point of view). Like the idea mentioned earlier that any subject can be taught to any child, Bruner's position on discovery learning is often misunderstood. He does not suggest that students should discover every fact or principle or formula they may need to know. Discovery is simply too inefficient a process to be used that widely, and learning from others can be as meaningful as personal discovery. Rather, Bruner argues that certain types of outcomes—understanding the ways in which ideas connect with one another, the possibility of solving problems on our own, and how what we already know is relevant to what we are trying to learn—are the essence of education and can best be achieved through personal discovery.

▶ Discover how ideas relate to each other and to existing knowledge

As an example of this discovery approach, Bruner describes an incident in which a student is asked to explain the purpose of a compass (the instrument used to draw perfect circles). When the student refers to it as a steadying tool, the other children in the class quickly think of other devices that serve the same purpose, such as a camera tripod or a cane. Another example is Bruner's approach to teaching geography in the elementary grades. Instead of having a group of fifth-graders memorize a set of geography facts, he gave them blank outline maps that showed the location of rivers, lakes, mountains, valleys, plains, and so on. Their task was to figure out where the major cities, railways, and highways might be located. The students were not permitted to consult books or other maps; they had to figure out locations on their own by drawing on their prior knowledge and reasoning ability.

Evaluations of the Discovery Approach   Discovery methods have been evaluated most often in the area of science education. Programs like *Elementary Science Study, Science—A Process Approach* and *Science Curriculum Improvement Study* stress hands-on activities in which students must use reasoning strategies in order to solve various problems. Since students work in small groups, these activities provide numerous opportunities for discussion and argument. Research at the elementary, junior high, and high school levels has produced mostly positive findings (see, for example, Bredderman, 1982; Glasson, 1989). On average, students in activity-based science programs scored at the 70th percentile on tests of science processes whereas students in traditional science classes scored at the 50th percentile. Low-achieving students gained the most from activity-based programs. They outscored the typical student in the comparison class on process tests by 34 percentile ranks (Bredderman, 1982).

A Constructivist View of Meaningful Learning

Many of Bruner's ideas about meaningful learning and the discovery approach can be found in a contemporary view of learning that we first mentioned in Chapter 1—**constructivism.** To understand the nature of constructivism consider first the opposite perspective, a view of learning that might be called *objectivism.* The objectivist view basically holds that all knowledge exists outside and independent of people, that some people (experts and teachers, for example) possess knowledge that others (novices and students, for example) do not, and that knowledge can be transferred from one person to another with such fidelity that the student comes to know what the teacher knows (Bednar et al., 1991).

The constructivist view of learning holds that meaningful learning is the active creation of knowledge structures (for example, concepts, rules, hypotheses, associations) from personal experience. In other words, each learner builds a personal interpretation of the world from his or her experiences. Additions to, deletions from, or modifications of these interpretations come from the sharing of multiple perspectives (Bednar et al., 1991). The constructivist view also holds that the essence of one person's knowledge can never be *totally* transferred to another person because knowledge is the result of a personal interpretation of experience that is influenced by such factors as the learner's age, gender, race, ethnic background, and knowledge base. In transferring knowledge from one person to another, some aspects of it are invariably "lost in translation." A clear example of constructivism can be seen in the area of musical performance. The meaning of a composition (be it classical, jazz, or popular) is constructed by each performer from such factors as his or her knowledge of the composer's personality and motives, the era in which the composer lived, the circumstances surrounding the composer's life, the nature of the instrument or instruments for which the composition was written, and the nature of the music itself. Since performers assign different meanings to such knowledge, different (yet equally valid) interpretations of the same composition result. Think, for example, of the many different ways in which you have heard the *Star Spangled Banner* sung. Although listeners may prefer one version over another, there is no one "correct" way to sing this song. Accordingly, and as Bruner argued some thirty years ago, students need to be provided with the conditions that will allow them to construct their own interpretation of key information and experiences.

> ► Constructivist view: meaningful learning due to personal interpretation of ideas, experiences

Conditions That Foster Constructivism   The conditions that constructivists typically mention include a cognitive apprenticeship between student and teacher, the use of realistic problems and conditions, and an emphasis on multiple perspectives (Bednar et al., 1991). The notion of a cognitive apprenticeship was illustrated in Chapter 9 when we described the reciprocal teaching program of Palincsar and Brown (1984). Its main feature is that the teacher models a cognitive process that the students are to learn and then gradually turns responsibility for executing the process over to the students as they become more skilled.

The second condition is that the students be given learning tasks that are set in realistic contexts. A realistic context is one in which the student must solve a meaningful problem by using a variety of skills and information. The example we provided earlier of requiring fifth-graders to specify the location of cities, railways, and highways by thinking as a geographer would is an example of this condition. Another example can be seen in the social studies program that Bruner helped to develop. The program was titled *Man: A Course of Study,* and it is often referred to as the MACOS curriculum. Here is Bruner's brief description of MACOS: "The content of the course is man: his nature as a species, the forces that shaped and continue to shape his humanity. Three questions recur throughout: What is human about human beings? How did they get that way? How can they be made more so?" (1966, p. 74).

In seeking answers to these questions, pupils study subjects considered to be significant in human social behavior: social organization, the management of prolonged childhood, parenthood, group relationships, and the concept of culture. Techniques used in presenting the MACOS curriculum include the following:

> MACOS techniques: contrast, guessing, participation, awareness

1. *Emphasizing contrast* (for example, contrasting human beings with animals, the modern human being with the prehistoric one, the adult with the child)

2. *Stimulating informed guessing* (for example, asking students to hypothesize how Eskimos decide which breathing holes to stalk when hunting seals and then showing a film to illustrate how they actually *do* decide)

3. *Encouraging participation* (for example, arranging for pupils to function as anthropologists by making observations, collecting data, and formulating and testing hypotheses)

4. *Arousing awareness* (for example, having students analyze how they are attempting to solve problems)

Bruner's approach to teaching—implicit in this description of a unit on human beings—is summarized in the following statement:

> To instruct someone in [a] discipline is not a matter of getting him to commit results to mind. Rather, it is to teach him to participate in the process that makes possible the establishment of knowledge. We teach a subject not to produce little living libraries on the subject, but rather to get a student to think mathematically for himself, to consider matters as an historian does, to take part in the process of knowledge-getting. Knowing is a process, not a product. (1966, p. 72)

Constructivism aided by cognitive apprenticeship, realistic tasks, multiple perspectives

The third condition fostering constructivism is that students should view ideas and problems from multiple perspectives. The rationale for this condition is twofold: Most of life's problems are multifaceted, and the knowledge base of experts is a network of interrelated ideas. The problem of becoming an effective teacher is a good example of the need for multiple perspectives. As we mentioned in Chapter 1, being an effective teacher requires the mastery of many skills and disciplines so that classroom problems (such as why a particular student does not perform up to expectations) can be analyzed and attacked from several perspectives. We have tried to help you develop an integrated knowledge base by constantly making cross-references throughout the text. For example, the topic of learning strategies is discussed primarily in Chapter 9 but is also mentioned in Chapters 7, 11, and 13 because of its relationship to instructional objectives, students' values, and the demands of classroom tests, respectively.

An instructional technique that is particularly well-suited to developing, comparing, and understanding different points of view is the classroom discussion (Schiever, 1991). Because this format also allows students to deal with realistic problems and to exercise cognitive skills taught by the teacher, it is an excellent general-purpose method for helping students construct (or discover, depending on your preference) a meaningful knowledge base. The Suggestions for Teaching in Your Classroom that follow provide some guidelines you might find helpful if and when you decide to use classroom discussion as part of a discovery/constructivist approach.

Suggestions for Teaching in Your Classroom

USING A DISCOVERY/CONSTRUCTIVIST APPROACH TO MEANINGFUL LEARNING

1. Prepare students for participation in classroom discussion by describing, modeling, and providing opportunities for students to practice classroom discussion skills.

2. Arrange the learning situation so that students are exposed to different perspectives of a problem or issue.
   a. Ask students to discuss familiar topics or those that are matters of opinion.
   b. Provide necessary background information by asking all students to read all or part of a book, take notes on a lecture, or view a film.

3. Structure discussions by posing a specific question, by presenting a provocative issue, or by asking students to choose topics or subtopics.
   a. In some cases, encourage students to arrive at conclusions already reached by others.
   b. In other cases, present a controversial topic for which there is no single answer.

4. If time is limited and if only one topic is to be covered, ask students to form a circle and have an all-class discussion.
   a. Ask questions that stimulate students to apply, analyze, synthesize, and evaluate.
   b. Allow sufficient time for initial responses, and then probe for further information (if appropriate).
   c. When selecting students to recite, use techniques likely to sustain steady but nonthreatening attention. At the same time, guard against the temptation to call primarily on bright, articulate, assertive pupils.

5. If abundant time is available and if a controversial or subdivided topic is to be discussed, divide the class into groups of five or so, and arrange for all members in each group to have eye contact with every other group member.
   a. Have students choose to be members of a group, or divide the class by rows or through a counting-off procedure.
   b. Ask the students to move chairs or desks to form circles in different parts of the room.

6. Consider appointing or having each group elect a moderator and a recorder.

7. As the groups engage in discussion, observe benignly but silently. Intervene only if it seems necessary to keep the discussion proceeding in a constructive manner.
   a. In most cases, avoid answering questions or participating actively in the discussion.

8. Ask the groups to share conclusions after they have had ample time to discuss the topic.
   a. Allow time at the end of the period for a spokesperson from each group to report on conclusions on specific points. Perhaps list these on the board and invite comments from the class.
   b. Consider asking each group to write a brief outline of their conclusions or to prepare a project or demonstration, and then to combine these into a notebook or culminating event.

---

1. Prepare students for participation in classroom discussion by describing, modeling, and providing opportunities for students to practice classroom discussion skills.

Group discussion is a skill that is composed of several components. Accordingly, discussion sessions are more likely to be productive if you invoke the constructivist principle of a cognitive apprenticeship and gradually teach students how to play the roles of listener, participant, recorder, and moderator. In the suggestions that follow, we describe and illustrate the types of behaviors that lead to useful exchanges of ideas and to meaningful learning.

The first step in helping students become skilled at the art of discussion is to describe the conditions and behaviors that produce a satisfying outcome. For example, you might tell students that they are more likely to find classroom discussions stimulating and informative if they are open to new ideas, make eye contact with the speaker, maintain an attentive posture, organize their thoughts, speak clearly, take notes, allow speakers to express their thoughts without interruption, refrain from monopolizing the conversation, and refrain from ridiculing other students' ideas. Then, over the course of a week or two, with different groups of four or five students conduct several brief (about 15 minutes) discussions in which these behaviors are modeled. As the rest of the class observes, point out when students exhibit the desired behaviors and when they do not. As the students become more skilled at conducting class discussions, allow them to function more independently and for longer periods of time. After several weeks they should be prepared to participate effectively in a full-length discussion.

2. Arrange the learning situation so that students are exposed to different perspectives of a problem or issue.

Handbook Heading:
Ways to Arrange for
Discovery to Take
Place

This is the crux of the discovery approach and the constructivist view of learning. The basic idea is to *arrange* and *guide* things so that students discover, or construct, a personally meaningful conception of a problem or issue. In some cases, you may present a topic that is a matter of opinion or one that all students are sure to know something about. In other cases, you might structure the discussion by exposing all participants to the same background information.

a. Ask students to discuss familiar topics or those that are matters of opinion.

Examples

"What are some of the techniques that advertising agencies use in television commercials to try to persuade us to buy certain products?"

"What do you think is the best book you ever read, and why do you think so?"

b. Provide necessary background information by asking all students to read all or part of a book, take notes on a lecture, or view a film.

Examples

After the class has read *Great Expectations,* ask, "What do you think Dickens was trying to convey when he wrote this novel? Was he just trying to tell a good story, or was he also trying to get us to think about certain kinds of relationships between people?"

"After I explain some of the principles of electrical currents, I'm going to ask you to suggest rules for connecting batteries in series and in parallel. Then, we'll see how well your rules work."

When using discussion techniques of instruction it is important to establish a relaxed, nonthreatening classroom atmosphere.
(Frank Siteman/Stock, Boston, Inc.)

"This film shows how beavers live. After it's over, we'll discuss ways that beaver behavior is similar to human behavior."

3. Structure discussions by posing a specific question, by presenting a provocative issue, or by asking students to choose topics or subtopics.

As the examples just noted indicate, it is important to structure a discovery session by giving students something reasonably specific to discuss. Otherwise, they may simply engage in a disorganized and desultory bull session. If you are going to function as a teacher, you should organize experiences so that more learning takes place under your direction than would occur if you left children entirely to themselves. You might supply direction in the following ways.

a. In some cases, encourage students to arrive at conclusions already reached by others.

Bruner's MACOS materials illustrate this approach. Thousands of books provide detailed answers to the questions "What is human about human beings? How did they get that way? How can they be made more so?" But Bruner believes that answers mean more when they are constructed by the individual, not supplied ready-made by others. As you look over lesson plans, therefore, you might try to select some questions for students to answer by engaging in discussion, rather than by reading or listening to what others have already discovered. In searching for such topics, you might take into account the techniques described by Bruner.

Here is a list of those techniques, together with an example of each one. In your Handbook you might describe similar applications that you could use when you begin to teach. Keep in mind that gaining insight depends on appropriate previous experience.

Emphasize contrast. In a sixth-grade social studies unit, on cultural diversity, say, "When you watch this film on Mexico, look for customs and ways of living that differ from ours. Then we'll talk about what these differences are and also try to figure out why they may have developed."

Stimulate informed guessing. In a junior high unit on natural science, you might say, "Suppose we wanted to figure out some kind of system to classify trees so that we could later find information about particular types. What would be the best way to do it?" After students have developed their own classification scheme, show them schemes developed by specialists.

Encourage participation. In a high school political science class, illustrate the jury system by staging a mock trial. (Note that the use of a simulation satisfies the constructivist criterion of realistic tasks and contexts. For additional information on the use of simulations, see the Suggestions for Teaching in Your Classroom section in Chapter 11.)

Stimulate awareness. In a high school English class, ask the students to discuss how the author developed the plot.

b. In other cases, present a controversial topic for which there is no single answer.

Discussions might center on provocative issues about which there are differences of opinion. One caution here is to avoid topics (such as premarital sex or legalized abortion) that parents may not want discussed in school, either because they are convinced it is their prerogative to discuss them with their children or because they feel that students may be pressured to endorse your opinion because you assign grades. You should not avoid controversy, but neither should you go out of your way to agitate pupils and their parents.

Another caution is to avoid selecting issues that provoke more than they instruct. You may be tempted to present a highly controversial topic and then congratulate yourself at the end of the period if most students engaged in heated discussion. But if they simply argued vociferously about something that had nothing to do with the subject you are assigned to teach, you could not honestly claim to have arranged an instructive exchange of ideas. A final caution relates to a characteristic of formal thought described in Chapter 2: There may be a tendency for secondary school students to engage in unrestrained theorizing when they first experience the thrill of being able to deal with hypotheses and possibilities. Thus it may be necessary to remind some students to take into account realities when they discuss controversial issues involving tangled background circumstances or conflicts of interest.

Examples

In a junior high school science class, ask students to list arguments for and against attempting to alter the genetic code of human beings.

In a high school political science class, ask students to list arguments for and against democratic forms of government.

4. If time is limited and if only one topic is to be covered, ask students to form a circle and have an all-class discussion.

Handbook Heading:
Ways to Supervise Discovery Sessions

You may sometimes wish to have the entire class discuss a topic. Such discussions are most likely to be successful if all students have eye contact with each other. The simplest way to achieve this is to ask all students to form a circle. Next invite responses to the question you have posed. As students make remarks, serve more as a moderator than as a leader. Try to keep the discussion on the topic, but avoid directing it toward a specific predetermined end result. If one or more students tend to dominate the discussion, say something like, "Maria and Jack have given us their ideas. Now I'd like to hear from the rest of you." If an aggressive student attacks or belittles something said by a classmate, say something like, "It's good to *believe* in a point of view, but let's be friendly as we listen to other opinions. This is supposed to be a discussion, not an argument or a debate."

In some instances, whole-class discussions work beautifully. A contribution by one student will spark a related one by another, and almost everyone will follow what is said with interest. On other occasions, however, the outcome can be deadly, disorganized, or both. Sometimes the first thing said by the first student will annihilate both the topic and the discussion. (An opinionated young man may say, for example, "There's absolutely no point in talking about that question. We can't change anything, so why waste time talking about it?") At other times, your bright and enthusiastic question, "Well, what do you think about that?" will be followed by complete silence, which in turn will be followed by nervous shuffling, much gazing out the window, and the like. (Just in case that happens, you should always have some sort of back-up activity planned for discussion periods.) Factors that lead to successful or unsuccessful discussions are often idiosyncratic, but there are certain procedures you might follow to increase the likelihood of success.

a. Ask questions that stimulate students to apply, analyze, synthesize, and evaluate.

When you first structure a discussion session, but also when it is under way, take care to ask questions likely to elicit different points of view. If you ask students to supply information (for example, "When did the Civil War begin?"), the first correct response will lead to closure. You may end up asking a series of questions leading to brief answers—the equivalent of a program or a fill-in exam. M. D. Gall (1970) reviewed dozens of studies of classroom recitation sessions and found consistent evidence that up to 80 percent of all questions asked by teachers stressed facts and knowledge. In some situations, such as review sessions before an exam, asking a series of questions that test knowledge is logical and desirable. But when one intends to encourage pupils to construct personally meaningful interpretations of the issues or to develop skills as deductive thinkers, it is preferable to ask questions likely to tap higher levels of thinking.

Examples

"You just learned how to calculate the area of a circle. Think of as many different ways as you can of how you might be able to use that bit of knowledge if you were a do-it-yourself home owner." (Application)

"What are possible reasons the Civil War took place when it did? Try to think of as many different possible causes as you can, and I'll list them on the board." (Analysis)

"Last month we read a novel by Dickens; this month we read a play by Shakespeare. What are some similarities in the way each author developed the plot of the story?" (Synthesis)

"We just read five short poems by Emily Dickinson. I'd like you to tell me which one you like the best and then explain why you preferred it to the others. What qualities did your favorite poem have that the others did not have, at least not to the same extent?" (Evaluation)

b. Allow sufficient time for initial responses, and then probe for further information (if appropriate).

Mary Budd Rowe (1974) found that many teachers fail to allow enough time for pupils to respond to questions. She discovered that quite often instructors would wait only one second before repeating the question or calling on another student. When teachers were advised to wait at least three seconds after asking a question, student responses increased in frequency, length, and complexity. Further, students seemed more confident (as reflected by the way they spoke and the kinds of statements they made), and more class members were inclined to participate.

One possible explanation for improved student recitation when teachers wait longer for a response is that reflective thinkers have an opportunity to figure out what they want to say. But even impulsive thinkers probably welcome a few more seconds of thinking time. It seems logical to expect that snap answers would be more superficial than answers supplied after even a few seconds of reflection.

In addition to giving students ample time to make an initial response, you should encourage them to pursue an idea. If it seems appropriate, probe for further information or clarification of a point by asking pupils who give brief or incomplete answers to explain how or why they arrived at a conclusion or to supply additional comments.

Examples

"Well, Margie, I'm sure a gardener might sometimes need to figure the area of a circle, but can you give a more specific example? If you can't think of one right away, put up your hand as soon as you can describe a specific situation where it would help to know the area of a circular patch of lawn or soil."

"Yes, John, it seems certain that differences of opinion about slavery had a lot to do with the Civil War. Let's pursue that a bit further. What were some of the economic and agricultural differences between the North and South that influenced feelings about slavery?"

c. When selecting students to recite, use techniques likely to sustain steady but nonthreatening attention. At the same time, guard against the temptation to call primarily on bright, articulate, assertive pupils.

In addition to asking questions during class discussions, you will need to decide who will recite. The way you moderate student contributions may not only determine how successful the discussion will be; it may also influence how pupils feel about themselves and each other. Jacob Kounin (1970) has pointed out that when a teacher first names a student and then asks a question, the rest of the class may tend to turn their attention to other things. The same tendency to "tune out" may occur if a teacher follows a set pattern of calling on students (for example, by going around a circle). To keep all the students on their toes, therefore, you might ask questions first and then, in an unpredictable sequence, call on those who volunteer to recite, frequently switching from one part of the room to another. As you look around the room before selecting a volunteer, remember Skinner's criticism that a few students may make all the discoveries. Guard against the temptation to call primarily on students you expect to give good or provocative answers. Repeatedly ignoring pupils who may be a bit inarticulate or unimaginative may cause them and their classmates to conclude that you think they are incompetent. If that occurs, those who are never given opportunities to express opinions or volunteer information are likely to lose interest in participating in discussions. They may totally ignore what is taking place.

5. If abundant time is available and if a controversial or subdivided topic is to be discussed, divide the class into groups of five or so, and arrange for all members in each group to have eye contact with every other group member.

Handbook Heading: Techniques for Arranging Small-Group Discussion

A major limitation of any kind of discussion is that only one person can talk at a time. This difficulty can be reduced by dividing the class into smaller groups before asking them to exchange ideas. A group of about five seems to work best. If only two or three pupils are interacting with each other, the exchange of ideas may be limited. If there are more than five, not all members will be able to contribute at frequent intervals.

a. Have students choose to be members of a group, or divide the class by rows or through a counting-off procedure.

One way to form groups, particularly if students have suggested subtopics, is to ask them to list in order their first three subject preferences. (Mention at the start that it is unlikely that all the students in the class will get their first choice.) Then you can divide by referring to the lists. One advantage of this technique is that students embark on a discovery session with the feeling that they have chosen to do so. Another advantage is that you can arrange group membership to a certain extent, since students won't know how many of their classmates listed a particular topic as first choice. You might break up potentially disruptive pairings (for example, two boys who often engage in wrestling matches, two girls who get the giggles whenever they are together, a high school couple who are passionately in love with each other) and also spread around talkative, creative, and thoughtful students.

Another way to divide the class, particularly if all groups are to discuss the same topic, is to ask all pupils in a row to form a group. Or have the class count off from one to five. After all students have counted off, ask all "ones" to move to one part of the room, "twos" to another part, and so on. There are often advantages to having different assortments of students discuss different topics. You can accomplish this goal by asking students to count off in different ways each time you divide the class.

b. Ask the students to move chairs or desks to form circles in different parts of the room.

Once the groups are formed, assign each one a particular part of the room. If the students do not form a circle of their own accord, urge them to arrange themselves so that they are all facing each other.

6. Consider appointing or having each group elect a moderator and a recorder.

Two of the most common problems of group discussion, regardless of the number of participants, are that one person will do most of the talking and that the members will stray from the original topic. When the class is divided into groups, both difficulties can be minimized if a moderator and a recorder are appointed or elected. Perhaps the simplest way to select them is to have students draw straws. Sometimes elections or appointments lead to hurt feelings, suspicion of favoritism, and the like.

The moderator should be instructed to keep the discussion on the topic and to make sure that everyone has a chance to speak. If the moderator seems too bossy, suggest that he or she ask the members of the group to vote on whether they are wandering away from the point. To make sure that everyone in the group has a chance to speak up and also to shut off a verbose or pushy talker, you might wait twenty minutes or so after the groups form and then say, "I think it is time for moderators to make sure that those who haven't said anything so far be given the chance to contribute ideas."

The role of the recorder is to list major points that the members of the group agree are important. If you do not ask a group to keep some sort of record of what is said or prepare some sort of answer to the question under discussion, the interchange of ideas is likely to dissolve into a bull session.

The aim of the constructivist approach is to produce some relatively specific insight in the minds of most, if not all, class members—in other words, to impel students to reorganize their perceptions in some fairly definite way so that they grasp new relationships and understand different perspectives. Therefore, completely open-ended discussions that trail off without any kind of conclusion are usually undesirable—unless, of course, the students are dealing with personal opinions and have been exposed to a variety of stimulating ideas.

7. As the groups engage in discussion, observe benignly but silently. Intervene only if it seems necessary to keep the discussion proceeding in a constructive manner.

Generally speaking, it seems preferable for the instructor to avoid participating in small-group discussion. Because of your roles as class leader, expert, and evaluator, whatever you say is likely to be accepted as the "right" answer. Accordingly, you may wish either to observe from your desk (perhaps while you correct exams or prepare a lesson) or to wander around the room, being careful not to hover around any group for a long time.

When students are invited to engage in small-group discussions, it may be necessary for the teacher to occasionally remind some groups to explore the assigned topic, not to engage in social chit-chat. (Elizabeth Crews)

a. In most cases, avoid answering questions or participating actively in the discussion.

After arranging many discovery sessions, Lawrence Shulman (1970) concluded that if a teacher answers a question posed by a member of a group, the ensuing interchange is likely to take the form of an "ask the expert" session. If you can keep a discussion going by answering a question, it is logical to do so, but for the most part it seems better to urge students to find their own answers. You should also try to control the tendency to lecture. If groups find that doing their own thinking is an effort, they may attempt to entice you into doing it for them. They may smile and act interested when you make a remark and shape your behavior to the point that you supply most of the information and ideas.

8. Ask the groups to share conclusions after they have had ample time to discuss the topic.

a. Allow time at the end of the period for a spokesperson from each group to report on conclusions on specific points. Perhaps list these on the board and invite comments from the class.

When all groups have been discussing the same topic, you may wish to pool ideas contributed by separate groups. One way to do this is to stand at the board and ask the recorder from group one to give a point from his or her list, then the recorder from group two to do the same, and so forth. Stress that each spokesperson should mention points not already noted, and continue inviting comments in order until all points are listed. Then use the final list as the basis for a class discussion.

b. Consider asking each group to write a brief outline of their conclusions or to prepare a project or demonstration, and then to combine these into a notebook or culminating event.

After each group has worked on its own project, arrange for all members of the class to learn about what others have discovered. In some cases, you might ask each group to prepare a written, illustrated report to be incorporated into a homemade textbook. Then a copy could be reproduced for each member of the class. In other cases, you might ask each group to prepare a display, demonstration, or skit to be presented on a particular day or days. If appropriate, you might treat the culmination as a gala occasion, complete with programs and refreshments.

Ausubel: The Importance of Meaningful Reception Learning

Like Jerome Bruner, David Ausubel stresses the importance of linking new information to existing knowledge schemes as a requirement for meaningful

Good expository teaching encourages interactive learning in which students participate in the learning process.
(Gary Bublitz/Dembinsky Photo Assoc.)

learning. In fact, on the flyleaf of *Educational Psychology: A Cognitive View* (1978), Ausubel states, "If I had to reduce all of educational psychology to just one principle, I would say this: the most important single factor influencing learning is what the learner already knows. Ascertain this and teach him accordingly." But while Bruner emphasizes the importance of discovery in meaningful learning, Ausubel emphasizes the importance of good-quality expository teaching. According to Ausubel, good-quality expository teaching involves presenting to the learner what is to be learned in more or less final form. In other words, the information (in a lecture or reading passage, for example) should be organized and stated in such a way that it can be easily related to students' existing knowledge schemes. Most of the behavioral learning techniques described in Chapter 8 are examples of good expository teaching. In programmed instruction or computer-assisted instruction, for instance, the material to be learned is organized and presented to the learner in a predetermined step-by-step fashion that allows for easy assimilation into existing knowledge schemes.

▶ Meaningful reception learning: integrate new ideas into existing knowledge schemes

This ease of assimilation is the goal of Ausubel's expository teaching, and he called that goal **meaningful reception learning** (that is, the integration of new ideas into existing knowledge schemes). Not all reception learning is meaningful, however. Rote, or nonmeaningful, learning occurs when students are presented with a mass of information for which few relationships are provided. In the study of history, for example, students often memorize the dates of certain events (such as the American Civil War), what happened during those events (battles between opposing armies, for example), and the roles of major figures (such as Abraham Lincoln, Jefferson Davis, Ulysses S. Grant, and Robert E. Lee). Ausubel maintains that while such material has meaningful components, it will not be learned as a meaningful whole so long as it remains unconnected to related knowledge schemes that the student already possesses. Hence, the components are memorized in more or less verbatim fashion and tend to be quickly forgotten. A reading passage or lecture that is designed to produce meaningful reception learning, on the other hand, would explain how these events were related to political, social, and economic factors as well as to something the student may already know (such as the circumstances surrounding a different civil war or a disagreement among family members).

When relationships are ignored, reception learning can be nonmeaningful

Having made a distinction between meaningful learning and rote learning and between reception learning and discovery learning, Ausubel points out some false beliefs regarding each type of learning. He notes that, contrary to arguments offered by some theorists, reception learning is not invariably rote learning and discovery learning is not necessarily meaningful. It is possible—and definitely desirable—for a student working through a program or studying a chapter in a text to search for meaning. In some forms of discovery learning, on the other hand, particularly where students are given a series of similar problems to solve in quick succession, they may unthinkingly apply a formula as they search for solutions.

Meaningful learning depends on nature of task, learner's set

Whether a student engages in meaningful rather than rote learning, Ausubel suggests, is a function of two factors: the nature of the learning task and the learner's intention, or learning set. A poorly written program *or* repetitive discovery projects may virtually force a student to resort to rote memorization or unthinking application of a formula. And many students may use a rote memorization approach to try to learn logically organized programs or to solve excellent discovery problems simply because they approach the task with the attitude that memorization is the only way to learn.

To understand why students adopt a rote or meaningful learning set, you will need to be aware of what they already know about a topic. This argument of Ausubel is similar to the information processing principle that any individual's perception of a stimulus will be a function of background experiences. It is also similar to Piaget's observation that every child's cognitive structure is unique. All of these views emphasize that teachers need to try to take into account a particular learner's thinking processes at a particular time and in a particular situation.

Advance organizer helps relate new ideas to existing schemes

To help students adopt a meaningful rather than rote learning set, Ausubel recommends that teachers use **advance organizers.** As the name suggests, advance organizers are introductory materials that provide an organizing structure to help students relate new information to existing knowledge schemes. Because no two students are likely to have identical cognitive structures, Ausubel maintains that advance organizers need to be more abstract, more general, and more inclusive than the material to be learned. Advance organizers usually are relatively brief passages written in familiar terms, although schematic diagrams and illustrations can also be used. Studies of advance organizers show that they have their strongest positive effects on measures of comprehension and problem solving rather than on measures of retention (Mayer, 1979).

Every theory has its potential limitations, and Ausubel's is no exception. The main weakness of meaningful reception learning is that the learner is largely responsible for establishing a meaningful learning set. Thus, it is possible for students to believe they have achieved a genuine understanding of something when in fact they have attained only a vague and superficial level of understanding. Students need to recognize those occasions when they do not understand the structure of a subject and be willing to do something about it. Students who have been trained to think strategically, as described in Chapter 8, are least likely to mistake superficial or rote learning for meaningful learning.

In summary, both Bruner and Ausubel agree that schools should promote meaningful learning. Bruner believes there is a legitimate place for good-quality texts and lectures just as Ausubel sees value in learning through discovery. The major difference between them and their advocates centers on how much in-school time students should devote to acquiring information created by others versus how much time they should devote to gaining experience solving problems. Bruner argues that children who gain considerable experience solving problems in school will be better equipped to solve problems outside of the classroom. And Ausubel argues (along with Skinner) that teachers are better off spending class time presenting subject matter as efficiently as possible. If problem-solving skills are deemed important, they should be taught systematically.

Regardless of which approach you favor, you will probably want to spend some time teaching your students how to be good problem solvers. Accordingly, this chapter next turns to a discussion of the nature of problem solving.

THE NATURE OF PROBLEM SOLVING

As with most of the topics covered in this book, an extensive amount of theorizing and research on problem solving has been conducted over the years. We will focus our discussion on the types of problems that students are typically required to deal with, the cognitive processes that play a central role in problem solving, and various approaches to teaching problem solving in the classroom.

Let's begin by asking what we mean by the terms *problem* and *problem solving*. According to Ellen Gagné, "a problem is said to exist when one has a goal and has not yet identified a means for reaching that goal" (1985, p. 138). **Problem solving,** then, is the identification and application of knowledge and skills that result in goal attainment. Gagné's definition encompasses a wide range of problem types, but there are three types that students frequently encounter both in school and out.

Three Common Types of Problems

▶ Well-structured
problems: clearly
stated, known solu-
tion procedures,
known evaluation
standards

In the first category are the well-structured problems of mathematics and science—the type of problems that students from kindergarten through junior high are typically required to solve. **Well-structured problems** are clearly formulated, can be solved by recalling and applying a specific procedure (called an *algorithm*), and result in a solution that can be evaluated against a well-known, agreed-upon standard (Frederiksen, 1984). Examples of well-structured problems are

$$5 + 8 = \underline{\qquad}, \quad 732 - 485 = \underline{\qquad}, \quad \text{and} \quad 8 + 3x = 40 - 5x$$

▶ Ill-structured prob-
lems: vaguely stated,
unclear solution pro-
cedures, vague evalu-
ation standards

In the second category are the ill-structured problems often encountered in everyday life and in disciplines like economics or psychology. **Ill-structured problems** are more complex, provide few cues pointing to solution procedures, and have less definite criteria for determining when the problem has been solved (Frederiksen, 1984). Examples of ill-structured problems are how to identify and reward good teachers, how to improve access for physically handicapped persons to public buildings and facilities, and how to increase voter turnout for primary and general elections.

▶ Issues: ill-structured
problems that arouse
strong feelings

The third category includes problems that are also ill structured but differ from the examples just mentioned in two respects. First, these problems tend to divide people into opposing camps because of the emotions they arouse. Second, the primary goal, at least initially, is not to determine a course of action but to identify the most reasonable position. These problems are often referred to as **issues** (Ruggiero, 1988). Examples of issues are capital punishment, gun control, and nondenominational prayer in classrooms. Beginning with the freshman year in high school, students usually receive more opportunities to deal with ill-structured problems and issues.

Helping Students Become Good Problem Solvers

Despite the differences that exist among well-structured problems, ill-structured problems, and issues, recent theory and research suggest that good problem solvers employ the same general approach when solving one or another of these problem types (see, for example, Bransford & Stein, 1984; E. Gagné, 1985; Gick, 1986; Krulik & Rudnick, 1988; Nickerson, Perkins & Smith, 1985; Ruggiero, 1988). When used to solve ill-structured problems or to analyze issues, this approach consists of five steps or processes (although the solution of well-structured problems may call for the implementation of only steps 2, 4, and 5):

1. Realize that a problem exists.
2. Understand the nature of the problem.
3. Compile relevant information.
4. Formulate and carry out a solution.
5. Evaluate the solution.

We will discuss each of these steps in the next few pages, along with some specific techniques that you can use to help your students become good problem solvers.

Step 1: Realize That a Problem Exists   Most people assume that if a problem is worth solving they won't have to seek it out—that it will make itself known. Like most assumptions, this one is only partly true. Well-structured problems are often thrust upon us by teachers, in the form of in-class exercises or homework, or by supervisors at work. Ill-structured problems and issues, on the other hand, often remain "hidden" from most people. It is a characteristic of good problem solvers that they are more sensitive to the existence of problems than most of their peers (Okagaki & Sternberg, 1990).

> Problem finding depends on curiosity, dissatisfaction with status quo

The keys to problem recognition, or *problem finding* as it is sometimes called, are curiosity and dissatisfaction. You need to question why a rule, procedure, or product is the way it is, or to feel frustrated or irritated because something does not work as well as it might. The organization known as Mothers Against Drunk Driving, for example, was begun by a woman who, because her daughter was killed in a traffic accident by a drunk driver, was dissatisfied with current, ineffective laws. This organization has been instrumental in getting state legislatures to pass laws against drunk driving that mandate more severe penalties. As another example, John Bransford and Barry Stein (1984) mention a business that, by taking a critical look at its record-keeping procedure, was able to eliminate the generation of 120 tons of paper per year.

Problem finding does not come readily to most people, possibly because schools emphasize solving well-structured problems and possibly because most people have a natural tendency to assume that things work as well as they can. Like any cognitive process, however, problem recognition can improve with instruction and practice. Students can be sensitized in a number of ways to the absence or flaws and shortcomings of products, procedures, rules, or whatever. We will make some specific suggestions about improving problem recognition and the other problem-solving processes a bit later in the Suggestions for Teaching in Your Classroom.

Step 2: Understand the Nature of the Problem   The second step in the problem-solving process is perhaps the most critical. The problem solver has to construct an *optimal* representation or understanding of the nature of a problem or issue. The preceding sentence stresses the word *optimal* for two reasons. First, most problems can be expressed in a number of ways. Written problems, for example, can be recast as pictures, equations, graphs, charts, or diagrams. Second, because the way we represent the problem determines the amount and type of solution-relevant information we recall from long-term memory, some representations are better than others. For obvious reasons, problem-solving researchers often refer to this process as **problem representation** or **problem framing.**

The most critical step in problem solving is determining and understanding the nature of the problem; some students need assistance with this task. (Martha Cooper)

▶ Problem framing depends on knowledge of subject matter, familiarity with problem types

To achieve an optimal understanding of a problem, an individual needs two things: a high degree of knowledge of the subject matter (facts, concepts, and principles) on which the problem is based, and familiarity with that particular type of problem. This background will allow the person to recognize important elements (words, phrases, and numbers) in the problem statement and patterns of relationships among the problem elements. This recognition, in turn, will activate one or more solution-relevant schemes from long-term memory. It is just this level of knowledge of subject matter and problem types that distinguishes the high-quality problem representations of the expert problem solver from the low-quality representations of the novice. Experts typically represent problems in terms of one or more basic patterns or underlying principles, whereas novices focus on limited or superficial surface features of problems.

To give you a clearer idea of the nature and power of an optimal problem representation, consider the following situation. When novices are given a set of physics problems to solve, they sort them into categories on the basis of some noticeable feature. For example, they group together all problems that involve the use of an inclined plane, or all the ones that involve the use of pulleys, or all those that involve friction; and then they search their memory for previously learned information. The drawback to this approach is that while two or three problems may involve the use of an inclined plane, their solutions may depend on the application of different laws of physics. Experts, on the other hand, draw on their extensive and well-organized knowledge base to represent groups of problems according to a common underlying principle such as conservation of energy or Newton's third law (Frederiksen, 1984; Gick, 1986).

As another example, consider the following apparent contradiction about American education: Over the last century, dozens of school reforms have been implemented; yet, in the view of many, little seems to have changed. According to Larry Cuban (1988), this contradiction can be resolved by understanding the difference between first-order changes and second-order changes. First-order changes seek to make existing structures and practices more efficient and effective. Second-order changes, by contrast, involve new goals, structures, and practices. Most of the second-order changes that altered the face of American education—the self-contained classroom, the graded curriculum, frequent testing, the fifty-minute period, teacher-led instruction, and the reliance on textbooks, for example—occurred roughly between 1850 and 1920. Since then, most changes have been of the first-order variety. New types of textbooks, new courses, new tests, a longer school year, and special programs were all designed to improve the quality of the existing structure. Reforms that were intended to produce second-order changes—reforms like nongraded schools, open classrooms, team teaching, and programmed instruction—either were altered to fit the existing structure or were discarded. Thus, although schools did change in this century, they also remained essentially the same, since the changes occurred at the margins. As Cuban points out, "defining problems carefully at the outset is far more important than generating clever solutions to ill-defined problems" (p. 343).

We have tried to show you in this section that an important aspect of the problem-solving process is the ability to activate relevant schemes (organized collections of facts, concepts, principles, and procedures) from long-term memory when they are needed. The more relevant and powerful the activated scheme, the more likely an effective problem solution will be achieved. But as many observers of education have pointed out, acquiring this ability is often easier said than done. John Bransford has argued that standard educational practices produce knowledge that is *inert*. That is, it can be accessed only under conditions that closely mimic the original learning context (Bransford et al., 1986). Richard Feynman, a Nobel Prize–winning physicist, made the same observation in describing how his classmates at the Massachusetts Institute of Technology failed to recognize the application of a previously learned mathematical formula: "They didn't put two and two together. They didn't even know what they 'knew.' I don't know what's the matter with people: they don't learn by understanding; they learn by some other way—by rote, or something. Their knowledge is so fragile!" (1985, p. 36).

| Inert knowledge due to learning isolated facts under limited conditions

To overcome this limitation of inert and fragile knowledge, teachers need to present subject matter in a highly organized fashion, and students need to learn more about the various conditions under which their knowledge applies. We have tried to achieve the same goals with our Suggestions for Teaching in Your Classroom sections and Handbook Headings feature.

Allow students ample time to gather information and share insights as they work toward a solution of a problem.
(Tony Savino/The Image Works, Inc.)

Step 3: Compile Relevant Information   For well-structured problems that are relatively simple and familiar (such as arithmetic drill problems), this step in the problem-solving process occurs simultaneously with problem representation. In the process of defining a problem, we very quickly and easily recall from long-term memory all the information that is needed to achieve a solution. As problems and issues become more complex, however, we run into two difficulties: The amount of information relevant to the solution becomes too great to keep track of mentally, and there is an increasing chance that we may not possess all the relevant information. As a result, we are forced to compile what we know in the form of lists, tables, pictures, graphs, and diagrams, and so on, and to seek additional information from other sources.

The key to using yourself as an information source is the ability to accurately retrieve from long-term memory information that will aid in the solution of the problem. We need to think back over what we have learned in other somewhat similar situations, make a list of some other form of representation of those ideas, and make a judgment as to how helpful that knowledge might be. Techniques for ensuring accurate and reliable recall were discussed in Chapter 8.

In addition to relying on our own knowledge and experience to solve problems, we can draw on the knowledge and experience of friends, colleagues, and experts. According to Vincent Ruggiero, "Investigating other people's views calls for little talking and a lot of careful listening. We do well, in such cases, to ask questions rather than make statements" (1988, p. 39). The main purpose of soliciting the views of others about solutions to problems and positions on issues is to identify the reasons and evidence those people offer in support of their positions. This skill of asking questions and analyzing responses is quite useful in debates and classroom discussions of controversial issues.

Step 4: Formulate and Carry Out a Solution   When you feel you understand the nature of a problem or issue and possess sufficient relevant information, you are ready to attempt a solution. The first step is to consider which of several alternative approaches is likely to be most effective. The literature on problem solving mentions quite a few solution strategies. We will discuss five that we think are particularly useful.

> Studying worked examples is an effective solution strategy

Study worked examples. This approach may strike you as so obvious that it hardly merits attention. But it is worth mentioning for two reasons. First, obvious solution strategies are the ones that are most often overlooked. Second, it is a very effective solution strategy. Mary Gick (1986) cites almost a dozen studies that showed improvements in solving a variety of problems as a result of studying similar problems whose solutions were worked out. The beneficial effect is thought to be due to the learner's acquisition of a general problem schema.

> Solve simpler version of problem first, then transfer process to harder problem

Work on a simpler version of the problem. This is another common and very effective approach. Geometry offers a particularly clear example of working on a simpler problem. If you are having difficulty solving a problem of solid geometry (which involves three dimensions), work out a similar problem in plane geometry (two dimensions) and then apply the solution to the three-dimensional example (Nickerson, Perkins & Smith, 1985; Polya, 1957). Architects and engineers employ this approach when they construct scaled-down models of bridges, buildings, experimental aircraft, and the like. Scientists do the same thing when they create laboratory simulations of real-world phenomena.

> Break complex problems into manageable parts

Break the problem into parts. The key to this approach is to make sure you break the problem into manageable parts. Whether or not you can do this will depend largely on how much subject matter knowledge you have. The more you know about the domain from which the problem comes, the easier it is to know how to break a problem into logical, easy-to-handle parts.

At least two benefits result from breaking a problem into parts: Doing so reduces the amount of information you have to keep in short-term memory to a manageable level, and the method used to solve one part of the problem can often be used to solve another part. Bransford and Stein (1984) use the following example to illustrate how this approach works.

Problem: What day follows the day before yesterday if two days from now will be Sunday?

1. What is today if two days from now will be Sunday? (Friday)

2. If today is Friday, what is the day before yesterday? (Wednesday)

3. What day follows Wednesday? (Thursday)

Work backward. This is a particularly good solution strategy to use whenever the goal is clear but the beginning state is not. Bransford and Stein (1984) offer the following example. Suppose you arranged to meet someone at a restaurant across town at noon. When should you leave your office to be sure of arriving on time? By working backward from your destination and arrival time (it takes about ten minutes to find a parking spot and walk to the restaurant; it takes about thirty minutes to drive to the area where you would park; it takes about five minutes to walk from your office to your car), you would more quickly and easily determine when to leave your office (about 11:15) than if you had worked the problem forward.

> Work backward when goal is clear but beginning state is not

Solve an analogous problem. If you are having difficulty solving a current problem, possibly because your knowledge of the subject matter is incomplete, it may be useful to think of a similar problem about a subject in which you are more knowledgeable. Solve the analogous problem, and then use the same method to solve the current problem. In essence, this is a way of making the unfamiliar familiar.

Although solving analogous problems is a very powerful solution strategy, it can be difficult to employ, especially for novices. In our earlier discussion of understanding the problem, we made the point that novices represent problems on the basis of superficial features whereas experts operate from knowledge of underlying concepts and principles. The same is true of using analogies. Novices are more likely than experts to use superficial analogies (Gick, 1986).

> Analogous problems must be very similar to target problem

A potential way around this problem is to provide students with good analogies. This approach does work, but in a limited way. For students to recognize the usefulness of the analogy, it must mimic the target problem in both structure and surface details. The evidence for this conclusion comes largely from a series of studies by Mary Gick and Keith Holyoak (for example, Gick & Holyoak, 1980, 1983; Holyoak & Koh, 1987).

In the initial experiments, college students read a story about a general who wanted to capture a fortress. If the general used his entire army, the attack would succeed. However, many of the surrounding villages would be destroyed during the attack because of mines planted along the roads leading to the fortress. This outcome was unacceptable. The general's solution was to divide his army into smaller groups that could slip through the minefields, send each group along a different road, and have them converge on the fortress at the same time. The students were then given a second story to read that concluded with a problem for them to solve. The second story was about a patient with an inoperable stomach tumor. The patient's doctor could destroy the tumor with a beam of high intensity x-rays, but healthy surrounding tissue would be destroyed in the process. Although a beam of lower intensity would not damage healthy tissue, neither would it destroy the tumor. The problem posed to the students was how to use radiation to destroy the tumor without destroying the healthy tissue at the same time. Only 30 percent of the students realized that just as the general solved his problem by dividing his forces and having them converge on the fortress simultaneously, the doctor could destroy the tumor by using several beams of low-intensity radiation aimed from different directions.

In the later study (Holyoak & Koh, 1987) students first read a story about a physics lab that used an expensive light bulb. The filament, enclosed in a permanently sealed bulb, was broken. It could be repaired with a high-intensity laser beam. This solution was unacceptable, however, because a high-intensity beam would also shatter the glass. The problem was solved by using several lower-intensity beams aimed at the filament. As before, students then read the inoperable-tumor story. Because the details of the light bulb and tumor stories were very similar, the outcome in this case was dramatically different. Almost 70 percent of these students were able to solve the tumor problem. This figure was increased to 75 percent when the subjects were told that the first story could help them solve the problem in the second story.

Step 5: Evaluate the Solution   The last step in the problem-solving process is to evaluate the adequacy of the solution. For relatively simple well-structured problems where the emphasis is on producing a correct response, two levels of evaluation are available to the problem solver. The first is to ask whether, given the problem statement, the answer makes sense. For example, if the problem reads 75 **x** 5 = ? and the response is 80, a little voice inside the problem solver's head should say that the answer cannot possibly be right. This signal should prompt a reevaluation of the way the problem was represented and the solution procedure that was used (for example, "I misread the times sign as a plus sign and added when I should have multiplied"). The second level of evaluation is to use an alternative algorithm (a fixed procedure used to solve a problem) to check the accuracy of the solution. This is necessary because making an error in carrying out an algorithm can produce an incorrect response that is "in the ballpark." For example, a common error in multiple-column subtraction problems is to subtract a smaller digit from a larger one regardless of whether the small number is in the minuend (top row) or the subtrahend (bottom row) (Mayer, 1987), as in

> Evaluate solutions to well-structured problems by estimating or checking

$$
\begin{array}{r}
522 \\
- \ 418 \\
\hline
116.
\end{array}
$$

Since this answer is off by only 12 units, it "looks right." The flaw can be discovered, however, by adding the answer to the subtrahend to produce the minuend.

The evaluation of solutions to ill-structured problems is likely to be more complicated and time consuming for at least two reasons. First, the evaluation should occur both before and after the solution is implemented. Although many flaws and omissions can be identified and corrected beforehand, some will slip through. There is much to be learned by observing the effects of our solutions. Second, because these problems are complex, often involving a dozen or

Students need many opportunities to practice problem-solving skills. (Tom Ives)

more variables, some sort of systematic framework should guide the evaluation. Vincent Ruggiero suggests a four-step procedure (1988, pp. 44–46). The first step is to ask and answer a set of basic questions. Imagine, for example, that you have proposed a classroom incentive system (a token economy, perhaps) to enhance student motivation. You might ask the following questions:

How exactly is it to be done, step by step?

By whom is it to be done?

When is it to be done (according to what timetable)?

Where is it to be done?

Who will finance it?

What tools or materials, if any, are to be used?

From what source will they be obtained?

How and by whom will they be transported?

Where will they be stored?

What special conditions, if any, will be required for the solution to be carried out?

The second step is to identify imperfections and complications. Is this idea, for example, safe, convenient, efficient, economical, compatible with existing policies and practices? The third step is to anticipate possible negative reactions from other people (such as your parents and your school principal). The last step is to devise improvements.

This discussion of problem solving has made clear that learning to solve problems means learning to find problems, represent them, draw on prior knowledge, formulate solutions, and evaluate solutions. In addition, students need opportunities to apply these processes to well-structured problems, ill-structured problems, and the analysis of issues. The Suggestions for Teaching in Your Classroom section that follows later in the chapter contains guidelines and examples that will help you improve the problem-solving skills of your students.

Mid-Chapter Review

The Nature of Meaningful Learning

Jerome Bruner urged teachers to stress the structure of a field of study (how fundamental ideas relate to each other) because of the positive effect a grasp of structure has on understanding and problem solving.

Because children represent knowledge in fundamentally different ways (that is, in the enactive, iconic, and symbolic modes) as they progress from childhood through adolescence, Bruner suggested the use of a spiral curriculum to foster meaningful learning. This type of curriculum reintroduces concepts in increasingly complex form as students move through the enactive, iconic, and symbolic modes of thought.

Bruner urged teachers to encourage students to discover how ideas relate to each other and to what they already know, since this is a very meaningful form of learning.

The constructivist view of learning holds that meaningful learning occurs when people make personal interpretations of ideas and experiences.

David Ausubel urged teachers to promote meaningful reception learning through lectures, handouts, textbooks, and the like, that students can easily relate to their existing knowledge schemes.

To help students relate new ideas to what they already know, Ausubel suggests that teachers provide advance organizers.

Problem Solving

Students should learn how to solve three general types of problems: well-structured problems (such as those in mathematics and science), ill-structured problems (such as those in politics, economics, and psychology), and issues (problems that tend to divide people into opposing camps because of the strong emotions they produce).

A general model of problem solving has five steps: Realize that a problem exists; understand the nature of the problem; compile relevant information; formulate and carry out a solution; evaluate the solution.

Suggestions for Teaching in Your Classroom

TEACHING PROBLEM-SOLVING TECHNIQUES

1. Develop a problem-solving orientation in students.
2. Teach students how to identify problems.
3. Teach students how to represent problems.
4. Teach students how to compile relevant information.
5. Teach several methods for formulating problem solutions.
6. Teach students the skills of evaluation.

---

1. Develop a problem-solving orientation in students.

Academic work (of which problem solving is a part) is often characterized as being a solitary, effortful, and "cold" activity. These characteristics are hardly likely to excite large numbers of people. Yet that is precisely where instruction in problem-solving techniques must start if it is to be successful. You must convince students that becoming skilled problem solvers is worth the time, the effort, the confusion, and the frustration that they will inevitably experience.

▶ Students are poor problem solvers because of too much TV, lack of reinforcement, lack of critical attitude

Contemporary students are seen as being poor problem solvers for one or more of the following reasons: Years of watching television have conditioned students to be passive observers with short attention spans; since the problem-solving process is rarely taught in schools or required at home, students rarely get rewarded for their problem-solving efforts; many students have come to believe that all opinions and sources of knowledge are equally valid; and many students accord feelings the same status as factual evidence or reasoned conclusions.

To help students develop a positive attitude toward learning and using problem-solving skills, Vincent Ruggiero (1988) suggests that teachers develop and reinforce the following dispositions in students:

Interest in the source of their own attitudes, beliefs, and values

Curiosity about their mental processes

Confidence in their ability

Willingness to make mistakes

Sensitivity to problems and issues

Positive attitude toward novelty

Interest in widening their experience

Respect for and willingness to use intuition when appropriate

Desire to reason well and base judgments on evidence

Willingness to subject ideas to scrutiny

Willingness to entertain opposing views

Curiosity about relationships among ideas

Passion for truth

Healthy attitude toward argumentation

2. Teach students how to identify problems.

As we pointed out earlier, identification is an often-overlooked part of the problem-solving process. Since the notion of finding problems is likely to strike students as an unusual activity, you may want to introduce this skill in gradual steps. One way to start is to have students list different ways in which problems can be identified. Typical responses are to scan newspaper and magazine articles, observe customer and employee behavior in a store, observe traffic patterns in the local area, and interview local residents, including, for instance, teachers, business owners, police, clergy, or government officials. A next step is to have students carry out their suggested activities in order to gain an understanding of the status quo and to find out how people identify problems. They may learn, for example, that a principal periodically has lunch with a teacher in order to learn of conditions that decrease the teacher's effectiveness. Finally, have students suggest improvements that could help solve problems they have identified.

3. Teach students how to represent problems.

The ability to construct a good representation of a problem is based on a command of the subject matter surrounding the problem and familiarity with the particular type of problem. As the work of Jerome Bruner and David Ausubel points out, students need to acquire a genuine understanding of many of the associations, discriminations, concepts, and rules of a discipline before they can effectively solve problems in that subject-matter area. Too often, pupils are taught to state principles on cue, but they reveal by further responses that they do not understand what they are saying. The classic illustration of this all too common trap was given by William James in his *Talks to Teachers:*

> A friend of mine, visiting a school, was asked to examine a young class in geography. Glancing at the book, she said: "Suppose you should dig a hole in the ground, hundreds of feet deep, how should you find it at the bottom—warmer or colder than on top?" None of the class replying, the teacher said: "I'm sure they know, but I think you don't ask the question quite rightly. Let me try." So, taking the book, she asked: "In what condition is the interior of the globe?" and received the immediate answer from half the class at once: "The interior of the globe is in a condition of igneous fusion." (1899, p. 150)

Comprehension of subject matter critical to problem solving

If these students had genuinely understood concepts and principles regarding the composition of the earth, instead of having simply memorized meaningless phrases, they would have been able to answer the original question.

Different problem types lend themselves to particular forms of representation. Verbal reasoning problems that are based on relationships among categories, for example, can usually be represented by a set of intersecting circles known as a Venn diagram.

Example Problem

The government wants to contact all druggists, all gun store owners, and all parents in a town. Based on the following statistics, how many people must be contacted?

Druggists   10

Gun store owners   5

Parents   3,000

Druggists who own gun stores   0

Druggists who are parents   7

Gun store owners who are parents   3

Solution Using Venn Diagram

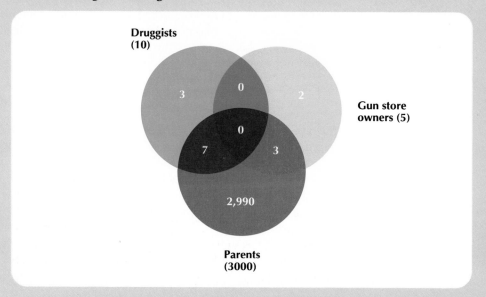

The total number of people who must be contacted is 2990 + 7 + 3 + 3 + 2 = 3,005 (adapted from Whimbey & Lochhead, 1986, p. 102).[1]

Verbal reasoning problems that describe transactions can take the form of a flow diagram.

Example Problem

Sally loaned $7.00 to Betty. But Sally borrowed $15.00 from Estella and $32.00 from Joan. Moreover, Joan owes $3.00 to Estella and $7.00 to Betty. One day the

---

1. Excerpts in this section adapted from *Problem Solving and Comprehension,* Fourth Edition, p. 272 by A. Whimbey and J. Lochhead, 1986. Hillside, New Jersey: Lawrence Erlbaum Associates, Inc., Publishers. Copyright 1986 by Lawrence Erlbaum Associates. Reprinted by permission of the publisher and authors.

women got together at Betty's house to straighten out their accounts. Which woman left with $18.00 more than she came with?

Solution Using Flow Diagram

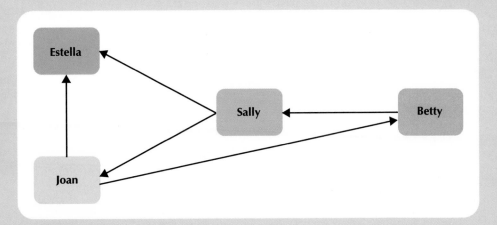

From the diagram, it is clear that Estella left with $18.00 more than she came with (adapted from Whimbey & Lochhead, 1986, p. 126).

4. Teach students how to compile relevant information.

Good problem solvers start with themselves when compiling information to solve a problem or evidence to support a position on an issue. They recognize the importance of recalling earlier-learned information (metacognitive knowledge) and are adept at doing so (cognitive skill). Poor problem solvers, by contrast, lack metacognitive knowledge, cognitive skills, or both. If their deficiency is metacognitive, they make little or no effort to recall solution-relevant memories, even when the information was recently learned, because they do not understand the importance of searching long-term memory for potentially useful knowledge. Even if a student poor in problem solving recognizes the value of searching long-term memory for relevant information, he or she may still be handicapped because of inadequate encoding and retrieval skills.

To minimize any metacognitive deficiency, make sure your instruction in problem-solving methods emphasizes the importance of retrieving and using previously learned knowledge. To minimize retrieval problems, make sure *you* recall and implement the Suggestions for Teaching in Your Classroom that we offered in the preceding chapter.

If a student does not possess all the relevant information needed to work out a solution or to analyze an issue, you will have to guide him or her toward individuals and sources that can help. In referring students to individuals, it is best to select people who are judged to be reasonably knowledgeable about the subject, are careful thinkers, and are willing to share their ideas (Ruggiero, 1988).

As an example, consider the issue of whether certain books (such as the novels *Catcher in the Rye* by J. D. Salinger and *Tom Sawyer* by Mark Twain) should be banned from a school's reading list. In interviewing an interested person, students might ask questions like the following, because they allow some insight into the individual's reasoning process and the evidence used to support his or her position:

What general effects do you think characters in novels who rebel against adult authority have on a reader's behavior?

Are certain groups of people, such as junior high and high school students, likely to be influenced by the motives and actions of such characters? Why do you think so?

Does a ban on certain books violate the author's right to free speech?

Does a book ban violate the principle of academic freedom? Why?

Is it the proper role of a school board to prevent or discourage students from exposure to certain ideas during school hours?

If a reasonably informed person is not available, recognized authorities can often be interviewed by phone. If a student chooses this tactic, Ruggiero suggests calling or writing in advance for an appointment, preparing questions in advance, and asking permission to tape-record the interview.

Obviously, in addition to or in lieu of personal interviews, students can find substantial information in a good library. For example, you can steer them toward books by recognized authorities, research findings, court cases, and interviews with prominent individuals in periodicals.

5. Teach several methods for formulating problem solutions.

Earlier we mentioned five methods for formulating a problem solution: study worked examples, work on a simpler version, break the problem into parts, work backward, and solve an analogous problem. Because of space limitations, we cannot present examples of each method. However, at the end of the chapter, under Resources for Further Investigation, we recommend several recently published books on problem solving that, taken together, provide numerous examples of each method. We also present the following example of a worked problem that breaks the problem into parts and incorporates working backward.

Example Problem

Paul owns 4 more than one-half as many books as Pete; Paul owns 32 books. How many books does Pete own?

Solution

Step 1. A diagram should be used to clarify the relationship between Paul's books and Pete's books. Starting with Pete's books, we take one-half of them.

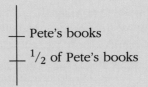

If we now add 4 books, we have Paul's books (which the problem says is 32 books).

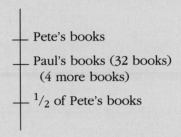

Step 2. To solve the problem, work backward. The diagram shows that if 4 books are taken from Paul he will have exactly one-half as many as Pete.

$$\text{Paul's books} - 4 = {}^1/_2 \text{ of Pete's books}$$
$$32 - 4 = 28 = {}^1/_2 \text{ of Pete's books}$$

Step 3. One half the number of books owned by Pete is 28. So Pete owns twice this number.

$$\text{Pete's books} = 2 \times 28 = 56$$

(adapted from Whimbey & Lochhead, 1986, p. 272)

6. Teach students the skills of evaluation.

Solutions to well-structured problems are usually evaluated by applying an estimating or checking routine. Such procedures can be found in any good mathematics text. The evaluation of solutions to ill-structured problems and analyses of issues, however, is more complex and is less frequently taught. Ruggiero (1988) lists the following twelve habits and skills as contributing to the ability to evaluate complex solutions and positions:

1. Open-mindedness about opposing points of view.
2. Selecting proper criteria of evaluation. Violations of this skill abound. A current example is the use of standardized achievement test scores to evaluate the quality of classroom instruction.
3. Understanding the essence of an argument. To foster this skill, Ruggiero recommends that students be taught how to write a *précis,* which is a concise summary of the original passage.
4. Evaluating the reliability of sources.

5. Proper interpretation of factual data (for example, recognizing that an increase in a state's income tax rate from 4 to 6 percent is an increase not of 2 percent but of 50 percent).

6. Testing the credibility of hypotheses. On the basis of existing data, hypotheses can range from highly improbable to highly probable.

7. Making important distinctions (for instance, between preference and judgment, emotion and content, appearance and reality).

8. Recognizing unstated assumptions (for example, that because two events occur close together in time, one causes the other; that what is clear to us will be clear to others; that if the majority believes something, it must be true).

9. Detecting fallacies (for instance, stereotyping, faulty analogies, straw-man arguments, or overgeneralizing).

10. Evaluating arguments.

11. Making sound judgments.

12. Recognizing when evidence is insufficient.

TRANSFER OF LEARNING

Throughout Chapters 8, 9, and 10, we have indicated that classroom instruction should be arranged in such a way that students independently apply the knowledge and problem-solving skills they learn in school to similar but new situations. This capability is typically valued very highly by educators. Referred to as **transfer of learning,** it is the essence of being an autonomous learner and problem solver. In this section, we will examine the nature of transfer and discuss ways in which you can help to bring it about.

The Nature and Significance of Transfer of Learning

The Theory of Identical Elements During the early 1900s, it was common practice for high school students and colleges to require that students take such subjects as Latin, Greek, and geometry. Because they were considered difficult topics to learn, mastery of them was expected to improve a student's ability to memorize, think, and reason. These enhanced abilities were then expected to facilitate the learning of less difficult subjects. The rationale behind this practice was that the human mind, much like any muscle in the body, could be exercised and made stronger. A strong mind, then, would learn things that a weak mind would not. This practice, known as the *doctrine of formal discipline,* constituted an early (and incorrect) explanation of transfer. In 1901, Edward L. Thorndike and Robert S. Woodworth proposed an alternative explanation of how transfer occurs. They argued that the degree to which knowledge and skills acquired in learning one task can help someone learn another task depends on how similar

▶ Early view of transfer based on degree of similarity between two tasks

Ideally, what is learned in the classroom should serve the learner in the future. (Bob Daemmrich/ Tony Stone Worldwide)

the two tasks are (assuming the learner recognizes the similarities). The greater the degree of similarity between the tasks' stimulus and response elements (as in riding a bicycle and riding a motorcycle), the greater the amount of transfer. This idea became known as the **theory of identical elements.**

Positive, Negative, and Zero Transfer   In time, though, other psychologists (among them Osgood, 1949; Ellis, 1965) identified different types of transfer and the conditions under which each type prevailed. A useful distinction was made between positive transfer, negative transfer, and zero transfer (Wingfield, 1979).

> Positive transfer: previous learning makes later learning easier

The discussion up to this point has been alluding to **positive transfer,** defined as a situation in which prior learning aids subsequent learning. According to Thorndike's analysis, positive transfer occurs when a new learning task calls for essentially the same response that was made to a similar, earlier learned task. The accomplished accordion player, for instance, probably will become a proficient pianist faster than someone who knows how to play the drums or someone who plays no musical instrument at all, all other things being equal. Similarly, the person who is fluent in French is likely to have an easier time learning Spanish than someone who speaks no foreign language.

> Negative transfer: previous learning interferes with later learning

Negative transfer is defined as a situation in which prior learning interferes with subsequent learning. It occurs when two tasks are highly similar but require different responses. A tennis player learning how to play racquetball, for example, may encounter problems at first because of a tendency to swing the racquetball racket as if it were a tennis racket. Primary grade children often experience negative transfer when they encounter words that are spelled alike but pronounced differently (as in "I will *read* this story now since I *read* that story last week").

Zero transfer is defined as a situation where prior learning has no effect on new learning. It can be expected when two tasks have different stimuli and

Students demonstrate positive specific transfer of capabilities when they apply skills acquired in one laboratory science, such as physics, to another laboratory science, such as chemistry. (Bob Daemmrich)

different responses. Learning to conjugate Latin verbs, for example, is not likely to have any effect on learning how to find the area of a rectangle.

Specific and General Transfer   The preceding description of positive transfer, while useful, is somewhat limiting because it is unclear whether the transfer from one task to another is due to specific similarities or to general or nonspecific similarities. Psychologists (as described by Ellis, 1978, pp. 249–250) decide whether transfer is due to specific or general factors by setting up learning tasks such as the following for three different but equivalent groups of learners:

	Initial Task	*Transfer Task*
Group 1	Learn French	Learn Spanish
Group 2	Learn Chinese	Learn Spanish
Group 3		Learn Spanish

> Specific transfer due to specific similarities between two tasks

> General transfer due to use of same cognitive strategies

If on a Spanish test Group 1 scores higher than Group 2, the difference is attributed to **specific transfer** of similarities between French and Spanish (such as vocabulary, verb conjugations, and sentence structure). On the other hand, if Groups 1 and 2 score the same but both outscore Group 3, the difference is attributed to nonspecific or **general transfer** of similarities between the two tasks, since Chinese shares no apparent specific characteristics with French or Spanish. In this case, it is possible that learners use cognitive strategies—such as imagery, verbal elaboration, and mnemonic devices—when learning a foreign language and that these transfer to the learning of other foreign languages. Such nonspecific transfer effects have also been demonstrated for other classroom tasks, like problem solving and prose learning (Ellis, 1978; Royer, 1979).

On the opening pages of his widely acclaimed book, *The Process of Education* (1960), Jerome Bruner made the following observations about specific and general transfer:

> "Learning should not only take us somewhere; it should allow us later to go further more easily . . . it should serve us in the future."

> One way that learning may have future value "is through its specific applicability to tasks that are highly similar to those we originally learned."

> A second way learning can serve us in the future "consists of learning not a skill, but a general idea, which can then be used as a basis for recognizing subsequent problems as special cases of the idea originally mastered."

> The second type of transfer is "dependent on the mastery of the structure of the subject matter," but it also involves "the development of an attitude toward learning and inquiry, toward guessing and hunches, toward the possibility of solving problems on one's own."

Contemporary Views of Specific and General Transfer

In the years since Bruner made these statements, psychologists have become more knowledgeable about the factors that produce specific and general transfer. Gavriel Salomon and David N. Perkins (1989), for example, offer a current treatment of these two forms of transfer under the labels **low-road transfer** and **high-road transfer,** respectively.

Low-Road Transfer   Low-road transfer refers to a situation where a previously learned skill or idea is almost automatically retrieved from memory and applied to a highly similar current task. For example, the student who has mastered the skill of two-column addition and correctly completes three-column and four-column addition problems with no prompting or instruction is exhibiting low-road transfer. Another example would be the student who learns how to tune up car engines in an auto shop class and then almost effortlessly and automatically carries out the same task as an employee of an auto-repair business.

Two conditions need to be present in order for low-road transfer to occur. One condition is that students have to be given ample opportunities to practice using the target skill. The second condition is that the practice has to occur with different materials and in different settings. The more varied the practice, the greater the range of tasks to which the skill can be applied. If, for example, you want students to be good notetakers, give them instruction and ample practice at taking notes from their biology, health, and English textbooks. Once they become accomplished notetakers in these subjects, they will likely apply this skill to other subjects in an almost automatic fashion. The auto mechanic who has learned to change the spark plugs in a Chrysler, a Toyota, and a Mercedes Benz should be able to do the same job as efficiently in a Ford, a Buick, or a Nissan. In essence,

Low-road transfer: previously learned skill automatically applied to similar current task

what we are describing is the behavioral principle of generalization. Since the transfer task is similar in one or more respects to the practice task, this type of transfer is also called *near transfer.*

In order to understand how people transfer prior knowledge and skills to new situations that look rather different from the original task, we need to explore the nature of high-road transfer.

▶ High-road transfer:
formulate rule from
one task and apply to
related task

High-Road Transfer   High-road transfer involves the conscious, controlled, somewhat effortful formulation of an "abstraction" (that is, a rule, a schema, a strategy, or an analogy) that allows a connection to be made between two tasks. For example, an individual who learns to set aside a certain number of hours every day in order to complete homework assignments and study for upcoming exams formulates the principle that the most efficient way to accomplish a task is to break it down into small pieces and work at each piece according to a set schedule. As an adult, the individual uses this principle to successfully deal with complex tasks at work and at home. As another example, imagine a student who, after much observation and thought, has finally developed a good sense of what school is and how one is supposed to behave there. In other words, this student has developed a "school schema." Such a schema would probably be made up of actors (teachers and students), objects (desks, chalkboards, books, pencils), and events (reading, listening, writing, talking, drawing). Since this is an idealized abstraction, actual classrooms may contain fewer or greater numbers of these characteristics in varying proportions. Even so, with this schema a student could walk into most any instructional setting (another school classroom, a training seminar, or a press briefing, for example) and readily understand what was going on, why it was going on, and how one should behave. Of course, with repeated applications of schemata, rules, strategies, and the like, the behaviors become less conscious and more automatic. What was once a reflection of high-road transfer becomes low-road transfer.

Salomon and Perkins refer to this deliberate, conscious, effortful formulating of a general principle or schema that can be applied to a variety of different-looking but fundamentally similar tasks as *mindful abstraction.* The *mindful* part of the phrase indicates that the abstraction must be thought about and fully understood for high-road transfer to occur. That is, people must be aware of what they are doing and why they are doing it. Recall our earlier discussion in this chapter (p. 447) of inert knowledge and Richard Feynman's observations of how his classmates at the Massachusetts Institute of Technology failed to recognize the application of a previously learned mathematical formula because it was initially learned for use only in that course.

Teaching for Low-Road and High-Road Transfer   To enhance both low-road and high-road transfer, Salomon and Perkins offer four suggestions:

▶ Low-road and
high-road transfer
produced by varied
practice at applying
skills, rules, memory
retrieval cues

1. Provide students with multiple opportunities for varied practice.

2. Give students opportunities to solve problems that are similar to those they will eventually have to solve.

3. Teach students how to formulate a general rule, strategy, or schema that can be used in the future with a variety of similar problems.

4. Give students cues that will allow them to retrieve from memory earlier learned information that can be used to make current learning easier.

If there is one thing we hope you have learned from this discussion of transfer of learning, it is this: *If you want transfer, teach for transfer.* As you can see, students have to be carefully prepared and coached to use the information and skills they learn in school. If you expect transfer, be it low-road or high-road, to occur on its own, you will be disappointed most of the time.

Applying Technology to Teaching

USING TECHNOLOGY TO IMPROVE PROBLEM-SOLVING SKILLS

A variety of well-designed computer programs exist that can help students acquire and refine one or more problem-solving skills. The 1991 edition of *Only the Best* (Neill & Neill, 1990) and the 1987 edition of *The Educational Software Selector* (EPIE Institute, 1986) describe several programs that you may want to consider using. We will briefly describe a few of them here to give you an idea of their goals and characteristics.

In *Blockers and Finders,* students attempt to move small animals called finders along a path on a 4 x 4 grid toward a particular destination. This seemingly straightforward task is complicated by hidden blockers, such as arrows and detours, that force the student to take a different path. The skill this program attempts to develop is inference. By using available information, the student can determine the best path to take. This program has different levels of difficulty that allow it to be used from the first grade on.

Solve It! is designed to foster the critical-thinking skills of students in grades four through twelve. Students read about a mystery and then probe a database for clues that will lead to a solution. The clues, which take the form of logic statements (for example, A and B, A or B, A but not B), allow students to eliminate suspects. Each game (there are six) can be played at three levels of difficulty.

Snooper Troops 1—G.P. Ghost is similar in nature to *Solve It!*. The Kim family has moved into an old mansion in which strange things happen. The student plays the role of detective and tries to figure out who is scaring the Kim family and why. Players question suspects, search houses for clues, and use something called the Snoopnet computer to gather information. This program can be used in grades three through twelve. An almost identical program for students in grades five through twelve, *Snooper Troops 2—Disappearing Dolphin,* is also available.

The Factory: Strategies in Problem Solving is a simulation that focuses on such problem-solving techniques as working backward, analyzing a process, and determining sequences. Intended for students in grades four through twelve, this program requires students to create products (geometric forms) on a simulated assembly line of their own design.

Comp-U-Solve contains a set of puzzles that have to be solved with the fewest possible moves. Intended for students in grades seven through twelve, this program provides instruction in logic and problem solving.

Resources for Further Investigation

Bruner on Education

Toward a Theory of Instruction (1966) is Jerome Bruner's most concise and application-oriented book on teaching. Chapter 1, "Patterns of Growth," and Chapter 3, "Notes on a Theory of Instruction," provide general descriptions of Bruner's view on teaching and learning. Chapter 4 describes how the MACOS materials were used to structure a discovery approach.

To learn more about Bruner, his ideas, and the circumstances that led him to study such topics as perception, concept formation, problem solving, cognitive development, and discovery learning, read *In Search of Mind: Essays in Autobiography* (1983).

Ausubel's Meaningful Reception Learning

David P. Ausubel provides detailed explanations of meaningful reception learning in *The Psychology of Meaningful Verbal Learning* (1963), *School Learning: An Introduction to Educational Psychology* (1969, Chapter 3), and *Educational Psychology: A Cognitive View* (2d ed., 1978, Chapters 2 and 4).

Problem-Solving Processes

In *Teaching Thinking Across the Curriculum* (1988), Vincent Ryan Ruggiero describes a model for solving problems and analyzing issues, discusses teaching objectives and methods, identifies obstacles to students' cognitive development, details assignments that can be used in a variety of courses, demonstrates how instructors can design additional course-specific thinking assignments, and offers guidelines for developing a thinking skills program. Many of the same topics are covered by Barry K. Beyer in *Practical Strategies for the Teaching of Thinking* (1988).

Diane F. Halpern describes several aspects of thinking and problem solving in *Thought and Knowledge: An Introduction to Critical Thinking* (2d ed., 1989).

Chapter 4, for example, describes the development of various reasoning skills (such as syllogistic, linear, and if-then skills) as well as reasoning in everyday contexts. Chapter 7 explains and illustrates with concrete examples how understanding probability helps us avoid fallacies in reasoning. And Chapter 9 details the development of problem-solving skills.

In Chapters 1, 2, and 3 of *Problem Solving: A Handbook for Elementary School Teachers* (1988), S. Krulik and J. A. Rudnick discuss the nature of problem solving, describe the nature and use of heuristics (general approaches to problem solving), and provide seventeen steps that teachers should follow when teaching problem solving. The remainder of the book provides a collection of strategy games (such as tic-tac-toe variations, blocking-strategy games, capture-strategy games), a collection of 178 nonroutine problems, a bibliography of problem-solving resources, ditto masters for selected problems, and ditto masters for strategy-game boards. Many of these games are simple enough for second- and third-graders.

In *Practical Strategies for the Teaching of Thinking* (1987), Barry K. Beyer describes techniques, principles, and strategies for teaching thinking in the classroom. Chapters 1 and 2 present a model of thinking and describe various thinking operations that teachers could elect to teach. Chapters 3–7 describe how to teach these operations in the context of almost any subject and at almost any grade level. Chapter 7 discusses how to teach thinking skills in such a way as to raise the likelihood that students will exhibit low-road and high-road transfer. In *Developing a Thinking Skills Program* (1988), Barry Beyer describes how to develop a thinking skills program. This book provides at least partial answers to such questions as What should we teach? Why? Where? How? and How will we know if we are successful?

SUMMARY

1. Jerome Bruner believes that meaningful learning occurs when students grasp the structure of a field of study (the nature of fundamental ideas and how they relate to one another) and when they discover these relationships themselves.

2. Bruner believes that fundamental ideas can be understood by children of any school age, provided the ideas are presented in a manner that is consistent with the child's current mode of mental representation (enactive, iconic, or symbolic). As children progress from one mode to the next, the same ideas can be presented a second or third time with increasing complexity and completeness, a technique referred to as the spiral curriculum.

3. The constructivist view holds that meaningful learning occurs when people make personal interpretations of ideas and experience.

4. Three conditions that support constructivism are a cognitive apprenticeship between teacher and student, the use of realistic learning tasks, and exposure to multiple perspectives.

5. David Ausubel believes that meaningful learning occurs when students receive information organized so that it can be easily related to their current knowledge schemes. Students also need to adopt a meaningful learning set.

6. To help students adopt a meaningful learning set, Ausubel suggests that teachers construct and provide advance organizers. An advance organizer is introductory material that is more ab-

stract, more general, and more inclusive than the material that is to be learned. It is intended to provide an organizing structure that helps students relate new ideas to existing knowledge schemes.

7. The types of problems that students most often come into contact with are well-structured problems, ill-structured problems, and issues. Well-structured problems are clearly stated and can be solved by applying previously learned procedures, and their solutions can be accurately evaluated. Ill-structured problems are often vaguely stated; they cannot always be solved by applying previously learned procedures, and their solutions cannot always be evaluated against clear and widely accepted criteria. Issues are like ill-structured problems, but with two differences: They arouse strong emotions that tend to divide people into opposing camps, and they require that one determine the most reasonable position to take before working out a solution.

8. A general problem-solving model is composed of five steps: Realize that a problem exists; understand the nature of the problem; compile relevant information; formulate and carry out a solution; evaluate the solution.

9. The keys to realizing that a problem exists are to be curious about why things are the way they are and to be dissatisfied with the status quo.

10. Understanding the nature of a problem, also known as problem representation or problem framing, requires a high level of knowledge about the subject matter surrounding the problem and familiarity with the particular type of problem.

11. Relevant information can be compiled by searching long-term memory, retrieving solution-relevant information, and representing that information as lists, tables, pictures, graphs, diagrams, and so on. In addition, friends, colleagues, and experts can be tapped for information.

12. Solutions can be formulated by studying worked examples, working on a simpler version of the problem, breaking the problem into parts, working backward, or solving an analogous problem.

13. Solutions for well-structured problems can be evaluated by estimating or checking. Solutions

for ill-structured problems can be evaluated by answering a set of basic questions that deal with who, what, where, when, why, and how; by identifying imperfections and complications; by anticipating possible negative reactions; and by devising improvements.

14. Transfer of learning occurs when the learning of new information or skills is influenced by previously learned information or skills.

15. An early view of transfer was based on Edward Thorndike and Robert Woodworth's theory of identical elements. This theory holds that transfer of learning is a function of how many elements two tasks have in common. The greater the similarity, the greater the degree of transfer.

16. Positive transfer occurs when a new learning task is similar to a previously learned task and calls for a similar response. Negative transfer occurs when a new learning task is similar to a previously learned task but calls for a different response. Zero transfer occurs when previously learned information or skills are so dissimilar to new information or skills that they have no effect on how quickly the latter will be learned.

17. Positive transfer that is due to identifiable similarities between an earlier learned task and a current one is referred to as specific transfer. Positive transfer that is due to the formulation, use, and carryover of cognitive strategies from one task to another is referred to as general transfer.

18. A current view of specific transfer is called low-road transfer. It is produced by giving students many opportunities to practice a skill in different settings and with different materials.

19. A current view of general transfer is called high-road transfer. It is produced by teaching students how to formulate a general rule, strategy, or schema that can be used in the future with a variety of problems that are fundamentally similar to the original.

KEY TERMS

structure *(426)*
spiral curriculum *(426)*
discovery learning *(427)*
constructivism *(428)*

DISCUSSION QUESTIONS

1. To foster meaningful learning (and guide students away from rote learning), Jerome Bruner has argued, teachers should help students discover how the basic ideas of a subject relate to each other and to what students already know. Can you recall a class where the instructor made use of discovery techniques? What did the instructor do? How did you react? Was the learning outcome as meaningful as Bruner suggests? How could you tell? How might you use similar techniques?

2. David Ausubel has argued that to steer students toward meaningful learning, teachers should provide information that has been organized so that it can be easily related to students' existing knowledge schemes. Can you recall one or more instances when a lecture or text was organized this way? How did you react? Was the learning outcome as meaningful as Ausubel suggests? How could you tell? How might you use similar techniques?

3. An important part of Ausubel's theory of meaningful reception learning is the establishment of a meaningful learning set. What should you do to establish such a set in yourself? How can you help your students do the same?

4. Critics of American education argue that contemporary students are poor problem solvers because they receive little systematic instruction in problem-solving processes. How would you rate the quantity and quality of the instruction you received in problem solving? In terms of the five steps discussed in this chapter, which ones were you taught? What can you do to ensure that your students become good problem solvers?

5. Many psychologists believe that the best way to determine if something has been meaningfully learned is to see whether the individual uses it to make future learning and problem solving easier (positive transfer of learning). Can you describe some personal instances of negative transfer? Can you explain these personal examples in terms of the behavioral and cognitive views of transfer presented in this chapter?

6. Educational psychologists who have studied transfer have said to teachers that if they want transfer, they should teach for transfer. What do you think this statement means?

Chapter 11

HUMANISTIC APPROACHES TO EDUCATION

AN EVALUATION OF HUMANISTIC EDUCATION

▶ Humanistic education emerged as a reaction against prevailing approaches

▶ Enthusiasm for humanistic education rises and falls as circumstances change

▶ Humanistic education made up of loosely related assumptions and techniques

▶ When appropriate, stress affective along with cognitive learning

▶ Preferable to be a helpful teacher rather than a friend

▶ Values clarification not likely to change students' habits or lives

SUGGESTIONS FOR TEACHING IN YOUR CLASSROOM

▶ Cardinal principle of humanistic education: give pupils choices

▶ Cardinal principle of communication: talk to situation, not to personality

▶ Encourage value development by taking advantage of object lessons

At the beginning of Chapter 8, we presented a brief preview of these chapters on learning, pointing out that three interpretations of learning would be discussed: behavioral theories, information processing theory and other cognitive theories, and humanistic approaches to education. These different approaches to learning derive from differences in basic assumptions, approaches to research, and interpretations of data. Behavioral theories, as you know, are based on observations of the ways in which overt behavior is influenced by forces in the external environment. Information processing and other

Enthusiasts for humanistic education argue that behavioral and cognitive psychologists have completely ignored the importance of emotions and feelings in school situations. (Gale Zucker)

cognitive theories, by contrast, are based on speculations about what goes on in the minds of students when they encode, store, and retrieve information, and solve problems. Finally, advocates of **humanistic education** are interested in how the affective (emotional and interpersonal) aspects of behavior influence learning.

One reason for studying learning from different perspectives is that as a teacher you will be interested in helping your students achieve diverse objectives in the cognitive, affective, and psychomotor domains, and to do so, you will want to use a variety of instructional techniques. Quite often you will ask your students to study individually as they read text and complete specific assignments. At other times you will want them to engage in class discussion or prepare group or individual projects. You will want to help them improve their efficiency as information processors. Finally, you will want them to respond to you and to schooling in positive ways and to develop positive feelings about themselves as individuals and students.

In sum, classroom learning is too complex a behavior to be fully understood from one point of view. It should be obvious by now that such concepts as reinforcement, feedback, shaping, modeling, encoding, retrieval from memory, analyzing, and planning complement one another even though they represent different perspectives. This chapter should be seen in the same light. Establishing an atmosphere that invites meaningful learning, cognitive growth, and a positive attitude toward self and others is as relevant to behavioral theory as it is to information processing and other cognitive theories.

To introduce the discussion of humanistic psychology, we will present a brief outline of the professional development and basic observations of three "elder statesmen" of this approach. Then we will outline other conceptions of humanistic education.

The three individuals who have had noteworthy impact on the emergence of humanistic psychology are Abraham H. Maslow, Carl R. Rogers, and Arthur Combs.

ARGUMENTS PROPOSED BY THE "ELDER STATESMEN" OF HUMANISTIC PSYCHOLOGY

Maslow: Let Children Grow

Maslow earned his Ph.D. in a psychology department that supported the behaviorist position. After he graduated, however, he came into contact with Gestalt psychologists, prepared for a career as a psychoanalyst, and became interested in anthropology. As a result of these various influences, he came to the conclusion that American psychologists who endorsed the behaviorist position had become so preoccupied with overt behavior and objectivity that they were ignoring some of the most important aspects of human existence. At the same time, Maslow became convinced that a strict Freudian view of behavior, which led to the conclusion that human beings desperately strive to maintain control of themselves, also had limitations, primarily because much of it was based on the behavior of neurotic individuals. When he observed the behavior of especially well-adjusted persons—or *self-actualizers,* as he called them—he concluded that healthy children *seek* fulfilling experiences. As an alternative to the behavioristic and psychoanalytic interpretations of behavior, Maslow proposed *third force* psychology.

In Chapter 15 of *Toward a Psychology of Being* (2d ed., 1968), Maslow describes forty-three basic propositions that summarize his views. Some of the most significant of these propositions are as follows: Each individual is born with an essential inner nature. This inner nature is shaped by experiences and by unconscious thoughts and feelings, but it is not *dominated* by such forces. Individuals control much of their own behavior. Children should be allowed to make many choices about their own development. Parents and teachers play a significant role in preparing children to make wise choices by satisfying their physiological, safety, love, belonging, and esteem needs, but they should do this by helping and letting children grow, not by attempting to shape or control the way they grow. (A more detailed outline of Maslow's view is presented in Chapter 12 in the discussion of motivation.)

▶ Maslow: teachers should help and let children grow and learn

Rogers: Learner-Centered Education

Carl R. Rogers had experiences quite similar to those of Maslow, and he came to similar conclusions. Rogers began his career as a psychotherapist who used psychoanalytic techniques. Eventually, he reached a conclusion identical to Maslow's: The psychoanalytic view sometimes made troubled human beings appear to be helpless individuals who needed the more or less constant help of psychotherapists to cope with their problems. Over a period of years, Rogers developed a new approach to psychotherapy. He called it *client-centered* (or *nondirective*) therapy, to stress the fact that the client, rather than the therapist, should be the central figure. (Or, as the term *nondirective* indicates, the therapist was not to tell the patient what was wrong and what should be done about it.) This view of therapy is a departure from psychoanalysis, in which the analyst is the central figure who makes interpretations and offers prescriptions. It is also based on rejection of the strict behaviorist view, since it assumes that the client will learn how to control his or her own behavior (and not merely be shaped by experiences).

As he practiced client-centered therapy, or the *person-centered* approach, as he eventually called it, Rogers came to the conclusion that he was most successful when he established certain conditions (1967, pp. 53–54). He did not attempt to put up a false front of any kind. He established a warm, positive, acceptant

Carl Rogers applied his ideas about client-centered psychotherapy to education. He believed that teachers could enhance student learning by not presenting a false front, by uncritically accepting students as they are, and by understanding students' feelings. (Douglas A. Land)

attitude toward his clients, and was able to empathize with them and sense their thoughts and feelings. Rogers concluded that these conditions set the stage for successful experiences with therapy because clients became more self-accepting and aware of themselves. Once individuals acquired these qualities, they were inclined and equipped to solve personal problems without seeking the aid of a therapist.

In addition to functioning as a therapist, Rogers served as a professor. Upon analyzing his experiences as an instructor, he concluded that the person-centered approach to therapy could be applied just as successfully to teaching. He thus proposed the idea of **learner-centered education**—that teachers should try to establish the same conditions as do person-centered therapists. Rogers sums up the qualities of a teacher who wants to use a learner-centered approach in this way:

> Perhaps the most basic of these essential attitudes is realness or genuineness. When the facilitator is a real person, being what she is, entering into the relationship with the learner without presenting a front or facade, she is much more likely to be effective. . . . She can be enthusiastic, can be bored, can be interested in students, can be angry, can be sensitive and sympathetic. Because she accepts these feelings as her own, she has no need to impose them on her students.
>
> There is another attitude that stands out in those who are successful in facilitating learning. . . . I think of it as prizing the learner, prizing her feelings, her opinions, her person. . . . It is an acceptance of this other individual as a separate person, having worth in her own right.
>
> A further element that establishes a climate for self-initiated, experiential learning is empathic understanding. When the teacher has the ability to understand the student's reactions from the inside, has a sensitive awareness of the way the process of education and learning seems _to the student,_ then again the likelihood of significant learning is increased. (1983, pp. 121–125)

> Rogers: teachers should be trusting, sincere; should prize students and empathize with them

Rogers argues (1980, pp. 273–278) that the results of learner-centered teaching are similar to those of person-centered therapy: Students become capable of educating themselves without the aid of teachers.

Combs: The Teacher as Facilitator

Arthur Combs became an enthusiastic advocate of the humanistic view after having experiences similar to those of Maslow and Rogers. He, too, became disenchanted with behaviorism and psychoanalysis and sought an alternative. Whereas Maslow based his conception of third force psychology on the study of motivation and Rogers based his view on his experiences as a psychotherapist, Combs used the cognitive view as a starting point for his speculations. He began with the assumption that "all behavior of a person is the direct result of his field of perceptions at the moment of his behaving" (1965, p. 12). From this assumption it follows that a teacher should try to understand any learning situation by speculating about how things seem from the students' point of view. This assumption also leads to the conclusion that to help students learn it is necessary to induce them to modify their beliefs and perceptions so that they will see things differently and behave differently. Some aspects of Combs's analysis of learning are similar to those of Bruner and other cognitive psychologists, but Combs placed less emphasis on cognitive aspects of learning and more on the personal perceptions of the learner.

Combs believed that the way a person perceives herself or himself is of paramount importance and that a basic purpose of teaching is to help each student develop a positive self-concept. He observed, "The task of the teacher is not one of prescribing, making, molding, forcing, coercing, coaxing, or cajoling; it is one of ministering to a process already in being. The role required of the teacher is that of facilitator, encourager, helper, assister, colleague, and friend of his students" (1965, p. 16). Combs elaborated on these points by listing six characteristics of good teachers: (1) They are well informed about their subject; (2) they are sensitive to the feelings of students and colleagues; (3) they believe that students can learn; (4) they have a positive self-concept; (5) they believe in helping all students do their best; and (6) they use many different methods of instruction (1965, pp. 20–23).

> Combs: teachers should be sensitive, trusting, confident, versatile

In collaboration with three colleagues, Combs (1974) later reaffirmed his belief in a humanistic approach to teaching and described how he developed a program to encourage the development of teachers with the characteristics just listed. He also offered evidence (pp. 175–181) to support the conclusion that teachers can be helped to increase their sensitivity to students' needs, develop self-confidence, and establish a positive classroom atmosphere.

Taken together, the observations of Maslow, Rogers, and Combs lead to a conception of education stressing that teachers should trust pupils enough to permit them to make many choices about their own learning. At the same time, teachers should be sensitive to the social and emotional needs of students, empathize with them, and respond positively to them. Finally, teachers should be sincere, willing to show that they, too, have needs, and experience positive feelings about themselves and what they are doing.

Maslow, Rogers, and Combs were the acknowledged leaders of the humanistic movement in American psychology, but several lesser-known colleagues also advocated humanistic education.

ARGUMENTS PROPOSED BY OTHER HUMANISTIC PSYCHOLOGISTS

Patterson: Humanistic Education as an Antidote

In *Humanistic Education* (1973), C. H. Patterson maintained that the crisis in American education perceived by such critics as Charles Silberman was due to too much stress on technological approaches to teaching. He urged teachers to

Humanistic educa-
tion proposed as anti-
dote to technological
approaches

use more human ways to facilitate subject-matter learning and also to pay more attention to affective aspects of learning. He offered both early and recent examples of humanistic education, outlined what he considered to be necessary changes in educational practices, and described the characteristics of humanistic teachers and the techniques they used (characteristics and techniques similar to those advocated by Rogers and Combs).

Brown: Confluent Education

Confluent education:
flowing together of
affective and cogni-
tive elements

In *Human Teaching for Human Learning* (1971), George Isaac Brown described **confluent education,** a flowing together of affective and cognitive elements in individual and group learning. He observed, "It should be apparent that there is no intellectual learning without some sort of feeling, and there are no feelings without the mind's being somehow involved" (p. 4). He described some basic affective techniques (for example, having individuals explore each other's faces with their hands or forming groups without speaking to one another) and outlined some classroom applications. A unit in ninth-grade social studies, for instance, was introduced with lectures by the instructor on theories of the nature of humankind. Then, students were asked to try to discover things about themselves by examining their thoughts, perceptions, and aspirations. Finally, they were asked to relate what they had discovered about themselves to what others had discovered about the nature of human beings in general. Toward the end of the book, Brown warned readers to proceed with caution; but he also urged teachers to try to avoid presenting affective learning as if it were isolated from the regular curriculum.

Gordon: Teacher Effectiveness Training (T.E.T.)

Thomas Gordon, who had studied with Carl Rogers, applied what he had learned about person-centered therapy to parent-child relationships in *Parent Effectiveness Training* (1970). The success of that book prompted him to write *Teacher Effectiveness Training* (1974), in which he stressed the importance of a favorable teacher-student relationship. He noted:

Teacher effectiveness
training stresses im-
portance of favorable
teacher-student rela-
tionship

> The relationship between a teacher and a student is good when it has (1) Openness or Transparency, so each is able to risk directness and honesty with the other; (2) Caring, when each knows that he is valued by the other; (3) Interdependence (as opposed to dependency of one on the other); (4) Separateness, to allow each to grow and to develop his uniqueness, creativity, and individuality; (5) Mutual Needs Meeting, so that neither's needs are met at the expense of the other's needs. (p. 24)

The basic technique Gordon recommends that teachers use is to discover who "owns" a problem. Gordon illustrates what he means by **problem ownership** with a rectangular diagram. A line across the top depicts an area indicating

▶ Solve classroom difficulties by determining who owns the problem

that a *student* owns a problem. A line across the bottom marks off a section representing that the *teacher* owns a problem. In between the two lines is the *teaching-learning no-problem* area, which ideally should be much larger than the other two areas. If the teacher is eager to instruct, well informed, and prepared, and if the students are cooperative and willing to learn, there is no problem. If the teacher is not prepared, or dislikes teaching, or is preoccupied with personal difficulties, she or he owns the problem and needs to seek a solution. If the students are addicted to doodling instead of paying attention or are afraid that they will not earn high enough grades to please their parents or have similar preoccupations, *they* own the problem. Gordon maintains that too often teachers use ineffective techniques, such as direct or indirect forms of blaming, when dealing with student-owned problems. Instead, teachers should indicate to students that they accept them as they are, by using techniques similar to those devised by Rogers for person-centered therapists. (These techniques, which are based on a basic *accept-reflect-clarify* strategy, are described in detail in *Teacher Effectiveness Training*.)

▶ I-messages tell how you feel about a situation, not about student characteristics

Gordon also recommends the use of **I-messages,** which convey how the teacher feels about a *situation,* not how she or he feels about students. If you find yourself getting angry because a class does not pay attention to a carefully planned presentation, for instance, Gordon suggests that you say, "I'm frustrated and disappointed because I worked for three hours last night getting this demonstration ready, and most of you are reading the school newspaper." Such a message describes how you feel, and is preferable to a message that criticizes student behavior, such as "You are acting like a bunch of spoiled brats who don't respond to anything other than violent action scenes in TV programs." Gordon argues that I-messages are more effective than you-messages because they make students realize that you are a real person and at the same time prevent you from attacking them personally. To be effective, I-messages should tell students in tangible and concrete ways what is creating the problem for the teacher and also make them aware of the teacher's feelings.

In *Teacher and Child* (1972) Haim Ginott offers a similar, but independently developed, presentation of many of the same techniques as those recommended by Gordon.

Purkey: Inviting School Success

William W. Purkey first called attention to the significance of the relationship between a student's self-concept and school achievement in a book of that title (*Self-Concept and School Achievement,* 1970) and later stressed the importance of students' positive self-perceptions in *Inviting School Success* (1984). Along with the other psychologists noted in this section, Purkey was bothered by what he called the *factory school* atmosphere engendered by too much stress on technological approaches to teaching. He was also impressed by research on the impact of teacher expectations (which is summarized in Chapter 13). He concluded that

Learning depends on how students perceive themselves

the way students respond in school depends to a significant extent on how they perceive themselves and that the way teachers react (or fail or react) influences student self-perceptions. (Erik Erikson, you may recall from Chapter 2, stresses that pupils should experience a sense of industry rather than inferiority.) To encourage students to experience feelings of positive self-worth, Purkey recommended that instructors develop and use skills of **invitational learning.**

Invitational learning: communicate to students that they are responsible, able, and valuable

Purkey defines an invitation as "a summary description of messages—verbal and nonverbal, formal and informal—continuously transmitted to students with the intention of informing them that they are responsible, able, and valuable" (p. 3). He outlines seven skills of invitational teachers:

1. Reaching each student (for example, learning names and having one-to-one contact)
2. Listening with care (for example, picking up subtle cues)
3. Being real with students (for example, providing only realistic praise)
4. Being real with oneself (for example, honestly appraising your own feelings and disappointments)

Invitational learning as described by Purkey involves communicating to students that they are responsible, able, and valuable. (Bob Daemmrich/Tony Stone Worldwide)

5. Inviting good discipline (for example, showing students you respect them)

6. Handling rejection (for example, not taking lack of student response in personal ways)

7. Inviting oneself (for example, thinking positively about oneself)

Purkey suggests that four student self-concept factors are likely to lead to school success: *relating* (to others), *asserting* (or experiencing a sense of self-control), *investing* (encouraging students to get involved with learning and with classmates), and *coping* (how well students meet school expectations). In the final chapter of *Inviting School Success*, Purkey suggests that teachers try to establish an atmosphere of warmth and a cooperative spirit, and that they convey positive expectations. Throughout the book, Purkey mentions anecdotes revealing how a single instance of personal interest, encouragement, or trust on the part of a teacher was reported to have changed a pupil's entire attitude toward self and toward school.

Taken together, the observations of Patterson, Brown, Gordon, and Purkey supplement the views of Maslow, Rogers, and Combs in calling attention to the importance of feelings, teacher-pupil relationships, and the desirability of having students develop positive feelings about themselves as they are given freedom to direct at least part of their own learning. Since this book is about ways to apply psychology to teaching, the discussion of humanistic approaches presented thus far has stressed the observations of psychologists. Brief mention should also be made, though, of popular humanistic techniques developed by educators.

HUMANISTIC TECHNIQUES DEVELOPED BY EDUCATORS

A Sampling of Humanistic Education Techniques

The *Humanistic Education Sourcebook* (1975), edited by Donald A. Read and Sidney B. Simon, serves as a comprehensive source of ideas for teachers who would like to put humanistic education into practice. Some of the techniques described in the *Sourcebook* involve *sensitivity training* and *encounter groups*. These techniques are essentially group therapy sessions, and they are intended to encourage participants to explore their emotions and feelings in highly personal ways. Other techniques are intended to encourage students to identify with others, empathize with them, and engage in vicarious experiences. Techniques of this type include role playing, psychodrama, sociodrama, and simulation games. Students may be asked to assume the roles of historical figures or act out situations (such as a teacher catching a student cheating), and then to reverse the roles. Or members of a group may be assigned roles and asked to follow detailed instructions for simulating a situation such as that involving world leaders at an arms control conference.

> Encourage pupils to identify by using role playing, simulation games

Values Clarification

Some of the most explicit instructions available to those who would like to use humanistic techniques of teaching are to be found in books on **values clarification.** This term, which is sometimes capitalized and sometimes abbreviated V.C., was originally applied to techniques proposed by Louis Raths for helping children become more aware of their values. The first book on the subject, *Values and Teaching* (1966) by Raths, Merrill Harmin, and Sidney B. Simon, described the basic strategies of values clarification. The authors proposed that students are likely to develop a set of values that will help them make confident and consistent choices and decisions if they engage in the following activities:

> Values clarification: encourage students to choose, prize, and act on beliefs

Choose their beliefs and behaviors by first considering and then selecting from alternatives.

Prize their beliefs and behaviors by cherishing and publicly affirming them.

Act on their beliefs repeatedly and consistently.

Values clarification strategies are intended to encourage individuals to choose, prize, and act on their beliefs. If students indicate during class discussions that everyone should help solve social problems, urge them to do something about them—such as raising money for AIDS research. (Spencer Grant/ Stock, Boston, Inc.)

Seventy-nine strategies for helping students engage in such activities are described in *Values Clarification: A Handbook of Practical Strategies for Teachers and Students* (1972) by Sidney B. Simon, Leland W. Howe, and Howard Kirschenbaum. Students are asked to choose their beliefs freely and from carefully considered alternatives—as in strategy 5, "Either-Or Forced Choice" (pp. 94–97). The teacher institutes this strategy by asking students, "Which do you identify with more, a Volkswagen or a Cadillac?" Pupils indicate their preference by walking to one side of the room or the opposite; they then team up with a classmate who made the same choice and explain the reasons for the choice. Students are encouraged to cherish and publicly affirm their beliefs by engaging in activities such as that presented in strategy 12, "Public Interview" (pp. 139–162). In this strategy, a student volunteers to be interviewed by the rest of the class and publicly affirms and explains her or his stand on various issues. Pupils are urged to act repeatedly and consistently on their beliefs when the teacher uses strategies such as number 42, "Letters to the Editor" (pp. 262–263), and asks each student in the class to write at least one letter to the editor of a newspaper or magazine. Copies of the letter and clippings from the paper or magazine (if available) are posted on a bulletin board, and at the end of the month pupils read their letters to the rest of the class and explain their reasons for speaking out on the issue they had selected.

Values clarification techniques can also be used to help motivate students to become more effective learning strategists. In addition to possessing a wide range of metacognitive knowledge, strategic skills, and tactical skills, good learning strategists hold certain values. Specifically, they believe that (1) the academic goals they choose to attain are meaningful and worthwhile, (2) the strategic and tactical skills they use to achieve their goals are useful and efficient, and (3) they are capable of effectively managing their cognitive resources. In other words, values clarification exercises can help students become aware of where they stand with respect to valuing the goals of strategic learning, the means of strategic learning, and their own intellectual characteristics (Paris, Lipson & Wixson, 1983).

Although values clarification techniques were devised to help students understand the source of their own motives and to make growth-oriented decisions, the same techniques can also help you meet multicultural education goals. As we pointed out in Chapter 6, misunderstandings between students and between student and teacher may be due to differences in how cultures value such things as the use of time, the expression of emotion, the obedience to authority, and the use of cooperation. The various values clarification strategies mentioned by Simon et al. (1972) can also be used to help students (and the teacher) realize that other points of view exist and to understand their origins. For example, it may be very instructive to have the white, Hispanic-American, and Asian-American students in a class listen to an African-American student explain how her or his values about obedience to authority and cooperation with peers were influenced by the civil rights protests led by Martin Luther King, Jr., and other African-American leaders of the 1960s.

Besides proposing that teachers use techniques such as those just summarized, humanistic educators recommended a change in grading practices. Even though grading policies are not methods of instruction, they merit mention here because they were an integral part of the humanistic education movement.

Emphasis on Pass/Fail Grading

▶ Humanistic educators argued that traditional grades should be abolished

Many humanistic educators (for example, Kirschenbaum, Simon & Napier, 1971) argued that traditional grading practices should be abolished because they interfered with achievement of the basic goals of that form of instruction. Humanistic education emphasized the development of positive feelings about self and others; stress on subject matter was to be replaced by stress on understanding of feelings, and teachers were to function as facilitators or friends. Traditional grading practices interfered with the achievement of those goals, it was argued, because students who received low grades were told, in effect, that they were inferior and incapable of learning. When students were graded "on the curve," critics pointed out, they were forced to compete against one another and to view classmates as "enemies." Teachers who assigned marks on exams, papers, and report cards were forced to function as authorities and judges rather than as facilitators and friends. For these and similar reasons, when humanistic education was at its peak of popularity during the early 1970s, the traditional letter-grade system was replaced in many schools, colleges, and universities by pass/fail or credit/no credit grading. When traditional grades *were* assigned, there was a tendency to relax standards and record many A's and B's on report cards.

Now that you are familiar with the nature of humanistic education, we are in a position to evaluate its effectiveness and current status.

AN EVALUATION OF HUMANISTIC EDUCATION

In order to evaluate humanistic education and speculate about how you might make constructive use of selected techniques in your classroom, you should know something of its history, implications for instruction, and likely effectiveness.

Humanistic Education in Different Social and Political Climates

Humanistic education emerged as a recognizable force in the late 1960s and reached its peak of popularity in the early 1970s. During that period of American history there was widespread dissatisfaction with our society and our schools. Riots and demonstrations in ghettos and on campuses were the most tangible signs of anger, disappointment, and frustration; but, more generally, many Americans experienced the feeling that something was wrong with our society

▶ Humanistic education emerged as a reaction against prevailing approaches

and that change was essential. Books attacking traditional forms of education became popular and led to interest in finding new approaches to schooling. Some parents were so convinced that public schools caused more harm than good that they formed so-called "free schools," in which pupils and teachers were treated as equals and students were allowed to decide what, when, and where they would study. Thus, the time was ripe for radical changes in educational techniques, and the advocates of humanistic education were so enthusiastic about that form of education that they won a substantial number of converts.

But within a short time after pupils, parents, and teachers embraced humanistic education with gusto, the social and political climate became more conservative. Furthermore, starting in the mid-1970s, the reports of declining achievement test scores, which contributed to the loss of enthusiasm for the discovery approach, had an even more damaging impact on humanistic education approaches. Just a few years after some critics had maintained that a "crisis" existed in American education that could be alleviated only by moving away from teacher-controlled instruction, other critics asserted that a new "crisis" was at hand and that it could be alleviated only through a "back to basics" movement. As you may be aware, American education is again being described in crisis terms. Over the past ten years, various reports, articles, and books have maintained that in comparison to certain European and Asian students, American students know less and are less skilled problem-solvers and critical thinkers. (Not everyone agrees with this assessment, however. For an alternative view, see "Why Can't They Be Like We Were?" by Gerald Bracey [1991]). This latest crisis has led to a call for classroom learning activities that are consistent with the humanistic theories discussed in this chapter as well as with the learning theories discussed in the previous three chapters—meaningful, hands-on activities that are embedded in familiar, everyday activities.

▶ Enthusiasm for humanistic education rises and falls as circumstances change

What we are trying to point out with this brief review is that, regardless of the political climate, it is possible to value and apply a mix of humanistic, cognitive, and other instructional methods to achieve affective and cognitive goals. Bruce Hall, Melvin Villern, and W. Wade Burley (1986) found in their research that beginning teachers who endorse humanistic outcomes in education (such as social and emotional development and clarification of social values) also tend to endorse such teacher-directed practices as the use of behavioral objectives, higher-order questions, and advance organizers. Thus, teachers who adopt or agree with a humanistic orientation do not necessarily oppose the recent emphasis on academic excellence. In fact, they probably believe that a humanistic orientation is more likely than a nonhumanistic orientation to produce high levels of classroom achievement.

Analyzing Separate Aspects of Humanistic Education

A second point to note about humanistic education is the one stressed at the beginning of this chapter: The term refers to a variety of assumptions and

▶ Humanistic education made up of loosely related assumptions and techniques

techniques. Some theorists stress basic assumptions about children, teachers, and the learning situation. Others describe attitudes of students and teachers or stress the significance of interpersonal relationships. Still others advocate the use of specific instructional techniques. Here is a summary of points emphasized by the various advocates of humanistic education mentioned in this chapter.

1. Assumptions about pupils and the basic nature of education.
   Maslow and Rogers: Teachers should trust children and let them make many of their own decisions; instruction should be learner-centered.

2. Characteristics of effective teachers.
   Rogers: Teachers should be trusting, sincere; should prize students and empathize with them.
   Combs: Teachers should be sensitive, trusting, confident, and versatile.

3. Affective factors should be explored as much as the cognitive side of subject matter.
   Brown: Confluent education should cause cognitive and affective elements of a learning situation to flow together.

4. Relationships between pupils and their teachers have an important impact on learning.
   Gordon: Teachers should try to establish positive relationships with pupils, determine who owns problems, use I-messages.

5. How students feel about themselves influences the way they learn.
   Purkey: Teachers should use invitational learning techniques by communicating to students that they are responsible, able, and valuable. Teachers should do everything possible to encourage students to develop positive feelings about themselves.

6. Teachers should use techniques to encourage pupils to explore their feelings and emotions.
   Suggested techniques: Sensitivity training, encounter groups

7. Teachers should use techniques for encouraging students to identify with others, empathize with them, and relate their own feelings to the feelings of the students.
   Suggested techniques: role playing, psychodrama, sociodrama, simulation games

8. Teachers should use techniques to help students become more aware of and act on their attitudes and values.
   Suggested techniques: values clarification strategies

9. Traditional grading practices should be replaced by pass/fail or credit/no credit evaluation procedures.

Are these techniques effective? After reviewing several dozen studies, John Swisher, Judith Vickery, and Peggy Nadenichek (1983) concluded that humanistic instructional techniques (for example, values clarification, role playing, and interpersonal relations training) were much more likely to produce positive outcomes than negative outcomes. Most of these studies reported gains for classroom management (reductions in problem behaviors and tardiness, increases in attendance), achievement, attitudes toward school, self-esteem, creativity, communication skills, and social awareness (an important outcome given the current emphasis on multicultural programs).

D. B. Matthews (1991) found that eighth-graders who learned in a relaxed atmosphere, where student suggestions about various school functions were sought, showed higher levels of intrinsic motivation for reading, social studies, and science than eighth-graders who learned in a more structured and teacher-directed environment.

Diann Musial (1986) examined how trusting and nontrusting environments affected the academic performance of college students. In one section of a course that she taught, she required students to sign an attendance roster and record their social security number for every class meeting; she took attendance at different times during class meetings to discourage students from attending only part of a class; and she gave, graded, and kept unannounced quizzes. For obvious reasons, this section was called the No Trust group. In the other section, called the Trust group, she never took attendance and allowed the students to grade and keep their quizzes. She examined the effect of these two environments on midterm exam scores, quality of classroom discussion, and quality of a term paper. The results were mixed. The No Trust group significantly outscored the Trust group on the 50-item midterm exam (39.24 vs. 34.27 items correct, respectively). On the other hand, the Trust group was rated as being more attentive during class discussion periods and as making more original statements than the No Trust group. There were no differences, however, for provocativeness, enthusiasm, or clarity. Lastly, the term papers of the Trust group students were given significantly higher creativity ratings than were the term papers of the No Trust students.

Despite the positive findings, there are good reasons for keeping some cautions in mind when implementing certain humanistic techniques. We discuss several of these next.

Using Humanistic Techniques Appropriately

1. *The assumptions that teachers should trust pupils and permit them to make many of their own decisions, and that instruction should center on the learner:* For reasons noted at the beginning of this section, these assumptions should probably be treated as appropriate only in qualified ways today. You might ask students to help you as much as possible in determining instructional objectives, and you might sometimes invite them to use the contract approach or to complete self-selected individual or group projects. Given the prevailing educational climate in this country, however, you should probably expect to make most of the decisions about what your students will learn and how they will learn it (or to implement decisions made by others, such as school boards and state education agencies). At the same time,

you should remember that teacher expectations often influence pupil behavior. Thus, you should try to communicate the feeling that you trust pupils, in the sense that you believe they are capable of learning.

2. *The assumption that teachers should show they are sincere, demonstrate sensitivity to the needs and feelings of pupils, and exhibit confidence and versatility:* All these characteristics are obviously desirable. There are a number of techniques you can use (such as I-messages) to demonstrate that you are genuine and sincere. You can also try to see things from a student's point of view. If you make careful plans to use a variety of techniques and follow the suggestions for developing a personal handbook and making an effort to become a better teacher (as described in the last chapter of this book), you should function as a versatile and confident teacher.

3. *The assumption that affective factors should be explored as much as the cognitive side of subject matter:* It may be unwise to stress the affective side of learning in the mid-1990s to the same extent that Brown recommended twenty years ago. It should be possible, though, to avoid making the presentation of subject matter too objective and sterile. When you think about how to structure class discussions or give individual or group assignments, you might look for ways to get students personally involved by considering affective, as well as cognitive, aspects of learning.

▶ When appropriate, stress affective along with cognitive learning

4. *The assumption that relationships between pupils and their teachers have an important impact on learning:* Behavioral theorists tend to concentrate on the most efficient ways to arrange learning situations; cognitive theorists are interested in the ways that students perceive relationships. Humanistic psychologists perform a valuable service when they call attention to the fact that *how* teachers present subject matter and interact with their students is often significant. You probably know from your own experience that you are more likely to respond to a teacher who makes an effort to establish a relaxed, positive classroom atmosphere and to treat you as an individual than to one who simply handles teaching chores in an impersonal way. There are many things you can do to establish positive relationships with your students, and you can handle classroom problems with a minimum of ill feeling if you take the trouble to think about problem ownership and use I-messages.

▶ Preferable to be a helpful teacher rather than a friend

At the same time, you should probably think of yourself as a teacher rather than as a friend. Those who have tried to teach by building an extremely close personal relationship with all pupils in a class have been unable to continue that kind of education for more than a year or two. Herbert Kohl, for example, described in *36 Children* (1967) how he used a highly personal, humanistic approach to teaching in an inner-city elementary school. After two years of that kind of instruction, he felt obliged to move to Spain to recuperate. And George Dennison, who described how he developed a humanistic school in *The Lives of Children* (1969), noted at the end of the book that the school closed its doors after two years. He explained, "It was not merely lack of money that closed the

Some humanistic educators maintain that teachers should do everything possible to encourage students to develop positive feelings about themselves. (Bob Daemmrich/The Image Works, Inc.)

school. We ourselves were not strongly enough motivated to make the sacrifices that would have been necessary to sustain it" (p. 273). He then noted that he returned to a full-time career as a writer after the school closed. You should also remember that, unlike the humanistic educators of the 1970s, you will almost certainly be expected to assign letter grades.

5. *The assumption that students' feelings about themselves influence the way they learn:* In *Inviting School Success*, Purkey summarizes research that supports this point, but you may be able to endorse it simply by examining your own reactions to teachers and schooling. Students are more likely to "put out" in a classroom if they feel their teachers like them, have faith in them, and believe they can learn. Thus, you should do everything possible to encourage your pupils to develop positive feelings about themselves as persons and learners.

6. *The assumption that teachers should encourage pupils to explore their feelings and emotions:* Of all the assumptions listed here, this one is probably most difficult to defend today. It would almost certainly be a mistake for you to devote in-class time to sensitivity training or encounter group sessions or to use psychodrama techniques in contemporary American classrooms.

7. *The assumption that teachers should use techniques to encourage students to identify with others, empathize with them, and relate their feelings to the feelings of others:* The remarks made in evaluating confluent education in point 3 above apply here as well. When aimed at increasing interest and involvement in subject matter, occasional use of role playing and simulation games can be effective. However, using such techniques only to make students aware of feelings, emotions, and interrelationships—independent of presenting subject matter— might lead to problems with parents and administrators.

8. *The assumption that teachers should make frequent use of values clarification strategies:* When values clarification strategies were first developed, lavish claims for the technique were made. In *Personalizing Education* (1975), for example, Leland and Mary Howe asserted that "if our values are clear, consistent, and soundly chosen, we tend to live our lives in meaningful and satisfying ways" (p. 17). Although they used the phrase "soundly chosen," the Howes joined with other values clarification enthusiasts in stressing that "Values Clarification is not an attempt to teach students 'right' and 'wrong' values. Rather, it is an approach designed to help students prize and act upon their own freely chosen values. Thus, V.C. is concerned with the process by which students arrive at their values, rather than the content of these values" (p. 19). There is no reason to assume, however, that students will automatically make sound choices when they engage in values clarification sessions. It is quite possible that when students are encouraged to develop clear and consistent values, they will choose those that focus on

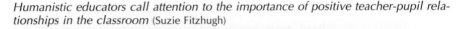

Humanistic educators call attention to the importance of positive teacher-pupil relationships in the classroom (Suzie Fitzhugh)

material possessions, power, self-indulgence, and the like. Considering the nature of high-pressure advertising in America and the kinds of individuals who achieve notoriety in our society, it would be surprising if such values were not favored by many young people. Simply because a person's values are made more consistent as a consequence of values clarification sessions, then, does not guarantee that the individual will live in a "meaningful and satisfying way." The opposite could be just as likely.

▶ Values clarification not likely to change students' habits or lives

Furthermore, if Piaget's description of cognitive development is taken into account, there is reason to doubt that very many pupils will actually develop a consistent value system through values clarification exercises. Many values clarification strategies are designed to be used with elementary school children who are at the concrete operations stage of cognitive development and unable either to grasp abstract concepts or to generalize. To cite just one example, when they are asked to indicate if they prefer ice cream, Jell-O, or pie for dessert (a question featured in a values clarification strategy intended to give children practice in choosing among alternatives), young children will probably react in a quite literal way. They will think about their favorite dessert but not about the principle of choosing among alternatives. There is no reason to believe that when they are faced with a choice involving values they will see any connection between picking a dessert and making a moral or ethical decision.

The same tendency to respond in literal ways is likely to be characteristic of many secondary school students as well, since the transition to formal thought is a gradual process. But even high school students who are capable of dealing with abstractions and hypothetical situations may not develop a realistic or workable set of values because novice formal thinkers tend to overlook realities. Secondary school students are also eager to impress others. If a high school girl volunteers to be interviewed by the class, for instance, she may supply glib and idealistic answers and be so preoccupied with making a good impression on classmates that there will be no carry-over to behavior outside of class. Simply because students can talk about positive values in discussing hypothetical situations does not mean that they will necessarily act that way when the chips are down. Because of factors such as these, it is unrealistic to expect that use of values clarification strategies will equip students with a value system that will lead to a "meaningful and satisfying life."

If you plan to use group discussion techniques fairly frequently, though, you may wish to examine books on values clarification and select strategies (keeping in mind the reservations just noted) that permit you to cover subject matter and clarify values at the same time. (Books you might consult will be noted in the Suggestions for Teaching in Your Classroom and the Resources for Further Investigation that follow.)

9. *The assumption that traditional grading practices should be replaced by pass/fail or credit/no credit evaluation procedures:* For reasons stated earlier, you will almost certainly be expected to assign (and defend) letter grades that reflect mastery of specific instructional objectives.

Mid-Chapter Review

Views of the "Elder Statesmen" of Humanistic Psychology

Humanistic psychology emerged when a number of theorists found that they were dissatisfied with behavioral and psychoanalytic interpretations of behavior, particularly the hypothesis stressed by Skinner and Freud that humans have little control over their own behavior. This hypothesis led to the assumption that it was essential for parents and teachers to shape behavior and control learning. An alternative view stressing that humans do control much of their own behavior, and that parents and teachers should allow freedom for children to explore and develop, was proposed by three eminent psychologists:

Abraham Maslow urged parents and teachers to trust children and let and help them grow.

Carl Rogers recommended that teachers be trusting and sincere, prize students, and empathize with them.

Arthur Combs maintained that teachers should be sensitive, trusting, confident, and versatile.

Proposals Made by Other Humanistic Psychologists and Educators

Psychologists who were bothered by the impersonal nature of technological and cognitive approaches to instruction proposed a variety of humanistic instructional techniques:

George Brown urged teachers to practice **confluent education,** in which cognitive and affective elements would flow together.

Thomas Gordon stressed that teachers should become effective in developing positive relationships with students. He urged teachers to think about **problem ownership** and to use **I-messages.**

William Purkey stressed that learning depends on how pupils perceive themselves and urged teachers to encourage **invitational learning** by communicating to students that they are responsible, able, and valuable.

Educators joined with psychologists in urging teachers to use humanistic approaches to instruction. Some recommended the use of role playing and simulation games; others advocated **values clarification,** whereby students were encouraged to choose, prize, and act on their beliefs. Still others argued that grades should be abolished, since low grades often cause students to feel inferior and incapable of learning.

Evaluating Humanistic Education

Humanistic education is difficult to evaluate because it is made up of loosely related assumptions and techniques. To understand why certain concepts and techniques were recommended, it should be noted that the humanistic movement emerged as a reaction against prevailing approaches. Enthusiasm for

(continued)

humanistic education peaked during a period of recent American history when there was widespread dissatisfaction with many aspects of our society as well as distrust of authority. Support for humanistic education declined when the social and political climate changed and as evidence accumulated revealing that American students exposed to student-centered instruction scored low on achievement tests.

Assumptions and techniques of humanistic education that still merit consideration, even with the present emphasis on subject-matter mastery, include:

Stress on affective as well as cognitive learning

Teacher sensitivity to student feelings and needs

Inviting students to think about values and attitudes

Suggestions for Teaching in Your Classroom

USING HUMANISTIC TECHNIQUES

1. Try to remain aware of the extent to which you direct and control learning. Whenever possible, permit and encourage students to make choices and to manage their own learning.

2. Establish a warm, positive, acceptant atmosphere. Do your best to communicate the feeling that you believe all the students in the class can learn and that you want them to learn.

3. When it seems appropriate, function as a facilitator, encourager, helper, and assister. But before attempting to function as a colleague or friend, think about possible complications.

4. If you feel comfortable doing it, occasionally show that you are a "real person" by telling students how you feel. When you express anger, however, comment on the situation, not on the personality traits of your students.

5. Do your best to help your students develop positive feelings about themselves. Empathize with them, and show that you are sensitive to their needs and feelings.

6. If appropriate, ask students to participate in role playing or simulation games.

7. If appropriate (and acceptable), make judicious use of values clarification strategies.

8. Do your best to provide learning experiences that will lead to the development of the habits and attitudes you want to foster.

9. Make use of object lessons. When illustrative incidents occur, take advantage of them.

10. Set a good example.

---

1. Try to remain aware of the extent to which you direct and control learning. Whenever possible, permit and encourage students to make choices and to manage their own learning.

> Cardinal principle of humanistic education: give pupils choices

Humanistic psychology developed as a reaction against strict behavioristic and psychoanalytic interpretations of behavior. Maslow, Rogers, and Combs ask educators to avoid the pitfalls of assuming that children are entirely shaped by experiences or that they need to be protected and guarded at all times. The cardinal principle of humanistic education is to give students opportunities to make choices and manage their own learning. It is neither logical nor possible, however, to give students complete freedom of choice. Immature children cannot anticipate what they will need to know in order to live in a technological society and cannot be expected to supervise or sustain all their own learning experiences. Furthermore, parents, school boards, and school administrators expect teachers to earn their salaries and produce tangible results. Even so, you should be able to offer your students many opportunities to participate in decisions about what will be studied, how it will be studied, and how classroom order will be maintained. As you plan lessons, you might ask yourself, "Am I setting up a controlled situation here because it is in the best interests of the students, or am I doing it because it's easier, because I like to feel that I'm indispensable, or because it gives me a sense of power?" If you are willing, you can find many ways to give students opportunities to make choices as they learn.

Examples

Handbook Heading: Ways to Give Pupils Choices

Ask the class to select topics to be covered (as noted in the suggestions for arranging group discussions presented in the preceding chapter).

Permit individual students to choose topics to be studied, perhaps by selecting from a suggested list or by proposing subjects on their own.

Arrange an open classroom situation so that students can engage in self-selected study of subjects of interest.

Invite students to participate in making decisions about class rules.

A number of strategies for providing opportunities for students to participate in decisions about what will be studied are described in *Personalizing Education* by Howe and Howe (1975). They describe a ten-step procedure outlined in Chapter 8 (pages 366–367) that involves preparation of a flow chart detailing steps to be followed.

Other ways to permit students a degree of choice, particularly when a prescribed curriculum must be covered, are described in Chapter 14 of *Personalizing Education.* One of these is the Student Self-Paced Style. In this approach, students are asked to study a prescribed topic, but they determine how fast, where, when, and with whom they will study. The Howes suggest that students correct their own work. For details of the Self-Paced Style, see pages 465–468 of *Personalizing Education.*

Handbook Heading:
Using Self-Paced and
Self-Selected Styles

An approach that gives students a bit more control over their own learning is called the Student Self-Selected Learning Style. It is similar to the Self-Paced Style, except for the first step: Instead of being given assigned work, students choose their own topics. One way to facilitate this approach is to prepare a large number of activity cards that give suggestions for studying different topics. The Howes suggest that these should include the following information: the name of the activity, the purpose, materials needed to complete the activity, steps to be followed, evaluation criteria to be used, and suggestions for follow-up activities. Many teachers' journals supply information that might be used in your preparation of such cards, or you might team up with other teachers and develop a combined set that could be reproduced. Another obvious way to accumulate such cards is to ask students to develop their own and then to save the best ones each year.

Still another variation of self-directed learning consists of the *contract approach,* which was described in Chapter 8 ("Behavioral Learning Theories").

2. Establish a warm, positive, acceptant atmosphere. Do your best to communicate the feeling that you believe all the students in the class can learn and that you want them to learn.

In their eagerness to persuade teachers to be efficient and objective, some advocates of the behaviorist view ignore the impact of the teacher's attitude. Humanistic psychologists call attention to the extent to which *how* you teach will influence the response of your students. At times you will want to be efficient and objective, but because successful learning experiences seem to depend to a significant extent on interpersonal relationships, you should not attempt to play the role of an impersonal authority or leader. You are more likely to get a positive response from your students if you exude warmth, enthusiasm, and high expectations. Remember the nature of the self-fulfilling prophecy, and communicate, as best you can, the attitude that every student in the class is capable of learning.

Examples

Learn pupils' names as fast as you can, and take an interest in them as individuals.

Try to show that you are intrigued, fascinated, excited, and enthusiastic about the things you present to the class.

Urge all students to do their best, and avoid forcing students to compete for a limited number of high grades. (Detailed instructions for doing this will be presented in the Learning for Mastery section of Chapter 13.)

Show that you are pleased (but not surprised) when students do well; don't act as if it bothers you to give high grades.

3. When it seems appropriate, function as a facilitator, encourager, helper, and assister. But before attempting to function as a colleague or friend, think about possible complications.

Even if you trust children and are convinced that they are often self-motivated, there are certain to be times when they will need and probably welcome prescriptions. There are also bound to be times when they will need to be coaxed or cajoled into completing even self-selected assignments. On the whole, however, you will probably get a better response from your pupils if they see you as a facilitator, encourager, and helper. This view of education is very similar to that proposed by advocates of the discovery approach, who stress that teachers should arrange lessons to permit students to gain insight. Even though you will sometimes prescribe, you can dispel an impression that you are a dictator or a manipulator by explaining why you are asking your pupils to learn certain things and by inviting students to help plan classroom activities. Before you make an effort to become a close friend to all your students, consider some of the problems likely to arise when you are required to assign grades, when you try to prevent jealousy or divide your in-class and at-home time among 30 to 150 "best friends," and when you must drop one crop of "friends" in favor of a new crop each report period or year. Teachers who take a genuine interest in their pupils and show that they like them almost invariably get a better response than those who are cold and aloof, but it is usually not advisable to replace the teacher-pupil relationship with a friend-to-friend relationship.

4. If you feel comfortable doing it, occasionally show that you are a "real person" by telling students how you feel. When you express anger, however, comment on the situation, not on the personality traits of your students.

Many advocates of humanistic education believe that students are more likely to examine their emotions if they observe a teacher doing the same. In addition, it is reasoned, students may become more sensitive to ways their behavior may hurt others. Accordingly, humanistic educators recommend that you not hesitate to show when you are pleased, angry, afraid, disappointed, and the like.

One of the first psychologists to propose this policy was Haim Ginott. In *Teacher and Child* (1972), he reasons that, given the realities of teaching, it is inevitable that teachers will become frustrated and angry. When this happens, the teacher is urged to be authentic and genuine (or, as Rogers puts it, a "real

▶ Cardinal principle of
communication: talk
to situation, not to
personality

person"). Ginott observes, "An enlightened teacher is not afraid of his anger, because he has learned to express it without doing damage. He has mastered the secret of expressing anger without insult" (p. 85). The "secret" is summed up by the cardinal principle of communication: "Talk to the situation, not to the personality and character" (p. 84). Ginott illustrates the secret and the principle by contrasting the response of two teachers who become angry when two boys throw pieces of bread at each other. The first attacks the boys' personalities by saying, "You two slobs! Clean it up now! You are not fit to live in a pigsty. I want to talk to your parents about your disgusting behavior!" (p. 87). The second expresses anger over the situation by saying, "I get angry when I see bread made into bullets. Bread is not for throwing. This room needs immediate cleaning" (p. 87). (As you can see, Ginott's "secret" is the same as Gordon's I-message technique.)

The degree to which you use this technique will be a function of your personality, the age of the pupils you teach, perhaps the subject you teach, and many other factors. But if you occasionally reveal your feelings, you may gain release of frustrations, show your students how they might do the same in similar situations, and make them more aware of how their actions may be unfair or damaging to others. If you have a very low level of frustration tolerance and reveal your feelings too often, however, your students may think of you not as a "real person" but as a chronic complainer or perhaps as someone with paranoid delusions of persecution. Whenever you do express anger, try to remember Ginott's cardinal principle and vent your hostility by using I-messages to comment on the situation, not on the personalities of your students.

5. Do your best to help your students develop positive feelings about themselves. Empathize with them and show that you are sensitive to their needs and feelings.

Just as your ability to express your feelings by talking to the situation rather than to the character of the student is partly a function of your personality, so is your ability to empathize with your students. A study by Sharon Morgan (1984) found that high-empathy teachers of emotionally disturbed children were only moderately sensitive to their own needs and feelings, had moderate feelings of self-worth, and were not fearful of spontaneously expressing their feelings. They depended on others for emotional support and were sensitive to the approval and disapproval of others. This seemed to heighten their awareness of the psychological needs of others. Even if you do not possess these characteristics, you can always try to see things from the student's point of view. Reflect on how you felt when you were a student, particularly when you felt insecure, ignorant, and frightened. Remain alert for things that you say or do that might embarrass, threaten, or belittle your students.

If you suspect that some of your students do not think highly of themselves, you might experiment with techniques for helping them develop positive self-concepts. Methods for doing this are described by John T. Canfield and Harold C. Wells in *100 Ways to Enhance Self-Concept in the Classroom* (1976) and in several strategies outlined in *Personalizing Education* (pp. 81–105) by Howe and Howe. One technique is to ask members of small groups to describe a successful accomplishment they achieved before they were ten years old. Another is to ask students to list things they are proud of. Still another is to ask members of a small group to "bombard" a selected classmate with all the strengths they see in her or him. In strategy 11 of *Values Clarification,* Simon, Howe, and Kirschenbaum suggest that students "whip around" the classroom telling what they are proud of, and in strategy 62 they provide words and music so that the same can be done in the form of a song.

Handbook Heading:
Ways to Help Students
Develop Positive Feel-
ings About Themselves

While techniques intended to help pupils develop positive feelings about themselves often produce tangible results, you should also keep in mind Erikson's observations on industry vs. inferiority. Perhaps the best way to make children and adolescents feel good about themselves is to help them master required subject matter and function as successful students. You might try to achieve that goal by using a number of different teaching techniques (so that you please some of your pupils some of the time), by using the motivational techniques described in Chapter 12, and by using the mastery approach described in Chapter 13.

6. If appropriate, ask students to participate in role playing or simulation games.

Some learning situations can be made more meaningful if students are encouraged to act out, identify with, or become involved in an activity. One way to do this is by asking students to engage in role playing.

Examples

Have elementary students act out the roles of George Washington, Abigail Adams, Benjamin Franklin, and so on, when they study the Revolutionary War period of American history.

Have junior high school students assume the roles of members of Congress debating some current issue.

In a high school business class, have students pretend they are job seekers and employers interviewing applicants for a position.

For more information on this technique see *Simulation Games and Learning Activities Kit for the Elementary School* (1977) by Jay Reese.

Simulation games feature the same basic techniques as role playing but present students with more structured and elaborate situations. A number of such games are available from publishers. One game of this type is "Generation Gap." Four to ten junior or senior high school students spend fifty minutes or so discussing interactions and conflicts between parents and an adolescent son or daughter. "Ghetto," as the name implies, stimulates students to spend two to four hours becoming involved in the problems of inner-city life. And "The College Game" helps high school seniors prepare for college. During a period of ninety minutes, they learn about course requirements, schedules, study habits and demands, and typical problems of first-year students. (Simulation games tend to be expensive. Accordingly, you might check your school district curriculum library to discover what is available or might be obtained. Also, you may want to examine the computer-based simulations mentioned in this chapter's Applying Technology to Teaching section.)

7. If appropriate (and acceptable), make judicious use of values clarification strategies.

The critique of humanistic education presented earlier in this chapter raised questions about the extent to which values clarification achieves the goals claimed by its proponents. Even though there are reasons to doubt that participating in values clarification sessions will cause children to develop a consistent set of values that will make their lives more meaningful and satisfying, the technique does possess advantages. For one thing, many of the strategies are provocative and interesting, and most students seem to enjoy them. For another, children may gain important insights as they carry out some of the activities. These insights may not merge into a coherent value system or be applied consistently when out-of-school value decisions are made, but they may occasionally influence behavior. Therefore, if you will be teaching in the elementary grades, you may wish to schedule values clarification sessions. At the secondary level, you might endeavor to work values clarification into lesson plans for courses in social studies, history, science, or home economics.

Handbook Heading:
Ways to Set Up Values
Clarification Sessions

Keep in mind, though, that values clarification is essentially a form of moral education. Thus, we repeat the same caution noted after the discussion of the theorizing of Piaget and Kohlberg in Chapter 2: Before using any values clarification strategies, check with your principal. You may be teaching in a school district where parents and/or school board members have expressed the view that the proper place for moral and values education is the home, not the school.

If you browse through books on values clarification to select your own strategies to supplement these examples, keep in mind Piaget's observations on cognitive development. Remember that elementary grade pupils are concrete thinkers and that secondary school students are prone to engage in unrestrained theorizing. For younger pupils, look for strategies that ask them to deal with familiar, concrete situations. For older students, avoid strategies that center on extreme hypothetical situations or issues that are remote from their daily lives. Quite a few values clarification strategies appear to have been devised by individuals who were eager to be imaginative and clever. Asking secondary school students to engage in debates about fanciful situations that are totally implausible or to offer solutions to global problems may be a way to use up thirty minutes of class time, but it is not likely to have any impact on their behavior.

To limit the possibility that values clarification will be thought of primarily as game time, several enthusiasts for the technique recommend that strategies become an integral part of the curriculum. Therefore, if you are impressed with values clarification, you might look for ways to work such strategies into lesson plans. Two excellent sources to consult for ideas about how to do this are *Readings in Values Clarification* (1973), edited by Kirschenbaum and Simon, and *Clarifying Values Through Subject Matter* (1972) by Harmin, Kirschenbaum, and Simon. Separate chapters in each of these volumes offer suggestions for working values clarification into the curriculum when teaching English, history, science, math, home economics, language, health education, and other subjects. The basic procedure recommended is to analyze a unit or course by listing points to be covered under three headings: facts, concepts, and values. If you are teaching a required unit on the Constitution, for example, Kirschenbaum and Simon suggest that you include under the *facts* category the list of the first ten amendments and why they were called the Bill of Rights. Under *concepts*, you might outline a discovery-session topic that would call attention to social injustices the Bill of Rights was intended to correct. Under *values,* you might insert a values clarification strategy that would ask students to form small groups and discuss the rights and guarantees they have in their families. (For additional examples of facts, concepts, and values to be taught in such a unit, see pages 114–116 of *Readings in Values Clarification.*)

8. Do your best to provide learning experiences that will lead to the development of the habits and attitudes you want to foster.

Refer to the taxonomy of affective objectives (pages 281–283) and prepare a list of value and attitude goals. Then think about how you might encourage such attitudes by using techniques other than values clarification strategies.

Examples

A kindergarten teacher tried to encourage perseverance by having her pupils begin the year with short-term projects and undertake more ambitious tasks toward the end of the year.

If you want to encourage students to be sensitive to the skills of artists, novelists, or composers, point out subtle details and particularly effective sections of their works.

To make students aware of the joys of good design, encourage them to look for everyday objects that are not only useful but attractive as well.

In your Handbook you might note some specific techniques for encouraging the development of the habits, attitudes, and values you listed earlier. (If you decide, for example, that you would like to encourage awareness of the importance of keeping informed, *how* might you do this?)

9. Make use of object lessons. When illustrative incidents occur, take advantage of them.

In attempting to inculcate attitudes and values, you may find that it is sometimes more effective to use natural situations than to devise formal presentations.

Examples

> Encourage value development by taking advantage of object lessons

If a national or international figure demonstrates his or her commitment to a value system (for example, a government official resigns from an influential and high-paying position to protest an unfair decision), invite the class to discuss the event.

If someone in the class does something especially thoughtful for a classmate (for example, sends a get-well card), ask the class to consider how pleased the recipient must have felt.

Use current events to illustrate the nature of certain kinds of behavior (for example, discuss the causes of riots or point out the importance of being informed about propositions on ballots).

10. Set a good example.

Some advocates of values clarification contend that systematic efforts to build attitudes are more likely to be effective than modeling because there is no way to determine which models will be imitated. While there may be a degree of

Use of values clarification strategies may encourage pupils to acquire desirable attitudes but positive values also are strengthened when students observe and imitate admirable models. (John Coletti/Tony Stone Worldwide)

validity to this argument, the fact remains that children acquire many types of behavior by imitating others and you will be one of the adult models they will have extended contact with. Therefore, the example you set may have an impact on your students, and you should make an effort to serve as a good model.

Examples

If you want your students to become sensitive to the feelings of others, show that you are sensitive to their feelings.

If you want your pupils to be tolerant of different opinions, show that you are willing to accept differences of opinion yourself.

If you want children to be trustworthy and considerate, show that you are trustworthy and considerate in your dealings with them.

If you would like your students to get assignments in on time, be prompt in evaluating and returning their work.

Applying Technology to Teaching

USING TECHNOLOGY TO SUPPORT HUMANISTIC EDUCATION

Including a section on the use of technology to support a humanistic approach to education may, at first glance, seem like a contradiction in terms. After all, we did note in the early section of this chapter that humanistic educators such as C. H. Patterson, George Isaac Brown, and William Purkey believed that behaviorally inspired approaches to instruction (for example, instructional objectives, teaching machines, and immediate reinforcement) emphasized efficiency in learning at the expense of feelings, attitudes, and values. While these observations have some validity, we ask you to keep two things in mind. First, humanistic educators do not advocate a total abandonment of technological approaches to instruction; they are simply looking for a better balance between the cognitive and affective domains. Second, technological approaches to instruction, particularly computer-based instruction, have developed far beyond the simple linear programs originally devised by B. F. Skinner. Indeed some computer programs fit nicely within a humanistic orientation because they deal with attitudes and values, are designed as simulations, and can be used by small groups of students.

In the next two paragraphs we will briefly describe several programs that you may find useful in pursuing humanistic goals. The programs described in the first paragraph deal directly with attitudes, values, and interpersonal relationships. If you decide to use them, you may want to enlist the help of your school guidance counselor. The programs described in the second paragraph are simulations that call for the use of role play, an activity that humanistic educators believe leads to meaningful learning because it involves both thinking and feeling. Information about the cost, hardware requirements, and availability of these programs can be obtained either from *The Educational Software Selector* (EPIE Institute, 1986) or from *Only the Best* (Neill & Neill, 1990).

The *Values Clarification Series* is composed of six programs designed to help students in grades seven to college identify their values. The titles of these programs are Student Interest Survey, Values Survey Program, Characteristic Survey Program, What Would You Do?, Do You Agree?, and What Do I Value? *Decision Making, Problem Solving* is a tutorial program for students in grades seven to college. It covers such topics as knowing one's absolutes, evaluating choices, positive and negative forces, attitude awareness, and attitude modification. *Who Am I?* is a tutorial program for students in grades seven through twelve that is designed to foster self-awareness. It includes a Money Values Inventory, a Parent Relationship Scale, a Self-Concept Inventory, and a Stress Management program. The *You and Others Series* is a simulation for students in grades nine to college that helps them explore relationships with classmates, teachers, and administrators. The program provides hypothetical situations and asks the student to indicate the most likely action or solution. The program then indicates the best response and explains its choice.

Seven Cities of Gold is a simulation for students in grades four through twelve that can be used either with small groups or with the entire class. This program lets students play the role of sixteenth-century Spanish conquistadors as they explore North and South America. *The Oregon Trail* is a similar simulation program for students in grades five through twelve. Students recreate the 2,000-mile journey by covered wagon from Missouri to Oregon taken by thousands of individuals in the mid-1800s. Activities include buying provisions; consulting an on-screen map; keeping track of weather conditions, illnesses, and food supplies; and deciding how fast to travel, where to stop, and where to cross rivers. These two simulations, and others like them, can be used to help students understand the values and motives of such historical figures as conquerors and pioneers as well as the feelings of the native peoples whose lands were conquered and settled.

Resources for Further Investigation

Maslow on Humanistic Education

If you would like to sample Abraham H. Maslow's observations on humanistic education, perhaps the best single book to read is *The Farther Reaches of Human Nature* (1971). In Part 4 of this book, you will find three articles on education, although articles in other sections may also be of interest to a future teacher. Two other books by Maslow that sum up his final observations on humanistic psychology are *Religions, Values, and Peak Experiences* (1970) and *New Knowledge in Human Values* (1970).

Rogers on Humanistic Education

Carl Rogers developed the technique of person-centered therapy over thirty years ago and has since applied the same basic idea of growth of the self to other aspects of living, including education. For a concise description of Rogers's philosophy, look for the essay "Learning to Be Free" in *Person to Person: The Problem of Being Human* (1967) by Rogers and Barry Stevens. The latter volume includes three more essays by Rogers, as well as related discussions by others who share his philosophy. In *Freedom to Learn for the 80s* (1983), Rogers presents his view of teaching, provides descriptions of actual classroom applications at the elementary, secondary, and college levels, and summarizes research on humanistic approaches to education. Rogers comments on "The Process of Education and Its Future" in Part 3 of *A Way of Being* (1980), published when he was seventy-eight. Howard Kirschenbaum describes Rogers's life and work in *On Becoming Carl Rogers* (1979).

Combs on Humanistic Education

Arthur Combs presented his views on humanistic education in *The Professional Education of Teachers* (1965); in a second edition of that book written in collaboration with Robert A. Blume, Arthur J. Newman, and Hannelore L. Wass, published in 1974; and in *Helping Relationships: Basic Concepts for the Helping Professions* (2d ed., 1978), written with D. L. Avila and William W. Purkey. Combs presents the argument that humanistic education is still worth providing—even at a time when there is stress on subject-matter mastery—in articles in the February 1981 issue of *Phi Delta Kappan* and the April 1982 issue of *Educational Leadership*.

Texts on Humanistic Education

Humanistic Education (1973) by C. H. Patterson and *Behavior Dynamics in Teaching, Learning, and Growth* (1975) by Don E. Hamachek are texts in educational psychology written from a humanistic point of view.

A Sampling of Books on Humanistic Education Techniques

Teacher Effectiveness Training (1974) by Thomas Gordon explains the rationale and use of problem ownership techniques and I-messages. *Teacher and Child*

(1972) by Haim Ginott provides a different analysis of essentially the same techniques. William W. Purkey and J. M. Novak describe "A Self-Concept Approach to Teaching and Learning" in *Inviting School Success* (2d ed., 1984).

Surveys of Humanistic Education

If you would like to sample a variety of descriptions and interpretations of humanistic education, examine *Readings in Values Clarification* (1973), edited by Howard Kirschenbaum and Sidney B. Simon, or *Humanistic Education Sourcebook* (1975), edited by Donald A. Read and Sidney B. Simon.

Values Clarification

For more information on values clarification and detailed instructions for putting values clarification strategies into practice, refer to *Values and Teaching* (1966) by Louis E. Raths, Merrill Harmin, and Sidney B. Simon; *Values Clarification: A Handbook of Practical Strategies for Teachers* (1972) by Sidney B. Simon, Leland W. Howe, and Howard Kirschenbaum; or *Personalizing Education: Values Clarification and Beyond* (1975) by Leland W. Howe and Mary Martha Howe.

SUMMARY

1. Humanistic approaches to education were extremely popular in the 1970s because of disenchantment with operant conditioning and its classroom applications as well as dissatisfaction with social and political conditions in the United States.

2. Humanistic approaches to education emphasize that learning is strongly influenced by the way students feel about themselves, the subjects they study, their teacher, and the process of schooling.

3. Based on his belief that healthy individuals seek fulfilling experiences, Abraham Maslow proposed that parents and teachers should let children grow intellectually, socially, and emotionally by satisfying their basic needs and allowing them to make choices about their own development.

4. Based on his experiences with client-centered therapy, Carl Rogers proposed that teachers be more learner-centered. This involves establishing a trusting, acceptant environment in which the teacher is genuine and empathizes with the student's point of view.

5. Arthur Combs proposed that teachers should try to understand learning tasks from the student's point of view and help each student develop a positive self-concept.

6. C. H. Patterson criticized the emphasis on technological approaches to teaching.

7. George Isaac Brown proposed that teachers practice confluent education, which he described as a flowing together of affective and cognitive elements in individual and group learning.

8. Thomas Gordon suggested that teachers use two humanistic techniques: determining who "owns" a problem and conveying I-messages. The point of both techniques is to indicate awareness and acceptance of feelings.

9. William Purkey suggested that teachers use the technique of invitational learning to encourage feelings of self-worth in students.

10. Classroom techniques suggested by humanistic educators include role playing, simulation games, values clarification, and pass/fail grading.

11. Values clarification exercises are intended to help students develop a set of personal values in order to give them a basis for making confident and consistent choices and decisions. The three steps in these exercises are to choose beliefs and behaviors, prize beliefs and behaviors, and act on beliefs.

12. Humanistic approaches to education are less popular now than they were in the 1970s because of a more stable sociopolitical climate and concern over declining achievement test scores. Nevertheless, research findings suggest that humanistic techniques lead to improvement in achievement, classroom behavior, self-esteem, attitudes toward school, and interpersonal relationships.

KEY TERMS

humanistic education   *(472)*
learner-centered education   *(475)*
confluent education   *(477)*
problem ownership   *(477)*
I-messages   *(478)*
invitational learning   *(479)*
values clarification   *(481)*

DISCUSSION QUESTIONS

1. Humanistic approaches to education are based partly on the assumption that students can be trusted to want to learn and become competent, productive members of society. Can you accept such an assumption? Why?

2. Can you recall any teachers who practiced the humanistic techniques suggested by Maslow, Rogers, Combs, and others? Did you like these teachers? Did you feel as if you learned as much from them as from other teachers? Would you model yourself after such teachers?

3. In response to humanistic techniques such as values clarification, some parents have said that the schools should stick to teaching cognitive knowledge and skills and leave values instruction to parents. How would you respond to a parent who made this argument to you?

Chapter 12
MOTIVATION

ACHIEVEMENT MOTIVATION THEORY

▶ Need for achievement encouraged by successful experiences

▶ Fear of success may be influenced by a variety of factors

▶ Low achievers attribute failure to lack of ability, success to luck

▶ High achievers attribute failure to lack of effort, success to effort, ability

THE IMPACT OF CLASSROOM ATMOSPHERE AND OF THE TEACHER

▶ Cooperative reward structures promote motivation, learning

▶ Competitive reward structures often discourage motivation

▶ Individual reward structures best suited to learning knowledge, simple skills

▶ Teacher attitudes derive from ability-evaluative, moral responsibility, or task mastery value systems

ENHANCING MOTIVATION FOR CLASSROOM LEARNING

▶ Optimal motivation likely when students have skills, value them

SUGGESTIONS FOR TEACHING IN YOUR CLASSROOM

▶ Students respond to activity, investigation, adventure, social interaction, usefulness

▶ Praise may influence pupil attitudes regarding ability to learn

The last four chapters told you about the various techniques you can use to accomplish Part 3 in the model of learning—namely, to help students achieve objectives. In the introduction to the first chapter in this part (Chapter 8, "Behavioral Learning Theories"), the point was made that if you will be teaching in the elementary grades, you will need to find ways to keep your pupils occupied for five hours each day. If you will be teaching in the secondary grades, you will need to arrange instructional activities for periods ranging from forty minutes to several hours.

Regardless of the grade or subject you teach, you will be concerned about keeping your students constructively busy.

Many techniques for achieving that goal have already been discussed. Providing your students with instructional objectives (as described in Chapter 7) gives them specific goals to shoot for. Many aspects of behavioral learning theories and information processing and other cognitive theories also suggest how you can arrange learning activities to keep students occupied. When you present students with computer-assisted learning materials, or ask them to discuss a provocative topic, or urge them to use information processing techniques to acquire specific bits of information, you are stimulating them to achieve objectives. Even so, most teachers discover, sooner or later, that they must frequently look for new and better ways to arouse and sustain interest in learning. That is why Part 3 concludes with this chapter on motivation. The importance of motivation was vividly pointed out by Larry Cuban (1990), whose name you may recall from Chapter 5. Larry Cuban is the Stanford University professor of education who returned to teach a high school class for one semester after a sixteen-year absence. Of this experience, he says: "If I wanted those students to be engaged intellectually, then every day—and I *do* mean *every* day—I had to figure out an angle, a way of making connections between whatever we were studying and their daily lives in school, in the community, or in the nation" (pp. 480–481).

Motivation is not a difficult concept to understand. It is typically defined as the forces that account for the arousal, selection, direction, and continuation of behavior. Nevertheless, many teachers have at least two major misconceptions about motivation that prevent them from using this concept with maximum effectiveness. One misconception is that some students are "unmotivated." Strictly speaking, that is not an accurate statement. As long as a student chooses goals and expends a certain amount of effort to achieve them, he or she is, by definition, motivated. What teachers really mean is that students are not motivated to behave in the way the teacher would like them to behave. The second misconception is that one person can directly motivate another. This view is inaccurate because motivation comes from within a person. What you *can* do with the help of the various motivation theories discussed in this chapter is create the circumstances that *influence* students to do what you want them to do. You can, for example, make your classroom attractive and stimulating, provide a variety of incentives, allow for the expression of inherent learning-related needs, and alter students' self-perceptions. Bear in mind, however, that attempts to influence motivation will not always be successful because the source of students' motivation will not always be clear. Consequently, you may find that, despite your best efforts, some students will avoid learning or engage in non-learning activities.

THE COMPLEX NATURE OF MOTIVATION

Motivation is a difficult subject to analyze because so many different factors influence the inclination to learn. To appreciate this point, examine the following dichotomies. Under headings that describe particular factors are two descriptions that summarize situations, students, or teachers that might be placed at either end of a continuum. The descriptions refer to extreme opposites; ordinarily, there would be many gradations in between.

The Nature of the Learning Task

Self-selected subject that has substantial built-in appeal.

Required subject with little intrinsic interest or appeal.

Subject that can be learned through often enjoyable group interaction.

Subject that must be learned through individual and often tedious effort.

Field trip to an ice cream plant.

Study period devoted to preparation for an exam on multiplication tables.

Dull subject that is presented in an interesting way.

Interesting subject that is presented in a dull way.

Characteristics of Individual Pupils

Pupil with many abilities and aptitudes.

Pupil with extremely limited abilities and aptitudes.

Pupil who has always earned high grades.

Pupil who has never earned a high grade.

Parents of student benefited from doing well in school and urge the pupil to do the same.

Parents of student had unrewarding experiences in school and are negative about education.

Student expects to benefit in a variety of ways from high grades.

Student is convinced that earning high grades will have no payoff value.

Student has had positive, rewarding experiences with a particular subject.

Student has had negative, embarrassing experiences with a particular subject.

Student admires adults and friends who are interested in a particular subject.

Student associates a particular subject with individuals who are feared or disliked.

Healthy, happy student.

Sickly, malnourished, unhappy student.

Pupil who feels physically comfortable and psychologically at ease in the classroom.

Pupil who feel physically uncomfortable, is anxious and insecure in the classroom.

Pupil with strong feelings of self-esteem.

Pupil with strong feelings of self-doubt.

Confident, successful pupil who attributes failure to lack of effort and reacts to failure by resolving to try harder.

Insecure, unsuccessful pupil who attributes failure to lack of ability and is convinced that failure will be inevitable if the task is attempted again.

Pupil with a strong desire to achieve, who regularly sets and meets goals.

Pupil with little desire to achieve, who either fails to set goals or daydreams about achieving impossible goals.

Pupil with parents who encourage but do not overemphasize academic achievement.

Pupil who resents parental pressure regarding academic achievement because of the feeling that he or she is working for *them*.

Pupil who welcomes competition because of the expectation of being a winner.

Pupil who dreads competition because of the expectation of being a loser.

Pupil who welcomes competition and feels that the rewards of being a winner are more important than relations with envious peers.

Pupil who avoids competition because of a feeling that being a winner will lead to problems with friends who may be less capable.

High school student who is a foreclosure or identity achievement type with clear academic goals.

High school student who is a moratorium or identity diffusion type with no clear academic goals.

Classroom Atmosphere

Classroom atmosphere is relaxed. There is emphasis on individual improvement. Those who fail on a first try are encouraged (and helped) to overcome limitations.

Classoom atmosphere is tense. There is emphasis on competition and public comparisons. Those who fail are penalized and often humiliated.

The Personality and Approach of the Teacher

Teacher is enthusiastic, pleasant, sympathetic, and understanding.

Teacher obviously dislikes subject (and teaching), is ill tempered and vindictive

Teacher takes personal responsibility for what happens in the classroom. When students experience difficulties, teacher seeks ways to help them learn.

Teacher thinks of teaching as "just a job." When students experience difficulties, teacher assumes that they lack ability and that nothing can be done to alter the situation.

Teacher plans ahead, is well organized, has ability to keep things going smoothly.

Teacher does little planning, is disorganized, flits from one activity to another.

Many factors determine whether the students in your classes will be motivated or not motivated to learn. You should not be surprised to discover that no single theoretical interpretation of motivation explains all aspects of student

Pupils are more likely to be motivated to learn when a teacher is pleasant, sympathetic, understanding, and well organized. (John Harding/Time Magazine)

interest or disinterest. Different theoretical interpretations do shed light, though, on particular reasons why some students in a given learning situation are more likely to want to learn than others. Furthermore, each theoretical interpretation can serve as the basis for developing techniques for motivating students in the classroom. Several theoretical interpretations of motivation—some of which are derived from discussions of learning presented earlier—will now be summarized.

THE BEHAVIORAL VIEW

Behavioral Interpretations of Motivation

Chapter 8 outlined the behavioral view of learning. Recall from that chapter that the experiments of B. F. Skinner called attention to the significance of reinforcement. After demonstrating that organisms tend to repeat actions that are reinforced and that behavior can be shaped by reinforcement, Skinner developed the technique of programmed instruction to make it possible for students to be reinforced for every correct response. Supplying the correct answer—and being informed that it *is* the correct answer—motivates the student to go on to the next frame; and as the student works through the program, the desired terminal behavior is progressively shaped.

Following Skinner's lead, many behavioral learning theorists perfected techniques of behavior modification. Students are motivated to complete a task by being promised a reward of some kind. Many times the reward takes the form of

Behavioral view of motivation: reinforce desired behavior

praise or a grade. Sometimes it is a token that can be traded in for some desired object; and at other times the reward may be the privilege of engaging in a self-selected activity.

Behavioral interpretations of learning help to reveal why some pupils react favorably to particular subjects and dislike others. For instance, some students may enter a required math class with a feeling of delight, while others might feel that they have been sentenced to prison. Skinner suggests that such differences can be traced to past experiences. He would argue that the student who loves math has been shaped to respond that way by a series of positive experiences with math. The math hater, on the other hand, may have suffered a series of negative experiences.

▶ Social learning view of motivation: identification and imitation

Social learning theorists, such as Albert Bandura, call attention to the importance of observation and imitation. A student who identifies with and admires a teacher of a particular subject may work hard partly to please the admired individual and partly to try to become like that individual. A student who observes an older brother or sister reaping benefits from earning high grades may strive to do the same. A pupil who notices that a classmate receives praise from the teacher after acting in a certain way may decide to imitate such behavior to win similar rewards.

Behavioral learning theory, therefore, can be used to explain the following aspects of motivation:

Why students may work on assignments that they would prefer not to do

Why students may persevere as they work toward a remote goal

Why some students will like a particular subject while others will hate it

Why a student may want to please certain teachers but not others

Why a student may want to be like an acquaintance who does well in a particular subject or in school generally

Limitations of the Behavioral View

While you may often want—or need—to use techniques of motivation based on behavioral learning principles, you should recognize certain disadvantages that come from overuse or misuse of such techniques. When pupils study in order to receive praise from a teacher, earn a high grade, or enjoy the privilege of doing something different, they experience **extrinsic motivation.** That is, the learner is seeking to earn something not related to the activity. Under ideal circumstances students should feel **intrinsic motivation:** They should study a subject for its own sake. Because of the influence of various factors, though, such learning may be the exception rather than the rule.

▶ Praise and rewards are extrinsic forms of motivation

This point will become clear if a few motivational aspects of the behavior of individuals in and out of school are contrasted. Students are motivated to learn by being awarded grades; individuals outside of school are motivated to engage in many activities because they hope to win certificates, badges, medals, public recognition, prizes, or admiration from others. Students are motivated to learn when they realize that grades in different courses can be "traded in" for a diploma that serves as an admission ticket to further education or job opportunities; individuals outside of school may compete for prizes that have a high payoff value. (An ice skater who wins a medal in the Olympics, to mention just one example, can "trade in" that medal for a high-paying job in an ice show and a lucrative contract to make television commercials.) Students may be persuaded to work at not-so-enjoyable learning tasks by being promised the chance to engage in a favorite activity when they finish the job; many adults work at jobs they do not enjoy so that they can earn enough money to engage in leisure-time activities that they *do* enjoy.

> Excessive use of rewards may lead to resentment, limit transfer, cause dependency

Even though you may often need to try to induce students to learn by offering rewards of different kinds, you should keep in mind that such an approach involves at least three potential dangers. First, students may feel that they are being manipulated and resent the fact that they must exert themselves in order to win your approval or gain a reward. Second, learning may be seen as a temporary means to an end. As soon as an exam is written or a course is completed, the extrinsic goal has been achieved and the student will tend to forget what was learned and perhaps even avoid the subject in the future. In such cases, little or no transfer will take place because the student is unlikely to receive any permanent benefit from learning and will be disinterested in seeking ways to apply what has been learned. Third, students may become too dependent on teachers.

> Intrinsic motivation undermined by rewarding performance, ignoring quality

> Intrinsic motivation enhanced when reward given according to predetermined standard

These dangers have been discussed and clarified by researchers. Mark Morgan (1984), for example, has analyzed the circumstances under which external rewards either undermine or enhance intrinsic motivation for school-type tasks. One of the most important of these circumstances concerns the perceived relationship between performance and reward. If students conclude, for example, that they will be rewarded simply for engaging in an activity and that quality of performance will be ignored, they are likely to show a decrease in intrinsic motivation for the task. The same effect is likely to occur when students receive greater or lesser amounts of a reward depending on rate of performance (such as number of problems completed on a worksheet or number of books read within a given period). On the other hand, there are two instances in which external rewards can enhance intrinsic motivation. First, when rewards are given according to some predetermined standard of excellence, when the task is moderately challenging, and when the reward is relatively large, intrinsic interest in the task is likely to increase. Second, intrinsic motivation can be enhanced when the task is moderately challenging and the size of the reward is consistent with the individual's perceived level of skill. If a student wins first prize in a science fair, for example, and believes that her project was truly superior to those of the other participants, a large reward may cause the student to maintain a strong interest in science.

Why do external rewards undermine intrinsic motivation when they are given just for performing a task? Morgan suggests two possibilities. One is that human beings have an innate drive to be competent (an idea we discuss in the next section), and rewards that are given irrespective of quality of performance say nothing about an individual's level of competence on moderately difficult tasks. The second possibility is that beginning in early childhood we learn to equate the promise of a reward with the performance of an unpleasant activity. Students may therefore come to believe that "if somebody promises me a reward to do something, it will probably be unpleasant." Furthermore, the type of reward seems to make no difference. Tangible rewards (such as toys and candy) and social rewards (such as praise and honors) can be equally effective in undermining or enhancing intrinsic motivation. These results strongly suggest that teachers should avoid the indiscriminate use of rewards for influencing classroom behavior, particularly when an activity seems to be naturally interesting to students. Instead, rewards should be used to provide students with information about their level of competence on tasks they have not yet mastered.

▶ Give rewards sparingly, especially on tasks of natural interest

THE COGNITIVE VIEW

▶ Cognitive view of motivation: arouse disequilibrium

The cognitive view stresses that human behavior is influenced by the way individuals perceive things. At any given moment, people are subjected to many forces that pull and push them in different directions. The direction that behavior takes is explained by assuming that individuals experience some sort of disequilibrium, which they feel impelled to overcome.

Cognitive Interpretations of Motivation

The techniques recommended by Jerome Bruner for structuring discovery sessions are intended to cause students to want to find out more about some topic or revise their perceptions. One such technique is to pose questions that cause pupils to recognize gaps in their thinking, which they are then eager to clarify or fill.

This view is related to Jean Piaget's principles of equilibration, assimilation, and accommodation. Piaget proposes that children possess an inherent desire to maintain a sense of organization and balance in their conception of the world (equilibration). A sense of equilibration may be experienced if a child assimilates a new experience by relating it to an existing scheme, or the child may accommodate by modifying an existing scheme.

Similar explanations have been offered by other psychologists. R. W. White (1959), for instance, prefers the words *competence* or *efficacy* over *equilibration*. White analyzed dozens of theories and hundreds of studies of motivation, some of which attempted to trace all urges to learn to biological needs. He concluded that many types of human behavior are not traceable to physiological drives, since there are some activities in which individuals engage when all their physical needs are satisfied. In other words, many of the things people do are motivated by curiosity, an urge to explore, or simply an impulse to try something for the fun of it.

Cognitive theory often highlights intrinsic motivation. Students who are intrinsically motivated value learning for its own sake. They try to get the intended benefit from every school task, regardless of expected outcome (for example, getting a reward), task characteristics (for example, an interesting subject), or their emotional state (for example, anxiety or fear of failure). They tend to exhibit a relaxed, persistent, task-involved state of mind, which in turn tends to increase their understanding of a topic or their level of cognitive skill (Brophy, 1983a). The advantage of such learning is that it is likely to transfer in both specific and general ways. What has been learned may have been selected because it represented a problem of personal concern, so the learner is likely to benefit from and remember it. And because the learner has successfully used self-discovery techniques that can be applied to other problems, an all-purpose technique has been acquired or strengthened.

Cognitive theory emphasizes intrinsic motivation

Cognitive theory, then, sheds light on the following aspects of classroom motivation:

Why it is not always necessary to offer rewards for learning

Why students may respond (or fail to respond) to class discussions or assignments that will have no impact on a grade

Why students may continue to seek an answer to a problem even though they have failed to experience reinforcement in early stages of exploration and inquiry

Why students will respond positively to one learning situation (because they experience a cognitive disequilibrium) but not respond to another

Why solving one problem may equip and stimulate a student to try to solve other problems

Limitations of the Cognitive View

Often difficult to arouse a cognitive disequilibrium

While cognitive theory appears promising as a means for motivating pupils, it has a major (and often debilitating) limitation: It is not always easy or even possible to induce students to experience a cognitive disequilibrium sufficient to stimulate them to seek answers. This is particularly true if an answer can be found only after comparatively dull and unrewarding information and skills are mastered. (How many elementary school pupils, for example, might be expected to experience a self-impelled urge to learn English grammar or to acquire skill in mathematics?) You are likely to gain some firsthand experience with the difficulty of arousing cognitive disequilibrium the first time you ask students to respond to what you hope will be a provocative question for class discussion. Some pupils may experience a feeling of intellectual curiosity and be eager to clarify their thinking, but others may stare out the window or do homework for another class.

THE HUMANISTIC VIEW

In Chapter 11, Abraham H. Maslow's views on humanistic education were briefly summarized. Recall that, while Maslow expressed varied opinions on education, his primary interest was motivation.

Maslow's Theory of Growth Motivation

A Hierarchy of Needs   Maslow described seventeen propositions, discussed in Chapter 1 of *Motivation and Personality* (3d ed., 1987), that he believed would have to be incorporated into any sound theory of *growth motivation* (or *need gratification*) to meet them. Referring to need gratification as "the most important single principle underlying all development," he added that "the single, holistic principle that binds together the multiplicity of human motives is the tendency for a new and higher need to emerge as the lower need fulfills itself by being sufficiently gratified (1968, p. 55). He elaborated on this basic principle by proposing a five-level hierarchy of needs. *Physiological* needs are at the bottom of the hierarchy, followed in ascending order by *safety, belongingness and love, esteem,* and *self-actualization* needs (see Figure 12.1). This order reflects differences in the relative strength of each need. The lower a need is in the hierarchy, the greater its strength—because when a lower-level need is activated (as in the case of extreme hunger or fear for one's physical safety), people will stop trying to satisfy a higher-level need (such as esteem or self-actualization) and focus on satisfying the currently active lower-level need (Maslow, 1987).

> People are motivated to satisfy deficiency needs only when those needs are unmet

The first four needs (physiological, safety, belongingness and love, and esteem) are often referred to as **deficiency needs** because they motivate people to act only when they are unmet to some degree. Self-actualization, by contrast, is often called a **growth need** because people constantly strive to satisfy it. Because it is at the top of the hierarchy, self-actualization is discussed more frequently than the lower-level needs. Basically, **self-actualization** refers to the need for self-fulfillment—the need to develop all of one's potential talents and capabilities. For example, an individual who felt he or she had the capability to write novels, teach, practice medicine, and/or raise children would not feel self-actualized until all of these goals had been accomplished to some minimal degree.

> Self-actualization depends on satisfaction of lower needs, belief in certain values

Maslow originally felt that self-actualization needs would automatically be activated as soon as the esteem needs were met, but he changed his mind when he encountered individuals whose behavior did not fit this pattern. He concluded that individuals whose self-actualization needs became activated held such values as truth, goodness, beauty, justice, autonomy, and humor in high regard (Feist, 1990).

In addition to the five basic needs that compose the hierarchy, Maslow described cognitive needs (such as the needs to know and to understand) and aesthetic needs (such as the needs for order, symmetry, or harmony). While not part of the basic hierarchy, these two classes of needs play a critical role in the

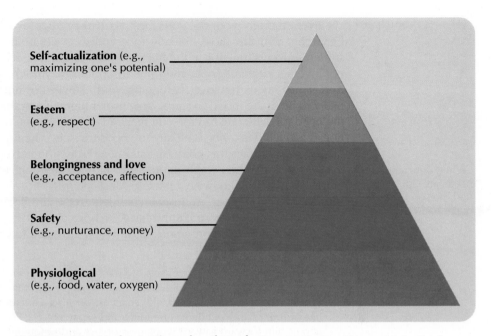

FIGURE 12.1   Maslow's Hierarchy of Needs (From "A Theory of Human Motivation," *Psychological Review,* vol. 50 (1943), pp. 370–396. Copyright 1943 by the American Psychological Association.)

satisfaction of basic needs. Maslow maintained that such conditions as the freedom to investigate and learn, fairness, honesty, and orderliness in interpersonal relationships are critical because their absence makes satisfaction of the five basic needs impossible. (Imagine, for example, trying to satisfy your belongingness and love needs or your esteem needs in an atmosphere characterized by dishonesty, unfair punishment, and restrictions on freedom of speech.)

Implications of Maslow's Theory

The implications of Maslow's theory of motivation for teaching are provocative. One down-to-earth implication is that a teacher should do everything possible to see that the lower-level needs of students are satisfied, so that they are more likely to function at the higher levels. Students are more likely to be primed to seek satisfaction of the esteem and self-actualization needs, for example, if they are physically comfortable, feel safe and relaxed, have a sense of belonging, and experience self-esteem. Since the satisfying of deficiency needs involves dependence on others, and since teachers have the primary responsibility for what takes place in the classroom, it is worth emphasizing again that you will play an important role in the need gratification of your students. The more effective you are in assisting them to satisfy their deficiency needs, the more likely they are to experience growth motivation.

Teachers are in a key position to satisfy deficiency needs

Even though you do your best to satisfy the lower-level needs in this hierarchy, you are most unlikely to establish a situation in which all of your students always function at the highest levels. A girl who feels that her parents do not love her or that her peers do not accept her may not respond to your efforts. And if her needs for love, belonging, and esteem are not satisfied, she is less likely to be in the mood to learn. Only under highly favorable circumstances does the need for self-actualization emerge; and only when the need for self-actualization is activated is a person likely to choose wisely when given the opportunity. Maslow emphasizes this point by making a distinction between *bad choosers* and *good choosers.* When some people are allowed freedom to choose, they seem consistently to make wise choices. Most people, however, frequently make self-destructive choices. An insecure student, for example, may choose to attend a particular college more on the basis of how close it is to home than on the quality of its academic programs. Maslow explains such apparent contradictions in this way:

> Every human being has [two] sets of forces within him. One set clings to safety and defensiveness out of fear, tending to regress backward, hanging on to the past, *afraid* to grow . . . , *afraid* to take chances, *afraid* to jeopardize what he already has, *afraid* of independence, freedom and separateness. The other set of forces impels him forward toward wholeness of Self and uniqueness of Self, toward full functioning of all his capacities, toward confidence in the face of the external world at the same time that he can accept his deepest, real, unconscious Self. (1968, pp. 45–46)

Growth, as Maslow sees it, is the result of a never-ending series of situations offering a free choice between the attractions and dangers of safety and those of growth. If a person is functioning at the level of growth needs, the choice will ordinarily be a progressive one. Maslow adds, however, that

> [i]n this process the environment (parents, therapists, teachers) is important in various ways, even though the ultimate choice must be made by the child:
> a. It can gratify his basic needs for safety, belongingness, love and respect, so that he can feel unthreatened, autonomous, interested and spontaneous and thus dare to choose the unknown.
> b. It can help by making the growth choice positively attractive and less danger-ous, and by making the regressive choice less attractive and more costly. (1968, pp. 58–59)

The first point emphasizes the suggestion made earlier that you should do everything possible to gratify deficiency needs and thus encourage growth. The second point can be clarified by a simple diagram Maslow uses to illustrate a situation involving choice (1968, p. 47):

▶ When deficiency needs are not satis-fied, person likely to make bad choices

Enhance the dangers		Enhance the attraction
Safety	⟵ person ⟶	Growth
Minimize the attractions		Minimize the dangers

▶ Encourage growth choices by enhancing attractions, minimizing dangers

This diagram emphasizes that if you set up learning situations that impress students as dangerous, threatening, or of little value, they are likely to play it safe, make little effort to respond, or even try to avoid learning. On the other hand, if you make learning appear appealing, minimize pressure, and reduce possibilities for failure or embarrassment, your students are likely to be willing, if not eager, to do an assigned task.

Maslow's theory can be used to explain or illuminate the following aspects of motivation:

Why pupils who feel uncomfortable because of hunger, ill health, or irritating physical conditions may not be interested in learning

Why pupils are more likely to be eager to learn in a relaxed, secure, inviting classroom than in a threatening, tense atmosphere

Why pupils who feel they are loved, accepted, and admired are more likely to be interested in learning than those who feel rejected, ignored, or mistreated

Why some pupils make wise choices when given opportunities to direct their own learning while others make self-destructive choices

Why some pupils may have a stronger desire to know and understand than others

Limitations of Maslow's Theory

While Maslow's speculations are thought-provoking, they are also sometimes frustrating. You may conclude, for instance, that awareness of his hierarchy of needs will make it possible for you to do an excellent job of motivating your pupils, only to discover that you don't know exactly how to apply what you have learned. Quite often, for example, you may not be able to determine precisely which of a pupil's needs are unsatisfied. Even if you *are* quite sure that a pupil lacks interest in learning because he or she feels unloved or insecure, you may not (as mentioned earlier) be able to do much about it.

Then again, there will be times when you can be quite instrumental in helping to satisfy certain deficiency needs. The development of self-esteem, for example, is closely tied to successful classroom achievement for almost all students. Although you may not be able to feed students when they are hungry or protect them from physical danger, you can always take steps to help them learn more effectively. To make that task easier, the next section describes a useful approach to motivation that revolves around the need to achieve.

ACHIEVEMENT MOTIVATION THEORY

The Need for Achievement

John W. Atkinson (1964) has developed a theory of motivation that combines the conception of *achievement motivation* proposed by David McClelland (1961)

David McClelland and J. W. Atkinson explain differences in the need for achievement by proposing that pupils who work diligently to earn high grades have had successful experiences reaching specific goals they have set for themselves. Those who lack the need for achievement have had experiences with failure, or have not set realistic goals, or both. (Erika Stone)

Need for achievement encouraged by successful experiences

with ideas about level of aspiration. McClelland believes that in the course of development, human beings acquire a *need for achievement,* and he has conducted research to demonstrate the degree to which this need varies among individuals. Atkinson hypothesizes that differences in the strength of the need for achievement can be explained by postulating a contrasting need to avoid failure. Some people, he suggests, are success oriented; others have a high degree of anxiety about failure. Through experimentation, Atkinson and George Litwin (1960) showed that success-oriented individuals are likely to set personal goals of intermediate difficulty (that is, they have a 50-50 chance of success), whereas anxiety-ridden persons set goals that are either very high or very low. (If anxiety-ridden individuals fail on the hard task, no one can blame them; and they are almost sure to succeed on the easy task.) Atkinson believes that the tendency to achieve success is influenced by the probability of success and the attractiveness of achieving it. A strong need to avoid failure is likely to develop in people who experience repeated failure and set goals beyond what they think they can accomplish.

The similarity of Atkinson's conception to Maslow's theory of motivation is apparent. Both emphasize that the fear of failure must be taken into account in arranging learning experiences. The same point has been stressed by William Glasser in *Control Theory in the Classroom* (1986) and *The Quality School* (1990). Glasser argues that for people to succeed at life in general, they must first experience success in one important aspect of their lives. For most children, that one important part should be school. But the traditional approach to education, which emphasizes comparative grading, allows only a minority of students to feel successful. Most students feel that they are failures, which depresses their motivation to achieve in other areas of their lives.

One of the most intriguing aspects of differences in need for achievement is that some individuals seem to "fear" success and others seem to be motivated to avoid it.

Fear and Avoidance of Success

Reading reports of research inspired by the work of McClelland and Atkinson, Matina S. Horner became intrigued by the finding that the need for achievement in males seemed to be more fully developed than in females. She decided to make this the subject of her Ph.D. dissertation (1968). Using a technique derived from studies by Atkinson, she asked 178 university students to write a four-minute story from this cue: "At the end of first-term finals Anne finds herself at the top of her medical school class." When she analyzed the stories, Horner found three recurrent themes: (1) fear that Anne would lose friends; (2) guilt about success; and (3) unwillingness to come to grips with the question of Anne's success (in some stories, the aforementioned cue was more or less ignored). She concluded that all three of these themes reflected a general *fear of success* and discovered that 65.5 percent of the stories written by women could be classified under this heading, as contrasted with only 9 percent of those written by men.

As a second part of her study, Horner placed men and women in competitive and noncompetitive situations. She found that women who wrote fear-of-success stories performed much better when working alone than when competing against others. She reasoned that fear of success motivates many women to avoid achievement, particularly in competitive situations.

Reports of Horner's study (1970) attracted attention, and a number of articles in newspapers and magazines led readers to believe that there is a well-established tendency for almost all women to fear success. Because of the publicity and topicality of the concept, over sixty studies derived from or similar to Horner's original research were carried out in the next three years. David Tresemer (1974, 1977) reviewed these and also analyzed the techniques used by Horner. He concluded that fear-of-success stories may be influenced by a variety of factors, including the type of cues supplied. For example, when a woman in a story is described as the best *psychology* student rather than as the best medical student, Tresemer reports, males write more fear-of-success stories than females.

▶ Fear of success may be influenced by a variety of factors

While some students may avoid success because they fear they will jeopardize their relationships with peers, others may have a weak need for achievement because of conflicts with parents. Irving B. Weiner (1980) proposes that many adolescents who seek counseling because of academic performance problems express resentment about parental demands, which they cannot or prefer not to meet. If the resentment is strong enough, the high school student may retaliate by deliberately earning low grades (perhaps as a means for establishing a negative identity).

Explanations of Success and Failure: Attribution Theory

Some interesting aspects of success and failure are revealed when students are asked to explain why they did or did not do well on some task. The four reasons most commonly given stress ability, effort, task difficulty, and luck. To explain a low score on a math test, for example, different students might make the following statements:

"I just have a poor head for numbers." (Lack of ability)

"I didn't really study for the exam." (Lack of effort)

"That test was the toughest I've ever taken." (Task difficulty)

"I guessed wrong about which sections of the book to study." (Luck)

(Because pupils *attribute* success or failure to the factors just listed, research of this type contributes to what is referred to as **attribution theory.**)

> Low achievers attribute failure to lack of ability, success to luck

Students with long histories of academic failure and a weak need for achievement typically attribute their success to easy questions or luck and their failures to lack of ability. Ability is a stable attribution (that is, people expect its effect on achievement to be pretty much the same from one task to another), while task difficulty and luck are both external attributions (in other words, people feel they have little control over their occurrence). Research has shown that stable attributions, particularly ability, lead to expectations of future success or failure, whereas internal attributions (those under personal control) lead to pride in achievement and reward attractiveness following success or lead to shame following failure (Nicholls, 1979; B. Weiner, 1979). Because low-achieving students attribute failure to low ability, future failure is seen as more likely than future success. In addition, ascribing success to factors beyond one's control diminishes the possibility of taking pride in achievement and placing a high value on rewards. Consequently, satisfactory achievement and reward may have little effect on the failure-avoiding strategies that poor students have developed over the years.

> High achievers attribute failure to lack of effort, success to effort, ability

Success-oriented students (high need achievers), on the other hand, typically attribute success to ability and effort, and failure to insufficient effort. Consequently, failure does not diminish expectancy of success, feelings of competence, or reward-attractiveness for these students. They simply resolve to work harder in the future.

It may be, then, that rewards will not motivate low need achievers to work harder so long as they attribute success to factors that are unstable and beyond their control. Such successes are seen as "flukes," which are unlikely to occur again and do little to instill a sense of pride and accomplishment. By contrast, because high need achievers expect to succeed and feel they are largely in control of their success, occasional failures do not greatly diminish their motivation for future learning.

This analysis suggests that programs designed to enhance motivation and achievement may need to include ways of altering perceived causes of performance. Quite often it is necessary for teachers to try to alter a poor student's self-concept, which may be a substantial undertaking requiring a concerted, coordinated effort. (An outline of procedures you might follow will be presented later in this chapter.)

Implications of Analyses of Achievement Motivation Theory

These various analyses of aspiration level and achievement help explain the following aspects of motivation:

Why some pupils have a higher level of aspiration than others

Why pupils with a low level of aspiration may fail to experience success because they set unrealistic goals

Why some pupils may almost seem to avoid success

Why high-achieving pupils may resolve to try harder after having a failure experience

Why low-achieving pupils may not really be encouraged by successful experiences

Limitations of Achievement Motivation and Attribution Theories

Perhaps the major limitation in speculating about aspirations, need for achievement, fear of success, and reactions to success and failure is that such forms of behavior are often difficult to observe or analyze. Another problem may be lack of consistency. In controlled situations, it may be possible to trace how and why students set goals. But in typical classroom settings, students may not have any clear idea about their level of aspiration, unless the teacher specifically asks them to set a particular standard for themselves. Furthermore, a pupil's level of aspiration may be bumped up or down by more or less chance circumstances. A student might do well on a first exam in a course, for example, because the teacher gave in-class time for study and happened to offer advice at a crucial point during the study period. The high score on that test might inspire the student to work for an A in that class. But if the second exam happened to be scheduled the day after the student had been ill, or if the teacher inadvertently snubbed him or her in class, the student might not prepare and could end up with a D grade. Poor performance on the second exam might then cause the student to forget about the A and concentrate instead on obtaining a C– with the least amount of effort.

It also seems likely that the aspiration level will vary with different subjects and courses. Tresemer found, for instance, that responses to fear-of-success stories depended on the kind of activity described. Thus, a girl might fear success in a "masculine" subject, such as physics, but not worry about being better than a boyfriend in a "neutral" subject, such as psychology, or a "feminine" subject, such as English. In addition, a high school student's level of aspiration or need for achievement is often intertwined in reciprocal fashion with feelings about identity. A foreclosure type who endorses parental attitudes regarding goals and values may have a very clear picture of what needs to be accomplished in school and may be motivated to achieve those goals. By contrast, moratorium or identity diffusion types, who may be in conflict with parents, uncertain about what to do after graduation, and/or confused about sex roles, may drift aimlessly through high school. Finally, students may find that they seem to have an affinity for certain subjects because of aptitudes, abilities, and past experiences. Other subjects may seem extraordinarily difficult to the same students because of lack of aptitude or absence of previous experience.

THE IMPACT OF CLASSROOM ATMOSPHERE AND OF THE TEACHER

As noted at various points in this discussion, the atmosphere of the classroom and the attitude and personality of the teacher can affect a student's motivation. These two topics will now be explored more systematically—before the implications for teaching are examined.

Classroom Atmosphere

Maslow's hierarchy of needs and his diagram illustrating the clash between safety and growth in situations involving choice call attention to the significance of classroom atmosphere. If students feel frightened, insecure, or rejected, they will find it difficult to concentrate on learning. If they feel that they will be penalized for failure or that there is little likelihood of success, they are more likely to make safety rather than growth choices. The impact on student behavior of different types of learning situations has been clarified by research on classroom reward structures.

Types of Classroom Reward Structures   According to James W. Michaels (1977), there are four basic classroom reward structures. Under the first structure, *individual competition,* only a small number of individuals can obtain the greatest rewards and, even then, only at the expense of other class members. One example of individual competition is the familiar "grading on a curve," which predetermines the percentage of A, B, C, D, and F grades. That is, regardless of the actual distribution of test scores, only a small percentage of the students in a class will receive A's. Under the second structure, *group competition,* groups of students cooperate among themselves in order to compete with other groups for the available rewards. Competition in this reward structure is defined as a situation where the actions of some students are seen as blocking the goal attainment of one or more other students.

Some researchers have argued that competitive reward structures lead students to focus on ability as the primary basis for motivation. This orientation is reflected in the question, "Am I smart enough to accomplish this task?" When ability is the basis for motivation, competing successfully in the classroom may be seen as relevant to self-esteem (since nobody loves a loser), difficult to accomplish (since only a few can succeed), and uncertain (success depends on how everyone else does). These perceptions may cause some students to avoid challenging subjects or tasks and give up in the face of difficulty (Ames & Ames, 1984; Dweck, 1986).

The third structure, *group reward,* is a true cooperative situation. In this case, rewards are distributed solely on the basis of the quality of the group's performance. An individual can obtain a reward (such as a high grade or a feeling of satisfaction for a job well done) only if the other group members are able to obtain the same reward. Also, all groups may receive the same rewards, provided they meet the teacher's criteria for mastery. In this case, cooperation is defined as a situation in which the actions of others are seen as promoting goal attainment. Cooperative structures lead students to focus on effort and cooperation as the primary basis of motivation. This orientation is reflected in the statement, "We can do this if we try hard and work together." In a cooperative atmosphere, students are motivated out of a sense of obligation: One ought to try, contribute, and help satisfy group norms (Ames & Ames, 1984). William Glasser, whose ideas we mentioned earlier, is a fan of cooperative learning. He points out that student motivation and performance tend to be highest for such activities as band, drama club, athletics, the school newspaper, and the yearbook, all of which require a team effort (Gough, 1987). We would also like to point out that cooperative learning and reward structures are consistent with the constructivist view of learning and teaching that we discussed in Chapters 1, 2, and 10, since they encourage inquiry, perspective sharing, and conflict resolution behaviors.

The fourth classroom reward structure is termed *individual reward*. In this situation, the accomplishments of and rewards received by one individual are completely independent of the accomplishments and rewards of other individuals. Thirty students working by themselves at computer terminals are functioning in an individual reward structure. According to Carole and Russell Ames (1984), individual structures lead students to focus on task effort as the primary basis for motivation (as in "I can do this if I try"). Whether or not a student perceives a task as difficult depends on how successful he or she has been with that type of task in the past. The obvious question at this point is, What is the relationship between these reward structures and motivation and achievement?

Reward Structures and Motivation Three of the leading writers on reward structures, David W. Johnson and Roger T. Johnson (1987, 1991) and Robert E.

Slavin (1991), have concluded that cooperative, competitive, and individualistic goal structures produce marked differences in student motivation and student achievement.

Students who learn cooperatively expect to succeed at classroom tasks, show a high degree of commitment to learning, are curious about a variety of subjects, are highly persistent, and demonstrate a high degree of intrinsic motivation for learning. (This statement echoes Morgan's conclusion that extrinsic rewards enhance intrinsic motivation when they tell us we are competent at something.) In comparison to competitive and individualistic arrangements, cooperative learning produces higher levels of achievement, particularly for tasks that involve some sort of problem-solving activity, self-esteem, and the liking of classmates (Johnson & Johnson, 1991; Slavin, 1990b, 1991). This last outcome should be of particular interest to those of you who expect to teach in areas that are marked by cultural diversity.

Effective cooperative-learning groups adhere to the following four principles, the first two of which are the most important (Slavin, 1990b):

1. *Team rewards.* The team rather than the individual earns the reward (such as a grade, a privilege, or a certificate).

2. *Individual accountability.* All team members must contribute to the assignment, be it a project, a problem-solving exercise, or mastery of a textbook chapter.

3. *Equal opportunities for success.* The top rewards are available to all students—provided each makes a significant contribution to the group effort. Since cooperative groups are heterogeneous with respect to ability, this goal is accomplished by requiring members to improve on their previous performance.

4. *Team competition.* Although cooperation within groups is required, competition between groups may be encouraged—provided all groups are able to obtain the top reward.

Johnson and Johnson (1991) suggest several reasons for the effectiveness of cooperative learning:

1. The discussion process promotes the discovery and development of higher-quality learning strategies.

2. The conflict among ideas, opinions, and conclusions of group members that is an inevitable part of the discussion process produces repetition, explanation, and integration of information, thereby enhancing retention and comprehension.

3. Group members provide valuable feedback, support, and encouragement of one another's efforts.

Many students who learn under a competitive reward structure have a low expectation for classroom success, show a low degree of commitment to learn-

> Cooperative reward structures promote motivation, learning

Competitive reward structures may inspire a small number of pupils to push themselves to their limits, but cooperative reward structures are more likely to motivate almost all students in a class to study and develop positive attitudes toward learning. (David Ryan/D. Donne Bryant Stock Photo)

▶ Competitive reward structures often discourage motivation

ing, are not curious about most subjects, do not persist at tasks for very long, and are more extrinsically than intrinsically motivated. Competition, as defined above, produces these negative motivational outcomes because it consistently produces the same "winners" and "losers." That is, those students with high levels of ability and prerequisite knowledge will almost always get the lion's share of classroom rewards, whereas their less fortunate peers will almost always reap failure, frustration, and a weak sense of self-esteem. As predicted by Maslow and Atkinson, students who experience chronic failure typically do whatever is necessary to avoid failure. Avoidance techniques may involve nonparticipation, low levels of effort, or very high or very low levels of aspiration.

Ames and Ames (1984) have pointed out some additional negative aspects of competitive reward structures. They found that children reward themselves only if they win a competition. The quality of the child's past performances on similar tasks tends to be seen as irrelevant. Furthermore, children who win in competitive situations tend to reward themselves more for winning than they reward others for winning, because of differences in attribution (for example, "My success was due to ability, but yours was due to luck").

Although competitive reward structures should be avoided during the initial phases of learning, since they emphasize preexisting differences among students, competition can be used in the classroom when all students have the ability to compete effectively. Thus, contests that center on the review of previously mastered knowledge (such as spelling words or definitions of terms) or similar levels of athletic skill can be highly motivating and enjoyable.

Disagreement exists about the effect of individual reward structures on motivation and achievement. Johnson and Johnson (1991) feel that when children are rewarded for their own efforts while working alone, they are likely to develop low expectations for success, a low commitment to learning, low persistence, and an extrinsic orientation to learning. Ames and Ames (1984), on the other hand, feel that individual reward structures may produce the greatest amount of intrinsic motivation and achievement. They found that children who performed academic tasks under an individual structure reported more effort-related, self-instructional, and self-monitoring types of thoughts than did children under a competitive structure (for example, "I will work carefully"; "I will take my time"; "I will make a plan"). These statements reflect metacognitive awareness and strategic behavior. Recall from Chapters 9 and 10 the importance of metacognition and strategic skills to learning, remembering, problem solving, and transfer. We will have more to say shortly on the relationship between information processing skills and motivation. Individual reward structures seem to be best suited to tasks that involve acquiring knowledge and simple skills.

> Individual reward structures best suited to learning knowledge, simple skills

On the basis of the above discussion, you may have begun to form a preference for a particular reward structure. That's fine so long as you realize two things: First, all of the reward structures have a legitimate place in the classroom. David and Roger Johnson (1991) estimate that under ideal circumstances a cooperative reward structure would be used 60 to 70 percent of the time, an individualistic reward structure 20 percent of the time, and a competitive reward structure 10 to 20 percent of the time. Second, other factors also influence motivation. The attitude and personality of the teacher, which we discuss next, is one such factor.

Teacher Attitude and Personality

To realize how much a teacher's attitude and personality may influence student motivation, examine some of your own experiences with different teachers. If you admired or had a crush on an elementary school teacher, for example, you probably were eager to earn that teacher's approval by performing well in class. If you disliked or feared a teacher in the elementary grades, you may have lost all interest in learning and simply endured school until the end of the year. If an elementary grade teacher obviously liked some subjects much better than others, you probably reacted in similar fashion. If you felt that a teacher was merely putting in time in the classroom, you likely did the same. In high school you may have chosen your college major because you admired the teacher of a particular subject. You may also have made a firm resolution never to take another course in a particular subject because you associated it with a disagreeable instructor. Some teachers probably made it clear that they disliked assigning high grades, while other teachers may have seemed genuinely pleased when they could legitimately award A's.

That these differences in teacher attitude and personality exist is undeniable. From where, however, do they originate? According to Carole and Russell Ames

Teacher attitudes derive from ability-evaluative, moral responsibility, or task mastery value systems

(1984), they originate largely from value systems that parallel the competitive, cooperative, and individualistic reward structures just discussed. These value systems, or systems of teacher motivation, are referred to as ability-evaluative, moral responsibility, and task mastery.

An ability-evaluative system, like competition, is based on winners and losers (good teachers and bad teachers). Thus, classroom conditions are arranged to maximize the appearance of high teaching ability and minimize the appearance of low teaching ability. This may take the form of unrealistically high student-performance standards and very tight control of the classroom. Under an ability-evaluative system, teachers attempt to maintain a sense of self-worth and competence by blaming students for failure and crediting themselves for success.

A moral responsibility motivational system is like a cooperative reward structure in that it revolves around such values as cooperation, dependability, and duty. The dominant question becomes "How can I help this student?" On the positive side, this orientation leads to a persistent teacher helping role. On the negative side, it could foster student dependency or teacher burnout. When teachers are motivated by a sense of moral responsibility, they tend to blame themselves for student failure and credit the student for success.

A task mastery motivational system is most like an individual reward structure. The focus is on identifying important learning tasks and determining how they can best be accomplished by students. Thus, teacher self-worth is more closely associated with student accomplishment than with the teacher's desire to appear able or responsible. Under this system, teacher ability and effort are seen as important determinants of student accomplishment.

ENHANCING MOTIVATION FOR CLASSROOM LEARNING

Most of the conceptions of motivation that have been discussed up to this point can be classified as *expectancy* or *performance* oriented because they describe what people expect to get for putting out a certain amount of effort. For example, operant conditioning and social learning theory suggest that people will work to achieve a goal if they expect to receive an appropriate reward. Likewise, humanistic theory holds that people will strive toward self-actualization if they expect their deficiency needs to be met. Achievement motivation theory holds that the level of excellence people work to attain depends on how they balance their level of aspiration against their fear of failure or fear of success. And attribution theory holds that the performance level people expect to attain depends on the perceived underlying causes of success and failure. According to an analysis by Jere Brophy (1983a), these approaches, while useful, are not likely by themselves to optimize student motivation because of the special nature of classrooms and academic work. Hence, they need to be supplemented with a "motivation to learn" theory that focuses on the *value* of learning for its own sake.

Brophy argues that classroom work has three characteristics that set it apart from other endeavors. First, it is primarily cognitive. Most academic tasks require such cognitive processes as attention, encoding, retrieval, organizing, and problem solving. Second, it is compulsory. Students rarely get to choose from among a set of tasks or to choose whether they will or will not perform a particular task. Third, classroom work is more or less publicly evaluated. It is very hard to hide the results of an exam, a book report, or a laboratory experiment from peers or parents.

Brophy discusses two implications that follow from his analysis. One is that the usual finding from achievement motivation research—that most students prefer situations in which there is about a 50 percent chance of success—is not likely to apply to the classroom. Given the above three characteristics of classroom tasks, most students would probably prefer easier tasks and a higher chance of success. Brophy cites supportive research showing that student motivation is enhanced when classroom success is the result of reasonable effort but is reduced when success results only from sustained effort. In addition, we know from Chapter 8 that learning occurs most smoothly and consistently when it is achieved through small, easy-to-master steps.

The second implication of Brophy's work is that performance levels are likely to be highest when motivation is optimal—relaxed but learning oriented—rather than when motivation is very high and intense. Again, given that classroom tasks are cognitive, compulsory, and publicly evaluated, motivation is likely to be optimal when students know they have the skills to master a task and value those skills. Very high motivation spurred by strong emotional arousal may well reduce performance. Thus, success experiences, effort attributions, achievement motives, or reward structures, by themselves, will not stimulate the best motivation for classroom learning. Students must also possess a sense of control over learning processes as well as a sense that classroom tasks provide valuable opportunities to use and refine those processes. The cognitive skills that are necessary to master most tasks and that contribute to this sense of control are the ones that were discussed in Chapter 9—metacognitive knowledge, strategic skills, and tactical skills.

In discussing how to produce an optimal level of motivation for classroom learning, Brophy makes several general suggestions that draw from most of the motivation theories discussed in this chapter. To begin with, the teacher needs to eliminate such impediments to motivation as negative attitudes, anxiety, and fear of failure. This can be done by using programmed materials to guarantee continuous progress and success, training students to set challenging but achievable goals, and training them to attribute failure to lack of effort rather than ability. Each of these approaches should have some positive effects, particularly if the level of task difficulty is appropriate for the student. If the task is too difficult, it may not be possible to set reasonable goals or to attribute failure to lack of effort rather than ability. This is not necessarily a trivial point; research has shown that many teachers give assignments that are too difficult for some students.

The next step is to produce positive motivation. Brophy offers several suggestions. First, make sure that the magnitude of a reward matches the quality of the work (this is the same point that Mark Morgan made earlier). Second, stimulate students to value a task because the knowledge or skills that it teaches

Optimal motivation likely when students have skills, value them

will be valuable in the future. You might mention, for example, that people who are knowledgeable and capable often are good problem solvers, are asked by others to help solve problems, hold positions of responsibility, and are quite satisfied with their position in life. This technique should be handled with care, though, because it can easily end up motivating out of fear and anxiety ("How are you going to get a job if you can't read or do math?" "You don't want people to think you are ignorant, do you?"). Third, help students to become more aware and appreciative of the knowledge and skills that they develop and to take pride in how they apply what they have learned. One way to further this goal is to provide students with clearly articulated objectives, so they will accurately recognize the level of skill or knowledge they have attained. Thus informed, they can gauge their progress toward higher, more distant goals. Fourth, stimulate students to value and enjoy the actual process of working on academic tasks. Presumably, as students gain better control over the processes of learning, they will find academic tasks more meaningful and intrinsically motivating.

In conclusion, Brophy points out that teachers need to do much work in this area. In one study of how elementary grade teachers presented tasks, it was found that only 28 percent of the teachers introduced tasks in a way that could be described as potentially fostering intrinsic motivation (as, for instance, when the teacher states that students are expected to enjoy the task and do well on it). In fact, one type of introduction in the intrinsic motivation category, called "self-actualization" (as when the teacher suggests that new knowledge or skill will bring pleasure or personal satisfaction), was *never* used by the teachers studied.

Now that you are familiar with interpretations of motivation, it is time to consider how the information and speculations just summarized can be converted into classroom practice. The following two lists provide some structure for this discussion. They highlight, on the left, reasons why students may lack motivation to learn and, on the right, how you might try to change or minimize those reasons. These lists not only serve as an outline of what follows; they may also function as a trouble-shooting checklist to which you might refer when you are baffled by lack of student interest in learning.

Why Student May Be Unmotivated	**Some Things You Might Do About It**
Subject is boring.	Try to make subject as interesting as possible; supply incentives to learn.
Subject is presented in a boring way.	Make a systematic effort to arouse and sustain interest.
Effort must be expended before mastery or enjoyment occurs.	Explain about delayed payoff; use behavior modification techniques to encourage perseverance; provide short-term goals.
Pupil would rather not exert self.	Specify objectives, rewards; attempt to make lack of effort seem unappealing.

Pupil doesn't know what to do.	State specific instructional objectives; explain how these can be met, what the rewards will be.
High school pupil has identity problems, lacks clear goals.	Urge pupil to select short-term goals, think about long-term goals.
Pupil lacks aptitude or ability.	Give less capable pupils individual help, more time to complete tasks; try different kinds of instruction.
Parents of pupil are neutral or negative about schooling.	Emphasize that learning can be enjoyable, that doing well in school opens up opportunities.
Pupil comes from a disadvantaged background, has limited experiences.	Check on range of experiences; supply necessary background information.
Pupil has had negative experiences in school or with a particular subject.	Make experiences in your classroom as positive as possible; make sure reinforcement occurs frequently.
Pupil associates subject with a disliked individual.	Try to be a sympathetic, responsive person so that pupil will build up positive associations.
Pupil dislikes subject because of envy or jealousy of those who do well at it.	Play down comparisons between pupils; urge self-improvement.
Pupil feels tired, hungry, uncomfortable.	Try to allow for or alleviate discomfort.
Pupil feels insecure, anxious, scared.	Make your classroom physically and psychologically safe.
Pupil experiences little sense of acceptance, belonging, esteem.	Show pupil that you respond positively, that pupil is worthy of esteem.
Pupil has never earned high grades, has been "punished" by low grades.	Avoid public comparisons; stress self-competition and individual improvement.
Pupil has low level of aspiration.	Urge pupil to set and achieve realistic goals.
Pupil has weak need for achievement.	Try to strengthen pupil's self-confidence; stress values of achievement.
Pupil is afraid to try because of fear of failure.	Arrange a series of attainable goals; help pupil achieve them.
Pupil assumes failure is due to lack of ability and that there is no point in trying.	Try to strengthen pupil's self-concept; set up a series of short-term goals; help pupil succeed after initial failure.

Pupil learns only when required or cajoled to learn	Invite pupil to participate in selecting goals, deciding how they will be met; encourage pupil to be self-directed.
Pupil resents learning only what others say must be learned	Invite pupil to participate in selecting instructional objectives.

Mid-Chapter Review

Views of motivation have been stated or implied by theorists who favor each of the views of learning described in Chapters 8, 9, 10, and 11.

The Behavioral View of Motivation

Behavioral theorists stress that individuals are motivated when their behavior is reinforced. Social learning theorists emphasize the impact of identification and imitation, pointing out that observing someone else benefiting from a certain type of behavior may motivate a person to do the same. Behavioral theorists urge teachers to reinforce students with praise and rewards of various kinds when correct or desired responses occur. Reinforcement practices can be effective, but they are *extrinsic* forms of motivation, inclining students to view learning as a means to an end—the earning of a reward. Excessive use of rewards may lead to resentment, limited transfer, dependence on teachers, and the undermining of intrinsic motivation.

The Cognitive View of Motivation

Cognitive theorists stress that individuals are motivated when they experience a *cognitive disequilibrium,* or a desire to find the solution to a problem. Arranging for pupils to experience a personal desire to find information or solutions is an *intrinsic* form of motivation whereby learning occurs for its own sake. Unfortunately, it is often difficult to arouse a cognitive disequilibrium in all, or even most, students.

The Humanistic View of Motivation

The humanistic psychologist Abraham Maslow proposed that human needs are arranged in hierarchical order. *Deficiency needs* (physiological, safety, belongingness and love, and esteem) must usually be satisfied and certain values must be held before self-actualization needs exert an influence. When the deficiency needs have been satisfied, the growth-motivated person seeks pleasurable tension and engages in self-directed learning. Teachers are in a key position to satisfy the deficiency needs; and they should remain aware that when the lower needs are not satisfied, students are likely to make either *safety* (nonproductive) choices or bad choices when they make decisions. Teachers can encourage pupils to make *growth* rather than safety choices by enhancing the attractiveness of learning situations likely to be beneficial and by minimizing the dangers of possible failure.

(continued)

Achievement Motivation Theory

Maslow's distinction between safety and growth choices is similar to the concept of *level of aspiration,* which stresses that people tend to want to succeed at the highest possible level while at the same time avoiding the possibility of failure. When students *are* successful, they tend to set realistic goals for themselves; and successful experiences, in turn, strengthen a *need for achievement.* It has been found, though, that some individuals (particularly females in certain situations) may experience a *fear of success,* in the sense that they worry that being successful may interfere with positive relationships with others.

Studies that led to the formulation of *attribution theory* revealed that low achievers tend to attribute failure to do well in school to lack of ability and therefore assume that there is no point in making greater efforts to succeed. When low achievers *are* successful, they tend to attribute it to luck. High achievers, on the other hand, attribute failure to lack of effort and assume they can succeed if they try harder.

The Impact of Classroom Atmosphere and of the Teacher

Classroom situations in which students are forced to compete against one another tend to discourage all but the very best students from trying. Cooperative reward situations, in which students work independently or cooperatively in noncompetitive ways to improve their mastery of subject matter, tend to promote motivation to learn in almost all students.

Enhancing Motivation for Classroom Learning

Because classroom learning tasks are cognitive, compulsory, and publicly evaluated, Jere Brophy argues that student motivation is at an optimal level when task difficulty is moderate (with a better than 50 percent chance of success), when students know they have the skills to master a task, and when they value those skills. To produce optimal levels of motivation, teachers need to help students eliminate negative attitudes, anxiety, and fear of failure and to value the processes and products of learning.

Suggestions for Teaching in Your Classroom

MOTIVATING STUDENTS TO LEARN

1. Try to make every subject interesting. Make study as active, investigative, "adventurous," social, and useful as possible.
2. Use behavior modification techniques to help students exert themselves and work toward remote goals.
3. Make sure that pupils know what they are to do, how to proceed, how they will know they have achieved goals.
4. Take into account individual differences in ability, background, attitudes toward school, and feelings about specific subjects.

5. Do everything possible to satisfy the deficiency needs—physiological, safety, belongingness, and esteem.
   a. Allow for the physical condition of your pupils and the classroom.
   b. Make your room physically and psychologically safe.
   c. Show your students that you take an interest in them and that they belong in your classroom.
   d. Arrange learning experiences so that all students can gain at least a degree of esteem.

6. Enhance the attractions and minimize the dangers of growth choices.

7. Direct learning experiences toward feelings of success in an effort to encourage a realistic level of aspiration, an orientation toward achievement, and a positive self-concept.
   a. Make use of objectives that are challenging but attainable.
   b. Provide knowledge of results by emphasizing the positive.
   c. Permit and encourage students to direct their own learning.

8. For students who need it, try to encourage the development of need achievement, self-confidence, and self-direction.
   a. Use achievement motivation training techniques.
   b. Use cooperative learning methods.

---

1. Try to make every subject interesting. Make study as active, investigative, "adventurous," social, and useful as possible.

Some subjects seem dull and boring to almost everyone; other subjects seem to have built-in appeal. If you don't plan motivational strategies, though, you might make a mildly boring subject deadly or convert a potentially interesting subject into one that is uninteresting. Lack of interest within the classroom often leads to a vicious circle. A dull presentation by the teacher causes students to show that they are bored and restless; and the lack of response from pupils causes the teacher to lose confidence and enthusiasm, and to assume that nothing can be done to arouse student interest. In short, the teacher's fatalistic reaction increases student boredom—and so on. For your own protection, then, as well as for the educational welfare of your students, you should endeavor to make what you teach as interesting as possible.

One way to figure out how to make almost *any* subject appealing is to analyze learning experiences that students respond to with interest when they are given opportunities to make free choices. May V. Seagoe surveyed reports on such experiences and concluded that students' interests very often result from successful experience and familiarity. Among the "points of appeal that emerge from studies of specific interests," she lists the following:

▶ Students respond to activity, investigation, adventure, social interaction, usefulness

(a) the opportunity for overt bodily *activity*, for manipulation, for construction, even for observing the movement of animals and vehicles of various sorts; (b) the opportunity for *investigation*, for using mental ingenuity in solving puzzles, for working problems through, for creating designs, and the like; (c) the opportunity for *adventure,* for vicarious experiences in makebelieve, in books, and in the mass media; (d) the opportunity for *social assimilation,* for contacts with others suitable to the maturity level of the child (ranging from parallel play to discussion and argument), for social events and working together, for human interest and humanitarianism, and for conformity and display; and (e) the opportunity for use of the new in real life, making the new continuous with past experience and projecting it in terms of future action. (1970, p. 25)

As you think about how you are going to organize your lesson plans for each day and each period, you might ask yourself: "Are there ways that I can incorporate activity, investigation, adventure, social interaction, and usefulness into this presentation?" Here are some examples of techniques you might use.

Activity

Handbook Heading:
Ways to Make Learning
Active

Have several students go to the board. Give a rapid-fire series of problems to be solved by those at the board as well as those at their desks. After five problems, have another group of students go to the board, and so on.

Arrange for all members of the class to go to the library and find information on some self-selected topic that is related to the subject being studied.

Arrange a field trip, particularly if it will have transfer value. Have a social studies class visit a district court, for instance.

Think of ways to move out of the classroom legitimately every now and then. Teach geometry, for instance, by asking the class to take several balls of string and lay out a baseball diamond on the side lawn of the school.

Seagoe found that students respond with interest to school situations that are active, investigative, adventurous, social, and useful. Having members of a fifth-grade class play the roles of state government officials is an activity that includes almost all these features. (Richard Hutchings)

Investigation

Handbook Heading:
Ways to Promote Investigation

In elementary grade classrooms (and in some secondary school classrooms), set up learning centers with provocative displays and materials, such as these suggested by C. M. Charles:

Appreciation center for observing paintings, poems, sculptures, arrangements, etc.

Art activity center equipped for drawing, painting, modeling, etc.

Communications center equipped for listening to, viewing, and dramatizing music, stories, and guided activities

Display center for showing and observing collections, projects, and hobbies

Games center where students can use instructional games, puzzles, and similar aids

Library and reading center containing both commercial and student-made reading materials

Science center equipped for observation and project work

Social science center stocked with maps, charts, documents, reference books, etc., along with materials and equipment for constructing (1972, p. 105)

(In secondary school classrooms, you might arrange centers that pertain to different aspects of a single subject. In a science class, for example, you might have an appreciation center stressing aesthetic aspects of science, a display center calling attention to new developments in the field, a library center consisting of attractive and provocative books, and so on.)

Invite the class to suggest a topic they want to investigate. Use techniques recommended by Howe and Howe, which were outlined in Chapter 10 (and which will be reviewed a bit later in these Suggestions).

Develop activity cards describing individual study projects, and ask students to investigate a topic of their own choice.

Adventure

Handbook Heading:
Ways to Make Learning Seem Adventurous

Occasionally, use techniques that make learning entertaining and adventurous. Such techniques might be particularly useful when you introduce a new topic. You might employ devices used by advertisers and the creators of "Sesame Street," for instance. Use intensity, size, contrast, and movement to attract attention. Make use of color, humor, exaggeration, and drama to introduce a new unit. Use audiovisual devices of all kinds—films, tapes, charts, models. Take students by surprise by doing something totally unexpected.

The night before introducing a new unit, redecorate part of the room. Then ask the class to help you finish it.

If you are going to introduce a unit on a famous historical or literary or scientific figure (and if you have always wanted to be an actor or actress), dress up in clothes similar to those worn by that person.

Consider using techniques such as these described by Albert Cullum in *Push Back the Desks* (1967). (Although Cullum's techniques were used with ele-

mentary school pupils, many of them could be adapted for use with older pupils.)

Arrange a "Parade of Presidents," in which each pupil selects a president of the United States and presents a State of the Union message to the rest of the class, each member of which takes the part of a member of Congress.

Teach geography by presenting "Adventure Hunts," in which the pupils imagine they are detectives trying to keep track of a person who travels to various parts of the United States.

Have the class build a replica of "King Tut's Tomb," and then encourage students to play the role of archaeologists. Instead of "digging" for mummies, however, the students use flashlights to find problems, puzzles, graphs, and other items dealing with numbers that are written on cards tacked to the inside walls of the tomb. Each problem has a number and a point score. After a student figures out an answer, he or she deposits it in a box designed as a sarcophagus. After each "dig," answers are discussed. At the end of the year, fancy certificates are presented to the archaeologists who, by accumulating sufficient points, made a specified number of successful digs.

Hand out dittoed sheets of twenty questions based on articles in each section of a morning newspaper. Each student is provided with a copy of the paper and competes against herself or himself to discover how many of the questions can be answered in the shortest period of time. (Typical questions: Why is the senator from Mississippi upset? Who scored the most points in the UCLA–Notre Dame basketball game? What did Lucy say to Charlie Brown?)

Create a "Renoir Room" (or the equivalent), in which reproductions of Renoir paintings are displayed on all the walls and the students are encouraged to find out as much as they can about the painter.

Have students read the poems of Longfellow and paint murals depicting scenes from the poems.

Social Interaction

Handbook Heading:
Ways to Make Learning
Social

Arrange small-group discussions, as described in Chapter 10.

Have two or more students team up and prepare a report.

Have students pair off and ask each other questions before an exam. Do the same with difficult-to-learn material by suggesting that pairs cooperate in developing mnemonic devices, preparing flashcards, and the like to help each other master information.

Organize an end-of-unit extravaganza where individuals and groups first present or display projects and then celebrate by having refreshments.

Use *role-playing* techniques and simulation games, as described in the discussion of humanistic education in Chapter 11.

Usefulness

Handbook Heading:
Ways to Make Learning
Useful

Continually point out that what is being learned can be used outside of class. Ask pupils to keep a record of how they use what they learn outside of class.

Develop exercises that make students aware that what they are learning has transfer value. Have students in an English class write a letter of application, for instance; have math students balance a checkbook, fill out an income tax form, or work out a yearly budget; have biology students think about ways they can apply what they have learned to avoid getting sick.

One approach that incorporates most or all of these techniques, and that can be used with preschool and primary grade children, is the project approach. Lillian Katz and Sylvia Chard (1989) define a project as an in-depth study of a particular topic that one or more children undertake and that extends over a period of days or weeks. Projects may involve an initial discussion that captures the students' interest (for example, discussing how a house is built); dramatic play; drawing, painting, and writing; group discussions; field trips; construction activities; and investigation activities. Because projects are based on children's natural interests and involve a wide range of activities, they are more likely to be intrinsically motivating.

2. Use behavior modification techniques to help students exert themselves and work toward remote goals.

Maslow's hierarchy of needs calls attention to reasons why few students come to school bursting with eagerness to learn. Only pupils with all their deficiency

Interest in learning may
be aroused or sustained
by occasional use of
role playing or dramatic
interpretations of different kinds. (Frank Siteman/
The Picture Cube)

needs satisfied are likely to experience a desire to know and understand. But
even growth-motivated students may follow the line of least resistance. It requires
much less effort to goof off than to work. Furthermore, hardly any pupils will
conclude on their own that they need to master certain basic skills before they
can engage in more exciting and rewarding kinds of learning. Accordingly, you
may often need to give your pupils incentives to learn. Techniques you might use
for this purpose were described in Chapter 8. They include shaping, modeling,
token economies, and contingency contracting.

Examples

Handbook Heading:
Using Behavior Modifi-
cation Techniques to
Motivate

Arrange for pupils to observe that classmates who persevere and complete a
task receive a reward of some kind. (It is probably better to let this occur
more or less naturally as opposed to publicly calling attention to star pupils.
In addition, it may be unwise to permit students who have finished an assignment to engage in self-chosen activities that are attention-getting or ostenta-
tiously enjoyable, since those who are still working on the assignment may
then become more inclined to think evil thoughts about their "lucky" classmates than to work on the task at hand.)

Draw happy faces on primary grade students' papers, give check marks as
students complete assignments, write personal comments acknowledging
good work, and assign bonus points.

Use tests and grades as motivating devices by relying on the mastery approach (to be described at the end of the next chapter).

Develop an individual reward menu, or contract with each pupil based on the Premack principle (Grandma's rule). After passing a spelling test at a particular level, for example, each student might be given class time to work on a self-selected project.

When making use of such motivational techniques, you might do your best to play down overtones of manipulation and materialism. Point out that rewards are used in almost all forms of endeavor to induce people to work toward a goal. Just because someone does something to earn a reward does not mean that the activity should never be indulged in for its own sake. (Athletes often compete to earn the reward of being members of the best team, for example, but they still enjoy the game.) To help students grasp the fact that rewards are a means to an end rather than an end in themselves, try suggesting that they use behavior modification techniques on themselves outside the classroom.

Examples

"I know that memorizing spelling words is not the most interesting thing in the world, but it's easier for us to understand each other if we all spell the same way. Besides, there is a school district requirement that you learn to spell the words on this list. I've just shown you some memorization techniques you might use, but you will also be rewarded with a chance to see that movie I mentioned when you reach the goal we just agreed on. If you find that you are able to work harder in school when you have a reward to shoot for, you might do the same thing outside of class. The next time you have a homework assignment or have to do some sort of chore, pick out a reward to give to yourself when you complete the job."

"It would be nice if you all wanted to read the text for this course for the sheer joy of it, because by the time you finish it, you will have acquired a lot of useful and interesting information. But since it isn't as exciting as a spy novel, I'm going to help you concentrate in class by letting you look at a videotape of a program from the 'Nova' series each time you pass an exam. To help yourselves concentrate when you study at home, you might follow the same procedure. After you have completed a homework assignment (or some household job), reward yourself by watching a favorite TV program."

3. Make sure that pupils know what they are to do, how to proceed, how they will know they have achieved goals.

Many times pupils do not exert themselves in the classroom because they say they don't know what they are supposed to do. Occasionally such a statement is merely an excuse for goofing off, but it may also be a legitimate explanation for lack of effort. Recall from Chapter 9 that knowing what one is expected to do is important information in the construction of a learning strategy. You should use the techniques described in Chapter 7 to take full advantage of the values of instructional objectives. The most important point about objectives—at least in terms of motivation—is that they should be clear, understood by all members of the class, and attainable in a short period of time. For reasons illustrated by behavioral theorists' experiments with different reinforcement schedules, pupils are more likely to work steadily if they are reinforced at frequent intervals. If you set goals that are too demanding or remote, lack of reinforcement during the early stages of a unit may derail students, even if they started out with good intentions. Whenever you ask students to work toward a demanding or remote goal, try to set up a series of short-term goals.

Examples

Handbook Heading:
Ways to Arrange
Short-Term Goals

"Here is a Mathematics Goal Card. It lists all of the mathematical skills you should learn by the end of the school year. As you achieve each of the goals on this card, you will receive a check mark. For every five check marks you earn, you will be rewarded with one of these cards. After you accumulate three cards, you will be able to trade them in for extra recess time. Since I want all of you to have extra recess time, I will give help if you need it and ask for it."

"This report period we are going to use what is called the personalized system of instruction. Here are lists of points I want you to concentrate on as you read each chapter of your text. As soon as you feel you know what the authors are emphasizing about each one of the points on a list, you can ask to take a quiz on that chapter. If you meet the criterion level for a passing grade the first time, you can go on to the next chapter. If you don't make it, you will be asked to study the material over and take the exam again. If you *do* have to study a chapter a second time, I will be available to answer questions and give study suggestions. As soon as you pass exams on all of the chapters, you will be given free time to work on your term project in class. If you take one exam a week, and if you pass each one the first time, you will have plenty of time to do an excellent term project without having to do any work after school."

4. Take into account individual differences in ability, background, attitudes toward school, and feelings about specific subjects.

As the descriptions at the beginning of the chapter reveal, students with high levels of ability whose parents are enthusiastic about education and provide many kinds of enriching experiences typically get off to a good start in school. If such students earn high grades the first time they are given report cards, they will be reinforced for studying and will be motivated to continue to earn high grades. If they have an occasional failure, they are likely to try harder the next time. They will also tend to set realistic goals for themselves and develop a strong need for achievement. On the other hand, students with limited academic ability or limited experiences who come from homes where parents take little or no interest in education are likely to have problems in school. If they receive low grades on their first report cards, get no encouragement from parents, and are unsuccessful when they try to earn higher grades, they are likely to become discouraged and fatalistic. They may approach many tasks with the expectation of failure, and if they do earn a high grade, they may attribute it to luck. They are also likely to set unrealistic goals for themselves and fail to experience a need to achieve.

In any class you are likely to find students who more or less fit each of those descriptions. Many others will be somewhere in between. Thus, some pupils in any class are likely to be essentially self-motivated; others will need a great deal of help and attention if they are to learn; most will need occasional assistance. Even highly motivated students, though, may find it difficult to study certain subjects. In any required high school or college course, for instance, there are likely to be some students who love the subject and can hardly wait to take advanced courses and others who detest the subject and cannot grasp how anyone could enjoy it. Thus, you will often need to consider general and specific differences in student desires to learn. To do so systematically, you might refer to the lists of dichotomies at the beginning of this chapter and also to the trouble-shooting checklist found just before these Suggestions for Teaching in Your Classroom. If you schedule a group or individual work period in class, look around the room and jot down the names (in a subtle way, so that your students are not aware they are being observed) of all the pupils who are obviously not concentrating on the task at hand.

If you realize before long that you are writing down the names of most pupils in the class, you probably should refer again to the suggestions for making learning active and interesting or use behavior modification techniques to sustain effort. But if only a few names are on your list, you might ask yourself questions such as these as you observe each unmotivated pupil:

Handbook Heading:
Ways to Analyze Motivation Problems

Is this assignment particularly boring or difficult for this student? What can I do to help him finish it? Should I team him with an excellent student so they could work on it together? Should I have him tutor a poor student? Should I urge him to pick out a personal reward activity that he can engage in when he finishes it?

Does this student understand what the assignment is and how to proceed? What can I do to make the goal more specific, and how can I make it more attractive?

Does this student lack background or experience in dealing with this assignment? Should I check on basic understanding and find materials that give background information, if needed? Should I give her a simpler assignment of the same type?

Has this student received a low grade recently? Should I go over and give her a pep talk and try to convince her that she *can* do well on this assignment? Should I divide the work up into a series of subassignments and reward her for completing each unit?

Does this student act as if he doesn't "belong" in this classroom? Should I go over and give him individual attention and provide as much personal encouragement as I can?

Does this student seem to resent it every time I give an assignment? Should I ask her to work out a learning contract with me so that she gets the feeling it's a mutual agreement?

5. Do everything possible to satisfy the deficiency needs—physiological, safety, belongingness, and esteem.
   a. Allow for the physical condition of your pupils and the classroom.

Examples

Handbook Heading:
Ways to Satisfy Physiological Needs

Be aware that your students may occasionally be hungry or thirsty. (This point sounds obvious, but it is frequently forgotten.) If conditions allow, permit snacks on an individual basis or have a routine—or occasional nonroutine—snack break.

Have a change of pace or a break when appropriate. With young children, make allowance for flexible nap time.

Schedule demanding activities when students are fresh; schedule relaxing activities toward the end of a period or day.

Be prepared for greater restlessness before lunch and just before dismissal time at the end of the day.

Be alert for physical annoyances, such as sunlight coming through a window and half-blinding a student or a draft by an open window. Try to eliminate the annoyance, or permit the student to move to another part of the room.

Make a habit of checking the room temperature. Ask students if the room is too warm or too cool.

b. Make your room physically and psychologically safe.

Handbook Heading:
Ways to Satisfy Safety Needs

The need for safety is likely to be satisfied by the general classroom climate you establish, although physical factors of safety may be involved, particularly with young pupils. In one kindergarten, for example, several children were worried about the possibility of fire after seeing television news coverage of a fire in a school. In most cases, however, you can best ensure safety by establishing a relaxed, secure classroom environment.

Examples

If you see that a pupil fears something (for example, being bullied by older pupils on the playground, fire, enclosed places), explain that you will offer protection or that adequate precautionary measures have been taken.

Establish a classroom atmosphere in which students know what to expect and can relax about routines. Do everything you can to make your room a place that is psychologically safe. Be alert to things you do that are unnecessarily threatening. Try to see things from your students' point of view in an effort to detect anxiety-producing situations.

As much as possible, establish classroom routines in which students can take the initiative. Don't require recitation; wait for students to volunteer. Don't force students to participate in new activities; let them try such activities when they feel ready.

A humiliating or embarrassing experience may generalize such that a student comes to hate or fear everything connected with a classroom. If a student does have such an experience, go out of your way to make him or her feel comfortable and secure. Try to arrange for the pupil to have a strong, positive experience in class to displace negative associations and build up positive ones.

Handbook Heading:
Ways to Satisfy Belong-
ingness Needs

c. Show your students that you take an interest in them and that they belong in your classroom.

Examples

Learn and use names as fast as you can.

Follow the open-education practice of keeping detailed records for individual pupils, and refer to accomplishments specifically.

Students are likely to be inclined to learn if you are enthusiastic, establish a positive atmosphere, and convey the impression that you take an interest in them and that they belong in your classroom. (Jeff Comella/courtesy of Mellon Bank Corporation)

Whenever possible, schedule individual tutorial or interview sessions so that you can interact with all students on a one-to-one basis. If a student is absent because of an extended illness, send a get-well card signed by the entire class.

To encourage class spirit, schedule group planning sessions or "sharing" activities; that is, invite students to talk about interesting experiences or to make announcements about after-school activities.

Handbook Heading:
Ways to Satisfy Esteem
Needs

d. Arrange learning experiences so that all students can gain at least a degree of esteem.

Examples

Play down comparisons; encourage cooperation and self-competition. (Evaluation techniques that encourage self-competition will be provided in the next chapter in an analysis of mastery learning.)

Permit students to work toward individual goals.

Provide opportunities to students who possess culture-specific talents (such as storytelling, singing, dancing, or weaving) to demonstrate and teach them to others.

Give individual assistance to students who are experiencing problems.

(Further suggestions for satisfying esteem needs will be presented with subsequent points.)

6. Enhance the attractions and minimize the dangers of growth choices.

When you first begin to teach, you might keep a copy of Maslow's diagram of a choice situation in your top desk drawer. Refer to it when the need arises and ask yourself, "Am I setting things up to encourage effort, or am I encouraging the student *not* to try?" If you establish situations that generate pressure, tension, or anxiety, your students will choose safety and do their best to remain uninvolved. But if you minimize risks and make learning seem exciting and worthwhile, even the less secure students may feel impelled to join in.

Examples

Don't penalize guessing on exams.

Don't impose restrictions or conditions on assignments if they will act as dampers. For example, avoid insisting that "You must hand in all papers typed, with no erasures or strikeovers." Some pupils may not even start a report under such conditions.

Avoid "do or die" situations, such as single exams or projects.

To encourage free participation, make it clear that you will not grade students on recitation.

Point out and demonstrate the values of learning and the limitations and disadvantages ("dangers") of not learning. For example, explain to students that knowing how to multiply and divide is necessary for personal bookkeeping and also that errors will lead to difficulties—perhaps making it necessary for someone else to do the work for them.

Remain aware of the disadvantages of inappropriate or excessive competition. If competition becomes excessive in a school situation, students may think of learning only as a means to an end (being better than others); as a result, they may become more interested in their relative position in a class than in their actual performance. Only a few students will be able to experience success, and the tendency to make safety rather than growth choices will be increased.

Handbook Heading:
Ways to Encourage
Self-Competition

To avoid these disadvantages, encourage students to compete against themselves. Try to give each pupil some experience with success by arranging situations in which all students have a fairly equal chance in a variety of activities, and make use of group competitive situations that stress fun rather than winning.

Examples

Have pupils set their own goals, and keep private progress charts.

Follow the open education technique of keeping a separate folder for each student rather than a grade book that indicates only relative performance.

Give recognition for such virtues as punctuality and dependability.

Give recognition for skill in arts and crafts and in music.

Use games such as "Spelling Baseball." Divide the class into two approximately equal teams. Each time a pupil spells a word correctly, award her or his team a base. Four bases, and the team has a run. Each misspelled word is an out. No team members are eliminated, and pressure is reduced considerably. If some unfortunate makes too many outs, throw an easy word the next time that person is at bat. In order to avoid overidentification with a particular team, use different players for each game. (If permanent teams are set up or if you overemphasize the competitive nature of the game by offering a prize, the technique may backfire.)

7. Direct learning experiences toward feelings of success in an effort to encourage a realistic level of aspiration, an orientation toward achievement, and a positive self-concept.

McClelland's theory of achievement motivation and Atkinson's development of it further emphasize how some people are success oriented and others anxiety ridden. Glasser maintains that for individuals to succeed at life in general, they must first experience success in one important part of their lives—particularly in school. All these theorists emphasize the vital importance of success. Students who experience early failure in any learning experience will either lose interest or actively avoid further learning, which could bring more failure. Thus, it is vital to try to arrange learning experiences in such a way that students will experience success. In order to feel successful, an individual must first establish goals that are neither so low as to be unfulfilling nor so high as to be impossible and must then know that the goals have been achieved. This is a two-step process: establishing goals and receiving knowledge of results.

a. Make use of objectives that are challenging but attainable.

The first step in the three-stage teaching strategy being stressed in this book is to state the desired terminal behavior. Those who favor behavioral approaches to instruction advocate the use of objectives stated in behavioral terms, primarily to make instruction more efficient; but they also suggest that objectives be used to arouse, sustain, and direct student interest. When objectives are used for purposes of motivation, however, it is especially important, as we pointed out in Chapter 11, to invite students to participate in their selection. You are likely to get a better reaction if, instead of simply stating objectives yourself, you invite your students to participate in selecting them—or at least to think along with you as you explain why the objectives are worthwhile. This will tend to shift the emphasis from extrinsic to intrinsic motivation.

Handbook Heading:
Ways to Encourage Students to Set Their Own Objectives

In developing objectives to serve a motivating function, you may want to use the techniques recommended by Mager to help shift the emphasis from teacher direction to student choice. Having a self-selected objective to shoot for is one of the best ways to arouse and sustain interest. You might assist your students in stating objectives in terms of a time limit, a minimum number of correct responses, the proportion of correct responses, or a sample of actions.

Examples

"How many minutes do you think you will need to outline this chapter? When you finish, we'll see that film I told you about."

"George, you got six out of ten on this spelling quiz. How many do you want to try for on the retest?"

"After reading this article on the laws of motion, see if you can state them in your own words and give two everyday examples of each."

The form of these examples implies that you are inviting students to participate in the development of their own objectives. Although this is a desirable policy to follow, sticking to it may not always be possible or appropriate. In many situations you may find it necessary to set goals yourself.

b. Provide knowledge of results by emphasizing the positive.

In order to experience success (as a basis for establishing a realistic level of aspiration), your students must receive detailed information about their performance. In a behavioral approach, feedback will be supplied automatically when students respond to a question in a computer program or compare their performance to criteria included in a set of instructional objectives. Knowledge of results may be vague or even absent if you attempt to arouse a cognitive disequilibrium, since there may not be any definite answer to a discussion topic. In discovery sessions—and in many other classroom situations—knowledge of performance may be supplied primarily by comments you make. If you make observations on recitation, ask questions in a discussion or on an exam, or provide comments on papers of various kinds, the kind of feedback you provide may make the difference between feelings of success and feelings of failure. Accordingly, you should do your best to comment favorably on successful performance and avoid calling attention to failure, particularly the kind that is already apparent.

Handbook Heading:
Ways to Supply Positive
Feedback

Some advocates of behavior modification suggest that teachers make broad use of praise as a reinforcer—to the point of suggesting that you shape your own behavior to increase your productivity as a praiser. Jere Brophy (1981), however, suggests that classroom teachers rarely use praise as an effective or desirable form of reinforcement. Behavioral theorists (O'Leary & O'Leary, 1977) have proposed that in order for praise to shape behavior, it should be provided only after performance of designated activities, it should be specific, and it should be sincere and credible. In reviewing records of actual teacher behavior in classroom situations, Brophy concluded that few teachers use praise in such ways. Most of the teachers who were observed used praise infrequently (less than 6 percent of the time), they did not wait until specified behavior had occurred before offering praise, and the favorable comments they made were more often general than specific. Accordingly, Brophy suggests that praise typically does not take the form of reinforcement; instead, it is likely to be a spontaneous reaction to student behavior. Quite often a teacher's behavior concerning praise is shaped by students rather than the reverse. Certain students *ask* for praise and reinforce the teacher by reacting positively when they receive it. Brophy found that in other cases students who aroused negative feelings in teachers for one reason or another received the most praise in classrooms. Apparently such pupils elicited praise from a teacher partly because they gave the impression of needing motivation and reassurance and partly because the teacher seemed to feel guilty about reacting negatively.

Brophy suggests that teachers tend to use praise in the following ways:

As a spontaneous expression of surprise or admiration ("Why, John! This report is really excellent!")

As compensation for criticism or vindication of a prediction ("After your last report, John, I said I knew you could do better. Well, you *have* done better. This is really excellent.")

As an attempt to impress all members of a class ("I like the way John just put his books away so promptly.")

As a transition ritual to verify that an assignment has been completed ("Yes, John, that's very good. You can work on your project now.")

As a consolation prize or to encourage students who are less capable than others ("Well, John, you kept at it and you got it finished. Good for you!")

Many of these uses of praise do not serve to reinforce student behavior in specific ways. Quite often, though, various forms of praise may influence a student's self-concept and attitude toward learning. In discussing the need for achievement and the concepts of attribution theory, earlier portions of this chapter acquainted you with differences in student reactions to failure. High achievers tend to attribute failure to lack of effort and resolve to try harder. Low achievers often attribute failure to lack of ability and assume nothing can be done about it. Brophy suggests that teachers may shape such reactions by the ways they supply praise (and criticism).

Praise may influence pupil attitudes regarding ability to learn

In an effort to help teachers become aware of some of the unexpected aspects of praise, Brophy drew up the guidelines for effective praise listed in Table 12.1. He also urges teachers to supplement verbal praise in the following ways:

Write specific favorable comments on students' work, taking into account individual expectations regarding performance.

Help students set appropriate goals, evaluate their own performance, and reinforce themselves for good work.

Encourage students to attribute outcomes to their own efforts and abilities rather than to external causes that are beyond their control.

(The last two points are discussed in detail in other sections of these Suggestions for Teaching in Your Classroom.)

c. Permit and encourage students to direct their own learning.

This suggestion has been made by both humanistic and behavioral psychologists. Many humanistic educators argue that when students are permitted to direct their own learning, teachers have fewer problems with motivation. To back up this argument, they (for instance, G. I. Brown, 1971) usually describe anecdotal reports written by teachers who used learner-centered approaches and were amazed by the enthusiasm of their students. It is true that when an individual or a group selects a topic of great intrinsic interest, and when the pieces in the puzzle fall together nicely, a great deal of enthusiasm is often generated. Unfortunately, such experiences tend to be rare. When some students are invited to direct their own learning, they become even more bored than when listening to a teacher. Others may select a topic that seems appealing at first glance but turns out on closer examination to be dull and unappealing. Furthermore, when students are first invited to work on topics of their own choice, the suggestion may be seen as a refreshing change. If the technique is used repeatedly, however, students may yearn for a teacher-directed session just for the sake of novelty.

Still another factor is that enthusiasm per se may not be a valid criterion for measuring success. Herbert Thelen's (1960) description of student-directed projects illustrates this point. The first project was a unit in the second grade called "How Do Different People Live?" The second was a television series produced by a high school class on the history of a community. The second-grade children,

TABLE 12.1 Guidelines for Effective Praise	
Effective Praise	**Ineffective Praise**
1. Is delivered contingently	1. Is delivered randomly or unsystematically
2. Specifies the particulars of the accomplishment	2. Is restricted to global positive reactions
3. Shows spontaneity, variety, and other signs of credibility; suggests clear attention to the student's accomplishment	3. Shows a bland uniformity, which suggests a conditional response made with minimal attention
4. Rewards attainment of specified performance criteria (which can include effort criteria, however)	4. Rewards mere participation, without consideration of performance process or outcomes
5. Provides information to students about their competence or the value of their accomplishments	5. Provides no information at all, or gives students information about their status
6. Orients students toward better appreciation of their own task-related behavior and thinking about problem solving	6. Orients students toward comparing themselves with others and thinking about competing
7. Uses students' own prior accomplishments as the context for describing present accomplishments	7. Uses the accomplishments of peers as the context for describing students' present accomplishments
8. Is given in recognition of noteworthy effort or success at tasks that are difficult (for *this* student)	8. Is given without regard to the effort expended or the meaning of the accomplishment (for *this* student)
9. Attributes success to effort and ability, implying that similar successes can be expected in the future	9. Attributes success to ability alone or to external factors such as luck or easy task
10. Fosters endogenous attributions (students believe that they expend effort on the task because they enjoy the task and/or want to develop task-relevant skills)	10. Fosters exogenous attributions (students believe that they expend effort on the task for external reasons—to please the teacher, win a competition or reward, etc.)
11. Focuses students' attention on their own task-relevant behavior	11. Focuses students' attention on the teacher as an external authority figure who is manipulating them
12. Fosters appreciation of and desirable attributions about task-relevant behavior after the process is completed	12. Intrudes into the ongoing process, distracting attention from task-relevant behavior

Source: Jere Brophy, "Teacher Praise: A Functional Analysis." *Review of Educational Research*, 51, No. 1 (1981), 5–32. Copyright © 1981. American Educational Research Association, Washington, D.C.

perhaps under the influence of a Walt Disney "True Life Adventure," chose to study *prairie dogs*, despite the efforts of the teacher to convert them to the Algonquin Indians (about whom she had a great deal of information from previous years). The dismay of the teacher turned to delight as the children not only came through with a smashing dramatic production about prairie dogs but also learned a great deal about how animals *and* people live. The TV series, on the other hand, generated much enthusiasm but no learning of subject matter.

Although it is desirable to encourage students to engage enthusiastically in class discussion, the topic should be chosen because it is likely to contribute to understanding, not simply because it is provocative. (Gale Zucker)

The students gained a lot of experience in taking photographs and lettering signs and solving lighting problems, but the production "incidentals" prevented them from thinking or learning about history. (This brings up an interesting question: If you endorse the argument made by some humanists [such as Combs, 1965] that how students *feel* about learning is more important than *what* they learn, what do you do when you have a bunch of committees working happily away on projects that have nothing to do with the curriculum? Is it better to have a class cheerfully laboring on incidentals or somewhat less enthusiastically engaged with genuine subject matter? This same point was raised earlier in the discussion of Cullum's technique for teaching math. Is it better to have students concentrate on learning to solve math problems or to spend considerable class time building a replica of King Tut's Tomb and crawling inside it with flashlights?)

At least part of the time, though, you might experiment with student-selected learning activities. An excellent source to consult when deciding how to arrange such activities is *Personalizing Education: Values Clarification and Beyond* (1975) by Leland W. Howe and Mary Martha Howe. In Part 3, "Personalizing the Curriculum," the Howes describe how you might encourage students to participate in selecting instructional objectives and be efficient self-directed learners. (These techniques were noted in Chapter 11.) After selecting a topic, students compile a flow chart, which lists anything related to the main topic that can be studied. Then the participants carry out a question census by listing all the questions they think would be important or useful in studying the topic. The next step is to identify available resources that can be used in seeking answers to these questions. The final stage of the process is to have students find answers to the questions and present a written or oral report. (For details and examples, see pp. 364–395 of *Personalizing Education*.)

Handbook Heading:
Ways to Permit Students to Direct Their Own Learning

To encourage individual pupils to direct their own learning, you might follow the suggestions offered by Raymond J. Wlodkowski (1978) for drawing up a personal contract. He recommends that such a contract should contain these four elements:

1. What the student will learn
2. How the student can demonstrate that she or he *has* learned
3. The degree of proficiency to be demonstrated
4. How the student will proceed

Wlodkowski offers this example (p. 57) of a contract that illustrates the four elements:

Date _____

1. Within the next two weeks I will learn to multiply correctly single-digit numbers ranging between 5 and 9—e.g., 5 x 6, 6 x 7, 7 x 8, 8 x 9, 9 x 5.
2. When I feel prepared, I will ask to take a mastery test containing 50 problems from this range of multiplication facts.
3. I will complete this contract when I can finish the mastery test with no more than three errors.
4. My preparation and study will involve choosing work from the workbook activities, number games, and filmstrip materials.

Signed _____

8. For students who need it, try to encourage the development of need achievement, self-confidence, and self-direction.

Despite your efforts to provide appropriate incentives, gratify deficiency needs, enhance the attractions of growth choices, and arrange learning experiences to produce a realistic level of aspiration and a feeling of success, some of your students will still lack confidence in their ability to learn. In such cases, you may try to help students acquire a general motive to achieve.

a. Use achievement motivation training techniques.

A technique described by Nicholls (1979) allows students opportunities to schedule their own classroom learning. For example, students can be given responsibility for deciding when to work on a particular assignment and for how long. This gives them the feeling they are working on a task because they want to, not because someone told them to. According to Nicholls, researchers have found greater continuing interest in learning tasks under self-evaluation and greater frequencies of assignment completion when opportunities for self-scheduling were increased.

Another technique for helping students to become better achievers was developed by J. S. Sorensen, E. A. Schwenn, and J. Barry (1970). They devised a checklist for self-ratings by elementary grade students on *prosocial behaviors* (see Figure 12.2). Students rated themselves and then participated in individual and small-group conferences with their teacher. During the conferences, the teacher defined each category on the list by recalling or identifying instances of the behavior described. Then each child was asked to select one or more types of behavior in which to improve and to check his or her present rating and desired rating. At the next conference, children rated themselves to determine if improvement had been achieved. The teacher supplied reinforcement in the form of praise for all improvement, kept a conference record to make note of progress and problems, and asked the pupils to describe reasons why working toward improvement would benefit them. Teacher ratings of student behavior after the program had been completed indicated that most students had made significant improvement in the types of behavior listed.

Sorensen, Schwenn, and Herbert J. Klausmeier (1969) used a similar approach to encourage elementary pupils to read more. Many books were made available in the classroom. Forms for reporting titles of books read were provided. Conferences with the teacher were arranged. At the conferences, teachers were urged to keep in mind four motivational procedures:

> Modeling: doing such things as telling the child that he (the adult) reads frequently and likes to read; being engaged in reading when the child comes in for the conference and starting to read a book as the child leaves the conference. . . .

A possible method for increasing intrinsic motivation is to allow students to choose and work on their own assignments. (Mike Greenlaw/The Image Works, Inc.)

FIGURE 12.2 Checklist of Prosocial Behaviors

(Reprinted from Herbert J. Klausmeier, Juanita S. Sorensen, and Elizabeth Ghatala, "Individually Guided Motivation Developing Self Direction and Prosocial Behaviors," *Elementary School Journal,* vol. 71 (March 1971), p. 344, with permission of the University of Chicago. Copyright © 1971 by the University of Chicago. All rights reserved.)

Name _____ Sex_____ Age_____ Date _____

Directions

Put an X under column 1 if you almost always have to be told to do the job.

Put an X under column 2 if you usually have to be told to do the job.

Put an X under column 3 if you sometimes do the job yourself and sometimes have to be told to do the job.

Put an X under column 4 if you usually do the job yourself.

Put an X under column 5 if you almost always do the job yourself.

	1	2	3	4	5
1. I listen to the teacher.					
2. I begin schoolwork right away.					
3. I correct mistakes.					
4. I work until the job is finished.					
5. I work when the teacher has left the room.					
6. If I make mistakes, I still keep working.					
7. I work on learning activities in free time.					
8. I get to class on time.					
9. I do extra schoolwork.					
10. I do my share in class projects.					
11. I read during free time.					
12. I ask questions about schoolwork.					
13. I have pencil, paper, and books ready when they are needed.					
14. I move quietly to and from my classes.					
15. I listen to the ideas of others.					
16. I help my classmates.					
17. I pick up when the work is finished.					
18. I take care of my clothing, books, and other things.					
19. I take care of the school's books, desks, and other things.					
20. I follow directions.					

Reinforcement: smiling, nodding affirmatively, saying "good," "fine," etc., when the student shows that he has independently read a book or pages in a book. The adult also reinforces positive attitude statements about reading either made spontaneously by the child or in response to questions.

Feedback: informing the child of progress by telling him how many books or pages in a book he has completed. Feedback was also given on any improvement in word recognition or comprehension skills.

Goal setting: helping the child select the next book of an appropriate difficulty level and length. The reading of the book or books then becomes the child's goal for the next conference. (1969, p. 351)

The reading frequency and achievement of almost all students increased as a result of this program, and even control pupils not included in the experiment showed improvement, indicating that the interest in reading became contagious.

If you despair at the lack of confidence, interest, or motivation of your students, you might encourage the development of the motivation to achieve by using variations of the techniques just discussed. With modifications, they could be used with all grade levels and with all types of students.

b. Use cooperative learning methods.

As we pointed out earlier in this chapter and previous ones, cooperative-learning methods have proven effective in increasing motivation for learning and self-esteem, redirecting attributions for success and failure, fostering positive feelings toward classmates, and increasing performance on tests of comprehension, reasoning, and problem solving (Johnson & Johnson, 1991; Slavin, 1990). Accordingly, you may want to try one or more of the cooperative-learning techniques described by David and Roger Johnson (1991) and Robert Slavin (1990). To familiarize you with these methods, we will briefly describe the Student Teams-Achievement Divisions (STAD) method devised by Robert Slavin and his associates at Johns Hopkins University.

STAD is one of the simplest and most flexible of the cooperative-learning methods, having been used in grades two through twelve and in such diverse subject areas as math, language arts, social studies, and science.

As with other cooperative-learning methods, students are assigned to four- or five-member groups that vary on such major characteristics as gender, ability level, and ethnic background so that each group mirrors the make-up of the class. Once these assignments are made, a four-step cycle is initiated: teach, team study, test, and recognition. The teaching phase begins with the presentation of material, usually in a lecture-discussion format. Students should be told what it is they are going to learn and why it is important. Lessons should emphasize comprehension of concepts, practice on working problems or preparing answers to questions, and providing feedback.

During team study, group members work cooperatively with teacher-provided worksheets and answer sheets.[1] The basic rules of team study are these:

1. Curriculum materials specifically designed for STAD can be obtained from the Johns Hopkins Team Learning Project, 3505 N. Charles Street, Baltimore, MD 21218.

(a) Each team member is responsible for ensuring that every other member has learned the material; (b) the task is not completed until all team members have mastered the assignment; (c) team members must ask one another for help before asking the teacher; and (d) team members may talk to one another, but softly.

When the study phase is completed, each student *individually* takes a quiz. After the quiz, the teacher collects and scores the papers. The scoring system ranges from 0 to 30 points and reflects degree of individual improvement over previous quiz scores. For example, 20 improvement points are awarded for quiz scores that match or exceed a "base" score by 10 points, and 30 improvement points are awarded for quiz scores that exceed the student's base score by more than 10 points.

Each team receives one of three recognition awards, depending on the average number of points earned by the team. For example, teams that average 15 to 19 improvement points receive a GOODTEAM certificate; teams that average 20 to 24 improvement points receive a GREATTEAM certificate; and teams that average 25 to 30 improvement points receive a SUPERTEAM certificate.

The cooperative methods developed by the Johnsons are similar to those developed by Slavin, but with two exceptions: They place a greater emphasis on teaching students how to productively work together; and they recommend using team grades, rather than certificates or other forms of recognition, as positive reinforcers.

Resources for Further Investigation

Surveys of Motivational Theories

If you would like additional information on one or more of the approaches to motivation mentioned in this chapter, a good place to start is a basic survey text. In *Human Motivation* (1985), David McClelland discusses the origin of motives, how they are learned, and what they are based on. Examined in detail are the achievement motive, the power motive, the affiliative motives, and the avoidance motives. Another text with the title *Human Motivation* (1980), by Bernard Weiner, surveys several theories of motivation, with an emphasis on attribution theory. *Motivation* (2d ed., 1986) by Herbert L. Petri, in addition to providing basic coverage of biological, behavioral, and cognitive approaches to motivation, includes an interesting chapter (14) on work motivation.

Achievement Motivation and Attribution Theory

J. W. Atkinson presents his views on achievement motivation in *Personality, Motivation, and Achievement* (1978), written with J. O. Raynor. *Motivation and Achievement* (1974), edited by Atkinson and Raynor, is a collection of articles by various authors. Another such collection is *Achievement and Achievement Mo-*

tives (1983), edited by Janet T. Spence. This latter volume contains chapters that look at achieving styles in men and women, achievement of children from one-parent households, and achievement of African-American children. Bernard Weiner provides an in-depth analysis of attribution theory in *An Attributional Theory of Motivation and Emotion* (1986).

Motivational Techniques

If you would like more information and ideas on classroom applications, peruse *Motivation and Teaching: A Practical Guide* (1978) by Raymond J. Wlodkowski; *Student Team Learning* (2d ed., 1988) by Robert E. Slavin; *Eager to Learn* (1990) by Raymond J. Wlodkowski; *Cooperative Learning: Theory, Research, and Practice* by Robert E. Slavin; and *Learning Together and Alone* (3d ed., 1991) by David W. Johnson and Roger T. Johnson.

Measuring Motivation

If you become interested in formally assessing your students' level of motivation, consult *Assessing Learning Motivation* (1988) by Richard W. Naccarato. This publication provides a critical review of thirty-four measures of academic motivation for students in grades one through twelve. In addition to technical information (for example, reliability, validity) about each measure, the author provides an address from which the instrument may be obtained.

SUMMARY

1. Motivation is the willingness to expend a certain amount of effort to achieve a particular goal. Motivation to master classroom tasks is affected by the nature of the learning task, the characteristics of the student, the classroom atmosphere, and the personality and approach of the teacher.

2. The behavioral view of motivation is based on the desire of individuals to attain a positive reinforcer (in the case of operant conditioning theory) or to imitate an admired individual (in the case of social learning theory). This view emphasizes extrinsic motivation.

3. When reinforcement is used excessively by teachers, some students may resent the teacher for being manipulative, learning may occur only when reinforcement is provided, some students may become dependent on the teacher, and intrinsic motivation for a task may be discouraged.

4. The cognitive view of motivation holds that people are inherently driven to overcome gaps or inconsistencies between what they know and what they experience. This view emphasizes intrinsic motivation.

5. One limitation of the cognitive view is that teachers may not always find it possible to induce a sense of disequilibrium in students.

6. The humanistic view of motivation, particularly Abraham Maslow's, is based on satisfying a hierarchical sequence of deficiency needs (physiological, safety, belongingness and love, and esteem) so that the individual can satisfy his or her self-actualization needs.

7. A limitation of the humanistic view is that the teacher may not always find it possible to identify a student's unmet deficiency needs or to satisfy them once they are identified.

8. The theory of achievement motivation posits that individuals are motivated by a need to achieve. Individuals with a high need to achieve aspire to goals of intermediate difficulty in order to balance success and failure. Individuals with a low need to achieve aspire either to very easy goals or to very difficult goals because they are motivated primarily by a fear of failure.

9. Some individuals, instead of being motivated by fear of failure, are motivated primarily by fear of success.

10. Research on the explanations people gave for their success and failure found marked differences between high achievers and low achievers. High achievers attribute success to ability and effort and failure to insufficient effort. Low achievers attribute success to luck or task difficulty and failure to lack of ability.

11. A limitation of the achievement motivation and attribution approaches to motivation is that they are difficult to observe and analyze.

12. The type of classroom reward structure that a teacher selects can encourage or discourage motivation. Four basic reward structures are individual competition, group competition, group reward (cooperation), and individual reward. For most classroom tasks, competitive reward structures discourage motivation and achievement, whereas cooperative and individual reward structures enhance motivation and achievement.

13. Teacher attitudes also influence student motivation. Some teachers are more concerned with giving the appearance of being a good teacher than with helping students. Other teachers are motivated by a sense of moral responsibility to help students learn. Finally, some teachers see improving student learning as a task they can master through ability and effort.

14. Because classroom learning is cognitive, compulsory, and publicly evaluated, motivation for learning is likely to be optimal when students know they possess learning skills and when they value those skills.

KEY TERMS

extrinsic motivation *(512)*
intrinsic motivation *(512)*
deficiency needs *(516)*
growth needs *(516)*
self-actualization *(516)*
attribution theory *(522)*

DISCUSSION QUESTIONS

1. At the beginning of this chapter, we drew a distinction between extrinsic motivation (doing something solely to obtain a reward offered by someone else) and intrinsic motivation (doing something solely because it brings pleasure or satisfaction). What percentage of your behavior do you think stems from intrinsic motivation? From extrinsic motivation? Do you think it is possible to change this ratio? How? Are any of your ideas applicable to the classroom?

2. Maslow states that for individuals to be motivated to satisfy self-actualization needs, the deficiency needs have to be satisfied first. Has this been the case in your own experience? If not, how was it different?

3. A limitation of Maslow's theory is that you may not always know when a student's deficiency needs are going unmet. How can you minimize the likelihood that you will be unaware of any student's deficiency needs?

4. Students with a high need to achieve usually attribute success to effort and ability, and failure to lack of effort. If you think of yourself as fitting this pattern, how did you get this way? Is there anything from your own experiences that you can use to help students develop this attributional pattern?

5. Have you ever experienced a competitive reward structure in school? Were your reactions to it positive or negative? Why? Would you use it in your own classroom? For what purpose and under what circumstances?

6. Have you ever experienced a cooperative reward structure in school? Were your reactions to it positive or negative? Why? Would you use it in your own classroom? For what purpose and under what circumstances?

Part 4

EVALUATING
PERFORMANCE

Chapter 13

MEASUREMENT AND EVALUATION OF CLASSROOM LEARNING

Key Points

THE NATURE OF MEASUREMENT AND EVALUATION

▶ Measurement: assigning numbers to things according to rules, to create a ranking

▶ Evaluation: making judgments about the value of a measure

TYPES OF MEASURES

▶ Performance tests measure skills under realistic conditions

▶ Performance tests can measure underlying skills or learned product

▶ Written tests measure degree of knowledge

REDUCING SUBJECTIVITY

▶ Pygmalion effect: impact of teacher expectations leads to self-fulfilling prophecy

▶ Limited effect of teacher expectancy on IQ scores

▶ Strong effect of teacher expectancy on achievement, participation

▶ Teachers respond favorably to females, compliance, neatness, achievement, attractiveness

SUGGESTIONS FOR TEACHING IN YOUR CLASSROOM

▶ Moderate testing produces more learning than no testing or frequent testing

▶ Necessary to obtain a representative sample of behavior when testing

▶ Table of specifications helps ensure an adequate sample of content, behavior

▶ Listing objectives and outcomes simplifies test preparation

▶ Formative evaluation: monitor progress, plan remedial instruction

▶ Summative evaluation: measure achievement, assign grades

▶ Younger pupils need more structure, repetition, feedback

▶ Use many formative tests with elementary school pupils

▶ Short-answer items easy to write but measure lower levels of learning

▶ Multiple-choice items measure different levels of learning but are hard to write

▶ Interpretive items measure reasoning but take time to construct

▶ Essay items measure complex learning but are hard to grade consistently

▶ Rating scales and checklists make evaluations of performance more systematic

▶ Item analysis tells about difficulty, discriminability of multiple-choice items

EVALUATION METHODS

▶ Norm-referenced grading: compare one student to others

▶ Norm-referenced grading based on absence of external criteria

▶ Norm-referenced grading can be used to evaluate advanced levels of learning

▶ Criterion-referenced grading: compare individual performance to stated criteria

▶ Criterion-referenced grades provide information about strengths and weaknesses

▶ Expectations of a normal distribution lead to low aspirations

▶ Mastery approach: gives pupils multiple opportunities to master goals at own pace

▶ Mastery learning has several potential limitations

▶ Mastery learning does not eliminate competition and comparisons

ALTERNATIVE PERFORMANCE-BASED APPROACHES TO CLASSROOM MEASUREMENT AND EVALUATION

▶ Alternative assessment methods are used to highlight the reasoning behind a response

Chapters 2 through 6 of this book acquainted you with information relating to Phase one of a theory of instruction or model of learning: taking into account what students are like and allowing for individual differences in characteristics and abilities. Chapter 7 was devoted to Phase two: specifying what is to be learned in the form of appropriate types of instructional objectives. Chapters 8 through 12 summarized information intended to assist you to achieve Phase three: helping students master instructional objectives by applying what psychologists have discovered about learning, cognitive strategies, and motivation. In this chapter, the fourth and final phase in the model of learning outlined in this book will be analyzed: determining whether students have achieved instructional objectives by measuring and evaluating performance.

THE NATURE OF MEASUREMENT AND EVALUATION

Measuring and evaluating student performance is something that every teacher has to do, usually quite frequently. Written test performances, book reports, research papers, homework exercises, oral presentations, science projects, and art works of various sorts are just some of the things that teachers must measure, with written tests accounting for about 45 percent of a typical student's course grade (Green & Stager, 1986/1987). No surprise, then, that in one study (Hiatt, 1979) 22 percent of a typical elementary school teacher's morning was taken up with various measurement activities. Yet despite the amount of time spent measuring and evaluating student performance, it is a task that most teachers dislike and that few do well. One reason is that many teachers have little or no in-depth knowledge of measurement and evaluation principles (Crooks, 1988; Hills, 1991; Stiggins, Griswold & Wikelund, 1989). Another reason is that the role of evaluator is seen as being inconsistent with the role of teacher (or helper). Since teachers with more training in measurement and evaluation use more appropriate measurement practices than teachers with less training (Green & Stager, 1986/1987), a basic goal of this chapter is to help you understand how such knowledge can be used to reinforce rather than work against your role as teacher. Toward that end, we begin by defining what we mean by the terms *measurement* and *evaluation*.

> Measurement: assigning numbers to things according to rules, to create a ranking

Measurement is the assignment of numbers to certain attributes of objects, events, or people according to a rule-governed system. For our purposes, we will limit the discussion to attributes of people. The rules that are used to assign the numbers will ordinarily create a ranking that reflects how much of the attribute different people possess (Gronlund & Linn, 1990). Thus, we can measure someone's level of typing proficiency by counting the number of words the person accurately types per minute, or someone's level of mathematical reasoning by counting the number of problems correctly solved.

> Evaluation: making judgments about the value of a measure

Evaluation involves using a rule-governed system to make judgments about the value or worth of a set of measures (Gronlund & Linn, 1990). What does it mean, for example, to say that a student answered 80 out of 100 earth science questions correctly? Depending on the rules that are used, it could mean that the student has learned that body of knowledge exceedingly well and is ready to progress to the next unit of instruction or, conversely, that the student has significant knowledge gaps and requires additional instruction.

Measurement and evaluation are often thought of as rather mechanical procedures that teachers go through to determine how much of something has been learned. Accordingly, they are usually seen as being largely, if not totally, unrelated to individual differences, learning, motivation, or instruction. This view is simply incorrect. Measurement and evaluation activities have a direct impact on various aspects of learning and instruction. As Terence J. Crooks (1988) has pointed out, for example, classroom evaluation guides students' "judgment of what is important to learn, affects their motivation and self-perceptions of competence, structures their approaches to and timing of personal study (e.g., spaced practice), consolidates learning, and affects the development of enduring learning strategies and skills. It appears to be one of the most potent forces influencing education" (p. 467).

TYPES OF MEASURES

Just as measurement can play several roles in the classroom, teachers have several ways to measure what students have learned. Which type of measure you choose will depend, of course, on the objectives you have stated. For purposes of this discussion, objectives can be classified in terms of two broad categories: *knowing how to do something* (for example, tie a square knot, dance the waltz, operate a microscope) and *knowing about something* (for example, that knots are used to secure objects, that dance is a form of social expression, that microscopes are used to study things too small to be seen by the naked eye). Measures that attempt to assess how well somebody can do something are often referred to as *performance* tests. And measures that attempt to assess the range and accuracy of someone's knowledge are usually called *written* tests.

The Nature of Performance Tests

Performance tests
measure skills under
realistic conditions

Performance tests attempt to measure how well people perform a particular skill or a set of skills under more or less realistic conditions. Deciding how realistic the conditions should be depends on such factors as time, cost, availability of equipment, and the nature of the skill being measured. Imagine, for example, that you are a third-grade teacher and one of your objectives is that students will be able to determine how much change they should receive after making a purchase in a store. If this is a relatively minor objective, or if you do not have a lot of props available, you might simply demonstrate the situation with actual money and ask the students to judge whether the amount of change received was correct. If, on the other hand, you consider this to be a major objective and you have the props available, you might set up a mock store and have each student make a purchase using real money (Gronlund, 1988).

Performance tests
can measure underly-
ing skills or learned
product

Performance tests may focus on a process (that is, the underlying skills that go into a performance), a product (an observable outcome such as a speech or a painting), or both. The measurement of process will often be emphasized for tasks that involve psychomotor skills. For example, a speech teacher may be more interested (at least initially) in assessing how well students use gestures, pauses, and changes in voice pitch and volume than in the content of their speeches (Gronlund & Linn, 1990). It is also possible to assess the processes underlying cognitive tasks. You may be just as interested in knowing which learning tactics students use to prepare for an exam and how well they use them as in knowing how much of the information they understand. At other times, the product will be more important than the process, perhaps because a variety of processes results in an equally good product. The quality of a drawing or the solution to a problem may be more important than the processes used to generate the end product.

Types of Performance Tests

Based on how closely each simulates real life, Norman Gronlund (1988) discusses four types of performance tests: paper-and-pencil performance, identification tests, simulated performance, and work sample.

Paper-and-Pencil Performance   These tests emphasize the application of knowledge or skill. In many instances, students are asked to construct something, such as a product map, a graph, a diagram, a short story, or a lesson plan. In other cases, paper-and-pencil performance tests are used to measure whether students are ready for a "hands-on" experience. For example, students may be asked to name and describe, from photographs or drawings, the functions of various switches, dials, and control mechanisms on a complex piece of electronic equipment before they are taught how to use it.

Identification Tests   These tests, which range from simple to complex, ask students to identify or describe things. For instance, anatomy students may be asked to identify the internal organs of an animal. Chemistry students might be asked to identify an unknown substance. Medical students may be asked to name

Performance tests assess how well students complete a task under realistic conditions.
(Gary Bublitz/Dembinsky Photo Assoc.)

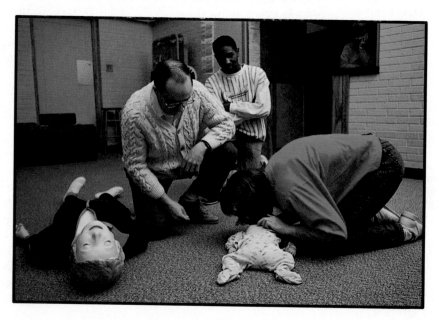

and describe the functions of surgical instruments. Automotive students may be asked to listen to a malfunctioning engine, identify the probable cause, and describe the best procedure for correcting it. Like the paper-and-pencil performance test, the identification test is often used to judge whether students are ready for a more true-to-life performance.

Simulated Performance   The emphasis in simulated performance is to reproduce exactly, under controlled conditions, the response that should be made under real-life conditions. Simulations can be used in virtually any area. Examples are seen in law (mock trials), teacher education (microteaching), counselor education (microcounseling), pilot training (cockpit simulators), emergency medical services (dummy patients, mock catastrophes), and national defense (war games).

Work Sample   The work sample usually reflects the highest degree of realism. Students perform a representative sample of behaviors for a particular task under realistic conditions. Two examples of the work sample are a driving test and student teaching.

Gronlund (1988) lists four steps in constructing a performance test: (1) Specify the outcomes to be measured; (2) select an appropriate degree of realism; (3) prepare instructions that clearly specify the test situation; and (4) prepare the observational form to be used in evaluating performance. Three main types of observational forms are used to measure performance: the product scale, the checklist, and the rating scale. Detailed discussions of the nature and uses of scales and checklists can be found in Airasian (1991), Gronlund (1988), and Popham (1990).

At the end of this chapter we will describe a slightly different approach to the use of performance-based measures that grew out of disenchantment with traditional written tests. In recent years, many teachers and measurement experts have complained that the typical written test reveals little or nothing of the depth of students' knowledge and how students use what they know to work through questions, problems, and tasks. In order to learn more about these capabilities, a number of alternative performance–based assessment methods have been developed. We will examine these on pages 612–614.

The Nature of Written Tests

Written tests measure degree of knowledge

As indicated at the beginning of this section, written tests attempt to measure how much people know about something. Since students learn mostly verbalized knowledge, such as facts, concepts, and principles, most of the tests they take are written.

Generally speaking, a written test is a set of written questions or statements to which the student must supply a written response. In the case of objective items (so called because the subjectivity that enters into scoring is minimal), the response is very brief and unambiguous. The most popular objective test items are multiple-choice, true-false, matching, and interpretive items. In the case of created-response items, the response is longer and potentially more ambiguous. Hence, these items allow for more subjectivity in scoring. The length of the created response may range from a word or two for short-answer items to several pages for essay items. Since most of your objectives as a teacher will revolve around how much students know about something, much of this chapter will deal with written tests. You should recognize, however, that many of the issues raised (such as the next one on reducing subjectivity) pertain equally to performance tests.

REDUCING SUBJECTIVITY

The foregoing reference to subjectivity calls attention to a problem you will have to deal with when you make judgments about others. It is likely that you yourself have experienced times when you felt that a teacher was less than objective, if not downright prejudiced. By becoming aware of some of the factors that influence one person's perceptions of others, you may be able to reduce subjectivity to a minimum in your own evaluations. Many of these factors are reflected in a phenomenon that has been intensively studied and is known variously as the *Pygmalion effect,* the *self-fulfilling prophecy,* and the *teacher expectancy effect.*

Awareness of the Impact of Teacher Expectations

In 1968 Robert Rosenthal and Lenore Jacobson published *Pygmalion in the Classroom,* in which they reported results of a study on the impact of teacher expectations. Rosenthal and Jacobson administered a little-known group test of intelligence (Flanagan's Test of General Ability) to children in grades one through six in a single San Francisco public school. The teachers of these children were not told the true name or nature of this test. Instead, they were told that the children had taken the "Harvard Test of Inflected Acquisition" and that, on the basis of the test results, certain pupils in each class were "likely to show unusual intellectual gains in the year ahead." In reality, however, there was no difference between the test performances of these "superior" pupils, who had been selected at random, and those of the other "average" children. At the end of the school year the same children took the Test of General Ability a second time.

Rosenthal and Jacobson reported in *Pygmalion in the Classroom* that the students who were labeled potential achievers showed significant gains in IQ and that the reason for these gains was that their teachers expected more of them. The authors referred to this phenomenon as the Pygmalion effect**,** because they felt that teacher expectations had influenced the students to become intelligent in thesame way that the expectations of the mythical Greek sculptor Pygmalion caused a statue he had carved to come to life. Another term frequently used for this phenomenon is **self-fulfilling prophecy,** because a prophecy about behavior is often fulfilled. If teachers communicate the "prophecy" that certain students will behave intelligently, those students may behave in the expected manner.

Pygmalion effect: impact of teacher expectations leads to self-fulfilling prophecy

The heroine of G. B. Shaw's Pygmalion, *the cockney flower girl Eliza Doolittle (Audrey Hepburn in the movie version of* My Fair Lady*) makes a grand entrance at a ball. The self-fulfilling prophecy is sometimes called the Pygmalion effect. As Eliza explains to her admirer Colonel Pickering, "The difference between a lady and a flower girl is the way she is treated, I shall always be a flower girl to Professor Higgins because he always treats me as a flower girl, and always will; but I know I can be a lady to you, because you treat me as a lady, and always will."* (Movie Still Archives)

When *Pygmalion in the Classroom* was first published, it attracted considerable attention. A number of writers on education proposed that it provided the key to revolutionizing the education of disadvantaged students. It was argued that the inadequate school performance of many students from poor backgrounds was due to low expectations on the part of teachers. If the teachers would simply communicate high expectations, it was reasoned, student performance would improve dramatically. Unfortunately, initial enthusiasm about the potency of the Pygmalion effect was soon replaced by doubts and qualifications. Some argued, for example, that Rosenthal and Jacobson's results did not strongly support their conclusions. Although the children in grades one and two who were identified as "intellectual bloomers" did score significantly higher than their "average" classmates on the IQ test at the end of the year, no such effect was found for the pupils in grades three through six. Others pointed out that just because positive expectations led to higher scores, it could not be assumed that negative expectations would cause low scores (Wineburg, 1987).

In the years following the publication of *Pygmalion in the Classroom,* hundreds of similar studies were carried out. Some attempted to replicate Rosenthal and Jacobson's findings, while others investigated the effects of teacher expectancy on other outcomes, such as classroom achievement and participation. Periodically, the results of these studies were reviewed and summarized (for example, by Braun, 1976; Brophy, 1983b; Brophy & Good, 1974; Cooper, 1979; Raudenbush, 1984; Rosenthal, 1985). One review found that the effect of teacher expectancy on IQ scores was essentially limited to first- and second-grade students, was moderate in strength at those grade levels, and occurred only when it was induced within the first two weeks of the school year (Raudenbush, 1984). Apparently, once teachers have had an opportunity to observe and interact with their own students, they view these experiences as more credible and informative than the results of a mental ability test. Reviews that have looked at the effect of teacher expectancy on classroom achievement and participation have generally found sizable positive *and* negative effects (for example, Braun, 1976; Brophy, 1983b; Cooper, 1979; Rosenthal, 1985). In addition, it appears that teacher expectations are more likely to maintain already existing tendencies than to drastically alter well-established behaviors. For example, primary grade teachers react differently to students in the fast-track reading group than to students in the slow-track group. When working with the more proficient readers, teachers tend to smile, lean toward the students, and establish eye contact more often. Criticism tends to be given in friendlier, gentler tones. The oral reading errors of proficient readers are often overlooked. When corrections are given, they are made at the end of the sentence or other meaningful unit rather than in the middle of such units. And comprehension questions are asked more often than factual questions as a means of monitoring students' attention to the reading selection. Less proficient readers, on the other hand, are corrected more often and in places that interrupt meaningful processing of the text, are given less time to decode difficult words or to correct themselves, and are asked low-level factual questions as a way of checking on their attention. Teachers' body posture is often characterized by frowns, pursed lips, shaking of the head, finger pointing, and sitting erect. In sum, through a variety of subtle ways, teachers communicate to students that they expect them to perform well or poorly and then create a situation that is consistent with the expectation. As a result, initial differences between good and poor readers either remain or widen over the course of the school career (Wuthrick, 1990).

In addition to documenting the existence of teacher expectancy effects and the conditions under which they occur, researchers have sought to identify the factors that might create high or low teacher expectations. Here is a list of some important factors taken from reviews by Braun (1976) and Brophy and Good (1974):

> **Limited effect of teacher expectancy on IQ scores**

> **Strong effect of teacher expectancy on achievement, participation**

> **Teachers respond favorably to females, compliance, neatness, achievement, attractiveness**

Attractive children are often perceived by teachers to be brighter, more capable, and more social than unattractive children.

Teachers tend to approve of girls' behavior more frequently than they approve of boys' behavior.

Female teachers tend to perceive the behavior of girls as closer to the behavior of "ideal students" than do male teachers.

Middle-class pupils are expected (by college students in education classes) to receive higher grades than lower-class students.

Teachers are more influenced by negative information about pupils (for example, low test scores) than they are by neutral or positive information.

Teachers appear to spend more time and to interact more frequently with high achievers than with low achievers.

High-achieving pupils receive more praise than low-achieving ones.

It is important to bear in mind that these factors (plus others such as ethnic background, knowledge of siblings, and impressions of parents) usually operate *in concert* to produce an expectancy. A teacher may be influenced not just by a single test score but by a test score, plus appearance, plus grades assigned by other teachers, and so forth. The task of objectively evaluating your students may be harder than you now realize. To help you minimize negative expectancies, we offer the following guidelines:

Handbook Heading:
Ways to Minimize Subjectivity

1. Try to control the influence of such factors as name, ethnic background, sex, physical characteristics, knowledge of siblings or parents, grades, and test scores. If you think you can be honest with yourself, you might attempt to describe your prejudices so that you will be in a position to try to guard against them. (Do you tend to be annoyed when you read descriptions of the exploits of members of a particular religious or ethnic group, for example?) Try to think of a pupil independently of her or his siblings and parents.

2. Make a well-planned effort to be fair and consistent in the way you interact with pupils. Perhaps keep a Question and Recitation Record to ensure that you call on all pupils in class about the same number of times. Strive to be consistently positive and enthusiastic when asking questions or responding to answers. (Don't hesitate or introduce vocal inflections when calling on less capable pupils. Such public signs of hesitation or lack of confidence may be communicated to the pupil and to classmates.) Refer to Table 12.1, page 421, to make your praise effective.

3. Perhaps keep a Positive Reinforcement Record in an effort to say favorable things about the work of all pupils. If, after keeping such a record for two weeks, you discover that you have not said a single positive thing to one or more students, make it a point to praise those pupils at least as regularly as others.

4. If you become aware of pupils' previous low grades or are presented with low test scores, give individuals identified as poor learners the benefit of the doubt. Use the information to try to help low-scoring pupils improve their classroom performance (by using techniques to be discussed later in this

chapter), and keep in mind that many factors (such as anxiety or misunderstanding instructions) may artificially lower test scores.

5. Strive to reduce the impact of distorted perceptions and negative expectations by taking advantage of the characteristics of tests.

Suggestions for Teaching in Your Classroom

EFFECTIVE MEASUREMENT TECHNIQUES

1. As early as possible in a report period, decide when and how often to give tests and other assignments that will count toward a grade.
   a. Consider distributing a course outline on the first day of class.
   b. Announce tests and other assignments well in advance. Give a detailed description of what will be covered, how it will be evaluated, and how much it will count toward a final grade.
   c. Schedule a moderate number of tests for each grading period.

2. Prepare a content outline and/or a table of specifications of the objectives to be covered on each exam, or otherwise take care to obtain a systematic sample.

3. Consider the purpose of each test or measurement exercise. Take into account the developmental characteristics of the pupils in your classes and the nature of the curriculum for your grade level.

4. Decide on the type of test items to use and write sufficient items to provide an adequate sample, measuring understanding at several levels of the taxonomies of educational objectives (if appropriate) and allowing for differences in cognitive styles.

5. Make up and use a detailed key.
   a. Evaluate each answer by comparing it to the key.
   b. Be willing and prepared to defend the evaluations you make.

6. During and after the grading process, analyze questions and answers in order to improve future exams.

---

1. As early as possible in a report period, decide when and how often to give tests and other assignments that will count toward a grade.
   a. Consider distributing a course outline on the first day of class.

In the opening pages of Chapter 7, "Devising and Using Objectives," you were urged to start at the end of an instructional sequence rather than just taking a stab at making a beginning. That is, you were asked to think about what you wanted your students to be able to do by the last day of class. You were also urged to write objectives that would specify or indicate how achievement would be evaluated. If you follow the suggestions for formulating objectives presented in that chapter, you should be able to develop a reasonably complete master plan that will permit you to devise a course outline even though you have only limited experience with teaching and/or a text or unit of study. If you announce at the beginning of a report period when you intend to give exams or set due dates for assignments, you not only give students a clear idea of what they will be expected to do, but you also give yourself guidelines for arranging lesson plans and devising, administering, and scoring tests. (If you will be teaching elementary grade students, it will be better to announce exams and assignments for a week at a time rather than providing a long-range schedule.)

Handbook Heading:
Outlining Units of
Study

> b. Announce tests and other assignments well in advance. Give a detailed description of what will be covered, how it will be evaluated, and how much it will count toward a final grade.

If you are coy, absent-minded, or vague about tests and assignments, you may discourage careful study. Consider these two announcements and imagine how you might react to each. "We'll have an exam in a week or so; it, uh, will cover, uh, everything we've discussed so far." "We'll have an exam next Wednesday; it will be on the material covered in class starting with the topic of _____ on pages 216 through 275 of the text. There will be five short-essay questions and a fifteen-item matching question based on the mimeographed outline of Key Points that I handed out." Which set of goals would look more attainable to you? Which would be more likely to motivate you to actually prepare for the exam? Suppose the first teacher then gave you a fifty-item true-false test on a 25-page section of the text (out of 400 pages covered so far), whereas the second gave you exactly the kind of test described. How would you feel about each class the next time an exam was scheduled? What would be your attitude toward doing a conscientious job of studying for each class?

For the most part, it is preferable to announce tests well in advance. Pop quizzes tend to increase anxiety and tension and to force students to cram on isolated sections of a book on a day-by-day and catch-as-catch-can basis. Simple homework assignments or the equivalent are more likely to encourage more careful and consistent study than pop quizzes. When tests are announced, it is comforting to students to know exactly what material they will be held responsible for, what kinds of questions will be asked, and how much it will count toward the final grade.

If you assign term papers or other written work, list your criteria for grading the papers (for example, how much emphasis will be placed on style, spelling and punctuation, research, individuality of expression). In laboratory courses most students prefer a list of experiments or projects and some description of how they will be evaluated (for example, ten experiments in chemistry, fifteen drawings in drafting, five paintings in art, judged according to posted criteria).

> c. Schedule a moderate number of tests for each grading period.

▶ Moderate testing
produces more learn-
ing than no testing or
frequent testing

Research has shown that students who take about three tests per grading period learn more than students who are tested less frequently or not at all. Don't assume, however, that if giving three tests is good, then giving five or six tests is better. A point of diminishing returns is quickly reached after the fourth test. The benefit of a moderate testing schedule appears to be due to three factors. First, a test cues students to attend to certain topics, skills, and details. Second, the students attend to the material one more time (thereby contributing to distributed practice). Third, the students process the material more meaningfully, particularly if they expect higher-level questions (Crooks, 1988).

2. Prepare a content outline and/or a table of specifications of the objectives to be covered on each exam, or otherwise take care to obtain a systematic sample.

If you have drawn up lesson plans, listed instructional objectives, or otherwise described the terminal behavior you are aiming for, you already have such an outline. If you have not done this by the time the first test is due, you are likely to make a resolution to be more conscientious next time. The more precisely and completely goals are described at the beginning of a unit, the easier and more efficient evaluation (and teaching) will be. Using a clear outline will help ensure an adequate sample of the most significant kinds of behavior.

▶ Necessary to obtain
a representative sam-
ple of behavior when
testing

When the time comes to assess the abilities of your pupils, you can't possibly observe and evaluate all relevant behavior. You can't listen to more than a few pages of reading by each first-grader, for example, or ask high school seniors to answer questions on everything discussed in several chapters of a text. Because of the limitations imposed by large numbers of students and small amounts of time, your evaluation will have to be based on a *sample* of behavior—a three- or four-minute reading performance and questions covering points made in only a few sections of text material assigned for an exam. It is therefore important to try to obtain a representative, accurate sample.

Handbook Heading:
Using a Table of Speci-
fications

Psychologists who have studied measurement and evaluation often recommend that as teachers prepare exams they use a **table of specifications** to note the types and numbers of test items to be included so as to ensure thorough and systematic coverage. You can draw up a table of specifications by first listing along the left-hand margin of a piece of lined paper the important topics that have been covered. Then insert appropriate headings from the taxonomy of objectives for the cognitive domain (or for the affective or psychomotor domains, if appropriate) across the top of the page. An example of such a table of specifications for the information discussed so far in this chapter is provided in Figure 13.1.

▶ Table of specifica-
tions helps ensure an
adequate sample of
content, behavior

Test specialists often recommend that you insert in the boxes of a table of specifications the percentage of test items that you intend to write for each topic and each type of objective. This practice forces you to think about both the number and the relative importance of your objectives before you start teaching or writing test items. Thus, if some objectives are more important to you than

Topic	Objectives					
	Knows	Comprehends	Applies	Analyzes	Synthesizes	Evaluates
Factors that lead to distorted perceptions						
Impact of teacher expectations						
Implications of research on expectations						
Characteristics of tests						

FIGURE 13.1   Example of a Table of Specifications for Material Covered So Far in This Chapter

others, you will have a way of ensuring that these are tested more thoroughly. On the other hand, if a test is going to be brief and emphasize all objectives more or less equally, you may wish to put a check mark in each box *as* you write questions. If you discover that you are overloading some boxes and that others are empty, you can take steps to remedy the situation. (For reasons to be discussed shortly, you may choose not to list all of the categories in the taxonomy for all subjects or at all grade levels. Tables of specifications that you draw up for your own use, therefore, may contain fewer headings across the top of the page than those in the table illustrated in Figure 13.1.)

Simply writing "knows," "applies," "analyzes," and so forth across the top of your table may not supply as much direction as you would like. Accordingly, you may find it helpful to refer to the tables of objectives and outcomes for the three taxonomies included in Chapter 7 (Tables 7.1, 7.2, and 7.3, pages 293–295). If you will take the trouble to flip back and examine those tables before reading further, you will realize that they provide a concise outline of all the basic objectives of each of the taxonomies, as well as specific-outcome verbs you can use when writing test questions or planning forms of evaluation. The same information for the cognitive taxonomy (derived once again from material discussed and summarized by Gronlund in *How to Write and Use Instructional Objectives,* 4th ed., 1991) is provided in different form below. (You might find it very useful to make copies of Tables 7.1, 7.2, and 7.3, as well as of Figure 13.1, and have them on your desk every time you map out general evaluation strategies or write test questions.)

> Listing objectives and outcomes simplifies test preparation

Knowledge Knows common terms, facts, rules, trends, classifications, criteria methods, procedures, principles, theories. (Ask students to *define, describe, identify, label, list, match, name, outline, reproduce, select, state.*)

Comprehension Comprehends facts and principles, interprets verbal or graphic material, translates from one form to another, estimates or predicts what might happen. (Ask students to *explain, generalize, give examples, state in their own words, paraphrase, rewrite, infer, predict.*)

Application Applies concepts and principles to new situations, applies laws and theories to practical situations, solves problems, constructs charts and graphs, demonstrates methods or procedures. (Ask students to *use, solve, prepare, draw, produce, construct, design, show, demonstrate.*)

Analysis Analyzes organization, identifies component parts. (Ask students to *organize, identify, subdivide, separate, differentiate, distinguish, illustrate, outline, select.*)

Synthesis Puts together separate ideas to form something new, relates one set of conclusions to another, formulates a new pattern. (Ask students to *organize, combine, compile, rearrange, plan, reconstruct, rewrite, summarize.*)

Evaluation Evaluates quality or value with reference to self-chosen or supplied criteria, makes judgments of adequacy or consistency. (Ask students to *arrange in order, compare, appraise, contrast, criticize, justify.*)

If you are inclined to write the general objectives recommended by Gronlund that we described in Chapter 7, you can subdivide the Objectives categories of Figure 13.1 into the specific outcomes that you intend to measure. Here, for example, is the knowledge-level objective noted in Chapter 7 that might be used in teaching sixth-grade music.

Knows musical instruments:

1. Names the instruments of an orchestra when pictures of each are displayed.
2. Identifies the instruments in an orchestra when pictures of each are displayed.
3. States differences between instruments of an orchestra and of a band.

The primary reason for using various types of instructional objectives to plan evaluation, for drawing up a table of specifications, or for referring to the lists just provided is to make your evaluations of student understanding and abilities comprehensive and systematic. Without some sort of rationale, you might simply make up questions on material that strikes you as testable.

You also might fall into the extremely common trap of writing questions that test a limited range of outcomes. Recall the statement made by Benjamin S. Bloom quoted in Chapter 7: "It is estimated that over 90 percent of test questions that U.S. public school students are *now* expected to answer deal with little more than information" (1984, p. 13). Bloom stressed the word *now* to emphasize that even though over one million copies of the taxonomy for the cognitive domain have been sold, very few teachers seem to be using them. A study of the test item–writing practices of thirty-six first- through twelfth-grade teachers (Stiggins, Griswold & Wikelund, 1989) found a similar but not quite as dramatic pattern. For science, social studies, and language arts, about 55 percent of the items were written at the recall level. About 19 percent were written at the comprehension and application levels, and about 16 percent were written at the analysis level. Only about 9 percent of the items reflected the two highest levels of Bloom's Taxonomy: synthesis and evaluation. The pattern for math, however, was quite different. For these tests, 72 percent of the items reflected Bloom's application level, followed by recall at 19 percent and synthesis at 9 percent. The researchers also found that teachers who had some in-service training in teaching and/or testing higher-order thinking skills wrote more higher-level questions and fewer recall questions than teachers with no in-service training.

If you take the trouble to be systematic about selecting and writing questions, you are much more likely to develop exams that are reliable and valid than if you simply dash off an assortment of test items. *Reliability,* as noted in Chapter 4, refers to the consistency of measurements and is concerned with questions such as these: If you gave the same exam a second time, would students earn essentially the same scores? If you prepare alternate-form exams on the same material, would students earn essentially the same scores on both exams? If you scored a short-answer or essay exam one night, would you end up with the same number of total points if you graded it two nights later? *Validity* refers to the extent to which a test measures what it is supposed to measure. If you want to find out if your students understand a chapter in a text, your test should give you an accurate indication that students who earn high scores understand the material better than students who end up with low scores. (The type of validity just described, you may recall, is called *content* validity, since it is concerned with how well a test measures the content of a subject of study. *Predictive* validity tells how well a test predicts future performance. For instance, you were probably asked to take the Scholastic Aptitude Test or the equivalent when you applied for admission to college because the admissions committee wanted to predict how well you would do. *Construct* validity indicates how well a test measures a particular construct or attribute. A test of musical aptitude, for example, should differentiate between students who respond quickly to instruction in music and those who do not.)

Test specialists who prepare standardized tests use a variety of statistical techniques to estimate reliability and validity and typically supply data permitting potential users to evaluate how well the test measures up in terms of consistency and accuracy. You will not have the time to use such techniques with your homemade exams; but as you prepare tests, you might attempt to ensure a satisfactory degree of reliability and validity by making up a sufficient number and variety of well-written questions on all aspects of a topic. Thus, perhaps the best way to endeavor to prepare reliable and valid exams is to do a conscientious job of following the suggestions in this chapter.

3. Consider the purpose of each test or measurement exercise. Take into account the developmental characteristics of the pupils in your classes and the nature of the curriculum for your grade level.

As you prepare your table of specifications, or otherwise plan a systematic testing procedure, think about the purpose of each evaluation exercise. Do you want to make an estimate of how much students understand or to place students at different levels (beginners, intermediate, advanced)? Do you want to monitor progress or plan remedial instruction (often called **formative evaluation** since the intention is to facilitate or form learning)? Do you want to discover how well instructional objectives have been met and/or determine a grade to be recorded on a report card (often called **summative evaluation,** since it sums up performance)? Do you want to try to identify sources of learning difficulties (referred to as *diagnostic* evaluation)? Do you want to combine several of these purposes? Depending on the purpose or purposes of a test, the form and content may vary. You should take this into account early in the testing sequence.

In addition to considering different uses of tests and other forms of evaluation when you plan evaluation strategies, you should think about the developmental characteristics of the students you plan to teach and the nature of the curriculum at your grade level. As noted in the discussion of Piaget's theory in Chapter 2, there are significant differences between preoperational, concrete operational, and formal thinkers. Furthermore, because primary grade children are asked to master a curriculum that is substantially different from the curriculum upper elementary and secondary school pupils are expected to learn, different forms of evaluation should be used at each level.

Primary grade children are asked to concentrate on learning basic skills, and their progress—or lack of it—will often be apparent even if they are not asked to take tests. A second-grader who can read only a few words, for instance, will reveal that inability each time he or she is asked to read. Upper elementary grade pupils are asked to improve and perfect their mastery of skills in reading, writing, and arithmetic and also to study topics in the sciences, social studies, and other subjects. Success in dealing with many subjects, learning materials, and tests often depends on skill in reading. A fifth-grader who is a slow reader, for instance, might not be able to get through an assigned chapter or answer all the questions on a multiple-choice test in the allotted time. Because performance in several subjects must be reported, many separate evaluations have to be made. In all of the elementary grades, there is usually an emphasis on helping as many students as possible master the curriculum. Thus tests may be used as much to diagnose weaknesses and chart improvement as to establish grades.

At the secondary level, students begin to move toward either a vocational or a college preparatory curriculum and to choose electives. Because courses in many subjects are often arranged in sequence, and because the process of identifying students most likely to go on to college begins at this time, comparisons of students become more systematic and direct. It is often desirable (or necessary) to discover if a student who takes Math I, for instance, is ready to go on to Math II. Colleges and universities may request that high schools establish particular grading standards in order to facilitate the selection of candidates who apply for admission. If a school does not maintain sufficiently high standards, graduates may encounter problems when they apply for admission to certain institutions of higher learning.

Formative evaluation: monitor progress, plan remedial instruction

Summative evaluation: measure achievement, assign grades

Two studies of the effectiveness of second- through fourth-grade teachers call attention to significant differences between younger and older pupils that should be considered when planning evaluation strategies.

Jere E. Brophy and Carolyn M. Evertson (1976) identified several second- and third-grade teachers who consistently seemed to do an especially effective job in the classroom. After observing the techniques used by these teachers and the impact they had on their pupils, Brophy and Evertson observed:

> Younger and less cognitively developed children seem to require more teacher structuring, smaller and more redundant steps in the learning process, more opportunities to practice and get corrective feedback, more attention to basic skills and factual knowledge, and the like. As they get older and/or more cognitively developed, they can begin to benefit increasingly from more indirect teaching, more verbal teaching, more opportunities for choice of assignments and independent work, more opportunities for group work and other student-to-student interaction, more challenging and faster paced instructional sequences, and the like. (p. 140)

The kinds of evaluation you might use if you teach in the first few grades, therefore, should be substantially different from those you might use at higher grade levels. Some primary graders will be preoperational thinkers and others will be embryonic concrete thinkers; all of them will benefit if they develop a sense of industry. Such children should have abundant opportunities to try out skills and receive immediate feedback. Instead of using weekly quizzes, you will find it preferable to have these students work on exercises daily. You can then

Younger pupils need more structure, repetition, feedback

There is some evidence that elementary school pupils who are provided with structured assignments score higher on standardized tests than those who attend classes that feature considerable self-direction. (Don & Pat Valenti/Tony Stone Worldwide)

supply feedback and also provide tangible evidence of progress. (Many texts and instructional materials designed for use in the early grades are accompanied by ready-made exercises of this type.)

▶ Use many formative tests with elementary school pupils

Upper elementary school pupils, most of whom will be concrete thinkers, might be given frequent formative examinations stressing knowledge and direct applications that can be derived from material recently presented in class. If you present a rule such as "*i* before *e* except after *c*," for instance, you might feature words that contain the letters *i* and *e* after *c* as well as after other letters. Instead of basing grades on a few summative tests, you might schedule frequent exams so that students can accumulate points as they work toward instructional objectives leading to a particular grade. And to promote feelings of industry rather than inferiority, provide remedial instruction to students who are experiencing difficulties and give them repeated opportunities to meet specific standards. (A comprehensive method for doing so will be described at the end of this chapter.)

After you have determined the purpose of a test, drawn up your table of specifications (or selected Key Points), and considered such factors as level of cognitive development and the curriculum, you will be faced with the task of deciding what kinds of test items to use. (If you have developed lists of specific learning outcomes, you will already know which types of items to write.)

4. Decide on the type of test items to use and write sufficient items to provide an adequate sample, measuring understanding at several levels of the taxonomies of educational objectives (if appropriate) and allowing for differences in cognitive styles.

Before beginning the actual composition of a test, you might first see if the publisher of the text you are using supplies examination questions. If test questions or evaluation exercises *are* available, you can use them exactly as provided or modify or supplement them with additional items of your own, so long as two conditions are met: The items should reflect your course objectives, and they should be well written. Since it is almost certain that you will need to write at least some of your own test questions, brief descriptions of different types of items will be presented in the next few pages. Each of the following sections describes the nature, advantages, and disadvantages of a particular type of question. Some guidelines for writing each type of item are also included.[1]

Short-Answer and Completion Items

Description: The student is asked to supply a brief answer consisting of a name, word, phrase, or symbol.

Example of a short-answer item: Robert Rosenthal did research on the impact of expectations. As a synonym for the term *self-fulfilling prophecy* he uses what term? (*Pygmalion effect*)

1. The general form and much of the content of the following sections are derived from material in Chapters 6 through 9 of *Measurement and Evaluation in Teaching* (6th ed., 1990) by Norman E. Gronlund and Robert L. Linn.

Example of a completion item: Robert Rosenthal did research on the impact of expectations. As a synonym for the term *self-fulfilling prophecy* he prefers the term *(Pygmalion effect)*.

Advantages: Easy to write. Can be written on the board or printed or typed on a single ditto master. Require pupil to *supply* the answer, not simply recognize it. Guessing and bluffing not likely to be too successful. Can ask many questions in a short period of time, get an extensive sample.

▶ Short-answer items easy to write but measure lower levels of learning

Disadvantages: Restricted to measuring simple learning at lower levels of the taxonomy of objectives for the cognitive domain. Unexpected (but plausible) answers may be difficult to prevent or score. If you teach more than one section of a course, students in one class will be able to tell friends in other classes many of the questions, which may mean that you will have to make up a different test for each class.

Guidelines:

1. Write the question so that the answer is brief and definite.
2. Guard against lifting phrases directly from the text.
3. As often as possible, use direct questions rather than incomplete statements (to facilitate grading and to reduce ambiguity).
4. If completion items are used, put blanks in a column on the right side of the paper. Or, if you print the questions on the board, have students list answers on a separate sheet of paper.

True-False or Alternative-Response Items

Description: The student is asked to identify the correctness of definitions, statements, facts, or principles or to distinguish between fact and opinion.

Examples: If the following statement is true, circle the T. If the statement is false, circle the F.

   (T)   F   The tendency for one characteristic to influence all impressions is called the halo effect.

If the following statement is a fact, circle the F. If it is an opinion, circle the O.

   (F)   O   A table of specifications is used to plan tests.

   F   (O)   Behavioral learning theory is more valuable to teachers than cognitive theory.

If the answer to the following question is yes, circle the Y. If it is no, circle the N.

   (Y)   N   Does *Pygmalion effect* mean the same as *self-fulfilling prophecy?*

   Y   (N)   Has Rosenthal's research on the impact of expectations been supported consistently by the research of other psychologists?

Advantages: it is possible to ask many questions in a short period of time. Answers are very easy to score. They can be an effective way to measure understanding of facts versus opinions.

Disadvantages: Restricted to measuring simple learning, usually at lowest levels of the taxonomy for the cognitive domain. Difficult to write items that can be reduced to absolute terms on other than trivial material. Items may penalize divergent thinkers. They may also permit and encourage guessing to the point that some students spend more time trying to figure out a pattern than analyzing questions. To offset the impact of guessing, need a very large number of items.

Guidelines:

1. Avoid broad general statements or statements that stress trivia.

2. Avoid use of long, complex sentences; restrict each statement to a single idea.

3. Write about an equal number of true and false statements, and make both types of statements approximately equal in length.

4. Try to avoid using words such as *always, never, sometimes,* and the like.

5. Write as many items as you think pupils can answer in allotted test time.

Matching Questions

Description: Pupil is asked to identify pairs of items to be associated.

Example: In the blank space next to each concept listed in the left-hand column, write the number next to the name of the appropriate individual listed in the right-hand column. A name may be used more than once.

_____ equilibration	1. Bandura
_____ operant conditioning	2. Erikson
	3. Gronlund
_____ growth needs	4. Mager
	5. Maslow
_____ identity vs. role confusion	6. Piaget
_____ anticipatory control	7. Sears
	8. Skinner
_____ assimilation	

Advantages: Compact form, can cover much material in a small amount of space. Teacher can print test on board, have students record answers on a slip of paper. Very easy to score. Can measure ability to distinguish between similar events or place them in order (if question is arranged to stress order).

Disadvantages: Restricted to measuring factual information at lowest levels of the taxonomy of objectives for the cognitive domain. Difficult to find homogeneous material or to avoid irrelevant clues. Easy for students in one class to tell friends in other classes what to study. May be simple for students to copy answers from others' papers.

Guidelines:

1. Try to stress items that are related in some way or are of the same type. Don't just throw together an assortment of miscellaneous information.

2. Include an unequal number of premises and responses. Tell students if a response can be used more than once. Do not list more than ten premises per question.

3. Keep the descriptions brief. Place short responses in the right-hand column.

4. Arrange responses in a logical order (alphabetically, chronologically.)

5. Do not have a matching question continue on a second page.

Multiple-Choice Items

Description: A statement (the *stem*) is followed by several alternative statements. One of these is the answer; the others are *distracters*. The form may involve a direct question or an incomplete statement, or it may ask for the best answer. Instructions at the top of the first page of the test booklet indicate how answers should be recorded.

Examples:

Which of the following is a definition of *projection?*

1. Tendency for expectations to influence perceptions

2. Tendency to ignore evidence that is inconsistent

3. Tendency for one characteristic to influence all impressions

(4.) Tendency to see own undesirable traits in others

Projection is said to occur when

1. expectations influence perceptions.

2. one characteristic of a person influences all impressions of that person.

3. inconsistent evidence is ignored.

(4.) someone sees his or her own undesirable traits in others.

Which of the following is the clearest and most accurate definition of projection?

1. Tendency for expectations to influence perceptions

2. Tendency to ignore evidence that is inconsistent with beliefs

3. Tendency for one characteristic to influence all impressions

(4.) Tendency to see own undesirable traits in others

Advantages: Can measure many types of understanding, including those at the middle and sometimes upper levels of the taxonomy for the cognitive domain. Can ask many questions in a class period; can thus get an excellent sample. Possible to reduce ambiguity often found in short-answer and true-false items. Very easy to grade, particularly when special answer sheets are used. Opportunity for guessing is reduced. Difficult for students in one class to pass on items to friends in other classes, so an exam can be used several times. Can give students experience with types of items that are commonly featured on standardized tests (such as those used in making decisions about college admission).

> Multiple-choice items measure different levels of learning but are hard to write

Disadvantages: Difficult and time-consuming to write items that measure more than knowledge. Under pressure to get a test ready, teacher may tend to write knowledge items. Students are asked to *recognize* correctness or incorrectness, not to supply information on their own. Often difficult to write a sufficient number of plausible distracters. Requires substantial time to type ditto masters, run off copies, collate, staple, number copies. May favor convergent thinkers, penalize divergent thinkers. Difficult to supply feedback for each question, thus tending to cause students to concentrate only on the score earned, not on which answers were correct and incorrect.

Guidelines:

1. Try to make the stem meaningful by itself and have it present a definite problem, without irrelevant material.

2. Try to avoid stems stated in negative terms (sometimes this is unavoidable).

3. Make sure all alternatives are grammatically consistent with the stem.

4. Try to ensure that the answer is clearly more correct than the distracters, but try to make the distracters plausible.

5. Arrange the alternatives in alphabetical order (to avoid establishing a pattern).

6. Use phrases such as *all of the above* or *none of the above* sparingly or not at all.

7. Make a deliberate effort to stress translation, interpretation, application, analysis, and evaluation when you write questions. Guard against writing too many knowledge questions. You might be tempted, for instance, to supply a definition in the stem and list four terms under it. Such a question merely asks the student to supply a label. A better way to write the question would be to put a *term* in the stem followed by four definitions. This format asks the student to think about what the term means (which is more useful than attaching a label). Better yet, ask students to *translate* the text definition of a term by selecting the best alternative description from four variations (perhaps expressed in slang terms). Students might be asked to *interpret* the term by choosing the best illustration of it from four supplied. They might be asked to *apply* it by selecting the best description of uses from four supplied. And they might be asked to *evaluate* it by picking out a strength or weakness from four descriptive statements.

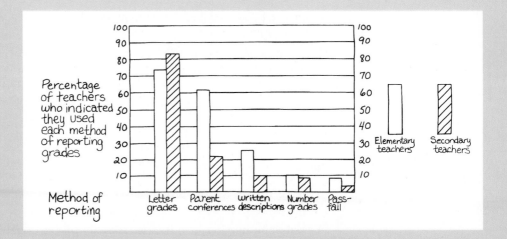

Interpretive Items

Description: A series of objective questions is based on a descriptive paragraph, a graph, diagram, map, cartoon, or illustration.

Example: The graph above indicates the percentage of teachers who reported (in a survey conducted by the National Education Association in 1970) using various types of grading procedures.

The statements that follow refer to the data recorded in the graph. Read each statement and mark your answer according to the following key:

Circle T if the graph data are sufficient to make the statement *true.*

Circle F if the data are sufficient to make the statement *false.*

Circle I if the graph data are *insufficient* to determine whether the statement is true or false.

T	F	(I)	Number grades were assigned by a greater number of elementary than secondary teachers.
(T)	F	I	About six-tenths of all elementary teachers reported grades in conferences.
T	F	(I)	Elementary grade teachers prefer letter grades to conferences or pass-fail grading procedures.
T	(F)	I	Fewer than one-tenth of the secondary teachers surveyed reported grades in parent conferences.
(T)	F	I	Four times as many secondary teachers assigned letter grades as participated in parent conferences.

Advantages: Measure student ability to interpret written or pictorial materials—an important form of cognitive behavior. Can measure complex learning, but in a more structured form than on an essay test. All students are supplied with identical data, which means that reasoning rather than memorization is stressed.

Disadvantages: Difficult and time-consuming to construct. Items based on written material favor good readers, penalize poor readers. Measure only the ability to solve problems that are presented in structured form. Pupils asked only to recognize correct answers, not to apply problem-solving skills on their own.

Guidelines:

1. Base questions on material that is new to pupils.

2. Write questions that are at an appropriate reading level.

3. Write questions that require analysis and interpretation of the material, not merely recognition of factual material.

4. Make the number of questions roughly proportional to the length of the material.

5. If the material permits, revise it as the questions are written (to make the questions less ambiguous or more challenging).

6. To simplify preparation of exams, write or draw the material on which the questions are based on the board, or project transparencies, or use an opaque projector.

Essay Items

Description: The student is asked to recall, organize, and integrate what is known about some topic.

Example: Compare behavioral learning theory and cognitive theory in terms of basic assumptions, typical research findings, and pedagogical applications.

Advantages: Can measure complex learning, particularly the abilities to analyze, synthesize, and evaluate. Student is asked to recall, select, and apply (not just recognize) what has been learned. Students gain experience in expressing their thoughts in writing—a skill required in many occupations. Because students reveal their train of thoughts in written form, it may be possible for the teacher to trace errors in understanding or reasoning. Questions can be written on the board; no need to prepare examination booklets.

Disadvantages: Teacher may be tempted to make up questions on the spur of the moment, not take into account instructional objectives in a systematic way. Extremely difficult, time-consuming, and tedious to grade. Extremely difficult to grade consistently. (The same teacher may give a substantially different grade if the papers are reread a few weeks later. Different instructors may give the same paper grades from A to D.) Because students can write on only a few topics in a typical class period, sample is very limited. Evaluator may be influenced by such factors as handwriting and spelling. If teacher does not take the trouble to avoid looking at the names of the students, may evaluate personalities rather than answers. Temptation to reward "pets" with

Interpretive items measure reasoning but take time to construct

Essay items measure complex learning but are hard to grade consistently

high grades, and to give low grades to students who antagonize or have registered dislike.

Guidelines:

1. Resist the temptation to dash off questions on the spur of the moment. Take time to devise questions that are related to instructional objectives.

2. Phrase the questions so that pupils have a clear idea what you want them to write about.

3. Tell students how many points each question will count; inform them that they will not be graded on spelling or grammar.

4. Immediately after you compose a question, write out your own answer. Use that answer to clarify the question and to grade papers. If possible and appropriate, indicate in your answer how many points you intend to award for each major idea correctly analyzed by students.

5. Have students write their names on the back of the last page of the exam so that you will be unaware of their identity as you grade papers. If you recognize handwriting, do your best to react to the answer, not to the student.

6. Consider asking pupils to write essay-type analyses in the form of term papers rather than under examination conditions.

Short-Essay Items

Description: Student is asked to recall, supply, apply, or explain information about a specific point or points.

Example: Describe and explain the values of three characteristics of tests.

Advantages: Student is asked to recall (not merely recognize), apply, explain, or analyze what has been learned—a more practical and realistic kind of behavior than responding to cues supplied by others (as in objective items). Student gains experience in expressing ideas in writing, but there is emphasis on conveying meaning succinctly. Test-preparation chores are not extreme: Three or four questions might be arranged on a page with room for answers, or questions can be written on the board. Teacher can grade answers by assigning points depending on quality of answers or by designating answers as plus or minus. Students reveal how much they understand; guessing and bluffing are reduced to a minimum since they either know the answer or don't know it. As the teacher reads papers, he or she acquires information that can be used to plan remedial instruction. It is possible to go over every question in class when exams are handed back.

Disadvantages: Take longer to score than objective tests. Scoring may not be consistent from one paper to another. Teacher may be influenced by such factors as handwriting and spelling. Teacher may be tempted to make up tests on the spur of the moment. Students in one class can tell friends in other classes what is on exams, thus possibly making it necessary to devise a different exam for each class. Provide a less complete sample than objective tests.

Guidelines:

1. Resist the temptation to make up tests on the spur of the moment. Try to choose a good sample of items derived from instructional objectives.

2. Immediately after you write an item, write out an acceptable answer. Use your answer to clarify the question and to grade answers.

3. Indicate the number of points each answer will count toward the total score.

4. To the extent possible, ask students to translate, interpret, apply, analyze, and evaluate what they have learned. Try to stress types of learning at the higher levels of the taxonomy for the cognitive domain.

5. Have students write their names on the back of the last page of the exam.

As you think about which types of questions to use in a particular situation, consider the pupil characteristics and curriculum differences noted earlier. In the primary grades, you may not use any tests in the strict sense. Instead you might ask your pupils to demonstrate skills, complete exercises (some of which may be similar to completion tests), and solve simple problems (often on worksheets). In the elementary grades you may need to use or make up dozens of measurement instruments since many subjects must be graded. Accordingly, it may be necessary to make extensive use of completion, short-answer, and short-essay items that can be printed on the board or on a ditto master. If you find it impossible or impractical to make up a table of specifications for each exam, at least refer to instructional objectives or a list of key points as you write questions. At the secondary level you might do your best to develop some sort of table of specifications for exams, not only to ensure measurement of objectives at various levels of the taxonomy but also to remind yourself to use different types of items.

Handbook Heading:
Using Different Types
of Test Items

The use of different types of test items allows you to balance their advantages and disadvantages. With older students, you may find that some questions are more appropriate than others for testing understanding at various levels of the taxonomy for the cognitive domain. In addition, you should try to allow for differences in cognitive style. As noted in Chapter 3, reflective thinkers perform better on tasks requiring analysis of details, whereas impulsive thinkers perform better on tasks requiring synthesis and evaluation. Some children memorize much more easily than others, whereas some are better able to concentrate on several factors at once (which would be an advantage when pondering matching or multiple-choice questions). Some pupils are convergent thinkers and tend to give conventional answers, but others are divergent thinkers and tend to respond to questions in idiosyncratic ways (which might lead to problems with objective test items). If you use different types of questions on tests, you may give all pupils a chance to deal with at least some problems that "fit" their cognitive style.

In certain elementary grade subjects and in skill or laboratory subjects at the secondary level, the types of questions just described may not be appropriate. At

▶ Rating scales and checklists make evaluation of performance more systematic

the primary grade level, for instance, you may be required to assign a report grade in oral reading. In a high school home economics class, you may grade pupils on how well they produce a garment or a soufflé. In a woodshop class, you may base a grade on how well students construct a piece of furniture. You may grade students in a music class on instrumental or vocal performance and those in a science class on how successfully they use laboratory equipment to carry out experiments. In such cases you can make evaluations more systematic and accurate by using *rating scales* and *checklists* and by attempting to equate (or at least take into account) the difficulty level of the performance to be rated.

To evaluate oral reading in the second grade, for instance, you might have pupils individually come to a quiet corner of the room and read the same passage. (If you simply went through a book, asking each pupil who came to you to read the next passage, some pupils would end up with much more difficult passages than others.) As they read, you might rate them on a five-point scale on such factors as pronunciation, clarity, fluency, absence of hesitation, and the like. Perhaps the best way to devise such rating scales is to listen to some sample readings of different material. As you listen, select aspects of the performance that strike you as important and ratable. Try to pick out types of behavior that can be described in specific terms and then write a description of each facet that you intend to rate.

To evaluate a product such as a garment or piece of furniture, you might use a checklist that you devised and handed out at the beginning of a course. Such a checklist should state the number of possible points that will be awarded for various aspects of the project—for example, accuracy of measurements and preparation of component parts, neatness of assembly, quality of finishing touches, final appearance, and so forth. To evaluate a performance, you might use the same approach, announcing beforehand how heavily you intend to weigh various aspects of execution. In music, for instance, you might note possible points to be awarded for tone, execution, accuracy, and interpretation. For both project and performance tasks, you might multiply the final score by a difficulty factor. (You have probably seen television coverage of Olympics events in which divers and gymnasts have their performance ratings multiplied by such a difficulty factor.)

Whenever you make ratings, you should try to allow for the sequencing of good and poor students. Any pupil who performs after the best student in a class is going to look poor by comparison. And anyone who follows the worst performer is going to look good. When making ratings you will need to try to avoid a tendency to rate all pupils at about the same level. Some raters start out with high ratings and then find they are unable to distinguish between good and excellent performers because the rating limit has been reached. Others tend to rate everyone as average.

Handbook Heading: Techniques for Evaluating Skills and Projects

If you will be teaching secondary school subjects that will involve evaluation of projects or performance, you might jot down in your Handbook techniques used by your own teachers. Note excellent evaluative approaches that you felt were fair and accurate as well as techniques to avoid at all costs.

5. Make up and use a detailed key.
   a. Evaluate each answer by comparing it to the key.

One of the most valuable characteristics of a test is that it permits comparison of the permanently recorded answers of all pupils to a fixed set of criteria. A complete key not only reduces subjectivity; it can also save you much time and trouble when you are grading papers and/or defending your evaluation of questions.

For short-answer, true-false, matching, or multiple-choice questions, you should devise your key as you write and assemble the items. With planning and ingenuity, you can prepare a key that will greatly simplify grading. First, arrange the test items (or a separate answer sheet) so that answers will be recorded in an orderly fashion (in a column on one side of the page, for example). Then, cut a manila folder in half (or take a piece of heavy paper of the same general consistency) and prepare a template in the following way: Take a piece of transparent paper and draw a circle or rectangle around the answer spaces. With carbon paper transfer these outlines to the heavier paper and punch or cut out openings. Print the word, phrase, or number of the answer next to each space. When the time comes to grade papers, place your template over each answer sheet and draw a red line through incorrect responses. All that remains is to tally the number of correct responses and record it on the answer sheet next to the pupil's name.

The onerous chore of grading papers can be speeded up and simplified if plus-minus grading is used. (Bob Daemmrich)

Handbook Heading:
Preparing a Detailed
Key

Preparing a key for essay or short-essay exams can be simplified if you follow the guidelines noted earlier in the analyses of these items. Perhaps the most important point to remember is to prepare answers *as* you write the questions. If you ask students to write answers to a small number of comprehensive essay questions, you are likely to maximize the consistency of your grading process by grading all answers to the first question at one sitting, then grading all answers to the second question, and so on. If a test consists of eight or ten short-essay items (which can usually be answered in a half-hour or so), you would have to do too much paper shuffling in order to follow such a procedure. One way to speed up the grading of short-essay exams (so that you can evaluate up to thirty tests in a single session of forty minutes or so) is to use plus-or-minus grading. If you use a point scale to grade short-essay answers, you will spend an agonizing amount of time deciding just how much a given answer is worth. But, with practice, you should be able to write short-essay questions and answers (on your key) that can be graded plus or minus. To develop skill in writing such questions, make up a few formative quizzes that will not count toward a grade. Experiment with phrasing questions that require students to reveal that they either know or don't know the answer. Prepare your key as you write the questions. When the time comes to grade papers, simply make a yes or no decision about the correctness of each answer. With a felt-tip pen make a bold check over each satisfactory answer on an exam, and simply tally the number of checks when you have read all the answers. (Counting up to eight or ten is obviously a lot quicker and easier than adding together various numbers of points for eight or ten answers.) Once you have developed skill in writing and evaluating short-essay questions that can be graded plus or minus, prepare and use summative exams. If you decide to use this type of exam, guard against the temptation to write items that measure only knowledge. Use a table of specifications or otherwise take steps to write at least some questions that measure skills at the higher levels of the taxonomy for the cognitive domain.

b. Be willing and prepared to defend the evaluations you make.

You will probably get few complaints if you have a detailed key and, when exams are returned, can explain to the class how each answer was graded. To a direct challenge about a specific answer to an essay or short-essay question, you might respond by showing complainers an answer that received full credit and invite them to compare it with their own.

A major disadvantage of multiple-choice items is that it is very difficult to go over a multiple-choice test in class. At least one student may have selected each of the wrong alternatives and will want to explain why, while the other members of the class doze or fume as they wait to give *their* explanations—or make out a list of right answers to pass on to someone in another section. Going over a fifty-item test could take hours. It could take hours with just one student, particularly if he or she is a divergent thinker or argumentative. Because of such factors, instructors often simply report or post scores on multiple-choice exams and make no offer to discuss individual questions with students. The unfortunate

When returning exams to students, be prepared to explain how each answer was graded. Distributing feedback booklets to students is a good way to encourage them to think about the information covered in the test, instead of concentrating only on their scores. (Jean-Claude Le-Juene)

result of such a policy is that it encourages students to think only about a score, not about what they have learned (or failed to learn). Students also reason that as soon as a test is completed, the purpose for learning what was covered on the exam has been served, and information might as well be forgotten.

Perhaps the best way to encourage students to think about what has been covered in multiple-choice questions, instead of concentrating only on the score, is to prepare a *feedback* booklet. As you write each multiple-choice question, also write a brief explanation as to why you feel the answer is correct and why the distracters are incorrect. If you follow this policy (which takes less time than you might expect), you can often improve the questions as you write your defense of the answer. If you go a step farther (to be described in the next point), you can obtain information to use in improving questions after they have been answered. This is a good policy to follow with any exam, multiple-choice or otherwise.

6. During and after the grading process, analyze questions and answers in order to improve future exams.

If you prepare sufficient copies of feedback booklets for multiple-choice exams, you can supply them to all pupils when you hand back scored answer sheets (and copies of the question booklets). After students have checked their papers and identified and examined questions that were marked wrong, invite them to select up to three questions that they wish to challenge. Even after they read your explanation in the feedback booklet, many students are likely to feel that they selected a different answer than you did for logical and defensible reasons. Permit them to write out a description of the reasoning behind their choices. If an explanation seems plausible, give credit for the answer. If several students chose the same questions for comment, you have evidence that the item needs to be revised.

If you follow the procedure of supplying feedback booklets, it is almost essential to prepare at least two forms of every exam. After writing the questions, arrange them into two tests. Make perhaps half of the questions the same, half unique to each exam. (If you have enough questions, you might prepare three forms.) If you teach multiple sections, give the first form to period 1, the next form to period 2, and thereafter use the forms in random order. This procedure will reduce the possibility that some students in later classes will have advance information about most of the questions on the test. (Having two or more forms also equips you to use a mastery approach, which will be described at the end of this chapter.)

Handbook Heading:
Analyzing Test Items

If you find that you do not have time to prepare feedback booklets, you might invite students to select three answers to defend *as* they record their choices when taking multiple-choice exams. This will supply you with information about ambiguous questions, even though it will not provide feedback to students. Allowing students to defend their answers to some or all of the items in other types of tests may also provide you with useful information about how well the items were written. If you discover, for example, that students supply a variety of wrong answers to a short-answer or completion item, you may conclude that the question was too ambiguous as written. (It's also possible that the information reflected in the item was not directly related to your objectives or was poorly taught.) As you read answers to essay and short-essay questions, you will often get quite direct insight into the word or phrase in a question that led students astray.

▶ Item analysis tells about difficulty, discriminability of multiple-choice items

Turning back to multiple-choice questions, you may also want to use simple versions of item-analysis techniques that measurement specialists use to analyze and improve this type of item. These techniques will allow you to estimate the difficulty level and discriminating power of each item. To do so, try the following steps suggested by Norman Gronlund (1988):

1. Rank the test papers from highest score to lowest score.

2. Select approximately the top one-third and call this the upper group. Select approximately the bottom one-third and call this the lower group. Set the middle group of papers aside.

3. For each item, record the number of students in the upper group and in the lower group who selected the correct answer and each distracter, as follows:

Item 1. Alternatives	A	B*	C	D	E
Upper Group	0	6	3	1	0
Lower Group	3	2	2	3	0

* = correct answer

4. Estimate item difficulty by calculating the percentage of students who answered the item correctly. The difficulty index for the above item is 40 percent (8/20 **x** 100). Note that the smaller the percentage the more difficult the item.

5. Estimate item discriminating power by subtracting the number in the lower group who answered the item correctly from the number in the upper group, and divide by one-half of the total number of students included in the item analysis. For the above example, the discrimination index is .40 (6 − 2 ÷ 10). When the index is positive, as it is here, it indicates that more students in the upper group than in the lower group answered the item correctly. A negative value indicates just the opposite.

As you can see, this type of item analysis is not difficult to do, nor is it likely to be very time consuming. In addition, it has several benefits that we will mention shortly. It is important to remember, though, that the benefits of item analysis can quickly be lost if you ignore certain limitations. One is that you will be working with relatively small numbers of students. Therefore, the results of item analysis are likely to vary as you go from class to class or from test to test with the same class. Because of this variation, you should retain items that a measurement specialist would discard or revise. In general, you should retain multiple-choice items whose difficulty index lies between 50 and 90 percent and whose discrimination index is positive (Gronlund, 1988). Another limitation is that you may have objectives that everyone must master. If you do an effective job of teaching these objectives, the corresponding test items are likely to be answered correctly by nearly every student. These items should be retained rather than revised to meet arbitrary criteria of difficulty and discrimination.

If you keep these cautions in mind, item analysis can help you accomplish several useful measurement goals. First, it provides a vehicle for discussing the test. Easy items can be discussed briefly, difficult items (those around the 50 percent level) can be explained more fully, and defective items can be discarded rather than defended as fair. Second, item analysis reveals common errors and misconceptions and can thus serve as a basis for reteaching and restudy. Third, item analysis helps you improve your test-writing skills and assign grades in a fair and meaningful fashion (Gronlund, 1988).

Mid-Chapter Review

Nature of Measurement and Evaluation

Whenever we assign numbers to certain attributes of people (such as typing ability or mathematical reasoning skills) according to a set of rules that allows us to rank people by how much of the attribute they possess, we are practicing measurement. Whenever we make judgments about the value or worth of the things we measure, we are practicing evaluation.

Types of Measures

The types of measures that most teachers use are performance tests and written tests. Performance tests are used to measure how well students perform a particular skill under somewhat realistic conditions. Depending on the teacher's objectives, they may be used to assess the adequacy of the underlying skills that go into a performance, the performance itself, or both.

Written tests are used to measure how much students know about some topic. Written test items are classified as objective or created-response depending on the type of response they require of the test taker and the resulting degree of subjectivity that enters into their scoring. Objective items include multiple-choice, true-false, matching, and interpretive. Created-response items include short-answer and essay.

Reducing Subjectivity

Pygmalion in the Classroom by Robert Rosenthal and Lenore Jacobson brought to light problems that subjectivity can create in measurement and evaluation of pupil performance. Rosenthal and Jacobson claimed that leading teachers to expect that certain pupils had untapped academic ability caused the teachers to treat those students differently, thereby causing their IQ scores to increase. Rosenthal and Jacobson called this phenomenon the *Pygmalion effect;* it is also known as *self-fulfilling prophecy* and the *teacher expectancy effect.* Subsequent research demonstrated very modest and limited teacher expectancy effects on IQ scores; but it showed much stronger and wider effects, both positive and negative, on classroom achievement and participation. Some of the factors that contribute to a teacher expectancy effect are gender, compliance, neatness, achievement, and attractiveness.

Effective Measurement and Evaluation Techniques

You can ensure effective measurement and evaluation practice by adhering to the following six steps:

1. As early as possible, decide when and how often to give tests and other assignments.

2. Prepare a table of specifications to ensure that you test all important subjects and outcomes.

3. Decide whether you want to test for the purpose of planning remedial instruction—a practice called *formative evaluation*—and/or for the purpose of determining how much was learned—a practice known as *summative evaluation.*

4. Decide whether you want to use objective items or created-response items, and which particular types of each.

5. Make up an answer key.

6. Analyze questions and answers to improve the quality of future exams.

EVALUATION METHODS

Once you have collected all the measures you intend to collect—for example, test scores, quiz scores, homework assignments, special projects, and laboratory experiments—you will have to give the numbers some sort of value (the essence of evaluation). As you probably know, this is most often done by using an A to F grading scale. Typically, a grade of A indicates superior performance; a B, above-average performance; a C, average performance; a D, below-average performance; and an F, failing. There are two general ways to approach this task. One approach involves comparisons among students. Such forms of evaluation are called *norm-referenced* since students are identified as average (or normal), above average, or below average. An alternative approach is called *criterion-referenced* because performance is interpreted in terms of defined criteria. (As you may recall, these concepts were initially discussed in Chapter 4.) Although both approaches can be used, we favor criterion-referenced grading for reasons we will mention shortly.

Norm-Referenced Grading

The norm-referenced approach assumes that classroom achievement will naturally vary among a group of heterogeneous students because of differences in such characteristics as prior knowledge, learning skills, motivation, and aptitude. Under ideal circumstances (hundreds of scores from a diverse group of students), this variation produces a bell-shaped or "normal" distribution of scores that ranges from low to high, has few tied scores, and has only a very few low scores and only a very few high scores. For this reason, norm-referenced grading procedures are also referred to as "grading on the curve."

The Nature of Norm-Referenced Grading   As with the interpretation of standardized test scores, course grades are determined by comparing each student's level of performance to the "normal" or average level of other, similar students in order to reflect the assumed differences in amount of learned material. The comparison may be to all other members of the student's class that year or it may be to the average performance of several classes stretching back over several years. It is probably better for teachers to use a broad base of typical student performance made up of several classes as grounds for comparison than to rely on the current class of students. Doing so avoids two severe distorting effects that can occur: When a single class contains many weak students, those with more well-developed abilities will more easily obtain the highest grades; and if the class has many capable students, the relatively weaker students are virtually predestined to receive low or failing grades (Hopkins & Antes, 1990; Kubiszyn & Borich, 1990).

The basic procedure for assigning grades on a norm-referenced basis involves just a few steps. First, determine what percentage of students will receive

> ▶ Norm-referenced grading: compare one student to others

which grades. If, for example, you intend to award the full range of grades, you may decide to give A's to the top 15 percent, B's to the next 25 percent, C's to the middle 35 percent, D's to the next 15 percent, and F's to the bottom 10 percent. Second, arrange the scores from highest to lowest. Third, calculate which scores fall in which category and assign the grades accordingly. Of course, many other arrangements are also possible. How large or small you decide to make the percentages for each category will depend on such factors as the nature of the students in your class, the difficulty of your exams and assignments, and your own sense of what constitutes appropriate standards. Furthermore, a norm-referenced approach does not necessarily mean that each class will have a normal distribution of grades or that anyone will automatically fail. For example, it is possible for equal numbers of students to receive A's, B's, and C's. A norm-referenced approach simply means that the grading symbols being used indicate one student's level of achievement relative to other students.

▶ Norm-referenced grading based on absence of external criteria

Proponents of norm-referenced grading typically point to the absence of acceptable external criteria for use as a standard for evaluating and grading student performance. In other words, there is no good way to externally determine how much learning is too little, just enough, or more than enough for some subject. And if there is no amount of knowledge or set of behaviors that must be mastered by all students, then grades may be awarded on the basis of relative performance among a group of students (Hopkins & Antes, 1990).

With these points in mind, let's turn now to a discussion of the advantages and disadvantages of norm-referenced grading.

Advantages and Disadvantages of Norm-Referenced Grading   There are at least two circumstances under which it may be appropriate to use norm-referenced measurement and evaluation procedures. You might, for example, wish to formulate a two-stage instructional plan, in which the first stage involves helping all students master a basic level of knowledge and skill in a particular subject. Performance at this stage would be measured and evaluated against a predetermined standard (such as 80 percent correct on an exam). Once this has been accomplished, you could supply advanced instruction and encourage students to learn as much of the additional material as possible. Since amount of learning during the second stage is not tied to a predetermined standard, and since it will likely vary because of differences in motivation and learning skills, a norm-referenced approach to grading can be used. This situation also fits Johnson and Johnson's (1991) guidelines for the use of competitive reward structures (discussed in Chapter 12), since everyone starts from the same level of basic knowledge.

▶ Norm-referenced grading can be used to evaluate advanced levels of learning

Norm-referenced measurement and evaluation are also applicable in cases where students with the best chances for success are selected for a limited-enrollment program from among a large pool of candidates. One example is the selection of students for honors programs who have the highest test scores and grade-point averages (Hopkins & Antes, 1990).

The main disadvantage of the norm-referenced approach to grading is that there are few situations in which the typical public school teacher can appropriately use it. Either the goal is not appropriate (as in such examples as mastery of certain material and skills by all students or diagnosis of an individual student's specific strengths and weaknesses) or the basic conditions cannot be met (classes are too small and/or homogeneous). When a norm-referenced approach is used in spite of these limitations, communication and motivation problems are often created. Consider the example of a group of high school sophomores having a great deal of difficulty mastering German vocabulary and grammar. The students may have been underprepared, the teacher may be doing a poor job of organizing and explaining the material, or both factors may be at work. At any rate, the top student averages 48 percent correct on all of the exams, quizzes, and oral recitations administered during the term. That student and a few others with averages in the high 40s will receive the A's. While these fortunate few may realize their knowledge and skills are incomplete, others are likely to falsely conclude that these students learned quite a bit about the German language since a grade of A is generally taken to mean superior performance. At the other extreme we have the example of a social studies class in which most of the students are doing well. Because the students were well prepared by previous teachers, used effective study skills, were exposed to high-quality instruction, and were strongly motivated by the enthusiasm of their teacher, the final test averages ranged from 94 to 98 percent correct. And yet the teacher who uses a norm-referenced scheme would assign at least A's, B's, and C's to this group. Not only does this practice seriously damage the motivation of students who worked hard and performed well; it also miscommunicates to others the performance of students who received B's and C's (Airasian, 1991).

Although higher standards generally lead to greater effort and more learning, students who perceive standards as unattainable are likely to become less motivated to learn. For the perennial low-achieving student or the student whose work is above average but not among the best, the A in a norm-referenced system is likely to be seen as unattainable. In addition, forcing students to compete for a limited number of top grades is antithetical to the goals of the cooperative-learning programs we described in earlier chapters and may have a negative impact on students' character development (Wynne & Walberg, 1985/1986). As one person who has studied this issue put it: "It is hard to see any justification before the final year or so of high school for placing much emphasis on using classroom evaluation for normative grading of student achievement" (Crooks, 1988, p. 468).

We will now describe a criterion-referenced approach that incorporates features that permit students to benefit from mistakes and to improve their level of understanding and performance. Furthermore, it establishes an individual (and sometimes a cooperative) reward structure, which fosters motivation to learn to a greater extent than do the competitive reward structures found in most norm-referenced approaches.

Criterion-Referenced Grading

▶ Criterion-referenced grading: compare individual performance to stated criteria

Under a criterion-referenced system, grades are determined by comparing the extent to which each student has attained a defined standard (or criterion) of achievement or performance. Whether the rest of the students in the class are successful or unsuccessful in meeting that criterion is irrelevant. Thus, any distribution of grades is possible. Every student may get an A or an F, or no student may receive these grades. For reasons we will discuss shortly, very low or failing grades tend to occur less frequently under a criterion-referenced system.

A common version of criterion-referenced grading assigns letter grades on the basis of the percentage of test items answered correctly. For example, you may decide to award an A to anyone who correctly answers at least 85 percent of a set of test questions, a B to anyone who correctly answers 75 to 84 percent, and so on down to the lowest grade. To use this type of grading system fairly, which means specifying realistic criterion levels, you would need to have some prior knowledge of the levels at which students typically perform. You would thus be using normative information to establish absolute or fixed standards of performance. however, although norm-referenced and criterion-referenced grading systems both spring from a normative data base (that is, from comparisons among students), the former system uses those comparisons to directly determine grades. The latter, by contrast, uses the same comparisons to establish criteria, and the extent to which the student masters the criteria determines the grade.

▶ Criterion-referenced grades provide information about strengths and weaknesses

Criterion-referenced grading systems (and criterion-referenced tests) have become increasingly popular in recent years primarily because of three factors. First, educators and parents complained that norm-referenced tests and grading systems provided too little specific information about student strengths and weaknesses. Second, educators have come to believe that clearly stated, specific objectives constitute performance standards, or criteria, that are best assessed with criterion-referenced measures. Third, and perhaps most important, contemporary theories of school learning claim that most, if not all, students can master most school objectives under the right circumstances. If this assertion is even close to being true, then norm-referenced testing and grading procedures, which depend on variability in performance, will lose much of their appeal. This third notion underlies a particular criterion-referenced approach to measurement and evaluation that is often referred to as *mastery learning* and stems in large part from the work of John B. Carroll (1963) and Benjamin Bloom (1968, 1976).

A Mastery Approach to Learning and Instruction

John B. Carroll (1963) supplied the impetus for the emergence of **mastery learning.** He proposed that the focus of instruction should be the *time* required for different students to learn a given amount of material. He suggested that teachers should allow more time and provide more and better instruction for students who learn less easily and less rapidly than their peers.

▶ Expectations of a
normal distribution
lead to low aspira-
tions

Benjamin Bloom (1968) used the Carroll model as the basis for a statement in favor of mastery learning. The traditional approach, he argued, promotes the concept that if a normal distribution of students (with respect to aptitude for a subject) is exposed to a standard curriculum, achievement after instruction will be normally distributed. This approach, Bloom maintains, causes both teachers and students to expect that only a third of all students will adequately learn what is being taught, and this expectation in turn leads to a disastrous self-fulfilling prophecy.

> This set of expectations, which fixes the academic goals of teachers and students, is the most wasteful and destructive aspect of the present educational system. It reduces the aspirations of both teachers and students; it reduces motivation for learning in students; and it systematically destroys the ego and self-concept of a sizeable group of students who are legally required to attend school for 10 to 12 years under conditions which are frustrating and humiliating year after year. (1968, p. 1)

Here is the alternative Bloom suggests:

> Most students (perhaps over 90 percent) can master what we have to teach them, and it is the task of instruction to find the means which will enable our students to master the subject under consideration. Our basic task is to determine what we mean by mastery of the subject and to search for the methods and materials which will enable the largest proportion of our students to attain such mastery. (1968, p. 1)

The widespread and effective use of mastery learning was stimulated by the formulation of desirable ways to devise instructional objectives (consider the work of Mager and Gronlund, for example), comprehensive descriptions of the hierarchical nature of learning (such as the various taxonomies of educational objectives), and complete instructional systems (such as computer-assisted instruction).

Ingredients of a Successful Mastery Approach   Carroll observed that "teaching ought to be a simple matter if it is viewed as a process concerned with the management of learning" (1971, p. 29). He suggested that the teacher's function is to follow this procedure:

▶ Mastery approach:
gives pupils multiple
opportunities to mas-
ter goals at own pace

Specify what is to be learned.

Motivate pupils to learn it.

Provide instructional materials [to foster learning].

[Present] materials at a rate appropriate for different pupils.

Monitor students' progress.

Diagnose difficulties and provide remediation.

Give praise and encouragement for good performance.

Give review and practice.

Maintain a high rate of learning over a period of time. (1971, pp. 29–30)

The following suggestions, which can be adapted for use at any grade level and in any subject area, are based on Carroll's outline:

Handbook Heading:
Making the Most of
Mastery Learning

1. Go through a unit of study, a chapter of a text, or an outline of a lecture and pick out what you consider to be the most important points—that is, those points you wish to stress because they are most likely to have later value or are basic to later learning.

2. List these points in the form of a goal card, instructional objectives (as described by Mager or Gronlund), Key Points, or the equivalent. If appropriate, arrange the objectives in some sort of organized framework, perhaps with reference to the relevant taxonomy of educational objectives.

3. Distribute the list of objectives at the beginning of a unit. Tell your students that they should concentrate on learning those points and that they will be tested on them.

4. Consider making up a study guide in which you provide specific questions relating to the objectives and a format that students can use to organize their notes.

5. Use a variety of instructional methods and materials to explain and illustrate objectives-related ideas.

6. Make up exam questions based on the objectives and the study guide questions. Try to write several questions for each objective.

7. Arrange these questions into at least two (preferably three) alternate exams for each unit of study.

8. Make up tentative criteria for grade levels for each exam and for the entire unit or report period (for example, A—not more than one question missed on any exam; B—not more than two questions missed on any exam; C—not more than four questions missed on any exam).

9. Test students either when they come to you and indicate they are ready or when you feel they have all had ample opportunity to learn the material. Announce all exam dates in advance, and remind students that the questions will be based only on the objectives you have mentioned. Indicate the criteria for different grade levels, and emphasize that any student who fails to meet a desired criterion on the first try will have a chance to take an alternate form of the exam.

10. Grade and return the exams as promptly as possible; go over questions briefly in class (particularly those that caused problems for more than a few students); and offer to go over exams individually with students. Allow for individual interpretations, and give credit for answers you judge to be logical and plausible, even if they differ from the answers you expected.

11. Schedule alternate exams and make yourself available for consultation and tutoring the day before. (While you are giving alternate exams, you can administer the original exam to students who were absent.)

12. If the students improve their score on the second exam but still fall below the desired criterion, consider a safety valve option: Invite them to provide you with a completed study guide (or the equivalent) when they take an exam the second time, or give them an open-book exam on the objectives they missed to see whether they can explain them in terms other than those of a written examination. If a student fulfills either of these options satisfactorily, give credit for one extra answer on the second exam.

13. To supplement exams, assign book reports, oral reports, papers, or some other kind of individual work that will provide maximum opportunity for student choice. Establish and explain the criteria you will use to evaluate these assignments, but stress that you want to encourage freedom of choice and expression. (Some students will thrive on free choice, but others are likely to feel threatened by open-ended assignments. To allow for such differences, provide specific directions for those who need them and general hints or a simple request that "original" projects be cleared in advance for the more independent thinkers.) Grade all reports Pass or Do Over, and supply constructive criticism on those you consider unsatisfactory. Announce that all Do Over papers can be reworked and resubmitted within a certain period of time. Have the reports count toward the final grade—for example, three reports for an A, two for a B, one for a C. (In addition, the student should pass each exam at the designated level.) You might also invite pupils to prepare extra papers to earn bonus points to be added to exam totals.

This basic technique will permit you to work within a traditional A to F framework, but in such a way that you should be able, without lowering standards, to increase the proportion of students who do acceptable work. It will also permit you to make the most of the procedures suggested by Carroll, and to use an individual reward structure.

Focus on Stating Objectives   One of the advantages of a criterion-referenced approach to grading is that it focuses attention on instructional objectives. Even if you try to be conscientious about drawing up a table of specifications when preparing exams in a norm-referenced approach, you may still fail to measure objectives in a systematic or comprehensive way. With a mastery approach, however, you are following the recommendations made by those who urge use of instructional objectives. Mager offered these guidelines:

Identify and describe the terminal behavior.

Define the important conditions under which the behavior is to occur.

Define the criterion of acceptable performance.

This is exactly the procedure you will follow if you use a mastery approach. Stating objectives in precise terms and focusing on specific terminal behavior at a specified level of performance also permits you to treat instruction as if it were a branching program. That is, some students may achieve unit objectives on their first try and go on to the next unit; but students who have problems reaching the

One of the advantages of mastery learning is that students may help each other learn because they are not competing against each other to earn high grades. (Elizabeth Crews)

desired criterion level on their first effort are given additional instruction and another opportunity to show that they can perform at an acceptable level. This approach is more likely to lead to understanding and to encourage transfer than any approach that permits only one try and reports results only in terms of relative position.

Criteria for Different Letter Grades One of the most crucial decisions in a mastery approach centers on the criteria you establish for different grade levels. If you hope to defend grades to parents, fellow teachers, and administrators, you should do everything possible to make sure that an A in your class is equivalent to an A in your colleagues' classes. James H. Block (1971) has reported that the proportion of A grades in mastery classes is typically higher than in traditional classes, not because of low standards but because more students are motivated to do A and B work. Therefore, you should be well prepared to defend your grades by retaining copies of exams and the keys used to evaluate them and by explaining the criteria for different grade levels. As Tom Kubiszyn and Gary Borich have pointed out, "it is a curious fact of life that everyone presses for excellence in education, but many balk at marking systems that make attainment of excellence within everyone's reach" (1990, p. 142).

In establishing criteria, refer to the discussion on instructional objectives in Chapter 7, particularly the observations of Mager (p. 289) and Gronlund (p. 291). You might set up standards for an exam in terms of the percentage of correct answers, the number of correct answers provided within a given time limit, or a sample of applications. An approach that has worked well in practice is to make up ten-question exams, grade each answer plus or minus, and use these standards: zero or one wrong—A, two wrong—B, three wrong—C, four wrong—D.

As noted earlier, plus or minus grading has definite advantages. It not only provides a definite number of correct and incorrect answers, but also simplifies and speeds up grading. If you make up exams with an equivalent number of questions but evaluate each on a 5-point scale, you will be forced to read each answer with great care and then make a studied judgment of its relative value. But if you use a plus-or-minus approach, you simplify both the judging and the totaling of the final score. In many cases, you will find that the answer is obviously right or wrong and that you can evaluate it in a matter of seconds. You can also read more carefully those answers that are marginal; and if you eventually do mark them minus, you can do so knowing that the student will have another chance. Finally, it is obviously much simpler to count the number of wrong answers than to add up ten scores ranging in value from 1 to 5. With practice, you may find grading exams so quick that you will be able to provide feedback the next day.

Limitations of Mastery Learning   On the basis of the evidence presented so far, you might be tempted to conclude that mastery learning is the ideal way to teach and to learn. While such optimism is understandable, it would also be somewhat premature and misplaced. The history of education is filled with innovative ideas (programmed instruction, discovery learning, and computer-assisted instruction, among others) that promised to maximize each student's achievements only to fall short of that goal. Given the complexity of school learning and the strong differences among students, it would have been truly amazing if any of these ideas had fully lived up to its promise. Nevertheless, many of the same ideas have made positive contributions to the improvement of learning. So it is with mastery learning. On the one hand, the research findings demonstrate that students taught under mastery conditions often learn more than students taught under nonmastery conditions. On a final exam, the typical student taught under mastery conditions outscores the typical nonmastery–taught student by about 23 percentile ranks (73rd percentile versus the 50th percentile, respectively). Although both low- and high-aptitude students benefit from a mastery approach, the improvement is greatest for low-aptitude students. Consequently, there is less variation in final exam scores in mastery classes than in nonmastery classes (Kulik, Kulik & Bangert-Drowns, 1990). On the other hand, mastery learning is not without its problems, any one of which may limit its effectiveness. Some of these problems are inherent in the technique and probably cannot be totally eliminated. The remaining problems are often the result of misconceptions as to what mastery learning can and cannot accomplish or of abuses of the technique due to an inadequate understanding of how it should be practiced. Taking the knowledge you now have about mastery learning (with respect to procedures for implementation and research findings) and considering the following problems, you will be able to make an informed decision as to whether or not to try it in your own classroom.

Some of these criticisms of mastery learning are derived from points made by D. J. Mueller (1973) and W. F. Cox and T. G. Dunn (1979):

▶ Mastery learning has several potential limitations

1. Mastery learning requires careful planning, preparation of several sets of evaluation materials, and extensive monitoring of student progress. Accordingly, it requires more teacher time and effort than conventional instruction.

2. The standard for mastery may be difficult to establish or defend.

3. Students may practice the "principle of least effort" by not studying for first exams on the assumption that they will pick up test-taking hints over time as they examine test questions. Accordingly, the teacher will have to administer and score several exams.

4. Since some students inevitably achieve mastery faster than others, it is necessary to devise alternative assignments for those who have passed tests at an acceptable level on the first try.

All of these limitations can be overcome, however, with effort and ingenuity.

Being Realistic About Mastery Learning   Although this discussion of mastery learning has been intended to make you enthusiastic about the approach, you should be aware that it is not a panacea. For one thing, some students will disappoint, if not infuriate, you by the lengths they will go to in trying to beat the system—even after you have done everything in your power to make the system fair, just, and sensible.

Under a mastery approach, you are most likely to be able to improve the learning, attitudes, and self-concept of the typical C student. Those who have previously felt incapable of competing for high grades might give it a try in a mastery scheme, and many who try are likely to learn more and earn higher grades than they ever have under norm-referenced educational practices. Students who find it difficult to learn, however, may feel even more inadequate under a mastery approach than under a traditional one. When every opportunity to learn is provided and slow students are still unable to respond and do as well as their classmates, it is more difficult for them to blame the system.

▶ Mastery learning does not eliminate competition and comparisons

Mastery learning reduces competition and comparisons, but it does not eliminate them. Students who learn easily will meet the criterion for an A with little effort; they are likely to go through the required sequence so rapidly that they have considerable time for independent study. But those who learn slowly will engage in a constant battle to keep up with the required work. Because fortunate students learn faster and can engage in more self-selected study, they will probably get further and further ahead of their less capable classmates. Despite suggestions that prestige colleges ought to practice open admissions, it is most unlikely that they will do so. Furthermore, the number of jobs at the top of a scale based on interest, pay, and influence will always be limited. A mastery approach cannot by itself alter the fact that students who learn easily and rapidly are still likely to be rewarded with admission to the best colleges and to get the best jobs. Even so, you may discover that a mastery approach is well worth the extra time, effort, and trouble it requires. A greater proportion of your students will probably learn more, enjoy school more, develop better attitudes toward learning, and feel more confident and proud of themselves than they would under comparative-grading techniques. Just don't expect miracles, and be prepared for the fact that some of your students—no matter how hard they try or how much assistance you give them—will still be unable to do as well as most of their classmates in the time available.

Converting Scores into Letter Grades

To gain some direct experience with criterion-referenced grading, assume that you either teach fourth grade or instruct five sections of tenth-grade social studies. Figure 13.2 depicts one way a teacher at *any* grade level might record grades when using mastery learning.

FIGURE 13.2   Page from a Teacher's Grade Book: Mastery Approach Featuring Point Grading

	1st Exam		2nd Exam		3rd Exam		Projects			Grade
	1st Try	2nd Try	1st Try	2nd Try	1st Try	2nd Try	1	2	3	
Adams, Ann	2	1	1		1		P	P	P	
Baker, Charles	4	3	4	3	5	3	P			
Cohen, Matthew	3		3		4	3	P			
Davis, Rebecca	2		2		2		P	P		
Evans, Deborah	3		4	3	3		P			
Ford, Harold	6	3	4	3	4	3	P			
Grayson, Lee	2	1	2	1	1		P	P	P	
Hood, Barbara	1		0		1		P	P	P	
Ingalls, Robert	3	2	2		3	2	P	P		
Jones, Thomas	5	4	4		4					
Kim, David	0		1		0		P	P	P	
Lapine, Craig	4	3	3		3		P			
Moore, James	3	2	2		2		P	P		
Nguyen, Tuan	3	2	3	2	3	2	P	P		
Orton, John	3	2	2		2		P	P		
Peck, Nancy	2	1	2	1	1		P	P		
Quist, Ann	3	2	4	2	2		P	P		
Richards, Mary	2	1	2	1	1		P	P	P	
Santos, Maria	4	2	3	2	3	2	P	P		
Thomas, Eric	2	1	1		1		P	P	P	
Wong, Yuen	4	3	3		3		P			
Vernon, Joan	5	3	4	3	4	3	P			
Zacharias, Saul	3	1	2	1	3	1	P	P	P	

Notice that there are two columns under each exam heading in this figure. The page has room for two scores because a mastery approach urges pupils to find out what errors they made on the first try on an exam, ask for clarification, study further (with or without teacher assistance), and take an alternate form of the exam in an effort to improve their score. The obvious advantage of this policy is that students who do less well than they had hoped on a first exam will feel motivated to try harder—instead of giving up, which is a common response when an exam is given only once.

You can figure grades using the data presented in Figure 13.2 by assuming that the following information was distributed to students on the first day of the report period.

Instructions for Determining Your Grade in Social Studies

Your grade in social studies this report period will be based on scores on three exams (worth 20 points each) and satisfactory completion of up to three projects.

Here are the standards for different grades:

A—Average of 18 or more on three exams, plus three projects at Pass level

B—Average of 16 or 17 on three exams, plus two projects at Pass level

C—Average of 14 or 15 on three exams, plus one project at Pass level

D—Average of 10 to 13 on three exams

F—Average of 9 or less on three exams

Another way to figure your grade is to add together points as you take exams. This may be the best procedure to follow as we get close to the end of the report period. Use this description of standards as a guide:

A—At least 54 points, plus three projects at Pass level

B—48 to 53 points, plus two projects at Pass level

C—42 to 47 points, plus one project at Pass level

D—30 to 41 points

F—29 points or less

If you are not satisfied with the score you earn on any exam, you may take a different exam on the same material in an effort to improve your score. (Some of the questions on the alternate exam will be the same as those on the original exam; some will be different.) Projects will be graded P (Pass) or DO (Do Over). If you receive a DO on a project, you may work to improve it and hand it in again. You may also submit an *extra* project,

(continued)

which may earn up to 3 points of bonus credit (and can help if your exam scores fall just below a cutoff point). As you take each exam and receive a Pass for each project, record your progress on this chart.

First Exam		Second Exam		Third Exam		Project 1	Project 2	Project 3	Extra Project	Grade
1st Try	2nd Try	1st Try	2nd Try	1st Try	2nd Try					

Instructions for Determining Your Grade in Social Studies

Your grade in social studies this report period will be based on scores on three exams and successful completion of up to three projects. The exams will consist of ten questions each, and your answers will be graded plus or minus. The projects will be graded P (Pass) or DO (Do Over). Here are the standards for different grades:

A—Miss not more than one question on any exam, three projects at Pass level

B—Miss not more than two questions on any exam, two projects at Pass level

C—Miss not more than three questions on any exam, one project at Pass level

D—Miss four questions on any exam

F—Miss five or more questions on all three exams

If you are not satisfied with the grade you earn on any exam, you may take a different form of the exam to try and improve your score. (Some of the questions on the alternate form of the exam will be the same as those on the original exam; some will be different.) You may hand in an extra project, which may earn up to two bonus points (and can help if you fall just below the cutoff point on one or two exams).

If you eventually attempt a mastery approach using techniques similar to those just described, keep in mind the following procedures:

Try to set aside a specified period one day each week for exams. When deciding how many exams to give, be sure to allow at least two days for each exam. If possible, also schedule at least one make-up exam day.

Grade and return papers and exams as soon as possible so that students will know whether or not to study for a second try. If you use a point-per-exam approach, it is preferable to make up multiple-choice exams that can be graded as quickly as students finish them. If you prefer short-essay questions, try using plus-or-minus grading. It is considerably simpler and faster than point grading.

On second-exam days, allow students who were satisfied with grades earned on the first try to work on projects or to engage in individualized study.

Start using grade standards that reflect the traditional pattern of 90 percent and above for an A, 80 to 89 percent for a B, and so forth. If it turns out that fewer than 10 percent of your pupils are earning A's after the first exam, it is possible that these standards are too high and should be lowered. Before drawing that conclusion, however, realize that there are several possible causes of poor test performance and low test grades, and that the other possibilities should be examined before you alter grading practices. You may find, for example, that several test items were vaguely worded, that some items did not adequately reflect course objectives, that the students did not prepare properly for the test, that they did not understand the material, or that you did not allow sufficient time for them to master the material. If you find that one or more of these factors could be responsible for lower than expected grades, apply corrective action and observe the effect on another exam before lowering your standards.

Try following either the first set of instructions to figure the grade for each pupil listed in Figure 13.2 or the second set of instructions to figure the grade for each pupil in Figure 13.3. Compare your mastery grades with those assigned by classmates to identify any arithmetic errors that might have been made. Finally, speculate about how students would respond to a mastery approach as compared to norm-referenced grading techniques.

IMPROVING YOUR GRADING METHODS: MEASUREMENT AND EVALUATION PRACTICES TO AVOID

Earlier in this chapter we noted that the typical teacher has little systematic knowledge of measurement and evaluation principles and, as a result, may engage in a variety of *inappropriate* testing and grading practices. We hope that the information in this chapter will help you to become more proficient than most of your colleagues at these tasks. (In addition, we strongly encourage you to take a course in classroom measurement and evaluation if you have not already done so.)

To reinforce what you have learned here, we will now describe some of the more common *inappropriate* testing and grading practices committed by teachers. The following list is based largely on the observations of Robert Lynn Canady and Phyllis Riley Hotchkiss (1989) and John R. Hills (1991).

1. *Worshiping averages.* Some teachers mechanically average all scores and automatically assign the corresponding grade, even when they know an unusually low score was due to an extenuating circumstance. Allowances can be made for physical illness, emotional upset, and the like either by allowing students to

	1st Exam		2nd Exam		3rd Exam		Exam	Projects			Grade
	1st Try	2nd Try	1st Try	2nd Try	1st Try	2nd Try	Total Points	1	2	3	
Adams, Ann	~~16~~	18	~~17~~	18	18			P	P	P	
Baker, Charles	~~13~~	14	14		~~10~~	14		P			
Cohen, Matthew	~~14~~	16	~~15~~	16	17			P	P		
Davis, Rebecca	19		19		20			P	P	P	
Evans, Deborah	~~16~~	18	~~17~~	18	~~16~~	18		P	P	P	
Ford, Harold	~~15~~	16	17		15			P	P		
Grayson, Lee	~~10~~	13	~~12~~	14	~~12~~	15		P			
Hood, Barbara	16		17		15			P	P		
Ingalls, Robert	~~16~~	18	16		15			P	P		
Jones, Thomas	~~11~~	14	~~12~~	16	15			P			
Kim, David	18		19		19			P	P	P	
Lapine, Craig	~~14~~	16	18		16			P	P		
Moore, James	17		17		17			P	P		
Nguyen, Tuan	~~17~~	18	19		~~16~~	17		P	P	P	
Orton, John	~~10~~	10	11		9						
Peck, Nancy	14		15		14			P			
Quist, Ann	~~16~~	18	~~17~~	18	18			P	P	P	
Richards, Mary	16		17		15			P	P		
Santos, Maria	13		15		14			P			
Thomas, Eric	~~15~~	16	~~15~~	17	15			P	P		
Wong, Yuen	14		15		16			P			
Vernon, Joan	~~11~~	14	~~13~~	14	~~12~~	14		P			
Zacharias, Saul	~~16~~	18	17		~~16~~	19		P	P	P	

FIGURE 13.3   Page from a Teacher's Grade Book: Mastery Approach Featuring + or − Grading

drop their lowest grade or by repeating the test on which they performed most poorly. While objectivity in grading is a laudatory goal, it should not be practiced to the extent that it prevents you from altering your normal procedures when your professional judgment indicates an exception is warranted. Another shortcoming of this practice is that it ignores measurement error. No one can construct the perfect test and no person's score is a true indicator of knowledge and skill. Test scores represent *estimates* of these characteristics. Accordingly, giving a student with an average of 74.67 a grade of D when 75 is the minimum needed for a C pretends the test is more accurate than it really is. This is why it is so important to conduct an item analysis of your tests. If you discover several items that are unusually difficult, you may want to make allowances for students who are a point or two from the next highest grade (and modify the items if you intend to use them again).

2. *Using zeros indiscriminately.* The sole purpose of grades is to communicate to others how much of the curriculum a student has mastered. When teachers also use grades to reflect their appraisal of a student's work habits or character, the validity of the grades is lessened. This occurs most dramatically when students receive zeros for assignments that are late (but are otherwise of good quality), incomplete, or not completed according to directions, and for exams on which students are suspected of cheating. This is a flawed practice for two reasons. First, and to repeat what we said in point 1, there may be good reasons why projects and homework assignments are late, incomplete, or different from what was expected. You should try to uncover such circumstances and take them into account. The second reason for not automatically giving zeros is that they cause communication problems. If a student who earns grades in the low 90s for most of the grading period is given two zeros for one or more of the reasons just mentioned, that student could easily receive a D or an F. Such a grade is not an accurate reflection of what was learned. If penalties are to be given for work that is late, incomplete, or not done according to directions and for which there are no extenuating circumstances, they should be clearly spelled out far in advance of the due date and they should not seriously distort the meaning of the grade. For students suspected of cheating, a different form of the exam can be given.

3. *Providing insufficient instruction before testing.* For a variety of reasons, teachers occasionally spend more time than they had planned on certain topics. In an effort to "cover the curriculum" prior to a scheduled exam, they may significantly increase the pace of instruction or simply tell students to read the remaining material on their own. The low grades that typically result from this practice will unfortunately be read by outsiders (and this includes parents) as a deficiency in students' learning ability when in fact they more accurately indicate a deficiency in instructional quality.

4. *Teaching for one thing but testing for another.* This practice takes several forms. For instance, teachers may provide considerable supplementary material in class through lecture, thereby encouraging students to take notes and study them extensively, but base test questions almost entirely on text material. Or, if they emphasize the text material during class discussion, they may take a significant number of questions from footnotes and less important parts of the text. A third form of this flawed practice is to provide students with simple problems or practice questions in class that reflect the knowledge level of Bloom's Taxonomy but to give complex problems and higher-level questions on a test. Remember what we said at the end of Chapter 11: If you want transfer, then teach for transfer.

5. *Using pop quizzes to motivate students.* If you recall our discussion of reinforcement schedules from Chapter 8, you will recognize that surprise tests represent a variable interval schedule and that such schedules produce a consistent pattern of behavior in humans under certain circumstances. Being a student in a classroom is not one of those circumstances. Surprise tests produce an undesirable level of anxiety in many students and cause others to simply give up. If you sense that students are not sufficiently motivated to read and study more consistently, consult the previous chapter for better ideas on how to accomplish this goal.

6. *Keeping the nature and content of the test a secret.* Many teachers scrupulously avoid giving students any meaningful information about the type of questions that will be on a test or what the items will cover. The assumption that underlies this practice is that if students have been paying attention in class, have been diligently doing their homework, and have been studying at regular intervals, they will do just fine on a test. But they usually don't—and the main reason why can be seen in our description of a learning strategy (Chapter 10). A good learning strategist first analyzes all of the available information that bears on attaining a goal. But if certain critical information about the goal is not available, the rest of the strategy (planning, implementing, monitoring, and modifying) will suffer.

7. *Keeping the criteria for assignments a secret.* This practice is closely related to the previous one. Students may be told, for example, to write an essay on what the world would be like if all diseases were eliminated, and to give their imagination free rein in order to come up with many original ideas. But when the papers are graded, equal weight is given to spelling, punctuation, and grammatical usage. If these aspects of writing are also important to you and you intend to hold students accountable for them, make sure that fact is clearly communicated to them.

8. *Shifting criteria.* Teachers are sometimes disappointed in the quality of students' tests and assignments and decide to change the grading criteria as a way to "shock" the students into more appropriate learning behaviors. For example, a teacher may have told students that mechanics will count for one-third of the grade on a writing assignment. But when the teacher discovers that most of the papers contain numerous spelling, punctuation, and grammatical errors, he may decide to let mechanics determine half of the grade. As we indicated before, grades should not be used as a motivational device or as a way to make up for instructional oversights. There are far better ways to accomplish these goals.

ALTERNATIVE PERFORMANCE-BASED APPROACHES TO CLASSROOM MEASUREMENT AND EVALUATION

In theory, both norm-referenced and criterion-referenced approaches to measurement and evaluation can take a variety of forms. In practice, however, a written test composed of such objective-item types as multiple-choice, short-answer, and true-false questions is the form that is most frequently used. While objective tests have certain advantages (such as standardization, ease of administration, and time and cost efficiencies), they also have certain inherent limitations. They do not, for example, allow teachers the opportunity to probe the reasoning behind a response. Accordingly, teachers are not likely to recognize when correct answers are based on little more than verbatim recall and when incorrect answers are the product of thoughtful but not-quite-accurate reasoning (Wiggins,1989). Because of this and other limitations of traditional written tests, measurement and evaluation specialists, in collaboration with classroom teachers, have recently proposed a number of alternative methods for assessing classroom learning. In the section that follows we will briefly describe three characteristics of **alternative assessment methods** that distinguish them from traditional written tests: the form they typically take, the type of preparation students are given, and the relationship between assessment and instruction.

> Alternative assessment methods are used to highlight the reasoning behind a response

Characteristics of Alternative Assessment

There are three alternative assessment methods commonly used to measure a student's performance: portfolios, actual performance, and interviews. The form most often used to assess prior performance is called *portfolio assessment*. A portfolio may contain one or more pieces of a student's work, some of which demonstrate different stages of completion. For example, a student's writing portfolio may contain an outline, rough draft, and final draft of a research paper; business letters; pieces of fiction; and poetry. Portfolios can also be constructed for math and science, as well as for projects that combine two or more subject areas. To measure current performance, the teacher may ask students to conduct an experiment, read a poem, give a speech, or solve a problem. Interviews can also be used to determine the depth of students' knowledge and the quality of their thinking. Although the use of interviews may seem to be a radical departure from normal testing methods, it is a practice that reflects the root meaning of the word *assessment*—to "sit with" a learner to be sure that his or her response to a question or task really means what it seems to mean (Wiggins, 1989).

A second feature characteristic of alternative assessment methods is that students know in advance what will be evaluated and how they will be evaluated. (As we pointed out in Chapter 9, students should be given this information prior to *any* test, since it makes strategic learning easier.) While this type of preparation is unfortunately not a common part of everyday classroom testing, it' is typically used in the performing arts, the studio arts, athletics, and vocational education. As Gene Maeroff (1991) has observed, "A young pianist who is asked to master Beethoven's 'Für Elise' becomes proficient by practicing the piece, knowing all the while that his examination will consist of playing it" (p. 274).

A third characteristic feature of alternative assessment methods is the close reciprocal relationship between testing and teaching: Not only is instruction influenced by the form and content of the assessment, but the assessment is consistent with how the curriculum is taught. For example, if in giving an oral book report a student is expected to speak loudly enough for everyone to hear, to speak in clear, complete sentences, to stay on the topic, and to use pictures or other materials to make the presentation interesting, the student needs to be informed of these criteria and classroom instruction should be organized around them. By the same token, the assessment of students' performances should be limited to just the criteria emphasized during instruction (Maeroff, 1991).

Current Developments and Future Prospects

Alternative assessment methods are currently being developed in Rhode Island, California, Connecticut, Kentucky, and Vermont, and are being planned in almost forty other states. Although most states are limiting themselves to writing samples at the present time, other states have gone further. Connecticut, for example, uses a range of performance-based assessments in science, foreign language, drafting, and small-engine repair. And Vermont is moving toward a portfolio-based assessment in writing and mathematics (Maeroff, 1991).

There is no question that alternative assessment methods have excited educators and will be used with increasing frequency in future years. But some of the same features that make these new assessment methods attractive also create problems that may or may not be solvable. For example, evaluating portfolios, performances, and interviews is time-consuming, labor intensive, and relatively imprecise. In fact, the problem of precision may be the most difficult one to solve. Obtaining reliable (meaning consistent) and valid (meaning accurate) measures of some characteristic by judging the quality of portfolios, performances, and interviews is difficult because there is as yet no consensus as to what a portfolio should include, how large a portfolio should be, what standards should be used to judge products and performances, and whether all students should be assessed under precisely the same conditions (Kirst, 1991; Maeroff, 1991). Accordingly, whether the portfolio, performance, and interview assessment methods we have described here eventually supplant objective, paper-and-pencil tests or simply become supplements to them is an open question.

Resources for Further Investigation

Suggestions for Writing Test Items

For specific suggestions on ways to write different types of items for paper-and-pencil tests of knowledge and on methods for constructing and using rating scales and checklists to measure products, performances, and procedures, consult one or more of the following books: *Measurement and Evaluation in Teaching* (6th ed., 1990) by Norman E. Gronlund and Robert L. Linn, *How to Construct Achievement Tests* (4th ed., 1988) by Norman E. Gronlund, *Educational Testing and Measurement* (3d ed., 1990) by Tom Kubisyzn and Gary Borich, and

Classroom Testing: Construction (2d ed., 1989) by Charles D. Hopkins and Richard L. Antes.

Writing Higher-Level Questions

As Benjamin Bloom and others have pointed out, teachers have a disappointing tendency to write test items that reflect the lowest level of the taxonomy—knowledge. To avoid this failing, carefully read Part II (pp. 62–200) of *Taxonomy of Educational Objectives, Handbook I: Cognitive Domain* (1956), edited by Benjamin Bloom. Each level of the taxonomy is clearly explained and followed by several pages of illustrative test items.

Making Up Sample Test Items

A good way to become aware of the difficulties and complexities of evaluation (as well as to understand different types of tests) is to devise some test questions. Compose several kinds of questions based on a chapter or two from this text or from a text in a subject you hope to teach. Refer to the guidelines in this chapter for writing different types of questions (and/or consult one of the books mentioned above). Be sure to make up your key as you write the questions. Then ask one or two classmates to take your test. Request that they not only record their answers but also add any critical remarks about the strengths and weaknesses of specific items. Summarize the answers and criticisms, and draw up a list of guidelines to follow when you construct classroom examinations.

Analyzing Test Items

Norman Gronlund briefly discusses item-analysis procedures for norm-referenced and criterion-referenced tests in Chapter 7 of *Constructing Achievement Tests* (4th ed., 1988). For norm-referenced multiple-choice tests, these include procedures for assessing the difficulty of each item, the discriminating power of each item, and the effectiveness of each alternative answer. For criterion-referenced tests, they include a measure for assessing the effects of instruction. More detailed discussions of item-analysis procedures can be found in Chapter 8 of *Educational Testing and Measurement* (3d ed., 1990) by Tom Kubiszyn and Gary Borich and in Chapter 13 of *Essentials of Educational Measurement* (4th ed., 1986) by Robert L. Ebel and David A. Frisbie.

Mastery Learning

If you would like to read comprehensive analyses of mastery learning, look for one of these books: *Human Characteristics and School Learning* (1976) by Benjamin S. Bloom; *All Our Children Learning* (1981) by Benjamin S. Bloom; *Improving Student Achievement Through Mastery Learning Programs* (1985), edited by Daniel H. Levine; and *Building Effective Mastery Learning Schools* (1989) by James H. Block, Helen E. Efthim, and Robert B. Burns.

SUMMARY

1. Measurement involves ranking individuals according to how much of a particular characteristic they possess. Evaluation involves making judgments about the value or worth of a set of measures.

2. Performance tests are used to measure how well people perform a particular skill or produce a particular product under somewhat realistic conditions. The main types of performance tests are paper-and-pencil, identification, simulation, and work sample.

3. Written tests are used to measure how much knowledge people have about some topic. Test items can be classified as objective (multiple-choice, true-false, matching, interpretive) or created-response (short-answer, essay).

4. The teacher expectancy effect, also known as self-fulfilling prophecy or the Pygmalion effect, occurs when teachers communicate a particular expectation about how a student will perform and the student's behavior changes so as to be consistent with the expectation.

5. Although the effect of teacher expectancy on IQ scores originally reported by Rosenthal and Jacobson has never been fully replicated, research has demonstrated that teacher expectancy strongly affects classroom achievement and participation in both positive and negative ways.

6. Factors that seem to play a strong role in producing a teacher expectancy effect include a student's gender, compliance, neatness, achievement, and attractiveness.

7. To be sure that the number of various types of items on a test is consistent with your instructional objectives, prepare a table of specifications.

8. To determine how well students are learning and whether any sort of remedial instruction is needed, use formative evaluation. To determine how much of a topic has been learned so that you can assign grades, use summative evaluation.

9. Checklists and rating scales are often used to measure the performance of a skill.

10. Item-analysis procedures exist to determine the difficulty and discriminability of multiple-choice items.

11. When grades are determined according to a norm-referenced system, each student's level of performance is compared to the performance of a group of similar students. Grading is competitive. A norm-referenced scheme is used by those who feel that external criteria for determining the adequacy of performance are unavailable.

12. In a criterion-referenced grading system, each student's level of performance is compared to a predetermined standard.

13. Related to criterion-referenced measurement and evaluation is the concept of mastery learning. As proposed by John Carroll and Benjamin Bloom, mastery learning holds that student achievement is largely a function of the amount of time a student is allotted for learning.

14. Alternative approaches to classroom assessment emphasize the use of such performance-based methods as portfolio assessment, performance of various tasks, and interviews in order to ascertain the depth of students' knowledge and how well they use what they know.

KEY TERMS

measurement *(564)*
evaluation *(564)*
self-fulfilling prophecy *(568)*
table of specifications *(574)*
formative evaluation *(578)*
summative evaluation *(578)*
mastery learning *(599)*
alternative assessment methods *(613)*

DISCUSSION QUESTIONS

1. Because students in American schools feel considerable pressure to obtain high grades, a significant number of them feel driven to cheat. Knowing that you will almost certainly have to give tests and assign grades on one basis or another, what might you do to reduce your students' tendency to cheat?

2. Over the last ten to twelve years you have probably taken hundreds of classroom tests. What types of tests best reflected what you learned? Why?

3. A norm-referenced approach to grading is often called grading on the curve. Have you ever taken a class in which grades were determined in this fashion? Did you feel that your grade accurately reflected how much you had learned? If not, explain why the grade was too low or too high.

4. Proponents of mastery learning argue that most students can master most subjects if they receive good-quality instruction and are allowed sufficient time to learn the material. On the basis of your own experience, would you agree with this assumption? Why or why not?

Part 5

MAINTAINING AN EFFECTIVE LEARNING ENVIRONMENT

Chapter 14

CLASSROOM MANAGEMENT

INFLUENCE TECHNIQUES

▶ Use supportive reactions to help students develop self-control

▶ Give criticism privately, then offer encouragement

I-MESSAGES AND THE NO-LOSE METHOD

▶ I-message: tell how you feel about an unacceptable situation

▶ No-lose method: come to mutual agreement about a solution to a problem

SUGGESTIONS FOR TEACHING IN YOUR CLASSROOM

▶ Be prompt, consistent, and reasonable when dealing with misbehavior

▶ First ignore misbehavior, then stress rewards; use punishment as a last resort

VIOLENCE IN AMERICAN SCHOOLS

▶ Violence most likely in inner-city junior high schools with weak administrators

▶ Male aggressiveness due to hormonal and cultural factors

▶ Junior–high–age boys with low grades may feel trapped

▶ Misbehavior of high school students may reveal lack of positive identity

▶ School violence can be reduced by improving student achievement levels

▶ Violence less likely when students invited to participate in making decisions

The discussion of classroom evaluation you just read completes the four-phase cycle of the model of learning that was outlined in Chapter 1. Part 1 asked you to take into account what students are like by becoming familiar with typical characteristics of pupils at different age levels as well as with pupil variability. Part 2 acquainted you with a variety of ways to state and use instructional objectives. Part 3 described methods for arranging instructional experiences by taking into account the research and speculations of behavioral, cognitive, and humanistic psychologists. In addition, it discussed ways to motivate students by considering each of those views. Part 4 outlined techniques for determining if students *have* learned and gave special emphasis to evaluating the mastery of objectives.

You are now equipped with information you can use to take into account pupil characteristics and make allowances for pupil variability. You can refer to the taxonomies, suggestions, and examples in Chapter 7 to make constructive use of instructional objectives. By drawing on the information provided in Part 3, you can prepare systematic sequences of learning experiences, arrange for students to make at least some of their own discoveries, and encourage awareness of the affective side of learning as well as sensitivity to interpersonal relationships. You are familiar with various views of motivation and with dozens of specific motivational techniques. The chapter you just finished acquainted you with ways to make efficient use of appropriate forms of evaluation to determine if your students have achieved objectives. Information in each of the chapters you have read so far, therefore, can help you build your skills as a teacher, but your effectiveness in the classroom is likely to be enhanced if you think about ways to *orchestrate* what you have learned and combine techniques in coordinated ways. The first part of this chapter describes guidelines you might follow in order to establish and maintain an effective learning environment in which you make coordinated use of the techniques described in earlier chapters.

Even if you do an excellent job of "getting it all together," however, certain factors and conditions will be beyond your control. Inevitably, some students will fail to respond to your efforts as positively as others. In addition to individual differences in responsiveness to you and to schooling, there are certain general characteristics or tendencies typical of pupils at different ages (and at all ages) that may lead to perennial kinds of classroom problems. Accordingly, you will occasionally need to deal with disruptive behavior. The second part of this chapter describes a variety of techniques you might use to handle such types of behavior and concludes with an analysis on the reasons for school violence. You should be able to prevent many problems, though, or at least nip them in the bud, by being prepared. That is why this chapter begins with a discussion of classroom management techniques.

TECHNIQUES OF CLASSROOM MANAGEMENT

Kounin's Observations on Group Management

Interest in the significance of classroom management was kindled when Jacob S. Kounin wrote a book titled *Discipline and Group Management in the Classroom* (1970). Kounin noted that he first became interested in group management when he reprimanded a college student for blatantly reading a newspaper in class. Kounin was struck by the extent to which the entire class responded to a reprimand directed at only one person, and he subsequently dubbed this the **ripple effect.** Chances are you can recall a situation when you were diligently

> Ripple effect: group response to a reprimand directed at an individual

working away in a classroom and the teacher suddenly became quite angry at a classmate who was disruptive. If you felt a bit tense after the incident (despite the fact that your behavior was blameless) and endeavored to give the impression that you were a paragon of student virtue, you have had personal experience with the ripple effect.

Once his interest in classroom behavior was aroused, Kounin supervised a series of observational and experimental studies of student reactions to techniques of teacher control. In analyzing the results of these various studies, he came to the conclusion that the following classroom management techniques appear to be most effective.

1. Show your students you are "with it." Kounin coined the term **withitness** to emphasize that teachers who prove to their students that they know what is going on in a classroom usually have fewer disciplinary problems than teachers who appear to be unaware of incipient disruptions. An expert at classroom management will nip trouble in the bud by commenting on potentially disruptive behavior before it gains momentum. An ineffective teacher may not notice such behavior until it begins to spread and then perhaps hopes that it will simply go away. At first glance, Kounin's suggestion that you show that you are "with it" might seem to be in conflict with the learning theorists' prediction that nonreinforced behavior will disappear. If the teacher's reaction is the only source of reinforcement in a classroom, ignoring behavior may cause it to disappear. In many cases, however, a misbehaving pupil gets reinforced by the reactions of classmates. Therefore, ignoring behavior is much less likely to lead to extinction of a response in a classroom than in controlled experimental situations.

> Teachers who show they are "with it" head off discipline problems

Jacob Kounin found that teachers who were "with it" and maintained smoothness and momentum in class activities had few discipline problems. (1992 David Pratt/Positive Images)

2. *Learn to cope with overlapping situations.* When he analyzed videotapes of actual classroom interactions, Kounin found that some teachers seem to have one-track minds. They are inclined to deal with only one thing at a time, and this way of proceeding causes frequent interruptions in classroom routine. One primary grade teacher observed by Kounin, for example, was working with a reading group when she noticed two boys on the other side of the room poking each other. She abruptly got up, walked over to the boys, berated them at length, and then returned to the reading group. By the time she returned, however, the children in the reading group had become bored and listless, and were tempted to engage in mischief of their own.

Kounin concluded that withitness and skill in handling overlapping activities seemed to be related. An expert classroom manager who is talking to children in a reading group, for example, might notice two boys at the far side of the room who are beginning to scuffle with each other. Such a teacher might in midsentence tell the boys to stop and make the point so adroitly that the attention of the children in the reading group does not waver. You might carry out a self-analysis of how you handle overlapping situations when you first begin to teach. If you find that you tend to focus on only one thing at a time, you might make an effort to develop skills in coping with two or more situations simultaneously.

3. *Strive to maintain smoothness and momentum in class activities.* This point is related to the previous one. Kounin found that some teachers cause problems for themselves by constantly interrupting activities without thinking about what they are doing. Some teachers whose activities were recorded on videotape failed to maintain the thrust of a lesson because they seemed unaware of the rhythm of student behavior (that is, they did not take into account the degree of student inattention and restlessness but, instead, moved ahead in an almost mechanical way). Others flip-flopped from one activity to another. Still others would interrupt one activity (for example, a reading lesson) to comment on an unrelated aspect of classroom functioning ("Someone left a lunch bag on the floor"). There were also some who wasted time dwelling on a trivial incident (making a big fuss because a boy lost his pencil). And a few teachers delivered individual, instead of group, instructions ("All right, Charlie, you go to the board. Fine. Now, Rebecca, you go to the board"). All these types of teacher behavior tend to interfere with the flow of learning activities. Each time pupils are interrupted they may be distracted and find it difficult to pick up the thread of a lesson. They may also be tempted to engage in mischievous activities. Kounin found greater pupil work involvement and less deviant behavior when teachers maintained momentum and smoothness instead of interrupting activities in the ways just described.

You might carry out a movement analysis of your own teaching from time to time. Think about how you handle a class for a period or a day, and see if you can recall incidents of this sort: (a) Your request for a change in activity seemed too abrupt. (b) You needlessly flip-flopped back and forth between activities. (c) You interrupted a lesson to comment on an unrelated situation that happened to come to your attention. (d) You made a mountain out of a molehill. (e) You gave

---

Being able to handle overlapping activities helps maintain classroom control

Handbook Heading: Learning to Deal with Overlapping Situations

Teachers who continually interrupt activities have discipline problems

Handbook Heading: Learning How to Maintain Momentum

instructions to individual pupils when it would have been simpler to address several at once. To counteract such tendencies, you might endeavor to maintain a smooth flow of activities in the following class periods and days. If you succeed in doing so, this smooth flow may become habitual.

4. *Try to keep the whole class involved, even when you are dealing with individual pupils.* Kounin found that some well-meaning teachers had fallen into a pattern of calling on students in a predictable order and in such a way that the rest of the class served as a passive audience. Unless you stop to think about what you are doing during group recitation periods, you might easily fall into the same trap. If you do, the "audience" is almost certain to become bored and may be tempted to engage in troublemaking activities just to keep occupied. Some teachers, for example, call on pupils to recite by going around a circle, or going up and down rows, or by following alphabetical order. Others call on a child first and then ask a question. Still others ask one child to recite at length (read an entire page, for example). All these techniques tend to spotlight one child in predictable order and cause the rest of the class to tune out until their turn comes. You are more likely to maintain interest and limit mischief caused by boredom if you use techniques such as the following:

▶ Keeping entire class involved and alert minimizes misbehavior

a. Ask a question, and after pausing a few seconds to let everyone think about it, pick out someone to answer it. With subsequent questions, call on students in an unpredictable order so that no one knows when she or he will be asked to recite. (If you feel that some students in a class are very apprehensive about being called on, even under relaxing circumstances, you can either ask them extremely easy questions or avoid calling on them at all.)

Handbook Heading: Ways to Keep the Whole Class Involved

b. If you single out one child to go to the board to do a problem, ask all other students to do the same problem at their desks and then choose one or two at random to compare their work with the answers on the board.

c. When dealing with lengthy or complex material, call on several students in quick succession (and in unpredictable order), and ask each to handle one section. In a primary grade reading group, for example, have one child read a sentence, then pick someone at the other side of the group to read the next sentence, and so on.

d. Use props in the form of flash cards, mimeographed sheets, or workbook pages to induce all students to respond to questions simultaneously. Then ask students to compare answers. (One ingenious elementary school teacher observed by Kounin had each pupil print the ten digits on cards that could be inserted in a slotted piece of cardboard. She would ask a question, such as "How much is 8 and 4?," pause a moment while the students arranged their answers in the slots, and then say, "All show!")

All these techniques are likely to be effective because they encourage participation by all students, introduce an element of suspense, and hold all students accountable for what is going on.

Student misbehavior can be minimized by providing changes of pace and introducing variety. (Elizabeth Crews)

5. *Introduce variety, and be enthusiastic, particularly with younger pupils.* After viewing videotapes of different teachers, Kounin and his associates concluded that some instructors seem to fall into a rut much more readily than others. At one end of the scale are teachers who follow the same procedure day after day, respond with the same, almost reflexive comments ("That's fine"), belabor a point, or continue a lesson so that it becomes almost unbearably tedious—perhaps out of lethargy or reluctance to think of something else for the class to do. At the other end of the scale are teachers who constantly seek to introduce variety, go out of their way to respond with enthusiasm and interest, and move quickly to new activities when they sense that students either have mastered or are satiated by a particular lesson. Apparently because of methodological complexities, Kounin failed to find statistical evidence that students responded differently to teachers at either end of such a scale. It seems logical to assume, however, that students would be more inclined to sleep, daydream, or get into mischief if they are exposed to dull, routine activities. Kounin pointed out, though, that variety may be most appropriate in elementary school classrooms because older students may be interested in thoroughly analyzing complex ideas and may be bothered if they are interrupted too frequently.

6. *Be aware of the ripple effect. When criticizing student behavior, be clear and firm, focus on behavior rather than on personalities, and try to avoid angry outbursts.* If you take into account the suggestions just made, you may be able to reduce the amount of student misbehavior in your classes. Even so, some behavior problems are certain to occur. When you deal with these, you can benefit from Kounin's research on the ripple effect. On the basis of observations, questionnaires, and experimental evidence, he concluded that "innocent" pupils in a class are more likely to be positively impressed by the way the teacher handles a misbehavior if the following conditions exist:

a. The teacher identifies the misbehaver and states what the unacceptable behavior is. ("George! Don't flip that computer disk at Henry.")

▶ Identify misbehavers, firmly specify constructive behavior

b. A suggestion is made that specifies more constructive behavior. ("Please put the computer disk back in the storage box.")

c. A reason is given explaining why the deviant behavior should cease. ("If the computer disk gets broken or dirty, no one else will be able to use it and we'll have to try to get a new one.")

d. The teacher is firm and authoritative and conveys a no-nonsense attitude.

e. The teacher does not resort to anger, humiliation, or extreme punishment. Kounin concluded that extreme reactions did not seem to make children behave better. Instead, anger and severe reprimands upset them and made them feel tense and nervous.

f. The teacher focuses on behavior, not on personality. This is the same point that Thomas Gordon emphasizes in *Teacher Effectiveness Training* (1974) and Haim Ginott stresses in *Teacher and Child* (1972).

University of Texas Studies of Group Management

Stimulated by Kounin's observations, members of the Research and Development Center for Teacher Education at the University of Texas at Austin instituted a series of studies on classroom management. The basic procedure followed in most studies was to first identify very effective and less effective teachers by using a variety of criteria (often stressing pupil achievement), ratings, and observations. Then classroom management techniques used by very effective teachers were analyzed in detail. In some studies (for example, Brophy, 1979; Good, 1982), basic characteristics of well-managed classrooms were described. They can be summarized as follows:

▶ Well-managed classroom: students complete clear assignments in busy but pleasant atmosphere

1. Students know what they are expected to do and generally experience the feeling that they are successful doing it.

2. Students are kept busy engaging in teacher-led instructional activities.

3. There is little wasted time, confusion, or disruption.

4. A no-nonsense, work-oriented tone prevails, but at the same time there is a relaxed and pleasant atmosphere.

These conclusions can be related to the information presented earlier. The first point stresses that students know what they are to do and generally feel successful doing it. This conclusion might be interpreted as supporting the use of instructional objectives stated in such a way that students know when they have achieved them. It might also be interpreted as supporting the use of mastery learning evaluation procedures. The next three points stress student productivity under teacher guidance and a no-nonsense, work-oriented atmosphere. These outcomes are more likely when teachers use procedures recommended by behavioral theorists than when they use forms of instruction advocated by cognitive and humanistic psychologists. It might be argued that such a conclusion

Clear communication of expectations and goals, paired with frequent feedback, leads to good classroom management. (Seth Resnick/Stock, Boston, Inc.)

could have been predicted, since student achievement was an important factor considered in selecting teachers classified as effective. Even so, because of the current emphasis on student achievement, it would appear that teachers who make frequent use of preplanned instructional activities are more likely to be perceived as effective managers than are teachers who use discovery approaches much of the time. Student-directed forms of learning not only tend to be less efficient than teacher-directed activities; they also increase possibilities for goofing off, mischief, or disruptive behavior. Elementary school boys working on a programmed workbook in math are less likely to get into mischief, for example, than the same boys working as a self-directed group arranging a bulletin board in the hallway outside the classroom.

Another set of studies carried out by the Texas researchers led to two recent books on group management, one for elementary school teachers (Evertson et al., 1989) and the other for secondary teachers (Emmer et al., 1989). You may wish to examine the appropriate book for your grade level (complete titles and names of authors are given in the Resources for Further Investigation), but for now we provide the following summary of basic keys to management success stressed in both volumes.

> Effective teachers plan how to handle classroom routines

1. On the very first day with a new class, very effective teachers clearly demonstrate that they have thought about classroom procedures ahead of time. They have planned first-day activities that make it possible for classroom routine to be handled with a minimum of confusion. They also make sure students understand why the procedures are necessary and how they are to be followed.

2. A short list of basic classroom rules is posted and/or announced, and students are told about penalties they will incur in the event of misbehavior.

> During first weeks, have students complete clear assignments under your direction

3. During the first weeks with a new group of pupils, the effective teacher has students engage in whole-group activities under his or her direction. Such activities are selected to make students feel comfortable and successful in their new classroom.

4. After the initial shakedown period is over, effective teachers maintain control by using the sorts of techniques described by Kounin: They show they are "with it," cope with overlapping situations, maintain smoothness and momentum, and avoid ignoring the rest of the class when dealing with individual pupils.

5. Effective teachers give clear directions, hold students accountable for completing assignments, and give frequent feedback.

Assertive Discipline

This list of factors calls attention to the importance of being thoroughly prepared the first days you meet with a new class. You should not only have thought about how you are going to handle classroom routine; you should also have planned learning activities likely to make students feel comfortable and successful. You should give students clear assignments, convey the message that they will be responsible for completing them, and provide positive feedback so that they are aware they have completed work successfully. A specific version of this general approach is the Assertive Discipline program of Lee Canter (1989).

Canter's program comprises three parts and is modeled after the classroom management practices of master teachers. The first part, *teaching students how to behave*, has two general steps. First, establish specific directions for each activity. For an all-class discussion, for example, you may want students to raise their hands and be recognized before speaking. For a cooperative learning session, you may want students to stay in their seats and to work quietly. Second, make sure the students know how to behave. You can accomplish this by writing the desired behaviors on the board, demonstrating them, asking students to restate them, questioning students to verify that they understand the rules, and immediately engaging them in the activity.

The second part of Assertive Discipline is *providing positive reinforcement*. Canter suggests that whenever you notice a student who is following the rules, point it out and make a positive comment. For example, if Maria has followed the rules laid down for a class discussion, you might say, "Maria raised her hand and patiently waited to be called on. Very good, Maria." Although this part of the program is either omitted or deemphasized by some teachers, Canter feels it is as important as the other two parts.

> Assertive Discipline: teach desired behaviors, give positive reinforcement, invoke discipline plan if necessary

The third and final part of the program is *invoking the discipline plan*. This involves the use of negative consequences, but only after the students have been taught the desired behaviors and positive reinforcement has been given. Canter suggests that teachers refrain from using negative consequences until at least two students have been positively reinforced for behaving appropriately. A discipline plan should include no more than five negative consequences for misbehavior, each of which is slightly more severe than the last one. For example, the first time a rule is broken, the student is warned. The second and third infractions result in ten-minute and fifteen-minute timeouts, respectively. The fourth infraction results in a call to the parents. And if the rule is broken a fifth time, the student must visit the principal. Although there are a variety of negative consequences that you can use, avoid those that might cause psychological or physical harm (ridicule and paddling, for example) for the reasons we gave in Chapter 8.

MANAGING THE JUNIOR HIGH AND HIGH SCHOOL CLASSROOM

Most of the classroom management techniques and suggestions we have discussed so far are sufficiently general that they can be used in a variety of classroom settings and with primary through secondary grade students. For example, Jacob Kounin's principles of withitness, learning to cope with overlapping situations, and striving to maintain smoothness and momentum in class activities are as applicable to the twelfth-grade physics instructor as they are to the first-grade teacher. The same can be said for the University of Texas studies of effective classroom management and Lee Canter's Assertive Discipline principles. Nevertheless, teaching adolescents is sufficiently different from teaching younger students that the management of a secondary classroom requires a slightly different emphasis and a few unique practices.

A second reason why classroom management has to be approached somewhat differently in the secondary grades is the segmented nature of secondary education. Instead of being in charge of the same twenty-five to thirty students all day, the typical secondary teacher is responsible for as many as five different groups of twenty-five to thirty students for about fifty minutes each. This arrangement results in a wider range of individual differences, a greater likelihood of seeing a wide range of behavior problems, and a greater concern with efficient use of class time.

Because of the special nature of adolescence, relatively short class times, and consecutive classes with different students, junior high and high school teachers must concentrate their efforts on preventing misbehavior. Edmund T. Emmer, Carolyn M. Evertson, Julie P. Sanford, Barbara S. Clements, and Murray E. Worsham (1989), in *Classroom Management for Secondary Teachers* (2d ed.), discuss how misbehavior can be prevented by carefully organizing the classroom environment, establishing clear rules and procedures, and delivering effective instruction.

According to Emmer and his associates, the physical features of the classroom should be arranged to optimize teaching and learning. They suggest an environment in which (a) high traffic areas—such as the teacher's desk and the pencil sharpener—are kept free of congestion, (b) the teacher can easily see all students, (c) frequently used teaching materials and student supplies are readily available, and (d) students can easily see instructional presentations and displays.

In too many instances, teachers spend a significant amount of class time dealing with misbehavior rather than with teaching and learning either because students are never told what is expected of them or because rules and procedures are not communicated clearly. Accordingly, Emmer et al. suggest that classroom rules be specifically stated, discussed with students on the first day of class, and, for seventh-, eighth-, and ninth-graders, posted in a prominent place. Sophomores, juniors, and seniors should be given a handout on which the rules are listed. Some examples of these basic rules follow:

Bring all needed materials to class.

Be in your seat and ready to work when the bell rings.

Respect and be polite to all people.

Do not talk or leave your desk when someone else is talking.

Respect other people's property.

Obey all school rules.

If you were impressed with the ideas of the humanistic educators (discussed in Chapter 11), you may want to allow some degree of student participation in rule setting. You can ask students to suggest rules, arrange for students to discuss why certain classroom rules are necessary, and perhaps allow students to select a few rules. This last suggestion should be taken up cautiously, however. Because secondary teachers teach different sets of students, having a different set of rules for each class is bound to cause confusion for you and hard feelings among some students. You may find yourself admonishing a student for breaking a rule that applies to a different class, and some students will naturally want to know why they cannot do something that is allowed in another class.

> Manage behavior of adolescents by making and communicating clear rules and procedures

In addition to rules, various procedures need to be formulated and communicated. Procedures differ from rules in that they apply to a specific activity and are usually directed at completing a task rather than completing a behavior. In order to produce a well-run classroom, you will need to formulate efficient procedures for beginning-of-the-period tasks (such as taking attendance and allowing students to leave the classroom), use of materials and equipment (such as the encyclopedia, dictionary, and pencil sharpener), learning activities (such as discussions, seatwork, and group work), and end-of-the-period tasks (such as handing in seatwork assignments, returning materials and equipment, and making announcements).

Much of what Emmer and his associates mention in relation to the characteristics of effective instruction has been described in earlier chapters. For example, they recommend that short-term (daily, weekly) and long-term (semester, annual) lesson plans be formulated and coordinated, that instructions and standards for assignments be clear and given in a timely manner, that feedback be given at regular intervals, and that the grading system be clear and fairly applied.

Suggestions for Teaching in Your Classroom

TECHNIQUES OF CLASSROOM MANAGEMENT

1. Show you are confident and prepared the first day of class.
2. Think ahead about how you plan to handle classroom routine, and explain basic procedures the first few minutes of the first day.
3. Establish and call attention to class rules.
4. Begin classwork the first day with an instructional activity that is clearly stated and can be completed quickly and successfully.
5. During the first weeks with a new group of students, have them spend most of their time engaging in whole-class activities under your direction.
6. Give clear instructions, hold students accountable for carrying them out, and provide frequent feedback.
7. Continually demonstrate that you are competent, well prepared, and in charge.
8. Be professional but pleasant, and try to establish a businesslike but supportive classroom atmosphere.

---

1. Show you are confident and prepared the first day of class.

The first few minutes with any class are often crucial. Your pupils will be sizing you up, especially if they know you are a new teacher. If you act scared and unsure of yourself, you will probably be in for trouble. Even after years of experience, you may find that confronting a roomful of strange pupils for the first time is a bit intimidating. You will be the center of attention and may feel the equivalent of stage fright. To switch the focus of attention and to begin to identify your pupils as individuals rather than as a threatening audience, you might consider using this strategy. Hand out 4-by-6-inch cards as soon as everyone is seated and ask your students to write down their full names, the names they prefer to be called, what their hobbies and favorite activities are, and a description of the most interesting experience they ever had. (For primary grade pupils who are unable to write, substitute brief oral introductions.) As they write, you will be in a position to make a leisurely scrutiny of your pupils as individuals. Recognizing that you are dealing with individuals should reduce the tendency to feel threatened by a group. Perhaps you have read about singers who pick out a single, sympathetic member of the audience and sing directly to her or him. The sea of faces as a whole is frightening. The face of the individual is not. Even if you are not bothered by being the center of attention, you might still consider using this card technique to obtain information that you can use to learn names rapidly and to individualize instruction. (More on this in suggestion 8.)

Whatever you do during the first few minutes, it is important to give the impression that you know exactly what you are doing. The best way to pull that off is to be thoroughly prepared.

2. Think ahead about how you plan to handle classroom routine, and explain basic procedures the first few minutes of the first day.

Handbook Heading:
Planning How to
Handle Routines

The Texas researchers found that very effective teachers demonstrated from the first moment with a new group of students that they knew how to handle the details of their job. They also conveyed the impression that they expected cooperation. In order to demonstrate that you are a confident, competent instructor, you should plan exactly how you will handle classroom routines. You will pick up at least some ideas about the details of classroom management during student teaching experiences, but it might be worth asking a friendly experienced teacher in your school for advice about tried and true procedures that have worked in that particular school. (You might also read one of the books on classroom management recommended at the end of this chapter.) You should try to anticipate how you will handle such details as taking attendance, assigning desks, handing out books and materials, what policy you intend to establish for permitting students to go to the restroom during class, and so forth. If you don't plan ahead, you will have to come up with an improvised policy on the spur of the moment, and that policy might turn out to be highly inefficient or in conflict with school regulations.

3. Establish and call attention to class rules.

▶ Establish and call
attention to class
rules the first day

Very effective teachers observed by the Texas researchers explained class rules the first day of school. Some teachers list standard procedures on a chart or bulletin board; others simply state them the first day of class. Either technique saves time and trouble later because all you have to do is refer to the rule when a transgression occurs. The alternative to this approach is to interrupt the lesson and disturb the whole class while you make a hurried, unplanned effort to deal with a surprise attack. Your spur-of-the-moment reaction may turn out to be clumsy and ineffective.

When you introduce rules the first day, take a positive, nonthreatening approach. If you spit rules out as if they were a series of ultimatums, the students may feel you have a chip on your shoulder, which the unwritten code of the classroom obligates them to try to knock off. One way to demonstrate your good faith is to invite the class to suggest necessary regulations and explain why they should be established. Whatever your approach, encourage understanding of the reasons for the rules. You can make regulations seem desirable rather than restrictive if you discuss why they are needed. Reasonable rules are much more likely to be remembered and honored than pronouncements that seem to be the whims of a tyrant.

Examples

"During class discussion, please don't speak out unless you raise your hand and are recognized. I want to be able to hear what each person has to say, and I won't be able to do that if more than one person is talking."

"During work periods, I don't mind if you talk a bit to your neighbors. But if you do it too much and disturb others, I'll have to ask you to stop."

"If you come in late, go to your desk by walking along the side and back of the room. It's disturbing—and not very polite—to walk between people who are interacting with each other."

4. Begin classwork the first day with an instructional activity that is clearly stated and can be completed quickly and successfully.

When selecting the very first assignment to give to a new class, refer to the suggestions for preparing instructional objectives proposed by Mager and Gronlund (Chapter 7), and arrange a short assignment that can be successfully completed before the end of the period. Clearly specify what is to be done, and perhaps state the conditions and criteria for determining successful completion. In addition, mention an activity (such as examining the assigned text) that students should engage in after they have completed the assignment. In the elementary grades, you might give a short assignment that helps students review material covered in the preceding grade. At the secondary level, pick out an initial assignment that is short, interesting, and does not depend on technical knowledge.

Examples

"Your teacher from last year told me that most of you were able to spell all of the words on the list I am going to read. Let's see if you can still spell those words. If you have trouble with certain ones, we can work together to come up with reminders that will help you remember the correct spelling."

"The first chapter in our natural science text for this fall is about birds. I want you to read the first ten pages and make a list of five types of birds that are described and prepare your own set of notes about how to recognize them. At 10:30 I am going to hold up pictures of ten birds, and I want you to see if you can correctly identify at least five of them."

In a junior high school English literature class, ask students to read an interesting short story and then write a brief synopsis of the plot.

In a high school history class, ask students to write a brief description of a movie they have seen that depicted historical events. Then ask them to indicate whether they felt the film interpretation was accurate.

5. During the first weeks with a new group of students, have them spend most of their time engaging in whole-class activities under your direction.

The very effective teachers observed by the Texas researchers followed the strategy just described, which makes sense when you stop to think about it. You can't expect students to adjust to the routine of a new teacher and classroom in just a few days. Accordingly, it would be wise to make sure students have settled down before asking them to engage in relatively unstructured activities like discovery learning. Furthermore, group discussions or group projects usually work out more successfully when the participants have a degree of familiarity with one another and a particular set of background factors (such as a chapter in a text). Thus, as you plan activities during the first weeks with a new class, prepare instructional objectives that ask students to complete assignments under your direction. Postpone using techniques recommended by cognitive and humanistic psychologists until later in the report period.

6. Give clear instructions, hold students accountable for carrying them out, and provide frequent feedback.

All three of these goals can be achieved by making systematic use of instructional objectives as described in Chapter 7 and by putting into practice the model of instruction described throughout this book.

7. Continually demonstrate that you are competent, well prepared, and in charge.

As students work at achieving instructional objectives, participate in group discussions, or engage in any other kind of learning activity, show them that you are a competent classroom manager. Arrange periods so that there will be a well-organized transition from one activity to the next, maintain smoothness and momentum, and don't waste time. Use a variety of teaching approaches so that you please some of your students some of the time, and use techniques recommended by behavioral, cognitive, and humanistic psychologists. Show you are "with it" by being alert for signs of mischief or disruptive behavior, and handle such incidents quickly and confidently by using the techniques described later in this chapter and in the "Becoming a Better Teacher" section of the next chapter.

8. Be professional but pleasant, and try to establish a businesslike but supportive classroom atmosphere.

Establish a business-like but supportive classroom atmosphere

If you establish classroom routines in a competent fashion and keep your students busy working to achieve clearly stated instructional objectives, you should be able to establish a no-nonsense, productive atmosphere. At the same time, you should strive to make your room an inviting and pleasant place to be. Keep in mind the observations of humanistic psychologists regarding the importance of taking into account feelings and interpersonal relationships. Put yourself in the place of students thrust into a strange classroom with an unfamiliar instructor. Try to identify with your students so that you can appreciate how they feel if they do or say something embarrassing, or have difficulty with classwork.

Students seem to respond more positively to schooling when they are treated as individuals, when their feelings and opinions are taken into account, and when they are invited to participate in making decisions. (Alan Levenson)

One of the best ways to get students to respond positively to you and make them feel welcome in your classroom is to learn their names as quickly as possible (even if you have five sections of secondary school students to teach). To accomplish this feat, refer to the cards mentioned in point 1 above. Use the information that the students have provided, perhaps supplemented by your own notes or sketches about distinctive physical and facial features, to establish associations between names and faces. Before and after every class period the first few days, flip through your pile of cards, try to picture the appearance of the students, and practice using their names. Refer to the description of mnemonic devices in the chapter on information processing. Once you have learned a pupil's name, use it as often as possible to maintain the memory trace. Greet pupils by name as they come in the door, use their names when asking them to recite or carry out some task, and speak to them personally when you hand back assignments.

Another way to make students feel at home in your classroom is to try to establish a feeling of class spirit. One way to do this is to have a brief *sharing* period—similar to the sharing time you may remember from your kindergarten days—at the beginning of each period. Invite students to describe recent interesting experiences they have had or to give announcements about extracurricular activities. If a member of the class is injured in an accident or suffers a lengthy illness, buy a get-well card and have every member of the class sign it before sending it off.

If you follow these procedures, you should be able to establish a well-managed classroom. As noted at the beginning of this chapter, however, you are likely to encounter occasional incidents of misbehavior—for reasons that often will be beyond your control. Even if you do everything possible to prevent problems from developing, you are still likely to have to deal with disruptive behavior. Therefore, techniques for handling disruptive behavior, the extent of disciplinary problems, and some of the factors that lead to misbehavior are topics that merit attention.

INFLUENCE TECHNIQUES

In *Mental Hygiene in Teaching* (1959), Fritz Redl and William W. Wattenberg describe a list of behavior management interventions called *influence techniques*. This list was modified by James E. Walker and Thomas M. Shea (1991). The following sections and subsections are based on the ideas of both sets of individuals.

Under each section, specific examples are offered, roughly reflecting a least-direct to most-direct ordering. Some are based on ideas noted by Redl and Wattenberg; some are based on the ideas of Walker and Shea; some are the results of reports by students and teachers; some are based on personal experience. You might use the Handbook Headings to pick out or devise techniques that seem most appropriate for your grade level or that you feel comfortable about.

Supporting Self-Control

Students should be encouraged to develop self-control. This first group of suggestions is designed to foster that trait.

Planned Ignoring   As we pointed out in Chapter 8, you might be able to extinguish inappropriate attention-seeking behaviors by merely ignoring them. Such behaviors include finger snapping, body movements, book dropping, hand waving, and whistling. If you plan to use this technique, make sure the student is aware that he or she is engaging in the behavior and that the behavior does not interfere with the efforts of other students.

Example

Carl has recently gotten into the habit of tapping his pencil on his desk as he works on an assignment as a way to engage you in a conversation that is unrelated to the work. The next several times Carl does this you neither look at him nor comment on his behavior.

Handbook Heading:
Signals to Use to Nip
Trouble in the Bud

Signals   In some cases a subtle signal can put an end to budding misbehavior. The signal, if successful, will stimulate the student to control him- or herself. (Note, however, that this technique should not be used too often, and that it is effective only in the early stages of misbehavior.)

Examples

> Clear your throat.
>
> Stare at the culprit.
>
> Stop what you are saying in midsentence and stare.
>
> Shake your head (to indicate no).
>
> Say "Someone is making it hard for the rest of us to concentrate" (or the equivalent).

> Use supportive reactions to help students develop self-control

Proximity Control   Place yourself close to the misbehaving student. This makes a signal a bit more apparent.

Examples

> Walk over and stand near the student.
>
> With an elementary grade pupil, it sometimes helps if you place a gentle hand on a shoulder or arm.

Interest Boosting   Convey interest in the misbehaver. This relates the signal to schoolwork.

Examples

> Ask the student a question, preferably related to what is being discussed. (Questions such as "Herman, are you paying attention?" or "Don't you agree, Herman?" invite wisecracks. *Genuine* questions are to be preferred.)

Signals such as staring at a misbehaving pupil are examples of influence techniques Redl and Wattenberg classify as "supporting self-control." (Junebug Clark/ Photo Researchers)

Go over and examine some work the student is doing. It often helps if you point out something good about it and urge continued effort.

Humor   Humor is an excellent, all-around influence technique, especially in tense situations. However, remember that it should be *good*-humored humor—gentle and benign rather than derisive. Avoid irony and sarcasm.

Examples

"Herman, for goodness' sake, let that poor pencil sharpener alone—I heard it groan when you used it just now."

Perhaps you have heard someone say, "We're not laughing *at* you; we're laughing *with* you." Before you say this to one of your pupils, you might take note that one second-grader who was treated to that comment unhinged the teacher by replying, "I'm not laughing."

Situational Assistance

Handbook Heading:
Ways to Supply Situational Assistance

Helping over Hurdles   Some misbehavior undoubtedly occurs because students do not understand what they are to do or lack the ability to carry out an assignment.

Examples

Try to make sure your students know what they are supposed to do.

Arrange for students to have something to do at appropriate levels of difficulty.

Have a variety of activities available.

Program Restructuring   In Chapter 1 we noted that teaching is an art because lessons do not always proceed as planned and must occasionally be changed in midstream. The essence of this technique is to recognize when a lesson or activity is going poorly and to try something else.

Examples

"Well class, I can see that many of you are bored with this discussion of the pros and cons of congressional term limits. Let's turn it into a class debate instead, with the winning team getting fifty points toward their final grade."

"I had hoped to complete this math unit before the Christmas break, but I can see that most of you are too excited to give it your best effort. Since today is the last day before the break, I'll postpone the lesson until school resumes in January. Let's do an art project instead."

Support from Routines   Trouble sometimes develops simply because students do not know what is expected of them. To avoid this in-limbo situation, it helps to establish a certain amount of routine, perhaps as part of the class rules (if you resort to such rules).

Examples

Establish a set pattern for getting started at the beginning of the day or period.

Make a specific routine of lining up for recess, lunch, and other activities.

At the beginning of gym classes (or the equivalent), when wild horseplay is at a maximum, establish a fixed procedure for taking roll (perhaps by having students stand on numbers painted on the floor), for determining activities to be participated in, and so on.

Antiseptic Bouncing   Sometimes a student will get carried away by restlessness, uncontrollable giggling, or the like. If you feel that this is nonmalicious behavior and due simply to lack of self-control, ask the student to leave the room. (You may have recognized that antiseptic bouncing is virtually identical to the *time-out* procedure described by behavior modification enthusiasts.)

Examples

"Herman, please go down to the principal's office and sit on that bench outside the door until you feel you have yourself under control."

Some high schools have "quiet rooms"—supervised study halls that take extra students any time during a period, no questions asked.

Physical Restraint   Students who lose control of themselves to the point of endangering other members of the class may have to be physically restrained. However, such restraint should be protective, not punitive; that is, don't shake or hit. This technique is most effective with younger children; such control is usually not appropriate at the secondary level.

Example

If a boy completely loses his temper and starts to hit another child, lead him gently but firmly away from the other pupils or sit him in a chair and keep a restraining hand on his shoulder.

Removing Seductive Objects   If certain objects or fellow students are too tempting for pupils, the wise thing to do is to put temptation behind them.

Examples

If an elementary grade pupil gets carried away using a projector, a stapler, a paper cutter, or whatever, put it away for a while.

If high school students in a shop or laboratory course seem unable to resist the temptation to fool around with expensive equipment, lock it up or erect a barrier of some kind (even a cloth cover will do).

Anticipatory Planning   Some classroom situations are particularly conducive to misbehavior. If a certain activity seems loaded with opportunities for mischief, try to prepare the class ahead of time and emphasize the need for control.

Example

When an elementary school class is going to visit the local newspaper plant or the equivalent, stress the importance of not touching anything, keeping away from the machines, and paying strict attention to the guide.

Reality and Value Appraisal

Handbook Heading:
Ways to Use Reality
and Value Appraisal

Most of the techniques described in the two preceding sections fall under the category of prevention. The following techniques involve prevention but also encourage more constructive behavior. As Redl and Wattenberg put it, "One of the goals of education is to enable people to increase the areas in which they can be guided by intelligence and conscience rather than by blind impulse, fear or prejudice" (1959, p. 358). The approaches presented here "appeal to children's sense of fairness and strengthen their ability to see the consequences of their actions" (p. 358).

Direct Appeals   When appropriate, point out the connection between conduct and its consequences. This is most effective if it is done concisely and if the technique is not used too often.

Examples

"We have a rule that there is to be no running in the halls. Herman forgot the rule, and now he's down in the nurse's office having his bloody nose taken care of. It's too bad Mr. Harris opened his door just as Herman went by. If Herman had been walking, he would have been able to stop in time."

"If everyone would stop shouting, we'd be able to get this finished and go out to recess."

Criticism and Encouragement   Sometimes it is necessary to criticize a particular student. It is preferable to do so in private, but often public criticism is the only possibility. (It also has the advantage of setting an example for other pupils.) In such cases you should do your best to avoid ridiculing or humiliating the student. Public humiliation may cause a child to hate you and school, to counterattack, or to withdraw. Because of the ripple effect, it may also have a negative impact on innocent students. One way to minimize the negative aftereffects of criticism is

▶ Give criticism privately, then offer encouragement

to tack on some encouragement in the form of a suggestion as to how the backsliding can be replaced by more positive behavior.

Examples

If a student doesn't take subtle hints (such as stares), you might say, "Herman, you're disturbing the class. We all need to concentrate on this." It sometimes adds punch if you make this remark when your back is turned while you are writing on the board or helping some other student. (This is one way to show that you are "with it.")

Act completely flabbergasted, as though the misbehavior seems so inappropriate that you can't comprehend it. A kindergarten teacher used this technique to perfection. She would say, "Herman! Is that you?" (Herman has been belting Lucy with a shovel.) "I can't believe my eyes. I wonder if you would help me over here." Obviously, this gambit can't be used too often, and the language and degree of exaggeration have to be altered a bit for older pupils. But indicating that you *expect* good behavior and providing an immediate opportunity for the backslider to substitute good deeds can be very effective.

Defining Limits   In learning about rules and regulations, children go through a process of testing the limits. Two-year-olds particularly, when they have learned how to walk and talk and manipulate things, feel the urge to assert their independence. In addition, they need to find out exactly what the house rules are. (Does Mommy *really* mean it when she says, "Don't take the pots out of the cupboard"? Does Daddy *really* mean it when he says, "Don't play with that hammer"?) Older children do the same thing, especially with new teachers and in new situations. The technique of defining limits includes not only establishing rules (as noted earlier) but also enforcing them.

Examples

Establish class rules, with or without the assistance of students, and make sure they are understood.

When someone tests the rules, show that they are genuine and that there *are* limits.

Postsituational Follow-Up   Classroom discipline occasionally has to be applied in a tense, emotion-packed atmosphere. When this happens, it often helps to have a postsituational discussion—in private, if an individual is involved; with the whole class, if it was a groupwide situation.

Examples

In a private conference: "Herman, I'm sorry I had to ask you to leave the room, but you were getting kind of carried away."

When confronted by a student, it is usually better to arrange for a private conference or appeal to an outside authority than to engage in a showdown in front of the class. (Bob Daemmerich)

"Well, everybody, things got a bit wild during those group work sessions. I want you to enjoy yourselves, but we practically had a riot going, didn't we? And that's why I had to ask you to stop. Let's try to hold it down to a dull roar tomorrow."

Marginal Use of Interpretation   Analysis of behavior can sometimes be made *while* it is occurring, rather than afterward. The purpose here is to help students become aware of potential trouble and make efforts to control it.

Example

To a restless and cranky prelunch class, you might say, "I know you're getting hungry and that you're restless and tired, but let's give it all we've got for ten minutes more. I'll give you the last five minutes for some free visiting time."

The value of these techniques is that they appeal to self-control and imply trust and confidence on the part of the teacher. However, they may become ineffective if used too often, and that is why so many different techniques have been noted. The larger your repertoire, the less frequently you will have to repeat your various gambits and ploys.

I-MESSAGES AND THE NO-LOSE METHOD

I-message: tell how you feel about an unacceptable situation

Handbook Heading:
Using I-Messages

Handbook Heading:
Speculating About
Problem Ownership

As noted in our discussion of humanistic teaching techniques in Chapter 11, Haim Ginott in *Teacher and Child* offers a cardinal principle of communication: "Talk to the situation, not to the personality and character" (1972, p. 84). Instead of making derogatory remarks about the personalities of two boys who have just thrown bread at each other, Ginott suggests that a teacher deliver an **"I-message"** explaining how he or she feels. Don't say "You are a couple of pigs"; say "I get angry when I see bread thrown around. This room needs cleaning." According to Ginott, guilty pupils who are told why a teacher is angry will realize the teacher is a real person, and this realization will cause them to strive to mend their ways. Ginott offers several examples of the cardinal principle of communication in Chapter 4 of *Teacher and Child.* And in Chapter 6 he offers some observations on discipline: Seek alternatives to punishment. Try not to diminish a misbehaving pupil's self-esteem. Try to provide face-saving exits.

A different analysis of many of the same points Ginott stresses is presented by Thomas Gordon in *T.E.T.—Teacher Effectiveness Training* (1974). In *T.E.T.,* teachers are urged to use I-messages, and to resort to authority and punishment only when absolutely necessary.

One procedure recommended by Gordon (and here we review points noted in Chapter 11) is for teachers to try to determine who *owns* a problem before they decide how to handle that problem. If a student misbehaves by doing something destructive (carving a desk top, for example), the teacher owns the problem and must respond by doing something to stop the destructive behavior. But if a student expresses anger or disappointment about some classroom incident (getting a low grade on an exam), that student owns the problem. Gordon suggests that failure to identify problem ownership may cause teachers to intensify difficulties unwittingly, even as they make well-intended efforts to diminish them. If a pupil is finding it difficult to concentrate on schoolwork because his or her needs are not satisfied, the situation will not be ameliorated if the teacher orders, moralizes, or criticizes. According to Gordon, such responses act as roadblocks to finding solutions to student-owned problems because they tend to make the pupil feel resentful and misunderstood. The preferred way to deal with a pupil who owns a problem is to use what Gordon calls **active listening.** The listener is *active* in the sense that interest is shown and the talker is encouraged to continue to express feelings; the listener does *not* actively participate by interpreting, explaining, or directing. The listener *does* respond, though, by recognizing and acknowledging what the student says.

For teacher-owned problems—those that involve misbehavior that is destructive or in violation of school regulations—Gordon agrees with Ginott that I-messages are appropriate. Instead of ordering, threatening, moralizing, using logic, offering solutions, or commenting on personal characteristics, Gordon urges teachers to explain why they are upset. Proof of the effectiveness of I-messages takes the form of anecdotes reported in *T.E.T.* provided by teachers who used them successfully. A principal of a continuation school for dropouts, for example, reported that a group of tough boys responded very favorably when he told them how upset he became when he saw them break some bottles against the school wall. Almost invariably the anecdotes reported in *T.E.T.* refer to the success of a teacher's first try at delivering an I-message. It seems likely that at least part of the technique's success the first time it is used could be attributed to surprise or novelty. But it is also possible that extensive use of the technique might stir up rather than calm down troublemakers. Instead of saying, "Gee! We never realized you felt that way!" they might say, "We're getting awfully tired of hearing about your troubles!"

Gordon urges teachers to try to resolve conflicts in the classroom by using the **no-lose method.** If either person in a conflict loses, there is bound to be resentment. If you tell a girl who is fooling around during a work period that she must settle down or stay after school, *she* loses. If you make a halfhearted and unsuccessful effort to control her and then try to cover up your failure by ignoring her and working with others, *you* lose. Gordon recommends that the preferred procedure is to talk over the problem and come up with a mutually agreeable compromise solution. He offers this six-step procedure for coming up with no-lose solutions, a procedure that is similar to the techniques recommended by Leland Howe and Mary Howe (1975) for choosing class discussion topics (noted in Chapters 10 and 11) and by Gyorgy Polya (1957) for using heuristics (described in Chapter 10). The teacher and student(s) come to mutual agreement by following this procedure:

In dealing with classroom conflicts, Thomas Gordon encourages teachers to use the no-lose method by which the teacher and students talk over a problem and resolve it in a mutually agreeable way. (1990 Frank Siteman/ Monkmeyer Press)

▶ No-lose method:
come to mutual
agreement about a
solution to a problem

1. Define the problem

2. Generate possible solutions

3. Evaluate the solutions

4. Decide which solution is best

5. Determine how to implement the solution

6. Assess how well the solution solved the problem (1974, p. 228)

To put this procedure into practice with an individual, you might approach a boy who is disruptive during a work period and engage in a dialogue something like this:

You: You're making such a ruckus over here by talking loudly and shoving others that I can't hear the group I'm working with. It looks as if you are having trouble settling down. Any ideas about how we can both do what we need to do?

Pupil: I think this workbook junk is stupid. I already know how to do these problems. I'd rather work on my science project.

You: Well, suppose we try this. You do one page of problems. If you get them all correct, we'll both know you can do them and you should be free to work on your science project. If you make some mistakes, though, that means you need more practice. Suppose you do a page and then ask me to check it. Then we can take it from there. How does that sound?

Handbook Heading:
Trying the No-Lose
Method

To put the no-lose method into effect when the entire class is upset about something, you would probably find it preferable to follow all six steps recommended by Gordon.

In certain situations Ginott's and Gordon's observations can be quite helpful. You might try to analyze what you say to pupils when you are upset to discover if you tend to mention character and personality instead of concentrating on the situation. If you find that you do criticize personal characteristics, make an effort to comment on the situation. You might also make an effort to determine who owns a problem before you decide how to deal with it. If a pupil is not behaving in the desired manner and appears to be unhappy or confused about it, you might try serving as an active listener. Encourage the student to talk about what is bothering him or her by serving as a sympathetic sounding board. In cases of defiant, disruptive, or destructive behavior, make occasional use of I-messages so that pupils learn you have feelings that ought to be respected. And if you find yourself confronted by a hostile student or class, you might use the no-lose method to find a mutually agreeable solution to the problem.

Even if you use the management techniques described earlier in this chapter, and attempt to allow for misbehavior by using techniques such as those just described, you are still likely to be faced with occasional incidents of disruption and/or defiance. Some general guidelines you might consider when you find it necessary to resort to disciplinary techniques appear in the Suggestions for Teaching in Your Classroom section that follows the Mid-Chapter Review.

Mid-Chapter Review

Techniques of Classroom Management

Interest in classroom management was stimulated in the early 1970s by the writings of Jacob Kounin. On the basis of observations and experiments, Kounin concluded that teachers who maintained effective control of student behavior possessed one or more of the following skills: (1) withitness, (2) ability to handle overlapping situations, (3) ability to maintain smoothness and momentum when teaching a lesson, (4) ability to keep the whole class involved in a lesson, (5) use of various materials and methods with an air of enthusiasm, and (6) ability to capitalize on the ripple effect by identifying the misbehaver and firmly specifying a more constructive behavior.

More recent studies at the University of Texas found that in well-managed classrooms, students have a clear idea of what they are expected to accomplish, are kept busy in a work-oriented but relaxed and pleasant atmosphere, and feel successful in carrying out their assigned tasks. These findings suggest that teachers should have a plan for handling classroom routine, should specify rules for classroom behavior, should provide understandable lessons that can be completed quickly and successfully, and should establish a businesslike but supportive classroom atmosphere.

Managing the Junior High and High School Classroom

You can productively manage the behavior of adolescents by arranging the classroom environment to optimize teaching and learning, by formulating and communicating clear rules for behavior, and by formulating and communicating clear procedures for starting and completing tasks. If possible, allow students to suggest rules and procedures, but make sure that you apply the same rules to all classes.

Influence Techniques

Fritz Redl and William Wattenberg recommend that teachers use a variety of influence techniques to manage classroom behavior. These include supporting self-control (through the use of such techniques as planned ignoring, proximity control, and humor), situational assistance (for example, helping students over hurdles, establishing routines, and removing seductive objects), and reality and value appraisal (for example, using criticism and encouragement, and defining limits).

I-Messages and the No-Lose Method

Haim Ginott proposed that teachers use I-messages when they confront students about misbehavior. By this he meant that the teacher should explain how he or she feels about the behavior of one or more students rather than denigrating the student's character.

Thomas Gordon suggested that teachers should help students determine who owns a particular problem, listen actively to student concerns, and adopt the no-lose method. The no-lose method calls for the teacher and misbehaving student to discuss the situation and formulate a mutually agreeable compromise solution.

Suggestions for Teaching in Your Classroom

HANDLING PROBLEM BEHAVIOR

1. Have a variety of influence techniques planned in advance.
2. Be prompt, consistent, and reasonable.
3. Avoid threats.
4. Whenever you have to deal harshly with a student, make an effort to reestablish rapport.
5. Consider making occasional use of behavior modification techniques.
6. When you have control, ease up—some.

---

1. Have a variety of influence techniques planned in advance.

You may save yourself a great deal of trouble, embarrassment, and strain if you plan ahead. When first-year teachers are asked which aspects of teaching bother them most, classroom control is almost invariably near the top of the list. Perhaps a major reason is that problems of control frequently erupt unexpectedly, and they often demand equally sudden solutions. If you lack experience, your shoot-from-the-hip reactions may be ineffective. Initial attempts at control that are ineffective tend to reinforce misbehavior, and you will find yourself trapped in a vicious circle. Yet this sort of trap can be avoided if specific techniques are devised ahead of time. Having in mind several methods of dealing with trouble will prepare you for the inevitable difficulties that arise.

However, if you find yourself forced to use prepared techniques too often, some self-analysis is called for. How can you prevent so many problems from developing? Frequent trouble is an indication that you need to work harder at motivating your class. You might refer to the list of causes of misbehavior in the preceding section for some specific troubleshooting suggestions. Also, check on your feelings when you mete out punishment. Teachers who really like students and want them to learn consider control techniques a necessary evil and use them only when they will provide a better atmosphere for learning. If you find yourself looking for trouble or perhaps deliberately luring pupils into misbehaving, or if you discover yourself gloating privately or publicly about an act of punishment, stop and think. Are you perverting your power to build up your ego or giving vent to sadistic impulses?

You will find an extensive list of *influence techniques* in the section that follows this discussion of general suggestions for maintaining classroom control.

*Handbook Heading:
Analyzing Feelings
After Dealing with
Troublemakers*

2. Be prompt, consistent, and reasonable.

▶ Be prompt, consistent, and reasonable when dealing with misbehavior

No attempt to control behavior will be effective if it is remote from the act that provokes it. If a troublemaker is to comprehend the relationship between behavior and counterreaction, one must quickly follow the other. Don't postpone dealing with misbehaving pupils or make vague threats to be put into effect sometime in the future (such as not permitting the pupils to attend an end-of-the-year event). By that time, most pupils will have forgotten what they did wrong. They then feel resentful and persecuted and may conclude that you are acting out of sheer malice. A frequent reaction is more misbehavior in an urge to "get even." (In such situations, guilty pupils are not likely to remember that you are the one doing the evening up.) On the other hand, retribution that is too immediate, that is applied when a student is still extremely upset, may also be ineffective. At such times, it is often better to wait a bit.

Handbook Heading:
Being Prompt, Consistent, and Reasonable in Controlling the Class

Being consistent about classroom control can save a lot of time, energy, and misery. Strictness one day and leniency the next, or roughness on one pupil and gentleness with another, invites all students to test you every day—just to see whether this is a good day or a bad day or whether they can get away with something more frequently than others do. Establishing and enforcing class rules is an excellent way to encourage yourself to be consistent.

Harshness in meting out retribution encourages rather than discourages more extreme forms of misbehavior. If pupils are going to get into a lot of trouble for even a minor offense, they will probably figure they should get their money's worth. In the early days of Merrie England all offenses—from picking pockets to murder—were punishable by death. The petty thief quickly became a murderer; it was a lot easier (and less risky) to pick the pocket of a dead man and, since the punishment was the same, eminently more sensible. The laws were eventually changed to make punishment appropriate to the degree of the offense. Keep this in mind when you dispense justice.

3. Avoid threats.

If at all possible, avoid a showdown in front of the class. In a confrontation before the whole group, you are likely to get desperate. You may start out with a "yes, you will"—"no, I won't" sort of duel and end up making a threat on the spur of the moment. Frequently, you will not be able to make good on the threat, and you will lose face. It's far safer and better for everyone to settle extreme differences in private. When two people are upset and angry with each other, they look silly at best and completely ridiculous at worst. You lose a great deal more than a student does when this performance takes place in front of the class. In fact, a student may actually gain prestige by provoking you successfully.

Perhaps the worst temptation of all is to try to get back at the entire class by making a blanket threat of a loss of privilege or detention. It hardly ever works and tends to lead to a united counterattack by the class. One elementary school teacher had the reputation of telling her class at least once a year that they would not be allowed to participate in the Spring Play-Day if they didn't behave. By the time pupils reached this grade, they had been tipped off by previous students that she always made the threat but never carried it out. They behaved accordingly. Suppose, in a fit of pique, you tell your class that they must "all stay forty-five minutes after school." What will you do when they start chattering in a chorus about bus schedules, car pools, music lessons, dentist appointments, and paper routes? You can usually avoid such nightmares by putting a stop to the problem before it begins to snowball.

4. Whenever you have to deal harshly with a student, make an effort to reestablish rapport.

Handbook Heading:
Ways to Establish Rapport

If you must use a drastic form of retribution, make a point of having a confidential conference with your antagonist as soon as possible. Otherwise, she or he is likely to remain an antagonist for the rest of the year. It's too much to expect chastised students to come to you of their own volition and apologize. You should set up the conference, then explain that the punishment has cleared the air as far as you are concerned and that they can start the next day with a clean slate. You shouldn't be surprised if a recalcitrant pupil doesn't respond with signs or words of gratitude. Perhaps some of the causes of misbehavior lie outside of school, and something you did or said may have been merely the last straw. Even if you get a sullen reaction, it is desirable at least to indicate your willingness to meet punished students more than halfway.

At the elementary level, you can frequently make amends simply by giving the child some privilege—for example, passing out paper or being hall monitor at recess. One teacher made it a point to praise a child for some positive action shortly after a severe reprimand.

5. Consider making occasional use of behavior modification techniques.

Many of the procedures that have been noted here—in particular, stating rules, using techniques planned in advance, and being prompt and consistent—are employed in a highly systematic fashion in the behavior modification approach to classroom control. In Chapter 8 you were acquainted with the techniques of behavior modification, including the suggestion that you follow this procedure when confronted by inappropriate behavior, as when two boys engage in a mild argument that stops and starts several times.

> First ignore misbehavior, then stress rewards; use punishment as a last resort

First, ignore the behavior. (It may extinguish because of lack of reinforcement.)

Second, remind the class that those who finish the assignment early will earn five bonus points and be allowed to see a film.

Third, approach the boys and tell them (privately and nicely) that they are disturbing others and making life difficult for themselves. If they do not complete the assignment in the allotted time, they will have to make it up some other time.

Fourth, resort to punishment by informing the boys (in a firm but not nasty way) that they must leave the classroom immediately and report to the vice-principal to be assigned to a study hall for the rest of the class period. Tell them they will have to complete the assignment when the rest of the class has free time.

Finish by pointing out that once the work is made up, they will be all caught up and in a good position to do satisfactory work for the rest of the report period.

Handbook Heading: Experimenting with Behavior Modification

The techniques just described are appropriate for secondary school students. The following behavior modification procedure for maintaining classroom control in the primary grades is recommended by Wesley C. Becker, Siegfried Engelmann, and Don P. Thomas:

1. Specify in a positive way the rules that are the basis for your reinforcement. Emphasize the behavior you desire by praising children who are following the rules. Rules are made important by providing reinforcement for following them. Rules may be different for different kinds of work, study, or play periods.

   Limit the rules to five or less.

   As the children learn to follow the rules, repeat them less frequently, but continue to praise good classroom behavior.

2. Relate the children's performance to the rules. Praise behavior, not the child.

   Be specific about behavior that exemplifies paying attention or working hard. . . .

   Relax the rules between work periods. . . .

3. Catch the children being good. Reinforce behavior incompatible with that which you wish to eliminate. Reinforce behavior that will be most beneficial to the child's development. . . .

4. Ignore disruptive behavior unless someone is getting hurt. Focus your attention on the children who are working well in order to prompt the correct behavior from the children who are misbehaving.

5. When you see a persistent problem behavior, look for the reinforcer. It may be your own behavior. (1971, p. 171)

6. When you have control, ease up—some.

It is extremely difficult, if not impossible, to establish a controlled atmosphere after allowing anarchy. Don't make the mistake of thinking you will be able to start out without any control and suddenly take charge. It may work, but in most cases you will have an armed truce or a cold war on your hands. It is far better to start out on the strict side and then ease up a bit after you have established control. Being strict doesn't mean being unpleasant or dictatorial; it simply means that all are aware that they are expected to respect the rights of others.

VIOLENCE IN AMERICAN SCHOOLS

The Safe School Study Report

Chances are, you have read reports about the extent of violence in American schools today and are understandably concerned about how dangerous teaching has become. At first glance, some of the statistics that have been reported are alarming, but closer scrutiny reveals that certain teachers are much more likely to be exposed to violence than are the majority. Because of increased reports of violence in American schools during the 1970s, the U.S. Department of Health, Education, and Welfare in 1978 issued a report titled *Violent Schools—Safe Schools: The Safe School Study Report to the Congress.* The report revealed that violence in American schools had reached a peak between 1965 and 1975 but was declining. Subsequent reports (summarized by Baker, 1985; Bauer, 1985) lead to the conclusion that a definite problem still exists for teachers in certain types of school situations.

Among the significant points noted in the *Safe School Study Report* were the following:

▶ Violence most likely in inner-city junior high schools with weak administrators

Factors associated with high levels of school violence included location of a school in a high crime area, large schools and classes, high proportion of male students, lack of firmness on the part of administrators, and perception of students that they had little control over what happened to them.

Most acts of violence took place in secondary schools, but attacks on pupils and teachers were about twice as frequent in *junior* high as in senior high schools.

The highest-risk areas in schools are stairways, hallways, cafeterias, and locker rooms. In all these places students are thrown together under crowded conditions. The safest places in schools were classrooms.

Administrators, teachers, and students all recommended firm discipline and supervision as the best single means for reducing violence. The authors of the report recommended greater "personalization" of schooling.

The problem of school violence still exists, particularly in inner-city schools. Julius Menacker, Ward Weldon, and Emanuel Hurwitz (1989) asked sixth- and eighth-grade students and teachers in four Chicago city public schools many of the same questions contained in the *Safe School Study Report.* Some of their main findings follow:

1. More than 50 percent of students reported that money, clothing, or personal property was stolen from them at least once during the school year.

2. Eight percent of students said they were threatened by someone with a gun or knife.

3. Four percent of students said that they were beaten so badly that they required medical attention.

4. Thirty-two percent of students said they had carried a weapon to school at least once, and 14 percent said they had done so more than once.

5. Fifteen percent of students reported hitting a teacher at least once during the school year.

6. Three percent of teachers said they were physically attacked by a student; 1 percent reported being threatened by a student with a weapon.

7. Forty-two percent of teachers said they were reluctant to confront misbehaving students out of fear for their own safety.

8. Thirty-nine percent of teachers reported damage to or theft of personal property during the school year.

Despite these figures, the authors characterize the schools as islands of relative safety since the incidence of violent crime in the surrounding community was even greater. They concluded that school violence will not markedly decline until the level of community order and safety increases.

Although these studies reveal a disquieting level of school violence, particularly in certain schools, they also suggest that you are likely to be physically safe in your own classroom. Nevertheless, school violence is a problem that directly or indirectly touches every student and teacher. Accordingly, you should be aware of the various explanations of school violence and the steps that can be taken to reduce its frequency. Those topics are the subjects of the next two sections.

Analyzing Reasons for Violence

The *Safe School Study Report* noted that the level of violence was highest in secondary schools with a high proportion of male students. One of the clear-cut sex differences that has been repeatedly supported by consistent evidence (reviewed by Parke & Slaby, 1983) is that males are more aggressive than females. While the causes of this difference cannot be traced precisely, it seems likely to be due to hormonal as well as cultural factors. *Hormone* in the Greek means "to arouse" or "to urge on," which reflects the fact that these substances are released in the bloodstream and arouse reactions in various parts of the body. The male sex hormone androgen arouses high energy and activity levels. Moreover, because of long-established cultural expectancies, males in our society are encouraged to assert themselves in physical ways. As a result, tendencies toward high energy and activity levels aroused by male sex hormones may be expressed in the form of aggressiveness against others.

► Male aggressiveness due to hormonal and cultural factors

As noted in the discussion of age-level characteristics in Chapter 3, there is also evidence that young girls in our society are encouraged to be dependent and to be eager to please adults, while young boys are encouraged to assert their independence (Block, 1973; Fagot, 1978). Furthermore, it appears that boys are more likely than girls to be reinforced for assertive and illegal forms of behavior. Martin Gold and Richard Petronio (1980, p. 524) speculate that delinquency in our society seems to have a masculine character. They suggest that the range of delinquent behavior that will be admired by peers is narrower for females than for males and that boys are more likely to achieve recognition by engaging in illegal acts. The same reasoning may well apply to disruptive behavior in the classroom. A boy who talks back to the teacher or shoves another boy in a skirmish in the cafeteria is probably more likely to draw a favorable response from peers than a girl who exhibits the same behavior. Thus, there are a variety of factors that predispose boys to express frustration and hostility in physical and assertive ways.

Boys also seem more likely than girls to experience feelings of frustration and hostility in school. For a variety of reasons (more rapid maturity, desire to please adults, superiority in verbal skills) girls earn higher grades, on the average, than boys do. A low grade almost inevitably arouses feelings of resentment and anger. In fact, any kind of negative evaluation is a very direct threat to a student's self-esteem. Thus, a junior or senior high school boy who has received an unbroken succession of low grades and is unlikely to graduate may experience extreme frustration and anger. Even poor students are likely to be aware that their chances of getting a decent job are severely limited by the absence of a high school diploma. At the same time, high school students who have never developed successful study habits and who are saddled with a low grade-point average may feel that it is impossible to do anything about the situation—unless there is a continuation school or the equivalent to attend. Older high school boys who do not have opportunities to attend special schools can escape further humiliation by dropping out of school; but junior high school boys cannot legally resort to the same solution, which may partially explain why violent acts are twice as frequent in junior as in senior high schools.

> Junior-high-age boys with low grades may feel trapped

Other explanations of disruptive classroom behavior are supplied by Erikson's observations on identity. A teenager who has failed to make a clear occupational choice, who is confused about sex roles, or who does not experience acceptance "by those who count" may decide to establish a negative identity. Instead of striving to behave in ways that parents and teachers respond to in positive ways, negative-identity teenagers may deliberately engage in opposite forms of behavior. James Marcia's identity status concept (1980, 1991) may also help you understand why certain pupils cause problems in class. Foreclosure types who have accepted parental values may well be model students. Moratorium types, who are experiencing identity crises of different kinds, may feel impelled to release frustration and anger. But even pupils who are not experiencing identity problems, either because they are too young to be concerned or because they have resolved their identity conflicts, may misbehave because they need to release frustration and tension.

> Misbehavior of high school students may reveal lack of positive identity

So far, we have mentioned the role of hormonal, academic, cultural, and personality factors in school violence. Each of these explanations places the responsibility for violent behavior largely or entirely on the individual. Other explanations focus instead on schools that are poorly designed and do not meet the needs of their students. Violent behavior, in this view, is seen as a natural (though unacceptable) response to schools that are too large, impersonal, and competitive; that do not enforce rules fairly or consistently; that use punitive ways of resolving conflict; and that impose an unimaginative, nonmeaningful curriculum on students (Zwier & Vaughan, 1984). Dona Kagan (1990) reports that students who are at risk of dropping out of school believe that their teachers neither care about them nor consider them capable of academic success. Ironically, the self-esteem and motivation of a large proportion of these students improve after they leave school to the extent that they enroll in General Equivalency Diploma or job training programs.

Evidence in support of the argument that the characteristics and climate of a school can lead to violence was noted earlier. Recall from Chapter 3, in our discussion of age-level characteristics at the high school level, that mention was made of negative reactions (such as vandalism) to schooling. In addition, Michael Rutter and several associates (1979) made a comprehensive study of twelve inner-city London schools. They found that the amount of misbehavior and damage to school property was significantly less in schools that had an academic emphasis, made incentives and rewards available, arranged good conditions for students, and provided opportunities for students to participate in decision making. The impact of school atmosphere was demonstrated by the fact that students who moved from "bad" elementary schools (characterized by considerable misbehavior) to secondary schools that fit the description just given exhibited a significant decrease in disruptive and destructive behavior.

Similar observations on the characteristics of schools that have low levels of violence were stressed by Eugene Howard, an authority on school climate and discipline, who wrote:

> Schools with positive climates are characterized by people-centered belief and value systems, procedures, rules, regulations, and policies. People care, respect, and trust one another, and the school, as an institution, cares, respects, and trusts people. In such a school, people feel a high sense of pride and ownership which comes from each individual having a role in making the school a better place. (1981)

Reducing School Violence

Classroom Tactics   The recommendations for improvement noted in the *Safe School Study Report,* the results of the Rutter study, and the conclusions reached by Howard suggest that academic achievement and school atmosphere can play a significant role in school violence. To foster respectable levels of achievement by as many students as possible, teachers can make effective use of carefully selected objectives, help students establish at least short-term goals, use efficient instructional techniques (such as those advocated by behavioral theorists), teach students how to use learning strategies, and implement a mastery approach. If you show that students who do not do well on the first try at an assignment will receive your help and encouragement to improve their performance, you may be able to convert at least some resentment into a desire to achieve.

School violence can be reduced by improving student achievement levels

At the same time, it appears that students should be invited to participate in making at least some decisions about what is to be studied and about school and classroom rules. Discovery techniques and the contract approach, for example, permit some self-direction by students. Such tactics may ease students' fears that schooling is impersonal and that they have no control over what happens to them. As humanistic psychologists have argued, students seem to respond more positively to schooling when they are treated as individuals, when their feelings and opinions are taken into account, and when they are invited to participate in making decisions about how the school and the classroom function.

Programs to Reduce Violence and Improve Discipline   Evidence from various sources (summarized by Baker, 1985; Bauer, 1985) that violent and disruptive acts are still common in many American schools prompted President Reagan to direct the Department of Justice and the Department of Education, in partnership with Pepperdine University, to form the National School Safety Center. (The center began operations in June 1984.) The same day he signed the directive, the president issued this statement: "I urge all federal, state, and local officials to assist this Center in addressing the needs of our nation's schools in the areas of school safety and restoration of discipline." As this message implies, the purpose of the center is to coordinate efforts to reduce violence and improve discipline in American schools.

Several states and many school districts have indeed initiated programs to make schools safer places for students and teachers. One such program is the Just Community at the Birch Meadow Elementary School in Reading, Massachusetts (Murphy, 1988). You may recall reading (at the end of Chapter 2) about the Just Community concept as an extension of Lawrence Kohlberg's work on moral reasoning. The goal of the Just Community at Birch Meadow was to help students take responsibility for reducing undesirable behaviors (such as petty bickering among students, the development of cliques, and graffiti on restroom walls) and promoting more desirable actions (such as cooperative learning, cleanup activities, and organizing fund-raising events).

Implementation of the Just Community concept involves two types of activities: circle meetings and student councils. Circle meetings are held in each

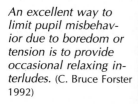

An excellent way to limit pupil misbehavior due to boredom or tension is to provide occasional relaxing interludes. (C. Bruce Forster 1992)

Violence less likely when students invited to participate in making decisions

classroom. The first meeting occurs on the first day of the school year and is devoted to establishing classroom rules and punishments. Subsequent meetings can be called at any time to deal with such issues as unfair treatment of some students by others (or by the teacher), classroom safety, and revisions of classroom rules. There were two student councils at Birch Meadow: one (the primary council) for kindergarten through grade three and the other (the intermediate council) for grades four and five. Each class selects a representative to serve on the council. The councils meet separately with the principal in alternating weeks to decide on ways to make the atmosphere of the school more enjoyable. For example, the primary council conducted a playground cleanup campaign and the intermediate council raised money to purchase an American flag for the school auditorium.

Milbrey McLaughlin and Joan Talbert (1990) describe three programs that differ in many respects but share the goal of the *Safe School Study Report* authors of a personalized school environment. One school was an alternative school for students with histories of school failure, substance abuse, and trouble with various forms of school authority. The second school was a performing arts magnet school with an ethnically and socioeconomically diverse student body. The third school was a vocational academy located within a large public high school. All three schools reported high attendance rates, a high level of academic success, few behavior problems, and strong positive feelings for the staff. The students attributed much of their success and positive feelings to the fact that the teachers recognized them as individuals and gave them positive support (a finding that supports the arguments of Dona Kagan and many humanistic theorists about why at-risk students drop out of school). All three schools were small in size and committed to a personalized environment. The specific techniques used to establish such an environment were quite varied. At one school, for example, teachers met for one period each day with about six students to review and discuss academic work and personal problems. Membership in these "core groups" remained stable for three years. At another school, after-hours activities such as softball games were scheduled. And in all three schools, cooperative-learning groups and whole-class discussion were used extensively. (For descriptions of other programs, see Nicholson et al., 1985.)

Resources for Further Investigation

Classroom Management

Even though it was published in 1959, the second edition of *Mental Hygiene in Teaching* by Fritz Redl and William W. Wattenberg includes a particularly clear, concise, and well-organized analysis of influence techniques. Many of the techniques described have been used by teachers for years and will continue to be used as long as an instructor is asked to supervise a group of pupils.

More recent analyses of classroom control techniques can be found in *Building Classroom Discipline* (3d ed., 1989) by C. M. Charles; *Classroom Management for Elementary Teachers* (2d ed., 1989) by Carolyn M. Evertson, Edmund T. Emmer, Barbara S. Clements, Julie P. Sanford, and Murray E. Worsham; *Classroom Management for Secondary Teachers* (2d ed., 1989) by Edmund T. Emmer, Carolyn M. Evertson, Julie P. Sanford, Barbara S. Clements, and Murray E. Worsham; *Behavior Management: A Practical Approach for Educators* (5th ed., 1991) by James E. Walker and Thomas M. Shea; and *Instructional Management for Detecting and Correcting Special Problems* (1991) by William H. Evans, Susan S. Evans, Robert A. Gable, and Rex E. Schmid.

Discussions of classroom management that emphasize particular approaches or techniques can also be found. For instance, James S. Cangelosi emphasizes the use of methods that foster student cooperation in *Classroom Management Strategies: Gaining and Maintaining Students' Cooperation* (1988); and William W. Purkey and David B. Strahan emphasize the use of invitational learning in *Positive Discipline: A Pocketful of Ideas* (1986).

School Violence

For information on how to reduce school violence through the use of behavior modification techniques, psychodynamic and humanistic interventions, and the teaching of prosocial values and behaviors, read *School Violence* (1984) by Arnold P. Goldstein, Steven J. Apter, and Berj Harootunian. *Victimization in Schools* (1985) by Gary D. Gottfredson and Denise C. Gottfredson describes research conducted at the Center for Social Organization of Schools at Johns Hopkins University on the nature and frequency of school violence; it also discusses possible solutions. And, finally, Amalia J. Cuervo, Joan Lees, and Richard Lacey describe how modifications in instructional techniques, curricula, school organization, student involvement, school-parent relationships, and school-community relationships can reduce school violence in *Toward Better and Safer Schools* (1984).

SUMMARY

1. Jacob Kounin, one of the early writers on classroom management, identified several effective classroom management techniques. Kounin emphasized the ripple effect, withitness, coping with overlapping activities, maintaining the momentum of a lesson, keeping the whole class involved in a lesson, using a variety of instructional techniques enthusiastically, focusing on the misbehavior of students rather than on their personalities, and suggesting alternative constructive behaviors.

2. Researchers at the University of Texas found that in well-managed classrooms students know what they are expected to do and do it successfully, are kept busy with teacher-designated activities, and exhibit little confusion or disruptive behavior. Such classrooms are marked by a work-oriented yet relaxed and pleasant atmosphere.

3. Lee Canter's Assertive Discipline program recommends that teachers teach students the behaviors they want them to exhibit, give them positive re-

inforcement, and, if the first two steps do not produce desirable results, invoke a discipline plan.

4. Fritz Redl and William Wattenberg first proposed their set of behavior management methods in 1959. These influence techniques are arranged by categories that roughly reflect a least-direct to most-direct ordering. These categories include supporting self-control, situational assistance, and reality and value appraisal.

5. Haim Ginott suggests that teachers use I-messages when responding to misbehavior. These are statements that indicate to students how the teacher feels when misbehavior occurs. The aim is to comment on the situation rather than on the personality and character of the student.

6. Thomas Gordon also suggests that teachers use I-messages. In addition, he recommends that teachers determine who "owns" a problem, use active listening when the student owns the problem, and resolve conflicts by using the no-lose method. The no-lose method involves discussing problem behaviors with the misbehaving student and formulating a mutually agreeable compromise solution.

7. While school violence seems to have peaked between 1965 and 1975, it is still a problem. It is most likely to occur in inner-city junior high schools with weak administrators. The school areas at highest risk for violent incidents are stairways, hallways, cafeterias, and locker rooms. The safest areas are classrooms.

8. Possible explanations for misbehavior and violence, particularly among boys at the junior high and high school levels, include high levels of the male sex hormone androgen, a culture that encourages male aggression and independence, feelings of resentment and frustration over low levels of achievement, and difficulty in establishing a positive identity.

9. Other explanations for school violence focus on the characteristics and atmosphere of schools that are so large that they seem impersonal, that emphasize competition, that do not enforce rules fairly or consistently, that use punishment as a primary means of resolving conflict, and that of-

fer a curriculum perceived as unimaginative and nonmeaningful.

10. Steps that classroom teachers can take to reduce school violence include providing students with well-conceived objectives, helping students set short-term goals, using instructional techniques derived from behavioral learning theories, teaching students how to use learning strategies, using a mastery approach, and allowing students to make some decisions about classroom rules and what is to be studied.

11. One schoolwide program that may reduce violence and improve behavior is the Just Community, where students are given responsibility for reducing undesirable behavior and increasing the frequency of desirable behavior.

KEY TERMS

ripple effect   *(622)*
withitness   *(623)*
I-messages   *(644)*
active listening   *(644)*
no-lose method   *(645)*

DISCUSSION QUESTIONS

1. Can you recall any classes where you experienced Kounin's ripple effect? Since this phenomenon simultaneously affects the behavior of several students, would you consider using it deliberately? Why?

2. Haim Ginott and Thomas Gordon recommend that teachers speak to the behavior and not the character of the student when responding to misbehavior. How often have you seen this done? If it strikes you as a good approach that is not practiced often enough, what steps will you take to use it as often as possible with your own students?

3. Do you agree with the argument raised earlier that school violence can be caused by a nonmeaningful, unimaginative curriculum? If so, what can you do to make the subjects you teach lively, interesting, and useful?

Chapter 15

BECOMING A
BETTER TEACHER

$\mathbf{A}$s you know from personal experience, some teachers are much more effective than others. Take a moment and think back to as many teachers as you can remember. How many of them were really outstanding in the sense that they established a favorable classroom atmosphere, were sensitive to the needs of students, and used a variety of techniques to help you learn? How many of them did an adequate, workmanlike job but left you bored or indifferent most of the time? How many of them made you dread entering their classrooms because they were either ineffective teachers or insensitive or even cruel in dealing with you and your classmates? Chances are you remember few outstanding teachers and had at least one incompetent or tyrant (and perhaps several of them). You probably know from your experiences as a student that ineffective or vindictive teachers are often dissatisfied with themselves and with their jobs. It seems logical to assume a circular relationship in such cases: Unhappy teachers often do a poor job of instruction; teachers who do a poor job of instruction are likely to be unhappy.

If you hope to be an effective teacher who enjoys life in the classroom (most of the time), you must be well prepared and willing to work. You will need a wide variety of skills, sensitivity to the needs of your pupils, and awareness of many instructional techniques. Each chapter in this book was written to help you acquire these various skills, sensitivities, and techniques. You are also likely to need two other general abilities if you hope to function as an above-average, successful, satisfied teacher: the ability to cope with frustrations and the ability to benefit from experience and improve your skills as an instructor. This last chapter offers some suggestions you might use to enhance such abilities.

COPING WITH FRUSTRATIONS

There are problems and frustrations in any profession or job, and teaching is no exception. If you hope to function effectively in the classroom, you will need to learn to cope with the many problems that are an inevitable feature of public school education. Here is a list of suggestions on how to cope with frustrations. With the exception of points 10, 11, and 13, the statements in italics are exact quotations from *Mental Hygiene in Teaching* (1959) by Fritz Redl and William W. Wattenberg, pages 494–497.

1. *Develop self-awareness.* The better people understand themselves, the less likely they are to be overwhelmed by events they cannot control. Furthermore, those who understand and accept themselves are usually able to accept and understand others. If you feel that you might benefit from developing greater self-awareness, consider enrolling in a college course intended to promote self-understanding.

2. *Recognize new possibilities in teaching.* If a "standard" technique for dealing with a problem is prohibited or not available to you, find a new and different way to do it.

3. *Evaluate dissatisfactions.* If you find yourself dissatisfied with certain aspects of teaching, try to select those portions of the problem that can be dealt with and become a relaxed fatalist about the rest. (Confucius put it in the form of the familiar prayer: Give me the strength to change what can be changed, the courage to accept what cannot be changed, and the wisdom to tell one from the other.)

4. *Re-evaluate total load.* If you are inundated by work and pressure mounts, try to eliminate or reduce certain tensions. For example, if you are driven to the brink by having to grade term papers for five classes of thirty pupils each, don't assign term papers until your teaching load is adjusted.

5. *Look for help on specific questions.* If you are hung up on a particular frustration, ask your principal, an older teacher, or a consultant for ideas. In

By openly communicating, sharing ideas, and solving problems with their colleagues, teachers can relieve stress and improve their teaching skills. (Stephen Frisch/Stock, Boston, Inc.)

some cases, all it takes is a little more experience or a different perspective to reveal a simple solution.

6. *Deliberately expose yourself to new experiences.* Anyone who is conscientious about teaching needs periods of rest and relaxation. Functioning as an inspirational instructor takes a lot out of a person. For this reason it may be wise to cultivate a noneducational hobby, take a nonteaching summer job, or make the most of that three-month vacation.

7. *Seek satisfactions elsewhere.* If conditions in school block the achievement of psychological needs, make a deliberate effort to find satisfaction outside the classroom. For example, one high school teacher felt unhappy about the lack of overt acceptance by and admiration from his students (not because he was a poor teacher but because high school students often make it a point not to show admiration openly). He became the scoutmaster of a Boy Scout troop. Another way to satisfy partly frustrated needs is to develop a creative hobby.

8. *Talk it over with friends.* One purpose of psychotherapy is to provide catharsis—the release of tension. You can get much the same result by talking over your problems with others. There is obviously a limit to how much you can impose on any one person, but an occasional legitimate gripe will rarely strain relationships with a spouse, friend, or colleague, especially if you spread the gripes around and act as a reciprocal "therapist." If you are upset about something (the furnace at home went on the blink at 3:00 A.M.), talk about it, and warn students that they had better look out for you that day.

9. *Stimulate group discussion.* A variation of the preceding point is "group therapy" sessions. Gripe sessions in a cafeteria or teachers' room are often an effective way to keep body and soul together, especially if there is an element of humor in them. (Looking for the humorous side of things is a fine, all-purpose method of dealing with frustrations in or out of the classroom.)

10. *Get physical release of tension.* When frustrations build up, you might indulge in recreational activities or physical work to gain release.

11. *Avoid taking out your frustrations on the class.* A primary reason for seeking release of tension through creative hobbies, gripes, or physical activities is to avoid punishing your students. When you find yourself frustrated, it is natural to want to take out your anger on those thirty scapegoats trapped in your room, especially if they have done more than their share in contributing to your frustration. In a sense, your students are so many sitting ducks. The temptation to shoot them down can be almost irresistible. A certain amount of righteous indignation is probably a reasonable reaction to genuinely guilty pupils, but too often an angry teacher is more at fault than the alleged provokers. If you are upset because of your own weaknesses or inabilities and compensate by bawling out the class or giving a spot quiz, the students will realize it. Frequently they will retaliate, and then you really *will* have some frustrations to cope with.

12. *Get professional help.* In some cases, personal problems are beyond the help that friends can give or are too extensive to be solved by any of the suggestions noted here. If you have reached this point, the sensible thing is to seek professional assistance. You should not regard the need for such help as an admission that you are a failure. Some frustrations may drive an individual to neurosis or psychosis. Individuals who recognize their need for help are often in better mental health than those who refuse to acknowledge the possibility.

13. *In extreme cases, execute a strategic withdrawal.* It sometimes happens that a teacher is caught in a bind. If you find yourself teaching in a school where you can see nothing but negative factors, it may be best to leave that field of forces. Unfortunate circumstances or personality conflicts may lead to an intolerable situation, in which case moving to a different school or a different district may be the sensible—rather than the cowardly—thing to do. If you discover, however, that your dissatisfactions are not with local conditions or people but that you simply do not enjoy teaching and that none of the preceding suggestions helps very much, it would be logical to look for a different kind of job. At stake is not only your own personal adjustment but also the well-being of your students.

Before discussing some suggestions that you might follow to improve your effectiveness as a teacher (and to avoid the necessity for resorting too often to the techniques just mentioned), we offer a few comments regarding consistency and control.

CONSISTENCY AND CONTROL

After making comprehensive observations of primary grade teachers over a period of time, Jere E. Brophy and Carolyn M. Evertson (1976) concluded: "For various reasons, most of them still unknown, many teachers are inconsistent from one year to the next in the degree of success they achieve in producing student learning gains, in the emotional responses they produce in students, and in their own emotional reactions and general behavior in the classroom" (1976, pp. 3–4). Brophy and Evertson further point out that new teachers, who often go through a process of trial and error when they first take over classrooms, are particularly inconsistent.

In interpreting these conclusions, you should take note that Brophy and Evertson observed primary grade teachers. Teachers of the first, second, and third grades not only have the same group of students for the entire school year; they also supervise the initial learning experiences of those pupils. Thus, they not only influence academic achievement but also shape attitudes toward learning. Quite a bit of variation between individual pupils and groups of pupils might therefore be expected during the first years of school. By contrast, teachers at the secondary level, who typically interact with several different groups of students for less than an hour a day during one report period, would probably not vary as much on measures of consistency. The subject and the primary instructional technique would also seem likely to influence the degree of variability from one year to the next. For instance, a high school teacher of a structured subject (such as math), who spent most class periods giving the same explanations, demonstrations, exercises, and tests year after year, would probably earn quite consistent ratings. But a teacher of a course such as social studies, who invited each class to suggest topics to be studied and who made frequent use of discussion techniques, would probably vary in rated effectiveness since the performance (and reactions) of each class would depend to a considerable extent on interactions between a unique group of students and the teacher.

If you expect to teach at the elementary level or plan to encourage student participation at the secondary level, you might prepare yourself for a degree of inconsistency. If you get off to a splendid start your first year in an elementary school, don't be surprised if things run less smoothly the next year. Conversely, if the first year turns out to be difficult, don't be discouraged. If you find that students in one section of a secondary grade course respond enthusiastically while those in another section seem sullen or hostile, recognize that variation is inevitable.

Differences in teaching effectiveness from year to year and from class to class may be inevitable, but that does not mean you cannot do anything about such variability. Perhaps the best way to put it is to say that you will have to work harder with some groups of students than with others. You should strongly resist the temptation to assume that some groups are simply going to be less responsive than others and that there is nothing you can do about it. You might use that assumption as an excuse for not putting out much effort. In their analysis of

Teachers of primary school children affect not only academic achievement but also attitudes toward learning. (C. Bruce Forster)

primary grade teachers, Brophy and Evertson concluded that those who were consistently effective perceived their job as interesting and worthwhile. They approached teaching with dedication and resourcefulness and took personal responsibility for what happened in their classrooms. If they realized that things were not going well with a particular class, they experimented industriously with different techniques until they found something that seemed to work. Ineffective and inconsistent instructors, by contrast, thought of teaching as "just a job." They tended to react to unresponsive classes by blaming the situation on causes beyond their control. They were likely to offer rationalizations to account for lack of learning.

You may recall from the discussion of motivation in Chapter 12 that high-achieving students tend to attribute failure to lack of effort and resolve to try harder. Low achievers, by contrast, tend to attribute failure to lack of ability and assume that they have no control over what happens. You may also recall from discussions of *learned helplessness* in Chapter 3 that individuals who feel that they have no control over their own behavior are likely to experience depression. Therefore, if you aspire to be a high-achieving teacher and are eager to experience (at least occasionally) a sense of exhilaration and accomplishment rather than feelings of depression, you should assume that what happens in your classroom is up to you.

Brophy and Evertson make the point that "effective teaching involves *orchestration* of a large number of factors, continually shifting teaching behavior to respond to continually shifting needs" (p. 139). They also note that "the most successful teachers looked upon themselves as diagnosticians and problem solvers" (p. 45). Taken together, these two observations emphasize the point that to be consistently effective you will almost certainly need to use different approaches with different groups of pupils. You also will want to seek ways to improve your instructional skills.

The remainder of this chapter offers some suggestions you might follow to develop versatility and resourcefulness in teaching.

IMPROVING YOUR SKILLS AS A TEACHER

There are a number of ways you can strive to become a more effective teacher. You might ask for students' evaluations or suggestions, use observation schedules, constantly use and revise your personal Handbook, or systematically analyze your technique by referring to the section on Becoming a Better Teacher: Questions and Suggestions presented at the end of this chapter. Each of these will be discussed separately.

Student Evaluations and Suggestions

In many respects, students are in a better position to evaluate teachers than anyone else. They may not always be able to analyze *why* what a teacher does is effective or ineffective (even an experienced expert observer might have difficulty doing so), but they know, better than anyone else, whether they are responding and learning. Furthermore, students form their impressions after interacting with a teacher for hundreds or thousands of hours. Most principals or other adult observers may watch a teacher in action for only a few minutes at a time. It makes sense, therefore, to pay attention to and actively solicit opinions from students. As a matter of fact, it will be virtually impossible for you to ignore pupil reactions. Every minute that school is in session, you will receive student feedback in the form of attentiveness (or lack of it), facial expressions, restlessness, yawns, sleeping, disruptive behavior, and the like. If you become aware that a particular lesson arouses either a neutral or a negative reaction, you may feel obliged, in self-defense, to seek a better way to present the same material in the future. If you find that you seem to be spending much of your time disciplining pupils, you may be driven to find other ways to teach.

In addition to analyzing the minute-by-minute reactions of your pupils, you may find it helpful to request more formal feedback. After completing a unit, you might ask, "I'd like you to tell me what you liked and disliked about the way this unit was arranged and give me suggestions for improving it if I teach it again next year."

A more comprehensive and systematic approach is to distribute a questionnaire or evaluation form and ask students to record their reactions anonymously. You might use a published form or devise your own. In either case, a common format involves listing a series of statements and asking students to rate them on a 5-point scale. Some of the published forms use special answer sheets that make

FIGURE 15.1   The Descriptive Ranking Form for Teachers

(From Don J. Cosgrove, "Diagnostic Rating of Teacher Performance," *Journal of Educational Psychology*, 1959, 50, p. 202. Copyright 1959 by the American Psychological Association.)

This form consists of 10 sets of phrases which are descriptive of instructor performance. Each set is composed of four phrases. Please consider the instructor you have for this course. In each set of phrases, rank the phrases from 1 to 4 as they apply to your instructor. Give a rank of 1 to the phrase which most applies, and 4 to the phrase which least applies, using Ranks 2 and 3 for intermediate ranks. Every phrase must be ranked. There can be no equal ranks.

Set a ———— Always on time for class [3]
———— Pleasant in class [2]
———— Very sincere when talking with students [4]
———— Well-read [1]

Set b ———— Contagious enthusiasm for subject [4]
———— Did not fill up time with trivial material [3]
———— Gave everyone an equal chance [2]
———— Made clear what was expected of students [1]

Set c ———— Classes always orderly [3]
———— Enjoyed teaching class [4]
———— Friendliness did not seem forced [2]
———— Logical in thinking [1]

Set d ———— Encouraged creativeness [4]
———— Kept course material up to the minute [1]
———— Never deliberately forced own decisions on class [2]
———— Procedures well thought out [3]

Set e ———— Authority on own subject [1]
———— Friendly attitude toward students [4]
———— Marked tests very fairly [3]
———— Never criticized in a destructive way [2]

Set f ———— Good sense of humor [4]
———— Spaced assignments evenly [3]
———— Students never afraid to ask questions in class [2]
———— Well organized course [1]

Set g ———— Accepted students' viewpoints with open mind [2]
———— Increased students' vocabulary by own excellent usage [1]
———— Students always knew what was coming up next day [3]
———— Students willingly worked for teacher [4]

Set h ———— Always knew what he was doing [3]
———— Appreciated accomplishment [4]
———— Did not ridicule wrong answers [2]
———— Well informed in all related fields [1]

Set i ———— Always had class material ready [3]
———— Covered subject well [1]
———— Encouraged students to think out answers [4]
———— Rules and regulations fair [2]

Set j ———— Always managed to get things done on time [3]
———— Course had continuity [1]
———— Made material significant [4]
———— Understood problems of students [2]

it possible to tally the results electronically. One disadvantage of many rating-scale evaluation forms is that responses may not be very informative unless you can compare your ratings to those of colleagues. If you get an overall rating of 3.5 on "makes the subject matter interesting," for example, you wouldn't know whether you need to work on that aspect of your teaching until you discover that the average rating of other teachers of the same grade or subject was 4.2. Another disadvantage is that published evaluation forms may not be very helpful unless all other teachers use the same rating scale. Fortunately, this may be possible in school districts that use a standard scale to obtain evidence for use in making decisions about retention, tenure, and promotion.

Another disadvantage of many rating scales is indicated by the phrase *leniency problem*. Pupils tend to give most teachers somewhat above-average ratings on most traits. Although leniency may soothe a teacher's ego, wishy-washy responses do not provide the information needed to improve pedagogical effectiveness. To get around the leniency problem and to induce pupils to give more informative reactions, forced-choice ratings are often used. Figure 15.1 shows a forced-choice rating form, the Descriptive Ranking Form for Teachers, developed by Don J. Cosgrove (1959). This form is designed to let teachers know how pupils perceive their skill in four areas of performance: (1) knowledge and organization of subject matter, (2) adequacy of relations with students in class, (3) adequacy of plans and procedures in class, and (4) enthusiasm in working with students. If you decide to use this form, omit the numbers in brackets that follow each statement when you prepare copies for distribution to students. On your own copy of the form, you should write in those numbers and use them to prepare your score in each of the four categories listed above.

To calculate your index of effectiveness in each category of the Descriptive Ranking Form for Teachers, assign a score of 4 to the phrase in each group that is ranked 1, a score of 3 to the phrase marked 2, and so on. Then add together the scores for all phrases identified by the parenthetical number 1, and do the same for the other sets of phrases. The cluster of phrases that yields the highest score is perceived by your students to be your strongest area of teaching; the cluster that yields the lowest score is considered to be your weakest. A total of 30 points for all phrases indicated by the parenthetical number 1, for example, means that you ranked high in category 1 (knowledge and organization of subject matter). If, however, you get only 12 points for phrases identified by the parenthetical number 4, you will need to work harder at being enthusiastic when working with students.

Quite often a homemade form that covers specific points regarding your personal approach to teaching will provide useful information. You might ask a series of questions about specific points (Were there enough exams? Did you think too much homework was assigned?). Or you can ask pupils to list the three things they liked best, the three things they liked least, and what they would suggest you do to improve the way a particular unit is taught. When you ask students to respond to questions like these, not only do you usually get feedback about teaching techniques, but you also get ideas you might use to improve your teaching skill. (On a rating scale, if rated below average on an item such as "Examinations are too difficult," you may not know *why* you were rated low or what you might do to change things for the better.)

Observation Schedules

While your students can supply quite a bit of information that can help you improve your teaching, they cannot always tell you about technical flaws in your instructional technique. This is especially true with younger pupils, but even sophisticated graduate students in college may not recognize why certain teaching techniques are ineffective. Accordingly, you may wish to submit to a detailed analysis of your approach to teaching. Several observation schedules have been developed for this purpose. *The Flanders Interaction Analysis Categories* (Flanders, 1970) is the most widely used teacher behavior schedule, but more than one hundred others are described in the multivolume *Mirrors of Behavior* (1970), edited by Anita Simon and E. G. Boyer. As the title of the Flanders schedule indicates, it stresses verbal interactions between teacher and pupils. The following ten categories are listed on a record blank: accepts feelings, praises or encourages, uses student ideas, asks questions, lectures, gives directions, criticizes, pupil talk-response, pupil talk-initiation, and silence or confusion. A trained observer puts a check mark opposite one of these categories every three seconds during a period when teacher and pupils are interacting verbally. Once the observation is completed, it is a simple matter to tally checks and determine the percentage of time devoted to each activity. Then, if a teacher discovers that a substantial amount of time was spent in silence or confusion and that only a tiny fraction of interactions involved praise or encouragement, a deliberate effort can be made to change for the better.

Perhaps the biggest problem with such observational approaches is the need for a trained observer. But it would be possible to team up with another teacher and act as reciprocal observers if you feel that a detailed analysis of your teaching style would be helpful.

Using Your Handbook to Improve Your Teaching

In Chapter 1 the point was made that this book has been written to be used in three ways: (1) as a text for a course in educational psychology, (2) as a source of practical ideas on how to apply psychology to teaching, and (3) as a means for improving your teaching effectiveness. The opening chapter also pointed out two types of marginal notes: (1) Key Points, to be referred to in order to grasp the essence of a chapter and to prepare for exams, and (2) Handbook Headings, to be used in preparing for teaching and for perfecting instructional techniques. You have probably referred to the Key Points already. If you expect to engage in student teaching in the near future, you may now find it valuable to refer to the Handbook Headings and to examine Becoming a Better Teacher: Questions and Suggestions. These two features were designed to complement each other, but they can also be developed and used separately and independently.

Successful teachers constantly analyze how students respond to classroom activities and assignments and strive to improve their effectiveness as instructors. The preparation of a personal Handbook and use of the Becoming a Better Teacher: Questions and Suggestions, should help you master and constructively modify your teaching skills. (Bob Daemmrich/ Stock, Boston, Inc.)

Given the nature of coursework, it is probable that you have thus far been asked to think of this book as a text. In particular, your instructor may have asked you to concentrate on sections of the book that he or she felt were of greatest significance and/or that fit a particular sequence of courses in a teacher education program. Once your coursework is completed, however, you may wish to use this book—on your own—in two ways: (1) as the basis for developing a personal Handbook of teaching, and (2) to identify and compensate for weaknesses in instructional technique.

The Handbook Headings offer a framework for you to use in developing your own set of guidelines for instruction. Before or during student teaching, you are urged to develop your own ideas about how to apply the information and techniques described in this book. If you take the trouble to put together your own concise Handbook, custom-tailored to fit the grade level and subjects you expect to teach, you should feel reasonably well prepared when you first take charge of a class. After a few weeks or months of experience, you might begin to make a systematic effort to analyze and improve your teaching technique. The information provided in Becoming a Better Teacher: Questions and Suggestions is offered as a means for achieving this goal. As noted in the opening chapter, these sections are based on points made in the text opposite the Handbook Headings. They are designed to call your attention to specific aspects of your teaching technique and to stimulate ideas you might use to improve your instructional skills. To help you relate questions to appropriate sections of the text, each Handbook Heading printed in the margin is listed in Becoming a Better Teacher: Questions and Suggestions. Under each heading is a question you might ask yourself. The question format is used on the assumption that it is the most direct way to call attention to particular facets of instruction. Then at least one "answer" to the question is provided, written as if it were a specific suggestion you might make to yourself. These suggestions might be used in two ways: (1) as troubleshooting aids when you are confronted with a specific, identifiable problem and (2) as a basis for systematic-rotation evaluations. To put the latter procedure into effect, make it a habit during the first year of your teaching career to set aside at least a few moments at the end of each school day for examining the Becoming a Better Teacher questions for one chapter. If you feel that you might improve your teaching by concentrating on techniques highlighted by a particular question, plan a step-by-step campaign. The next day, peruse the questions for the next chapter, and so on. If you follow this procedure for a few weeks, you should systematically evaluate all aspects of teaching discussed in this book and also become thoroughly familiar with every section of your Handbook. Then, when you become aware of the need for improving some phase of instruction, you will know where to look for help, and you will have a good start toward devising your own step-by-step plan for solving a particular problem.

Suggestions for Developing a Personal Handbook

Perhaps the best way to begin creating your Handbook is to purchase a three-ring binder and a generous supply of lined paper. Then, as soon as possible after you complete this course (but definitely before you are scheduled to student teach), go through the chapters of this book and prepare your own personalized versions of the information and teaching suggestions that have been provided here. You might also examine other books for supplementary suggestions. (Titles of books that provide practical tips for teachers on a variety of topics will be noted at appropriate points in the following guidelines.)

Once you have a general outline, you might insert additional teaching ideas you remember having observed, ask acquaintances to do the same, and observe effective teachers to pick up some of their particular tricks of the trade. Finally, use your Handbook to organize ideas you pick up during methods courses. If you follow most of these suggestions, you should have a source book of ideas on how to handle many of the teaching problems you are likely to encounter when you first take charge of a classroom.

Here are some guidelines you might follow as you begin to develop your Handbook, arranged with references to each chapter of the text.

Chapter 2 Stage Theories of Development

Suggestions for making use of Erikson's description of psychosocial stages:

1. Under the heading "Stages of Psychosocial Development," describe the stages that relate to pupils of the age level you expect to teach (pp. 43–45).

2. If you expect to be teaching high school students, record brief definitions and comments on *identity, sex roles, occupational choice, psychosocial moratorium, negative identity,* and *identity statuses* (pp. 45–54). Record points about each of these concepts that you feel might be of value when the time comes to try to understand how and why adolescents behave as they do.

3. Examine the Suggestions for Teaching in Your Classroom: Applying Erikson's Theory on pages 55–57. Select points that relate to the pupils you expect to teach, and prepare your own summary. If you expect to teach preschool pupils, examine points opposite the Handbook Heading on page 55. For points that relate to elementary or secondary school students, look opposite the Handbook Headings on page 55.

4. If you expect to be teaching any junior or senior high school courses in which you will have opportunities to work with students on an individual basis, you might examine *Skill-Streaming the Adolescent: A Structured Learning Approach to Teaching Prosocial Skills* (1980) by A. P. Goldstein, R. P. Sprafkin, N. J. Gershaw, and R. Klein. Summarize the techniques they recommend.

Suggestions for making use of Piaget's description of stages of cognitive development:

1. List and write your own definition of the basic principles of Piaget's theory: *organization, scheme, assimilation, accommodation, equilibration* (pp. 58–61).

2. Describe the Piagetian stages for the pupils you expect to teach. In most cases you should describe at least *two* stages since it is unlikely that pupils at any grade level will exhibit characteristics of only one stage. (Refer to the descriptions on pages 61–68.)

3. Describe how you might use Vygotsky's zone of proximal development to aid students' cognitive development (pp. 69–70).

4. Examine Suggestions for Teaching in Your Classroom: Applying Piaget's Theory (pp. 71–73). Select points opposite the Handbook Heading for the appropriate grade level on page 72, and prepare your own summary. Leave room for additional points to be added later. If you will be teaching preschool or primary grade pupils, read *The Piaget Handbook for Teachers and Parents: Children in the Age of Discovery, Preschool–Third Grade* (1986) by Rosemary Peterson and Victoria Felton-Collins for additional suggestions. If you will be teaching elementary grade pupils, consult *Children's Thinking and Learning in the Elementary School* (1989) by Peter Langford, *Children's Thinking* (2d ed., 1991) by Robert S. Siegler, or *Piaget for the Classroom Teacher* (2d ed., 1980) by Barry Wadsworth.

Suggestions for encouraging moral development:

1. Prepare your own capsule summary of differences between the *morality of constraint* and the *morality of cooperation* (Table 2.1).

2. Prepare your own capsule summary of Kohlberg's stages of moral reasoning (Table 2.2).

3. Prepare your own capsule summary of Gilligan's analysis of the difference between male and female adolescent moral development (pp. 81–83).

4. Examine Suggestions for Teaching in Your Classroom: Encouraging Moral Development (p. 85). Select points opposite the Handbook Heading: Ways to Encourage Moral Development that you think might help you foster moral development in the students you expect to teach. For more detailed suggestions, consult *Promoting Moral Growth* (1979) by Richard Hersh, Diana Paolitto, and Joseph Reimer; *The Moral Child* (1988) by William Damon; or *Promoting Social and Moral Development in Young Children* (1986) by Carolyn Pope Edwards.

Chapter 3 Age-Level Characteristics

Go through the section of this chapter that describes characteristics of the pupils you expect to teach. Prepare your own list of characteristics and describe how you might allow for each. Pay particular attention to sections opposite Key Points and Handbook Headings.

For additional information on specific topics, you might examine the following books:

Preschool and primary grade teaching: *Teachers of Young Children* (3d ed., 1981) by Robert D. Hess and Doreen J. Croft

Handling differences of opinion, emotional outbursts, hostile behavior: *Teacher's Handbook of Special Learning Problems and How to Handle Them* (1977) by Muriel S. Karlin

Junior high and high school teaching: *Adolescent Stress* (1991), edited by Mary Ellen Colten; *Adolescents at Risk: Prevalence and Prevention* (1990) by Joy G. Dryfoos.

Chapter 4 Assessing Pupil Variability

1. Under the heading "Criteria for Evaluating Standardized Tests," record your own brief definitions of the following: *reliability, content validity, predictive validity, construct validity, norms* (pp. 148–152).

2. Under the heading "Types of Standardized Tests," describe the nature of each of the following: *achievement tests, diagnostic tests, aptitude tests, individual tests, competency tests* (pp. 152–154; see also the Mid-Chapter Review on pp. 170–172).

3. Under the headings "Types of Standardized Tests" and "Interpreting Standardized Test Scores" record brief descriptions of the following types of scores: *norm-referenced, criterion-referenced, raw score, percentile rank, z score, T score, stanine score* (pp. 152–159; see also the Mid-Chapter Review on pp. 170–172).

4. Under the heading "The Nature and Measurement of Intelligence," record a brief definition of *intelligence* and state ways in which you can use the results of intelligence tests to improve student achievement.

5. Examine the Suggestions for Teaching in Your Classroom: Using Standardized Tests (pp. 172–176), and prepare your own list of points to remember. Pay particular attention to the list of test-taking skills (p. 173) to explain to your students before they take standardized tests.

Chapter 5 Dealing with Pupil Variability

1. Record your own brief description of the provisions of Public Law 94-142 (pp. 188–189). Be sure to describe these provisions: *development of an individualized education program, least restrictive environment* (including a definition of *mainstreaming*), *due process, protection in evaluation procedures*.

2. List characteristics of mildly retarded students (pp. 201–202), and then outline teaching techniques summarized in the Suggestions for Teaching in Your Classroom: Instructing Students with Mild Retardation (pp. 202–206). Include points noted under these Handbook Headings:

   Helping Mildly Retarded Pupils Deal with Frustration

   Combating the Tendency to Communicate Low Expectations

   Giving Mildly Retarded Students Simple Assignments

   Using Overlearning with Mildly Retarded Students

   Giving Mildly Retarded Students Proof of Progress

3. List characteristics of pupils classified as learning disabled (pp. 207–209), and then outline the points summarized in the Suggestions for Teaching in Your Classroom: Instructing Pupils with Learning Disabilities (pp. 210–213). Be sure to note techniques under these Handbook Headings:

   Preparing Your Own Versions of IEPs

   Arranging the Classroom Environment to Facilitate Learning

4. List characteristics of emotionally disturbed students (pp. 213–216). Under the Handbook Heading: Activities and Materials That Encourage Cooperation (p. 217), note techniques for encouraging withdrawn students to interact with classmates.

5. Examine the Suggestions for Teaching in Your Classroom: Instructing Gifted and Talented Students on pages 226–230. Draw up your own list of guidelines, including points noted under these Handbook Headings:

Providing Horizontal and Vertical Enrichment

Individualized Study for the Gifted and Talented

Urging Gifted Students to Develop Creative Hobbies and Interests

Chapter 6 Understanding Cultural Diversity

1. If you expect to teach in a part of the country that contains students from one or more ethnic minority groups (such as African-American, Native American, Puerto Rican, and Asian-American), read about and take notes on the history, values, customs, and behavior patterns of each group.

2. Locate and visit a school that has a successful multicultural education program. Take note of both its positive and negative features. Indicate how you will implement the former and avoid the latter.

3. Reread the Suggestions for Teaching in Your Classroom: Instructing Disadvantaged Students on pages 247–252. Draw up your own list of guidelines, including points noted under the Handbook Heading: Using Productive Techniques of Teaching (p. 249).

4. Examine Suggestions for Teaching in Your Classroom: Promoting Multicultural Understanding (pp. 263–265). Draw up your own list of techniques for teaching students from diverse cultural backgrounds, including points noted under these Handbook Headings:

Ways to Promote Awareness of Contributions of Ethnic Minorities

Ways to Help Students Explore Conflicts Between Cultures.

Chapter 7 Devising and Using Objectives

1. Prepare your own capsule summary of the main headings of the taxonomies for the cognitive (pp. 279–281), affective (pp. 281–283), and psychomotor (pp. 283–284) domains.

2. Summarize Mager's suggestions for stating specific objectives (pp. 289–291).

3. Summarize Gronlund's suggestions for stating general objectives followed by lists of specific learning outcomes (pp. 291–292).

4. Print, type, or photocopy the lists of general objectives and specific outcome action verbs listed in Tables 7.1 (p. 293), 7.2 (p. 294), and 7.3 (p. 295).

5. Examine Suggestions for Teaching in Your Classroom: Using Instructional Objectives (pp. 303–314), and prepare your own list of procedures to follow in order to make effective use of instructional objectives.

Chapter 8 Behavioral Learning Theories

1. Write a brief description of each of these basic principles of operant conditioning: *positive reinforcement, negative reinforcement, punishment, time-out, extinction, generalization, discrimination* (pp. 328–332).

2. Describe how and why you might set up a learning situation according to each of these reinforcement schedules: *fixed interval, variable interval, fixed ratio, variable ratio* (pp. 333–334).

3. Describe how you would use each of the following techniques to modify student behavior: *shaping, token economy, contingency contracting, extinction, time-out, response cost* (pp. 340–343).

4. Outline the four basic processes of observational learning (pp. 347–349).

5. Examine Suggestions for Teaching in Your Classroom: Applying Behavioral Theories in the Classroom (pp. 353–366). Then use the following Handbook Headings to organize your own list of applications. Refer to the examples following most points for specific ideas and techniques, selecting those that are most appropriate for the grade level and subject(s) you expect to teach.

   Checking on Causes of Behavior

   Ways to Supply Specific and Immediate Feedback

   Ways to Supply Delayed Feedback

   Ways to Supply Different Types of Reinforcement

   Ways to Use Schedules of Reinforcement

   Describing Terminal Behavior

   Ways to Encourage Perseverance

   Ways to Use Behavior Modification to Maintain Control

6. Describe the nature and purpose of each of the following types of computer-assisted instruction programs: *drill and practice, tutorial, problem solving* (pp. 367–368).

7. Prepare a list of features commonly found in CAI programs that violate basic operant conditioning principles (p. 369). Prepare a second list that contains the features of a well-designed CAI program (pp. 370–371).

Chapter 9 Information Processing Theory

1. Write a brief description of each of the following structures: *sensory register* (p. 382), *short-term memory* (p. 384), *long-term memory* (p. 387).

2. Note factors that influence *recognition* and *attention* as well as ways that attending can be encouraged (pp. 382–384).

3. Describe how *maintenance rehearsal* (p. 384) differs from *elaborative rehearsal* (pp. 384–385).

4. Describe how *organization* (p. 385) and *meaningfulness* (p. 385–387) help people store information in long-term memory.

5. Explain how *schemata* in long-term memory influence learning and recall (pp. 387–390).

6. Write a brief description of *metacognition* (pp. 390–391) and explain its role in learning.

7. Prepare a list of *memory-directed tactics* and *comprehension-directed tactics* that you might help your students learn to use (p. 393–394).

8. Describe the components of a *learning strategy* and how you might help your students learn to formulate them (pp. 400–401).

9. Examine Suggestions for Teaching in Your Classroom: Helping Your Students Become Efficient Information Processors (pp. 405–416), and note procedures you might follow, including points relating to each of these Handbook Headings:

Techniques for Capturing Attention

Techniques for Maintaining Attention

Techniques for Increasing Attention Span

Ways to Use Chunking to Facilitate Learning

Organizing Information into Related Categories

Ways to Stress Meaningfulness

Way to Teach Memory Tactics

Ways to Teach Comprehension Tactics

Ways to Teach Learning Strategies

Chapter 10 Cognitive Learning Theories and Problem Solving

1. Briefly describe the significance of *structure* (p. 426), the *spiral curriculum* (p. 426), and *discovery* (pp. 426–428) in Bruner's thinking about learning and teaching.

2. List and record examples of the various techniques Bruner developed for use in presenting the MACOS curriculum (pp. 429–430).

3. Examine Suggestions for Teaching in Your Classroom: Using a Discovery/Constructivist Approach to Meaningful Learning (pp. 430–443), and prepare your own outline of ideas to try in your classroom. Include the following Handbook Headings in your own set of applications:

Ways to Arrange for Discovery to Take Place

Ways to Supervise Discovery Sessions

Techniques for Arranging Small-Group Discussions

4. Explain the relationship of *expository teaching* to *meaningful reception learning* (pp. 440–443).

5. Describe and provide an example of *well-structured problems* (p. 444), *ill-structured problems* (p. 444) and *issues* (p. 444).

6. List techniques you might use to improve students' skills on each of the following problem-solving steps (pp. 444–453):

Realize that a problem exists.

Understand the nature of the problem.

Compile relevant information.

Formulate and carry out a solution.

Evaluate the solution.

7. Describe the conditions that lead to *positive transfer* (p. 461) as well as those that lead to *negative transfer* (p. 461).

8. Describe the essence of *specific transfer, general transfer, low-road transfer,* and *high-road transfer* (pp. 462–465).

Chapter 11 Humanistic Approaches to Education

1. Briefly summarize the basic philosophies of education espoused by Maslow (p. 473), Rogers (pp. 474–475), and Combs (pp. 475–476).

2. Summarize the basic ideas presented by Gordon in *Teacher Effectiveness Training* (pp. 477–478), and note how you might determine problem ownership and use I-messages.

3. List techniques you might use to put into practice *invitational learning* as described by Purkey (pp. 478–480).

4. Describe the essence of the *values clarification* approach (pp. 481–483).

5. Refer to Suggestions for Teaching in Your Classroom: Using Humanistic Techniques on pages 492–501, and prepare your own outline of procedures to follow. Include notes relating to each of these Handbook Headings:

Ways to Give Pupils Choices

Using Self-Paced and Self-Selected Styles

Ways to Communicate Interest in Pupils as Individuals

Ways to Set Up Values Clarification Sessions

Chapter 12 Motivation

1. Write brief summaries of the *behavioral* and *social learning* views of motivation (pp. 511–512). Then note some possible disadvantages of overuse of behavioral techniques (pp. 512–514).

2. Write a brief summary of the *cognitive* view of motivation (pp. 514–515). Then note limitations of this approach to motivating students (p. 515).

3. Record your interpretation of Maslow's *hierarchy of needs* (pp. 516–517). Then note educational implications of Maslow's theory (pp. 517–519) and possible limitations of such interpretations (p. 519).

4. Note different ways that students may respond to success and failure (pp. 522–523).

5. Summarize findings regarding the impact of *competitive* and *cooperative* reward structures (pp. 524–528).

6. Summarize Brophy's argument about the significance of valuing learning for motivation (pp. 529–531).

7. Prepare your own version of the troubleshooting checklist on pages 531–533, or note the page numbers on that list so that you will be able to turn directly to that section of the text when you want to try to identify possible causes of lack of student interest in learning.

8. Examine Suggestions for Teaching in Your Classroom: Motivating Students to Learn (pp. 534–557). Use the following Handbook Headings to organize your own set of applications:

Ways to Make Learning Active

Ways to Promote Investigation

Ways to Make Learning Seem Adventurous

Ways to Make Learning Social

Ways to Make Learning Useful

Using Behavior Modification Techniques to Motivate

Ways to Arrange Short-Term Goals

Ways to Analyze Motivation Problems

Ways to Satisfy Physiological Needs

Ways to Satisfy Safety Needs

Ways to Satisfy Belonging Needs

Ways to Satisfy Esteem Needs

Ways to Encourage Self-Competition

Ways to Encourage Students to Set Their Own Objectives

Ways to Supply Positive Feedback

Ways to Permit Students to Direct Their Own Learning

Chapter 13 Measurement and Evaluation of Classroom Learning

1. Write your own definitions of *measurement* and *evaluation* (p. 564).

2. Describe the different types of *performance tests,* and explain the purpose for using each one (pp. 566–567).

3. Describe the purpose of *written tests* and the various types of items that can be used in written tests (pp. 567–568).

4. Prepare a list of the kinds of factors (such as attractiveness) that have been found to influence teacher reactions to pupil behavior and performance, referring to the conclusions of Brophy and Good, and Braun (pp. 570–571).

Then summarize guidelines to follow in efforts to minimize your own tendency to be influenced by such factors, using (if appropriate) the Handbook Heading: Ways to Minimize Subjectivity.

5. Examine Suggestions for Teaching in Your Classroom: Effective Measurement Techniques (pp. 572–594). Use the following Handbook Headings to draw up your own list of guidelines:

   Outlining Units of Study

   Being Considerate in Scheduling

   Using a Table of Specifications

   Guidelines for Writing Test Questions

   Using Different Types of Test Items

   Techniques for Evaluating Skills and Projects

   Preparing a Detailed Key

   Analyzing Test Items

6. Explain the rationale for using a *norm-referenced* approach to determining grades, and summarize the procedures for doing so (pp. 596–598).

7. Explain the rationale for using a *criterion-referenced* approach to determining grades, and summarize the procedures for doing so (p. 599).

8. Examine the suggestions for using a *mastery learning* approach (pp. 599–602). Write a brief description of how you might proceed if you decide to use this approach.

Chapter 14 Classroom Management

1. Draw up your own list of guidelines based on Kounin's *Discipline and Group Management in the Classrooms* summarized on pp. 622–627). Use the following Handbook Headings:

   Learning to Deal with Overlapping Situations

   Learning How to Maintain Momentum

   Ways to Keep the Whole Class Involved

2. Outline the characteristics of a well-managed classroom reported by University of Texas researchers (p. 627). Include points relating to this Handbook Heading: Planning How to Handle Routines.

3. Examine the section on Influence Techniques (pp. 637–643), the discussion of I-messages and the no-lose method (pp. 644–646), and the Suggestions for Teaching in Your Classroom: Handling Problem Behavior (pp. 648–651). Draw up your own list of classroom control techniques, using the following Handbook Headings:

   Signals to Use to Nip Trouble in the Bud

Ways to Supply Situational Assistance

Ways to Use Reality and Value Appraisal

Using I-Messages

Speculating About Problem Ownership

Trying the No-Lose Method

Analyzing Feelings After Dealing with Troublemakers

Being Prompt, Consistent, and Reasonable in Controlling the Class

Ways to Establish Rapport

Experimenting with Behavior Modification

4. Summarize the reasons given for the occurrence of school violence (pp. 653–655). Then make a list of suggestions for reducing school violence (pp. 655–657).

Becoming a Better Teacher: Questions and Suggestions

The purpose of the following lists of questions and suggestions is to make it possible for you to engage in a systematic attempt to improve your teaching effectiveness after you have actually embarked on your career in the classroom. The points noted in these pages are presented in the form of questions and suggestions so that you can analyze your teaching style on a point-by-point basis. They are organized with reference to the Handbook Headings printed in the margins, the same headings that you have been urged to use as the basis for sections of your Handbook. The reasoning behind this dual use of Handbook Headings is that if you become aware of a weakness in your teaching technique as you examine the questions that follow, you will know exactly where to turn for specific ideas about how to overcome it (provided you have prepared a comprehensive personal Handbook).

When you first begin to teach, it is recommended that you spend a few minutes at the end of each school day referring to these questions and suggestions. If you follow a procedure of systematically working through the entire list, you will not only analyze many facets of your teaching style; you will also become familiar with where you can find leads to help you when you later encounter various kinds of teaching problems.

In some of the sections that follow, observational or other exercises are described. You might use these exercises to obtain information about certain types of pupil behavior or to plan group and individual instructional activities. If you are asked to assign grades for "citizenship" or "work habits," you might use the observational techniques described to make your evaluations as systematic and objective as possible.

Chapter 2 Stage Theories of Development

Am I providing plenty of opportunities for younger pupils to develop a sense of autonomy? What else can I do to foster independence? Am I doing my best to minimize the emergence of feelings of doubt or shame? Suggestion: Check on how often I give children ample time to complete something on their own, how often I finish a task *for* a child.

With older pupils, am I making it possible for feelings of initiative and accomplishment to emerge? Do I make pupils feel guilty by imposing unnecessary restrictions or regulations? Suggestion: Keep a record of how much time I spend directing activities and how much time I permit pupils to engage in self-selected activities.

Am I arranging learning experiences so that pupils can complete assignments successfully and in such a way that they acquire feelings of genuine accomplishment? What can I do to minimize feelings of inferiority on the part of those who don't do as well as others? Suggestion: Arrange learning situations so that pupils compete against themselves and frequently experience a sense of successful achievement. Use mastery learning techniques described in Chapter 13.

What can I do to foster the development of a sense of identity? Do I take enough personal interest in individual students so that they feel they are being recognized as individuals? Suggestion: Keep a record of the number of times I recognize—say hello to, call on, smile at, talk with—each student in my classes. If I discover I have ignored some students, make it a point to address them by name and comment favorably on their work.

Is there anything I can do in the courses I teach to help students begin to think about occupational choice? Can I provide specific job skills, or should I concentrate on helping pupils get ready for college, not only by learning subject matter but by becoming skilled students? Suggestion: Make a list of job skills—academic *and* nonacademic—that I can teach in my classes.

Is it appropriate in the courses I teach to encourage analysis of sex roles so that each individual can develop a personal philosophy of how to deal with sex differences? Suggestion: Check to see if it will be appropriate to set up a discussion of male and female attitudes and achievement in the field of study I teach.

Should I explain the concept of *psychosocial moratorium* to students and point out that there is no reason to panic if they are not positive about occupational choice by the time they graduate? Suggestion: Point out that some of the famous people in almost any field of endeavor floundered around before they settled on that particular career.

How can I be tolerant of students who have chosen a negative identity? What can I do to avoid confirming a student's negative identity by reacting too harshly to impertinent or disruptive behavior? If I really have to put down a trouble-maker, do I try to give him or her a chance to do something praiseworthy immediately afterward? Suggestion: Keep a record of what I say and whom I say it to when I really criticize students. Then write out some guidelines for doing a more effective, positive job of handling the next incident involving a disruptive student. (Check Chapter 14 for ideas.)

Ways to Apply Piaget's Theory (Preschool and Elementary Grades)

Am I remaining aware of the fact that many of my pupils may be thinking in preoperational terms—that is, that they tend to think of only one quality at a time and are incapable of mentally reversing actions? What can I do to arrange learning experiences that stress only one thing at a time and also feature physical manipulation of objects rather than mental manipulation of symbols? Suggestion: Ask veteran teachers about teaching materials and techniques that stress manipulation.

What can I do to set up learning experiences so that pupils can learn through their own activities and also explain things to each other? Suggestion: Next week, set up some learning centers (tables with books, objects, and instructional materials in various areas of study and interest), and invite pupils to make and share discoveries.

How can I avoid having students acquire merely verbal learning (that is, memorizing statements that they do not really understand)? What can I do to encourage students to concentrate on concepts and ideas they thoroughly comprehend? Suggestion: Give pupils frequent opportunities to explain ideas in their own way.

Should I ask individual pupils to carry out some of the Piaget experiments so that I can estimate if they are thinking at the preoperational level and also develop insight into how young children think? Suggestion: Pick out appropriate Piaget experiments that are described in Resources for Further Investigation (pp. 86–92), and obtain and prepare the necessary materials so that I will be equipped to evaluate how my students think.

When confronted by a tattletale or when discussing classroom rules, do I keep in mind that pupils of this age are moral realists and that they will need separate rules for different situations and tend to concentrate on consequences rather than intentions? Suggestion: If students get needlessly upset over minor rule infractions, point out that sometimes it is better to change the rules slightly; then go on to another topic.

Ways to Apply Piaget's Theory (Secondary Grades)

What can I do to allow for the fact that most pupils shift from concrete to formal thinking around the sixth grade or so and that they will sometimes think one way, sometimes the other? Should I use some of Piaget's experiments or class exercises to estimate how many pupils are capable of formal thinking? Suggestion: Pick out appropriate Piaget experiments that are described in Resources for Further Investigation (pp. 86–92), and obtain and prepare the necessary materials so that I will be equipped to evaluate how my students think.

When students show that they are capable of formal thought, how can I teach problem-solving skills? Suggestion: Make a list of promising ways to teach problem solving after examining the section on that topic in Chapter 10, pages 443–453.

Should I avoid presenting far-out hypothetical situations in order to hold down the tendency for inexperienced formal thinkers to concentrate more on possibilities than realities? How can I encourage novice theorists to take realities into account? Suggestion: When selecting discussion topics, choose those that require students to deal with actual conditions and realistic problems, and avoid those that more or less *force* far-out theorizing.

Ways to Encourage Moral Development

Am I taking into account differences between the moral thinking of younger and older pupils? Suggestion: Refer to Tables 2.1 and 2.2 on pages 62 and 75 of the text, or consult my own Handbook versions of those tables. Think about the kind of moral reasoning likely to be used by the pupils I teach.

Am I taking into account differences between the moral thinking of male and female adolescents? Suggestion: Review Gilligan's analysis of adolescent moral development, and incorporate issues of interpersonal understanding and caring into classroom exercises and discussions of morality.

Is it possible and appropriate for me—in the next few days—to introduce a classroom discussion of some aspect of morality? Suggestion: Refer to the techniques for arranging such discussions on page 85 of the text.

Chapter 3 Age-Level Characteristics

Preschool and Kindergarten

Active Games

What games and exercises can I use to permit pupils to be active in reasonably controlled ways? Suggestion: Ask veteran teachers for energetic but safe game ideas.

Riot-Stopping Signals and Activities

What signals can I use to gain immediate attention, even when the noise and activity level is excessively high? What activities and games can I use to calm down pupils when they begin to get carried away? Suggestions: Pick out some piano chords to use as an "Attention!" signal. Select two or three calming activities to use.

Allowing for Large-Muscle Control

Am I requiring pupils to spend too much time working at finicky activities? Are the pencils, crayons, brushes, and tools we have in the classroom large enough, or do pupils seem to have difficulty manipulating them? Suggestion: Make an inventory of objects that are held in the hand, and check to see if some of them seem hard for children to manipulate.

How Much Control Is Necessary?

Am I exerting too much control over my pupils? If I keep insisting on quiet play, am I doing it primarily for my own convenience? Should I stipulate that once a child gets out some blocks, finger paints, or the equivalent, he or she must play with these materials for at least a specified period of time? How can I help children become conscientious about cleaning up after they have engaged in activities that involve equipment? Suggestion: Keep a record of the amount of time pupils spend engaging in particular self-selected activities, and note what they do when they switch from one activity to another.

Suggested Form for Activities Record Sheet

Activity	Pupil	Date and Time	Termination Behavior
Easel painting	Mary	4/9/93 9:35–9:45	Put messy brushes on easel tray and went over to join Nancy in doll corner.

Encouraging Girls to Achieve, Boys to Be Sensitive

Are there books in our classroom library that depict girls or older females as weak and submissive and destined to become only housewives? If so, should I dispose of them? Are there plenty of books that depict females engaging in a wide variety of careers? If girls in the class persist in playing with dolls, should I try to encourage them to engage in other activities? Suggestion: Carry out a time-sampling study to determine the proportion of girls and boys who engage in sex-stereotyped activities, such as girls playing with dolls. (Use the time-sampling form outlined above.)

Helping Pupils Understand Anger

The last time a pupil became angry about something and hit someone, or the like, did I simply intervene and punish, or did I try to help the child understand the behavior? Should I use Ginott's technique of taking the child aside and asking questions intended to help him or her realize why the angry outburst occurred and, if possible, suggesting less destructive ways of letting off steam? Suggestion: Make a resolution to try Ginott's technique the next time I deal with an angry child.

Ways to Avoid Playing Favorites

Am I reacting more positively to some pupils than to others and inadvertently causing jealousy and resentment? Do I respond more favorably to attractive, obedient students who show that they like me and less favorably to unattractive, troublemaking, or indifferent pupils? What can I do to be more positive toward pupils I find difficult to like? Should I make a systematic effort to spread my smiles and praise around more equitably so that all pupils get approximately the same number of positive reactions? Suggestion: Keep a record of the number of times I respond positively to each child in the class. If some children don't have a check mark opposite their names after one week, make sure they do by the end of the next week.

Handling Sharing

Do all pupils get to participate in sharing? If not, how can I encourage shy children to gain some experience talking in front of others? Am I prepared in case someone starts to share the wrong things? Suggestion: Keep a record of sharing participation—who speaks up, what they say, how long they talk, how confident they are.

Suggested Form for Sharing Record Sheet

Name	Date	Topic	Duration	Attitude and Manner	Notes
Jane	10/14	Kittens	30 seconds	Spoke so softly it was difficult to hear what she had to say. Looked at floor whole time.	Encourage her talk more in small-group situations.

Encouraging Competence

Am I using techniques likely to lead my pupils to develop feelings of competence and self-confidence? How often and how successfully do I

Interact with individual pupils?

Show interest in what children say and do?

Permit and encourage independence?

Urge pupils to strive for more mature and skilled ways of doing things?

Establish firm and consistent limits?

Explain why restrictions are necessary?

Show pupils that their achievements are admired and appreciated?

Communicate sincere affection?

Serve as a model of competence?

Suggestion: List these points on a sheet of paper, and try to keep a tally of the number of times I behave in the way described. Then concentrate on one or two points, and make a deliberate effort to do a better job using that type of behavior.

Suggested Form for Analyzing Effectiveness in Encouraging Competence

Individual Interaction			
Name	**Date**	**Time**	**Nature of Interaction**
Jimmy	11/16	2 min.	Noticed Jimmy was standing in center of room sucking his thumb. Asked him if he had looked at any new books. Took him over to book corner and helped him pick out a book. Asked him to tell me about it later.

(Notes of this type could be jotted down immediately after interactions of various kinds. Similar records could be kept for other activities likely to encourage competence.)

Primary Grades

Building Activity into Classwork

Am I forcing students to sit still for too long? What can I do to give pupils legitimate reasons for moving around as they learn? Suggestion: Keep a record of the amount of "seat time" pupils have to put in before they are given the chance to move around.

Safe but Strenuous Games

Am I encouraging pupils to engage in safe but strenuous games during recess? When I am on playground duty, do I remain alert for reckless play? Have I found out the procedure to follow if a child is injured? Suggestion: Keep a time-sampling record of recess activities.

Using Sociometric Techniques

Should I use sociometric techniques to become more aware of isolates? Should I try to help isolates develop skill and confidence in social situations by pairing them with popular children? Suggestion: Make lists of children *I* think are popular and those I think are isolates. Then ask children, individually, to tell me who they like best, record their choices on a target diagram, and compare the sociometric responses to my predictions.

Enjoyable Team Games

At recess time, do students engage in frequent arguments about rules? If so, what team games might be used to arouse interest but minimize quarrels? Should I ask pupils for their favorite games or consult books describing team games of various kinds? Should I find out what teachers of other grades do during recess in order to avoid duplication of recess activities? Suggestion: Ask the class to suggest games they would like to play.

Handling Feuds and Fights

Am I alert for the possibility of feuds in the classroom? If I discover that some pupils seem to delight in antagonizing each other, what can I do to effect a truce? Have I thought about how to handle an honest-to-goodness fight? Suggestion: Keep a record of arguments and fights. If some pupils get into an excessive number of altercations, try to persuade them to find other ways to let off steam.

Avoiding Sarcasm and Extreme Criticism

Do I tend to use sarcasm with pupils who may take what I say too literally? Have I recently been excessively critical of individual pupils or the entire class? Have I ever ridiculed or publicly humiliated a pupil? If so, what can I do to prevent myself from engaging in such activities in the future? Suggestion: At the end of each day, analyze any extreme or critical statements I have made. (If I can't remember all critical remarks, make it a policy to write them down.) Ask myself if my anger was justified. Try to remember how the victim (or victims) reacted.

Spreading Around Responsibilities

Do I use a fair rotation scheme so that all pupils—not just favorites—get a chance to handle enjoyable responsibilities? Do I give pupils enough chances to help out? What other classroom responsibilities can I add to those already assigned?

Suggestion: Ask the class to suggest ways to spread around enjoyable responsibilities. Keep a Responsibility Record to make sure every pupil gets a fair share of the most popular responsibilities.

Ways to Handle Wrong Answers

Have I used an effective technique recently for handling hopelessly wrong answers? If not, what should I say the next time this occurs? Suggestion: Ask veteran teachers how they handle wrong answers.

Elementary Grades

Helping Pupils Adjust to the Growth Spurt

Do any pupils seem to be upset about the timing of the growth spurt—fast-maturing girls or slow-maturing boys in particular? Is there anything I can do to help them adjust (for example, explain about the spurt, point out that things will eventually even out, urge them to engage in activities that do not depend on size or strength)? Suggestion: Pick out the three most mature and least mature girls and boys, and check to see if they seem bothered by their atypicality.

Encouraging Creative Expression

Do I give my pupils chances to engage in art and craft activities and to display their work? How can I encourage pupils to work at original craft and art projects? Are there ways I can encourage students to sing, act, dance, or play an instrument if they want to do so before an audience? Suggestion: Consider setting up a Friday afternoon amateur hour.

Ways to Promote Social Sensitivity

Are there certain pupils who seem to lack social skills to the point that they offend others? Suggestion: Privately, and as subtly as possible, talk to such pupils about how what they do influences the reactions of others. Urge them to make an effort to take into account the feelings of others.

Encouraging Participation in Rule Making

Have I given the pupils in my classes opportunities to participate in the formulation of class rules? Suggestion: Invite students to offer their ideas on class rules, but set up the discussion so that concrete thinking and moral realism are controlled. That is, don't ask them to supply *all* of the rules, and don't ask them to determine how rule violators should be punished.

Encouraging Girls to Excel in Math and Science

Am I treating girls as if they are not capable of mastering math and science? Is there anything I can do to encourage girls to consider a career that is based on math or science? Suggestion: Complete a list of women who have become prominent in math or science-based careers, and emphasize the employment opportunities that exist for women who are interested in these areas.

Allowing for Differences in Cognitive Style

What can I do to allow for differences in cognitive style? Suggestion: Follow the suggestions made by Robert J. Sternberg (pp. 119–122).

Junior High

Helping Early and Late Maturers Cope

Have I paid any attention to the behavior of late-maturing boys and early-maturing girls? Suggestion: Make it a point to pick out the least mature boys and most mature girls in the class. Observe them to determine if they seem to exhibit the sorts of behavior reported in Table 3.7, page 123. If late-maturing boys or early-maturing girls seem bothered, try to give them opportunities to gain status and self-confidence by succeeding in schoolwork or by taking on classroom responsibilities.

Ways to Reduce Vandalism

Is vandalism a problem in our school? Suggestion: Use the techniques that Rutter found to be associated with lower levels of vandalism. Show students that I appreciate them, make my room as comfortable as possible, permit students to participate in making decisions, emphasize academic achievement, serve as a model to be imitated, function as an efficient class manager.

High School

Helping Students Overcome Depression

Do some of the pupils in my classes seem extremely depressed most of the time? Suggestion: Make it a point to show such pupils that I care about them. Use teaching techniques to encourage them to work toward—and achieve—a series of personal, short-term goals.

Chapter 4 Assessing Pupil Variability

Using Standardized Tests

Am I going to need to administer any standardized tests to my students during this report period? Suggestion: Find out if any tests are scheduled. A few days before any test is to be given, review Suggestions for Teaching in Your Classroom: Using Standardized Tests on pp. 172–176. Review those Suggestions once again before looking over test profiles and discussing scores with students.

Explaining Test-Taking Skills

Is a standardized test scheduled to be given in the near future? Suggestion: The day before the test is scheduled, explain test-taking skills to the class by covering the points noted on page 173.

Interpreting Test Scores

Do I understand my students' test scores well enough to avoid misinterpreting and misusing them? Suggestion: Review the user's manual of the test your students took, as well as a basic text on standardized testing, and compare each student's score with the work he or she has done in class over a period of several weeks.

Chapter 5 Dealing with Pupil Variability

Helping Mildly Retarded Pupils Deal with Frustration

Do I pay enough attention to the kinds of frustrations faced by mildly retarded pupils? Suggestion: Make it a point to observe how mildly retarded children in class react when instructional activities tend to call attention to differences in learning ability. If the poorest learners in the group seem disappointed or upset, try to figure out ways to help them cope with inability to do schoolwork as easily as others.

Combating the Tendency to Communicate Low Expectations

Do I tend to communicate the impression that mildly retarded students are not really capable of learning? Suggestion: Examine the list of tendencies and antidotes included under point 2 on page 203. If I recognize that I tend to react in some of the ways listed as tendencies, use the antidote suggested to combat that tendency.

Giving Mildly Retarded Students Simple Assignments

When I assign class work, do I take into account that mildly retarded pupils cannot cope with complex tasks? Suggestion: Prepare some cards that outline simple tasks that can be completed quickly, and ask children with retardation to work on such assignments when more capable students are involved with more complex tasks.

Using Overlearning with Mildly Retarded Students

Am I remaining aware that mildly retarded students may need to go over material many times in order to master it? Suggestion: Set up individual or small-group study sessions to expose mildly retarded pupils repeatedly to basic material. Try to introduce some variety into such drill sessions, but remember that pupils should be aware that they are learning the same material, even if it is presented in different ways.

Giving Mildly Retarded Students Proof of Progress

Have I set up lessons in such a way that mildly retarded students will know that they have made at least some progress? Suggestion: Develop a chart or personal learning diary so that students can record tangible indications of progress as they complete assignments.

Preparing Your Own Versions of IEPs

Do any of my students need special kinds of instruction, even though they do not qualify as handicapped under PL 94-142? Suggestion: With the cooperation of each student involved, try preparing an individualized education program by noting objectives, describing teaching practices and assignments, and listing criteria for determining achievement.

Arranging the Classroom Environment to Facilitate Learning

Do some of my students seem to have a particularly difficult time getting to work or persevering once they get started? Suggestion: Refer to the suggestions on pages 212–213 for arranging the classroom environment so that distractions are minimized.

Activities and Materials That Encourage Cooperation

Do any of my students keep to themselves even though classmates try to interact with them? Suggestion: Instead of lecturing or guiding a discussion, use simulations and games that require cooperation among participants.

Getting Students to Initiate Interaction with a Withdrawn Child

Am I too busy to help withdrawn students become more outgoing? Suggestion: Have a high-achieving, outgoing student tutor a withdrawn student in a subject that gives the withdrawn student difficulty.

Providing Horizontal and Vertical Enrichment

Have I been doing an effective job of supplying both horizontal and vertical enrichment? Suggestion: In drawing up lesson plans, write down some horizontal and vertical enrichment ideas to use with pupils who finish assignments faster than others.

Individualized Study for the Gifted and Talented

Am I doing a conscientious job of planning individualized study projects for gifted and talented learners? Suggestion: The next time I ask students to work on a project, explain the contract approach, and invite gifted and talented learners (in particular) to discuss independent learning with me individually.

Urging Gifted Students to Develop Creative Hobbies and Interests

Am I doing anything to encourage gifted and talented students who have extra study time on their hands to develop hobbies or interests in creative ways? Suggestions: Pick out pupils who always seem to finish assignments ahead of time or who have exceptional abilities in some area of interest. Urge them to convert a hobby or interest into a specialized field of investigation. At the elementary level, urge pupils to really get involved with a hobby. At the secondary level, encourage pupils to prepare projects for competitions of various kinds.

Chapter 6 Understanding Cultural Diversity

Using Productive Techniques of Teaching

Am I using teaching techniques with disadvantaged pupils that have been found to be productive? Suggestion: Examine the lists of most and least productive teaching techniques on page 249. Make a systematic effort to use productive techniques, and avoid those that do not seem to be effective.

Ways to Promote Awareness of Contributions of Ethnic Minorities

Do my students seem to be poorly informed about the contributions made to society by different ethnic groups? Suggestion: Implement the suggestions on page 263 for increasing awareness of the contributions of ethnic minorities.

Ways to Help Students Explore Conflicts Between Cultures

Are my students puzzled and dismayed by conflicts among such ethnic groups as African-Americans, Korean-Americans, Jewish-Americans, Native Americans, and Hispanic-Americans? Suggestion: Have students prepare and present reports on the history, values, customs, and behavior patterns of each group. Then use this information in an all-class discussion to explain why such conflicts occur, whether they are productive, and how destructive conflicts can be avoided in the future.

Chapter 7 Devising and Using Objectives

Ways to Use Instructional Objectives

Am I making effective use of instructional objectives? Suggestion: When planning teaching units, look over Mager's suggestions for stating specific objectives and Gronlund's ideas on stating general objectives with specific learning outcomes. Then figure out the best way to state instructional objectives for each unit.

Using the Taxonomy of Cognitive Objectives

Have I consulted the Taxonomy of Educational Objectives: Cognitive Domain when drawing up lesson plans? Suggestion: The next time I plan a unit, refer to the headings and questions listed in the abridged version of the taxonomy for the cognitive domain presented on pages 279–281. Make an attempt to list the kinds of things I would like students to learn, using the headings of the taxonomy to organize them. Also, check the list of categories and specific-outcome verbs in Table 7.1, page 293.

Using the Taxonomy of Affective Objectives	Am I making a systematic approach to identify affective objectives? Suggestion: Look over the Taxonomy of Educational Objectives: Affective Domain (pp. 281–283), and list some of the habits and attitudes I should try to foster. Then describe specific ways I might encourage students to achieve those affective objectives. Also, check the list of categories and specific outcome verbs in Table 7.2, page 294.
Using the Taxonomy of Psychomotor Objectives	Am I being systematic about teaching psychomotor skills? Suggestion: Look over the Taxonomy of Educational Objectives: Psychomotor Domain (pp. 283–284), and list some of the psychomotor skills I should try to foster. Also, check the list of categories and specific outcome verbs in Table 7.3, page 295.

Chapter 8 Behavioral Learning Theories

Checking on Causes of Behavior	Did I do anything today that shaped undesirable forms of student behavior? Suggestion: The next time the class is listless or uncooperative or the next time a student is rebellious, analyze what I said and did before and after I noticed the behavior to try to determine if I inadvertently shaped it. If it appears that I *did* cause problems for myself, resolve to avoid making the same mistake again.
Ways to Supply Specific and Immediate Feedback	The last time I asked the class to learn factual material, did I supply specific and immediate feedback? Suggestion: The next time I plan a lesson that requires students to supply many right answers, make it a point to arrange things so that feedback is frequent, specific, and immediate.
Ways to Supply Delayed Feedback	Am I taking into account that with meaningful material it may be preferable to supply delayed feedback? Suggestion: The next time I ask students to wrestle with "thought" questions, give them a chance to reason out, revise, and augment their answers before giving feedback.
Ways to Use Schedules of Reinforcement	Am I overusing certain types of reinforcement, thereby causing them to become ineffective? Suggestion: Make a list of dozens of different ways I can supply reinforcement. Then try to recall at the end of the day which ones I used and did not use in an effort to become a versatile rather than a mechanical reinforcer.
Describing Terminal Behavior	Am I being systematic enough about describing precisely what students should achieve when they complete an assignment or unit? Suggestion: The next time I draw up lesson plans, describe the terminal behavior and figure out what students will need to know or do in order to achieve it.
Ways to Encourage Perseverance	Am I taking advantage of the Premack principle (Grandma's rule)? Suggestion: Invite students to draw up their own reward menus, and then let them reinforce themselves after they have completed tedious tasks or tough assignments.
	Is it feasible and appropriate for me to use learning contracts? Suggestion: During the next report period or when we start a new unit, explain the contract

system, and ask if any students would like to work on individual projects instead of carrying out standard assignments.

Ways to Use Behavior Modification to Maintain Control

Can I do a more effective job of controlling the class if I use behavior modification techniques? Suggestion: Pick out a common type of discipline problem (for example, two students scuffling), and plan how to handle it using behavior modification techniques. Then the next time that kind of trouble occurs, try out the planned techniques, and make any adjustments that seem necessary.

Chapter 9 Information Processing Theory

Techniques for Capturing Attention

Do I make sure I have everyone's attention before I present a lesson? Do I use innovative ways to present something new? Suggestion: Experiment with attention-getting techniques such as those described on pages 406–407. Spend a few moments when getting ready to present something new by trying to come up with a distinctive grabber.

Techniques for Maintaining Attention

Am I able to maintain everyone's attention once I get it? Suggestion: Use a variety of teaching methods and materials—flash cards, board work, student teams, class projects, problems that require unusual forms of thinking—to keep interest and attention at high levels.

Techniques for Increasing Attention Span

Can my students learn to increase their attention spans? Suggestions: Experiment with games such as those described on page 408. Play two taped messages simultaneously and ask the students to listen to one while ignoring the other. Then see how well they can answer factual questions about the message they were supposed to be listening to.

Ways to Use Chunking to Facilitate Learning

Am I presenting hard-to-learn material in small enough chunks and in study periods of appropriate duration? Suggestion: Examine hard-to-learn material to see if it can be divided into chunks. Set up distributed study periods so that students can learn material in bite-size chunks.

Organizing Information into Related Categories

Are there sets of information my students need to learn that can be grouped into related categories? Suggestion: Examine text chapters and lesson plans, and look for ways to organize material that needs to be memorized into groups so that one item leads to an association with other items.

Ways to Stress Meaningfulness

Are my students searching for meaning as they learn, or do they seem to resort to rote memorization? Suggestion: Give a brief explanation of elaborative rehearsal, and present students with a planned exercise so that they get practice elaborating on new information by relating it to what they already know. Then have students tell each other how they searched for meaningful associations, and then urge them to use the same technique on their own.

Ways to Teach Memory Tactics

Do my students have difficulty recalling important information for discussions, oral presentations, and tests? Suggestions: Schedule a series of sessions on how to memorize. Explain how experts use memory aids, and give an example of each of the mnemonic devices listed in my Handbook. Whenever possible, supply mnemonics to help students learn. Ask students to develop mnemonics on their own, and ask them to share these with the rest of the class.

Ways to Teach Comprehension Tactics

Do my students have difficulty understanding the meaning of what they read or of what I present in class? Suggestions: Schedule a series of sessions on how to study. Explain the purpose and mechanics of summarizing, self-questioning, and notetaking (see pp. 413–414). Provide opportunities for students to practice these skills on material they have been assigned to read. Give corrective feedback as needed. Also consider preparing graphic displays of ideas like the concept maps in the Study Guide that accompanies this text.

Ways to Teach Learning Strategies

Are my students likely to benefit from the use of learning strategies? Suggestion: Read the description of learning strategies on pages 400–401. If it seems likely that my students will be able to formulate a strategy as described or a variation of it, explain the basic procedures and have them give it a try. After they have experimented with the strategy, ask them to discuss how it worked and how it might be improved.

Chapter 10 Cognitive Learning Theories and Problem Solving

Ways to Arrange for Discovery to Take Place

When I set up a discovery session, do I arrange the situation so that it helps students gain insight? Suggestion: The next time I plan a discovery session, think about how to present background information, or otherwise arrange things so that students are likely to grasp new relationships.

Ways to Supervise Discovery Sessions

Am I doing an effective job supervising all-class discussions? Suggestion: Make up a checklist of steps to follow in supervising discovery sessions that involve the entire class. Include such things as how to arrange desks and chairs, what sorts of questions to ask, a reminder to wait at least three seconds for students to respond, phrases to use when probing for more complete or revealing answers, and a strategy for calling on students so that everyone remains alert but no one feels threatened or ignored.

Techniques for Arranging Small-Group Discussion

Am I doing an effective job arranging small-group discussions? Suggestion: Make up a checklist of steps to follow in setting up and supervising small-group discussions. Include ideas on how to organize the groups, how to select a moderator and recorder, what to do while the groups interact, and guidelines for when to intervene.

Chapter 11 Humanistic Approaches to Education

Ways to Give Pupils
Choices

Am I giving my students plenty of opportunities to participate in making deci-sions and the freedom to choose among alternatives? Suggestion: Try out the ten-step procedure recommended by Howe and Howe for permitting pupils to participate in planning a teaching unit.

Using Self-Paced and
Self-Selected Styles

Should I introduce self-direction by first using self-paced and then self-selected styles of learning? Suggestion: Set up a unit in such a way that students can work at their own pace. Then set up a unit whereby students can choose from a variety of topics (perhaps presented on activity cards). If the activity cards work out, look for additional activities in teachers' journals. Also ask pupils to make up activities to add to an "Independent Project File."

Ways to Help Students
Develop Positive Feel-ings About Themselves

Have I recently used any techniques designed to encourage students to feel good about themselves? Suggestion: Try out a values clarification strategy that encour-ages pupils to describe things they have done that they are proud of.

Ways to Set Up Values
Clarification Sessions

Should I use any values clarification strategies during the next two weeks? Suggestion: Read the section on values clarification in Chapter 11 and/or one of the recommended books consisting of V.C. strategies, and pick out at least one to try out next week.

Chapter 12 Motivation

Ways to Make Learning
Active

Am I giving my students enough chances to be active as they learn? Suggestion: Examine the examples of active learning on page 536, and plan ways to use one or more of such techniques during the next few days.

Ways to Promote Inves-tigation

Are there ways that I can give my students greater opportunities to *investigate?* Suggestions: Consider the possibility of setting up investigation centers in the room. Take the entire class to the library and have them select books in an area of interest. Ask the class to suggest possible field trips or guest lecturers.

Ways to Make Learning
Seem Adventurous

Are there ways that I can legitimately and effectively use some "show biz" tech-niques in my classroom? Suggestions: As I plan each new unit, think about dramatic or unexpected ways to introduce it. Examine the techniques devised by Cullum (pp. 537–539) to see if identical or similar activities might fit into lesson plans.

Ways to Make Learning
Social

Am I giving my students opportunities to engage in social interaction as they learn? Suggestions: Have students team up and study for exams or prepare reports. Consider the use of role playing or simulation games.

Ways to Make Learning
Useful

Am I making sure that my students are aware that what they are learning is useful or potentially useful? Suggestions: Frequently point out how what is being learned can be used. Devise class exercises that demonstrate the potential value of what is being learned.

Using Behavior Modification Techniques to Motivate

Am I making use of behavior modification techniques to help students stick with material that is not intrinsically interesting? Suggestions: Consider setting up a series of tasks so that students are aware of their progress. Supply positive reinforcement in the form of verbal and written comments. Encourage students to use behavior modification techniques on themselves by following procedures similar to those described on pages 540–541.

Ways to Arrange Short-term Goals

Am I expecting my students to work toward remote goals? Suggestion: Try developing the equivalent of a goal card, or use some variation of contingency contracting.

Ways to Analyze Motivation Problems

Am I being systematic about analyzing motivation problems? Suggestion: Follow the procedures described on pages 543–544. Make it a point to observe how students respond to assignments; then speculate about causes of lack of motivation by referring to the trouble-shooting checklist on pages 531–533.

Ways to Satisfy Physiological Needs

Am I taking into account the physiological needs of my students? Suggestions: List specific ways to make sure students' physiological needs are satisfied. For example, let students go to the bathroom as often as they (legitimately) need to. At frequent intervals, ask students if the room seems too cold or warm. And consider scheduling snack time, or urge students to have a snack between classes.

Ways to Satisfy Safety Needs

Am I doing something that causes students to worry about their physical or psychological safety? Suggestion: Make up a list of safety-need dos and don'ts. For example, don't make students attempt any activity if they act apprehensive. But do make it a point to be sympathetic and supportive after students have had a bad experience.

Ways to Satisfy Belonging Needs

Do my students give the impression that they feel welcome, relaxed, and accepted when they enter my classroom? Suggestion: Next month, schedule some sort of activity, such as a brief personal planning session, that gives me a chance to interact individually with every pupil in class.

Ways to Satisfy Esteem Needs

Am I inadvertently putting down some of my students? Suggestions: Look for ways to play down public comparisons. Consider using cooperative learning and mastery learning arrangements. Try to individualize assignments so that all students can improve.

Ways to Encourage Self-Competition

Am I remembering the disadvantages of competitive reward structures? Suggestions: Have pupils keep private progress charts. Give recognition for good performance in a variety of activities. Follow the suggestions under the next two headings for encouraging pupils to set their own goals and finding a variety of ways to supply positive feedback.

Ways to Encourage Students to Set Their Own Objectives

Am I permitting my students to participate in setting individual objectives? Suggestion: Urge students to set goals for themselves by stating objectives in terms of a time limit, a number or proportion of correct responses, or a sample of actions. (Refer to the examples on page 548).

Ways to Supply Positive Feedback

Am I supplying plenty of positive feedback—in the most effective ways? When I use praise, do I use techniques that Brophy suggests are likely to be effective? Suggestion: Over a period of days, keep a record of how I use praise. Then analyze those praise responses with reference to the points raised by Brophy and the information summarized in Table 12.1 (p. 551).

Ways to Permit Students to Direct Their Own Learning

Am I being too dictatorial in determining what we will study and how we will learn it? Suggestions: Consider using the procedures for student-selected topics proposed by Howe and Howe (p. 552), the method for setting up a personal contract devised by Wlodkowski (p. 553), or the Check List of Prosocial Behaviors developed by Sorenson, Schnwenn, and Bavry (p. 555).

Chapter 13 Measurement and Evaluation of Classroom Learning

Ways to Minimize Subjectivity

Have I thought about ways to reduce the impact of factors that lead to the creation of a self-fulfilling prophecy? Suggestion: Consult the guidelines for reducing subjectivity on pages 571–572. Try out techniques that seem promising.

Outlining Units of Study

The last time I introduced a unit, did I explain what would be covered and tell students what they would be expected to do? Suggestion: The next time I plan a unit, make out a syllabus to be distributed the first day. Outline what will be covered, and explain how the grade will be determined.

Being Considerate in Scheduling

Have I ever asked pupils for their reactions when I announce when exams will be scheduled or papers will be due? Suggestion: Each time I announce an exam or a project deadline, ask the class if there are any reasons I have overlooked that may make it difficult for them to meet those deadlines.

Using a Table of Specifications

Have I thought about using a table of specifications when I prepare exams? Suggestion: Look over the description of how to use a table of specifications on pages 574–575. If it appears that using such techniques will help improve exams in the subjects(s) I teach, experiment with them when preparing the next exam.

Guidelines for Writing Test Questions

Have I examined the analysis of different types of test questions in Chapter 13? Suggestion: Read pages 580–588, and draw up my own list of guidelines for writing different types of test items. After writing the first draft of questions for the next exam, analyze each item with reference to the advantages and disadvantages listed in the item descriptions in the text. Use those points to improve the questions.

Using Different Types of Test Items

Am I using a variety of test items on my exams? Suggestions: Analyze all recent tests I have given, and prepare a record of which types of items I have used. If I have overemphasized some types and ignored others, prepare a table of specifications for the next exam to make sure that I use a variety of items.

Techniques for Evaluating Skills and Projects

Am I going to evaluate skills for projects within a few weeks? Suggestions: Before asking students to prepare projects or demonstrate their ability to perform a skill, plan how I will evaluate their productions or performance in a fair and practical way. Ask experienced teachers how they evaluate projects and performance.

Preparing a Detailed Key

The last time I corrected an exam, did I use a complete key? Suggestion: The next time I write exam questions, include a key that I can use in evaluating those questions. Then put myself in the position of a pupil, and check to see if the question clearly asks for the information listed in the key.

Analyzing Test Items

Have I analyzed the items on exams to weed out confusing or ineffective items and identify particularly good ones? Suggestion: The next time I give an exam, ask students to help me identify good and bad questions. Do the same as I grade papers. Identify or record on index cards questions that seem to be particularly effective.

Making the Most of Mastery Learning

Have I considered using a mastery approach? Suggestion: Read the section on mastery learning on pages 599–602. Think about the possibility of using a mastery approach. If it will not be in conflict with school regulations, try out a mastery grading system some time this report period.

Chapter 14 Classroom Management

Learning to Deal with Overlapping Situations

Am I "with it" in terms of knowing what is going on in my classroom, or do I have a one-track mind? Suggestions: Carry out a self-analysis of how I deal with simultaneous activities. Make it a point to look around the room continually as I carry out one activity, and keep an eye out for signs of incipient problems. Practice ways to handle more than one thing at a time. List some techniques to use to prove I'm "with it": If I see two boys starting to shove each other just before I turn to write something on the board, tell them to stop as I write with my back turned. Start a sentence, insert a comment directed at the troublemaker, and go right on with the rest of the sentence.

Learning How to Maintain Momentum

Do I flip-flop from one activity to another or unnecessarily interrupt the flow of an activity? Suggestions: The next time I am tempted to interrupt what we are doing to comment on some unrelated incident or activity, fight down the impulse and keep things flowing. Also, make an effort to build momentum into class activities as I draw up plans for the day or period.

Ways to Keep the Whole Class Involved

Am I using techniques that tend to cause some members of the class to tune out? Suggestions: Make up a list of ways to keep everybody involved. Call on pupils in unpredictable order. Ask questions first, and then call on pupils. Ask several pupils to respond in quick succession. Have all pupils in the class respond to questions one way or another.

Planning How to Handle Routines

Have I made a conscious effort to anticipate and plan for how I tend to handle class routines? Suggestion: Ask an experienced teacher to describe typical classroom routines in our school and explain how he or she handles them. Then draw up my own detailed description of how I intend to manage my classroom.

Signals to Use to Nip Trouble in the Bud

What signals might I use to communicate to potential troublemakers that I am with it? Suggestions: Clear my throat. Pause a few seconds in midsentence, and stare at the misbehaving pupils. Move and stand near troublemakers. Direct a question at a pupil who is beginning to engage in disruptive behavior. Make a lighthearted remark about what is going on.

Ways to Supply Situational Assistance

What techniques can I use to help potential troublemakers control themselves? Suggestions: Remind them of what they are supposed to be doing. Set up routines designed to minimize temptation. Send a pupil who seems on the verge of getting into trouble on an errand. Prepare the class and stress the need for control when a potentially explosive activity is imminent.

Ways to Use Reality and Value Appraisal

How can I help pupils become aware of how their misbehavior regularly affects them and others? Suggestions: Take advantage of object lessons to illustrate why certain rules are necessary and logical. If a student must be criticized, follow up with encouragement, conveying the idea that improved behavior is expected. Ask the class to help establish rules, or at least talk about why rules are necessary and logical. After a tense and disagreeable experience, allow a cooling-off period; then analyze what happened and explain why it must not happen again. Help pupils gain understanding when they show signs of losing control.

Using I-Messages

Am I applying Ginott's fundamental principle of communication, and am I using I-messages? Suggestion: Just after I reprimand pupils, jot down what I said. Then check to see if I criticized personality or character rather than the situation. If I *did* tell students they were lazy or sloppy or something similar, make a resolution to deliver an I-message the next time I face a similar situation; in short, tell the student or the class how I feel about it.

Speculating About Problem Ownership

Have I ever tried to figure out who "owns" a problem before dealing with it? Suggestion: Starting tomorrow, try to classify the ownership of problems as soon as I become aware of them. If students are doing something disruptive or destructive, use an appropriate influence technique to handle it in an authoritative way. If the problem seems to be due to feelings of confusion, inadequacy, or incompetence, try active listening.

| Trying the No-Lose Method | Am I trying to seek compromises when conflicts develop, or am I being too dictatorial? Suggestion: The next time I run into a conflict with an individual pupil or the entire class, try the no-lose method. That is, define the problem, ask for and propose solutions, and come to mutual agreement about a solution. |

Analyzing Feelings After Dealing with Troublemakers

How do I feel after I really have to put down a student? Suggestion: The next time I deal harshly with a pupil, make it a point to examine the emotional aftereffects I experience. If I am pleased and smug, should I be? If I am upset, what might I do to avoid experiencing similar emotional tension in the future?

Being Prompt, Consistent, and Reasonable in Controlling the Class

Am I being prompt, consistent, and reasonable in my efforts to maintain control of the class? Suggestions: Carry out a personal survey of how prompt and consistent I am as a disciplinarian. Perhaps ask the class to tell me in anonymous statements if they think punishments are reasonable.

Ways to Establish Rapport

The last time I sharply criticized a pupil, did I later make a move to effect a reconciliation? Suggestion: The next time I have to deal harshly with a pupil, make it a point to tell or show the individual that, as far as I am concerned, bygones are bygones and I am not holding a grudge. Then try to give that pupil a chance to do something constructive.

Experimenting with Behavior Modification

Have I tried using a behavior modification approach to handle discipline problems? Suggestions: Write down and put into practice a series of steps to follow when dealing with classroom misbehavior. State rules or a description of what needs to be done in order to gain reinforcement. Perhaps invite pupils to prepare individual reward menus. Praise those who are doing what they should be doing. If negative behavior does not extinguish when it is ignored, point out unfortunate consequences that might occur if that behavior continues. At the same time, stress the desirability of completing the task and gaining reinforcement.

Resources for Further Investigation

Coping with Frustrations

The frustrations you will need to cope with when you begin to teach will be similar to those that teachers have faced for decades. Thus, even though *Mental Hygiene in Teaching* by Fritz Redl and William W. Wattenberg was published in 1959, it is still one of the clearest and most sympathetic discussions of ways teachers might cope with personal and professional problems they are likely to experience.

Solving Problems

As you approach the end of your first year of teaching, you might find it of interest and value to read *Teaching Is Tough* (1980) by Donald R. Cruikshank and several associates. The book discusses common teaching problems under five headings: affiliation, control, parent relationships and home community conditions, student success, and time. You would do well to postpone reading this book until after you have taught for several months because it contains a teacher problems checklist that you can use to assess your skill at solving problems in each of the areas just noted and to plan how to correct inadequacies. The book also outlines a twelve-step problem-solving process and describes detailed techniques for handling each of the basic types of problems.

Glossary

Accommodation Tendency to revise an existing scheme as the result of a new experience.

Achievement motivation Motive to achieve characterized by a desire to be successful; set of techniques designed to encourage students to strive to be successful.

Achievement test Standardized test designed to measure how much has been learned about a particular subject.

Acronym Mnemonic device made up of the first letters of a set of several words to be memorized.

Acrostic Mnemonic device made up of a sentence consisting of words that begin with the same first letter, as a set of words to be memorized.

Active listening Recognizing and acknowledging what a talker is saying, and encouraging continued expression of feelings.

Adaptation Basic human tendency to adjust to the environment.

Adolescent egocentrism Tendency of adolescents to assume that their thoughts and actions are as interesting to others as to themselves.

Advance organizers Introductory materials that provide an organizing structure to help students relate new information to existing schemes.

Affective domain The domain whose taxonomy concentrates on attitudes and values.

Affective objectives Instructional objectives that stress attitudes, feelings, and values.

Alternative assessment methods Methods of assessing classroom learning that deviate from traditional written tests by emphasizing various types of performances and the collection of previous work into portfolios.

Androgyny Possessing both male and female characteristics.

Aptitude test Standardized test designed to supply an estimate of a student's potential ability in a particular area of study.

Assimilation Tendency to fit a new experience into an existing scheme.

Associative play Disorganized play, with no assignment of activities or roles.

Attention Focusing on a portion of currently available information

Attribution theory Explanations of ways that students respond to success or failure by attributing their performance to interactions among ability, effort, luck, and task difficulty.

Authoritarian parents Parents who lack warmth, make demands, and wield power, without taking into account the child's point of view.

Authoritative parents Parents who are confident in their abilities as parents and therefore provide their children with a model of competence.

Aversive control Principle of behavior whereby students behave in a desired way in order to avoid having to do something disagreeable.

Behavioral learning theories Sets of principles based on observations of overt behavior.

Behavior disorder Term that is essentially synonymous with *emotional disturbance*. Preferred by many theorists because it calls attention to behavior that needs to be changed.

Behavior modification Technique of shaping behavior by reinforcing desirable responses, ignoring undesirable responses.

Between-class ability grouping Classroom grouping of students with similar intelligence and achievement test scores.

Branching program A form of written instruction in which the subject matter is broken down into a series of relatively large, logically arranged steps called frames and through which there are multiple paths depending on a learner's pattern of correct and incorrect responses.

Chunking Cognitive process in which unrelated bits of information are grouped in some way.

Classical conditioning Form of learning first studied by Ivan Pavlov wherein a reflexive (or elicited) response becomes associated with a new stimulus (also called *Pavlovian conditioning*).

Cognitive domain   The domain whose taxonomy stresses knowledge and intellectual skills.

Cognitive objectives   Instructional objectives that stress knowledge and intellectual abilities and skills.

Cognitive style   A marked tendency to repeatedly respond to tasks and problems in a particular way.

Cognitive theories   Sets of principles proposed by psychologists to account for what happens in the minds of students as they learn.

Competency test   Test designed to determine if individuals (such as potential high school graduates) possess minimum basic skills.

Competitive reward structure   Classroom arrangement where only the best pupils earn rewards in the form of high grades.

Computer-assisted instruction   Use of computers to present programs or otherwise facilitate or evaluate learning.

Confluent education   Form of humanistic education stressing the flowing together of cognitive and affective elements.

Conservation   Ability to recognize that properties of objects stay the same despite a change in appearance.

Constructive play   Manipulating objects in order to construct or create something.

Constructivism   A view of learning which holds that meaningful learning occurs when people make personal interpretations of ideas and experiences.

Construct validity   How accurately a test measures a particular attribute (or psychological construct).

Content validity   How well the items that make up a test sample (or measure) a particular type of ability or understanding.

Contingency contracting   Agreement that a teacher will supply a specified reward when a student completes a mutually agreed-upon assignment.

Convergent thinker   Individual who tends to respond to questions and stimuli in predictable, conventional ways.

Cooperative learning   Technique of instruction whereby students work together in small groups.

Cooperative play   An organized form of play in which leadership and other roles are assigned; may involve some form of coordinated enterprise.

Cooperative reward structure   Classroom arrangement whereby students are encouraged to help one another learn.

Criterion-referenced test   Test in which a student's performance is evaluated with reference to specified criteria or to that individual's previous level of performance.

Culture   A term used to describe how a group of people perceives the world; formulates beliefs; evaluates objects, ideas, and experiences; and behaves.

Cumulative rehearsal   A memory tactic in which a constantly changing set of items is repeated by continuously adding new items and dropping old ones.

Decentration   Ability to think of more than one quality at a time.

Deficiency needs   The lower needs (physiological, safety, belongingness and love, esteem) in Maslow's hierarchy.

Disadvantaged pupils   Pupils whose out-of-school experiences may fail to equip them for adequate academic performance.

Discovery learning   Form of instruction in which a teacher arranges the learning environment so that students can find their own answers.

Discrimination   Responding in different ways to different stimuli.

Distributed practice   The scheduling of short study periods at frequent intervals.

Divergent thinker   Individual who tends to respond to questions and stimuli in unpredictable, unconventional ways.

Dramatic play   Use of an imaginary situation during play.

Due process   Legal procedures and safeguards intended to protect the rights of the pupil.

Egocentrism   Assumption that others see things the same way; inability to imagine another's point of view.

Elaborative rehearsal   Information processing techniques in which stored information is used to aid memorization; facilitation of information transfer from short-term to long-term memory.

Emotional disturbance   Condition characterized by chronic inability to learn, relate to others, or overcome depression (also referred to as *behavior disorder*).

Epigenetic principle   A biological principle that describes the sequence of development of the various parts of the fetus.

Equilibration Tendency for children to seek cognitive coherence and stability.

Ethnic group A collection of people who identify with one another on the basis of ancestral country, race, religion, language, values, political interests, economic interests, and/or behavior patterns.

Evaluation The use of a rule-governed system to make judgments about the value or worth of a set of measures.

Extinction Tendency for a conditioned response to disappear if not reinforced from time to time.

Extrinsic motivation Doing something to earn some sort of reward or because it is required.

Fear of failure An extreme degree of anxiety over the prospect of failure that motivates people to attempt to accomplish tasks that are either very easy or very difficult.

Fear of success Tendency of individuals to worry about being more successful than others because of fear of jeopardizing interpersonal relationships.

Fixed interval schedule Reinforcement supplied according to a fixed interval of time.

Fixed ratio schedule Reinforcement supplied according to a fixed pattern of responses.

Foreclosure type Adolescent who has unquestioningly endorsed the goals and values of his or her parents.

Formative evaluation Monitoring progress and planning remedial instruction as a way of facilitating learning.

Frames Individual steps of a teaching-machine program.

Functional play Making simple repetitive movements with or without the use of objects.

Games with Rules Using prearranged rules to play a game.

Generalization Tendency for a learned response to be aroused by any stimulus similar to a stimulus that was coupled with reinforcement (more specifically referred to as *stimulus generalization*).

General objectives Objectives that describe the types of behavior students should exhibit in order to demonstrate what they have learned, accompanied by a sample of specific learning outcomes.

General transfer Transfer due to the use of the same cognitive strategies in working two tasks.

Gifted and talented A term applied to children and youth who give evidence of high performance capabilities and who require services or activities not normally provided by the school in order to fully develop such capabilities.

Grade equivalent score Score on a standardized test that indicates level of performance with reference to average performance at different grade levels.

Growth need The upper-most need (self-actualization) in Maslow's hierarchy.

Growth spurt A period of unusually rapid physical growth between the sixth and ninth grades.

Heuristics Methods or techniques of problem solving.

High-road transfer Formulation of a rule or strategy from one task and application to generally similar tasks.

Horizontal enrichment Enrichment technique that consists of giving a rapid learner who has finished an assignment before the rest of the class more material at the same general level of difficulty.

Humanistic education Approach to instruction that stresses attitudes, values, personal fulfillment, and relationships with others.

Identity Sense of psychosocial well-being produced by acceptance of one's appearance, clear goals, recognition from others.

Identity achievement type Adolescent who has made satisfying self-chosen commitments regarding sex role and occupational choice.

Identity diffusion type Adolescent who avoids thinking about goals, roles, and values.

Ill-structured problems Problems that are vaguely stated, have unclear solution procedures, and are subject to vague evaluation standards.

I-message A teacher's explanation of how he or she feels regarding an unsatisfactory situation (a technique recommended by Haim Ginott).

Individualized education program (IEP) Specially planned program of instruction and evaluation designed for a particular handicapped child (as required by Public Law 94–142).

Individual reward structure A situation in which the rewards received by students are determined solely on the basis of each individual's accomplishments.

Information-processing theory Study of the ways sensory input is transformed, stored, recovered, and used.

Intelligence quotient (IQ) Score on an intelligence test (originally computed by dividing chronological age by mental age, with 100 representing average performance).

Interdisciplinary assessment team A group of personnel required under PL 94–142, consisting of a school psychologist, guidance counselor, classroom teacher, school social worker, learning disability specialist, speech therapist, physician, and/or psychiatrist.

Interindividual variation Differences between individuals at a given point in time.

Interpersonal reasoning The ability to understand the relationship between motives and behavior among a group of people.

Intraindividual variation Differences within an individual over time and across different situations.

Intrinsic motivation Doing something for its own sake; the accomplishment of a task as its own reward.

Invitational learning Form of humanistic education in which teacher communicates to students that they are responsible, able, and valuable.

Irreversibility Inability to understand that one can return to the starting point of a sequence of mental or physical actions by performing the actions in reverse order.

Issues Ill-structured problems that arouse strong feelings.

Item analysis A quantitative method of determining the difficulty level and discriminating ability of multiple-choice items.

Joplin Plan A variation of "regrouping" whereby students with the same achievement test scores but from different grades are grouped together into one classroom.

Keyword method Mnemonic device used to learn a foreign-language word by forming a visual image or link with an English word.

Learned helplessness Feelings of helplessness and lack of control over one's life, learned through experiences and from the reactions of others.

Learner-centered education An approach in which the teacher tries to be genuine and to establish a trusting, acceptant, empathetic attitude toward the student.

Learning More or less permanent change in behavior as a result of experiences.

Learning disabilities Disorders in basic processes that lead to learning problems not due to other causes.

Learning strategy A general plan for improving one's ability to learn, encompassing metacognitive knowledge, strategic skills, and tactical skills.

Learning tactic A specific technique for memorizing and/or understanding information to be learned.

Least restrictive environment Provision of PL 94–142 that directs school districts to place handicapped students in the most normal educational setting that the student's handicapping condition will allow.

Level of aspiration Tendency of individuals to set goals in an effort to succeed at the highest possible level while avoiding failure.

Linear program A form of written instruction in which the subject matter is broken down into a series of relatively small, logically arranged steps called frames in order to eliminate incorrect responses and to which the learner supplies a written response beginning with the first frame and proceeding in sequence to the last frame.

Long-term memory (LTM) Storehouse of permanently recorded information in one's memory.

Low-road transfer A situation in which a previously learned skill or idea is automatically applied to a highly similar current task.

Mainstreaming Policy of placing handicapped pupils in regular classes for part or all of the school day.

Maintenance rehearsal Information processing technique intended to help learners hold information for immediate use.

Massed practice Scheduling long study periods at infrequent intervals.

Mastery learning Technique of instruction whereby pupils are given multiple opportunities to master a series of exams, evaluated with reference to specified criteria.

Meaningful reception learning The integration of new ideas into existing knowledge schemes.

Measurement The assignment of numbers to certain attributes of objects, events, or people according to a rule-governed system.

Melting pot A term describing the assimilation of diverse ethnic groups into one national mainstream.

Mental retardation Below-average intelligence (defined by an IQ score of 67 or lower) accompanied by adaptive problems.

Metacognition Knowledge of how one's mind works; thinking about ways to improve one's ability to memorize and learn.

Mnemonic device Memory aid or system designed to improve recall.

Morality of constraint Moral thinking typical of children up to the age of ten or so, characterized by sacred rules and permitting neither exceptions nor allowance for intentions (also called *moral realism*).

Morality of cooperation Moral thinking typical of children twelve years and older characterized by flexible rules, mutual agreements, and allowance for intentions.

Moratorium type Adolescent who is suffering an identity crisis because of confusion or indecision about sex role and/or occupational choice.

Motivation Arousal, selection, direction, and continuation of behavior.

Multicultural education Teaching practices that show understanding, acceptance, and encouragement of culturally diverse behavior and thinking patterns.

National Assessment of Educational Progress A periodic assessment of the achievement levels of nine-, thirteen-, seventeen-, and twenty-six through thirty-five-year-old American children and young adults in various subject matter areas.

Negative identity Adopting forms of behavior opposite to those regarded as desirable by parents and most adults.

Negative reinforcement Strengthening a desired behavior by removing a negative stimulus after the behavior occurs.

Negative transfer A situation in which prior learning interferes with subsequent learning.

No-lose method Method of conflict resolution in which two individuals come to a mutual agreement about a solution to a problem.

Normal curve Theoretical distribution that takes the form of a symmetrical, bell-shaped curve.

Norm group A sample of individuals reflecting the larger population for which a test is intended; the norm group's scores serve as the standard of comparison for all other scores.

Norm-referenced test Test in which a student's performance is evaluated by comparing it to the performance of others.

Observational learning Acquisition of a new form of behavior as a result of observing another person benefit from using that behavior (also called *modeling*).

Onlooker behavior Behavior characteristic of children, who spend most of their time watching others.

Open education An approach to education derived from Jean Piaget's theory of cognitive development and characterized by self-selected learning activities, interaction among students, individual and small-group instruction, and informal methods of evaluation.

Operant conditioning Form of learning first studied by B. F. Skinner wherein a voluntary (or emitted) response is strengthened when it is reinforced.

Organization Basic human tendency to systematize and combine processes into coherent systems.

Parallel play A form of play whereby children play beside, but not really with, other children, perhaps using the same toys, but in an independent way.

Peer tutoring Technique of instruction involving the teaching of one child by another.

Peg-word method Mnemonic device that involves associating a new item with a previously learned item.

Percentile rank Score that indicates the percentage of students taking a test who are at or below a particular raw score.

Perceptual centration Tendency to focus attention on only one characteristic of an object or aspect of a problem or event at a time.

Performance test A measure of how well people perform a particular skill or set of skills under more or less realistic conditions.

Positive reinforcement Strengthening a desired behavior by presenting a positive stimulus after the behavior occurs.

Positive transfer A situation in which prior learning aids subsequent learning.

Premack principle Principle whereby students are allowed to engage in a self-selected activity after they complete assigned work (also called *Grandma's rule*).

Problem representation/framing That part of the problem-solving process in which the learner attempts to determine precisely the type of problem with which he or she is confronted.

Problem solving Identification and application of knowledge and skills that result in goal attainment.

Programmed instruction Form of instruction wherein material is organized into a series of small steps (frames) and feedback is supplied after each response.

Prosocial behavior Forms of behavior that involve understanding the needs and feelings of others, getting along with others, or functioning well in group situations.

Psychological androgyny Ability of an individual to assume masculine *or* feminine roles without difficulty or self-consciousness.

Psychomotor domain The domain whose taxonomy focuses on physical abilities and skills.

Psychosocial moratorium Period of delay of commitment or postponement of occupational choice.

Puberty The point in physical development when secondary sex characteristics appear and sexual reproduction first becomes possible.

Punishment A behavior modification technique that seeks to eliminate or suppress an undesired behavior by administering an aversive stimulus to an individual whenever he or she exhibits the undesired behavior.

Recognition Noting key features of a stimulus and relating them to stored information.

Reflective teaching Teaching that blends artistic and scientific elements.

Regrouping Grouping into one classroom students of the same age, ability, and grade but from different classrooms.

Reinforcement A behavior modification technique that seeks to strengthen a desired response either by presenting a positive stimulus after the behavior has been exhibited or by withdrawing an aversive stimulus after the behavior has been exhibited.

Reinforcement menu A behavior modification technique wherein students choose a positive reinforcer from a list of reinforcers whenever a desired behavior has been exhibited.

Reliability The degree to which scores are consistent if the same test is given to the same students a second time.

Response cost Withdrawal of positive reinforcement following undesired behavior.

Ripple effect Group response to a reprimand directed at an individual.

Role confusion Having no clear conception of appropriate types of behavior that others will react to favorably.

Schemata Abstract structures of organization.

Scheme Organized pattern of behavior or thought.

Self-actualization The need to develop all of one's potential talents and capabilities.

Self-fulfilling prophecy Tendency for individuals to behave in ways they are expected to behave (essentially the same as *Pygmalion effect*).

Self-reinforcement Giving oneself a positive reinforcer whenever one's behavior meets or exceeds personal standards.

Sensory register First memory structure that holds information for possible processing.

Serial position effect The tendency to remember items at the beginning and end of a long list.

Shaping Reinforcement of actions that move progressively closer to the desired result (or terminal behavior).

Short-term memory (STM) "Working" memory, or information temporarily stored in one's memory.

Skinner box Device developed by B. F. Skinner to study operant conditioning.

Social class An indicator of an individual's or family's relative standing in society.

Social learning theory Form of behavioral learning theory attributing changes in behavior to observation and imitation.

Sociometric techniques Methods of assessing friendships, cliques, and levels of popularity among students in a classroom.

Solitary play Type of play whereby children play alone, making no attempt to interact with others within speaking distance.

Specific objectives Objectives that specify the behavior to be learned, the conditions under which it will be exhibited, and the criterion for acceptable performance.

Specific transfer Transfer due to specific similarities between two tasks.

Spiral curriculum Teaching an idea in simplified form early in schooling and then reteaching it later in more complex form.

Spontaneous recovery The occasional reappearance of behaviors undergoing extinction.

Standard deviation Statistic that indicates the degree to which a particular score deviates from the mean of a distribution.

Standardized test Test prepared for nationwide use by a testing corporation that establishes norms by presenting a carefully selected set of items to a representative sample of students.

Stanine score Score that indicates a pupil's position in a distribution divided into nine one-half standard deviation units.

Structure The basic or fundamental ideas of a subject and how they relate to each other.

Summative evaluation Evaluation of student's performance in an attempt to discover how well instructional objectives have been met and/or to determine a grade.

Table of specifications Chart of types and numbers of test items to be included in an exam to ensure thorough and systematic coverage of a unit of study.

Target behavior A designated activity to be shaped through behavior modification (also referred to as a *terminal behavior*).

Task analysis Description of the elements or components of a task or skill.

Taxonomy Comprehensive classification scheme in which categories are arranged in hierarchical order.

Terminal behavior Desired result preselected by an experimenter or programmer who intends to shape behavior by applying operant conditioning principles.

Theory of identical elements The greater the degree of similarity between the stimulus and response elements of two tasks, the greater the amount of transfer.

Time-out Behavior modification technique in which undesirable behavior is weakened by temporarily removing positive reinforcement.

Token economy Reinforcing students through use of behavior modification procedures by supplying tokens (such as check marks) that can later be traded in for some reward.

Transfer of learning Ability of individuals to apply what they learn in one situation to other situations.

T score How far a raw score is from the mean in numerical terms, calculated by using a mean of 50 and a standard deviation of 10.

Unoccupied behavior Nonplay behavior in which children stand around and watch others or engage in aimless activities.

Validity How well a test appropriately measures what its users intend to measure.

Values clarification Set of techniques of humanistic education designed to help students choose, prize, and act on their beliefs.

Variable interval schedule Reinforcement supplied after sporadic or unpredictable intervals of time.

Variable ratio schedule Reinforcement supplied according to a variable pattern of responses.

Vertical enrichment Enrichment technique that consists of giving a rapid learner who has finished an assignment before the rest of the class more advanced work of the same general type.

Vicarious reinforcement Imitating a modeled behavior that was positively reinforced in the expectation of receiving the same reinforcement.

Well-structured problems Problems that are clearly stated, can be solved using known solution procedures, and can be evaluated based on known standards.

Within-class ability grouping Dividing a single class of students into two or three groups, according to ability in a specific subject.

Withitness Describes a teacher who demonstrates to students constant awareness of their behavior.

Zero transfer A situation in which prior learning has no effect on new learning.

Zone of proximal development The difference between what a child can do on his or her own versus what can be accomplished with some assistance.

Z score How far a raw score is from the mean in standard deviation units.

Bibliography

Achenbach, T. M., & Edelbrock, C. S. (1983). *Manual for the child behavior checklist and revised child behavior profile*. Burlington, VT: University of Vermont.

Adelson, J. (1971). The political imagination of the young adolescent. *Daedalus, 100*(4), 1013–1049.

Adelson, J. (1972). The political imagination of the young adolescent. In J. Kagan & R. Coles (Eds.), *Twelve to sixteen: Early adolescence*. New York: Norton.

Adelson, J. (Ed.). (1980). *Handbook of adolescent psychology*. New York: Wiley.

Adelson, J. (1986). *Inventing adolescence: The political psychology of everyday schooling*. New Brunswick, NJ: Transaction Books.

Ainsworth, M. D. S., & Wittig, B. A. (1972). Attachment and exploratory behavior of one-year-olds in a strange situation. In B. M. Foss (Ed.), *Determinants of infant behavior* (Vol. 4). New York: Wiley.

Airasian, P. W. (1991). *Classroom assessment*. New York: McGraw-Hill.

Almy, M. C., Chittenden, E., & Miller, P. (1966). *Young children's thinking*. New York: Columbia University, Teacher's College.

Ames, C., & Ames, R. (1984). Systems of student and teacher motivation: Toward a qualitative definition. *Journal of Educational Psychology, 76*(4), 535–556.

Anastasi, A. (1988). *Psychological testing* (6th ed.). New York: Macmillan.

Anderson, R. C. (1984). Some reflections on the acquisition of knowledge. *Educational Researcher, 13*(9), 5–10.

Anderson, T., & Boyer, M. (1978). *Bilingual schooling in the United States* (2nd ed.). Austin, TX: National Educational Laboratory.

Andre, M. E. D. A., & Anderson, T. H. (1978–1979). The development and evaluation of a self-questioning study technique. *Reading Research Quarterly, 14*, 605–623.

Andre, T., & Phye, G. D. (1986). Cognition, learning, and education. In G. D. Phye & T. Andre (Eds.), *Cognitive classroom learning*. Orlando, FL: Academic Press.

Annis, L., & Annis, D. (1979, April). *A normative study of students' preferred study techniques*. Paper presented at the annual meeting of the American Educational Research Association, San Francisco.

Anthony, E. J. (1970). Behavior disorders. In P. H. Mussen (Ed.), *Carmichael's manual of child psychology* (3d ed., Vol. 2). New York: Wiley.

Appleton, N. (1983). *Cultural pluralism in education*. New York: Longman.

Archer, S. L. (1991). Identity development, gender differences in. In R. M. Lerner, A. C. Peterson, & J. Brooks-Gunn (Eds.), *Encyclopedia of Adolescence*. New York: Garland Publishing.

Armbruster, B. B., Echols, C. H., & Brown, A. L. (1982). The role of metacognition in reading to learn: A developmental perspective. *The Volta Review, 84*(5), 45–56.

Atkinson, J. W. (1964). *An introduction to motivation*. Princeton, NJ: Van Nostrand.

Atkinson, J. W., & Litwin, G. H. (1960). Achievement motive and test anxiety conceived as motive to approach success and motive to avoid failure. *Journal of Abnormal and Social Psychology, 60*, 52–63.

Atkinson, J. W., & Raynor, J. O. (Eds.). (1974). *Motivation and achievement*. Washington, DC: Winston.

Atkinson, J. W., & Raynor, J. O. (1978). *Personality, motivation, and achievement*. Washington, DC: Hemisphere.

Atkinson, R. C. (1975). Mnemotechnics in second language learning. *American Psychologist, 30*, 821–828.

Atkinson, R. C., & Raugh, M. R. (1975). An application of the mnemonic keyword method to the acquisition of a Russian vocabulary. *Journal of Experimental Psychology: Human Learning and Memory, 104*, 126–133.

Atkinson, R. C., & Shiffrin, R. M. (1968). Human memory: A proposed system and its control processes. In K. W. Spence & J. T. Spence (Eds.), *The psychology of learning and motivation* (Vol. 2). New York: Academic Press.

Ausubel, D. P. (1963). *The psychology of meaningful verbal learning*. New York: Grune & Stratton.

Ausubel, D. P., Novak, J. D., & Hanesian, H. (1978). *Educational psychology: A cognitive view* (2d ed.). New York: Holt, Rinehart & Winston.

Ausubel, D. P., & Robinson, F. G. (1969). *School learning: An introduction to educational psychology*. New York: Holt, Rinehart & Winston.

Baker, K. (1985). Research evidence of a school discipline problem. *Phi Delta Kappan, 66*, 482–487.

Baldwin, A. Y. (1991). Ethnic and cultural issues. In N. Colangelo & G. A. Davis (Eds.), *Handbook of gifted education*. Boston: Allyn & Bacon.

Bandura, A. (1986). *Social foundations of thought and action: A social cognitive theory*. Englewood Cliffs, NJ: Prentice-Hall.

Bandura, A., Ross, D., & Ross, S. (1961). Transmission of aggression through imitation of aggressive models. *Journal of Abnormal and Social Psychology, 63*, 375–382.

Bandura, A., Ross, D., & Ross, S. (1963a). Imitation of film mediated aggressive models. *Journal of Abnormal and Social Psychology, 66*, 3–11.

Bandura, A., Ross, D., & Ross, S. (1963b). A comparative test of the status envy, social power, and secondary reinforcement theories of identificatory learning. *Journal of Abnormal and Social Psychology, 67*, 527–534.

Bandura, A., & Walters, R. H. (1963). *Social learning and personality development*. New York: Holt, Rinehart & Winston.

Bangert-Drowns, R. L., Kulik, C-L. C., Kulik, J. A., & Morgan, M. T. (1991). The instructional effect of feedback in test-like events. *Review of Educational Research, 61*(2), 213–238.

Bangert-Drowns, R. L., Kulik, J. A., & Kulik, C-L. C. (1985). Effectiveness of computer-based education in secondary schools. *Journal of Computer-Based Instruction, 12*(3), 59–68.

Banks, J. A. (1991). *Teaching strategies for ethnic studies* (5th ed.). Boston: Allyn & Bacon.

Bartlett, F. C. (1932). *Remembering.* London: Cambridge University Press.

Bauer, G. L. (1985). Restoring order to the public schools. *Phi Delta Kappan, 66,* 488–490.

Baumrind, D. (1971). Current patterns of parental authority. *Developmental Psychology Monographs, 1,* 1–103.

Baumrind, D. (1991). Parenting styles and adolescent development. In R. M. Lerner, A. C. Peterson, & J. Brooks-Gunn (Eds.), *Encyclopedia of adolescence.* New York: Garland Publishing.

Beck, A. T. (1970). *Depression: Causes and treatment.* Philadelphia: University of Pennsylvania Press.

Becker, W. C., Englemann, S., & Thomas, D. R. (1971). *Teaching: A course in applied psychology.* Chicago: Science Research Associates.

Bednar, A. K., Cunningham, D., Duffy, T. M., & Perry, J. D. (1991). Theory into practice: How do we link? In G. J. Anglin (Ed.), *Instructional technology: Past, present, and future.* Englewood, CO: Libraries Unlimited.

Bee, H. (Ed.). (1978). *Social issues in developmental psychology* (2d ed.). New York: Harper & Row.

Beirne-Smith, M. (1991). Peer tutoring in arithmetic for children with learning disabilities. *Exceptional children 57*(4), 330–337.

Bellezza, F. S. (1981). Mnemonic devices: Classification, characteristics, and criteria. *Review of Educational Research, 51,* 247–275.

Bem, S. L. (1975). Sex-role adaptability: One consequence of psychological androgyny. *Journal of Personality and Social Psychology, 31,* 634–643.

Bem, S. L. (1976). Sex-typing and androgyny: Further explorations of the expressive domain. *Journal of Personality and Social Psychology, 34*(5), 1016–1023.

Benbow, C. P. (1991). Mathematically talented children: Can acceleration meet their educational needs? In N. Colangelo & G. A. Davis (Eds.), *Handbook of gifted education.* Boston: Allyn & Bacon.

Bennett, C. I. (1990). *Comprehensive multicultural education: Theory and practice* (2d ed.). Boston: Allyn & Bacon.

Bergen, D. J., & Williams, J. E. (1991). Sex stereotypes in the United States revisited: 1972–1988. *Sex Roles, 24*(7/8), 413–423.

Berko, J. (1958). The child's learning of English morphology. *Word, 14,* 150–177.

Berliner, D. C. (1986). In pursuit of the expert pedagogue. *Educational Researcher, 15*(7), 5–13.

Best, R. (1983). *We've all got scars.* Bloomington, IN: Indiana University Press.

Beyer, B. K. (1987). *Practical strategies for the teaching of thinking.* Boston: Allyn & Bacon.

Beyer, B. K. (1988). *Developing a thinking skills program.* Boston: Allyn & Bacon.

Blais, D. M. (1988). Constructivism: A theoretical revolution in teaching. *Journal of Developmental Education, 11*(3), 2–7.

Blatt, M., & Kohlberg, L. (1978). The effects of classroom moral discussion upon children's level of moral development. In L. Kohlberg & E. Turcel (Eds.), *Recent research in moral development.* New York: Holt, Rinehart & Winston.

Block, J. H. (1971). Operating procedures for mastery learning. In J. H. Block (Ed.), *Mastery learning: Theory and practice.* New York: Holt, Rinehart & Winston.

Block, J. H. (1973). Conceptions of sex role: Some cross-cultural and longitudinal perspectives. *American Psychologist, 28,* 512–529.

Block, J. H. (1976). Issues, problems and pitfalls in assessing sex differences. *Merrill-Palmer Quarterly, 22,* 283–308.

Block, J. H., Efthim, H. E., & Burns, R. B. (1989). *Building effective mastery learning schools.* New York: Longman.

Bloom, B. S. (1968). Learning for mastery. *Evaluation Comment, 1*(2), Los Angeles: University of California, Center for the Study of Evaluation of Instructional Programs.

Bloom, B. S. (1976). *Human characteristics and school learning.* New York: McGraw-Hill.

Bloom, B. S. (1981). *All our children learning.* New York: McGraw-Hill.

Bloom, B. S. (1984). The two sigma problem: The search for methods of group instruction as effective as one-to-one tutoring. *Educational Researcher, 13*(6), 4–16.

Bloom, B. S., Englehart, M. B., Furst, E. J., Hill, W. H., & Krathwohl, D. R. (Eds.). (1956). *Taxonomy of educational objectives. The classification of educational goals. Handbook I: Cognitive domain.* New York: McKay.

Blumenthal, S. J., & Kupfer, D. J. (1988). Overview of early detection and treatment strategies for suicidal behavior in young people. *Journal of Youth and Adolescence, 17*(1), 1–22.

Blythe, T., & Gardner, H. (1990). A school for all intelligences. *Educational Leadership, 47*(7), 33–37.

Bolin, F. S. (1990). Helping student teachers think about teaching: Another look at Lou. *Journal of Teacher Education, 41*(1), 10–19.

Borker, S. R. (1987). Sex roles and labor force participation. In D. B. Carter (Ed.), *Current conceptions of sex roles and sex typing.* New York: Praeger.

Bower, G. H., Clark, M. C., Lesgold, A. M., & Winzenz, D. (1969). Hierarchical retrieval schemes in recall of categorized word lists. *Journal of Verbal Learning and Verbal Behavior, 8,* 323–343.

Bowman, B. T. (1989). Educating language-minority children: Challenges and opportunities. *Phi Delta Kappan, 71*(2), 118–120.

Boyer, C. B., & Hein, K. (1991). Sexually transmitted diseases in adolescence. In R. M. Lerner, A. C. Peterson, & J. Brooks-Gunn (Eds.), *Encyclopedia of adolescence.* New York: Garland Publishing.

Boyer, E. L. (1983). *High school.* New York: Harper & Row.

Bracey, G. W. (1983). On the compelling need to go beyond minimum competency. *Phi Delta Kappan, 64*(10), 717–721.

Bracey, G. W. (1988). Selective retention. *Phi Delta Kappan, 69*(5), 379–380.

Bracey, G. W. (1991). Why can't they be like we were? *Phi Delta Kappan, 73*(2), 104–117.

Braddock, J. H., II. (1990). Tracking the middle grades: National patterns of grouping for instruction. *Phi Delta Kappan, 71*(6), 445–449.

Bragstad, B. J., & Stumpf, S. M. (1987). *A guidebook for teaching study skills and motivation* (2d ed.). Boston: Allyn & Bacon.

Braithwaite, E. R. (1959). *To sir, with love.* Englewood Cliffs, NJ: Prentice-Hall.

Bransford, J. D. (1979). *Human cognition: Learning, understanding, and remembering.* Belmont, CA: Wadsworth.

Bransford, J. D., Sherwood, R., Vye, N., & Rieser, J. (1986). Teaching thinking and problem solving: Research foundations. *American Psychologist, 41*(10), 1078–1089.

Bransford, J. D., & Stein, B. (1984). *The IDEAL problem solver: A guide for improving thinking, learning, and creativity.* San Francisco: Freeman.

Brantlinger, E. A., & Guskin, S. L. (1985). Implications of social and cultural differences for special education with specific recommendations. *Focus on Exceptional Children, 18*(1), 1–12.

Braun, C. (1976). Teacher expectations: Sociopsychological dynamics. *Review of Educational Research, 46*(2), 185–213.

Bredderman, T. (1982). Activity science—the evidence shows it matters. *Science and Children, 20*(1), 39–41.

Brittain, C. V. (1968). An exploration of the bases of peer compliance and parent-compliance in adolescence. *Adolescence, 2,* 445–458.

Broadbent, D. E. (1958). *Perception and communication.* New York: Pergamon Press.

Brody, E. B., & Brody, N. (1976). *Intelligence: Nature, determinants, and consequences.* New York: Academic Press.

Bronfenbrenner, V. (1970). *Two worlds of childhood.* New York: Russell Sage Foundation.

Brooks, J. G. (1990). Teachers and students: Constructivists forging new connections. *Educational Leadership, 47*(5), 68–71.

Brooks-Gunn, J. (1987). Pubertal processes: Their relevance for developmental research. In V. B. van Hasselt & M. Hersen (Eds.), *Handbook of adolescent psychology.* New York: Pergamon Press.

Brooks-Gunn, J., & Furstenberg, F. F., Jr. (1989). Adolescent sexual behavior. *American Psychologist, 44*(2), 249–257.

Brophy, J. E. (1979). Teacher behavior and its effects. *Journal of Educational Psychology, 71,* 733–750.

Brophy, J. E. (1981). Teacher praise: A functional analysis. *Review of Educational Research, 51*(1), 5–32.

Brophy, J. E. (1983a). Conceptualizing student motivation. *Educational Psychologist, 18*(3), 200–215.

Brophy, J. E. (1983b). Research on the self-fulfilling prophecy and teacher expectations. *Journal of Educational Psychology, 75*(5), 631–661.

Brophy, J. E., & Alleman, J. (1991). Activities as instructional tools: A framework for analysis and evaluation. *Educational Researcher, 20*(4), 9–23.

Brophy, J. E., & Good, T. L. (1974). *Teacher-student relationships: Causes and consequences.* New York: Holt, Rinehart & Winston.

Brown, A. L., Campione, J. C., & Day, J. D. (1981). Learning to learn: On training students to learn from text. *Educational Researcher, 10*(2), 14–24.

Brown, C. A. (1982). Sex typing in occupational preferences of high school boys and girls. In I. Gross, J. Downing, & A. d'Heurle (Eds.), *Sex role attitudes and cultural change.* Dordrecht, Holland: D. Reidel Publishing Company.

Brown, G. I. (1971). *Human teaching for human learning: An introduction to confluent education.* New York: Viking Press.

Brown, R. (1973). *A first language: The early stages.* Cambridge, MA: Harvard University Press.

Broverman, I. K., Vogel, S. R., Broverman, D. M., Clarkson, F. E., & Rosenkrantz, P. S. (1972). Sex-role stereotypes: A current appraisal. *Journal of Social Issues, 28*(2), 59–78.

Bruner, J. S. (1951). Personality dynamics and the process of perceiving. In R. R. Blake & G. V. Ramsey (Eds.), *Perception: An approach to personality.* New York: Ronald Press.

Bruner, J. S. (1960). *The process of education.* New York: Vintage Books.

Bruner, J. S. (1966). *Toward a theory of instruction.* New York: Norton.

Bruner, J. S. (1971). *The relevance of education.* New York: Norton.

Bruner, J. S. (1983). *In search of mind: Essays in autobiography.* New York: Harper & Row.

Bruner, J. S., Goodnow, J. J., & Austin, G. A. (1956). *A study of thinking.* New York: Wiley.

Bryant, P. E. (1984). Piaget, teachers, and psychologists. *Oxford Review of Education, 10*(3), 251–259.

Bryson, J. E., & Bentley, C. P. (1980). *Ability grouping of public school students: Legal aspects of classification and tracking methods.* Charlottesville, VA: Michie Company.

Burnett, C., Mendoza, G., & Secunda, S. (1975). *What I want to be when I grow up.* New York: Simon & Schuster.

Bybee, R. W., & Sund, R. B. (1982). *Piaget for educators* (2d ed.). Columbus, OH: Charles E. Merrill.

Byrd, D. E. (1990). Peer tutoring with the learning disabled: A critical review. *Journal of Educational Research, 84*(2), 115–118.

Canady, R. L., & Hotchkiss, P. R. (1989). It's a good score! Just a bad grade. *Phi Delta Kappan, 71*(1), 68–71.

Canfield, J. T., & Wells, H. C. (1976). *100 ways to enhance self-concept in the classroom: A handbook for teachers and parents.* Englewood Cliffs, NJ: Prentice-Hall.

Cangeolsi, J. S. (1988). *Classroom management strategies: Gaining and maintaining students' cooperation.* New York: Longman.

Canter, L. (1989). Assertive discipline—more than names on the board and marbles in a jar. *Phi Delta Kappan, 71*(1), 57–61.

Carrasquillo, A. L. (1991). *Hispanic children and youth in the United States: A resource guide.* New York: Garland Publishing.

Carroll, J. B. (1963). A model of school learning. *Teachers College Record, 64,* 723–733.

Carroll, J. B. (1971). Problems of measurement related to the concept of learning for mastery. In J. H. Block (Ed.), *Mastery learning: Theory and practice.* New York: Holt, Rinehart & Winston.

Carter, D. B. (1987). The role of peers in sex role socialization. In D. B. Carter (Ed.), *Current conceptions of sex roles and sex typing.* New York: Praeger.

Case, R. (1975). Gearing the demands of instruction to the developmental capacities of the learner. *Review of Educational Research, 45*(1), 59–88.

Cassidy, J., & Johnson, N. (1986). Federal and state definitions of giftedness: Then and now. *Gifted Child Today, 9*(6), 15–21.

Cazden, C. (1968). The acquisition of noun and verb inflections. *Child Development, 39,* 433–438.

Chalfant, J. C. (1989). Learning disabilities: Policy issues and promising approaches. *American Psychologist, 44*(2), 392–398.

Charles, C. M. (1972). *Educational psychology: The instructional endeavor.* St. Louis, MO: Mosby.

Chesler, M., & Fox, R. (1966). *Role playing methods in the classroom.* Palo Alto, CA: Science Research Associates.

Chinn, P. C., & Plata, M. (1987/1988). Multicultural education: Beyond ethnic studies. *Teacher Education and Practice, 4*(2), 7–10.

Clausen, J. (1975). The social meaning of differential physical and sexual maturation. In S. Dragastin & G. H. Elder, Jr. (Eds.), *Adolescence in the life cycle.* New York: Wiley.

Coates, D. L., & van Widenfeldt, B. (1991). Pregnancy in adolescence. In R. M. Lerner, A. C. Peterson, & J. Brooks-Gunn (Eds.), *Encyclopedia of adolescence.* New York: Garland Publishing.

Cohen, P. A., Kulik, J. A., & Kulik, C-L. C. (1982). Educational outcomes of tutoring: A meta-analysis of findings. *American Educational Research Journal, 19*(2), 237–248.

Coleman, J. C. (1980). Friendship and the peer group in adolescence. In J. Adelson (Ed.), *Handbook of adolescent psychology.* New York: Wiley.

Collins, A. (1991). The role of computer technology in restructuring schools. *Phi Delta Kappan, 73*(1), 28–36.

Colten, M.E., & Gore, S., eds. (1991). *Adolescent stress.* NY: Aldine de Gruyter.

Combs, A. W. (1965). *The professional education of teachers.* Boston: Allyn and Bacon.

Combs, A. W. (1981). Humanistic education: Too tough for a tender world? *Phi Delta Kappan, 62,* 446–449.

Combs, A. W. (1982). Affective education or none at all. *Educational Leadership, 39*(7), 494–497.

Combs, A. W., Avila, D. L., & Purkey, W. W. (1978). *Helping relationships: Basic concepts for the helping professions* (2d ed.). Boston: Allyn and Bacon.

Combs, A. W., Blume, R. A., Newman, A. J., & Wass, H. L. (1974). *The professional education of teachers* (2d ed.). Boston: Allyn and Bacon.

Conger, J. J. (1991). *Adolescence and youth* (4th ed.). New York: Harper Collins.

Conger, J. J., & Miller, W. C. (1966). *Personality, social class, and delinquency.* New York: Wiley.

Conoley, J. C., & Kramer, J. J. (Eds.). (1989). *Tenth mental measurements yearbook.* Lincoln, NE: Buros Institute of Mental Measurements.

Consortium for Research on Black Adolescence (1990). *Black adolescence: Current issues and annotated bibliography.* Boston: G. K. Hall.

Cook, L. K., & Mayer, R. E. (1983). Reading strategies training for meaningful learning from prose. In M. Pressley & J. R. Levin (Eds.), *Cognitive strategy research: Educational applications.* New York: Springer-Verlag.

Cooper, H. M. (1979). Pygmalion grows up: A model for teacher expectation, communication, and performance influence. *Review of Educational Research, 49*(3), 389–410.

Cosgrove, D. J. (1959). Diagnostic ratings of teacher performance. *Journal of Educational Psychology, 50,* 220–224.

Council for Exceptional Children (1991). *Education of the Handicapped Act Amendments of 1990: Summary of major changes to current law.* Reston, VA: Council for Exceptional Children, Office of Governmental Relations.

Covington, M. V. (1985). Strategic thinking and the fear of failure. In J. W. Segal, S. F. Chipman, & R. Glaser (Eds.), *Thinking and learning skills* (Vol. 1). Hillsdale, NJ: Lawrence Erlbaum.

Cox, W. F., Jr., & Dunn, T. G. (1979). Mastery learning: A psychological trap? *Educational Psychologist, 14,* 24–29.

Craighead, W. E., Kazden, A. E., & Mahoney, M. J. (1981). *Behavior modification* (2d ed.). Boston: Houghton Mifflin.

Craik, F. I. M., & Lockhart, R. S. (1972). Levels of processing: A framework for memory research. *Journal of Verbal Learning and Verbal Behavior, 11,* 671–684.

Crockett, L. J. (1991). Sex roles and sex-typing in adolescence. In R. M. Lerner, A. C. Peterson, & J. Brooks-Gunn (Eds.), *Encyclopedia of adolescence.* New York: Garland.

Cronbach, L. J. (1990). *Essentials of psychological testing* (5th ed.). New York: Harper & Row.

Crooks, T. J. (1988). The impact of classroom evaluation practices on students. *Review of Educational Research, 58*(4), 438–481.

Cruickshank, D. R., & Associates (1980). *Teaching is tough.* Englewood Cliffs, NJ: Prentice-Hall.

Csikszentmihalyi, M., & Larson, R. (1984). *Being adolescent.* New York: Basic Books.

Cuban, L. (1986). *Teachers and machines: The classroom use of technology since 1920.* New York: Teachers College Press.

Cuban, L. (1988). A fundamental puzzle of school reform. *Phi Delta Kappan, 69*(5), 340–344.

Cuban, L. (1990). What I learned from what I had forgotten about teaching: Notes from a professor. *Phi Delta Kappan, 71*(6), 479–482.

Cuervo, A. G., Lees, J., & Lacey, R. (1984). *Toward better and safer schools.* Alexandria, VA: National School Boards Association.

Cullum, A. (1967). *Push back the desks.* New York: Citation Press.

Cziko, G. A. (1992). The evaluation of bilingual education. *Educational Researcher, 21*(2), 10–15.

Damon, W. (1988). *The moral child.* New York: Free Press.

Daniels, S. (1967). *How 2 gerbils, 20 goldfish, 200 games, 2000 books, and I taught them how to read.* Philadelphia: Westminster Press.

Dar, Y., & Resh, N. (1986). *Classroom composition and pupil achievement.* New York: Gordon and Breach.

Dasen, P., & Heron, A. (1981). Cross-cultural tests of Piaget's theory. In H. C. Triandis & A. Heron (Eds.), *Handbook of cross-cultural psychology, developmental psychology* (Vol. 4). Boston: Allyn & Bacon.

Dawe, H. A. (1984). Teaching: A performing art. *Phi Delta Kappan, 65*(8), 548–552.

Dawson, M. M. (1987). Beyond ability grouping: A review of the effectiveness of ability grouping and its alternatives. *School Psychology Review, 16*(3), 348–369.

Dempster, F. N. (1988). The spacing effect: A case study in the failure to apply the results of psychological research. *American Psychologist, 43*(8), 627–634.

Dennison, G. (1969). *The lives of children.* New York: Vintage.

Devine, T. G. (1987). *Teaching study skills: A guide for teachers* (2d ed.). Boston: Allyn & Bacon.

DiMartino, E. C. (1989). Understanding children from other cultures. *Childhood Education, 66*(1), 30–32.

diSibio, M. (1982). Memory for connected discourse: A constructivist view. *Review of Educational Research, 52*(2), 149–174.

Doll, C. A. (1987). *Evaluating educational software.* Chicago: American Library Association.

Douvan, E., & Adelson, J. (1966). *The adolescent experience.* New York: Wiley.

Doyle, R. P. (1989). The resistance of conventional wisdom to research evidence: The case of retention in grade. *Phi Delta Kappan, 71*(3), 215–220.

Doyle, W. (1983). Academic work. *Review of Educational Research, 53*(2), 159–200.

Dryfoos, J. G. (1990). *Adolescence at risk: Prevalence and prevention.* NY: Oxford University Press.

Duchastel, P. C., & Merrill, P. F. (1973). The effects of behavioral objectives on learning: A review of empirical studies. *Review of Educational Research, 43*(1), 53–69.

Duell, O. K. (1986). Metacognitive skills. In G. D. Phye & T. Andre (Eds.), *Cognitive classroom learning.* Orlando, FL: Academic Press.

Durkin, K. (1985). *Television, sex roles and children.* Milton Keynes, England: Open University Press.

Dusek, J. B. (1987a). *Adolescent development and behavior.* Englewood Cliffs, NJ: Prentice-Hall.

Dusek, J. B. (1987b). Sex roles and adjustment. In D. B. Carter (Ed.), *Current conceptions of sex roles and sex typing.* New York: Praeger.

Dweck, C. S. (1986). Motivational processes affecting learning. *American Psychologist, 41*(10), 1040–1048.

Dweck, C. S., & Bush, E. S. (1976). Sex differences in learned helplessness: I. Differential debilitation with peer and adult evaluators. *Developmental Psychology, 12,* 147–156.

Dwyer, C. A. (1982). The role of schools in developing sex role attitudes. In I. Gross, J. Downing, & A. d'Heurle (Eds.), *Sex role attitudes and cultural change.* Dordrecht, Holland: D. Reidel Publishing.

Ebel, R. L., & Frisbie, D. A. (1991). *Essentials of educational measurement* (5th ed.). Englewood Cliffs, NJ: Prentice-Hall.

Edmunds, R. D. (Ed.). (1980). *American Indian leaders: Studies in diversity.* Lincoln, NE: University of Nebraska Press.

Edwards, A. J. (1971). *Individual mental testing, part I: History and theories.* Scranton, PA: Intext Educational Publishers.

Edwards, C. P. (1986). *Promoting social and moral development in young children.* New York: Teachers College Press.

Elkind, D. (1989). Developmentally appropriate practice: Philosophical and practical implications. *Phi Delta Kappan, 71*(2), 113–117.

Elkind, D. (1981). *Children and adolescents: Interpretive essays on Jean Piaget* (3d ed.). New York: Oxford University Press.

Ellis, H. C. (1965). *The transfer of learning.* New York: Macmillan.

Ellis, H. C. (1978). *Fundamentals of human learning, memory, and cognition* (2d ed.). Dubuque, IA: Wm. C. Brown.

Ellis, H. C., & Hunt, R. R. (1989). *Fundamentals of human memory and cognition* (4th ed.). Dubuque, IA: Wm. C. Brown.

Emmer, E. T., Evertson, C. M., Sanford, J. P., Clements, B. S., & Worsham, M. E. (1989). *Classroom management for secondary teachers* (2d ed.). Englewood Cliffs, NJ: Prentice-Hall.

EPIE Institute. (1986). *TESS: The educational software selector.* New York: Teachers College Press.

Epstein, H. T. (1980). Brain growth and cognitive functioning. In D. R. Steer (Ed.), *The emerging adolescent: Characteristics and educational implications.* Columbus, OH: National Middle School Association.

Erdelyi, M. H., & Goldberg, B. (1979). Let's now sweep repression under the rug: Towards a cognitive psychology of repression. In J. Kihlstrom & F. Evans (Eds.), *Functional disorders of memory.* Hillsdale, NJ: Lawrence Erlbaum.

Ericsson, K. A., Chase, W. G., & Faloon, S. (1980). Acquisition of a memory skill. *Science, 208,* 1181–1182.

Erikson, E. H. (1963). *Childhood and society* (2d ed.). New York: Norton.

Erikson, E. H. (1968). *Identity: Youth and crisis.* New York: Norton.

Evans, J. (1985). *Teaching in transition: The challenge of mixed ability grouping.* Milton Keynes, UK: Open University Press.

Evans, R. I. (1967). *Dialogue with Erik Erikson.* New York: Harper & Row.

Evans, W. H., Evans, S. S., Gable, R. A., & Schmid, R. E. (1991). *Instructional management for detecting and correcting special problems.* Boston: Allyn & Bacon.

Evertson, C. M., Emmer, E. T., Clements, B. S., Sanford, J. P., & Worsham, M. E. (1989). *Classroom management for elementary teachers* (2d ed.). Englewood Cliffs, NJ: Prentice-Hall.

Fagot, B. I. (1978). The influence of sex of child on parental reactions to toddler children. *Child Development, 49,* 459–465.

Fagot, B. I., & Leinbach, M. D. (1987). Socialization of sex roles within the family. In D. B. Carter (Ed.), *Current conceptions of sex roles and sex typing.* New York: Praeger.

Fantuzzo, J. W., Polite, K., & Grayson, N. (1990). An evaluation of reciprocal peer tutoring across elementary school settings. *Journal of School Psychology, 28*(4), 309–323.

Fantuzzo, J. W., Riggio, R. E., Connelly, S., & Dimeff, L. A. (1989). Effects of reciprocal peer tutoring on academic achievement and psychological adjustment: A component analysis. *Journal of Educational Psychology, 81*(2), 173–177.

Faw, H. W., & Waller, T. G. (1976). Mathemagenic behaviors and efficiency in learning from prose materials. *Review of Educational Research, 46,* 691–720.

Feather, N. T. (1980). Values in adolescence. In J. Adelson (Ed.), *Handbook of adolescent psychology.* New York: Wiley.

Feingold, A. (1988). Cognitive gender differences are disappearing. *American Psychologist, 43*(2), 95–103.

Feist, J. (1990). *Theories of personality* (2d ed). Fort Worth, TX: Holt, Rhinehart & Winston.

Fernald, G. (1943). *Remedial techniques in basic school subjects.* New York: McGraw-Hill.

Feynman, R. P. (1985). *"Surely you're joking, Mr. Feynman."* New York: Norton.

First, J. M. (1988). Immigrant students in U.S. public schools: Challenges with solutions. *Phi Delta Kappan, 70* (3), 205–210.

Flanders, N. A. (1970). *Analyzing teacher behavior.* Reading, MA: Addison-Wesley.

Flavell, J. H. (1976). Metacognitive aspects of problem solving. In L. B. Resnick (Ed.), *The nature of intelligence.* Hillsdale, NJ: Lawrence Erlbaum.

Flavell, J. H. (1979). Metacognition and cognitive monitoring: A new area of cognitive-developmental inquiry. *American Psychologist, 34*(10), 906–911.

Flavell, J. H. (1987). Speculations about the nature and development of metacognition. In F. E. Weinert & R. H. Kluwe (Eds.), *Metacognition, motivation, and understanding.* Hillsdale, NJ: Lawrence Erlbaum.

Flinders, D. J. (1989). Does the "art of teaching" have a future? *Educational Leadership, 46*(8), 16–20.

Foot, H. C., Shute, R. H., & Morgan, M. J. (1990). Theoretical issues in peer tutoring. In H. C. Foot, M. J. Morgan, & R. H. Shute (Eds.), *Children helping children.* Chichester, England: John Wiley & Sons.

Foster, D. W. (1982). *Sourcebook of Hispanic culture in the United States.* Chicago: American Library Association.

Franca, V. M., Kerr, M. M., Reitz, A. L., & Lambert, D. (1990). Peer tutoring among behaviorally disordered students: Academic and social benefits to tutor and tutee. *Education and Treatment of Children, 13*(2), 109–128.

Frasier, M. M. (1987). The identification of gifted black students: Developing new perspectives. *Journal for the Education of the Gifted, 10*(3), 155–180.

Frasier, M. M. (1991). Disadvantaged and culturally diverse gifted students. *Journal for the Education of the Gifted, 14*(3), 234–245.

Frederiksen, N. (1984). Implications of cognitive theory for instruction in problem solving. *Review of Educational Research, 54*(3), 363–408.

Friedenberg, E. Z. (1963). *Coming of age in America: Growth and acquiescence.* New York: Vintage Books.

Furst, E. J. (1981). Bloom's taxonomy of educational objectives for the cognitive domain. *Review of Educational Research, 51*(4), 441–453.

Furstenberg, F. F., Jr., Lincoln, R., & Menken, J. (Eds.). (1981). *Teenage sexuality, pregnancy, and childbearing.* Philadelphia: University of Pennsylvania Press.

Furth, H. G. (1970). *Piaget for teachers.* Englewood Cliffs, NJ: Prentice-Hall.

Furth, H. G., & Wachs, H. (1975). *Thinking goes to school.* New York: Oxford University Press.

Gage, N. L. (1984). What do we know about teaching effectiveness? *Phi Delta Kappan, 66*(2), 87–93.

Galbraith, R. E., & Jones, T. M. (1976). *Moral reasoning.* Minneapolis, MN: Greenhaven Press.

Gall, M. D. (1970). The use of questions in teaching. *Review of Educational Research, 40,* 707–721.

Gall, M. D., Gall, J. P., Jacobsen, D. R., & Bullock, T. L. (1990). *Tools for learning: A guide to teaching study skills.* Alexandria, VA: Association for Supervision and Curriculum Development.

Gallagher, J. J. (1985). *Teaching the gifted child* (3d ed.). Boston: Allyn and Bacon.

Gallatin, J. (1980). Political thinking in adolescence. In J. Adelson (Ed.), *Handbook of adolescent psychology.* New York: Wiley.

Gallimore, R., & Tharp, R. (1990). Teaching mind in society: Teaching, schooling, and literate discourse. In L. C. Moll (Ed.), *Vygotsky and education: Instructional implications and applications of sociohistorical psychology.* Cambridge, England: Cambridge University Press.

Galton, F. (1890). Statement made in footnote to an article by J. M. Cattell, Mental tests and measurement. *Mind, 15,* 373.

Gardner, H. (1983). *Frames of mind: The theory of multiple intelligences.* New York: Basic Books.

Gardner, H., & Hatch, T. (1989). Multiple intelligences go to school. *Educational Researcher, 18*(8), 4–10.

Garfinkel, B. D., Crosby, E., Herbert, M. R., Matus, A. L., Pfeifer, J. K., & Sheras, P. L. (1988). *Responding to adolescent suicide.* Bloomington, IN: Phi Delta Kappa Educational Foundation.

Gelman, R., & Baillargeon, E. E. (1983). A review of some Piagetian concepts. In J. H. Flavell & E. M. Markman (Eds.), *Handbook of child development: Vol. III. Cognitive development* (4th ed.). New York: Wiley.

Getzels, J. W., & Jackson, P. W. (1962). *Creativity and intelligence.* New York: Wiley.

Gick, M. L. (1986). Problem-solving strategies. *Educational Psychologist, 21*(1,2), 99–120.

Gick, M. L., & Holyoak, K. J. (1980). Analogical problem solving. *Cognitive Psychology, 12,* 306–355.

Gick, M. L., & Holyoak, K. J. (1983). Schema induction and analogical transfer. *Cognitive Psychology, 15,* 1–38.

Gilligan, C. (1982). *In a different voice: Psychological theory and women's development.* Cambridge, MA: Harvard University Press.

Gilligan, C. (1988). Exit-voice dilemmas in adolescent development. In C. Gilligan, J. Ward, J. Taylor, & B. Bardige (Eds.), *Mapping the moral domain: A contribution of women's thinking to psychological theory and education.* Cambridge, MA: Harvard University Press.

Ginott, H. (1965). *Between parent and child.* New York: Macmillan.

Ginott, H. (1972). *Teacher and child.* New York: Macmillan.

Ginsburg, H. P., & Opper, S. (1988). *Piaget's theory of intellectual development* (3d ed.). Englewood Cliffs, NJ: Prentice-Hall.

Glaser, R. (1976). Components of a psychology of instruction: Toward a science of design. *Review of Educational Research, 46*(1), 1–24.

Glasser, W. (1986). *Control theory in the classroom.* New York: Harper & Row.

Glasser, W. (1990). *The quality school.* New York: Harper & Row.

Glasson, G. E. (1989). The effects of hands-on and teacher demonstration laboratory methods on science achievement in relation to reasoning ability and prior knowledge. *Journal of Research in Science Teaching, 26*(2), 121–131.

Gold, M., & Petronio, R. J. (1980). Delinquent behavior in adolescence. In J. Adelson (Ed.), *Handbook of adolescent psychology.* New York: Wiley.

Goldstein, A. P., Apter, S. J., & Harootunian, B. (1984). *School violence.* Englewood Cliffs, NJ: Prentice-Hall.

Goldstein, A. P., Sprafkin, R. P., Gershaw, N. J., & Klein, P. (1980). *Skillstreaming the adolescent: A structured learning approach to teaching prosocial skills.* Champaign, IL: Research Press.

Goldstein, H., & Seigle, D. M. (1971). *A curriculum guide for teachers of the educable mentally handicapped: The Illinois plan for special education for exceptional children.* Danville, IL: Interstate Printers and Publishers.

Goldstein, K. M., & Blackman, S. (1978). *Cognitive style.* New York: Wiley.

Gollnick, D. M., & Chinn, P. C. (1990). *Multicultural education in a pluralistic society* (3d ed.). Columbus, OH: Charles E. Merrill.

Good, T. (1982). *Classroom research: What we know and what we need to know* (R&D Report No. 9018). Austin, TX: University of Texas, Research and Development Center for Teacher Education.

Gordon, S., & Gilgun, J. F. (1987). Adolescent sexuality. In V. B. van Hasselt & M. Hersen (Eds.), *Handbook of adolescent psychology.* New York: Pergamon Press.

Gordon, T. (1970). *PET: Parent effectiveness training.* New York: Wyden.

Gordon, T. (1974). *TET: Teacher effectiveness training.* New York: McKay.

Gorman, R. M. (1972). *Discovering Piaget: A guide for teachers.* Columbus, OH: Charles E. Merrill.

Gottfredson, G. D., & Gottfredson, D. C. (1985). *Victimization in schools.* New York: Plenum.

Gottlieb, J. (Ed.). (1980). *Educating mentally retarded persons in the mainstream.* Baltimore: University Park Press.

Gough, P. B. (1987). The key to improving schools: An interview with William Glasser. *Phi Delta Kappan, 68*(9), 656–662.

Gould, S. J. (1981). *The mismeasure of man.* New York: Norton.

Grabe, M. (1986). Attentional processes in education. In G. D. Phye & T. Andre (Eds.), *Cognitive classroom learning.* Orlando, FL: Academic Press.

Green, K. E. (1991). Teachers and standardized testing of students. In K. E. Green (Ed.), *Educational testing: Issues and applications.* New York: Garland Publishing.

Green, K. E., & Stager, S. F. (1986–1987). Testing: Coursework, attitudes, and practices. *Educational Research Quarterly, 11*(2), 48–55.

Gronlund, N. E. (1959). *Sociometry in the classroom.* New York: Harper & Row.

Gronlund, N. E. (1988). *How to construct achievement tests* (4th ed.). Englewood Cliffs, NJ: Prentice-Hall.

Gronlund, N. E. (1991). *How to write and use instructional objectives* (4th ed.). New York: Macmillan.

Gronlund, N. E., & Linn, R. L. (1990). *Measurement and evaluation in teaching* (6th ed.). New York: Macmillan.

Grossman, E. J. (Ed.). (1977). *Manual on terminology and classification in mental retardation* (3d ed.). Washington, DC: American Association on Mental Retardation.

Grossman, H. J. (Ed.). (1983). *Classification in mental retardation.* Washington, DC: American Association on Mental Deficiency.

Gruber, E., & Vonèche, J. J. (Eds.). (1977). *The essential Piaget: An interpretive reference and guide.* New York: Basic Books.

Guerin, G. R., & Maier, A. S. (1983). *Informal assessment in education.* Palo Alto, CA: Mayfield.

Guilford, J. P. (1967). *The nature of human intelligence.* New York: McGraw-Hill.

Guralnick, M. J. (1986). The peer relations of young handicapped and nonhandicapped children. In P. S. Strain, M. J. Guralnick, & H. M. Walker (Eds.), *Children's social behavior: Development, assessment, and modificaton.* Orlando, FL: Academic Press.

Gutek, G. L. (1988). *Education and schooling in America* (2d ed.). Englewood Cliffs, NJ: Prentice-Hall.

Hakuta, G., & Gould, L. J. (1987). Synthesis of research on bilingual education. *Educational Leadership, 44*(6), 38–45.

Hakuta, K., & Garcia, E. E. (1989). Bilingualism and education. *American Psychologist, 44*(2), 374–379.

Hall, B. W., Villem, M. G., & Burley, W. W. (1986). Humanistic orientation and selected teaching practices among 1st-year teachers. *Journal of Humanistic Education and Development, 25*(1), 12–17.

Hall, E. (1983, June). A conversation with Erik Erikson. *Psychology Today,* pp. 22–30.

Hall, G. S. (1904). *Adolescence: Its psychology and its relations to physiology, anthropology, sociology, sex, crime, religion, and education* (2 vols.). New York: Appleton.

Hall, R. V., Axlerod, S., Foundopoulos, M., Shellman, J., Campbell, R. A., & Cranston, S. S. (1971). The effective use of punishment to modify behavior in the classroom. *Educational Technology, 11,* 24–26.

Halmi, K. A. (1987). Anorexia nervosa and bulimia. In V. B. Van Hasselt & M. Hersen (Eds.), *Handbook of adolescent psychology.* New York: Pergamon Press.

Halpern, D. F. (1984). *Thought and knowledge: An introduction to critical thinking.* Hillsdale, NJ: Erlbaum.

Hamachek, D. E. (1975). *Behavior dynamics in teaching, learning, and growth.* Boston: Allyn and Bacon.

Hammill, D., Leigh, J., McNutt, G., & Larsen, S. (1981). A new definition of learning disabilities. *Learning Disability Quarterly, 4*(4), 336–342.

Hansgen, R. D. (1991). Can education become a science? *Phi Delta Kappan, 72*(9), 689–694.

Harmin, M., Kirschenbaum, H., & Simon, S. B. (1972). *Clarifying values through subject matter.* Minneapolis: Winston.

Hartshorne, H., & May, M. A. (1929). *Studies in service and self-control.* New York: Macmillan.

Hartshorne, H., & May, M. A. (1930a). *Studies in deceit.* New York: Macmillan.

Hartshorne, H., & May, M. A. (1930b). *Studies in the organization of character.* New York: Macmillan.

Hartup, W. W. (1989). Social relationships and their developmental significance. *American Psychologist, 44*(2), 120–126.

Hassett, J. (1984). Computers in the classroom. *Psychology Today, 18*(9), 22–28.

Hengeller, S. W. (1989). *Delinquency in adolescence.* Newbury Park, CA: Sage Publications.

Herndon, J. (1968). *The way it spozed to be.* New York: Simon & Schuster.

Herndon, J. (1971). *How to survive in your native land.* New York: Simon & Schuster.

Hersh, R. H., Paolitto, D. P., & Reimer, J. (1979). *Promoting moral growth: From Piaget to Kohlberg*. New York: Longman.

Hess, R. D., & Croft, D. J. (1981). *Teachers of young children* (3d ed.). Boston: Houghton Mifflin.

Hess, R. D., & Shipman, V. (1965). Early experiences and the socialization of cognitive modes in children. *Child Development, 36,* 869–886.

Hiatt, D. B. (1979). Time allocation in the classroom: Is instruction being short changed? *Phi Delta Kappan, 61*(4), 289–290.

Higbee, K. L. (1979). Recent research on visual mnemonics: Historical roots and educational fruits. *Review of Educational Research, 49,* 611–630.

Highet, G. (1957). *The art of teaching*. New York: Vintage Books.

Hill, J. P. (1987). Research on adolescents and their families: Past and prospect. In C. E. Irwin, Jr. (Ed.), *Adolescent social behavior and health*. San Francisco: Jossey-Bass.

Hills, J. R. (1991). Apathy concerning grading and testing. *Phi Delta Kappan, 72*(7), 540–545.

Hobbs, N. (1975). *The futures of children*. San Francisco: Jossey-Bass.

Hoffman, L. W. (1972). Early childhood experiences and women's achievement motives. *Journal of Social Issues, 28*(2), 129–156.

Hoffman, M. L. (1980). Moral development in adolescence. In J. Adelson (Ed.), *Handbook of adolescent psychology*. New York: Wiley.

Hoge, R. D. (1988). Issues in the definition and measurement of the giftedness construct. *Educational Researcher, 17*(7), 12–16, 22.

Holmes, C. T. (1989). Grade level retention effects: A meta-analysis of research studies. In L. A. Shepard & M. L. Smith (Eds), *Flunking grades: Research and policies on retention*. London: Falmer Press.

Holyoak, K. J., & Koh, K. (1987). Surface and structural similarity in analogical transfer. *Memory & Cognition, 15*(4), 332–340.

Homme, L., & Tosti, D. (1971). *Behavior technology: Motivation and contingency management*. San Rafael, CA: Individual Learning Systems.

Hopkins, C. D., & Antes, R. L. (1989). *Classroom testing: Construction*. Itasca, IL: Peacock.

Horan, J. J., & Straus, L. K. (1987). Substance abuse in adolescence. In V. B. van Hasselt & M. Hersen (Eds.), *Handbook of adolescent psychology*. New York: Pergamon Press.

Horner, M. S. (1968). *Sex differences in achievement motivation and performance in competitive and non-competitive situations*. Unpublished doctoral dissertation, University of Michigan, Ann Arbor.

Horner, M. S. (1970). Femininity and successful achievement: A basic inconsistency. In J. M. Bardwick, E. Douvan, M. S. Horner, & D. Guttman (Eds.), *Feminine personality and conflict*. Belmont, CA: Brooks/Cole.

Horowitz, F., & O'Brien, M. (1986). Gifted and talented children: State of knowledge and directions for research. *American Psychologist, 41*(10), 1147–1152.

Howard, E. R. (1981, Fall). *School climate improvement—Rationale and process*. Illinois School Research and Development.

Howe, L. W., & Howe, M. M. (1975). *Personalizing education: Values clarification and beyond*. New York: Hart.

Hughes, F. P., & Noppe, L. D. (1991). *Human development across the life span*. New York: Macmillan.

Hyde, J. S. (1986). Gender differences in aggression. In J. S. Hyde & M. C. Linn (Eds.), *The psychology of gender*. Baltimore: Johns Hopkins University Press.

Hyman, I. A., & D'Alessandro, J. (1984). Good, old-fashioned discipline: The politics of punitiveness. *Phi Delta Kappan, 66*(1), 39–45.

Illich, I. (1971). *Deschooling society*. New York: Harper & Row.

Irwin, C. E., Jr., & Millstein, S. G. (1991). Risk-taking behaviors during adolescence. In R. M. Lerner, A. C. Peterson, & J. Brooks-Gunn (Eds.), *Encyclopedia of adolescence*. New York: Garland Publishing.

Jackson, S., & Bosma, H. (1990). Coping and self in adolescence. In H. Bosma & S. Jackson (Eds.), *Coping and self-concept in adolescence*. New York: Springer-Verlag.

James, W. (1899). *Talks to teachers on psychology: And to students on some of life's ideals*. New York: Holt. (Reprinted in *The Works of William James,* 1983, Cambridge, MA: Harvard University Press).

Jensen, A. R. (1980). *Bias in mental testing*. New York: Free Press.

Jessor, S., & Jessor, R. (1975). Transition from virginity to nonvirginity among youth: A social-psychological study over time. *Developmental Psychology, 11,* 473–484.

Johnson, D. W., & Johnson, R. T. (1987). *A meta-analysis of cooperative, competitive, and individualistic goal structures*. Hillsdale, NJ: Lawrence Erlbaum.

Johnson, D. W., & Johnson, R. T. (1991). *Learning together and alone: Cooperative, competitive, and individualistic learning* (3d ed.). Englewood Cliffs, NJ: Prentice-Hall.

Johnson, R. E. (1975). Meaning in complex learning. *Review of Educational Research, 45*(3), 425–460.

Jones, M. C. (1957a). The later career of boys who were early or late maturing. *Child Development, 28,* 113–128.

Jones, M. C. (1957b). Physical ability as a factor in social adjustment in adolescence. *Journal of Educational Research, 39,* 287–301.

Jones, M. C. (1965). Psychological correlates of somatic development. *Child Development, 36,* 899–911.

Kagan, D. M. (1990). How schools alienate students at risk: A model for examining proximal classroom variables. *Educational Psychologist, 25*(2), 102–125.

Kagan, J. (1964a). *Developmental studies of reflection and analysis*. Cambridge, MA: Harvard University Press.

Kagan, J. (1964b). Impulsive and reflective children. In J. D. Krumbolz (Ed.), *Learning and the educational process*. Chicago: Rand McNally.

Kail, R. (1984). *The development of memory in children* (2d ed.). San Francisco: Freeman.

Kalbaugh, P., & Haviland, J. M. (1991). Formal operational thinking and identity. In R. M. Lerner, A. C. Peterson, & J. Brooks-Gunn (Eds.), *Encyclopedia of adolescence*. New York: Garland Publishing.

Kamii, C. (1984). Autonomy: The aim of education envisioned by Piaget. *Phi Delta Kappan, 65*(6), 410–415.

Kaplan, J. S. (1991). *Beyond behavior modification: A cognitive-behavioral approach to behavior management in the school* (2d ed.). Austin, TX: Pro-Ed.

Karlin, M. S. (1977). *Teacher's handbook of special learning problems and how to handle them*. West Nyack, NY: Parker Publishing.

Karnes, F., & Collins, E. (1980). *Handbook of instructional resources and references for teaching the gifted*. Boston: Allyn and Bacon.

Katz, L. G., & Chard, S. C. (1989). *Engaging children's minds: The project approach*. Norwood, NJ: Ablex Publishing.

Kaufman, B. (1964). *Up the down staircase*. New York: Avon.

Kazdin, A. E. (1989). Developmental psychopathology: Current research, issues, and directions. *American Psychologist, 44*(2), 180–187.

Keller, F. S. (1954). *Learning: Reinforcement theory*. New York: Random House.

Kellett, M. C. (1980). *Memory power*. New York: Sterling.

Kellogg, J. B. (1988). Forces of change. *Phi Delta Kappan, 70*(3), 199–204.

Kelly, M. L., & Carper, L. B. (1988). Home-based reinforcement procedures. In J. C. Witt, S. N. Elliott, & F. M. Gresham (Eds.), *Handbook of behavior therapy in education*. New York: Plenum Press.

Kennedy, R. E. (1991). Delinquency. In R. M. Lerner, A. C. Peterson, & J. Brooks-Gunn (Eds.), *Encyclopedia of adolescence*. New York: Garland Publishing.

Kerr, M. M., & Nelson, C. M. (1989). *Strategies for managing behavior problems in the classroom* (2d ed.). Columbus, OH: Merrill.

Keyser, D. J., & Sweetland, R. C. (Eds.). (1984–1991). *Test critiques* (Vols. 1–8). Austin, TX: Pro-Ed.

Kiewra, K. A. (1985). Investigating notetaking and review: A depth of processing alternative. *Educational Psychologist, 20*(1), 23–32.

Kiewra, K. A. (1988). Cognitive aspects of autonomous notetaking: Control processes, learning strategies, and prior knowledge. *Educational Psychologist, 23*(1), 39–56.

Kindel, S., & Benoit, E. (1984, April 23). Hello, Mr. Chips. *Forbes*, pp. 132–136.

Kirk, S., & Chalfant, J. (1984). *Developmental and academic learning disabilities*. Denver: Love.

Kirk, S. A., & Gallagher, J. J. (1989). *Educating exceptional children* (6th ed.). Boston: Houghton Mifflin.

Kirschenbaum, H. (1979). *On becoming Carl Rogers*. New York: Dell.

Kirschenbaum, H., & Simon, S. B. (Eds.). (1973). *Readings in values clarification*. Minneapolis: Winston.

Kirschenbaum, H., Simon, S. B., & Napier, R. W. (1971). *Wad-ja-get? The grading game in American education*. New York: Hart.

Kirst, M. W. (1991). Interview on assessment issues with James Popham. *Educational Researcher, 20*(2), 24–27.

Klatzky, R. L. (1980). *Human memory: Structures and processes* (2d ed.). San Francisco: Freeman.

Klauer, K. (1984). Intentional and incidental learning with instructional texts: A meta-analysis for 1970–1980. *American Educational Research Journal, 21*(2), 323–339.

Klausmeier, H. J., Sorensen, J. S., & Ghatala, E. (1971). Individually guided motivation: Developing self-direction and prosocial behaviors. *Elementary School Journal, 71*, 340–350.

Kohl, H. (1967). *36 children*. New York: New American Library.

Kohlberg, L. (1963). The development of children's orientations toward a moral order: I. Sequence in the development of moral thought. *Vita Humana, 6*, 11–33.

Kohlberg, L. (1969). Stage and sequence: The cognitive-developmental approach to socialization. In D. A. Goslin (Ed.), *Handbook of socialization theory and research*. Chicago: Rand McNally.

Kohlberg, L. (1976). Moral stages and moralization: The cognitive-developmental approach. In T. Lickona (Ed.), *Moral development and behavior: Theory, research, and social issues*. New York: Holt, Rinehart & Winston.

Kohlberg, L. (1978). Revisions in the theory and practice of moral development. In W. Damon (Ed.), *New directions for child development: Moral development* (No.2). San Francisco: Jossey-Bass.

Kohlberg, L. (1985). The just community approach to moral education in theory and practice. In M. W. Berkowitz & F. Oser (Eds.), *Moral education: Theory and application*. Hillsdale, NJ: Lawrence Erlbaum.

Komoski, P. K. (1984). Educational computing: The burden of insuring quality. *Phi Delta Kappan, 66*(4), 244–248.

Kounin, J. S. (1970). *Discipline and group management in classrooms*. New York: Holt, Rinehart & Winston.

Kovacs, M. (1989). Affective disorders in children and adolescents. *American Psychologist, 44*(2), 209–215.

Kozma, R. B. (1991). Learning with media. *Review of Educational Research, 61*(2), 179–212.

Kozol, J. (1967). *Death at an early age*. Boston: Houghton Mifflin.

Krathwohl, D. R., Bloom, B. S., & Masia, B. B. (1964). *Taxonomy of educational objectives. Handbook II: Affective domain*. New York: McKay.

Krulik, S., & Rudnick, J. A. (1988). *Problem solving: A handbook for elementary school teachers*. Boston: Allyn and Bacon.

Kubiszyn, T., & Borich, G. (1990). *Educational testing and measurement: Classroom application and practice* (3d ed.). Glenview, IL: Scott, Foresman/Little, Brown.

Kulhavy, R. W., Schwartz, N. H., & Peterson, S. (1986). Working memory: The encoding process. In G. D. Phye & T. Andre (Eds.), *Cognitive classroom learning*. Orlando, FL: Academic Press.

Kulik, C-L., Kulik, J. A., & Bangert-Drowns, R. L. (1990). Effectiveness of mastery learning programs. *Review of Educational Research, 60*(2), 265–299.

Kulik, J. A., & Kulik, C-L. (1984). Effects of accelerated instruction on students. *Review of Educational Research, 54*(3), 409–426.

Kulik, J. A., & Kulik, C-L. (1988). Timing of feedback and verbal learning. *Review of Educational Research, 58*(1), 79–98.

Kulik, J. A., Kulik, C-L., & Bangert-Drowns, R. L. (1985). Effectiveness of computer-based education in elementary schools. *Computers in Human Behavior, 1*, 59–74.

Lambert, B. G., & Mounce, N. B. (1987). Career planning. In V. B. van Hasselt & M. Hersen (Eds.), *Handbook of adolescent psychology*. New York: Pergamon Press.

Langford, P. (1989). *Children's thinking and learning in the elementary school*. Lancaster, PA: Technomic Publishing.

Langone, J. (1990). *Teaching students with mild and moderate learning problems*. Boston: Allyn & Bacon.

Larsen, L. F. (1972). The influence of parents and peers during adolescence: The situation hypothesis revisited. *Journal of Marriage and the Family, 34,* 67–74.

Leadbeater, B. (1991). Relativistic thinking in adolescence. In R. M. Lerner, A. C. Peterson & J. Brooks-Gunn (Eds.), *Encyclopedia of adolescence.* New York: Garland Publishing.

Lepper, M. R., & Chabay, R. W. (1985). Intrinsic motivation and instruction: Conflicting views on the role of motivational processes in computer-based education. *Educational Psychologist, 20*(4), 217–230.

Lepper, M. R., & Gurtner, J-L. (1989). Children and computers: Approaching the twenty-first century. *American Psychologist, 44*(2), 170–178.

Lerner, J. (1993). *Learning disabilities: Theories, diagnosis, and teaching strategies* (6th ed.). Boston: Houghton Mifflin.

Levin, J. R. (1982). Pictures as prose-learning devices. In A. Flammer & W. Kintsch (Eds.), *Advances in psychology: Vol. 8. Discourse processing.* Amsterdam: North-Holland.

Levin, J. R., Shriber, L. K., Miller, G. E., McCormick, C. B., & Levin, B. B. (1980). The keyword method in the classroom: How to remember states and their capitals. *Elementary School Journal 80* 185–191.

Levine, D. U. (Ed.). (1985). *Improving student achievement through mastery learning programs.* San Francisco: Jossey-Bass.

Levine, D. U., & Havighurst, A. J. (1989). *Society and education* (7th ed.). Boston: Allyn & Bacon.

Lickona, T. (1976). Research on Piaget's theory of moral development. In T. Lickona (Ed.), *Moral development and behavior: Theory, research, and social issues.* New York: Holt, Rinehart & Winston.

Linn, M. C., & Hyde, J. S. (1991). Cognitive and psychosocial gender differences, trends in. In R. M. Lerner, A. C. Peterson, & J. Brooks-Gunn (Eds.), *Encyclopedia of adolescence.* New York: Garland Publishing.

Little, J. K. (1967). The occupations of non-college youth. *American Educational Research Journal, 4,* 147–153.

Livingston, C., & Borko, H. (1989). Expert-novice differences in teaching: A cognitive analysis and implications for teacher education. *Journal of Teacher Education, 40*(4), 36–42.

Livson, N., & Peskin, H. (1980). Perspectives on adolescence from longitudinal research. In J. Adelson (Ed.), *Handbook of adolescent psychology.* New York: Wiley.

Lockwood, A. (1978). The effects of values clarification and moral development curricula on school age subjects: A critical review of recent research. *Review of Educational Research, 48*(3), 325–364.

Loftus, E. F., & Loftus, G. R. (1980). On the permanence of stored information in the brain. *American Psychologist, 35*(5), 409–420.

Long, J. D., Frye, V. H., & Long, E. W. (1985). *Making it till Friday* (3d ed.). Princeton, NJ: Princeton Book.

Lorayne, H., & Lucas, J. (1974). *The memory book.* New York: Ballantine Books.

Lovitt, T. C. (1989). *Introduction to learning disabilities.* Boston: Allyn & Bacon.

Luria, A. R. (1968). *The mind of a mnemonist: A little book about a vast memory.* New York: Ballantine Books.

Lynch, J. (1986). *Multicultural education: Principles and practice.* London: Routledge & Kegan Paul.

Maccoby, E. E., & Jacklin, C. N. (1974). *Psychology of sex differences.* Stanford, CA: Stanford University Press.

Maeroff, G. I. (1991). Assessing alternative assessment. *Phi Delta Kappan, 73*(4), 272–281.

Mager, R. F. (1962). *Preparing instructional objectives.* Palo Alto, CA: Fearon.

Mager, R. F. (1984). *Preparing instructional objectives* (rev. 2d ed.). Belmont, CA: Pitman Learning.

Magnusson, D., Duner, A., & Zetterblom, G. (1975). *Adjustment.* New York: Wiley.

Maker, C. (1982). *Curriculum development for the gifted.* Rockville, MD: Aspen Systems.

Manni, J. L., Winikur, D. W., & Keller, M. R. (1984). *Intelligence, mental retardation, and the culturally different child: A practitioner's guide.* Springfield, IL: Thomas.

Marcia, J. E. (1966). Development and validation of ego identity status. *Journal of Personality and Social Psychology, 3*(5), 551–558.

Marcia, J. E. (1967). Ego identity status: Relationship to change in self-esteem, "general adjustment," and authoritarianism. *Journal of Personality, 35* (1), 119–133.

Marcia, J. E. (1980). Identity in adolescence. In J. Adelson (Ed.), *Handbook of adolescent psychology.* New York: Wiley.

Marcia, J. E. (1991). Identity and self-development. In R. M. Lerner, A. C. Peterson, & J. Brooks-Gunn (Eds.), *Encyclopedia of adolescence.* New York: Garland Publishing.

Marsh, H. W. (1991). Failure of high-ability high schools to deliver academic benefits commensurate with their students' ability levels. *American Educational Research Journal, 28*(2), 445–480.

Marshall, S. P., & Smith, J. D. (1987). Sex differences in learning mathematics: A longitudinal study with item and error analysis. *Journal of Educational Psychology, 79*(4), 372–381.

Marton, F. (1988). Describing and improving learning. In R. R. Schmeck (Ed.), *Learning strategies and learning styles.* New York: Plenum Press.

Maslow, A. H. (1943). A theory of human motivation. *Psychological Review, 50,* 370–396.

Maslow, A. H. (1968). *Toward a psychology of being* (2d ed.). Princeton, NJ: Van Nostrand.

Maslow, A. H. (1970a). *Religions, values, and peak experiences.* New York: Viking.

Maslow, A. H. (1970b). *New knowledge in human values.* New York: Harper & Row.

Maslow, A. H. (1971). *The farther reaches of human nature.* New York: Viking.

Maslow, A. H. (1987). *Motivation and personality* (3d ed.). New York: Harper & Row.

Mastropieri, M. A., Scruggs, T. E., & Levin, J. R. (1987). Mnemonic instruction in special education. In M. A. McDaniel & M. Pressley (Eds.), *Imagery and related mnemonic processes.* New York: Springer-Verlag.

Matarazzo, J. D. (1972). *Wechsler's measurement and appraisal of adult intelligence* (5th ed.). New York: Oxford University Press.

Matthews, D. B. (1991). The effects of school environment on intrinsic motivation of middle-class children. *Journal of Humanistic Education and Development, 30*(1), 30–36.

Mayer, R. E. (1987). Learnable aspects of problem solving: Some examples. In D. E. Berger, K. Pezdek, & W. P. Banks

(Eds.), *Applications of cognitive psychology: Problem solving, education, and computing.* Hillsdale, NJ: Lawrence Erlbaum.

Mayer, R. E. (1979). Can advance organizers influence meaningful learning? *Review of Educational Research, 49,* 371–383.

McClelland, D. C. (1961). *The achieving society.* Princeton, NJ: Van Nostrand.

McClelland, D. C. (1985). *Human motivation.* Glenview, IL: Scott, Foresman.

McConnell, S. R., & Odom, S. L. (1986). Sociometrics: Peer-referenced measures and the assessment of social competence. In P. S. Strain, M. J. Guralnick, & H. M. Walker (Eds.), *Children's social behavior: Development, assessment, and modification.* Orlando, FL: Academic Press.

McLaughlin, M. W., & Talbert, J. (1990). Constructing a personalized school environment. *Phi Delta Kappan, 72*(3), 230–235.

McLaughlin, T. F., & Williams, R. L. (1988). The token economy. In J. C. Witt, S. N. Elliott, & F. M. Gresham (Eds.), *Handbook of behavior therapy in education.* New York: Plenum Press.

Mehan, H., Hertweck, A., & Meihls, J. L. (1986). *Handicapping the handicapped: Decision making in students' educational careers.* Stanford, CA: Stanford University Press.

Mehrens, W. A., & Lehman, I. J. (1987). *Using standardized tests in education* (4th ed.) Longman: New York.

Melton, R. F. (1920). Resolution of conflicting claims concerning the effect of behavioral objectives on student learning. *Review of Educational Research, 48,* 291–302.

Menacker, J., Weldon, W., & Hurwitz, E. (1989). School order and safety as community issues. *Phi Delta Kappan, 71*(1), 39–40, 55–56.

Mercer, C. D., & Mercer, A. R. (1985). *Teaching students with learning problems* (2d ed.). Columbus, OH: Merrill.

Mercer, J. R. (1975). Psychological assessment and the rights of children. In N. Hobbs (Ed.), *Issues in the classification of children* (Vol. 1). San Francisco: Jossey-Bass.

Mercer, J. R. (1977). *Labelling the mentally retarded.* Berkeley, CA: University of California Press.

Messick, S. (1989). Meaning and values in test validation: The science and ethics of assessment. *Educational Researcher, 18*(2), 5–11.

Messick, S. (1976). *Individuality in learning.* San Francisco: Jossey-Bass.

Michaels, J. W. (1977). Classroom reward structures and academic performance. *Review of Educational Research, 47,* 87–98.

Miller, B. C., Higginson, R., McCoy, J. K., & Olson, T. D. (1987). Family configuration and adolescent sexual attitudes and behavior. *Population and Environment, 9*(2), 111–123.

Miller, G. A. (1956). The magical number seven, plus or minus two: Some limits on our capacity for processing information. *Psychological Review, 63,* 81–97.

Miller, G. A., Galanter, E., & Pribram, K. H. (1960). *Plans and the structure of behavior.* New York: Holt, Rinehart & Winston.

Miller, N. E., & Dollard, J. (1941). *Social learning and imitation.* New Haven: Yale University Press.

Miller, P. H. (1983). *Theories of developmental psychology.* San Francisco: Freeman.

Miller, P. Y., & Simon, W. (1980). The development of sexuality in adolescence. In J. Adelson (Ed.), *Handbook of adolescent psychology.* New York: Wiley.

Mitchell, J. V., Jr. (Ed.). (1985). *Ninth mental measurements yearbook.* Highland Park, NJ: Gryphon Press.

Molnar, A., & Lindquist, B. (1989). *Changing problem behavior in schools.* San Francisco: Jossey-Bass.

Morgan, M. (1984). Reward-induced decrements and increments in intrinsic motivation. *Review of Educational Research, 54*(1), 5–30.

Morgan, S. R. (1984). An illustrative case of high-empathy teachers. *Journal of Humanistic Education and Development, 22*(4), 143–148.

Morris, P. (1977). Practical strategies for human learning and remembering. In M. J. A. Howe (Ed.), *Adult Learning.* New York: Wiley.

Morris, R. B. (Ed.). (1961). *Encyclopedia of American history.* New York: Harper & Row.

Mortimer, J. T. (1991). Employment. In R. M. Lerner, A. C. Peterson, & J. Brooks-Gunn (Eds.), *Encyclopedia of Adolescence.* New York: Garland Publishing.

Moss, H. A. (1967). Sex, age, and state as determinants of mother-infant interaction. *Merrill-Palmer Quarterly, 13,* 19–36.

Mueller, D. J. (1973). The mastery model and some alternative models of classroom instruction and evaluation: An analysis. *Educational Technology, 13*(5), 5–10.

Murphy, D. F. (1988). The just community at Birch Meadow Elementary School. *Phi Delta Kappan, 69*(6), 427–428.

Murphy, J. (1987). Educational influences. In V. B. van Hasselt & M. Hersen (Eds.), *Handbook of adolescent psychology.* New York: Pergamon Press.

Musial, D. (1986). In search of excellence: Applying the principles of trust to education. *Contemporary Education, 58*(1), 42–44.

Myers, C. R. (1970). Journal citations and scientific eminence in contemporary psychology. *American Psychologist, 25,* 1041–1048.

Naccarato, R. W. (1988). *Assessing learning motivation.* Portland, OR: Northwest Regional Educational Laboratory.

Nagy, P., & Griffiths, A. K. (1982). Limitations of recent research relating Piaget's theory to adolescent thought. *Review of Educational Research, 52*(4), 513–556.

National Advisory Committee on Handicapped Children. (1968). *First annual report, U.S. Senate subcommittee on education of the committee on labor and public welfare.* Washington, DC: U.S. Government Printing Office.

Neill, S. B., & Neill, G. W. (1990). *Only the best: Preschool-grade 12.* New York: R. R. Bowker.

Neisser, U. (1982). *Memory observed.* San Francisco: Freeman.

Newcomer, S., & Udrey, J. R. (1987). Parental marital status effects on adolescent sexual behavior. *Journal of Marriage and the Family, 49*(2), 235–240.

Nicholls, J. G. (1979). Quality and inequality in intellectual development: The role of motivation in education. *American Psychologist, 34,* 1071–1084.

Nicholson, G., Stephens, R., Elder, R., & Leavitt, V. (1985). Safe schools: You can't do it alone. *Phi Delta Kappan, 66,* 491–496.

Nickerson, R. S., Perkins, D. N., & Smith, E. E. (1985). *The teaching of thinking.* Hillsdale, NJ: Lawrence Erlbaum.

Nolen, S. B. (1988). Reasons for studying: Motivational orientations and study strategies. *Cognition and Instruction, 5*(4), 269–287.

Norman, D. A., & Rumelhart, D. E. (1970). A system for perception and memory. In D. A. Norman (Ed.), *Models of human memory*. New York: Academic Press.

Northway, J. L. (1940). A method for depicting social relationships obtained by sociometric testing. *Sociometry, 3*, 144–150.

Novak, M. (1971). Rise of unmeltable ethnics. In M. Friedman (Ed.), *Overcoming middle class rage*. Philadelphia: Westminster Press.

Nuttall, E. V. (1987). Survey of current practices in the psychological assessment of limited-English-proficiency handicapped children. *Journal of School Psychology, 25*(1), 53–61.

Nye, R. D. (1979). *What is B. F. Skinner really saying?* Englewood Cliffs, NJ: Prentice-Hall.

Oakes, J. (1985). *Keeping track: How schools structure inequality*. New Haven: Yale University Press.

Ochse, R., & Plug, C. (1986). Cross-cultural investigation of the validity of Erikson's theory of personality development. *Journal of Personality and Social Psychology, 50*(6), 1240–1252.

Offer, D. (1969). *The psychological world of the teenager: A study of normal adolescent boys*. New York: Basic Books.

Offer, D., & Offer, J. B. (1975). *From teenage to young manhood: A psychological study*. New York: Basic Books.

Ohanian, S. (1990). PL 94–142: Mainstream or quicksand? *Phi Delta Kappan, 72*(3), 217–222.

Okagaki, L., & Sternberg, R. J. (1990). Teaching thinking skills: We're getting the context wrong. In D. Kuhn (Ed.), *Developmental perspectives on teaching and learning thinking skills*. Basel, Switzerland: S. Karger.

O'Leary, K., & O'Leary, S. (Eds.). (1977). *Classroom management: The successful use of behavior modification* (2d ed.). New York: Pergamon Press.

Ornstein, A. C., & Levine, D. U. (1993). *Foundations of education* (5th ed.). Boston: Houghton Mifflin.

Osgood, C. E. (1949). The similarity paradox in human learning: A resolution. *Psychological Review, 56*, 132–143.

Ovando, C. J., & Collier, V. P. (1985). *Bilingual and ESL classrooms: Teaching in multicultural contexts*. New York: McGraw-Hill.

Overton, W. F., & Byrnes, J. P. (1991). Cognitive development. In R. M. Lerner, A. C. Peterson, & J. Brooks-Gunn (Eds.), *Encyclopedia of Adolescence*. New York: Garland Publishing.

Padilla, A. M., Fairchild, H. H., & Valadez, C. M. (Eds.). (1990). *Bilingual education: Issues and strategies*. Newbury Park, CA: Sage Publications.

Palincsar, A., & Brown, A. L. (1984). Reciprocal teaching of comprehension-fostering and comprehension-monitoring activities. *Cognition and Instruction, 1*(2), 117–175.

Pallas, A. M., Natriello, G., & McDill, E. L. (1989). The changing nature of the disadvantaged population: Current dimensions and future trends. *Educational Researcher, 18*(5), 16–22.

Paris, S. G., Cross, D. R., & Lipson, M. Y. (1984). Informed strategies for learning: A program to improve children's reading awareness and comprehension. *Journal of Educational Psychology, 76*(6), 1239–1252.

Paris, S. G., Lipson, M. Y., & Wixson, K. K. (1983). Becoming a strategic reader. *Contemporary Educational Psychology, 8*, 293–316.

Paris, S. G., & Oka, E. R. (1986). Children's reading strategies, metacognition, and motivation. *Developmental Review, 6*, 25–56.

Parke, R. D., & Slaby, R. G. (1983). The development of aggression. In E. M. Hetherington (Ed.), *Handbook of child psychology: Socialization, personality, and social development* (Vol. 4). New York: Wiley.

Parten, M. B. (1932). Social participation among preschool children. *Journal of Abnormal and Social Psychology, 27*, 243–269.

Patterson, C. H. (1973). *Humanistic education*. Englewood Cliffs, NJ: Prentice-Hall.

Patterson, G. R., DeBaryshe, B. D., & Ramsey, E. (1989). A developmental perspective on antisocial behavior. *American Psychologist, 44*(2), 329–335.

Pauk, W. (1984). *How to study in college*. Boston: Houghton Mifflin.

Peeck, J., Bosch, A. B. van Den, & Kreupling, W. J. (1982). Effect of mobilizing prior knowledge on learning from text. *Journal of Educational Psychology, 74*(5), 771–777.

Peltier, G. L. (1991). Why do secondary schools continue to track students? *The Clearing House, 64*(4), 246–247.

Pendarvis, E. A., Howley, A. A., & Howley, C. B. (1990). *The abilities of gifted children*. Englewood Cliffs, NJ: Prentice-Hall.

Penfield, W. (1969). Consciousness, memory, and man's conditioned reflexes. In K. Pribram (Ed.), *On the biology of learning*. New York: Harcourt Brace Jovanovich.

Peskin, H. (1967). Pubertal onset and ego functioning. A psychoanalytic approach. *Journal of Abnormal Psychology, 72*, 1–15.

Peskin, H. (1973). Influence of the developmental schedule of puberty on learning and ego functioning. *Journal of Youth and Adolescence, 2*, 273–290.

Peterson, A. C. (1988). Adolescent development. In M. R. Rosenzweig & L. W. Porter (Eds.), *Annual review of psychology, 39*, 583–607.

Peterson, A. C., & Taylor, B. (1980). The biological approach to adolescence. In J. Adelson (Ed.), *Handbook of adolescent psychology*. New York: Wiley.

Peterson, L. R., & Peterson, M. J. (1959). Short-term retention of individual verbal items. *Journal of Experimental Psychology, 58*, 193–198.

Peterson, R., & Felton-Collins, V. (1986). *The Piaget handbook for teachers and parents: Children in the age of discovery, preschool–third grade*. New York: Teachers College Press.

Petri, H. L. (1986). *Motivation: Theory and research*. Belmont, CA: Wadsworth.

Petti, T. A., & Larson, C. N. (1987). Depression and suicide. In V. B. van Hasselt & M. Hersen (Eds.), *Handbook of adolescent psychology*. New York: Pergamon Press.

Phillips, J. L., Jr. (1981). *Piaget's theory: A primer*. San Francisco: Freeman.

Piaget, J. (1948). *The moral judgment of the child* (M. Cabain, Trans.). Glencoe, IL: Free Press. (Original work published 1932.)

Piaget, J. (1952a). *The language and thought of the child*. London: Routledge & Kegan Paul.

Piaget, J. (1952b). *The origins of intelligence in children.* New York: International Universities Press.

Piaget, J., & Inhelder, B. (1956). *The child's conception of space.* London: Routledge & Kegan Paul.

Piaget, J., & Inhelder, B. (1969). *The psychology of the child.* New York: Basic Books.

Piechowski, M. M. (1991). Emotional development and emotional giftedness. In N. Colangelo & G. A. Davis (Eds.), *Handbook of gifted education.* Boston: Allyn & Bacon.

Polya, G. (1957). *How to solve it* (2d ed.). Princeton, NJ: Princeton University Press.

Popham, W. J. (1990). *Modern educational measurement: A practitioner's perspective* (2d ed.). Englewood Cliffs, NJ: Prentice-Hall.

Power, C. (1981). Moral education through the development of the moral atmosphere of the school. *Journal of Educational Thought, 15*(1), 4–19.

Power, C. (1985). Democratic moral education in the large public high school. In M. W. Berkowitz & F. Oser (Eds.), *Moral education: Theory and application.* Hillsdale, NJ: Lawrence Erlbaum.

Premack, D. (1959). Toward empirical behavior laws: 1. Positive reinforcement. *Psychological Review, 66,* 219–233.

Pressley, M., Levin, J. R., & Delaney, H. D. (1982). The mnemonic keyword method. *Review of Educational Research, 52,* 61–91.

Privacy rights of parents and students. (1975). *Federal Register, 40*(3), 1208–1216.

Purkey, W. W. (1970). *Self concept and school achievement.* Englewood Cliffs, NJ: Prentice-Hall.

Purkey, W. W., & Novak, J. M. (1984). *Inviting school success* (2d ed.). Belmont, CA: Wadsworth.

Purkey, W. W., & Strahan, D. B. (1986). *Positive discipline: A pocketful of ideas.* Columbus, OH: National Middle Schools Association.

Quay, H. C. (1986). Classification. In H. C. Quay & J. S. Werry (Eds.), *Psychopathological disorders of childhood* (3d ed.). New York: Wiley.

Ramsey, P. G. (1987). *Teaching and learning in a diverse world: Multicultural education for young children.* New York: Teachers College Press.

Raths, L., Harmin, M., & Simon, S. B. (1966). *Values and teaching.* Columbus, OH: Merrill.

Ratner, C. (1991). *Vygotsky's sociohistorical psychology and its contemporary applications.* New York: Plenum Press.

Raudenbush, S. W. (1984). Magnitude of teacher expectancy effects on pupil IQ as a function of the credibility of expectancy induction: A synthesis of findings from 18 experiments. *Journal of Educational Psychology, 76*(1), 85–97.

Raugh, M. R., & Atkinson, R. C. (1975). A mnemonic method for learning a second-language vocabulary. *Journal of Educational Psychology, 67,* 1–16.

Read, D. A., & Simon, S. B. (Eds.). (1975). *Humanistic education sourcebook.* Englewood Cliffs, NJ: Prentice-Hall.

Redl, F., & Wattenberg, W. W. (1959). *Mental hygiene in teaching* (2d ed.). New York: Harcourt Brace Jovanovich.

Reese, J. (1977). *Simulation games and learning activities kit for the elementary school.* West Nyack, NY: Parker Publishing.

Reid, M. I., Clunies-Ross, L. R., Goacher, B., & Viles, C. (1981). *Mixed ability teaching: Problems and possibilities.* Windsor, UK: NFER-Nelson.

Rennie, S., & Grimstad, K. (1975). *The new woman's survival sourcebook.* New York: Knopf.

Resnick, L. B. (1987). Learning in school and out. *Educational Researcher, 16*(9), 13–20.

Reynolds, C. R., Gutkin, T. B., Elliot, S. N., & Witt, J. C. (Eds.). (1984). *School psychology: Essentials of theory and practice.* New York: Wiley.

Richards, M., & Peterson, A. C. (1987). Biological theoretical models of adolescent development. In V. B. van Hasselt & M. Hersen (Eds.), *Handbook of adolescent psychology.* New York: Pergamon Press.

Robinson, H. A. (1983). *Teaching reading, writing, and study strategies* (3d ed.). Boston: Allyn and Bacon.

Rogers, C. R. (1967). Learning to be free. In C. R. Rogers & B. Stevens (Eds.), *The problem of being human.* Lafayette, CA: Real People Press. (Reprinted from S. Farber & R. H. L. Wilson, Eds., 1963, *Conflict and creativity: Control of the mind,* New York: McGraw-Hill.)

Rogers, C. R. (1980). *A way of being.* Boston: Houghton Mifflin.

Rogers, C. R. (1983). *Freedom to learn for the 80's.* Columbus, OH: Merrill.

Rogers, D. (1972). *The psychology of adolescence* (2d ed.). New York: Appleton-Century-Crofts.

Rohwer, W. D., Jr. (1984). An invitation to an educational psychology of studying. *Educational Psychologist, 19*(1), 1–14.

Rollock, B. (1988). *Black authors and illustrators of children's books.* New York: Garland Publishing.

Rose, T. L. (1984). Current uses of corporal punishment in American public schools. *Journal of Educational Psychology, 76*(3), 427–441.

Rosen, B. M., Bahn, A. K., & Kramer, M. (1964). Demographic and diagnostic characteristics of psychiatric clinic outpatients in the USA, 1961. *American Journal of Orthopsychiatry, 24,* 455–467.

Rosenshine, B. (1976). Classroom instruction. In N. L. Gage (Ed.), *The psychology of teaching methods. The 75th Yearbook of the National Society for the Study of Education, Part I.* Chicago: University of Chicago Press.

Rosenthal, R. (1985). From unconscious experimenter bias to teacher expectancy effects. In J. B. Dusek (Ed.), *Teacher expectations.* Hillsdale, NJ: Lawrence Erlbaum.

Rosenthal, R., & Jacobson, L. (1968). *Pygmalion in the classroom.* New York: Holt, Rinehart & Winston.

Rosenthal, T., & Zimmerman, B. (1978). *Social learning and cognition.* New York: Holt, Rinehart & Winston.

Rotheram-Borus, M. J., & Koopman, C. (1991). AIDS and adolescents. In R. M. Lerner, A. C. Peterson, & J. Brooks-Gunn (Eds.), *Encyclopedia of adolescence.* New York: Garland Publishing.

Rowe, M. D. (1974). Wait-time and rewards as instructional variables, their influence on language, logic, and fate control: Part one—wait-time. *Journal of Research in Science Teaching, 11,* 81–94.

Royer, J. M. (1979). Theories of the transfer of learning. *Educational Psychologist, 14,* 53–72.

Royer, J. M., & Cable, G. W. (1975). Facilitated learning in connected discourse. *Journal of Educational Psychology, 67,* 116–123.

Royer, J. M., & Cable, G. W. (1976). Illustrations, analogies, and facilitative transfer in prose learning. *Journal of Educational Psychology, 68,* 205–209.

Rubin, K. H., Maioni, T. L., & Hornung, M. (1976). Free play behavior in middle- and lower-class preschoolers: Parten and Piaget revisited. *Child Development, 47,* 414–419.

Rubin, L. J. (1985). *Artistry in teaching.* New York: Random House.

Ruggiero, V. R. (1988). *Teaching thinking across the curriculum.* New York: Harper & Row.

Rutter, M. (1980). *Changing youth in a changing society: Patterns of adolescent development and disorder.* Cambridge, MA: Harvard University Press.

Rutter, M. (1990). Changing patterns of psychiatric disorders during adolescence. In J. Bancroft & J. M. Reinisch (Eds.), *Adolescence and puberty.* New York: Oxford University Press.

Rutter, M., Maughan, B., Mortimore, P., Ousten, J., & Smith, A. (1979). *Fifteen thousand hours: Secondary schools and their effects on children.* Cambridge, MA: Harvard University Press.

Rutter, M., Tizard, J., & Whitmore, K. (Eds.). (1981). *Education, health, and behavior.* Huntington, NY: Krieger. (Original work published 1970.)

Ryan, K., & Cooper, J. M. (1991). *Those who can, teach* (6th ed.). Boston: Houghton Mifflin.

Sadker, M. P., & Sadker, D. M. (1982). *Sex equity handbook for schools.* New York: Longman.

Sadker, M. P., & Sadker, D. M. (1991). *Teachers, schools, and society* (2d ed.). New York: Random House.

Salomon, G., & Perkins, D. N. (1989). Rocky roads to transfer: Rethinking mechanisms of a neglected phenomenon. *Educational Psychologist, 24*(2), 113–142.

Sameroff, A. J., & Chandler, M. J. (1975). Reproductive risk and the continuum of caretaking causality. In F. D. Horowitz (Ed.), *Review of child development research* (Vol. 4). Chicago: University of Chicago Press.

Samuda, R. J., Kong, S. L., Cummins, J., Pascual-Leone, J., & Lewis, J. (1989). *Assessment and placement of minority students.* Toronto: C. J. Hogrefe.

Sanders, N. M. (1966). *Classroom questions: What kinds?* New York: Harper & Row.

Saunders, M. (1983). *Multicultural teaching: A guide for the classroom.* New York: McGraw-Hill.

Sauve, D. (1985). *Guide to microcomputer courseware for bilingual education* (rev. & exp.). Rosslyn, VA: National Clearinghouse for Bilingual Education.

Scarcella, R. (1990). *Teaching language minority students in the multicultural classroom.* Englewood Cliffs, NJ: Prentice-Hall.

Scarr, S., Weinburg, R. A., & Levine, A. (1986). *Understanding development.* San Diego, CA: Harcourt Brace Jovanovich.

Schiever, S. W. (1991). *A comprehensive approach to teaching thinking.* Boston: Allyn & Bacon.

Schlaefli, A., Rest, J. R., & Thoma, S. J. (1985). Does moral education improve moral judgment? A meta-analysis of intervention studies using the Defining Issues Test. *Review of Educational Research, 55*(3), 319–352.

Schon, D. A. (1987). *Educating the reflective practitioner.* San Francisco: Jossey–Bass.

Schon, I. (1980). *A Hispanic heritage: A guide to juvenile books about Hispanic people and cultures.* Metuchen, NJ: Scarecrow Press.

Schultz, T. (1989). Testing and retention of young children: Moving from controversy to reform. *Phi Delta Kappan, 71*(2), 125–129.

Schunk, D. H. (1981). Modeling and attributional effects on children's achievement: A self-efficacy analysis. *Journal of Educational Psychology, 73*(1), 93–105.

Schunk, D. H. (1987). Peer models and children's behavioral change. *Review of Educational Research, 57*(2), 149–174.

Schunk, D. H. (1991). *Learning theories: An educational perspective.* New York: Macmillan.

Seagoe, M. V. (1970). *The learning process and school practice.* Scranton, PA: Chandler.

Seagoe, M. V. (1975). *Terman and the gifted.* Los Altos, CA: Kaufmann.

Seligman, M. E. P. (1975). *Helplessness: On depression, development, and death.* San Francisco: Freeman.

Selman, R. L. (1976a). Social-cognitive understanding: A guide to educational and clinical practice. In T. Lickona (Ed.), *Moral development and behavior: Theory, research, and social issues.* New York: Holt, Rinehart & Winston.

Selman, R. L. (1976b). Toward a structural analysis of developing interpersonal relations concepts. In A. Pick (Ed.), *Minnesota symposia on child psychology* (Vol. 10). Minneapolis: University of Minnesota Press.

Selman, R. L. (1980). *The growth of interpersonal understanding: Developmental and clinical analyses.* New York: Academic Press.

Selmes, I. (1987). *Improving study skills.* London: Hodder and Stoughton.

Serafica, F. C., & Rose, S. (1982). Parents' sex role attitudes and children's concepts of femininity and masculinity. In I. Gross, J. Downing, & A. d'Heurle (Eds.), *Sex role attitudes and cultural change.* Dordrecht, Holland: D. Reidel Publishing Co.

Shepard, L. A., Smith, M. L., & Vojir, C. P. (1983). Characteristics of pupils identified as learning disabled. *American Educational Research Journal, 20*(3), 309–332.

Shook, S. C., LaBrie, M., Vallies, J., McLaughlin, T. F., & Williams, R. L. (1990). The effects of a token economy on first grade students' inappropriate social behavior. *Reading Improvement, 27*(2), 96–101.

Shrable, K., & Sassenrath, J. M. (1970). Effects of achievement, motivation, and test anxiety on performance in programmed instruction. *American Educational Research Journal, 7,* 209–220.

Shulman, L. (1970). The hidden group in the classroom. *Learning and Development, 2*(3), 1–6.

Shulman, L. S. (1986). Those who understand: Knowledge growth in teaching. *Educational Research, 15*(2), 4–21.

Shulman, L. S. (1987). Knowledge and teaching: Foundations of the new reform. *Harvard Educational Review, 57*(1), 1–32.

Siegel, E., & Gold, R. (1982). *Educating the learning disabled.* New York: Macmillan.

Siegel, O. (1982). Personality development in adolescence. In B. B. Wolman (Ed.), *Handbook of developmental psychology.* Englewood Cliffs, NJ: Prentice-Hall.

Siegler, R. S. (1983). Information processing approaches to development. In P. H. Mussen (Ed.), *Handbook of child psychology: Vol. 1. History, theory, and methods* (4th ed.). New York: Wiley.

Siegler, R. S. (1991). *Children's thinking* (2d ed.). Englewood Cliffs, NJ: Prentice-Hall.

Sigelman, C. K. & Shaffer, D. R. (1991). *Life-span human development.* Pacific Grove, CA: Brooks Cole.

Simon, A., & Boyer, E. G. (Eds.). (1970). *Mirrors for behavior: An anthology of classroom observation instruments continued.* Philadelphia: Research for Better Schools.

Simon, S. B., Howe, L. W., & Kirschenbaum, H. (1972). *Values clarification: A handbook of practical strategies for teachers and students.* New York: Hart.

Simpson, E. J. (1972). *The classification of educational objectives: Psychomotor domain.* Urbana, IL: University of Illinois Press.

Simpson, M. L. (1984). The status of study strategy instruction: Implications for classroom teachers. *Journal of Reading, 28*(2), 136–143.

Simpson, R. L. (1962). Parental influence, anticipatory socialization, and social mobility. *American Sociological Review, 27,* 517–522.

Sizer, T. R. (1985). *Horace's compromise: The dilemma of the American high school.* Boston: Houghton Mifflin.

Skinner, B. F. (1948). *Walden two.* New York: Macmillan.

Skinner, B. F. (1951). How to teach animals. *Scientific American, 185*(6), 26–29.

Skinner, B. F. (1968). *The technology of teaching.* New York: Appleton-Century-Crofts.

Skinner, B. F. (1976). *Particulars of my life.* New York: Knopf.

Skinner, B. F. (1979). *The shaping of a behaviorist.* New York: Knopf.

Skinner, B. F. (1983). *A matter of consequences.* New York: Knopf.

Skinner, B. F. (1984). The shame of American education. *American Psychologist, 39*(9), 947–954.

Skinner, B. F. (1986). Programmed instruction revisited. *Phi Delta Kappan, 68*(2), 103–110.

Slavin, R. E. (1987). Ability grouping and student achievement in elementary schools: A best-evidence synthesis. *Review of Educational Research, 57*(3), 293–336.

Slavin, R. E. (1988). *Educational psychology: Theory into practice* (2d ed.). Englewood Cliffs, NJ: Prentice-Hall.

Slavin, R. E. (1989). PET and the pendulum: Faddism in education and how to stop it. *Phi Delta Kappan, 79*(10), 752–758.

Slavin, R. E. (1990a). Achievement effects of ability grouping in secondary schools: A best-evidence synthesis. *Review of Educational Research, 60*(3), 471–500.

Slavin, R. E. (1990b). *Cooperative learning: Theory, research, and practice.* Englewood Cliffs, NJ: Prentice-Hall.

Slavin, R. E. (1991). Synthesis of research on cooperative learning. *Educational Leadership, 48*(5), 71–82.

Smilansky, S. (1968). *The effects of sociodramatic play on disadvantaged preschool children.* New York: Wiley.

Smilansky, S., & Shefatya, L. (1990). *Facilitating play: A medium for promoting cognitive, socio-emotional and academic development in young children.* Gaithersburg, MD: Psychological and Educational Publications.

Smith, D. D. (1989). *Teaching students with learning and behavior problems* (2d ed.). Englewood Cliffs, NJ: Prentice-Hall.

Smith, K., Johnson, D. W., & Johnson, R. T. (1981). Can conflict be constructive? Controversy versus concurrence seeking in learning groups. *Journal of Educational Psychology, 73*(5), 651–663.

Smith, M. L., & Shepard, L. A. (1987). What doesn't work: Explaining policies of retention in the early grades. *Phi Delta Kappan, 69*(2), 129–134.

Snow, R. E. (1986). Individual differences and the design of educational programs. *American Psychologist, 41*(10), 1029–1039.

Snowman, J. (1986). Learning tactics and strategies. In G. D. Phye & T. Andre (Eds.), *Cognitive classroom learning: Understanding, thinking, and problem solving.* New York: Academic Press.

Snowman, J. (1987, October). *The keys to strategic learning.* Paper presented at the annual meeting of the Mid-Western Educational Research Association, Chicago, IL.

Soar, R. (1973). *Follow Through classroom process measurement and pupil growth, 1970–71* (Final report). Gainesville, FL: University of Florida, College of Education.

Soldier, L. L. (1989). Cooperative learning and the Native American student. *Phi Delta Kappan, 71*(2), 161–163.

Sonenstein, F. L., & Pittman, K. J. (1984). The availability of sex education in large school districts. *Family Planning Perspectives, 16,* 19–25.

Sorensen, J. S., Schwenn, E. A., & Barry, J. (1970). *The use of individual and group goal-setting conferences as a motivational device to improve student conduct and increase student self-direction: A preliminary study* (Tech. Rep. No. 520). Madison, WI: University of Wisconsin, Wisconsin Research and Development Center for Cognitive Learning.

Sorensen, J. S., Schwenn, E. A., & Klausmeier, H. J. (1969). *The individual conference: A motivational device for increasing independent reading in the elementary grades* (Practical Paper No. 8). Madison, WI: University of Wisconsin, Wisconsin Research and Development Center for Cognitive Learning.

Sorenson, R. C. (1973). *Adolescent sexuality in contemporary America: Personal values and sexual behavior.* New York: World.

Spence, J. T. (Ed.). (1983). *Achievement and achievement motives.* San Francisco: Freeman.

Sprinthall, N. A., & Sprinthall, R. C. (1987). *Educational psychology: A developmental approach* (4th ed.). New York: Random House.

Stallings, J. A., & Kaskowitz, D. H. (1974). *Follow Through classroom observation and evaluation, 1972–1973.* Menlo Park, CA: Stanford Research Institute.

Standing, L. (1973). Learning 10,000 pictures. *Quarterly Journal of Experimental Psychology, 25,* 207–222.

Standing, L., Conezio, J., & Haber, R. (1970). Perception and memory for pictures: Single trial learning of 2500 visual stimuli. *Psychonomic Science, 19,* 73–74.

Sternberg, R. J. (1984). Toward a triarchic theory of human intelligence. *Behavioral and Brain Sciences, 7,* 269–287.

Sternberg, R. J. (1988). *The triarchic mind: A new theory of human intelligence*. New York: Viking.

Sternberg, R. J. (1990). Thinking styles: Keys to understanding student performance. *Phi Delta Kappan, 71*(5), 366–371.

Stiffman, A. R., Earls, F., Robins, L. N., Jung, K. G., & Kulbok, P. (1987). Adolescent sexual activity and pregnancy: Socioenvironmental problems, physical health, and mental health. *Journal of Youth and Adolescence, 16*(5), 497–509.

Stiggins, R. J., Griswold, M. M., & Wikelund, K. R. (1989). Measuring thinking skills through classroom assessment. *Journal of Educational Measurement, 26*(3), 233–246.

Stitt, B. A. (1988). *Building gender fairness in schools*. Carbondale, IL: Southern Illinois University Press.

Stronge, J. H., Lynch, C. D., & Smith, C. R. (1987). Educating the culturally disadvantaged gifted student. *The School Counselor, 34* (5), 336–344.

Strother, D. B. (1986). Suicide among the young. *Phi Delta Kappan, 67*(10), 756–759.

Sulzer-Azaroff, B., & Mayer, G. R. (1986). *Achieving educational excellence: Using behavioral strategies*. New York: Holt, Rinehart & Winston.

Susman, E. J. (1991). Stress and the adolescent. In R. M. Lerner, A. C. Peterson, & J. Brooks-Gunn (Eds.), *Encyclopedia of adolescence*. New York: Garland Publishing.

Suter, D. P., & Wolf, J. S. (1987). Issues in the identification and programming of the gifted/learning disabled child. *Journal for the Education of the Gifted, 10*(3), 227–237.

Swisher, J. F., Vickery, J. R., & Nadenichek, P. (1983). Humanistic education: A review of research. *Journal of Humanistic Education and Development, 22*(1), 8–15.

Taba, J., & Elkins, D. (1966). *Teaching strategies for the culturally disadvantaged*. Chicago: Rand McNally.

Tanner, J. M. (1972). Sequence, tempo, and individual variation in growth and development of boys and girls aged twelve to sixteen. In J. Kagan & R. Coles (Eds.), *Twelve to sixteen: Early adolescence*. New York: Norton.

Taylor, C. A. (1989). *Guidebook to multicultural resources 1989–1990 Edition*. Madison, WI: Praxis Publications.

Thelen, H. A. (1960). *Education and the human quest*. New York: Wiley.

Thoma, S. J. (1986). Estimating gender differences in the comprehension and preference of moral issues. *Developmental Review, 6,* 165–180.

Thomas, M. (1974). *Free to be you and me*. New York: McGraw-Hill.

Thorndike, E. L., & Woodworth, R. S. (1901). The influence of improvement in one mental function upon the efficiency of other functions. *Psychological Review, 8,* 247–261.

Thurlow, M. L., & Ysseldyke, J. E. (1979). Current assessment and decision making practices in model LD programs. *Learning Disability Quarterly, 2,* 15–24.

Tidwell, R. (1989). Academic success and the school dropout: A minority perspective. In G. L. Berry & J. K. Asamen (Eds.), *Black students: Psychosocial issues and academic achievement*. Newbury Park, CA: Sage Publications.

Tonemah, S. (1987). Assessing American Indian gifted and talented students' abilities. *Journal for the Education of the Gifted, 10*(3), 181–194.

Tresemer, D. (1974). Fear of success: Popular but unproven. *Psychology Today, 7*(10), 82–85.

Tresemer, D. (1977). *Fear of success*. New York: Plenum.

Triandis, H. C. (1986). Toward pluralism in education. In S. Modgil, G. K. Verma, K. Mallick, & C. Modgil (Eds.), *Multicultural education: The interminable debate*. London: Falmer.

Trost, J. E. (1990). Social support and pressure and their impact on adolescent sexual behavior. In J. Bancroft & J. M. Reinisch (Eds.), *Adolescence and puberty*. New York: Oxford University Press.

Trubowitz, S. (1968). *A handbook for teaching in the ghetto school*. Chicago: Quadrangle.

Tudge, J., & Rogoff, B. (1989). Peer influences on cognitive development: Piagetian and Vygotskian perspectives. In M. H. Bornstein & J. S. Bruner (Eds.), *Interaction in human development*. Hillsdale, NJ: Lawrence Erlbaum.

Tulving, E., & Pearlstone, Z. (1966). Availability vs. accessibility of information in memory for words. *Journal of Verbal Learning and Verbal Behavior, 5,* 381–391.

Tuma, J. M. (1989). Mental health services for children: The state of the art. *American Psychologist, 44*(2), 188–199.

Turnure, J. E., & Lane, J. F. (1987). Special educational applications of mnemonics. In M. A. McDaniel & M. Pressley (Eds.), *Imagery and related mnemonic processes*. New York: Springer-Verlag.

Udrey, J. R. (1990). Hormonal and social determinants of adolescent sexual initiation. In J. Bancroft & J. M. Reinisch (Eds.), *Adolescence and puberty*. New York: Oxford University Press.

U.S. Committee for the White House Conference on Education. (1956). *A report to the president*. Washington, DC: U.S. Government Printing Office.

U.S. Department of Health, Education, & Welfare. (1978). *Violent schools—safe schools. The safe school report to the Congress* (Vol. 1). Washington, DC: U.S. Government Printing Office.

Valente, W. D. (1987). *Law in the schools* (2d ed.). Columbus, OH: Merrill.

van der Voort, T. H. A. (1986). *Television violence: A child's-eye view*. Amsterdam: North-Holland.

van Hasselt, V. B., & Hersen, M. (Eds.). (1987). *Handbook of adolescent psychology*. New York: Pergamon Press.

Vargas, J. (1986). Instructional design flaws in computer-assisted instruction. *Phi Delta Kappan, 67*(10), 738–744.

Vasquez, J. A. (1990). Teaching to the distinctive traits of minority students. *The Clearing House, 63*(7), 299–304.

Vitz, P. C. (1990). The use of stories in moral development: New psychological reasons for an old educational method. *American Psychologist, 45*(6), 709–720.

Voyat, G. (1983). *Cognitive development among Sioux children*. New York: Plenum Press.

Vygotsky, L. S. (1986). *Thought and language* (A. Kozulin, Trans.). Cambridge, MA: MIT Press. (Original work published 1934.)

Wadsworth, B. J. (1980). *Piaget for the classroom teacher* (2d ed.). New York: Longman.

Wadsworth, B. J. (1989). *Piaget's theory of cognitive and affective development* (4th ed.). New York: Longman.

Walberg, H. J. (1990). Productive teaching and instruction: Assessing the knowledge base. *Phi Delta Kappan, 71*(6), 470–478.

Walberg, H. J., Schiller, D., & Haertel, G. D. (1979). The quiet revolution in educational research. *Phi Delta Kappan, 61*(3), 179–182.

Walker, D. F. (1983). Reflections on the educational potential and limitations of microcomputers. *Phi Delta Kappan, 65*(2), 103–107.

Walker, J. E., & Shea, T. M. (1991). *Behavior management: A practical approach for educators* (5th ed.). New York: Macmillan.

Waterman, A. S. (1988). Identity status theory and Erikson's theory: Communalities and differences. *Developmental Review, 8,* 185–208.

Wechsler, D. (1967). *Wechsler Preschool and Primary Scale of Intelligence.* New York: Psychological Corporation.

Wechsler, D. (1974). *Wechsler Intelligence Scale for Children—Revised.* New York: Psychological Corporation.

Wechsler, D. (1975). Intelligence defined and undefined: A relativistic appraisal. *American Psychologist, 30*(2), 135–139.

Wechsler, D. (1981). *Wechsler Adult Intelligence Scale—Revised.* New York: Psychological Corporation.

Weiner, B. (1979). A theory of motivation for some classroom experiences. *Journal of Educational Psychology, 71,* 3–25.

Weiner, B. (1980). *Human motivation.* New York: Holt, Rinehart & Winston.

Weiner, B. (1986). *An attributional theory of motivation and emotion.* New York: Springer-Verlag.

Weiner, I. B. (1975). Depression in adolescence. In F. F. Flach & S. C. Draghi (Eds.), *The nature and treatment of depression.* New York: Wiley.

Weiner, I. B. (1980). Psychopathology in adolescence. In J. Adelson (Ed.), *Handbook of adolescent psychology.* New York: Wiley.

Werner, E. E., Bierman, J. M., & French, F. E. (1971). *The children of Kauai: A longitudinal study from the prenatal period to age ten.* Honolulu; University of Hawaii Press.

West, D. J., & Farrington, D. P. (1973). *Who becomes delinquent?* London: Heinemann.

Wheatley, G. H. (1991). Constructivist perspectives on science and mathematics learning. *Science Education, 75*(1), 9–21.

Whimbey, A., & Lochhead, J. (1986). *Problem solving and comprehension* (4th ed.). Hillsdale, NJ: Lawrence Erlbaum.

White, B. L., & Watts, J. C. (1973). *Experience and environment: Major influences on the development of the young child.* Englewood Cliffs, NJ: Prentice-Hall.

White, R. W. (1959). Motivation reconsidered: The concept of competence. *Psychological Review, 66,* 297–333.

Whitmore, J. (1987). Conceptualizing the issue of underserved populations of gifted students. *Journal for the Education of the Gifted, 10*(3), 141–153.

Wicks-Nelson, R., & Israel, A. C. (1991). *Behavior disorders of childhood* (2d ed.). Englewood Cliffs, NJ: Prentice-Hall.

Wiggins, G. (1989). A true test: Toward more authentic and equitable assessment. *Phi Delta Kappan, 70*(9), 703–713.

Wilen, D. K., & Sweeting, C. (1986). Assessment of limited English proficiency Hispanic students. *School Psychology Review, 15*(1), 59–75.

Williams, J. E., & Best, D. L. (1990). *Measuring sex stereotypes: A multination study* (rev. ed.). Newbury Park, CA: Sage.

Willig, A. C. (1985). A meta-analysis of selected studies on the effectiveness of bilingual education. *Review of Educational Research, 55*(3), 269–318.

Willis, J., Hovey, L., & Hovey, K. G. (1987). *Computer simulations: A source book to learning in an electronic environment.* New York: Garland Publishing.

Wineburg, S. S. (1987). The self-fulfillment of the self-fulfilling prophecy. *Educational Researcher, 16*(9), 28–37.

Wingfield, A. (1979). *Human learning and memory.* New York: Harper & Row.

Wlodkowski, R. J. (1978). *Motivation and teaching: A practical guide.* Washington, DC: National Education Association.

Wlodkowski, R. J., & Jaynes, J. H. (1990). *Eager to learn.* San Francisco: Jossey-Bass.

Wolfgang, C., & Glickman, G. (1980). *Solving discipline problems: Alternative strategies for classroom teachers.* Boston: Allyn and Bacon.

Wong, B. Y. L. (1985). Self-questioning instructional research: A review. *Review of Educational Research, 55*(2), 227–268.

Wood, F. W., & Zabel, R. H. (1978). *Making sense of reports on the incidence of behavior disorders/emotional disturbance in school populations.* Unpublished manuscript, University of Minnesota, Minneapolis.

Woodring, P. (1957). *A fourth of a nation.* New York: McGraw-Hill.

Wright, H. F. (1960). Observational child study. In P. H. Mussen (Ed.), *Handbook of research methods in child development.* New York: Wiley.

Wuthrick, M. A. (1990). Blue jays win! Crows go down in defeat! *Phi Delta Kappan, 71*(7), 553–556.

Wynn, R. L., & Fletcher, C. (1987). Sex role development and early educational experiences. In D. B. Carter (Ed.), *Current conceptions of sex roles and sex typing.* New York: Praeger.

Wynne, E. A., & Walberg, H. J. (1985/1986). The complementary goals of character development and academic excellence. *Educational Leadership, 43*(4), 15–18.

Yao, E. L. (1988). Working effectively with Asian immigrant parents. *Phi Delta Kappan, 70*(3), 223–225.

Yates, F. A. (1966). *The art of memory.* London: Routledge & Kegan Paul.

Yates, M. R., Saunders, R., & Watkins, J. F. (1980). A program based on Maslow's hierarchy helps students in trouble. *Phi Delta Kappan, 61*(10), 712–713.

Ysseldyke, J. E., & Algozzine, B. (1990). *Introduction to special education* (2d ed.). Boston: Houghton Mifflin.

Zelnick, M., & Shah, F. K. (1983). First intercourse among young Americans. *Family Planning Perspectives, 15,* 64–70.

Zelniker, T., & Jeffrey, W. E. (1976). Reflective and impulsive children: Strategies of information processing underlying differences in problem solving. *Monographs of the Society for Research in Child Development, 41*(5, Serial No. 168).

Zimmerman, B. J., & Blotner, R. (1979). Effects of model persistence and success on children's problem solving. *Journal of Educational Psychology, 71*(4), 508–513.

Zimmerman, B. J., & Ringle, J. (1981). Effects of model persistence and statements of confidence on children's self-efficacy and problem solving. *Journal of Educational Psychology, 73*(4) 485–493.

Zwier, G., & Vaughan, G. M. (1984). Three ideological orientations in school vandalism research. *Review of Educational Research, 54*(2), 263–292.

Author/Source Index

Subject Index

STUDENT RESPONSE FORM

What do you think of this book? The authors and publisher would like to know what you think of this seventh edition of *Psychology Applied to Teaching*. Your comments will help us not only in improving the next edition of this book but also in developing other texts. We would appreciate very much if you would take a few minutes to respond to the following questions. When you have indicated your reactions, please send this form to: College Marketing, Houghton Mifflin Company, One Beacon Street, Boston, MA 02108.

1. On a ten-point scale, with 10 as the highest rating and 1 as the lowest, how do you rate the following features of *Psychology Applied to Teaching?*
   Overall rating compared to all other texts you have read _____
   Interest level compared to all other texts you have read _____
   Readability compared to other texts _____
   Clarity of presentation of concepts and information _____
   Value of the *Key Points* as a learning aid _____
   Helpfulness of *Mid-Chapter Reviews* _____
   Helpfulness of summary *tables* and *diagrams* _____
   Interest level and pedagogical effectiveness of the *illustrations* _____
   Usefulness of the *Resources for Further Investigation* _____
   Usefulness of *Applying Technology to Teaching* _____
   Usefulness of the *Handbook Headings* and *Suggestions for Developing a Personal Handbook* _____
   Usefulness of *Becoming a Better Teacher: Questions and Suggestions* _____

2. Do you intend to sell this book _____ or keep it for future reference _____?
   (Please insert an X in the appropriate space.)

3. Have you used (or do you intend to refer to) *Becoming a Better Teacher: Questions and Suggestions* to improve your teaching effectiveness?
   Yes _____ No _____

4. Please turn to the table of contents and list here the numbers of all chapters that were assigned by your instructor.

   _____

5. If not all chapters were assigned, did you read any others on your own? Please indicate chapter numbers you read on your own.

   _____

6. Were there any topics that were not covered that you thought should have been covered?

   _____

7. Please indicate the number of each of the following types of exams that your instructor asked you to take:
   multiple choice ____ short-answer ____ essay ____ oral ____ other
   (please specify)_____

8. Did your instructor give you the opportunity to compare your test answers to the answers provided by the person who wrote the questions? Yes _____ No _____

9. Were you required to write a term paper _____ or complete some sort of term project? (Please specify the nature of the term project.)_____

10. Did you use the Study Guide? Yes _____ No _____
On a ten-point scale, how do you rate the usefulness of the Study Guide? _____

Did your instructor ask you to use the Study Guide _____ or did you obtain it on your own _____?

11. Are you attending a 2-year college _____, 4-year college _____, university _____?

12. What was your class standing at the time you took the course in educational psychology?
Freshman _____ Sophomore _____ Junior _____ Senior _____ Graduate _____

13. Is your college or university on the quarter system _____ or the semester system _____?

14. If you had the chance to talk to the authors of this book just before they started to prepare the next edition, what suggestions would you give them for improving *Psychology Applied to Teaching?*

Index to Suggestions for Teaching in Your Classroom

Index to Applying Technology to Teaching